Unconcealed

Sophie Richard

Unconcealed

The International Network of Conceptual Artists 1967–77
Dealers, Exhibitions and Public Collections

Edited by Lynda Morris

Published by Ridinghouse

Produced in association with
Norwich University College of the Arts

For Lucie

Sophie used to talk about her thesis as if it were a child. She was expecting a baby when she graduated and, as such, she realised two of her dreams at virtually the same time. But she didn't live long enough to enjoy the fruits of her hard work nor to delight in watching her child grow up. She died, aged only 31, three months after her graduation in Norwich and a matter of weeks after the birth of our daughter Lucie.

Sophie could not have chosen a better metaphor but for the fact that the intellectual gestation of her thesis proved not only to be longer but more difficult than her pregnancy. Sophie dedicated seven years of her life to her research on Conceptual art. For many, this book will tell the exciting story of the Conceptual art network in Europe. For me, it will always serve as a reminder of those happy years in Paris and in Sheffield.

I am very grateful to Lynda Morris who edited Sophie's research and to all those who made this publication possible. That this book should survive Sophie does not make her death any easier to accept. But for those who were so fond of her it will be a comfort to know that she left a legacy. It is right that this book be dedicated to Lucie because both their destinities are linked.

Tom Reisen

Contents

Appendices

Appendix 4 Conversations

'Unconcealment' is the English translation of *Entborgenheit*, a term used by Martin Heidegger. He wrote about art as a form of disclosing, of the artist's ability to come closer to meanings buried underneath the words appropriated by mythology, religions, empires, science and politics. He wrote about art as a means of 'enabling what is to be'.[1]

'Unconcealment' can be applied on two different levels to Sophie Richard's research on the Conceptual art of the late 1960s and early 1970s. Firstly, it refers to the way in which Conceptualism encouraged the analysis of structures and meanings. The Conceptual artists took the formal language of documents and images, and turned them in upon themselves, in what I described at the time as 'self-referential ideas'.[2] Secondly, Richard has disclosed the network behind Conceptual art during the first decade of the movement. The business of Conceptual art, or more precisely the accrual of value, is discussed as one of the layers of meaning buried within the work.

Richard's PhD Thesis *International Network of Conceptual Artists: Dealer Galleries, Temporary Exhibitions and Museum Collections (Europe 1967–1977)*, was presented at Norwich School of Art and Design,[3] an Associate College of Anglia Ruskin University, Cambridge, in September 2006. Sadly, Richard died seven weeks after giving birth to her daughter Lucie, in November 2007, before she had time to prepare her thesis for publication. For me, her death was a personal and professional tragedy. I was her supervisor for the four years of her research, and as a participant in some of the events of the Conceptual network, I had handed over my knowledge of this period to her. This is how I came to edit her thesis and prepare it for publication.

1 David Farrell Krell (ed.), *Martin Heidegger Basic Writings*, London: Routledge & Kegan Paul, 1978.

2 For example in Lynda Morris, 'Douglas Huebler', *Studio International*, April 1973, p.198 and 'Art et Language Lynda Morris annotated by Art & Language', *Art Press*, March 1974.

3 Norwich School of Art and Design became Norwich University College of the Arts in 2009.

Although Richard's first language was Luxembourgish, she worked with me in English on this thesis.[4] She also spoke French, German and Flemish/Dutch. This enabled her to undertake documentary research in museums and archives across Europe. Her data centred on the triangle between the Rhineland cities of Düsseldorf and Cologne, Amsterdam, Brussels and Gent. Ten of the cities prominent in early exhibitions of Conceptual art are in this triangle. Cities rather than countries were key to the development of the Conceptual network in the first decade.

The methodology that I handed on to Richard was to work initially, and at length, on primary documents of the period, especially art magazines, taking as much notice of the adverts as the editorials. She consulted my archives in Norwich regularly. She received a research grant from the Henry Moore Institute in Leeds and also worked at the Tate Archive, the Casino in Luxembourg and the Anton and Annick Herbert archive in Gent. A grant from the Goethe Institute enabled her to consult archives in Germany, including that of Konrad Fischer, the key dealer of Conceptual art. She also sought out existing recorded interviews with the leading figures. She defined the groups of artists, dealers and exhibitions for her study so that she could begin the construction of the databases, which are published in the appendices of this book. Her data concentrates on public collections and those private collections that have been accessioned in recent years by museums. She chose not to collect data on sales to other private collections during this period. The data therefore focuses on the relationship between the artists, dealers and public collections. She was unable for financial reasons to continue her research in the US.

Half of the artists in Richard's databases are from the US and half from Europe. Conceptual art was the first post-1945 art movement to treat American and European artists equally. We discussed the extent to which recent US books on Conceptual art had altered this balance. Richard was at the conference for the Tate exhibition, *Open Systems*, 2005, when I questioned Alexander Alberro about the omission of Seth Siegelaub's July/August 1970 issue of *Studio International* from his book *Conceptual Art and the Politics of Publicity*, 2003.[5] Richard took up this argument on subsequent occasions and in the introduction and conclusion of this book. She grasped the bias in perspectives constructed

4 Prior to undertaking this thesis, Richard had completed an MPhil thesis (DEA), *Harald Szeeman et les expositions d'art contemporain* at L'Université de Paris 1 Panthéon-Sorbonne in 2000.
5 Richard also took part in the conference *New Research into Conceptualism in Europe* at the Norwich Gallery in February 2005.

20 or 30 years after the events in recently published and academic histories. Richard was then equipped to interview the key figures of the movement. She transcribed her own interviews, remembering W. H. Auden's idea that you understand more by writing out texts rather than by reading or listening.

Richard devised the databases at an early stage of her research although she continued to add to them throughout. She requested access to accession files and information on purchases from museums and information in exhibition archives, persistently overcoming the reluctance of museums to release this information. As a result of EU Freedom of Information Legislation, The Stedelijk Museum, Amsterdam, and Tate, London, allowed her access to their accession files and the prices they paid for works. Other European museums gave information regarding the dealers from whom a work was purchased. The Stedelijk and Tate prices enable readers to estimate the prices being paid for other works. Richard's databases can be compared with the prices quoted by Willi and Linde Bongard's Kunstkompass chart of the top 100 contemporary artists, some of which are reprinted in the appendices of this book.[6]

Prices have been kept in their original currencies in the databases because of the difficulty of establishing actual exchange rates on sales that often took public museums 12 or more months to complete in a period of economic turbulence. I have prepared an additional chart of the exchange rate fluctuations between the Pound, the Dollar and the Deutschmark during the period 1967–77. Sterling floated between 1969 and 1971, bringing to an end the Bretton Woods System of pegged exchange rates. Currencies further fluctuated in the early 1970s with inflation. The instability increased with the escalation of the Vietnam War and the Oil Crisis resulting from OPEC price increases after two Arab Israeli wars, terrorism and the riots of alienated youth. The Pound was decimalised in 1969: 240 pence in a Pound meant that each new penny was worth 2.4 old pence and was considered to have caused inflation and undermined the Pound. In the late 1970s, an Exchange Rate Mechanism – the ERM – was introduced in Europe.[7]

Richard chose not to illustrate her thesis, but I started to develop with her the idea of an exhibition to mark the eventual publication of the thesis. This exhibition was to bring together three artists whose work addressed the internal

6 For example, between 1972 and 1976 Richard Long rose from 74 to 41 in the Kunstkompass. See pp.350–359.

7 I remember that by 1976 a loaf of bread in Germany cost £3. In London it cost less than 50p.

COMPARISON OF EXCHANGE RATES $–£–DM, 1967–1979

	1967	1968	1969	1970	1971	1972	1973	1974	1975	1976	1977	1978	1979
$1 = DM	4.01	3.98	3.66	3.65	3.48	3.19	2.65	2.58	2.46	2.52	2.32	2.00	1.83
$1 = £					.4166	.3846	.4348	.4545	.4348	.4166	.6250		
£1 = DM	11.22	9.63	8.83		8.35	8.29	6.09	5.68	5.65	6.04	3.71		

Figures taken from R.L. Bidwell, *Currency Conversion Tables: 100 Years of Change*, London: Rex Collings, 1970

contradictions of radical Conceptual art: André Cadere, who colonised other people's exhibitions with his 'round bar of wood'; Ian Wilson, whose *Conversations* were a psychoanalysis of his audience; and Jacques Charlier. For this publication, I have worked with Charlier to select 40 of his 600-plus *Vernissage des Expositions* photographs from 1974–75, made for his exhibition at the Palais des Beaux Arts, Brussels, alongside On Kawara.[8] Charlier's catalogue for his exhibition was of the photographs taken at its vernissage. It is an extraordinary photographic record of the heyday of the 'network of Conceptual art'.

My introduction is based on an analysis of the databases that Richard created for her thesis. The use of databases is appropriate to a study of Conceptualism, because the revelation of information through data was one of the ways in which Conceptualism defined itself. Future users of Richard's databases will be able to consider the extent to which economic factors have influenced the direction of recent art that is usually viewed as aesthetically independent.

Conceptual art in the first decade was a true avant-garde and this period was marked by a corresponding emergence of a new generation of young dealers who developed innovative means of distribution, and they frequently worked as curators of exhibitions in public galleries and museums. An analysis of Richard's data suggests that there was a correlation between these exhibitions curated by dealers and the subsequent purchase of the artists' work by museums. The questions raised by Richard's data are for the public sector to analyse.

8 See pp.269–289. Images courtesy of Galerie Nadjar Vilenne, Liège.
9 *Studio International*, February 1971.

Private-sector dealers of radical contemporary art are there to sell their artists' work, and there is no conflict in that. This was less of an ethical dilemma then, when the environment was less commercial.

The databases concentrate on 14 dealer galleries. My introduction discusses the most dramatic story, that of Konrad Fischer. He started his career as an artist and then opened a space in Düsseldorf, selling to museums in Germany, the Netherlands and the UK. In the mid to late 1960s, young Germans were on a mission to work with US artists. Germany was the front line of the Cold War and NATO was its protection. In an interview with Jorge Jappe, Fischer said: 'When I was an artist everything was so far away; Warhol, Lichtenstein and all those were great unattainable men. But when you know them, you can have a beer with them and get rid of your inferiority complex. I insist that the artist has to be there when I show his work, ... Palermo and Richter ... two of the German artists who have exhibited with me, have now been to New York, and they felt at home there because they had already met artists like Andre and LeWitt over here ...'[9]

In a chart compiled to introduce the interview with Jappe, Fischer listed his record of 'firsts':

EXHIBITIONS AT KONRAD FISCHER GALLERY, DÜSSELDORF

First one-man shows:
Darboven, Sandback, Long, Fulton, McLean, Gilbert & George, Ruthenbeck
First European one-man shows:
Andre, Artschwager, LeWitt, Nauman, Ryman, Smithson, Weiner, Huebler, Wilson
First German one-man shows:
Dibbets, Rinke, Buren, Merz, Law
Other exhibitions:
Bechers, Palermo, Polke, Richter, Rückriem, Sladden, Panamarenko
One-man shows in museums arranged by Konrad Fischer:
Andre, Darboven (Museum Mönchengladbach); Long, Sandback, LeWitt, Dibbets (Museum Haus Lange, Krefeld); Palermo (Museum Wuppertal Studio).
Collective exhibitions arranged by Konrad Fischer:
Prospect 68 and Prospect 69, Städtische Kunsthalle, Düsseldorf; *Konzeption/Conception*, Städtisches Museum, Leverkusen, October 1969.[10]

Fischer did not explain in the *Studio International* interview the relationship between his 'firsts' and his network. His strategy was to gain a small percentage from sales to galleries across Europe. This enabled him to have the time to co-curate museum shows to increase his artists' reputation. The best interests of his artists were served by enabling sales from galleries in different cities, from which he gained only a small commission. This also explains Fischer's ability to co-curate museum shows. He thought the job of the dealer was to do the work for museum curators in order to show his artists. This was more important than individual sales. Richard's research demonstrates that this business concept underpins the early success of Conceptualism in Europe and was at the heart of its development in the first decade. What Richard's databases reveal is the increasingly central role economics plays in recent art history.

I have made an additional list of the defining mixed exhibitions of Conceptual art in both public galleries and museums and in dealer galleries (see pp17–19). I have highlighted those exhibitions that were organised by what I have called 'dealer curators'. It shows that more than 50 per cent of the defining exhibitions of Conceptual art in public galleries, museums and dealer galleries were organised by 'dealer curators'. Half of that 50 per cent were organised by Fischer. This reinforces the correlation between a dealer curating exhibitions and sales made to public collections.

I discussed with Richard an example, from my own experience, of Fischer's central, but concealed role. I worked at the Institute of Contemporary Arts in London as the touring exhibition *When Attitudes Become Form*, organised by Harald Szeemann, was installed there in 1969.[11] It was the experience of working with artists rather than objects that I have sought to pass onto future generations with the EAST*international* exhibitions in Norwich. Many of the artists in *When Attitudes Become Form* had been in Fischer's Prospect 68 in Düsseldorf. A letter to Fischer from Charles Harrison, the curator of the ICA showing, thanks him for his assistance in the preparation of *When Attitudes Become Form* for the ICA and asks for instructions on how to install the work of a number of artists.[12] Szeemann was busy organising *Happenings and Fluxus* for the Kunsthalle and Kunstverein in Cologne and he only arrived in London in time to make the opening speech. Harrison was also busy, teaching at St Martins and working at *Studio*

10 *Ibid.*
11 I had started work at the ICA in July 1969, after studying Fine Art at Canterbury College of Art, where I had attended two short courses run by Terry Atkinson of Art & Language.
12 Konrad Fischer Archive, Düsseldorf. Letter dated 22 July 1969.

DEFINING GROUP EXHIBITIONS OF CONCEPTUAL ART IN EUROPE, 1967–77 (AND GROUP EXHIBITIONS BEYOND EUROPE THAT INCLUDE EUROPEAN ARTISTS)

* Exhibitions curated by dealers
Exhibitions curated by Konrad Fischer in bold

1966 *Primary Structures*, Jewish Museum, New York. Curator: Kynaston McShine.

1967 **Serielle Formationen*, Studio Gallery, Frankfurt am Main. Curators: Paul Maenz and Peter Roehr.

**Dies alles Herzchen wird einmal dir gehoren, 19:45–21:55*, Galerie Dorothea Loehr, Frankfurt. Curator: Paul Maenz.

*First Kunstmarkt, Kunsthalle and Kunstverein, Cologne. Annually 1967–1974. Initiated by Hein Stünke and Rudolf Zwirner.

Arte Povera–Im Spazio, Galleria La Bertesca, Genoa. Curator: Germano Celant.

1968 Documenta 4, Kassel. Director: Arnold Bode. Curator (Painting): Jan Leering.

**Minimal Art*, Gemeentemuseum, The Hague. Curators: Enno Develing and John Weber.

***Prospect 68*, Städtische Kunsthalle Düsseldorf**. Curators: Konrad Fischer and Hans Strelow.

1969 **Number 7*, Paula Cooper Gallery, New York. Curator: Lucy R. Lippard.

Earth Art, Andrew Dickson White Museum of Art, Cornell University, Ithaca. Curator: Willoughby Sharp.

**Ecologic Art*, John Gibson Gallery, New York. Curator: John Gibson.

**One Month*. Publication/calendar. Curator: Seth Siegelaub.

Op Losse Schroeven, Stedelijk Museum, Amsterdam. Curator: Wim Beeren. Also shown at Folkwang Museum, Essen (under the title *Verborgene Structuren*).

When Attitudes Become Form, Kunsthalle Bern; Museum Haus Lange, Krefeld; Institute of Contemporary Arts, London. Curators: Harald Szeemann, Paul Wember (Krefeld) and Charles Harrison (London).

Place and Process, The Edmonton Art Gallery, Edmonton, Alberta. Curators: Willoughby Sharp and Evander Schley.

Art by Telephone, Museum Contemporary Art, Chicago. Curator: Jan van der Marck.

**A 379089*, Antwerp. Institute founded by: Geert Bekaert, James Lee Byars, Marcel Broodthaers, Jef Cornelis, Herman Daled, Anny De Decker, Isi Fiszman, Bernd Lohaus, Hubert Peeters. Artisic Coordinator: Kasper König.

**July–August–September 1969*. Exhibition took place simultaneously at 11 locations around the world. Curator: Seth Siegelaub.

557,087, Seattle Art Museum, Seattle. Curator: Lucy R. Lippard. Also shown at Vancouver Art Gallery, Vancouver (under the title *955,000*) and Centro de Arte y Comunicación, Buenos Aires (as *3,549,000*).

***Prospect 69*, Städtische Kunsthalle, Düsseldorf**. Curators: Konrad Fischer and Hans Strelow.

**Land Art*. Films broadcast on SFB on April 15th, 1969, in Germany. Curator: Gerry Schum.

***Konzeption/Conception*, Städtisches Museum, Leverkusen**. Curators: Konrad Fischer and

Rolf Wedewer.
Pläne und Projekte als Kunst, Kunsthalle, Bern. Curator: Felix Zdenek.
Concept: Harald Szeemann.
1970 *Conceptual Art and Conceptual Aspects*, New York Cultural Center, New York.
Curator: Donald Karshan.
18 Paris IV.70, rue Mouffetard, Paris. Curator: Michel Claura.
Conceptual art, Arte povera, Land art, Galleria Civica d'Arte Moderna, Turin.
Curator: Germano Celant.
*First Basel Art Fair.
projectsproposalsvision, Midland Group, Nottingham. Curator: Tim Threlfall.
**Studio International*, July/August, vol. 180 no.924, London. Also published as a book.
Curators: David Antin, Germano Celant, Michel Claura, Charles Harrison,
Lucy R. Lippard, Seth Siegelaub, Hans Strelow.
Idea Structures: Survey '70, Camden Arts Centre, London. Curator: Charles Harrison.
Information, Museum of Modern Art, New York. Curator: Kynaston McShine.
**Wall Show*, Lisson Gallery, London. Curator: Nicholas Logsdail.
1971 ***Formulation*, Addison Gallery of American Art, Phillips Academy, Andover.**
Curators: Konrad Fischer and Gian Enzo Sperone.
6th Guggenheim International Exhibition 1971, Solomon R. Guggenheim Museum,
New York. Curator: Diane Waldman.
***Das Konzept ist die Form*, Westfälischen Kunstverein, Münster.**
Curators: Klaus Honnef, Paul Maenz and Konrad Fischer.
Sonsbeek 71, Sonsbeek Park, Arnhem. Curators: Wim Beerens (Chair), Geert van Beijeren.
***Prospect 71*: Projection, Städtische Kunsthalle, Düsseldorf.**
Curators: Konrad Fischer and Hans Strelow.
In Another Moment, Gallery SKG, Belgrade. Curators: Braco and Nena Dimitrijevic.
*Kölner Kunstmarkt, Kunsthalle und Kunstverein, Cologne.
*IKI/Internationale Kunst-und Informationsmesse, Belgisches Haus und Volkshochschule,
Cologne.
Roadshow XI, Bienal de Sao Paulo. Curator: John Dunbar.
**Actualité d'un Bilan*, Yvon Lambert, Paris. Curators: Michel Claura and Yvon Lambert.
1972 ***'Konzept'-Kunst*, Kunstmuseum, Basel**. Curator: Konrad Fischer.
***De Europa*, John Weber Gallery, New York**. Curators: Konrad Fischer and Gian Enzo
Sperone.
36th Biennale di Venezia: Esposizione Internationale d'Art, Venice.
***Documenta 5*, Museum Fridericianum and Neue Galerie, Kassel.**
General Secretary: Harald Szeemann.
Conceptual Art 'Idee+Idee/Licht'. Curators: Konrad Fischer and Klaus Honnef.
The New Art, Hayward Gallery, London. Curator: Anne Seymour. Assistant: Nicholas Serota.
**The Book as Artwork 1960–1972*, Nigel Greenwood Inc. Ltd., London. Curators: Germano
Celant and Lynda Morris.
1973 **Deurle 11/7/73*, Museum Dhont-Dhaenens, Deurle. Curators: Anny De Decker,
Paul Maenz and Fernand Spillemaeckers.

Contemporanea, Parking of the Villa Borghese, Rome. Curator: Achille Bonito Oliva.
***Prospect 73, *Malers Painters Peintres*, Städtische Kunsthalle, Düsseldorf.** Curators: Konrad Fischer and Hans Strelow.
16 Place Vendôme, private apartment, Paris. Also shown at Städtisches Museum, Mönchengladbach; Kaiser Wilhelm Museum, Krefeld and Internationaal Cultureel Centrum (ICC), Antwerp. Curators: Michel Claura and René Denizot.

1974 Palais des Beaux-Arts, Brussels. Various exhibitions 1973–1974. Curator: Yves Gevaert.
**Project 74, Kunst bleibt Kunst*, Wallraf-Richartz Museum, Kunsthalle, Cologne. Curator/staff: Paul Maenz.

1976 ***Prospect/Retrospect, Europa 1946–1976*, Kunsthalle, Düsseldorf.** Curators: Konrad Fischer and Hans Strelow.

1977 *Skulptur Ausstellung in Münster*, citywide, Münster. Curators: Klaus Bussmann and Kasper König.
Documenta 6, Museum Fridericianum, Kassel. Curator: Manfred Schneckenburger.

International during the installation. The person who had his coat off, rolled up his sleeves and worked with the artists and the installation teams until Harrison arrived in the afternoon was Fischer.

Hans Strelow defended Fischer's role as a dealer-curator. Together, they curated the Düsseldorf series of Prospect exhibitions in 1968, 1969, 1971, 1973 and 1976. In an interview with Brigitte Kölle, Strelow said: 'We had 20,000 Marks at our disposal for the first exhibition ... Konrad and I prepared the show for months, without being paid a fee ... Konrad and I compiled a list of artists we thought should take part in the exhibition and then sent the list to the jury ... We organised the exhibition in a public institution and we felt obliged to objectivity. Therefore, commerce played no part whatsoever'.[13]

In spring 1969, Fischer went to New York to prepare the Prospect 69 exhibition for the Kunsthalle and Kunstverein in Düsseldorf. He made a good impression. A letter dated 7 May 1969, quoted by Richard, from Marilyn Fischbach to Fischer concerning Robert Ryman suggests: 'You could be the central European gallery connection ... and you could distribute the work in Europe ... The commission could be 25 per cent to you, which leaves little to us, actually only 15 per

13 Brigitte Kölle (ed.), *Okey Dokey Konrad Fischer*, Cologne: Walther König, 2007. Richard met Kölle in Düsseldorf, but she died before Kölle's important book appeared in early 2008.

cent'.[14] However, an agreement was not reached. In the autumn, Ryman had exhibitions with the European dealers Heiner Friedrich, Françoise Lambert, Yvon Lambert, Franz Dalem and Gian Enzo Sperone. This shows the development of a network for US artists across Europe, linked to Düsseldorf. Richard's databases show fewer sales for Ryman than for LeWitt and Nauman: their prices averaged $3–4,000, while Ryman's averaged $15–16,000. The Italian collector Giuseppe Panza bought 17 works by Ryman between 1971 and 1974, probably spending well over $250,000 at early 1970s prices.

Fischer's influence in the US can also be illustrated by another example. In November 1969, the curator Diane Waldman wrote to Fischer that she was planning a research trip to see younger German artists for a Guggenheim exhibition in New York. Waldman lists Joseph Beuys, Reiner Ruthenbeck, Bernd and Hilla Becher, Jörg Immendorff, Klaus Rinke, Gerhard Richter and Sigmar Polke. Her *Guggenheim International* opened in February 1971 and included 11 of the artists on Fischer's *Studio International* list of 'Firsts'. None of the artists on her original list survived her consultation with Fischer.

An important exhibition curated by Fischer, with Klaus Honnef, was section 17 of Documenta 5, *Idee+Idee/Licht* of 1972. It was a small section of the show, but as Honnef discussed with Richard in an interview in 2005:

> My feeling was that I could still learn a few things and I opted to work with Fischer ... It was a very intense collaboration. I worked very intensively with him on exhibitions in Münster, and he cooperated with me very closely on the book [*Concept Art*, Phaidon, 1971] ... For Harald Szeemann it wasn't his favourite section ... he thought it was a bit too cerebral ... Of course the specialists, the insiders, thought that our section – that big room with the *Circle* by Richard Long in the middle, and Darboven and Sol LeWitt opposite, and also Agnes Martin – was the Cathedral of Documenta, along with Richard Serra, who was in the next room ... Fischer was very meticulous about the budget. We only had a little B&B on the outskirts.

Johannes Cladders discussed the issues around the dealer-curator with Brigitte Kölle:

14 Konrad Fischer Archive, Düsseldorf.

BK: Wasn't it a bit disreputable that Konrad, as a gallery owner, conceived a section of the Documenta and also displayed artists from his own gallery?
JC: Konrad was appointed a chaperone, Klaus Honnef ... [*laughs*] I'm not aware that anyone objected ... Of course he was interested in selling ... But selling was not his main intention.[15]

Richard's meticulous research shows us that because he was a dealer, Fischer's role has been concealed behind 'the objectivity of curators' like Szeemann, Honnef and Cladders.

I have also made a comparative chart from Richard's data on dealer sales to museums between 1967 and 1980 (see pp.23–25). This shows, at least from the data available to Richard, that Fischer controlled a quarter of all sales to public collections of Conceptualism in Europe in the first decade. However, I would argue that Fischer was building on the model of Marcel Duchamp's role as an artist/dealer/curator.

An exchange of letters between Fischer and Sol LeWitt in November 1967, reproduced in chapter one, reveals the percentage arrangements not only between artist and dealer but also to other dealers across various European cities. The US artists were passed around the European galleries in a franchise arrangement. On 22 November 1967 Fischer writes: 'The Percentage: 50 per cent for the artist, 50 per cent for the gallery, 30 per cent for the other gallery and 50 per cent for you ... when the show is taken to another place. I think there should be 20 per cent for my gallery'.[16] However, this only applied to the works shown by Konrad Fischer.

In Brigitte Kölle's book *Okey Dokey Konrad Fischer*, Bruce Nauman discusses the relationship between American and European galleries: 'Carl [Andre] and Sol [LeWitt] both had shows in the States but nobody bought anything. They were much more accepted in Europe ... Konrad still sold more work in Europe than was sold in the US. Prices were very low. I think the fact my dealers – Dick Bellamy and Leo Castelli – had my work in New York gave me a lot of credibility.'[17]

There are differences between US and European perceptions of the development of Conceptual art, influenced by diverging cultural agendas. There are also significant differences in the order in which work was seen on either side of the

15 B. Kölle, *op. cit.*
16 Konrad Fischer Archive, Düsseldorf.
17 B. Kölle, *op. cit.*

SUMMARY OF DATA FROM APPENDICES 1.4–1.7: SALES TO PUBLIC MUSEUM COLLECTIONS IN EUROPE, 1967–80

DEALER	ARTIST	SALE	TOTAL SALES	MARKET SHARE %
ACE	Bruce Nauman	2	2	0.57
AFA	Carl Andre	4	4.5*	1.29
	Douglas Huebler	.5*		
Art & Project	Hanne Darboven	3	29	8.29
	Jan Dibbets	15		
	Gilbert & George	2.5		
	Joseph Kosuth	.5*		
	Sol LeWitt	5		
	Richard Long	1		
	Mario Merz	1		
	Lawrence Weiner	1		
Artist Direct Sales	Carl Andre	3	34	9.71
	Marcel Broodthaers	2.5		
	Daniel Buren	3		
	Hanne Darboven	2		
	Jan Dibbets	3		
	Douglas Huebler	1		
	Sol LeWitt	7		
	Richard Long	8		
	Bruce Nauman	2		
	Robert Ryman	.5*		
	Lawrence Weiner	2		
Artist Gift	Marcel Broodthaers	3	33	9.43
	Hanne Darboven	8		
	Gilbert & George	12		
	Sol LeWitt	12		
Richard Bellamy	Bruce Nauman	3	3	0.86
Galerie Bernier	Mario Merz	1	1	0.28

DEALER	ARTIST	SALE	TOTAL SALES	MARKET SHARE %
Bruno Bischofberger	Bruce Nauman	1	1	0.28
René Block	Carl Andre	1	1	0.28
Galerie Borgmann	Marcel Broodthaers	1	1	0.28
Galerie Isy Brachot	Marcel Broodthaers	1	1	0.28
Eugenia Butler	Bruce Nauman	1	1	0.28
Leo Castelli	Jan Dibbets	1	18	5.13
	Douglas Huebler	.5*		
	Joseph Kosuth	.5*		
	Bruce Nauman	15		
	Lawrence Weiner	1		
Castelli/Sonnabend Tapes & Films, Inc.	Bruce Nauman	6	7	2.00
	Lawrence Weiner	1		
Galerie Durand-Dessert	Hanne Darboven	1	1	0.28
Konrad Fischer	Carl Andre	16	95.5	27.23
	Hanne Darboven	7		
	Jan Dibbets	6		
	Gilbert & George	1		
	Douglas Huebler	2		
	Sol LeWitt	17		
	Richard Long	11		
	Mario Merz	2		
	Bruce Nauman	22		
	Robert Ryman	8.5		
	Lawrence Weiner	3		
Heiner Friedrich	Carl Andre	3	11	3.14
	Marcel Broodthaers	2		
	Bruce Nauman	3		
	Robert Ryman	2		
Nigel Greenwood	Marcel Broodthaers	1	5.5	1.57
	Gilbert & George	4		
	Joseph Kosuth	.5*		

DEALER	ARTIST	SALE	TOTAL SALES	MARKET SHARE %
Galerie Felix Handschin	Marcel Broodthaers	1	2	0.57
	Mario Merz	1		
Françoise Lambert	Richard Long	1	2	0.57
	Robert Ryman	1		
Yvon Lambert	Jan Dibbets	1	7	2.00
	Robert Ryman	3		
	Lawrence Weiner	3		
Lisson Gallery	Sol LeWitt	2	6	1.71
	Richard Long	4		
Paul Maenz	Joseph Kosuth	2	2	0.57
MTL	Joseph Kosuth	.5*	0.5	0.14
Rolf Preisig	Jan Dibbets	1	5	1.43
	Douglas Huebler	1		
	Sol LeWitt	1		
	Robert Ryman	1		
	Lawrence Weiner	1		
Public Galleries:			6	1.71
Kunstmuseum Bern/	Richard Long	1		
Städtisches Museum, Mönchengladbach/	Marcel Broodthaers	2		
Kunstmuseum Basel/		1		
MOMA Oxford		2		
Rolf Ricke	Bruce Nauman	2	2	0.57
Alfred Schmela	Carl Andre	4	4	1.14
Videogalerie Schum/ Projektion Ursula Wevers	Gilbert & George	.5	1.5	0.43
	Mario Merz	1		
Galerie Seriaal	Marcel Broodthaers	1	2	0.57
	Daniel Buren	1		

DEALER	ARTIST	SALE	TOTAL SALES	MARKET SHARE %
Ileana Sonnabend	Gilbert & George	1	7	2.00
	Mario Merz	1		
	Bruce Nauman	5		
Sotheby's	Bruce Nauman	1	1	0.28
Gian Enzo Sperone	Carl Andre	2	17	4.86
	Jan Dibbets	3		
	Douglas Huebler	2		
	Joseph Kosuth	1		
	Richard Long	3		
	Bruce Nauman	1		
	Robert Ryman	3		
	Lawrence Weiner	2		
Sperone-Westwater-Fischer	Carl Andre	4	4	1.14
Galerie Stampa	Marcel Broodthaers	1	1	0.28
Michael Werner	Marcel Broodthaers	1	1	0.28
John Weber	Carl Andre	7	18	5.14
	Jan Dibbets	1		
	Sol LeWitt	1		
	Richard Long	2		
	Robert Ryman	7		
Wide White Space	Carl Andre	3	8.5	2.43
	Marcel Broodthaers	2.5		
	Daniel Buren	3		
Rudolf Zwirner	Hanne Darboven	2	3	0.86
	Sol LeWitt	1		

Notes:
Data extracted from: Appendices/Databases: 1.4, 1.7 (see pp. 314–338). The period for the data is 1967–1980. Several galleries opened after 1967 and some closed before 1980. This data is based on the number of sales to public museum collections and not on the value of those sales. The data only includes public museum collections and those private collections that are now part of public museum collections. Other sales in this period to private collections and museums outside Europe are not included.
* The figure '.5' refers to occasions where a purchase has been made from two dealer galleries.

Atlantic between 1968 and 1973. Anti-American demonstrations at the Venice Biennale and Documenta in 1968 asked: 'What else remains for the artists of a nation which wages such a criminal war as that in Vietnam but to produce Minimal art?' Europe continued to show American Minimal sculpture, especially those sculptors whose critical and theoretical writings blended into radical language-based and documentary photographic and video Conceptualism. Minimal painting was not shown a great deal in Europe until after 1973.[18] The American understanding of the development of formalist Minimalism into Conceptualism was therefore different to the European understanding of a combination of Fluxus and Pop developing into a theoretical, political conceptualism.

When Prospect 73, subtitled *Malers Painters Peintres*, opened in Düsseldorf in 1973, it shocked those of us who had thought of Prospect as an idealistic and progressive force for radical Conceptualism. A survey of painting over the previous 15 years, it included the European premiere of Emile de Antonio's film *Painters Painting, The New York Art Scene 1940–1970* (1972), which reinforced the idea of a continuous development from American abstraction to Pop to Minimalism.[19] This was the first time I heard the term 'Conceptual painting' used. Prospect 73 focused attention not only on Robert Ryman, Brice Marden, Dorothea Rockburne and Agnes Martin, but also on the painters with whom Fischer had studied at the Düsseldorf Akademie in the early 1960s: Gerhard Richter with his new Minimalist colour-chart paintings and Sigmar Polke with his large-scale montage paintings.

The prices quoted in Richard's databases give us this clear example of commercial interests controlling the direction of contemporary art. It could be argued that Fischer had developed radical Conceptual art in Europe with Prospect in 1968, 1969 and 1971, but had then betrayed it with a return to Minimal painting in 1973. In mitigation, Fischer appears to have used the profits from the sales of works by US Minimalist painters to develop the careers of his European artists.[20]

I worked for Nigel Greenwood from July 1971 to May 1974 and I saw Fischer frequently in London and at art fairs and openings across Europe and New York throughout the 1970s. I met him again in 1993, when he came to Norwich to select the third EAST exhibition for me. This gave me the opportunity to ask

18 I organised the first two exhibitions of US Minimalism in Britain: *Strata*, Royal College of Art, London, 14 January–1 February 1974 and the related small *Agnes Martin* exhibition at the Scottish National Gallery of Modern Art, Edinburgh, 23 February–17 March 1974.

19 *Painters Painting: The New York Art Scene, 1940–1970*. Dir. Emile de Antonio, 1973. Runtime: 116 min. Country: USA. I actually carried the film in my luggage from New York to Prospect in Düsseldorf.

20 David Tremlett mentioned that when the Tate bought his *Spring Recordings* from Fischer in Düsseldorf, after it had been shown at Documenta 5, the latter did not take his dealer percentage. Lynda Morris in conversation with David Tremlett, Autumn 2008.

him about the difference between my memories of Conceptualism and recent published accounts. As a result of those conversations, I began to trust my memories. However, I knew that my knowledge of Fischer's role would not be accepted as an objective record. The years spent working with research students like Moseley and Richard since Fischer's death in 1996 have meant that my account has been thoroughly examined and verified by the facts; 'unconcealed' by a new generation of art historians in archives, documents and interviews.

I will finish by summarising the points I have made as a result of my analysis of Richard's databases. There is a correlation between a dealer curating mixed exhibitions in public spaces and their sales to public collections in the period between 1967 and 1977 shown by a comparison of the two aggregate databases created for my introduction. This suggests museums thought as much about the dealer they were buying from, as the work they were acquiring. Museums believed artists made their best work for dealers who also curated exhibitions for public spaces. Richard has collected significant evidence that 'dealer curators' represented the private galleries that museums acquired the most works from in the period 1967 to 1977.

The early success of Conceptual art was based on the co-ordination of European tours for US artists. Galleries shared expenses and also in some cases shared the commission on sales. This idea appears to have been developed by Konrad Fischer in Düsseldorf with Heiner Friedrich in Munich and John Weber at Dwan Gallery in New York. The sales of work by US artists allowed European dealers to support the careers of less established European artists. European artists were included in mixed museum exhibitions of Conceptual art co-curated by dealers. Dealers were able to arrange exhibitions for their less established European artists in the European network created for US artists. Finally the funds European dealers acquired from sales of US artists to European museums enabled them to support the careers of younger European artists.

Sophie Richard's unconcealing of the economic-critical history of Conceptual art is a new step in the research of this important period. I am sure that Richard's study will inspire future generations of curators and art historians and inform the development of professional standards in museums and public galleries, as they delve deeper into the history of Conceptual art.

Unconcealed

Introduction

Since the 1990s, Conceptual art has been the object of increasing academic and curatorial attention, as demonstrated by the number of books and exhibitions on the subject. Most publications have been concerned with general Conceptual art histories,[1] whereas shows have dealt with specific aspects of the movement, such as Conceptual art in Britain or the significance of Conceptual art documents.[2]

What is it that makes this movement so appealing, 40 years after its beginnings in the late 1960s? And why, as the artist Lawrence Weiner wondered in a recent conversation, have the works of this generation of artists endured to this day and why are they still successful?[3]

Firstly, the Conceptualists were the first generation of artists since the Second World War to radically change the understanding and acceptance of what an artwork could be. Suddenly, a work could be a walk in nature (Richard Long), a striped wall (Daniel Buren) or a phrase (Weiner). These artists also developed the notion that the concept on which a work is based can prevail over its physical realisation. Contemporary academics see Conceptual art as a reaction against the accepted definitions of an artwork as established by Clement Greenberg's modernist critique.[4] Technological innovations contributed to the new art. Contemporary art production continues to be based on the opening up of the field of art that began in the late 1960s. Moreover, the new art led to the formation of innovative exhibition and dealing practices. These working methods, privileging the ideas of artists over material objects, are still being used today.

Secondly, there seems to be an awareness of the need to study the period

1 For instance: Michael Newman and Jon Bird (eds), *Rewriting Conceptual Art*, Reaktion Books, London, 1999; Alexander Alberro and Blake Stimson (eds), *Conceptual Art. A Critical Anthology*, The MIT Press, Cambridge, Massachussets, 1999; Anne Rorimer, *New Art in the 60s and 70s. Redefining Reality*, Thames & Hudson, London, 2001; Peter Osborne (ed.), *Conceptual Art*, Phaidon Press, London, 2002; Michael Corris (ed.), *Conceptual Art: Theory, Myth and Practice*, Cambridge University Press, Cambridge, 2004.

2 For example: Clive Phillpot and Andrea Tarsia, *Live in Your Head. Concept and Experiment in Britain, 1965–75* (exh. cat.), Whitechapel Art Gallery, London, 2000; Catherine Moseley (ed.), *Conception. Conceptual Documents 1968 to 1972* (exh. cat.), Norwich Gallery, Norwich; Article Press, 2001 (MPhil, Norwich School of Art and Design, 2001); Ann Goldstein and Anne Rorimer (eds), *Reconsidering the Object of Art: 1965–1975* (exh. cat.), The Museum of Contemporary Art, Los Angeles, The MIT Press, Cambridge, Mass. and London, 1995; Suzanna Héman, Jurrie Poot and Hripsimé Visser (eds), *Conceptual Art in the Netherlands and Belgium, 1965–1975* (exh. cat.), Stedelijk Museum, Amsterdam; NAi Publishers, Rotterdam, 2000.

3 Lawrence Weiner in conversation with the author, Graz, 10 June 2006, manuscript notes.

4 See: Osborne, *Conceptual Art*, *op. cit.*, p.18; Blake Stimson, 'The promise of conceptual art', in Alberro and Stimson, *Conceptual Art: A Critical Anthology*, *op. cit.* p.xl–xli; Rorimer, *New Art in the 60s and 70s*, *op. cit.*, p.12.

5 For example: Peter Braunstein and Michael William Doyle (eds),

while the participants are still alive. In recent years numerous artists, curators and critics whose names are linked with Conceptual art have died. These include Mario Merz (1925–2003), Donald Karshan (1930–2003), Nigel Greenwood (1941–2004), Johannes Gachnang (1939–2005), Konrad Fischer (1939-1996), Harald Szeemann (1933–2005), Edy de Wilde (1919–2005), Geert van Beijeren (1933–2005), Jan Leering (1934–2005) and Peter Townsend (1919–2006).

Conceptual art arose in a broader context of social unrest, paralleling the discourse around May 1968. There currently seems to be a renewed fascination with this period in which unprecedented collective and political changes occurred. Numerous books continue to be published on subjects such as the hippie movement and the counterculture.[5]

Recent studies of the movement include firsthand interviews, such as Stefan Römer's film *Conceptual Paradise. There is a place for sophistication* (2005, 110 minutes),[6] based on interviews with international artists and art theorists of Conceptualism, and also reflecting upon the documentary as a genre. Among the curatorial and academic interest in Conceptual art, one particular tendency, the study of dealers and 'art enablers' of the period, emerges. One can mention Alexander Alberro's study of the curator Seth Siegelaub entitled *Conceptual Art and the Politics of Publicity*[7] and Stefan Urbaschek's research on the dealer Heiner Friedrich and the Dia Art Foundation.[8] I wrote an MPhil thesis on a curator of the period: *Harald n et les expositions d'art contemporain* (Harald Szeemann and the exhibitions of Contemporary art), a survey of thc new types of exhibitions and independent curatorial activities set up by Szeemann from the 1960s until 2000.[9]

Several doctoral theses on the the study of art dealers have recently been written and there are others currently being undertaken. Brigitte Kölle submitted a thesis on the dealer Konrad Fischer in 2005: *The art of exhibiting. Investigations on the work of the artist and art agent Konrad Lueg/Fischer (1939–1996).*[10] This analyses Fischer's role in establishing new ways to present and mediate contemporary art. It also tries to demonstrate the fact that Fischer's activities as an artist and as a dealer led to an 'art of exhibiting'.[11] Barbara Hess is currently researching a PhD on the formation of a new type of gallery for contemporary art in West Germany during the 1960s and early 1970s in the

Imagine Nation, The American Counterculture of the 1960s & '70s, Routledge, New York and London, 2002; Barry Miles, *Hippie*, Cassell Illustrated, London, 2003.

6 One can also mention the following publications: Moseley, *Conception, op. cit.*; Alexander Alberro and Patricia Norvell, *Recording Conceptual Art, Early Interviews with Barry, Huebler, Kaltenbach, LeWitt, Morris, Oppenheim, Siegelaub, Smithson, Weiner*, University of California Press, Berkeley, Los Angeles and London, 2001.

7 Alexander Alberro, *Conceptual Art and the Politics of Publicity*, The MIT Press, Cambridge, Mass. and London, England, 2003 (PhD, Northwestern University, Evanston, Illinois, 1996).

8 Stefan Urbaschek, *Dia Art Foundation, Institution und Sammlung 1974–1985*, Tectum Verlag, Marburg, 2003 (PhD, Humboldt University, Berlin, 2002).

9 Sophie Richard, *Harald Szeemann et les expositions d'art contemporain*, unpublished MPhil thesis (D.E.A.), Université de Paris I Panthéon-Sorbonne, Paris, 2000.

10 Brigitte Kölle, *Die Kunst des Ausstellen. Untersuchungen zum Werk des Künstlers und Kunstvermittlers Konrad Lueg/Fischer (1939–1996)*, PhD, University of Hildesheim, Hildesheim, 2005. [Editor's note: Now published as: Brigitte Kölle, *Okey Dokey Konrad Fischer*, 2007, Verlag der Buchhandlung Walther König, Cologne.]

11 This study does not focus on Konrad Fischer's business interests. However, as we will see in the present research, particularly in Chapter 5, the dealer was a fine strategist and an efficient art seller.

12 Barbara Hess, *Handeln für die Avantgarde. Die Herausbildung*

context of Minimal and Post-Minimal art.[12] At the University of Gent, Wanner De Clercq recently started work on a doctoral thesis on the MTL gallery.

While there are a number of studies dedicated to individual protagonists of the art world, a study of the formation of the international network of Conceptual art in Europe during the late 1960s and 1970s is lacking. Furthermore, the development of private and public collections at the time has never been analysed. There is a gap in knowledge regarding the support and dealing network that was being established for Conceptual art. This research aims to address this omission. Whilst a number of previous studies have looked at the aesthetic issues, this study looks at the art market and its background.[13]

In the late 1960s and early 1970s, artists such as Art & Language, Marcel Broodthaers, Joseph Kosuth, Douglas Huebler and Lawrence Weiner were concerned with definitions of what constitutes a work of art. These artists were challenging the accepted value of art objects through increasingly conceptualised artistic practices. For instance, Art & Language produced philosophical texts, Huebler presented maps and photographs as documents of performances, and Weiner gave instructions for works "to be realised or not". The rejection of the art object in favour of an emphasis on the conceptual process led to internal contradictions within the Conceptual art market.

Conceptualism, because of its dematerialisation, seemed to challenge the work's value as economic exchange. It suggested a hostile relationship to the market and the commodification of art. However, as early as 1973, Lucy Lippard expressed her disillusion with such contradictions:

> Hopes that 'conceptual art' would be able to avoid the general commercialization, the destructively 'progressive' approach of modernism were for the most part unfounded ... the major conceptualists are selling work for substantial sums here and in Europe; they are represented by (and still more unexpected – showing in) the world's most prestigious galleries. Clearly, whatever minor revolutions in communication have been achieved by the process of dematerializing the object ... art and artists in a capitalist society remain luxuries.[14]

Recently published theoretical discourses, especially Alexander Alberro's

neuer Produktionsformen und Funktionsweisen westdeutscher Galerien für zeitgenössische Kunst in den 60er und frühen 70er Jahren (Dealing for the Avant garde. The formation of new methods of production and of functioning by West German dealer galleries of contemporary art in the 1960s and early 1970s), PhD, University of Cologne, Cologne.

13 There currently seems to be a general interest in the art market, as recent exhibitions and conferences demonstrate: 'The Business of Art: Evidence from the Art Market' (Getty Research Institute, Getty Center, Los Angeles, 21 March–13 June 2004) and 'The London Art Market, 1870 to the Present' (Tate Britain, 6–7 October 2006).

14 Lucy Lippard (ed.), *Six Years: The Dematerialization of the Art Object from 1966 to 1972: a cross-reference book of information on some aesthetic boundaries: consisting of a bibliography into which are inserted a fragmented text, art works, documents, interviews, and symposia, arranged chronologically and focused on so-called conceptual art or information or idea art with mentions of such vaguely designated areas as minimal, anti-form, systems, earth, or process art, occurring in the Americas, Europe, England, Australia, and Asia (with occasional political overtones)*, University of California Press, Berkeley and Los Angeles, 1997 (2nd edition), p.263. First edition published in 1973.

15 Alberro, *Conceptual Art and the Politics of Publicity*, *op. cit.*

16 Lynda Morris, 'Introduction to the Conference: New Research into Conceptualism in Europe', in *New Research into Conceptualism in Europe*, Dispatch 114, Norwich Gallery, Norwich School of Art and Design, Norwich, 2005, unnumbered pages.

17 *Ibid.* Peter Osborne sees a difference between 'art-critical

study of Seth Siegelaub,[15] have underlined the paradoxical status of Conceptual art, which on one hand challenged the traditional frameworks of the art world, but on the other hand was dependent on marketing and advertising.

This research makes a distinction between the 'mode of production' and the 'mode of dissemination' of Conceptual art. The focus is on the infrastructure and the display of Conceptual works of art rather than the nature and the interpretation of objects. Thus the relationship between the work and the network is represented as integrated rather than confrontational.

Furthermore, there appear to be two major characteristics that emerge from recent academic studies and curatorial projects on Conceptualism: an American focus, and what might be called an 'idealist' focus. For several reasons, both are partial and problematic. This research attempts to redress this balance.

Lynda Morris argues that there is a difference between American and European accounts of Conceptual art, which is linked to the political and geographical context of the period.[16] In America, there was an overlap between Minimal and Conceptual art, but in Europe, the social unrest of the late 1960s and early 1970s meant that there were few shows of American Minimalism, particularly painting. Furthermore, America's neighbouring countries are Central and South America, whereas Western Europe's neighbours were behind the Iron Curtain. If Minimalist painting and South American artists 'are clearly represented then the account has an American emphasis'.[17]

Moreover, Conceptual art events that occurred in Europe have been left out of recent publications – another demonstration of their American emphasis. The recent Phaidon book, *Minimalism*, edited by James Meyer, does not mention the crucial *Minimal Art* exhibition organised at the Gemeentemuseum in The Hague in 1968.[18] Alberro's *Conceptual Art and the Politics of Publicity* does not consider Seth Siegelaub's important magazine exhibition in *Studio International*[19] (*July–August 1970*) or the *16 Place Vendôme* painting show that he set up with Michel Claura in Paris in 1973.[20]

There also seems to be a debatable broadening of the scope of Conceptual art resulting from a contemporary reading of art historical facts. In recent studies one notices the expansion of the geographical range into South America and Japan. This is the case, for instance, in the writings of Peter Osborne and

cultures of Europe and the US East coast, on the one hand, and the West coast, on the other'. His argument rests on the fact that shows such as *Global Conceptualism* (Queens Museum of Art, 1999) have been preoccupied with issues of classification, whereas exhibitions like *Reconsidering the Object of Art, 1965–1975* (Museum of Contemporary Art, Los Angeles, 1995) have favoured a more empiricist historiography. See: Osborne, *Conceptual Art*, *op. cit.*, p.48.

18 James Meyer (ed.), *Minimalism*, Phaidon, London, 2000. For a discussion of this show, see: Chapter 2.1.

19 Lynda Morris, *New Research into Conceptualism in Europe*, *op. cit.*

20 For an account of these exhibitions, see: Chapters 3.1. and 3.3.

21 See: Osborne, *Conceptual Art*, *op. cit.*; Alexander Alberro, 'Reconsidering conceptual art, 1966-1977', in Alberro and Stimson, *Conceptual Art: A Critical Anthology*, *op. cit.*; Alexander Alberro, 'A Media Art: Conceptualism in Latin America in the 1960s', in Newman and Bird, *Rewriting Conceptual Art*, *op. cit.*

22 *Global Conceptualism: Points of Origin, 1950s–1980s* (exh. cat.), Queens Museum of Art, New York, 1999.

23 The recent exhibition, *Open Systems: Rethinking Art c. 1970*, organised in 2005 at Tate Modern, London, further demonstrates a tendency to apply contemporary approaches and analyses to Conceptual art. See: Donna De Salvo (ed.), *Open Systems: Rethinking Art c. 1970*, Tate Publishing, London, 2005.

24 See, for example: Rorimer, *New Art in the 60s and 70s*, *op. cit.*, p.7. Michael Corris defends an Anglo-American scope of Conceptualism,

Alberro.[21] The exhibition *Global Conceptualism: Points of Origin, 1950s–1980s* organised in 1999 at the Queens Museum of Art in New York was particularly broad in focus.[22] Conceptual art practices in all five continents were broached, from Australia to South Korea to Eastern Europe. This approach gives an unprecedented international dimension to Conceptualism, and moves away from the manner in which the art movement was actually perceived in its first decade.[23]

The present study is based on the long-established notion that Conceptual art was first of all a Western European and American movement,[24] and that there was equality between European and American artists. But because European and US Conceptual artists first gained acceptance in European dealer galleries and museums, and because this study aims to discuss the original support and dealing network, it has a European focus. Although the events that took place in America are not completely absent from the study, they are viewed from the perspective of the European art world.[25]

The study discusses the original international network of Conceptual artists from its beginnings in the late 1960s to its commercial assimilation in the late 1970s. The starting point is 1967. This date corresponds to the first showings of Conceptual artworks in Europe, via exhibitions organised by Paul Maenz in Frankfurt and the opening of Konrad Fischer's gallery in Düsseldorf. The research ends in 1977, and thus constitutes a discussion of the first decade of Conceptualism. It focuses on three main aspects that led to the formation and evolution of the movement, namely dealer galleries, temporary exhibitions in exhibition spaces and museums, and the setting up of museum collections. These three stages functioned as stepping stones in the development of the Conceptual artists' careers.[26]

The term 'Conceptual art' is problematic because it has been used to group together a variety of sub-movements, such as Land art and Arte Povera. The use of 'Conceptual art' to designate a group of artists who started their careers in the mid-to-late 1960s had already become generally accepted by the early 1970s.[27] By then, critics had noted that what seemed to bring these artists together was a common belief in the importance of the idea over its physical realisation.[28] But, as Peter Osborne suggests, the 'established dominance of the term "conceptual art" is less the retrospective victory of one particular artistic faction over its rivals

although he recognises that 'recent work on the scope of so-called global conceptualism' has altered irrevocably our understanding of the movement. See: Michael Corris, 'An Invisible College in an Anglo-American World', in Corris, *Conceptual Art: Theory, Myth and Practice*, *op. cit.*, p.10.

25 At the beginning of this research project, I delimited the geographical focus of the study by adding 'Northern Europe' to the title. Possible confusion over whether or not this referred only to Scandinavia led me to change it to 'Europe'.

26 John Baldessari suggested that I should call my study 'The Dark Side of Conceptual Art'. John Baldessari in conversation with the author, Graz, 10 June 2006, manuscript notes.

27 See, for example, the following early publications: Klaus Honnef, *Concept art*, Phaidon, Cologne, 1971; Ursula Meyer, *Conceptual Art*, Dutton, New York, 1972. One can also mention the *Conceptual Art, Conceptual Aspects* show organised in 1970 at the New York Cultural Centre. There were, however, other terms that were being used at the time, such as 'Process Art', 'Anti-Art', 'ABC Art' and 'Non-Art'. The origin of the term is contested by several protagonists of the movement, such as Edward Kienholz and Joseph Kosuth. However, Sol LeWitt is generally accepted as being the first to use and define the term in his 'Paragraphs on Conceptual Art', first published in 1967. See: Sol LeWitt, 'Paragraphs on Conceptual Art', *Artforum*, vol.5, no.10, summer 1967, p.79–84. See also: Benjamin H.D. Buchloh, 'De l'esthétique d'administration à la critique institutionnelle (Aspects de l'art conceptuel, 1962–1969)', in Claude Gintz (ed.),

(as some complain) than the consequence of a deeper need for historical intelligibility.'[29] Indeed, it appears that the term has been retained mainly for practical reasons.

In this book, the term 'Conceptual art' is used as a label for the art developments that occurred in Europe in the late 1960s and 1970s. It covers artists who were part of the same group and who exhibited in the same dealer galleries and museums, but who were producing different kinds of works: for example, Joseph Kosuth (Conceptual art), Sol LeWitt (Minimal art), Richard Long (Land art) and Mario Merz (Arte Povera). The movement placed an emphasis on real experience as opposed to theory or electronically mediated and automatic experiences. In the late 1960s, Conceptual art was a form of protest but was not involved in everyday politics. However, the creation of an independent network of artists was already a political statement. Conceptualists rejected old values and were driven by a sense of the 'international' and the 'collective' in an idealist Marxist sense. Conceptual artists used the art world to express a set of principles different from those of the mainstream.

All the protagonists agree[30] on the fact that the international Conceptual network brought together a small group of people who subsequently became friends.[31] These include many different categories: artists, dealers, curators, museum directors, private collectors and art critics. These individuals all contributed to the development and official recognition of the movement. Although all those connected with the network were important, for the purposes of this study, boundaries had to be set in order to define its focus. It seemed that a dozen European and American Conceptual artists would constitute a reasonable sample of the network.[32] The most representative of those artists who had international careers and who exhibited in key exhibitions and dealer galleries were chosen. It was also important to select artists of different generations (Marcel Broodthaers was born in 1924, Richard Long in 1945). Another important factor was to select artists who came from different European countries and different American cities (Bruce Nauman from the West Coast, for example). In addition, a major consideration was that a wide range of media should be represented. Thus, to name but a few, the following types of work were included: writings and teaching (Art & Language), photographic works within

L'art conceptuel: une perspective (exh. cat.), Musée d'Art moderne de la Ville de Paris, Paris, 1989, p.25.

28 See, for instance: Honnef, *Concept Art*, *op. cit.*, p.30.

29 Osborne, *Conceptual Art*, *op. cit.*, p.17–18.

30 See, for instance: Annick and Anton Herbert in conversation with the author, Gent, 15 November 2004, audio-tape recording (Appendix 4.8); Klaus Honnef in conversation with the author, Bonn, 21 March 2005, audio-tape recording (Appendix 4.9); Rudi Fuchs in conversation with the author, Amsterdam, 25 April 2005, audio-tape recording (Appendix 4.6).

31 As an indication, Jan Dibbets's *'Project for Art & Project'* from 1969 lists 196 people. For a discussion of the piece, see Chapter 2.2.

32 In the end, 15 artists were selected: eight European artists: Art & Language, Marcel Broodthaers, Daniel Buren, Hanne Darboven, Jan Dibbets, Gilbert & George, Richard Long and Mario Merz, and seven American artists: Carl Andre, Douglas Huebler, Joseph Kosuth, Sol LeWitt, Bruce Nauman, Robert Ryman and Lawrence Weiner.

33 Dealer galleries: Art & Project (Amsterdam), Konrad Fischer (Düsseldorf), Heiner Friedrich (Munich), Nigel Greenwood (London), Françoise Lambert (Milan), Yvon Lambert (Paris), Lisson Gallery (London), MTL (Brussels), Paul Maenz (Cologne), Rolf Preisig (Basel), Ileana Sonnabend (Paris), Gian Enzo Sperone (Turin), Jack Wendler (London) and Wide White Space (Antwerp). Temporary exhibition spaces and museums: Städtisches Museum (Mönchengladbach), Kunsthalle (Düsseldorf), Kunstverein (Münster), Ludwig Museum (Cologne), Kunstmuseum (Basel), Kunstmuseum (Lucerne), Stedelijk

conceptual frameworks (Jan Dibbets, Douglas Huebler), paintings within conceptual frameworks (Daniel Buren, Robert Ryman), sculptures (Carl Andre, Sol LeWitt) and videos (Bruce Nauman).

The selection of dealer galleries, temporary exhibition spaces and museums was straightforward as the Conceptual artists all exhibited in the same places and group exhibitions during the late 1960s and 1970s. Fourteen European dealer galleries and 11 public institutions were chosen.[33] Some were of particular significance because they had never been studied before; these included Nigel Greenwood, Françoise Lambert, Yvon Lambert, MTL, Rolf Preisig and Jack Wendler.

The choice of private collectors and critics followed on from the choice of artists and galleries; key Conceptual artists' works were collected by the same people, and articles and books were written by the same critics. The European Conceptual art collectors have never previously been discussed in detail, nor their contribution to the network studied. To this core group one has to add various satellite locations and settings where relevant. Identifying this central group of people and places also enabled me to determine the countries that were of particular significance to the network – namely, Germany, Belgium, the Netherlands, England, France, Switzerland and Italy.[34]

European countries did not all have the same status in the network of Conceptual art. Germany, for instance, was a country of artists and dealer galleries; Switzerland was a country of museums and private collectors; Belgium was a country of collectors and dealer galleries. Moreover, some countries established closer relationships with US artists than others. Germany, as the centre of the dealing structure, was very close to US artists. Weiner, an American artist, lived in Amsterdam. US artists felt at home in the UK due to the English language. Importantly, much of the knowledge that American artists had of Europe was based on the experience gained by US soldiers after the Second World War. GIs stationed in Europe, including Elvis Presley in Germany, were key to the ideas of Capitalist Realism.

The study places itself within the radical documentary tradition used by Conceptual artists in the late 1960s and 1970s to investigate the underlying structures of society.[35] Thus the form of the book is appropriate to its content.[36]

Museum (Amsterdam), Stedelijk Van Abbemuseum (Eindhoven), Palais des Beaux-Arts (Brussels), Museum of Modern Art (Oxford), Tate Gallery (London).

34 As we will see, this also determined the countries to which I chose to travel to undertake original research.

35 The study deals with artists whose works reveals underlying structures of contemporary capitalist societies. For instance, in general terms, Hanne Darboven's obsessive writing related to increasing bureaucratisation; Gilbert & George worked on the stylistics of England, Art & Language used language and philosophy as a pattern to discuss the look of language and its use in art, and Douglas Huebler documented his works with photographs, maps and lists.

36 It was Catherine Moseley's research on Conceptual art documents that led me to contact the Norwich School of Art and Design to undertake a research degree with her supervisor Lynda Morris, who has also worked on documentary traditions from 1930 to 1950 as well as Conceptual art. See: Moseley, *Conception*, *op. cit.* See also: Lynda Morris, *The Story of the Artists' International Association 1933–1953*, Modern Art Oxford, Oxford, 1983.

37 Lippard, *Six Years*, *op. cit.*

38 I was able to double-check and cross-reference the data myself to ensure consistency and comprehensiveness.

39 See: Appendices 1.1 and 1.2. The difference between group exhibitions and solo shows is important. The idea of the development of Conceptual artists' careers is based on the following progression:

Its conceptual framework follows a documentary and factual structure that provides accurate information on the movement. This way of working had already been adopted in the early 1970s by the art critic Lucy Lippard for her book *Six Years*, which documented the 'dematerialisation of the art object' from 1966 to 1972.[37] This publication was a compendium of Lippard's files; in this way she tried to find an analogy between her documentation on the art world and its presentation.

The research process was carried out by first developing a set of databases. These resulted from the aim to uncover and document the idea of a stepladder of Conceptual artists' careers, that developed from dealer galleries to mixed temporary exhibitions, to museum solo shows and on to museum purchases. These exhaustive databases constitute an unprecedented source of information on the formation of a support and dealing network around Conceptual artists in Europe and thus constitute a valuable and reliable tool.[38]

A first database on artists' shows in dealer galleries and a second one on exhibitions in public institutions were assembled from documentation on individual artists. These records enabled me to see clearly how the artists moved around, how dealers collaborated with one another and how the artists' careers developed internationally from the late 1960s to the late 1970s.[39] In order to clarify the latter, a supplementary database in the form of a chronological list of shows was set up for every artist.[40]

A second set of databases was developed for museum purchases.[41] The first in this set records the Conceptual works acquired by European institutions during the period studied. This enabled me to determine the collecting procedure of each museum and also to study the underlying strategies of the dealers. A supplementary database on the prices of the works allowed me to establish the value of the pieces in comparison with other goods during a period of exchange rate turbulence, and as percentages of museums' purchasing budgets.

During the research, it emerged that the role of private collectors was more important than originally thought. Because most collections remain in the private domain, the database was confined to those private collections that entered public museum collections.[42] This also enabled me to compare the development of private and public collections at the time.

solo shows in dealer galleries, group shows in temporary exhibition spaces, solo shows in temporary exhibition spaces, group shows in museums, and finally, solo shows in museums.

40 See: Appendix 1.3.

41 See: Appendix 1.6 and 1.7. These databases were difficult to establish because most museums conceal concrete information on the provenance of the artworks in their permanent collections. Negotiations and perseverance finally enabled me to obtain the information I needed in order to compile the records on museum purchases.

42 See: Appendix 1.4 and 1.5.

43 My knowledge of French, German, English and to some extent Dutch enabled me to carry out original research in a variety of countries. Research in Germany was completed thanks to a research grant from the DAAD (Deutscher Akademischer Austauchdienst), which I was awarded in 2004. Trips to France, Belgium and the Netherlands were financed in part by the Norwich School of Art and Design.

44 The restricted access to the archives of most dealer galleries led me to put much emphasis on Konrad Fischer because I had open access to the archive of his gallery. As my research on museum purchases confirmed his leading role and importance, this emphasis was largely justified. Some archives, such as that of Art & Project (Netherlands Institute for Art History) and Nigel Greenwood (Tate Library and Archive), will only become available to researchers in the coming years.

45 For example, the Getty Research Institute in Los Angeles holds

The databases constitute a concrete structure and an architectural framework that I was able to use as a basis for carrying out further research on primary sources. Factual research in documentary archives kept in Europe constituted the next step of the investigation.[43] I was able to get access to the archives of many private and public institutions considered in the study. These included galleries such as Konrad Fischer, MTL and Wide White Space, as well as numerous museums: Städtisches Museum, Mönchengladbach; Kunstverein Münster; Museum Ludwig, Cologne; Kunsthalle Düsseldorf; Kunstmuseum Basel; Stedelijk Museum, Amsterdam and Tate Gallery, London.[44] For financial and practical reasons, I was unable to travel to research US archives.[45]

The knowledge I gained from this fieldwork allowed me to enter into revealing discussions with 28 important protagonists of the movement.[46] The resulting interviews with artists, dealers, curators, museum directors, private collectors and critics were carried out between 2003 and 2006.[47] Regrettably, two dealers who were central figures in the network, Konrad Fischer (1939–96), and Fernand Spillemaeckers (1938–78) from Galerie MTL, were no longer alive when this research was carried out.[48]

The next stage of the research process was to compare and analyse my own data with information from contemporary sources. Looking chronologically through art magazines of the period gave me a sense of the development of the movement, especially via advertisements and articles on mixed and solo shows.[49] Books and exhibition catalogues of the late 1960s and 1970s were also very useful.[50]

Contemporary literature on Conceptualism was then used. While the quantity and range of publications were helpful in getting a grasp of the movement and in locating the 'gaps' in knowledge, the amount of existing literature on the support and dealing network is relatively small.[51] The publications that come the closest to my own approach are those that concentrate on Conceptual art in a circumscribed geographical area, such as the Netherlands and Belgium,[52] or America and England,[53] and not only describe artists' works, but also consider the reception and promotion of Conceptualism in these countries. This is a further justification of the value of undertaking research about networks surrounding art movements rather than the art itself.

the archives of the Paul Maenz Gallery, Cologne, and of the Italian private collector Giuseppe Panza.

46 Sixteen discussions are reproduced as Appendix 4.

47 See the 'References' section for a full list of interviews undertaken.

48 Fernand Spillemaeckers died in 1978 and Konrad Fischer died in 1996.

49 *Artforum*, *Avalanche*, *Data*, *Flash Art* and *Studio International* were important sources.

50 Research assistance funding awarded by the Henry Moore Institute allowed me to spend two weeks in 2004 in Leeds, researching in their extensive library. The National Art Library, the Tate Library (both in London) and the Kunst- und Museumsbibliothek der Stadt Köln (Cologne) were also important sources.

51 Examples of the publications on dealer galleries during the period studied include: Gerd De Vries (ed.), *Paul Maenz Köln 1970–1980–1990, Eine Avant-garde Galerie und die Kunst unserer Zeit, An Avant-garde Gallery and the Art of our Time*, DuMont Buchverlag, Cologne, 1991; Yves Aupetitallot (dir.), *Wide White Space, Hinter dem Museum, 1966–1976, Behind the Museum* (exh. cat.), Palais des Beaux-Arts, Brussels; Richter Verlag, Düsseldorf, 1994; Anna Minola, Maria Cristina Mundici, Francesco Poli and Maria Teresa Roberto (eds), *Gian Enzo Sperone, Torino Roma New York, 35 anni di mostre tra Europa e America* (2 vols.), Hopefulmoster editore, Turin, 2000.

52 Héman, Poot and Visser, *Conceptual Art in the Netherlands and Belgium, 1965–1975*, *op. cit.* One can also mention the recent un-

The catalogue of the exhibition *Conceptual Art in the Netherlands and Belgium, 1965–1975*, which was held in 2000 at the Stedelijk Museum in Amsterdam, can also be compared with my own way of structuring this document.[54] It focuses on a given number of artists, and documents chronologically important publications, exhibitions and events that took place between the mid-1960s and the mid-1970s.[55] The publication also gives a chronological list of artists' solo shows in Dutch and Belgian private and public institutions.[56]

Other books provided examples of investigations of networks and art markets in connection with different movements, such as late nineteenth- and early twentieth-century art in France.[57] Nicholas Serota's book *Experience or Interpretation: The Dilemma of Museums of Modern Art* is an insightful study into the changing relationship between galleries and artists in the twentieth-century modern art museum.[58]

My methodology (databases, primary sources, first-hand interviews, secondary sources) enabled me to isolate and link all the facts in order to develop the research and to constitute my conceptual framework. These models also helped me to portray relationships between theories. The study is mostly based on inductive research, but occasionally deductive approaches were used. Thus it constitutes a socio-historical study from which conceptual conclusions can be drawn. The investigation could have been developed further. First of all, more Conceptual artists could have been interviewed, but geographical distances and time constraints did not allow this.[59] Secondly, additional research into dealer gallery archives would have been useful for gaining a broader perspective on the dealing network. The private nature of most of these archives did not permit these supplementary investigations. These two points, however, demonstrate the potential for future investigations in this area.

To summarise, this research project is a unique study that gives fresh insight into a new generation of young dealers who developed original working methods appropriate to the new kinds of works being produced by young artists. It also shows how these innovative working methods were later institutionalised as they were taken up by museum curators and directors. Moreover, it highlights the great number of private and public collections of Conceptual art put together at the time. As an original and unprecedented study of an unconventional and

published PhD by Paula Feldman, *Made to Order: American Minimal Art in the Netherlands, Late 1960s to Early 1970s*, Courtauld Institute of Art, London, 2005.

53 Thomas Dreher, *Konzeptuelle Kunst in Amerika und England zwischen 1963 und 1976*, Peter Lang, Europäische Hochschulschriften, Kunstgeschichte, Frankfurt/Main, Bern, New York, Paris, 1992 (PhD, University of Heidelberg, Heidelberg, 1988).

54 Héman, Poot and Visser, *Conceptual Art in the Netherlands and Belgium, 1965–1975, op. cit.*

55 The show was subtitled 'artists, collectors, galleries, documents, exhibitions, events'.

56 Héman, Poot and Visser, *Conceptual art in the Netherlands and Belgium, 1965–1975, op. cit.*, p.100–105.

57 See: Harrison C. White and Cynthia A. White, *Canvases and Careers: Institutional Change in the French Painting World*, J. Wiley & Sons, New York, 1965; Malcolm Gee, *Dealers, Critics and Collectors of Modern Painting: aspects of the Parisian art market between 1910 and 1930*, Garland Pub., New York, 1981.

58 Nicholas Serota, *Experience or Interpretation: The Dilemma of Museums of Modern Art*, Thames & Hudson, London, 1996.

59 For example, correspondence with Long about a possible interview ended in a missed meeting due to agenda constraints. Although I met Darboven during my stay in Düsseldorf in April 2005, her fragile health prevented a real discussion from taking place.

alternative microcosm, this research brings significant supplementary understanding and new insight to the history of Conceptual art. Many of the key dealers and artists in the Conceptual network have remained active throughout the 1980s and 1990s to the present day. Furthermore, the new dealing and curating methods, strategies and techniques developed in the late 1960s and 1970s are still used in the contemporary art world. The model of investigation adopted here, including the setting up of databases, could therefore be applied to subsequent art movements and later forms of networking in contemporary art, while the Appendices can serve as an encyclopaedic tool for further research on Conceptualism and for curatorial studies in general.

Part 1: Support structure

Historical background

In order to look at the beginnings of the Conceptual network in the late 1960s in Europe, the background of American art after the Second World War and its links with Europe should be considered. US art in the postwar period had a major influence on European dealer galleries and museums.

The 1950s

During the 1950s, recovering from the devastation of the war, Europe looked towards America, which seemed culturally more advanced. By the end of the 1940s and beginning of the 1950s, Abstract Expressionism was confirmed as the major new art movement, with New York as the centre of the art world. With the support of critics, dealers and museums, Abstract Expressionist painters became the heirs of the European avant-garde that the United States had welcomed during the war.[1] The rapid international success enjoyed by the Abstract Expressionists was also due to the postwar strategy of promoting the American cultural model in Europe. With the escalation of the Cold War, art became a way for the US to promote the cultural 'freedom' of the West, in opposition to the 'controlled' Socialist Realism of the East. It was this idea of freedom which Americans promoted in postwar Europe.

The American Authorities, through bodies such as the International Council of the Museum of Modern Art in New York, organised travelling exhibitions of American artists in Europe, with the ideological motivation of counteracting the influence of the Eastern bloc in the arts.[2] In 1958, for example, the travelling exhibition of Abstract Expressionism, *Die Neue Amerikanische Malerei* (The New American Painting), was shown at the Kunsthalle in Basel.[3] The involvement of

1 Among European artists living in exile in New York were Max Ernst, Marc Chagall, Fernand Léger, André Breton, Piet Mondrian, Jacques Lipchitz and Marcel Duchamp.

2 The International Council of the Museum of Modern Art, a non-profit membership corporation of art collectors, patrons and community leaders, was founded in 1953 to give the museum's international programme both national and international cooperation and support. See: Helen M. Franc, 'The early years of the International Program and Council', in *The Museum of Modern Art in the Mid Century, At Home and Abroad*, MoMA, New York, 1994, pp.109–149.

3 The Arts Council of Great Britain organised similar exhibitions at the Tate Gallery.

MOMA in American foreign policy at the time has been highlighted by Eva Cockcroft.[4] During the early 1950s, MOMA even purchased the American pavilion at the Venice Biennale, taking sole responsibility for the shows from 1954 to 1962, and thus supporting Abstract Expressionism.

American art was able to take the lead after the war because of the strength of the US art market. Some very influential galleries had opened in New York during the war, including Peggy Guggenheim's Art of This Century (1942). It acted as a meeting place for young American and exiled European artists, and became a platform for the international avant-garde. In the aftermath of the war, many dealer galleries were launched, including Samuel Kootz (1945), Charles Egan (1946) and Betty Parsons (1946). Parsons took over most of the artists shown by Peggy Guggenheim when the latter left for Europe. These included Barnett Newman, Jackson Pollock, Mark Rothko and Ad Reinhardt. One can also mention Sydney Janis (1949), Tibor de Nagy (1950), André Emmerich and Leo Castelli (both in 1957). In the postwar period, there were about 150 art galleries in New York, whereas there were only 40 when the war broke out.[5] On the West Coast, Virginia Dwan opened a gallery in Los Angeles in 1959, supporting artists such as Robert Goodnough and Harry Nadler.

The power of American art and its market did not prevent developments in the European art world. On the contrary, the high cost of transporting large canvases of Abstract Expressionism from America to Europe encouraged dealers to look for a new generation of European artists. Thus, a number of dealer galleries that largely focused on modern European artists opened in Europe. In Paris, Denise René launched her gallery in 1945 and made her reputation by supporting kinetic artists (Victor Vasarely, Jesús-Rafael Soto). A few years later, in 1956, the flamboyant Iris Clert launched her gallery space, promoting Yves Klein, Arman and Jean Tinguely. Clert became known for letting the artists use the gallery space for experimental shows, such as Klein's *Le Vide* (The Void) in 1958 and Arman's *Le Plein* (The Full) in 1960.[6]

In London, the Marlborough Gallery dominated the art scene in the late 1940s and 1950s. It was launched in 1946 by Frank Lloyd and Harry Fischer; the latter had immigrated to England from Vienna. Two years later, they were joined by David Somerset. During the 1950s, the gallery hosted numerous shows of

4 For an extensive discussion of the links between MOMA, the CIA and American Cold War politics, see: Eva Cockcroft, 'Abstract Expressionism, Weapon of the Cold War', *Artforum*, June 1974, pp.38–41.

5 Serge Guilbaut, *Comment New York vola l'idée d'art moderne*, J. Chambon, Nîmes, 1989, p.120.

6 At that time, the American art world began to show interest in contemporary French artists. In Los Angeles, Virginia Dwan showed Yves Klein (1961), Arman (1962), Niki de Saint-Phalle (1964) and Martial Raysse (1964).

French Impressionists (Edgar Degas, Auguste Renoir). In the 1960s, Marlborough focused on modern British artists (Henry Moore, Barbara Hepworth) and opened up to young contemporary artists such as Francis Bacon and Jackson Pollock. It was one of the few European galleries that could afford to import large-scale paintings from the United States. In the 1960s, the wealth of the enterprise allowed for the establishment of Marlborough Graphics and a branch in New York.

In Switzerland, the postwar period saw the opening of a few galleries oriented towards classic modern art (Pablo Picasso, Alberto Giacometti). These included Ernst and Hildy Beyeler in Basel (1951), Eberhard Kornfeld in Bern (1951), and later Jan Krugier in Geneva (1962). In Italy, one can mention the Apollinaire Gallery, Milan, run by Guido Le Noci from 1957. He focused his gallery programme on Nouveau Réalisme, exhibiting Yves Klein (1957) and Christo (1963).

In the 1950s, several dealer galleries were launched in Germany. Otto van de Loo opened a space in 1957 in Munich, specialising in Cobra, L'Art Informel and Situationism. Alfred Schmela (born 1918) was a committed avant-garde dealer and an established figure in Düsseldorf since 1957.[7] In Germany, he was the first to exhibit Klein (1957), Antoni Tàpies (1957), Otto Piene (1959), Günther Uecker (1961), Kenneth Noland (1962) and Robert Morris (1964). He also worked with young artists living and working in the Rhine area. Thus he gave the first solo shows to Konrad Fischer-Lueg, Gerhard Richter (both in 1964) and Joseph Beuys (1965). Schmela was involved in the Fluxus movement, a small international network of artists, composers and designers who developed performative and literary forms of art. Beuys (1921–86) can be seen as a key link between Fluxus and Conceptualism.

The 1960s

In the 1960s, economic growth facilitated the development of the art world and numerous dealer galleries opened. Early in the decade, Pop art took the lead as the most avant-garde art movement. Leo Castelli (1910–99) was seen as the one dealer in New York defining the movement, being the main dealer of Pop artists such as Robert Rauschenberg, Roy Lichtenstein, Jasper Johns and Andy Warhol.[8] There were number of collectors of Pop art in the United States, notably the

7 For an overview of the exhibitions organised by Alfred Schmela, see: Karl Ruhrberg (ed.), *Alfred Schmela, Galerist, Wegbereiter der Avantgarde,* Vienna and Cologne, 1996, pp.24–83.

8 For a comprehensive overview of exhibitions organised by Leo Castelli, see: 'Exhibition Chronology', in Barbara Jakobson (Ed.), *Leo Castelli, gentle snapshots: An exhibition in honour of the twenty-fifth anniversary of Leo Castelli Gallery* (exh. cat.), Galerie Bruno Bischofberger, Zurich, 1982, pp.63–76.

insurance broker Leon Kraushar, the art-book publisher Harry Abrams and the yellow cab fleet owner Robert Scull. Additionally, prominent European collectors such as Peter Ludwig (born 1925) and Giuseppe Panza (born 1923) purchased Pop art from Castelli in the early 1960s. Perhaps the stardom of the Pop artists, as well as the young and triumphant image of the movement, flattered the individualist egos of these successful businessmen.[9]

The economic boom in the 1960s engendered a growing market for new art. From 1960 to 1965, the number of dealer galleries in New York increased from about 150 to 250.[10] In New York, Marilyn Fischbach (1960), Richard Bellamy (1961) and Klaus Kertess (Bykert Gallery, 1966) opened galleries around this time. In Los Angeles, there were the galleries of Douglas Chrismas (ACE Gallery, 1961) and Nicholas (Nicky) Wilder (1965), son of the film director Billy Wilder.

During the 1960s, Abstract Expressionism and Pop art made their way into European dealer galleries. In 1962, Ileana Sonnabend (born 1914), Castelli's ex-wife, opened a gallery in Paris (Quai des Grands-Augustins) with her second husband Michael Sonnabend (born 1900). Castelli and Sonnabend established transatlantic business links. She exhibited American Pop artists in Paris and promoted their careers all over Europe.[11] She also showed the work of contemporary European artists, such as Konrad Klapheck (1965).

In West Germany, by the mid-1960s, numerous dealer galleries focusing on contemporary European and American artists had been set up. Rudolf Zwirner (born 1933), the Secretary of Documenta 2 in 1959, launched his space in 1960 in Essen (Ruhr area), showing artists such as Morris Louis, Kenneth Noland and George Segal. In 1963, Michael Werner, together with Benjamin Katz, launched the Werner & Katz Galerie in Berlin with the first solo show of Georg Baselitz. In 1964, he opened his own space, giving first shows to the German artists A.R. Penck and Markus Lüpertz (both 1968).

Heiner Friedrich (born 1938) and Franz Dahlem (born 1944) launched a shared gallery in Munich in July 1963 with an exhibition of the German painter Peter Schubert. In 1964, they first presented the work of artists such as Richter and Cy Twombly. A year later, in 1965, Dahlem left the collaboration to open his own gallery in Darmstadt, where he became the adviser of the private collector Karl Ströher.[12] Friedrich established himself as an important dealer by showing

9 Max Kozloff, 'American Painting during the Cold War', *Artforum*, May 1973, pp.52–53.

10 Steven Naifeh, *Culture Making: Money, Success, and the New York Art World*, Princeton University Press, Princeton, 1976, p.96.

11 In 1964, Leo Castelli published an advertisement in *Art International* showing a map of Europe with little flags indicating shows of his artists all over the continent. See: *Art International*, July 1964. Ileana Sonnabend set up the exhibition 'The Popular Image' at the Institute of Contemporary Arts in London in October–November 1963. It included works by Pop artists such as Rauschenberg, Johns, Dine and Lichtenstein.

12 'Franz Dahlem', *Kunstforum International*, vol.104, November–December 1989, pp.243–244. For a discussion of Karl Ströher's collection, see Chapter 4.1.

young German artists such as Blinky Palermo (1966), Franz Erhard Walther and Konrad Fischer-Lueg (both in 1967).[13]

Rolf Ricke launched his gallery in 1964 in Kassel, a city close to the East-West border of Germany that hosted the Documenta exhibitions.[14] He first showed young unknown European artists, before he began dealing with New York galleries. During a trip to America, he got to know the Bianchini Gallery and the Green Gallery.[15] Consequently, Ricke organised exhibitions of Pop artists such as Allan d'Arcangelo and Jim Dine (both 1967). He gave American artists Richard Serra, Keith Sonnier and Peter Young solo shows in Germany, before they were known in New York.

René Block (born 1942) opened a dealer gallery in September 1964 in Berlin with a show entitled *Neodada, Pop, Decollage, Kapitalistischer Realismus*. This first exhibition included works by Richter, Sigmar Polke, Fischer-Lueg and Wolf Vostell. Through contacts with Vostell and Beuys, Block became a promoter of Fluxus and Happenings. The early performances at the gallery included actions by Stanley Brouwn and Beuys (October and December 1964 respectively).[16] He continued to promote Capitalist Realism, and organised a solo show of paintings by Fischer-Lueg in 1966, *Waschlappen und Handtücher* (Face Cloths and Towels).[17]

Great Britain also developed its art market in the early 1960s. The Robert Fraser Gallery (1962, Duke Street) and Kasmin Ltd. (1963, New Bond Street) contributed to the 'Swinging Sixties' London art scene. Fraser was close to the rich and famous, especially the Rolling Stones and the Beatles. Fraser (1937–86) showed European and American contemporary artists, including Peter Blake and Bridget Riley, Andy Warhol and Jim Dine. John Kasmin (born 1934) supported British artists such as David Hockney, Robyn Denny and Anthony Caro, and US artists like Kenneth Noland and Jules Olitski.

At the same time, the abstract painter and historian of Cubism, John Golding, launched the Axiom Gallery in London to promote British abstract painters. From about 1965, it was run and managed by one of his students, Nigel Greenwood (1941–2004).[18] During the 1960s, the gallery hosted shows of artists such as John McLean, John Walker and Malcolm Carder.

Another notable gallery to emerge at this time was the Ad Libitum Gallery

13 The archive of the Galerie Heiner Friedrich is closed to the public. Some documents, donated by the dealer's ex-wife Six Friedrich in 1996–97, are kept by the Zentralarchiv des internationalen Kunsthandel, Cologne (File A47). For a comprehensive outline of exhibitions organised by Heiner Friedrich, see: Urbaschek, *Dia Art Foundation*, *op. cit.*

14 The Documenta exhibition series, which took place every four years, was launched in 1955 by the art professor and designer Arnold Bode. The first Documenta focused on art since 1945. Since 1972, the exhibition has been held every five years.

15 Phyllis Tuchman, 'American Art in Germany, The History of a Phenomenon', *Artforum*, November 1970, pp.61–68.

16 'René Block', *Kunstforum International*, vol.104, November–December 1989, pp.256–257.

17 See: Thomas Kellein (ed.), *Ich nenne mich als Maler Konrad Lueg* (exh. cat.), Kunsthalle, Bielefeld, 1999, p.176.

18 Judy Greenwood in an e-mail to the author, 22 February 2006. See also: Nicholas Serota, 'Nigel Greenwood, Influential gallerist who helped shape contemporary British art', *The Guardian*, 21 April 2004.

in Antwerp (1960), owned by Jacqueline Trouillard-Reydams[19] and showing Nouveau Réaliste artists (François Dufrêne, Raymond Hains) and the Zéro Group (Uecker, Piene). There were also Galerie Bruno Bischofberger in Zurich in 1963, Galerie Rijke Swart in Amsterdam in 1964 and Lucio Amelio's Modern Art Agency in Naples in 1965.

In the mid-1960s, the European art world benefited from further developments. For instance, the London-based art magazine *The Studio* became *Studio International* in 1964. The addition of the word 'international' was significant since it characterised Peter Townsend's (1919–2006) editorship from 1965 to 1975.[20] This also reflected the way in which the European art world was developing. Townsend, who had spent a decade in China (1940 to early 1950s), reinvigorated the publication. He found new contributors and assistant editors. He also favoured foreign reports and caught the voices of a diverse art community. Townsend turned *Studio International* into one of the most important contemporary art magazines in Europe.[21] Another influential magazine, *Art and Artists*, was launched by the critic and curator Mario Amaya (Andy Warhol's one-time partner) in London in 1966.

In 1967, the first Conceptual art events in Europe took place. A chronological discussion of the setting up of the network of Conceptual artists will clearly show the connection between dealer galleries, temporary exhibition spaces, museums and art magazines.

19 During the 1960s, Flanders, and particularly Antwerp, was a prosperous area thanks to the flourishing diamond business. Walloonia's mining industries, on the other hand, were slowly declining. Moreover, in Belgium, the 1960s were dominated by national struggles between the Flemish and the Walloons. A linguistic border had been set up in 1962, along with the partition devised by the Ministry of Education and Cultural Affairs.

20 Jo Melvin is currently researching towards a PhD on *Studio International* at University College London: *Studio International Magazine: Peter Townsend's Editorial Papers 1965–1975*.

21 See: Tim Hilton, 'Peter Townsend, he survived China's revolution to start his own as an arts editor in Bloomsbury', *The Guardian*, 26 July 2006. See also: 'Obituary, Peter Townsend 1919–2006', *Art Monthly*, no.299, September 2006, pp.14–16.

Chapter 1

The beginnings of the network of Conceptual artists: 1967 and earlier

1.1 Seeds of the network: 1967

Paul Maenz's inaugural exhibitions in Germany

In Europe, the key event that first presented Conceptual artworks to a general audience was the exhibition *Serielle Formationen* (Serial Formations) organised by Paul Maenz and Peter Roehr in Frankfurt in May–June 1967.[22] Maenz (born 1939) worked in advertising for the American company Young & Rubicam. As the company's art director in New York from 1965–67, he got to know people such as Willoughby Sharp, with whom he founded the art information periodical *Kineticism Press*.[23]

In 1966, the *Primary Structures* exhibition organised at the Jewish Museum by Kynaston McShine (born 1935), curator of Painting and Sculpture,[24] and the *10* show at the Dwan Gallery, New York, had helped Maenz discover Minimal art.[25] Subsequently, he became friends with Minimal artists such as Carl Andre, Sol LeWitt and Agnes Martin.[26] On his return to Germany, he and his friend the artist Peter Roehr (1944–68) decided to exhibit these artists and to explore the diversity of serial art production, a subject that Roehr explored in his own practice.

Serielle Formationen was organised in the studio gallery of the University of Frankfurt. It included 62 works by established artists such as Serra and Vasarely, alongside pieces by young artists like Charlotte Posenenske, Markus Raetz and Fischer-Lueg. Above all, the show presented for the first time in Germany works by American artists such as Andre, LeWitt, Martin and Donald Judd. It was also the first time that the work of the young Dutch artist Jan Dibbets was exhibited

22 *Serielle Formationen*, Studio Galerie, Frankfurt/Main, 22 May–30 June 1967. Artists: Andre, Arman, Bayrle, Bladen, Breder, Castellani, Christo, Dibbets, Fastnacht, Fiebig, Flavin, Girke, Goepfert, Gonschior, Haacke, Henderikse, Hilgemann, Höke, Judd, Kolář, Kusama, Leblanc, Lenk, LeWitt, Fischer-Lueg, Luther, Manzoni, Martin, Mavignier, Peeters, Poons, Posenenske, Raetz, Riley, Roehr, Rot, Schlenker, Schmidt, Schoonhoven, Staudt, Steiner, Stella, Talman, Uecker, Vasarely, De Vries, Warhol and the Gruppe X. See: Peter Roehr and Paul Maenz (eds), *Serielle Formationen* (exh. cat.), Studio Galerie, Studentenschaft der Johann Wolfgang Goethe Universität, Frankfurt/Main, 1967.

23 *Kineticism Press* would evolve into the art magazine *Avalanche*, which Sharp founded with Liza Béar in 1970. Sharp later became a video artist. He was married briefly to Renate Sharp, who was Jürgen Harten's assistant at the Kunsthalle Düsseldorf from 1969.

24 *Primary Structures: younger American and British sculptors*, Jewish Museum, New York, 27 April–12 June 1966. Artists: Andre, Annesley, Artschwager, Bell, Bladen, Bolus, Caro, DeLap, De Maria, Doyle, Flavin, Forakis, Frazier, Gerowitz, Gorski, Gray, Grosvenor, Hall, Huebler, Judd, Kelly, King, Kipp, Laing, LeWitt, McCracken, Matkovic, Morris, Myers, Phillips, Pinchbeck, Romano, Scott, Smith, Smithson, Todd, Truitt, Tucker, Van Buren, Von Schlegell, Witkin and Woodham.

25 *10*, Dwan Gallery, New York, 4–29 October 1966. Artists: LeWitt, Baer, Reinhardt, Smithson, Andre, Martin, Flavin, Morris, Steiner and Judd. See: Meyer, *Minimalism*, *op. cit.*, pp.76–79. In 1965, Virginia

in Germany (*Demontabele Multiples*; Demountable Multiples, 1967).[27] Andre was represented by a small drawing, *Words* (1967) and LeWitt by an early black wooden structure, *First Modular Cube* (1965), which Maenz had bought in the artist's New York studio in 1966.[28]

In September 1967, Maenz organised another show that was essential to the beginnings of Conceptual art in Europe. The performance-exhibition *Dies alles Herzchen wird einmal dir gehören, 19:45–21:55, September 9th, 1967, Frankfurt, Germany* (Someday, Sweetheart, All this Will be Yours)[29] was organised in Niederursel, outside Frankfurt, in the former stables of the Galerie Dorothea Loehr.[30] It presented ephemeral works by eight young European artists: Dibbets, Fischer-Lueg, Posenenske, Roehr, Barry Flanagan, Bernhard Höke, John Johnson and Richard Long.

The show included young British artists unknown in Germany. The contact with and suggestion to include these artists was made by Dibbets. In 1967, he had been awarded a British Council grant to study at St Martin's School of Art in London. There he got to know Long and Flanagan, and also George Pasmore (later of Gilbert & George). They could not come over for the show and therefore their work was realised according to instructions they had sent. For instance, Long's piece consisted of marking out the shape of an exhibition room with loosely touching pieces of wood. The work, *Sculpture corresponding to another one in England*, was repeated outdoors in Bristol.[31]

The First Cologne Kunstmarkt

A few days later, on 12 September 1967, the first Kunstmarkt (Art Fair) was held in Cologne.[32] The idea of organising a fair to centralise and promote the art market in Germany was initiated in 1966 by Hein Stünke (Galerie Der Spiegel, Cologne) and Rudolf Zwirner (Cologne).[33] Their intention was twofold: to promote the German art market internationally, specifically young artists, without being dependent on imports from foreign galleries, and to interest a broad audience in contemporary art through the programmes of avant-garde galleries.[34] The Verein Progressiver Deutscher Kunsthändler (VPDK, Organisation of Progressive German Art Dealers) was founded by 18 German dealers, including René Block (Berlin), Alfred Schmela (Düsseldorf) and Rolf Ricke

Dwan had opened a second gallery in New York with an exhibition of Edward Kienholz.

26 'Paul Maenz', *Kunstforum International*, vol.104, November–December 1989, p.283. See also: Paul Maenz, 'Before 1970', in *Paul Maenz Köln 1970–1975*, Paul Maenz, Cologne, 1975, pp.11–12.

27 Roehr and Maenz met Jan Dibbets while hitchhiking to Cologne. See: Jan Dibbets in conversation with the author, Amsterdam, 28 April 2005, audio-tape recording (Appendix 4.5). See also: 'Paul Maenz', *Kunstforum International*, *op. cit.*, p.283.

28 Paul Maenz, *Art is to change ..., Skizzen aus der Umlaufbahn*, Lindinger + Schmid, Regensburg, 2002, pp.41–42. See also: Maenz, 'Before 1970', in *Paul Maenz Köln 1970–1975*, *op. cit.*, p.11.

29 The title refers to a scene in the film *Lawrence of Arabia* (1962), where a sheikh shows his son a landscape of dunes. See: Maenz, *Art is to change*, *op. cit.*, p.14.

30 *Dies alles Herzchen wird einmal dir gehören, 19:45–21:55, September 9th, 1967, Frankfurt, Germany*, Galerie Dorothea Loehr, Frankfurt/Main, 9 September 1967. See: Astrid Kießling, *Die Galerie Dorothea Loehr in Frankfurt am Main, Das erste Jahrzehnt*, unpublished Master's dissertation, Kunstgeschichtliches Institut der Johann Wolfgang Goethe-Universität, Frankfurt/Main, 1995, pp.83–88.

31 See: Maenz, 'Before 1970', in *Paul Maenz Köln 1970–1975*, *op. cit.*, pp.12–13. For a detailed account of the works in the exhibition, see: Dibbets in conversation with the author, *op. cit.* Dibbets conceived a 'Perspective Correction' in the form of a sawdust oval that was

(now in Cologne). The organisation set up the Kunstmarkt and only its members were allowed to have a stand.

The first Kölner Kunstmarkt (Cologne Art Fair) was a completely German event.[35] It promoted itself as a fair for 'progressive' galleries, and was therefore attacked by those who had not been invited. The outsiders protested that this selection procedure made them appear as second-class galleries.[36] In protest, Heiner Friedrich, Munich, organised a counter exhibition, *Demonstrative 67*, in the nearby Studio Dumont. He presented the works of artists in his gallery, including Palermo, Polke, Richter and Fischer-Lueg.[37]

In September 1967, the Cologne Kunstmarkt attracted between 15,000 and 16,000 visitors and produced an overall turnover of 1 million Deutschmarks.[38] From the point of view of the organisers, the fair was a financial and cultural success. It was decided to continue the fair on an annual basis, but without significantly increasing the number of exhibitors.[39] The Kunstmarkt is generally seen as the event that established Cologne as an art metropolis. Since the war and the partition of Germany, and thus the division of Berlin, the country had had no art capital. The desire to establish a new art centre in West Germany was another reason for choosing Cologne as the venue.[40]

Konrad Fischer, Düsseldorf

About a month later, in October 1967, Konrad Fischer (1939–96) opened a gallery in Düsseldorf. From 1958 to 1962 he had studied, with Richter and Polke, at the Kunstakademie in Düsseldorf,[41] and as we have seen, he had previously been known as an artist, exhibiting under his mother's maiden name of Lueg with the group 'Capitalist Realism'. From 1963, he had had solo shows in several galleries across Germany, including Schmela (1964), Block (1966) and Friedrich (1967). He had also exhibited in the key group shows set up by Paul Maenz in 1967. This gave rise to his interest in the work of American and European artists such as Andre, LeWitt, Posenenske, Dibbets and Long.

Both Dibbets and Maenz recall that it was during *Dies alles Herzchen* (September 1967) that Fischer told them of his plan to open a gallery.[42] The idea had originated when Schmela invited him to start a second Schmela gallery for young artists.[43] From the summer of 1967, it became clear to Fischer that he

perceived by the viewer as a circle.

32 Kunstmarkt Köln, Gürzenich, Cologne, 12–17 September 1967.

33 In the mid-1960s, Rudolf Zwirner moved his gallery from Essen to Cologne. In September 1966, he had given his first European one-man show to the American Minimal artist Dan Flavin. The whole show had been purchased by Giuseppe Panza. See: Michael Govan and Tiffany Bell, *Dan Flavin, A Retrospective* (exh. cat.), Yale University Press, New Haven and New York, 2004, p.119. See also: *Art of the Fifties, Sixties and Seventies, The Panza Collection*, Antique Collector's Club, Jaca Book, Milan, 1999, p.302.

34 Volker Rattemeyer and Renate Penzinger (eds), *20 Jahre Kunstmarkt 1967–1986*, Bundesverband Deutscher Galerien, Cologne, 1986, p.8.

35 Dealer Galleries : Galerie Änne Abels (Cologne), Galerie Appel & Fretsch (Frankfurt/Main), Galerie Block (Berlin), Galerie Brusberg (Hannover), Galerie Gunar (Düsseldorf), Galerie Müller (Stuttgart), Galerie Neuendorf (Hamburg), Galerie Niepel (Düsseldorf), (op)-art Galerie (Essling), Galerie Ricke (Cologne), Galerie Schmela (Düsseldorf), Galerie Der Spiegel (Cologne), Galerie Springer (Berlin), Galerie Stangl (Munich), Galerie Thomas (Munich), Galerie Tobiès & Silex (Cologne), Galerie van de Loo (Munich) and Galerie Zwirner (Cologne). See: *Kunstmarkt 1967* (exh. cat.), Verein progressiver deutscher Kunsthändler, Cologne, 1967, unnumbered pages.

36 Dieter Delus, 'Kartell am Kunstmarkt', Saarbrücker Zeitung, 14 March 1967, in File A1 XIII 1, Zentralarchiv des internationalen Kunsthandel, Cologne (hereafter Zadik).

wanted to promote the work of young artists who were unknown in Germany and, more generally, in Europe.[44] When preparing for the opening of his dealer gallery in Düsseldorf, he contacted Kasper König in New York, asking him for his help.[45] It appears from his letter dated 8 July 1967 that it was Robert Morris who was his first choice for the inaugural show at the gallery, and not LeWitt and Andre as is commonly believed:[46]

> I am planning big things. For these big things, however, I urgently need your help.
>
> I am opening a dealer gallery. In September. I already have the space, very beautiful ...
>
> So far everything is fine; now, however, I need your help. The first exhibition?! – I have heard, that you will come to Europe in September to Doberman with Robert Morris and another artist, whose name I can't remember, and here I want to kindly ask you to speak with Bob Morris and to convince him to do something in the Galerie 'Konrad Fischer' ...
>
> Dear Kaspar [*sic*], I absolutely want to make a progressive gallery, in which good young artists, also unknown, would exhibit, but you will understand that I have the highest ambition that an outstanding artist like Robert Morris will open my gallery. You know the situation in Germany and I believe, that you too will welcome a new good dealer gallery here ...
>
> Who is the other artist? I am further interested in Carl Andre, Donald Judd, Sol LeWitt, Agnes Martin, Ronald Bladen. You will certainly also know a few good, young people there, whose names are not known to me yet and who I could exhibit here.[47]

Fischer did not in fact exhibit Morris (born 1931) until 1973.[48] In 1967, Morris was represented by Leo Castelli in New York; soon afterwards, in 1968, he was to be represented by Sonnabend in Paris. It is likely that these dealers did not want him to exhibit with another dealer in Europe. Moreover, Morris had received a solo show at Schmela in October 1964, which had been a collaboration with Richard Bellamy's Green Gallery.[49]

In the end, it was with one of his other choices, Carl Andre (born 1935), that

37 See: 'Ganz am Anfang / How it all began, Richter, Polke, Lueg & Kuttner', Sediment, Zadik, Cologne, no.7, 2004, pp.107–109. See also: Kellein, *Ich nenne mich als Maler Konrad Lueg*, *op. cit.*, pp.158–159.

38 Statistics of the 1967 art fair, in CD-Rom, 'Kunstmarkt Köln '67, Entstehung und Entwicklung der ersten Messe für moderne Kunst, 1967–1974', *Sediment*, Zadik, Cologne, no.6, 2003. Even *The New York Times* published an article about the first Cologne Kunstmarkt. See: 'Big Cologne Exhibition Seeks to Focus German Art Market', *The New York Times*, 19 September 1967, in File A1 XIII 1, Zadik.

39 Minutes of the Organisation's annual meeting in Cologne dated 9 October 1967 (Protokoll der Sitzung des Vereins progressiver deutscher Kunsthändler), in File C2 IV 15, Zadik.

40 For a discussion of Cologne's role as an art centre, see: Wulf Herzogenrath and Gabriele Lueg (eds), *Die 60er Jahre, Kölns Weg zur Kunstmetropole – Vom Hapenning zum Kunstmarkt* (exh. cat.), Kölnischer Kunstverein, Cologne, 1986.

41 In 1963, Polke, Richter, Fischer-Lueg and Manfred Kuttner founded the Kapitalistischer Realismus (Capitalist Realism), a political German Pop art movement. [Editor's note: Fischer 1958–62, Richter 1961–63, Polke 1961–67: dates at Düsseldorf Kunstakademie]. They were very much influenced by Andy Warhol, from whom they got the idea of painting from performance portraits and photography. See: Stephan Strsembski, 'Kapitalistischer Realismus?', in 'Ganz am Anfang / How it all began', *Sediment*, *op. cit.*, pp.47–59. See also: Hans Strelow, 'Vivre avec Pop, Une démonstration en faveur du Réalisme Capitaliste de Konrad Lueg et Gerhard Richter

Fischer launched his space. Although Andre had been included in *Serielle Formationen*, he had only been represented by a small drawing. Fischer must have seen more of Andre's work in reproduction in art magazines. Even if König was central in conveying information from the New York art world, Fischer also acknowledged the importance of photographs in getting to know the work of American artists.[50]

It was König, however, who contacted Andre regarding the show at Fischer's.[51] Because Fischer did not have enough money to pay for the shipping and insurance of artworks from America, he sent the artist a cheap ticket and had him fly over to make the work for the show in Düsseldorf. He explained:

> Minimal Art was unknown in Europe, and I saw an opening. I thought it was important, and I knew it only from photographs. So I thought I'd try to get through to the artists – I was one myself after all – and I said to myself 'If someone sends them a plane ticket, they'll come.' So I sent one to Andre.[52]

The idea of having the artist fly over rather than transport the works was a novel one at the time, engendering the creation of in-situ works.[53] Fischer considered dealers part of the process of producing art, and the exhibition was the result of a genuine collaboration between the dealer and the artist.[54] At the time, specialised manufacturing companies, such as the metalwork firm Nebato run by the engineer Dick van der Net in Bergeyk, South Holland, appeared.

Carl Andre

In October–November 1967, Andre's first European solo show took place at Konrad Fischer, Düsseldorf.[55] The space was a small alley that ran through an apartment building in the old part of the city, the Altstadt (Neubrückstraße), located between the Kunsthalle and Kunstverein and the Kunstakademie.[56] The configuration of the floor sculpture corresponded to the proportions of the gallery space. Andre's work was a rectangle of 5 by 20 units of hot-rolled steel (0.5 × 250 × 1000 cm).[57] It was named *5 × 20 Altstadt Rectangle (Düsseldorf, 1967)*, underlining its physical characteristics, place and date of production.[58]

As Andre later pointed out, the Düsseldorf art scene was not completely

Düsseldorf 1963', in Bernd Klüser and Katharina Hegewisch (eds), *L'Art de l'Exposition*, Editions du Regard, Paris, 1998, pp.295–301.

42 Jan Dibbets in conversation with the author, *op. cit.* See also: 'Interview with Jan Dibbets', in Moseley, *Conception*, *op. cit.*, p.126. Compare with: Suzaan Boettger, 'The lost contingent: Paul Maenz's prophetic 1967 event and the ambiguities of historical priority', *Art Journal*, vol.62, no.3, Spring 2003, pp.34–47.

43 'Konrad Fischer interviewed by Georg Jappe', *Studio International*, vol.181, no.930, February 1971, p.69. See also: 'Konrad Fischer', *Kunstforum International*, vol.104, November–December 1989, p.279.

44 For a comprehensive outline of exhibitions of Conceptual artists at the gallery, see: Database 1, Section Konrad Fischer (Appendix 1.1). For an overview of all the exhibitions organised by Fischer, see: *Ausstellungen bei Konrad Fischer, Düsseldorf, Oktober 1967–Oktober 1992* (exh. cat.), Edition Marzona, Bielefeld, 1993, pp.5–11. See also: Appendix 3.10.

45 Kasper König (born 1943), then a young German art historian, studied anthropology at the New School of Social Research in New York from 1965 to 1968. In 1967, he founded a publishing house with his brother Walther, Verlag Gebrüder König, Cologne – New York, producing art books about Franz Erhard Walther, Robert Filliou, Fluxus and others. König had met Fischer in the early 1960s, when the latter was studying at the Kunstakademie in Düsseldorf. They were close friends and König became the 'eyes and ears' of Fischer in the USA. Lynda Morris in conversation with the author. See also:

unknown in New York at the time.[59] Robert Morris and his partner the dancer Yvonne Rainer had visited the city for the artist's show at Schmela in 1964. Further, Eva Hesse (born in Hamburg in 1936), who had immigrated to New York with her family in 1938, spent 1964–65 in Kettwig an der Ruhr with her husband the sculptor Tom Doyle, under the patronage of the textile manufacturer and art collector Friedrich Arnhard Scheidt. Moreover, Maenz and König had spent time in New York. Thus, from the mid-1960s, there were connections between the New York and German art worlds, particularly the Rhine-Ruhr area. This further contributed to the development of the nearby cities of Düsseldorf and Cologne as the new centres of art in Germany.

There were also connections between New York and other European countries, notably the UK. In 1966, Michael Baldwin (born 1945) and Terry Atkinson (born 1939), who would be among the founders of the Art & Language group in 1968, met at Lancaster Polytechnic. In March 1966, Baldwin made contact with LeWitt and in July 1967, Atkinson went to New York, where he met LeWitt, Andre, Dan Graham, Robert Smithson and Weiner. He travelled across the US before departing in September 1967. In May–June 1968, work by Art & Language was included in a group show, also featuring work by Andre and Weiner, at the Dwan Gallery, New York.[60]

Hanne Darboven

From July 1966, the German artist Hanne Darboven (born 1941) lived in New York. In December 1966, her work was included in the show *Working Drawings and Other Visible Things on Paper Not Necessarily Meant to be Viewed as Art* at the School of Visual Arts Gallery, New York, organised by the artist Mel Bochner, who taught art history there.[61] The exhibition consisted of four white wooden pedestals bearing binders for visitors to leaf through, of Xerox copies of working drawings and other material by artists such as Judd, Hesse, Graham, LeWitt, Smithson and Dan Flavin.

Darboven's work was also included in the opening exhibition of the Lannis Museum of Normal Art launched by Joseph Kosuth (born 1945) and Christine Kozlov in New York. The exhibition, held in November 1967, included works by Andre, Bochner, Darboven, Judd, Kosuth, Kozlov, LeWitt, Morris, Smithson,

'Two-women show as good as one-man show, Ein Gespräch mit Kasper König', in Kölle, *Die Kunst des Ausstellen*, *op. cit.*, pp.35–49.

46 Carl Andre, 'Footnote to a 25 year old gallery', in *Ausstellungen bei Konrad Fischer*, *op. cit.*, p.3.

47 Letter from Konrad Fischer to Kasper König dated 8 July 1967, in Galerie Korrespondenz 1967–[1969], Archive Konrad Fischer Galerie, Düsseldorf (hereafter AKFGD) (author's translation). Although the archive of the early period of Konrad Fischer's gallery is kept privately by his widow Dorothee Fischer in Düsseldorf, she allowed me access to it.

48 'Robert Morris', Konrad Fischer, Düsseldorf, 17 February–16 March 1973. See: *Ausstellungen bei Konrad Fischer*, *op. cit.*, p.87.

49 Monika Schmela, 'Erinnerungen', in Ruhrberg, *Alfred Schmela*, *op. cit.*, p.202. Richard Bellamy (1927–98) inaugurated the Green Gallery in 1961, promoting artists such as Larry Poons (1962) and James Rosenquist (1963). He organised the first solo shows of the Minimal artists Donald Judd (December 1963–January 1964) and Dan Flavin (November–December 1964).

50 'Konrad Fischer interviewed by Georg Jappe', *Studio International*, *op. cit.*, p.68. Andre himself thinks that Fischer had seen pictures and comments about his work in *Artforum*. See: 'My life as an artist would have ended long ago ... A written conversation with Carl Andre', in Kölle, *Die Kunst des Ausstellen*, *op. cit.*, p.222.

51 Andre, 'Introduction to a 25 Year old Gallery', in *Ausstellungen bei Konrad Fischer*, *op. cit.*, p.3.

52 'Konrad Fischer interviewed by Georg Jappe', *Studio*

On Kawara, Walter De Maria, Robert Ryman and Frank Stella.[62]

A month later, in December 1967, Fischer organised Darboven's first solo exhibition in Düsseldorf.[63] Maenz recalled that the artist came to Frankfurt after *Dies alles Herzchen* to show him her work on the recommendation of LeWitt.[64] Fischer also acknowledged LeWitt's role as an intermediary in acquainting him with Darboven.[65] In parallel with drawings by Darboven, Fischer exhibited works by another German female artist, Charlotte Posenenske (1930–85). Fischer knew her architectural work, having exhibited with her in Frankfurt at *Serielle Formationen* and *Dies alles Herzchen* earlier in 1967.[66]

America–West Germany connections

The first exhibitions organised by Fischer at his gallery demonstrate that he was setting up a programme of both American Minimal artists and the European artists who were to become known as Conceptualists. In comparison with what had happened in the postwar period, there was a 'sudden shift around 1967 from "international" – meaning American artists in Europe – to "international" meaning equality between American and European artists'.[67] Indeed, the Conceptual network in Europe included both young European artists and their American counterparts. Although the American artists were not completely unknown in the US, they received greater recognition in Europe. In 1969, Lippard saw Europe as being 'more fertile for new ideas and new ways of disseminating art than the United States'.[68]

In 1967, the major events that launched the Conceptual network in Europe occurred in Germany. Lynda Morris suggests that Conceptualism in the late 1960s and early 1970s was led by West Germany:

> It was led by Germany for two reasons; firstly the US, UK and French military had occupied West Germany since 1945. West Germany was the front line of the West, the battlefield on which any further nuclear confrontation between USA and USSR would take place ... West Germany continued to be an occupied nation not because of the 1939–45 War, but because of the Cold War and the physical manifestation of the Iron Curtain, the Berlin Wall, until 1989 ... If they were to avoid the violence of terrorism, the postwar generation of

International, *op. cit.*, p.69.

53 Fischer was not the only European dealer to fly over American artists in the late 1960s, but he was the one who would do it most systematically. Rolf Ricke, for instance, had the American artist Gary Kuehn travel to Kassel during the summer of 1967 to prepare an exhibition.

54 'Konrad Fischer interviewed by Georg Jappe', *Studio International*, *op. cit.*, p.70.

55 'Carl Andre', Konrad Fischer, Düsseldorf, 21 October–28 November 1967. See: *Ausstellungen bei Konrad Fischer*, *op.cit.*, p.13. See also: Database 3, Section Carl Andre (Appendix 1.3). Compare with: *Carl Andre, Sculptor 1996, Krefeld at Home, Wolfsburg at Large* (exh. cat.), Oktagon Verlag, Stuttgart, 1996, p.242. In America, Andre had had solo shows at the Tibor de Nagy Gallery, New York (1965, 1966) and at the Dwan Gallery, Los Angeles (1967).

56 Konrad Fischer's Neubrückstraße gallery space was reconstructed in 1997 in Norwich during the East exhibition by the artists Liesbeth Bik and Jos van der Pol, *Proposition for Reclaiming a Space* (1997). See: Norwich Gallery, Norwich, Dispatch 036, 1997, unnumbered pages.

57 At this time, companies began to specialise in the fabrication of structures for artists. These included the metalwork firm Nebato, run by the engineer Dick van der Net in Bergeyk, South Holland, or the Bernstein Brothers Factory in New York. Nebato was first asked to fabricate metallic structures for Sol LeWitt in 1968. Andre's *Altstadt Rectangle* was produced by a local company that had also

young Germans in the mid 1960s needed to find a way to talk to and to work with their contemporaries amongst the nuclear nations occupying the Western half of their country. They were able to have that dialogue with the conceptual artists from the USA and from the UK and other European countries.[69]

Sol LeWitt

Fischer's German contacts with America, Maenz and König, were also the go-betweens between the dealer and Sol LeWitt in late 1967. In a letter to Fischer, dated 10 November 1967, LeWitt wrote:

> Dear Sir,
> Both Paul Maenz and Kasper König have contacted me with the offer of a show in your gallery. Carl Andre has also spoken very highly of you and your gallery. I would like very much to have a show there. The cost of manufacture would have to be borne by the gallery. (I have been told there is a place in Holland which would do this.) Also the transportation costs and a place to stay in Dusseldorf. After the show at the Galerie Fischer would the work be available for shows elsewhere in Europe? I would like to show the work wherever there is interest in it. I have had an offer of a show in Zurich at the Gallery Bischofberger in the spring of 1968.
>
> Could you write and tell me if this is OK and when you would like me to come over (my classes are over where I teach on December 21). Also I would like to know who would own the work when completed. And what is the percentage that the gallery would get on the sales and the % I would get. If the work is shown in other galleries in Europe, what % would the Galerie Fischer get, and what % the other gallery.
>
> I look forward to hearing from you and eventually meeting you personally.
> Sincerely,
> Sol LeWitt[70]

LeWitt's letter reveals the artist's confidence and his determination to become better known in Europe. He was older (born 1928) than many of the other Conceptual artists and by the end of 1967 had already held a number of

made the doors for Fischer's gallery space. See Dorothee Fischer, quoted in Kölle, *Die Kunst des Ausstellen*, *op. cit.*, p.140.

58 Andre's work was for sale for DM 4,000. It was purchased jointly by Kasper König and Konrad Fischer. See: 'Ich kann die Wolken im Himmel verkaufen, Ein Gespräch mit Johannes Cladders' and 'Two-women show as good as one-man show, Ein Gespräch mit Kasper König', in Kölle, *Die Kunst des Ausstellen*, *op. cit.*, pp.229–240. The work was acquired in 1974 by the Italian collector Giuseppe Panza. See: Database 5 on the Panza Collection (Appendix 1.5). See also: *Art of the Fifties, Sixties and Seventies, The Panza Collection*, *op. cit.*, p.299. As we will see in Chapter 2.1, soon after the show, the Dutch collectors Mia and Martin Visser commissioned Andre to make a similar work for their home. Later, the Kunstmuseum in Basel (1974) and the Stedelijk Museum in Amsterdam (1976) acquired '*Altstadt*' pieces conceptually similar to the work that appeared in this first solo exhibition. See: Database 6 on purchases of Conceptual art by European museums (Appendix 1.6).

59 Andre, 'Introduction to a 25 Year old Gallery', in *Ausstellungen bei Konrad Fischer*, *op. cit.*, p.3.

60 'Language II (Andre, Art & Language, Darboven, De Maria, Flavin, Heizer, Kawara, Kosuth, Morris, Weiner', Dwan Gallery, New York, 25 May–22 June 1968. See: Lippard, *Six Years*, *op. cit.*, pp.17–30. See also: *Terry Atkinson*, Norwich Gallery, Norwich, Dispatch 022, 1996, unnumbered pages.

61 'Working Drawings and Other Visible Things on Paper not necessarily meant to be viewed as Art', School of Visual Arts Gallery,

solo exhibitions in America. His first one-man show took place in May 1965 at the Daniels Gallery, New York, which was then directed by Dan Graham.[71] Moreover, LeWitt had been represented by the Dwan Gallery since his solo show in New York in May–June 1966.[72] However, Fischer declared that: 'Sol LeWitt came here quite independently of Dwan.'[73] This is also what the artist's letter suggests.

In his letter to Fischer, LeWitt had frankly raised issues of other European exhibitions, possession of the works and percentages on sales. On 22 November, Fischer replied to the artist:

> Dear Sir,
> I am glad to hear from you that you are ready to come to Düsseldorf in December. I will surely find out a place, you can do your work or where it could be done, either in Holland or in a factory here in Düsseldorf, all cost, concerning the manufacture and the material, your coming and, of course, your staying in Germany will be taken by the gallery.
>
> Naturally I am too very much interested, that your show goes to some good places, as well as in Germany as in other parts of Europe. You asked me who will own the pieces, when they are completed: I am sure we'll sell them, if not, we'll see. The percentage: 50% for the artist, 50% for the gallery, when the show is taken to another place, I think there should be 20% for my gallery, 30% for the other gallery and 50% for you. If there is any other question about these commercial things, please ask Kasper.
>
> You know the Den Haag Museum will do a show of 10 US sculptors in March 68 and I think you'll do some pieces for this museum, when you are in Europe.
>
> Please come as soon as possible between Christmas and New Year, I think so we can start your exposition at the beginning of 68. If you could send me some photographs of your works and biographical notes before you are coming, I would be able to prepare the invitation cards in advance.
>
> I'm looking forward to your coming to Düsseldorf with pleasure and I hope you'll have a good time here.
>
> Sincerely,
> Konrad Fischer[74]

New York, December 1966. For an extensive discussion of this early exhibition, see: James Meyer, 'The Second Degree, Working drawings and other visible things on paper not necessarily meant to be viewed as art', in Corris, *Conceptual Art: Theory, Myth and Practice*, *op. cit.*, pp.108–122. See also: Meyer, *Minimalism*, *op. cit.*, pp.112–113.

62 See: Lippard, *Six Years*, *op. cit.*, pp.30–31.

63 'Hanne Darboven', Konrad Fischer, Düsseldorf, starting 5 December 1967. See: *Ausstellungen bei Konrad Fischer*, *op. cit.*, p.14. See also: Database 3, Section Hanne Darboven (Appendix 1.3).

64 Maenz, 'Before 1970', in *Paul Maenz Köln 1970–1975*, *op. cit.*, p.14.

65 'Konrad Fischer interviewed by Georg Jappe', *Studio International*, *op. cit.*, p.70.

66 In 1969, Posenenske came to the conclusion that art could not contribute to the solution of social problems. She therefore ended her artistic career in order to become a sociologist.

67 Morris, 'Introduction to the Conference', *New Research into Conceptualism in Europe*, *op. cit.*, unnumbered pages. See also: Thomas Kellein, 'It's the Sheer Size: European Responses to American Art', in Christos M. Joachimides, *American Art in the 20th Century*, Prestel Verlag, Munich, 1993, p.188.

68 Lippard, *Six Years*, *op. cit.*, p.8.

69 Morris, 'Introduction to the Conference', *New Research into Conceptualism in Europe*, *op. cit.* There were, however, terrorists groups in Germany in the early 1970s, such as the Movement 2 June and the Rote Armee Faction (RAF, Red Army Faction), commonly

Fischer did not refer to the artist's invitation to exhibit at Bischofberger's gallery in Zurich in the spring of 1968. His insistence that LeWitt should come over to Düsseldorf as quickly as possible and his desire to prepare the invitation card in advance demonstrate the dealer's desire to secure the first showing of LeWitt in his own gallery. Indeed, LeWitt's debut European solo exhibition opened on 6 January 1968 at Konrad Fischer.[75]

The artist came to Düsseldorf on 7 December and realised works in Europe specifically for the exhibition. The pieces on show were five *Cubes with Hidden Cubes* (1967) and six earlier pieces from *Serial Project No.1 (ABCD)* (1966). In addition to the sculptures, LeWitt arranged to make some other small pieces and drawings that could possibly be sold. The artist further insisted that the pieces should be shown elsewhere in Europe.[76] Subsequently, LeWitt had two further solo shows in early 1968 in Europe, one at Bruno Bischofberger (Zurich) and one at Heiner Friedrich (Munich).

Fischer's correspondence with the latter two dealers reveals that he made himself the main contact for LeWitt in Europe. He took care of the production of the works by the manufacturer Nebato, and helped to set up the shows in Munich and Zurich. Bischofberger acknowledged Fischer's help in organising the LeWitt show at his gallery. Further, he paid one-third of the artist's travel costs from New York to Düsseldorf.[77] Although Bischofberger had invited LeWitt early on, it seems that it was with Friedrich that Fischer worked most closely.[78] Le Witt's exhibition in Munich was titled *Five Cubes* and the works on show were the same as in Düsseldorf.[79] Fischer had pieces produced by Nebato specifically for the Munich show. Friedrich also contributed a third of the cost of the artist's ticket from New York to Germany, as well as half of the works' production costs.[80]

Fischer's leading role

This example reveals how, very early on, Fischer secured his position as the primary dealer of Conceptual artists and how he networked with other like-minded dealers in Europe.[81] Kasper König recalled that if: 'an artist had already exhibited elsewhere, Konrad was no longer interested. He wanted to be the first one and to have direct contact with the artists.'[82] Moreover, the gallery became a meeting place where American artists, who may not have met in the US, could

known as the Baader-Meinhof group.

70 Manuscript letter from LeWitt to Fischer dated 10 November 1967, in Korrespondenz mit Künstlern 1969–1970, AKFGD. The manufacturer in Holland mentioned by LeWitt was Nebato in Bergeyk.

71 *Sol LeWitt*, Daniels Gallery, New York, 4–29 May 1965. From this first show onwards, LeWitt's work was collected by people such as Dorothy and Herbert Vogel. See: *Works from the Collection of Dorothy and Herbert Vogel* (exh. cat.), The University of Michigan Museum of Art, Ann Arbor, Michigan, 1977, unnumbered pages. LeWitt had also established himself as a key theorist with his 'Paragraphs on Conceptual Art'. See: LeWitt, 'Paragraphs on Conceptual Art', *Artforum*, *op. cit.*, pp.79–84.

72 'Sol LeWitt', Dwan Gallery, New York, 10 May–June 1966. For LeWitt's early exhibition history, see: Alicia Legg (ed.), *Sol LeWitt* (exh. cat.), The Museum of Modern Art, New York, 1978. For a chronology of exhibitions held at the Los Angeles and New York galleries, see: Virginia Dwan, *Art Minimal et Conceptuel, Earthworks, New York, Les années 60–70* (exh. cat.), Galerie Montaigne, Paris, 1991, unnumbered pages. The archives of the Virgina Dwan Gallery have been kept since 1996 by the Archives of American Art, Smithsonian Institute, Washington and the Center for Curatorial Studies, Bard College, Annandale-on-Hudson.

73 'Konrad Fischer interviewed by Georg Jappe', *Studio International*, *op. cit.*, p.69.

74 Manuscript letter from Fischer to LeWitt dated 22 November

get to know each other.[83]

Several works from LeWitt's exhibition in Düsseldorf were purchased by private collectors; some were purchased by other dealers. Three were bought by Alfred Schmela (*4 part set ABCD 5*, *4 part set ABCD 9* and *3 part set 789 B*).[84] It seems that the Dutch collectors Mia and Martin Visser acquired two metallic structures (*9 part set B* and *9 part set D*).[85]

LeWitt was very interested in the way in which his career developed in Europe. He had a clear vision of the development of an artist's publicity and subsequent prices and sales of works. He wrote to Fischer on 18 January 1967, when his exhibition was still on:

> Good to hear from you. Everything seems very Okey Dokey ... The reasons for making the prices are: 1) to make more money, 2) so that American collectors would not go to Europe – bypassing the Dwan Gallery here, 3) once a collector has a piece he will not want another and there are only a limited no. of collectors, 4) it is better to sell less work now because next year it will be easier to sell work in Europe because I will have more publicity etc. What do you think? When will you come to New York? What happened about Multiple? Hans Mayer wanted to make a large (150 cm) one. This is a mistake. If someone buys this, then they will not buy a large piece. Perhaps you can talk to him. I would still like to sell it out right (no percentages) ...
>
> Please write and tell me what you think. Also tell me what prices you charged Schmela & English guy (what was his name) and Ilse. Maybe you should wait to sell things until summer when The Hague show and Documenta (if I will be in it) will provide more publicity to sell for higher prices.
>
> I think you should use Nebato as much as possible but if taxes are too high in Holland do you think you can find a factory that will do as well in Germany? It should be very high quality.[86]

John Weber, who had directed the Dwan Gallery since 1962, first in Los Angeles and then in New York, wrote to Fischer on 1 February 1968, a couple of days before the end of LeWitt's show in Düsseldorf:

1967, in Korrespondenz mit Künstlern 1969–1970, AKFGD. The Den Haag exhibition referred to by Fischer is *Minimal Art*, a show that was organised by Enno Develing at the Gemeentemuseum from 23 March to 26 May 1968. See: Chapter 2.1 for an account of this show.

75 *Sol LeWitt*, Konrad Fischer, Düsseldorf, 6 January–3 February 1967. See: *Ausstellungen bei Konrad Fischer*, *op. cit.*, p.16. See also: Database 3, Section Sol LeWitt (Appendix 1.3).

76 Manuscript letter from LeWitt to Fischer dated 27 November 1967, in Korrespondenz mit Künstlern 1969–1970, AKFGD.

77 Undated letter from Fischer to Bischofberger of 1968, and Letter from Bischofberger to Fischer dated 27 April 1968, in Galerie Korrespondenz 1967–69, AKFGD.

78 In 1965, Friedrich first travelled with his wife Six to America in order to get to know the art scene there. During their six-week stay, they established contacts with Walter De Maria (whom they got to know via the dealer Dick Bellamy), La Monte Young and Marian Zazeela. Friedrich financially supported these artists from that moment on, although he would not show De Maria's *Earth Room* until September 1968, nor Young and Zazeela's *Dream House* until July 1969. See: Heiner Friedrich in conversation, in Urbaschek, *Dia Art Foundation*, *op. cit.*, p.68. See also: 'Six Friedrich', *Kunstforum International*, vol.104, November–December 1989, p.247. For an overview of exhibitions of Conceptual artists at Friedrich's gallery, see: Database 1, Section Heiner Friedrich (Appendix 1.1) and Appendix 3.11.

79 *Sol LeWitt, Five Cubes*, Galerie Heiner Friedrich, Munich, 1968.

> My compliments to you on the series of exhibitions which you have had in your newly inaugurated gallery. We are very pleased with the results of the exhibition; I understand from both Sol and Carl that sales have been going very well. Sol was worried over one point, however, and I believe it is a point that he has discussed with you in writing. This is the phenomena of other German art dealers purchasing his work for resale at a higher price. The price of Sol's pieces was very low for American standards. They were set at a low price so that they could get out into public collections. It would perhaps be best if you confined your sales to museums and private individuals rather than dealers.[87]

Weber was not taking percentages on European sales of his artists.[88] This strategy led to benefits for both Weber and the European dealers. On the one hand, it enabled European dealers to have access to the American market and to split the money directly with the artists. On the other, Weber took advantage of the promoting of his artists in Europe, which was also profitable to their careers in America. However, both Weber and LeWitt were keen to maintain the artist's prices and to establish a European market that would be independent and not competing with the American marketplace.

Nevertheless, Fischer seems to have continued to sell to other dealers, as he declared in 1971: 'More than 50 per cent of what I sell goes to other galleries.'[89] He had been doing so as early as 1968, an indication that Conceptual artworks were seen as profitable. But the dealers who acquired works for resale were those with whom Fischer had not established close business relations and who were outside of the network of Conceptual art that was starting to take shape.

Heiner Friedrich, Munich

A dealer with whom Fischer particularly collaborated at that time was Heiner Friedrich, Munich (Maximilianstrasse). Indeed, one of Friedrich's artists, Blinky Palermo (pseudonym of Peter Schwarze, 1943–77) was the next artist to be exhibited at the Düsseldorf gallery in February–March 1968.[90] Fischer knew his work from the *Demonstrative 67* exhibition in which they had both exhibited. Friedrich had been Palermo's main dealer since he had given him his first solo show in

80 Letter from Fischer to Friedrich dated 29 January 1968, and Letter from Fischer to Friedrich dated 8 February 1968, in Galerie Korrespondenz 1967–69, AKFGD.

81 The numerous articles published by the art critics Georg Jappe and Hans Strelow, notably in the *Frankfurter Allgemeine Zeitung*, contributed greatly to establishing the reputation of Fischer's gallery. See, for instance: Hans Strelow, 'Hundert Stahlplatten gleich eine Plastik, Konrad Fischer eröffnet seine Galerie mit dem Amerikaner Carl Andre', *Rheinische Post*, 20 October 1967, and: Georg Jappe, 'Bodenplatten und Neon, Düsseldorfer Galerien im November', *Frankfurter Allgemeine Zeitung*, 20 November 1967.

82 'Two-women show as good as one-man show, Ein Gespräch mit Kasper König', in Kölle, *Die Kunst des Ausstellen*, *op. cit.*, p.241. [Editor's note: now published in Kölle, *Okey Dokey Konrad Fischer*, Verlag der Buchhandlung Walther Koenig Köln, 2007] (author's translation).'

83 Bruce Nauman for instance, remembered meeting Carl Andre and Sol LeWitt in Düsseldorf. See: 'Bruce, here is some paper and some pencils. You should make some drawings. Don't just sit here! A conversation with Bruce Nauman', in *Ibid.*, p.246.

84 Letter from Konrad Fischer to Sol LeWitt dated 15 January 1968, in Korrespondenz mit Künstlern 1969–70, AKFGD.

85 Letter from Konrad Fischer to Heiner Friedrich dated 8 February 1968, in Galerie Korrespondenz 1967–69, AKFGD. The Vissers were early purchasers from the new art galleries that emerged in Europe at the time. In 1967, they also purchased works by Manzoni from

May–July 1966 in Munich.[91] He was very protective of Palermo and it is revealing that he let him have a one-man show in Düsseldorf.[92] The exchange of artists also took place the other way round. Carl Andre, for instance, exhibited at Friedrich's gallery from 16 March to 18 April 1968 (*22 Steel Row*).[93]

In the late 1960s, agreements between dealers were central in setting up a network of Conceptual artists in Europe. Contacts with artists were also important in getting to know other Conceptual artists. 'There is no doubt that good artists respect other good artists', noted Fischer.[94] LeWitt and Andre appear to have particularly influenced the dealer.[95] Moreover, Dorothee Fischer (born 1937), his wife, recalls that the contact with the USA was made through the artists themselves.[96]

Andre played a key role in introducing Fischer to the American Conceptual art world. In February 1968, when Fischer was preparing for his first trip to New York that April,[97] the artist wrote to him: 'You will be very welcome in New York. Many fine artists wish to show you their work. I have told them that you are a fine fellow, an artist, not a stuffy dealer.'[98] He travelled with Andre and spent time with some other artists, especially with LeWitt, Flavin, Judd and König.[99] The costs of Fischer's trip to America were shared with Friedrich, who was thus able to take advantage of Fischer's gallery visits and contacts for his own Munich gallery.[100]

From the outset of his career as a dealer, Fischer focused the programming of his gallery equally on young American and European artists whose work was largely unknown in Europe. It was important for him to forge links between US and European artists because it created contacts for them when they were travelling overseas.[101] A characteristic of the gallery was that he called it '*Ausstellungen bei Konrad Fischer*' (exhibitions at Konrad Fischer's), without using the word 'Gallery'.[102] This shows his independence and confidence in being an art enabler rather than a traditional dealer. In addition, the invitations to the gallery were postcards conceived by the artists.[103] Fischer developed a new type of gallery in which everything was done in close partnership with the artist. He had trained and worked as an artist himself before becoming a dealer. Curiously, he showed exactly the opposite kind of art to that he had produced himself: sculpture rather than painting, Minimal and Conceptual art rather than Pop. Concerning his

Wide White Space. See: 'Interview Yves Aupetitallot, Anny De Decker, Bernd Lohaus', in Aupetitallot, *Wide White Space*, *op. cit.*, p.32.

86 Manuscript letter from Sol LeWitt to Konrad Fischer dated 18 January 1968, in Korrespondenz mit Künstlern 1969–70, AKFGD.

87 Letter from John Weber, Dwan Gallery New York, to Konrad Fischer dated 1 February 1968, in Galerie Korrespondenz 1967–69, AKFGD.

88 Urbaschek, *Dia Art Foundation*, *op. cit.*, p.68.

89 'Konrad Fischer interviewed by Georg Jappe', *Studio International*, *op. cit.*, p.71.

90 'Palermo, Rot-Blau', Konrad Fischer, Düsseldorf, 6 February–1 March 1968. See: *Ausstellungen bei Konrad Fischer*, *op. cit.*, p.17.

91 'Blinky Palermo, Bilder und Zeichnungen', Galerie Heiner Friedrich, Munich, 24 May–5 July 1966.

92 Anny De Decker from the Wide White Space complained that she never managed to exhibit Palermo because of resistance from Heiner Friedrich. See: 'Interview Yves Aupetitallot, Anny De Decker, Bernd Lohaus', in Aupetitallot, *Wide White Space*, *op. cit.*, p.49.

93 See: list of shows organised by Heiner Friedrich, in Urbaschek, *Dia Art Foundation*, *op. cit.*, p.233.

94 'Konrad Fischer interviewed by Georg Jappe', *Studio International*, *op. cit.*, p.70.

95 'Two-women show as good as one-man show, Ein Gespräch mit Kasper König', in Kölle, *Die Kunst des Ausstellen*, *op. cit.*, p.240.

96 Dorothee Fischer in conversation with the author, Düsseldorf, April 2005, manuscript notes.

transformation from artist to dealer, Fischer declared: 'I was called differently and I became another person.'[104]

From 1967, Conceptualism in Europe was led by West Germany. However, Germany's central role in establishing the network of Conceptual art was strengthened through its connections with America, particularly New York. What was important was not from which side of the Atlantic the artists came, but that they were producing works that resulted from the same interests and questions.

Arte Povera in Italy

Italy was also culturally significant for the Conceptual network in 1967. In spring of that year, Giancarlo Politi launched the magazine *Flash Art*, which was to become important to Conceptual art. The first manifestations of Arte Povera were also emerging. In October 1967, the art critic Germano Celant (born 1940) organised two separate exhibitions, *Arte Povera – Im Spazio*, at the Galleria La Bertesca, Genoa.[105] Contributors included Alighiero Boetti, Luciano Fabro and Jannis Kounellis.[106] At the same time, Arte Povera artists also appeared at the Galleria Sperone in Turin. In December 1967, the gallery hosted the group show *Con temp l'azione*, featuring artists such as Boetti, Fabro, Michelangelo Pistoletto, Gilberto Zorio and Giovanni Anselmo.[107]

97 'Konrad Fischer interviewed by Georg Jappe', *Studio International*, *op. cit.*, p.69.

98 Manuscript letter from Carl Andre to Konrad Fischer dated 13 February 1968, in Korrespondenz mit Künstlern, 1969–1970, AKFGD. We have seen that Heiner Friedrich went to New York in 1965, but he did not exhibit the US artists he had met before 1968.

99 'Konrad Fischer', *Kunstforum International*, *op. cit.*, p.279. One should point out here that some of the Minimal artists had known each other since the late 1950s and early 1960s, when they worked at the MoMA, New York. LeWitt had worked as a night-desk assistant. Ryman and Flavin had both worked as guards. The art critic Lucy Lippard also worked there as a library assistant. See: Lippard, *Six Years*, *op. cit.*, p.viii.

100 Kölle, *Die Kunst des Ausstellen*, *op. cit.*, p.49.

101 'Konrad Fischer interviewed by Georg Jappe', *Studio International*, *op. cit.*, p.70.

102 The current name, Konrad Fischer Galerie, was chosen by Dorothee Fischer after the dealer's death in 1996. Although they had separated in 1981, they remained business partners and continued to work together at the gallery.

103 For examples of postcard mailings, see: 'Konrad Fischer interviewed by Georg Jappe', *Studio International*, *op. cit.*, pp.69–71.

104 Heinz-Norbert Jocks, 'Einseitig muss man sein, damit etwas weitergeht', *Kunstforum*, vol.127, July-September 1994, p.402 (author's translation).

105 *Arte Povera – Im Spazio*, Galleria La Bertesca, Genoa, October

1.2 Conclusion

The postwar European art world developed steadily. The economic boom of the 1960s enhanced the art market. From 1967, the development of the art world in Europe gained momentum as a result of close connections with America. The first showings of American Conceptual artists in Europe were paralleled by exhibitions in the US (Andre, LeWitt). However, shows of European Conceptualists only occurred in Europe (Dibbets, Long, Darboven).

In 1968 and 1969, Conceptual art would continue to develop strongly in Europe. An international support and dealing network of Conceptual artists also built up steadily. This meant more dealer galleries were launched across the continent and the first group shows were organised in temporary exhibition spaces and public museums.

Technical improvements and social unrest

By 1967, the notion that the world was changing was important. Technological improvements revolutionised everyday life. Political and social unrest was latent. Peace and counter-culture movements were coming into being. Western youth became more daring and outspoken; issues with which they became concerned included the denouncement of the Vietnam War and anti-nuclear campaigns. Travelling and communication became easier and faster. In April 1967, the first Boeing 737 made its maiden flight. Thanks to charter flights, air travel was an increasingly popular and affordable mode of public transport. The development of electronic telephone exchanges and the use of satellites made international phone calls more feasible. The first colour television broadcast in Europe took place in Britain in 1967. The black and white video camera and video recorder were popularised by low-priced and easy-to-use machines such as Sony's Portapack (1965). The invention of the Xerox machine allowed the unlimited reproduction of documents. Developments in compositing made printing easier and faster, with the use of off-set presses and computers. As a result, the manufacture of magazines and books, postcards and posters expanded.

Throughout most of the 1960s, America was deeply engaged in the Vietnam

1967. Artists: Boetti, Fabro, Kounellis, Paolini, Pascali and Emilio Prini. La Bertesca Gallery was founded in 1966 by Francesco Masnata. The first shows were dedicated to American Pop artists.

106 Lippard, *Six Years*, *op. cit.*, p.30.

107 *Con temp l'azione*, Galleria Sperone, Turin, starting 4 December 1967. Artists: Alviani, Anselmo, Boetti, Fabro, Mondino, Nespolo, Piacentino, Pistoletto, Scheggi, Simonetti and Zorio. See: Minola, Mundici, Poli and Roberto, *Gian Enzo Sperone*, *op. cit.*, pp.114–491.

War. From 1967 onwards, numerous marches against the conflict were organised, notably in San Francisco and New York.[108] That year, race riots took place all over the country. This was the period of the 'Summer of Love', when the so-called 'hippie movement' came to full fruition in San Francisco. The movement advocated counter-culture, communal living and ecological awareness.

In Germany, 1967 marked the beginnings of the student protest movement. The German Student Movement demonstrated against the Vietnam War and the conservative university system. In Düsseldorf, Joseph Beuys set up the *Deutsche Studenten Partei* (German Student Party), which argued for worldwide disarmament and educational reform.

108 Lynda Morris is undertaking research into the involvement of American artists in wars. None appear to have fought in the Vietnam War (1965–73). Judd, Flavin and Morris, who were from an older generation, had been GIs in South-East Asia. Douglas Huebler (1924–97), who was much older than most of the artists considered in this study, had been a marine in the Korean War (1950–53). Richard Tuttle was in Japan at a formative stage. Seth Siegelaub points out that many of the younger Conceptual artists came from the upper-middle class and, hence, could avoid enlistment as front-line soldiers; most Conceptual artists were registered in the officer class. Seth Siegelaub in conversation with the author, Amsterdam, 27 April 2005, audio-tape recording (Appendix 4.14), and Lynda Morris in conversation with the author.

Chapter 2

The growth of the network and temporary exhibitions: 1968–69

2.1 1968

1968 marked an internationalisation of the art world, with communication between different countries and cities. The organisation of temporary group exhibitions secured Conceptual art as a new and innovative movement within the art world.

Minimal art in Europe

At that time, Minimalism and Conceptualism were connected. Minimalism was seen by certain people as a continuity of mainstream American Formalism, related through the work of artists such as Frank Stella to the tradition of post-war American abstract art. Because Minimal art was shown in Europe, American Minimalists were among the original agents of the Conceptual network.

In March 1968, a major show *Minimal Art* was curated for the Gemeentemuseum, The Hague, by Enno Develing (1933–99).[1] The event was organised in collaboration with John Weber, Director of the Dwan Gallery, who made all the arrangements in New York since Develing could not travel to the United States.[2] Works by American artists such as Sol LeWitt, Carl Andre and Robert Morris were presented. In Europe, the show assumed the role played by *Primary Structures* in New York in 1966, in the sense that it presented Minimal artists as a movement in a public institution.[3]

1 *Minimal Art*, Haags Gemeentemuseum, The Hague, 23 March–26 May 1968. Artists: Andre, Bladen, Flavin, Grosvenor, Judd, LeWitt, Morris, Smith, Smithson and Steiner. From 17 January to 23 February 1969, the exhibition was shown at the Kunsthalle, Düsseldorf, and from 23 March to 5 May 1969 at the Akademie der Künste, Berlin. The show was also intended to travel to the Musée d'Art moderne de la ville de Paris to run from 18 June to 11 August 1968, but it was cancelled due to the May 1968 revolts.

2 Letter from Enno Develing to *Studio International*, in 'Correspondence', *Studio International*, vol.177, no.912, June 1969, p.256.

3 The American critic Barbara Reise (1940–78) edited a special issue on Minimalism in *Studio International* in April 1969 which was also important in introducing Minimalism to a European audience. See: Barbara Reise, 'Aspects of art called "minimal"', *Studio International*, vol.177, no.910, April 1969, pp.165–189. In 1966, Reise had received a Fulbright Scholarship to study at the Courtauld Institute and she lived in London from that moment on. In 1968, she became Senior Lecturer at Coventry College of Art and Design. In 1969 she also became a contributing editor to *Studio International*.

4 'Carl Andre, Robert Barry, Lawrence Weiner', Laura Knott Gallery, Bradford Junior College, Massachusetts, 4 February–2 March 1968. Seth Siegelaub had founded his dealer gallery 'Seth Siegelaub Contemporary Art' in 1964. The first shows combined oriental rugs with paintings and sculptures by artists such as Pierre Clerk, Michael Eastman, Denis McCarthy and Lawrence Weiner. The gallery closed

Seth Siegelaub and Lucy R. Lippard

At about the same time, the first mixed exhibitions of Conceptual art were organised in the US. In February–March 1968, Seth Siegelaub (born in the 1940s) organised *Carl Andre, Robert Barry, Lawrence Weiner* at the Laura Knott Gallery of the Bradford Junior College (Massachusetts).[4] The venue may have been suggested by the artist Douglas Huebler (1924–97) who had been teaching at the Bradford College since 1957. He had known Siegelaub, who had been promoting his art as a private dealer since 1966.[5]

Chuck Ginnever, who had seen this exhibition and who was teaching at the Windham College, Putney (Vermont), invited Siegelaub to make a follow-up show in April–May 1968.[6] As the college did not have a gallery, the artists worked outdoors on site-specific sculptural installations. The works were realised with materials from the area and were meant to last only for the duration of the exhibition.[7] Andre, for instance, presented *Joint*, a sculpture made from 183 units of baled hay placed end to end from the woods into a field. Both shows were held in colleges and were followed by public symposia with the artists.[8] The first debate was moderated by Siegelaub, the second by Dan Graham. These public discussions held in educational surroundings demonstrate the will to engage with the audience and to present these artists as a group identified with one dealer.

In February 1968, the American critic Lucy Lippard (born 1937) published with John Chandler the article 'The Dematerialisation of the Art Object', which was to become a key document in defining the phenomenon of Conceptual art.[9] She pointed out that Conceptual artists executed their works outside the studio, thus underlining that it was the artists who were now travelling, rather than the works. Lippard, who was Siegelaub's partner at the time, emerged as a major art critic for Conceptualism.[10]

Gian Enzo Sperone, Turin

In early 1968, the Arte Povera group continued to develop in Northern Italy. Following the first mixed shows that had established the movement in late 1967, the Galleria De' Foscherari, Bologna, presented an Arte Povera group show in March–April 1968 including Boetti, Pistoletto and Mario Merz.[11] This exhibition was curated by Germano Celant in association with the Italian art dealer Gian

down in 1966, but Siegelaub continued to deal privately (Weiner, Huebler). Thus Siegelaub had known Weiner since the opening of his New York gallery in 1964. About the same time, he got to know Robert Barry who was in a nearby corporate gallery. Barry introduced him to Andre. See: Siegelaub in conversation with the author, *op. cit.* See also: Alberro, *Conceptual Art and the Politics of Publicity*, *op. cit.*, pp.11–12.

5 'Truro, Massachusetts, October 11–14, 1992', in *Douglas Huebler, «Variable», etc.* (exh. cat.), FRAC Limousin, Limoges, 1993, pp.126–127.

6 'Andre, Barry and Weiner', Windham College, Putney, Vermont, 30 April–31 May 1968.

7 This outdoor exhibition related to the emerging phenomenon of Land Art in America (Walter De Maria, Michael Heizer).

8 Lippard, *Six Years*, *op. cit.*, pp.40–48. See also: Alberro, *Conceptual Art and the Politics of Publicity*, *op. cit.*, p.16–24.

9 Lucy Lippard and John Chandler, 'The Dematerialization of Art', *Art International*, vol.2, no.12, February 1968, pp.31–36.

10 Lippard had contributed an essay to the exhibition catalogue of the Den Haag *Minimal Art* exhibition. See: Lucy R. Lippard, '10 Structurists in 20 Paragraphs', in *Minimal Art* (exh. cat.), Haags Gemeentemuseum, The Hague, 1968, pp. 25–31.

11 'Arte Povera', Galleria De' Foscherari, Bologna, 24 February–15 March. Artists: Anselmo, Boetti, Ceroli, Fabro, Kounellis, Merz, Paolini, Pascali, Piacentino, Pistoletto, Prini and Zorio. See: Germano Celant, *Arte Povera* (exh. cat.), De' Foscherari, Bologna, 1968. See also: Carolyn Christov-Bakargiev, *Arte Povera*, Phaidon, London

Enzo Sperone (born 1939).[12]

From this moment, Sperone became a central figure in the promotion of Arte Povera artists. From the spring of 1968, he supported the Deposito d'Arte Presente in Turin, an old factory that became an informal meeting place and gallery for artists. This artist-run space was organised by Pistoletto, Piero Gilardi and the collector Marcello Levi, and was used by artists such as Boetti, Kounellis, Merz, Pistoletto and Zorio.[13] These were mostly artists who were already, or were soon to be, exhibiting at the Galleria Sperone in Turin (Via Cesare Battisti). For example, Gilardi, Pistoletto and Pino Pascali had been represented by the gallery since 1966. In 1967, they were joined by Marisa Merz and Zorio. In January 1968, Mario Merz (1925–2003) had a solo show at the gallery.[14] It was followed by shows of Anselmo (April 1968) and Kounellis (December 1968).

May 1968: France and Italy

In Spring 1968, the student and youth protests that had started in 1967 reached their high point in what has become known as 'May '68'. In France, Germany, Italy, Britain and the Netherlands, demonstrations against elitism, institutional authority and higher education's submission to business interests took place.[15] Many peace demonstrations against the Vietnam War were held. Rapidly, the youth movement drew closer to the working class with claims of equality and social rights. Occupation of faculties and public meetings led to violent confrontations with the police. These were particularly brutal in Paris, where barricades were built in the Latin Quarter. These uprisings had a great impact on European societies. Access to higher education was broadened. Feminism, advocating the pill and abortion, and ecological awareness became popular. Advances in working conditions such as reduced working hours, minimum salary and equality, were fought for by unions.

1968 Venice Biennale

The impact of social unrest on culture was apparent during the summer of 1968 at the Venice Biennale and at Documenta 4.[16] The opening of the Venice Biennale on 22 June 1968 became a focus for artist and student protests.[17] Artists including Otto Piene complained about the authoritarian selection procedure

and New York, 1999, pp.28–54.

12 From 1962 to 1964, Gian Enzo Sperone directed the Il Punto Gallery in Turin. In May 1964, he launched his own gallery space in Turin with a group show of Rotella, Mondino, Pistoletto and Lichtenstein. At the time, Italian Arte Povera and American Pop art were the main focuses of his gallery. Through his connections to Ileana Sonnabend, he exhibited many Pop artists such as Rauschenberg (June 1964) and Warhol (February 1965). The archive of the Galleria Sperone is closed to the public. For a comprehensive outline of exhibitions of Conceptual artists at the gallery, see: Database 1, Section Gian Enzo Sperone (Appendix 1.1). For a comprehensive overview of the exhibitions organised by Sperone, see: Minola, Mundici, Poli and Roberto, *Gian Enzo Sperone*, *op. cit.*, pp.491–499. See also: Appendix 3.13.

13 See: Minola, Mundici, Poli and Roberto, *Gian Enzo Sperone*, *op. cit.*, pp.26–32. See also: Christov-Bakargiev, *Arte Povera*, *op. cit.*, p.53.

14 Mario Merz, Galleria Gian Enzo Sperone, Turin, from 19 January 1968. See: Minola, Mundici, Poli and Roberto, *Gian Enzo Sperone*, *op. cit.*, pp.118–119. See also: Database 3, Section Mario Merz (Appendix 1.3). Merz had his first solo show in 1954 at the Galleria La Bussola, Turin.

15 Students found the expression of their discontent in the writings of the philosopher Herbert Marcuse (*One-dimensional Man*, 1964) and of the writer and filmmaker Guy Debord (*La Société du Spectacle*, 1967). Jean-Paul Sartre's Existentialism also had some influence on the youth movements of the late 1960s, with its Marxist social

and the system of prices at an art event they considered 'capitalistic'. The Argentine artist Julio Le Parc led demonstrations against American art and was later deported from France. Protesters were brutally attacked by riot police on the Piazza San Marco.[18] As a demonstration of their disapproval against this 'police biennale', the Swedes closed their pavilion. The French artists also withdrew their work and most Italian artists went on strike.[19]

However, the other pavilions remained unchanged. The national selections of artists were not particularly innovative or daring. Artists on show included Horst Janssen (Germany), Carel Visser (Holland), Arman (France) and Leonard Baskin (USA).[20] One of the most politically critical works was shown by David Lamelas (born 1946) in the Argentine pavilion. His *Office of Information about the Vietnam War at Three Levels: The Visual Image, Text and Audio* was a news agency in which a ticker-tape machine brought live the latest news on the Vietnam War. While this work was a representation of the artist's political position, it was also questioning the structures by which information was disseminated. Perhaps most important were the discussions initiated about the structure of international art shows and their organisers' methods of selecting artists.

Documenta 4

Documenta 4 opened five days after the Venice Biennale, on 27 June 1968, in Kassel.[21] Its new structure and the selection of participants denoted the changing cultural interests in Germany: it demonstrated a concern with contemporary art rather than with the past. The Artistic Director Arnold Bode (1900–77) was backed by a council of 24 art world professionals. The German representation was strong. However, the council did include prominent figures from outside Germany, such as Jan Leering, the Director of the Stedelijk Van Abbemuseum in Eindhoven, who was in charge of the painting section. He included American Minimal artists: Andre, LeWitt (*47 Three part variations on three different kinds of cubes*), Morris and Flavin.[22] The show was popular, attracting 207,000 visitors.[23]

Student demonstrations in Europe and a dockers' strike in America caused severe transport problems for artists trying to get their works to Kassel; these were paralleled by organisational and installation difficulties. The domination and interference of American dealers in the selection and hanging procedure

implications and political commitment (*Critique de la raison dialectique*, 1965).

16 In America too, social unrest had repercussions on the art world. In 1968, Paula Cooper launched the first art gallery in New York's Soho district with an exhibition to benefit the Student Mobilization Committee to End the War in Vietnam. The show included works by Andre, Flavin, Judd, Mangold and Ryman, among others, as well as LeWitt's first wall drawing.

17 *Venezia Biennale 1968, LXXXIV Esposizione Biennale Internationale d'Arte Venezia*, Venice, 22 June–20 October 1968. For a discussion of the politicalisation of artists at the Venice Biennale, see: Therese Schwartz, 'The Politicalization of the Avant-Garde', *Art in America*, November–December 1971, pp.103–105.

18 This event was reported by *Studio International*. See: Jean Clay, 'Art Tamed and Wild', *Studio International*, vol.177, no.912, June 1969, pp.262–265.

19 Leif Nylen, 'Suddenly last summer', *Art and Artists*, vol.4, no.5, August 1969, pp.58–61. These troubles would eventually result in the creation of a new statute for the Biennale in 1973.

20 Carel Visser is the brother of the Dutch private collector Martin Visser. Grand Prizes were awarded to Bridget Riley (painting), Nicolas Schöffer (sculpture) and Horst Janssen (engraving).

21 *Documenta 4*, Museum Fridericianum, Kassel, 27 June–6 September 1968.

22 In spring 1968, the Stedelijk Van Abbemuseum in Eindhoven had presented a show of works in Dutch private collections, including

was denounced,[24] as were their business-focused interests: 'On their ground floor stands, American dealers displayed outsize works which could be acquired in the basement in miniature versions, as lithographs, sketches, micro-sculptures, etc.'[25]

German artists demonstrated against the fact that a third of the approximately thousand works on show were by American artists ('Documenta Americana'). Jörg Immendorff and Wolf Vostell condemned Documenta's inability to incorporate Happenings and Fluxus. As an expression of dissent against the politics of exclusion, they set up – together with Friedrich Heubach, a research assistant in psychology at the University of Cologne – the art magazine *Interfunktionen*. The first issue focused on the Documenta 4 controversies and featured material on Fluxus and Happenings (Nam June Paik, Jörg Immendorff, Wilhelm Kagel, Wolf Vostell).[26] *Interfunktionen* presented itself as a new form of art publication, one that questioned the conventional art critical and art information system.

Wide White Space, Antwerp

American dealers such as Leo Castelli and German dealers like Rolf Ricke, Rudolf Zwirner and Heiner Friedrich all lent to Documenta 4.[27] Anny De Decker and Bernd Lohaus from Wide White Space gallery organised a parallel exhibition in the nearby Parkhotel Hessenland in Kassel. In two conference rooms, they presented works from their artists: Marcel Broodthaers (born 1924), Joseph Beuys, Christo, Piero Manzoni and Panamarenko.[28] The opening of this exhibition coincided with the Documenta that Beuys and Christo exhibited in. De Decker explained: 'We'd been going for two years, which was no time at all, and that presentation was a very good way of making ourselves known.'[29] Indeed, this parallel exhibition of Documenta artists did much to establish their reputation.

The art historian Anny De Decker and her partner the German artist Bernd Lohaus (born 1940) had opened a gallery space in Antwerp (Plaatsnijders-straat) in March–April 1966 to show the work of Belgian artists such as Panamarenko, Hugo Heyrman (both March–April 1966) and Broodthaers (May–June 1966).[30] Lohaus had studied at the Kunstakademie in Düsseldorf, where fellow students included Fischer-Lueg and Richter. He also knew Beuys, who had been teaching

that of Mia and Martin Visser (Andre, Broodthaers, Darboven). See: *Three Blind Mice, The collectors Visser (Bergeyk, Antwerpen), Peeters (Bruges) and Becht (Hilversum)* (exh. cat.), Stedelijk Van Abbemuseum, Eindhoven, 1968.

23 Manfred Schneckenburger (ed.), *Documenta, Idee und Institution, Tendenzen-Konzepte-Materialien*, Bruckmann, Munich, 1983, p.90.

24 Frank Whitford and Robert Kudielka, 'Documenta 4: a critical review', *Studio International*, vol.176, no.903, September 1968, pp.74–76.

25 Clay, 'Art Tamed and Wild', *Studio International, op. cit.*, p.263.

26 See: 'documenta – documentation', *Interfunktionen*, no.1, 1968. See also: Gloria Moure (ed.), *Behind the facts. Interfunktionen 1968–1975* (exh. cat.), Poligrafa, Barcelona, 2004, p.47.

27 Tuchman, 'American Art in Germany, The History of a Phenomenon', *Artforum, op. cit.*, p.60.

28 See: Aupetitallot, *Wide White Space, op. cit.*, p.250.

29 'Interview Yves Aupetitallot, Anny De Decker, Bernd Lohaus', in *Ibid.*, p.45.

30 The archive of Wide White Space remains in the possession of Anny De Decker and Bernd Lohaus and is private. Some docu-ments, such as leaflets and posters, are kept by the Archives de l'Art Contemporain en Belgique, Brussels (File Fonds divers: Documentation presse Wide White Space, Anvers, no inventory number; hereafter AACBB). For a comprehensive outline of exhibitions of Conceptual artists at the gallery, see: Database 1, Section Wide White Space (Appendix 1.1). For a review of all the shows organised by the

in Düsseldorf since 1961. The links to Düsseldorf led De Decker and Lohaus to establish dealing relations with Alfred Schmela.[31]

Documenta 4 coincided with solo exhibitions of American Conceptual artists in Europe. Dealers took advantage of the artists visiting Europe to arrange showings in their galleries. From 3 to 25 May 1968, Andre had a solo exhibition at Wide White Space.[32] After his shows at Fischer and Friedrich, this was the artist's third solo exhibition in Europe. De Decker and Lohaus discovered Andre's work during his first European exhibition in Düsseldorf in October 1967, and it was Fischer who put them in touch with the artist.[33] Similarly, in May 1968, Dan Flavin had a solo show at Heiner Friedrich, Munich.[34]

Bruce Nauman

On 10 July 1968, the first European solo exhibition of Bruce Nauman (born 1941) was held at Konrad Fischer's in Düsseldorf.[35] It appears that it was again Kasper König who put Fischer in contact with the artist. König got to know Nauman's work at Richard Bellamy's gallery in New York and subsequently visited his studio in San Francisco.[36] Fischer wrote to Nauman on 25 May 1968:

> This is the first time you get a word from me. But I think we had a good connection via my friend Kasper.
>
> Now I want to say you very concrete things. But at first I would be very glad and proud if you would come to Düsseldorf, and I know that many people are very interested in your work.
>
> I want to send you a 21 days ticket California–Düsseldorf–California. With this ticket you can start to New York, if you want, at the 21 of June, but you cannot go over the Atlantic before the 24 of June. But I think that is a good time to come, for then you can go with me to the Documenta opening (26–27). (I have booked a place in a hotel for you.) You can fetch the ticket in the middle of June (12–14) at your next Lufthansa office, and they will write you too I think.
>
> It would be very nice, if you take some videos with you to Germany, so that I can sell some pieces of yours. Excuse me, I am not only thinking in selling, but I think it is good if you earn some money here, and me too, for the ticket is

Wide White Space, see: *Ibid.*, pp.226–338. See also: Appendix 3.14. Broodthaers was one of the first Conceptual artists to have been exhibited by the Wide White Space, from 1966 onwards. See: Database 3, Section Marcel Broodthaers (Appendix 1.3). See also: *Ibid.*, p.229.

31 *Ibid.*, pp.229–230.

32 *Carl Andre*, Wide White Space, Antwerp, 3–25 May 1968. See: *Ibid.*, p.249.

33 'Interview Yves Aupetitallot, Anny De Decker, Bernd Lohaus', in *Ibid.*, p.41.

34 'Dan Flavin, two primary series and one secondary', Galerie Heiner Friedrich, Munich, 9 May–5 June 1968.

35 'Bruce Nauman, 6 day week – 6 sound problems', Konrad Fischer, Düsseldorf, 10 July–8 August 1968. See: *Ausstellungen bei Konrad Fischer*, *op. cit.*, p.21. See also: Database 3, Section Bruce Nauman (Appendix 1.3). Nauman had received his first solo shows at the Nicholas Wilder Gallery, Los Angeles, in 1966 and at Leo Castelli, New York, from 27 January to 17 February 1968.

36 'Two-women show as good as one-man show, Ein Gespräch mit Kasper König', in Kölle, *Die Kunst des Ausstellen*, *op. cit.*, p.240.

37 Manuscript letter from Fischer to Nauman, California, dated 25 May [1968], in Korrespondenz mit Künstlern 1969–1970, AKFGD. In a letter to Fischer, LeWitt also mentioned Kasper König as providing the contact to Nauman. See: Letter from LeWitt to Fischer dated 27 April 1968, in Korrespondenz mit Künstlern 1969–70, AKFGD.

very expensive for me. I hope you understand.
I hope you will have a good time in Europe and a successful show at my place.
Please let me know (via Lufthansa) when you arrive.[37]

It seems that Nauman's show was conceived on the spot since it consisted of a sound installation of six different loops of noises made by the artist in the gallery (walking, bouncing two balls, etc). One loop was made for each day of the week.

Because this was Nauman's first gallery exhibition in Europe, Fischer was considered his main dealer there. Thus the artist wrote to him after the show, in September 1968: 'Nick Wilder wants to assume you are my German dealer and Ileana Sonnabend can have pieces with that understanding. So perhaps we can do something again if you like.'[38] Subsequently, Nauman had his second European solo show at Sonnabend, Paris, in November–December 1968.[39] On this occasion, however, it was probably Castelli rather than Fischer who made the arrangements. Moreover, it seems that Castelli tried to put Fischer off by imposing other German connections. Indeed, Nauman wrote to Fischer in October 1968, a month before his show at Sonnabend:

> I don't know how things will work out because although everything is fine with Nick, Leo would rather deal with Zwerner [sic] in Germany and perhaps only some special arrangements with you. I think it is something I will not have too much control over – though he was also interested in Richard and I told him not to do that especially and he said OK. I hope it can be worked out.[40]

In 1968, already a year after opening his gallery, Fischer was considered a potential rival in Europe for the transatlantic Castelli-Sonnabend links.[41] Moreover, Rudolf Zwirner had established a serious reputation in Cologne by exhibiting Minimal artists such as Flavin and by launching the Cologne Art Fair in 1967.

38 Manuscript letter from Bruce Nauman, New York, to Konrad Fischer dated 15 September 1968, in Korrespondenz mit Künstlern 1969–70, AKFGD. In 1965, Nicholas Wilder (1937–89) launched his gallery in Los Angeles with exhibitions of Agnes Martin (1965), John McCracken (1965), Dan Flavin (1966) and Bruce Nauman (1966).

39 'Bruce Nauman', Galerie Ileana Sonnabend, Paris, 25 November–15 December 1968. For a comprehensive outline of exhibitions of Conceptual artists at the gallery, see: Database 1, Section Ileana Sonnabend, Paris (Appendix 1.1). See also: Appendix 3. 8.

40 Manuscript letter from Bruce Nauman to Konrad Fischer dated 6 October 1968, in Korrespondenz mit Künstlern 1969–70, AKFGD.

41 The Sonnabend-Fischer rivalry concerning Nauman's representation in Europe continued in 1969. Indeed, in April 1969, Fischer wrote to the artist that he would like to have a further show with him after the one he was planning at Sonnabend. But he complained that there was a rumour that Nauman would be showing with Rolf Ricke, who in exchange would give Sonnabend a show of Richard Serra. He added that he did not approve of this situation, expressing a hope that Nauman would decide for himself where to show in Germany. See: Letter from Fischer to Nauman dated 29 April 1969, in Korrespondenz mit Künstlern 1969–70, AKFGD. Nauman had his second show at Sonnabend in December 1969 and at Fischer in February–March 1970. Both dealers continued to represent Nauman throughout the 1970s. See: Database 3, Section Bruce Nauman (Appendix 1.3).

Jan Dibbets

During Documenta 4, in August 1968, the first German solo exhibition of Jan Dibbets (born 1941) was held by Fischer.[42] Fischer and Dibbets knew each other from the 1967 exhibitions *Serielle Formationen* and *Dies alles Herzchen* in Frankfurt. In April 1968, six months after the opening of Fischer's space, Dibbets had contacted the dealer, asking about the possibility of an exhibition:

> Since Frankfurt I have not heard much from you. I read quite a lot about your gallery (Andre). The exhibition in Frankfurt was even more important than one could think. It was the first exhibition of what one now calls 'sensorial art' (Long, Flanagan, Pasmore, etc) ...
>
> What I wanted to ask you is if it would be possible for me to do an installation at your gallery of grass, sand and little tree trunks. I send you for information [on] a slightly older grass piece.
>
> If you are interested then send me information about your gallery (dimensions etc). Then I will send you a map with what I could do. By agreement I will come to execute this.
>
> It's a pity about the 200 mistakes I made in German but the main point is that you can read it.[43]

On 27 April, Fischer replied to Dibbets, writing that it was a good idea to do an installation in his space. He also pointed out that 'sensorial art' was very promising.[44] Two days later, on 29 April, Dibbets answered:

> I think sensorial art could be a European answer to American Minimal Art. Sonnabend works on it behind the screens.[45]
>
> An exhibition at your place would be very good to show some of my things in Germany. As far as I am aware, your gallery is long and small. That would be very good for me. If you send me plans of your gallery I will send you the different possibilities. I don't know if there is something to earn but I am sure that there will be something to see. (Grass? Wood? Sand? Water?).[46]

Dibbets's comment on Sonnabend further demonstrates that she was

42 'Jan Dibbets, Rasenrolle, Holzbündel, Wasserpfütze', Konrad Fischer, Düsseldorf, 15 August–17 September 1968. See: *Ausstellungen bei Konrad Fischer*, *op. cit.*, p.22. Dibbets had had his first exhibitions (serial paintings) at the Galerie 845 (1965) and Galerie Swart (1966, 1967) in Amsterdam.

43 Letter from Dibbets to Fischer dated April 1968, in Korrespondenz mit Künstlern 1969–70, AKFGD (author's translation).

44 Letter from Fischer to Dibbets dated 27 April 1968, in Korrespondenz mit Künstlern 1969–70, AKFGD.

45 Dibbets was not a fluent German speaker. He probably meant 'behind the scenes'.

46 Letter from Dibbets to Fischer dated 29 April 1968, in Korrespondenz mit Künstlern 1969–70, AKFGD (author's translation).

47 Minola, Mundici, Poli and Roberto, *Gian Enzo Sperone*, *op. cit.*, p.18.

48 'Konrad Fischer interviewed by Georg Jappe', *Studio International*, op. cit., p.70.

49 Letter from Konrad Ficher to Richard Long, Bristol and London [2 letters] dated 18 August 1968, in Korrespondenz mit Künstlern 1969–70, AKFGD.

50 Manuscript letter from Long, London, to Fischer dated 22 August [1968], in Korrespondenz mit Künstlern 1969–70, AKFGD.

51 *Richard Long*, Konrad Fischer, Düsseldorf, 21 September–18 October 1968. See: *Ausstellungen bei Konrad Fischer*, *op. cit.*, p.23.

52 'Konrad Fischer', *Kunstforum International*, *op. cit.*, p.280.

53 The archive of Art & Project is held at the Netherlands Institute

making great efforts to establish herself as the key dealer for new progressive art in Europe. From 1967, she had initiated business links with Sperone to exhibit Arte Povera artists in Paris: Gilardi (1967), Zorio and Anselmo (both 1969).[47]

Richard Long

At the time of Dibbets's show in August 1968, Fischer contacted another artist whom he had known since the 1967 Frankfurt performance exhibition, Richard Long (born 1945). The dealer declared: 'I have never felt so spontaneously enthusiastic about anyone as I did about Long.'[48] He wrote on 18 August 1968:

> Dear Richard Long,
> Since one year nearly I have a small gallery in Düsseldorf. Jan Dibbets just has a show here. Jan spoke a lot about you and in a very high way. I saw one piece of yours (branches) in Frankfurt last year. I would like to give you a show if you are interested.
>
> I did the following shows till now: Carl Andre, C. Posenenske + H. Darboven, Sol LeWitt, Ruthenbeck, Palermo, Fred Sandback, Richard Artschwager, Bruce Nauman, Jan Dibbets. I send you some invitation cards of these shows and a map of the place. You can do here whatever you like to show. The next date the space is free is the 18th of September, for one month. If it is possible for you I would like if you could do a show then.
>
> I have a studio, where you can live and work for some days; also I'll pay some money for your trip to Düsseldorf.
>
> I hope very much you are interested! Please let me know soon. Looking forward to your answer.
>
> With best regards,
> Konrad Fischer[49]

A few days later, on 22 August 1968, Long replied:

> Dear Konrad Fischer
> Thank you very much for your letter, and your offer. I am very interested in using your gallery and I would like to know the colour and composition of

for Art History, The Hague (Rijksbureau voor Kunsthistorische Documentatie). In accordance with a contract with the owners, it will not be open to the public until 2008.

54 Rudolf W.D. Oxenaar, 'On art and museum policies in the Netherlands', *Studio International*, vol.185, no. 955, May 1973, pp.203–204.

55 Christophe Cherix, 'Un entretien avec les éditeurs du Art & Project Bulletin (Février-Mars 2003)', in Press Release, 'Art & Project Bulletin, Amsterdam, 1968–1989', Cabinet des Estampes, Musée d'art moderne et contemporain, Geneva, 2003. See also: 'Interview Andriaan van Ravesteijn', in Moseley, *Conception*, *op. cit.*, p.151.

56 'Charlotte Posenenske', Art & Project, Amsterdam, 20 September–16 October 1968. See: *Art & Project Bulletin*, no.1, 17 September 1968. For a comprehensive outline of exhibitions of Conceptual artists at the gallery, see: Database 1, Section Art & Project (Appendix 1.1). For an extensive overview of exhibitions organised by Art & Project see: Appendix 3.1.

57 All the Bulletins were recently presented in the exhibition 'Art & Project Bulletin, Amsterdam 1968–1989' held at the Cabinet des Estampes, Musée d'art moderne et contemporain, Geneva (21 October–25 January 2004) and at the Centre National de l'Estampe et de l'Art imprimé, Chatou/Paris (October 2004–30 January 2005).

58 Cherix, 'Un entretien avec les éditeurs du Art & Project Bulletin (Février-Mars 2003)', in Press Release, *op. cit.* (author's translation).

59 Prospect 68, Kunsthalle, Düsseldorf, 20–29 September 1968.

60 Hans Strelow was a primary-school friend of Fischer. See:

your floor. Also, would it be possible to divide the gallery in two parts, so that the back door was not used during the exhibition. I will, of course, provide the invitation cards myself, so how many do you suggest I get? It may be more convenient to have them printed in Dusseldorf, so I will send them as soon as possible.

I would like to have about 5 days in which to prepare my exhibit. Please send my correspondence arriving on or after September 1 to my British address.

Once again, many thanks,
Yours sincerely,
Richard Long[50]

Long's first one-man show opened on 21 September 1968.[51] It included *Sculpture at Konrad Fischer, Düsseldorf* (1968), an in-situ floor installation made of 1,318 wooden sticks from the River Avon Gorge. For the duration of the show, Long travelled daily to the nearby city of Wuppertal, where he realised a sculpture in the lawn of a garden.[52]

Art & Project, Amsterdam

In 1968, Adriaan van Ravesteijn (born 1938) and Geert van Beijeren Bergen en Henegouwen (1933–2005) launched a new progressive art gallery in Amsterdam (Richard Wagnerstraat). The gallery, called Art & Project, was located on the ground floor of their house in the suburbs.[53] The Netherlands was very dynamic culturally at this time. There were over 500 museums in the country and numerous local dealer galleries in Amsterdam.[54] Van Beijeren had worked as a librarian at the Stedelijk Museum, Amsterdam, since 1966, and had connections with the art world. Their friendship with Rijke Swart was central in their decision to open a gallery, and also in getting to know artists such as Dibbets and Ger van Elk.[55] The gallery's first exhibition opened on 20 September 1968 and was dedicated to Charlotte Posenenske.[56] This was an artist with whom Dibbets had exhibited in Frankfurt in 1967, and it is possible that it was he who approached her. Posenenske had exhibited at Konrad Fischer in December 1967.

Right from the beginning, the Art & Project Bulletin,[57] conceived as an

'Konrad Fischer', *Kunstforum International*, *op. cit.*, p.277.

61 *Prospect 68, Katalog-Zeitung zur internationalen Vorschau auf die Kunst in den Galerien der Avantgarde* (exh. cat.), Städtische Kunsthalle Düsseldorf, 1968.

62 *Prospect 68* (brochure), Städtische Kunsthalle Düsseldorf, 1968 (author's translation).

63 Other cities, such as Nuremberg, also proposed to host the art fair. See: Letter from Dietrich Mahlow, Institut für Moderne Kunst, Nuremberg, to the VPDK dated 16 November 1967, in File C2 IV 15, Zadik.

64 Letter from Otto van de Loo to Karl Ruhrberg dated 25 November 1967, and Letter from Ruhrberg to Van de Loo dated 11 December 1967, in File C2 IV 15, Zadik.

65 Undated and unsigned letter from the VPDK, in File C2 IV 15, Zadik.

66 Letter from Otto van de Loo to all members of the VPDK dated 25 April 1968, in File A1 VIII 6, Zadik.

67 See the document entitled 'Das Auswahlkomitee entschied sich für folgende Galerien' (the jury chose the following dealer galleries), in File IV 29371–138, Archive Kunsthalle Düsseldorf, Stadtarchiv, Düsseldorf (hereafter AKDSD). The document is reproduced as Appendix 2.1.

68 Strelow underlined that all the votes were submitted by post. See: 'Wie können wir die interessantesten Künstler in Düsseldorf zeigen ohne Geld zu haben? Ein Gespräch mit Hans Strelow', in Kölle, *Die Kunst des Ausstellens*, *op. cit.*, p.233.

information letter and a work of art realised by the artists, was distributed in parallel with the shows. Adriaan van Ravesteijn explained:

> One has to remember that cultural Europe was in full agitation at the moment of the launching of Art & Project. A period marked by anti-conformism reached its apogee in Paris in 1968. Everything had to be changed, even the usual art gallery. Thus the name 'Art and Project' did not include the word 'gallery', a simple leaflet replaced the sending out of glossy invitation cards. The participation of the public also became important in the realisation of the work of art. We did not invent these things, they were in the air! The attention we paid to the bulletin was due to our isolated geographical situation. Information given in advance could, we hoped, encourage the public to leave the city centre and to pay us a visit. The two inside pages were given to the invited artists to display their ideas, in relation or not to an exhibition in the gallery.[58]

Prospect 68

On 20 September 1968, the first of the Prospect exhibitions at the Kunsthalle in Düsseldorf opened.[59] The event was set up by Fischer and the art critic Hans Strelow as a reaction to the first Cologne Art Fair in 1967.[60] Prospect was neither a group show nor an art fair. It was rather, as the exhibition catalogue stated, an 'international preview of art from the avant-garde galleries'.[61]
The Kunsthalle's brochure explained:

> ... the information on the current trends on the international art scene is necessary, because the art lover ought to know what is really up-to-date, what he can expect to see in the coming season in the galleries of the world, the first intermediaries between the new art and the public.[62]

The success of the first Cologne Art Fair had attracted the interest of the nearby Düsseldorf art community. In November 1967, shortly after the Cologne event, Karl Ruhrberg, the director of Kunsthalle Düsseldorf, contacted Otto van de Loo, Head of the VPDK, the Organisation of Progressive German Art Dealers

69 Letter from Otto van de Loo to Karl Ruhrberg dated 13 July 1968, in File A1 VIII 6 56, Zadik. See also: Letter from Friedrich to Ruhrberg dated 5 July 1968, in File IV 29371–138, AKDSD. The exhibition catalogue of Prospect 68 included an advertisement for the 'Kunstmarkt Köln 68' and one for Galerie Heiner Friedrich, Munich. It also included a list of the first ten exhibitions held at Konrad Fischer, Düsseldorf.

70 As Castelli and Sonnabend were collaborating, they could be represented at both events. Castelli held a stand in Cologne, while Sonnabend had one in Düsseldorf.

71 [Editor's note: This may have been because the galleries had to cover their own costs.]

72 Galleries: Galleria Apollinaire (Milan), Axiom Gallery (London), Galerie Bischofsberger (Zurich), Galerie Iris Clert (Paris), Dwan Gallery (New York), Mathias Fels & Cie (Paris), Robert Fraser Gallery (London), Kasmin Limited (London), Galerie Yvon Lambert (Paris), Galleria Del Naviglio (Milan, Venice), Galerie Ileana Sonnabend (Paris), Galeria Sperone (Turin), Rijke Swart (Amsterdam), Galerie M.E. Thelen (Essen), Wide White Space (Amsterdam) and Galerie René Ziegler (Zurich).

73 Artists on show were: Abrams, Adzak, Alviani, Andre, Anselmo, Arakawa, Atwell, Avedisian, Bannard, Beuys, Blake, Boetti, Bonalumi, Bonies, Brenner, Brô, Broodthaers, Brusse, Buren, Calzolari, Capogrossi, Carder, Caulfield, Ceroli, César, Christo, D'Arcangelo, Dekkers, Doyle, Pierre de Maria, Walter De Maria, Denny, Dine, Evison, Farrell, Flavin, Grisi, Harris, Haworth, Held, Hide, Hodgkin,

in Cologne, proposing to host the 1968 art fair in Düsseldorf.[63] During its annual meeting, however, the organisation made the decision to hold the event in Cologne again.[64] Although Ruhrberg specifically mentioned in his letter that there was no 'Kunstmarkt Krieg' (art fair war), a rivalry between the two cities was created with the launching of Prospect 68.

What annoyed the VPDK most about Prospect was not just its existence as another exhibition set up by German dealers, but its intention to invite international dealer galleries. VPDK believed that the presence of renowned international galleries such as Sidney Janis or Marlborough would take away potential business from German dealers, and that in the long run, especially if these foreign galleries established contacts with museums and private collectors, this could cause the downfall of the German art market.[65]

In order to counteract the Düsseldorf project, the VPDK decided to invite to Cologne international dealer galleries that might be interested in the rival event. The condition would be that the foreign dealers should associate with the German galleries promoting the same artists.[66] Foreign dealers had to choose between the two events.

Prospect was based on an original concept. An international jury selected the dealer galleries rather than the artists to be invited. The galleries were free to present the works of any artists. The jury of the 1968 event was composed of seven representatives of various groups within the art world structure. These were museum curators Enno Develing (Gemeentemuseum, The Hague), Paul Wember (Kaiser Wilhelm Museum, Krefeld) and Pontus Hulten (Moderna Museet, Stockholm); art critics Alan Bowness (London) and Kurt Meyer (Zurich); and private collectors Martin Visser (Bergeyk) and Hubert Peeters (Bruges).

The jury voted on a shortlist of 56 European and American dealer galleries.[67] It appears that the members of the jury could vote for a maximum of 25 galleries each, but not all votes had to be used.[68] Several progressive European dealer galleries that showed or would soon show Conceptual art were included in this original choice: Sperone, Friedrich, Wide White Space and Fischer. Sperone and Wide White Space were included in the exhibition; Fischer and Friedrich were not. Fischer was probably excluded because he only got one vote from Wember, but it also may have been because he was one of the organisers. Friedrich

House, Jacquet, Jensen, Kienholz, King, Kitaj, Klasen, Koetsier, Laing, Lamelas, Latham, LeWitt, Lijn, Lin, Lohaus, Lohse, Luginbühl, Luther, Malaval, Manders, Matiello, McEwen, Mario Merz, Meylan, Monchâtre, Monro, Morris, Nauman, Palermo, Panamarenko, Piacentino, Price, Prini, Raynaud, Reusch, Rieti, Ross, Ruthenbeck, Sandback, Sanejouand, Scanavino, Self, Smith, Scheggi, Smithson, Snelson, Steiner, Stevenson, Struycken, Thek, Toyofuku, Tucker, Uriburu, Venet, Volten, Walker, Yasuda and Zorio.

74 In October 1968, Buren had his first solo show, presenting an in-situ installation of vertical stripes at the Galleria Apollinaire, Milan. See: *Daniel Buren, Mot à Mot* (exh. cat.), Editions du Centre Georges Pompidou, Editions Xavier Barral, Editions de la Martinière, Paris, 2002, p.G 02–G 03. In Paris, on 3 January 1967, Daniel Buren, Olivier Mosset, Michel Parmentier and Niele Toroni (BMPT group) had organised their *Manifestation 1* at the Salon de la Jeune Peinture in Paris. During the opening of the Salon, they each realised a painting bearing visual signs that would become their signature: vertical stripes for Buren, a small black circle for Mosset, horizontal bands for Parmentier and imprints of paint brushes for Toroni. At the same moment, they distributed a tract which included the words: 'Nous ne sommes pas peintres' (We are not painters). As a protest against art's reactionary position, they withdrew their work from the show on the following day. See: *Ibid.*, p.M 05.

75 See: Photographs kept in Box Prospect 68, Archive Städtische Kunsthalle Düsseldorf, Düsseldorf (hereafter ASKDD).

76 Barbara Hess, '30 Jahre Ausstellungen bei Konrad Fischer 1967–

received four votes, which would have secured his position. However, because of the rivalry with the Cologne Art Fair, he had to choose between the two events.[69] This restriction, imposed by Cologne, led to the exclusion of several galleries, despite the votes achieved: Castelli (six votes),[70] Müller (five votes), Schmela (four votes) and Zwirner (five votes). However, it is unclear why Richard Bellamy (six votes) and the Pace Gallery (four votes) did not take part, since neither participated in the Cologne Art Fair.[71]

In the end, 16 international dealer galleries were represented by their artists at the Düsseldorf event.[72] They mostly came from France, Italy, Britain and Switzerland, but there were also others from the Netherlands, Belgium and Germany. Dwan was the only American gallery. Although all galleries presented innovative art tendencies, only a few showed works by Conceptual artists.[73] The Galleria Apollinaire (Milan) presented work by Daniel Buren (born 1938).[74] Wide White Space exhibited many artists, including Broodthaers, Beuys, Christo and David Lamelas. Sperone showed Arte Povera artists such as Boetti and Prini. Sonnabend presented notably Nauman and Morris, Mario Merz and Zorio. The Dwan Gallery showed works by Andre, LeWitt, Smithson and Flavin.

Prospect 68 was held from 20–29 September, a month before the Cologne Art Fair. Photographs of the opening demonstrate that it attracted important people from the art world, who would become key protagonists of the Conceptual art network, such as Schum, Cladders and Szeemann.[75] That the enterprise was a success is evidenced by the fact that the Kunsthalle had to close at one point during the opening to prevent overcrowding, and over its ten-day run[76] it was visited by 15,000 people.[77] The press reported the presence of an international audience.[78] This event played an important part in developing the Conceptual art network because it enabled further contacts to be established. For instance, De Decker, Lohaus and Yvon Lambert met Buren there.[79] Nigel Greenwood from the Axiom Gallery, London, was able to make many contacts which would be useful for the opening of his own gallery.

1968 Cologne Kunstmarkt

The Cologne Kunstmarkt was held from 15–20 October 1968 in the Kunsthalle.[80] In comparison with the previous year, the event was a great success, attracting

1997', *Sediment*, Zadik, no.2, 1997, p.25. The party with free 'beer and beat' contributed to drawing many people to the Kunsthalle.

77 Letter from Karl Ruhrberg to all the participating dealer galleries dated 11 October 1968, in File IV 29371– 138, AKDSD.

78 See, for instance: Anna Klapheck, 'Blick in die neue Kunstszene', *Rheinische Post*, 20 September 1968.

79 'Interview Yves Aupetitallot, Anny De Decker, Bernd Lohaus', in Aupetitallot, *Wide White Space*, *op. cit.*, pp.53–98.

80 'Kunstmarkt 1968', Kunsthalle, Cologne, 15–20 October 1968.

81 Statistics of the 1968 art fair, in CD-Rom, 'Kunstmarkt Köln '67', *Sediment*, *op. cit.*

82 See: *Kunstmarkt 1968* (exh. cat.), Verein progressiver deutscher Kunsthändler, Cologne, 1968, unnumbered pages.

83 In December 1968 in New York, the show *9 at Leo Castelli* presented works of Arte Povera artists alongside international contemporary artists. The show was organised at the suggestion of Robert Morris. *9 at Leo Castelli*, Castelli Warehouse, New York, December 1968. Artists: Anselmo, Bollinger, Hesse, Kaltenbach, Nauman, Saret, Serra, Sonnier and Zorio. See: Christov-Bakargiev, *Arte Povera*, *op. cit.*, p.61.

84 *Arte povera e Azione povere*, Arsenali della Repubblica, Amalfi, 4–6 October. Artists (selection): Ableo, Anselmo, Boetti, Camoni, Dibbets, Fabro, Ferrara, Gilardi, Icaro, Kounellis, Lista, Long, Marotta, Martelli, Henry Martin, Mario and Marisa Merz, Paolini, Pascali, Piacentino, Pistoletto, Prini, Rumma, Sauzeau-Boetti, Trini, Celant, Van Elk and Zorio.

more than twice the number of visitors (between 30,000 and 50,000, compared with 15,000–16,000 in 1967). It also produced a turnover of two million Deutschmarks, double the amount of the year before.[81] But while the Kunstmarkt was certainly a successful and profitable enterprise, it was not concentrated on Conceptual art. Friedrich showed works by Palermo and Walter De Maria; Ricke showed Flavin; Block showed Reiner Ruthenbeck; Müller showed Robert Mangold.[82] But since none of the young Conceptual dealer galleries had been invited, Conceptualism was not comprehensively represented. The place for Conceptual art in the alternative network was Prospect in Düsseldorf.

Arte povera e Azione povere

In the same month, October 1968, the first show to present the Italian Arte Povera artists alongside their international peers took place.[83] *Arte povera e Azione povere* was organised by Marcello Rumma and curated by Germano Celant in Amalfi (near Naples).[84] It was a three-day event presenting various discussions, performances and collective works by artists and writers including Boetti, Dibbets, Long, Merz, Ger van Elk and Zorio.[85] Long made a performance entitled *Shaking hands with passers-by*.

Carl Andre, Städtisches Museum, Mönchengladbach

The organisation of group shows of progressive artists in public spaces and the setting up of early solo shows went together. On 18 October 1968, Andre's first European one-man show in a public institution opened at the Städtisches Museum, Mönchengladbach.[86] At the time, the museum was a small city-owned provincial institution in the Rhine-Ruhr area. Since 1967, it had been directed by Johannes Cladders (born 1924). He had previously been Paul Wember's assistant at the Kaiser Wilhelm Museum in Krefeld. In 1967, the exhibition budget was DM 10,000, but that had increased to DM 24,000 in 1968. In 1968, 6,356 visitors came to see the temporary exhibitions.[87]

By October 1968, Andre had exhibited at Fischer (October–November 1967), Friedrich (March–April 1968) and Wide White Space (May 1968). Cladders remembered that he got to know Andre at Documenta 4 (June–September 1968), where he had been fascinated by his concrete-block floor sculpture.[88] The show

85 See: *Ibid.*, pp.56–60.

86 'Carl Andre', Städtisches Museum, Mönchengladbach, 18 October–15 December 1968. For an overview of the exhibitions of Conceptual artists at the museum, see: Database 2, Section Mönchengladbach (Appendix 1.2).

87 Questionnaire filled out by the Städtisches Museum, Mönchengladbach, in 1975, in File C5 VI 2, Zadik. Compare with: Marlis Grüterich, 'Mönchengladbach', *Studio International*, vol.193, no.985, January–February 1977, pp.27–29.

88 Walter Grasskamp, *Johannes Cladders*, Kunststiftung NRW, DuMont, Cologne, 2004, p.41.

89 Susanne Wischermann, *Johannes Cladders, Museumsmann und Künstler*, Peter Lang, Europäische Hochschulschriften, Kunstgeschichte, Frankfurt/Main, 1997, p.38 (PhD, Cologne University, 1996).

90 The help of Dwan and Fischer as Andre's main American and European dealers respectively was acknowledged in the exhibition catalogue. See: *Carl Andre* (exh. cat.), Städtisches Museum, Mönchengladbach, 1968. Cladders developed an original concept for the exhibition catalogues, which were small boxes in which sheets of papers with texts or any other kind of object could be included. In the case of Andre, the catalogue-box contained a sort of narrow tablecloth.

91 At Cladders's request, Andre's steel pieces were realised for free by the company Mannesmann, whose director, Dr Wlaschekl, was a member of the cultural committee of the City of Mönchengladbach.

in Mönchengladbach comprised a wooden sculpture and six site-specific steel floor pieces, the *Mönchengladbach Squares*.[89] Fischer, as the artist's main dealer, was central in setting up this first museum exhibition.[90] Although he did not plan the realisation of the pieces on show,[91] he took care of the other arrangements, including the contribution by the Mönchengladbach museum to Andre's travel expenses.

Organising public showings of artists was central to reaching a wider public, and also to the official recognition of Conceptual art. Museum exhibitions were likely to be paralleled by purchases for the permanent collection.[92] On this matter, Fischer declared: 'It is fundamental for me to care for my artists, foremost, that they exhibit in other galleries. Not in Cologne of course. I wouldn't find that great – it's too close – but in Milan, London, Munich. And then it's important that they go into museums!'[93]

Robert Ryman

On 29 October 1968, Heiner Friedrich held the first European solo show of the American Minimal painter Robert Ryman (born 1930).[94] At about the same time, from 21 November 1968, Ryman had another one-man show at Konrad Fischer.[95] It is likely that both dealers got to know Ryman's work through their US connections.[96] The two German shows were planned and organised alongside each other. It seems that Friedrich was the first to propose a show to the artist and that Fischer took advantage of his being over in Europe to invite him to Düsseldorf.[97]

Ryman was one of the rare Minimalist painters to be exhibited as early as 1968 in Europe.[98] The artist himself sent over the works from his New York studio.[99] In order to ensure a distinction between the shows, Ryman chose not to mix the media.[100] The Munich exhibition comprised recent paintings on canvas that were from 1967–68, including *Adelphi*, *Orrin*, *Aacon*, *Exeter*, *Impex*, *Essex* and *Medway*.[101] The show in Düsseldorf included paintings on handmade paper from the *Classico* series (1968).

Although Ryman's exhibition at Heiner Friedrich opened before the one at Konrad Fischer, the latter imposed himself as the artist's main European dealer. Correspondence between Marilyn Fischbach, Ryman's dealer in New York,[102]

See: Grasskamp, *Johannes Cladders*, *op. cit.*, p.41. See also: Letter from Cladders to Fischer dated 12 December 1968, in File Ausstellungen: Andre/Darboven/La Cédille [1968–69], Archive Städtisches Museum, Mönchengladbach (hereafter ASMM).

92 This aspect will be studied in Chapter 5. Only a few months later, Darboven had her first museum exhibition in Mönchengladbach. *Hanne Darboven, Ausstellung mit 6 Filmprojektoren nach 6 Büchern über 1968*, Städtisches Museum, Mönchengladbach, 25 February–7 April 1969. She had her second solo show at Fischer's from 22 October to 15 November 1968. See: *Ausstellungen bei Konrad Fischer*, *op. cit.*, p.24.

93 'Konrad Fischer', *Kunstforum International*, *op. cit.*, pp.279–280 (author's translation).

94 'Robert Ryman', Galerie Heiner Friedrich, Munich, 29 October–November 1968. See the list of shows organised by Heiner Friedrich, in Urbaschek, *Dia Art Foundation*, *op. cit.*, p.233. See also: Manuscript letter from Ryman to Fischer dated 12 September 1968, in Korrespondenz mit Künstlern 1969–70, AKFGD. Robert Ryman had his first solo show in April–May 1967 at the Paul Bianchini Gallery, New York. He was married to Lucy Lippard from 1961 to 1966.

95 *Robert Ryman*, Konrad Fischer, Düsseldorf, 21 November–17 December 1968. See: *Ausstellungen bei Konrad Fischer*, *op. cit.*, p.25. This exhibition has wrongly been considered Ryman's first European solo show.

96 We have seen above that Friedrich had enjoyed connections with the American art world since 1965. Fischer had spent some time

and Fischer provided a record of the negotiations between the two galleries organising the artist's European shows. In May 1969, six months after Ryman's first exhibition in Düsseldorf, Fischbach wrote:

> [I] hope that in co-operation with you, we can work together for Ryman in Europe and in the United States. We only feel that it should be done together, so that there is some consistency in all the arrangements ...
>
> What would you think of the following: You could be the central European gallery connection, on communication to us, and then you could distribute the work in Europe, and most of the European arrangements could be made directly with you ...
>
> The commission could be 25% to you, which leaves very little to us, actually, only 15% ... It is essential that Bob exhibits in Germany, France and Italy as much as possible.[103]

Although Ryman vetoed this arrangement,[104] this letter is interesting. First, it shows the percentages dealers received at the time. Second, it shows that Fischer was seen as the right person to represent the artist in Europe. Lastly, it demonstrates the importance of Europe to American dealer galleries.

American Conceptual artists in America

More temporary exhibitions of Conceptual artists were organised in America, especially through the activities of Siegelaub. In November 1968, he set up the debut New York solo exhibition of Huebler.[105] *Douglas Huebler: November, 1968* was the first show to exist solely as a catalogue, in which the works and documentation were reproduced in a neutral way.[106] Huebler explained: 'The existence of each sculpture is documented by its documentation. The documentation takes the form of photographs, maps, drawings and descriptive language.'[107] For Huebler, a construction in language can work as a sculpture equally as well as a fabricated object.

Weiner came to the same conclusion at the same time. In December 1968, Siegelaub prepared a catalogue-exhibition of Weiner's work entitled *Statements*.[108] It contained 24 works: one statement per page described a simple

in New York in April 1968, notably spending time with LeWitt. LeWitt knew Ryman from having worked with him at the MoMA in the early 1960s. It is possible that it was he who introduced the two men.

97 Undated letter from Fischer to Ryman dated 1968, in Korrespondenz mit Künstlern 1969–70, AKFGD.

98 In the late 1960s, Minimal sculpture was shown in Europe (Andre, LeWitt, Flavin), but not Minimal painting. Sculpture seemed to be part of Conceptual art because it was linked with theoretical and philosophical texts. Marden, Mangold and Twombly were not exhibited in Europe until the early 1970s. This aspect will be discussed in Chapter 3.4.

99 Meyer, *Minimalism*, *op. cit.*, p.158.

100 Manuscript letter from Ryman to Fischer dated 1 August 1968, in Korrespondenz mit Künstlern 1969–70, AKFGD.

101 Fischer brought back *Orrin* from a New York trip for the Dutch collectors Herman and Henriette van Eelen. See: Herman and Henriette van Eelen in conversation with the author, Amsterdam, 27 April 2005, audio-tape recording (Appendix 4.17). See also: Chapter 4.3.

102 Marilyn Fischbach (1931–2003) launched her gallery in 1960, exhibiting artists such as Ronald Bladen, Eva Hesse and Alex Katz.

103 Letter from Fischbach to Fischer dated 7 May 1969, in Galerie Korrespondenz 1967–69, AKFGD.

104 [Editor's note: Dorothee Fischer in conversation with Lynda Morris, February 2009.]

105 Huebler had received his first one-man shows at the Philips

action to alter the physical environment. It included 'general statements' and 'specific statements', as in 'one aerosol can of enamel sprayed to conclusion directly upon the floor'.[109]

Xerox Book

The concept of organising exhibitions of works that did not need a physical realisation was further enhanced in the *Xerox Book*, also known as *Carl Andre, Robert Barry, Douglas Huebler, Joseph Kosuth, Sol LeWitt, Robert Morris, Lawrence Weiner*.[110] This publication functioned as a group exhibition as well as a work of art. It was edited by Seth Siegelaub and the collector and businessman Jack Wendler.[111] Each artist was given a 25-page section to realise a work that could be easily duplicated by the newly available technique of mass reproduction: the Xerox photocopy machine. This project allowed Siegelaub to promote the artists associated with him and to show them in a new form of exhibition that he had invented. Further, the layout and media used created a neutral and equal way of presenting artists.[112]

In 1968, a number of temporary exhibitions in Europe and the United States produced and confirmed an awareness within the art world that Conceptual artists constituted a group. This group was particularly associated with certain dealers, such as Fischer, Sperone and Siegelaub, who set up these shows. The development of the Conceptual network was paralleled by the development of the European art world, with the founding of new dealer galleries for example. In Amsterdam, in addition to Art & Project, there was also the Galerie Seriaal, which specialised in prints and editions.[113] One can also mention Daniel Templon in Paris, who launched a gallery for contemporary French artists such as Ben (Vautier), Christian Boltanski and LeGac.

Gallery, Detroit, in 1953 and at the Obelisk Gallery, Boston, in 1968. His sculptural work had been shown in 1966 in the *Primary Structures* exhibition at the Jewish Museum, New York.

106 The publication of the catalogue was financially supported by the young American stockbroker and art patron Raymond Dicks. See: Alberro, *Conceptual art and the Politics of Publicity*, *op. cit.*, p.190, note 41.

107 *Douglas Huebler: November 1968*, Seth Siegelaub, New York, 1968, unnumbered pages.

108 *Lawrence Weiner, Statements*, Seth Siegelaub, The Louis Kellner Foundation, New York, 1968.

109 See: Osborne, *Conceptual Art*, *op. cit.*, p.125. See also: Alberro, *Conceptual Art and the Politics of Publicity*, *op. cit.*, p.95.

110 *Xerox Book: Carl Andre, Robert Barry, Douglas Huebler, Joseph Kosuth, Sol LeWitt, Robert Morris, Lawrence Weiner*, Seth Siegelaub and John W. Wendler, New York, 1968.

111 In 1967, Seth Siegelaub and Jack Wendler had set up a service company, Image. Art Programs for Industry, Inc., which presented itself as a public-relations specialist for programmes involving the fine arts. See: Alberro, *Conceptual art and the Politics of Publicity*, *op. cit.*, pp.12–13.

112 For an extensive discussion of the works included in the *Xerox Book*, see: *Ibid.*, pp.136–148.

113 Mia Visser (Editions Bergeyk-Bergeyk), Wies Smals (Galerie Smals, Amsterdam) and Ritsaert ten Cate (Galerie Mickery, Loenersloot) combined to set up the Galerie Seriaal in Amsterdam,

2.2 1969

The Rhineland area

The growth of the European art world continued in 1969. In Germany, the Rhineland area increasingly established itself as an art centre. Düsseldorf appeared to be a city of artists, mainly due to the activities of the Kunst-akademie.[114] Fischer had been an artist before opening a gallery, and Alfred Schmela was a painter. The renowned Paris dealer Denise René, together with Hans Mayer, launched a space in Düsseldorf in 1969.[115] Nevertheless, Cologne increasingly became the city of the dealer galleries. Following Rudolph Zwirner and Rolf Ricke, Michael Werner moved his gallery from Berlin to Cologne. In 1960, there had been very few galleries in Cologne; by 1970, there were nearly 50.[116]

Daniel Buren

On 17 January 1968, Buren's first solo show in a European Conceptual art gallery, opened at Wide White Space.[117] De Decker and Lohaus had invited Buren to do the show after meeting him at Prospect 68. The artist conceived the show on the spot when he arrived at the gallery. The result was an in-situ installation of green-and-white striped papers that were pasted inside and outside the gallery on the lower part of the walls.[118] The striped paper was used for the invitations as well as the work of art. Critics such as Michel Claura and Otto Hahn and private collectors including Herman Daled attended the opening.[119] De Decker recalls the show:

> ... at his first exhibition, Buren had stuck up his papers, then said we had to do a price list. I asked him if it was for sale. He said that if anyone wanted an intervention at their own house it would be done for a fixed sum, whether it was big or small. It was like a kind of fee.[120]

Subsequently Mia and Martin Visser, who had been buying Conceptual art in Europe from the early days, invited Buren to carry out an intervention in their

a sort of sales centre for mass-produced works of art.

114 Joseph Beuys was a teacher at the Kunstakademie, Düsseldorf from 1961 to 1972. Bernd and Hilla Becher (born 1931 and 1934 respectively) taught photography from the mid-1970s.

115 Hans Mayer had established his first gallery in Esslingen (near Stuttgart) in 1965. Not long afterwards, in 1967, Denise René and Hans Mayer had opened a gallery together in Krefeld.

116 Georg Jappe, 'Young artists in Germany', *Studio International*, vol.183, no.941, February 1972, p.65.

117 *Daniel Buren*, Wide White Space, Antwerp, 17 January–6 February 1969. See: Aupetitallot, *Wide White Space*, *op. cit.*, pp.176–255.

118 'Interview Yves Aupetitallot, Daniel Buren', in *Ibid.*, pp.88–92.

119 Michel Claura was the half brother of Daniel Buren. He was a lawyer and became a central art critic for BMPT (Buren, Mosset, Parmentier, Toroni) and Conceptual art in France between 1967 and 1971.

120 De Decker in conversation with the author, Antwerp, 16 November 2004, audio-tape recording (Appendix 4.4) (author's translation).

121 'Interview with Yves Aupetitallot, Daniel Buren', in Aupetitallot, *Wide White Space*, *op. cit.*, pp.96–97.

122 *Earth Art*, Andrew Dickson White Museum, Cornell University, Ithaca, New York, 19 February–16 March 1969. Artists: Dibbets, Haacke, Jenny, Long, Medalla, Morris, Oppenheim, Smithson and Uecker. One should underline here that this was another

home in Bergeyk. *Papier collé blanc et vert* was realised in February–March 1968 on one of the main walls of their Rietveld house.[121]

European Conceptual artists in America

If 1968 saw the showing of American artists in Europe, 1969 saw the showing of European artists in America. Long and Dibbets travelled to America in February 1969 to participate in the *Earth Art* show organised by the editor Willoughby Sharp at the Andrew Dickson White Museum at Cornell University, Ithaca, New York.[122] This was the first time that they had exhibited their work in the US alongside that of American artists such as Morris and Smithson.

During his stay in New York, Long was offered his first solo show in America by John Gibson in February–March 1969.[123] The artist explained to Fischer how things worked out:

> One day before I was due to fly back to Europe, after the Cornell exhibition I saw John Gibson and he suggested I had a show in New York immediately, so we did. It is much better to do it suddenly like this. I am not showing sculpture (he only has a small gallery, which is really an office) but large blow up photographs of some of my sculptures done in England, and I think it is very useful information.[124]

One Month

In March 1969, Long and other European Conceptual artists participated in an international show, *One Month*, organised by Seth Siegelaub.[125] Each artist was invited to make a work on each day of the month. This 'calendar exhibition' included pieces by Terry Atkinson and Michael Baldwin (Art & Language) and Barry Flanagan, along with works by Andre, Kosuth, Huebler, LeWitt, Nauman, Weiner and Wilson. This 'group exhibition' took place in the catalogue since the 31 works consisted only of verbal information. The catalogue was distributed worldwide free of charge. Siegelaub explained his position: 'People who have galleries can show their objects only in one place at a time. I'm not limited. I can have my ideas in 20 different places at once. Ideas are faster than tedious objects.'[126]

contemporary art show in the USA to be organised in a university.

123 *Richard Long*, John Gibson Gallery, New York, 22 February–14 March 1969.

124 Manuscript letter from R Long, New York, to Dorothee and Konrad Fischer dated [February 1969], in Korrespondenz mit Künstlern 1969–70, AKFGD.

125 *One Month*, also known as *March 1–31, 1969*, 1–31 March 1969. Artists: Andre, Asher, Atkinson, Baldwin, Barry, Barthelme, Baxter, Byars, Chamberlain, Cooper, Flanagan, Flavin, Hay, Huebler, Huot, Kaltenbach, Kawara, Kosuth, Kozlov, LeWitt, Long, Morris, Nauman, Oldenburg, Oppenheim, Ruppersberg, Ruscha, Smithson, Valentine, Weiner and Wilson.

126 David Shirey, 'Impossible Art – What Is It?', *Art in America*, May–June 1969, p.39.

127 Sol LeWitt, 'Sentences on Conceptual Art', 0–9, no.5, January 1969, pp.3–5. For the manuscript and genesis of this text, see: Héman, Poot and Visser, *Conceptual art in the Netherlands and Belgium 1965–1975*, *op. cit.*, pp.48–73.

128 *January 5–31, 1969* (exh. cat.), Seth Siegelaub, New York, 1969, unnumbered pages. The exhibition *January 5–31, 1969* (Barry, Huebler, Kosuth and Weiner) was organised by Seth Siegelaub and was held in an office in the McClendon Building, New York.

129 We have seen in Chapter 1.1. that Walther König launched a publishing house in 1967 with his brother Kasper König, the Verlag Gebrüder König, Köln–New York.

130 Gabriele Lueg, 'Gespräch mit Walther König', in Herzogenrath

1969 saw the radicalisation of the position of certain American Conceptual artists. LeWitt published his 'Sentences on Conceptual Art' in the art magazine *0–9* and simultaneously in *Art-Language* Volume 1 Number 1, May 1969. In it, he declared: 'Since no form is intrinsically superior to another, the artist may use any form, from an expression of words (written or spoken) to physical reality, equally.'[127] Weiner meanwhile formulated his 'Statement of Intent', which would be consistently repeated in relation to all of his work:

> 1. The artist may construct the piece, 2. The piece may be fabricated, 3. The piece need not to be built. Each being equal and consistent with the intent of the artist, the decision as to condition rests with the received upon the occasion of receivership.[128]

Walther König's bookshop, Cologne

The increasing importance of artists' texts, books and catalogues at this time was further highlighted when Walther König, Kasper König's brother, opened a bookshop in Cologne in March 1969. He specialised in all kinds of progressive art publications.[129] He had previously worked as an assistant at the Bücherstube beim Dom, where he was responsible for the art section. He left the shop to establish his own business when his boss Hans Meyer died. From 1967, under König's initiative, the Bücherstube had a stand at the Cologne Art Fair and also at Documenta 4 in 1968.[130] From 1969, he had a stand at many art fairs.

Op Losse Schroeven* and *When Attitudes Become Form

In March 1969, two key group exhibitions of international Conceptual artists took place in Europe. *Op Losse Schroeven, Situaties en cryptostructuren* (Square Pegs in Round Holes, Situations and Cryptostructures)[131] was the first to open, on 15 March 1969 at the Stedelijk Museum, Amsterdam.[132] At the time, Edy de Wilde (1919–2005) was the director of the Museum, a position he had held since 1963. He had previously been the director of the Stedelijk Van Abbemuseum, Eindhoven. He had focused the museum's programming on Abstract Expressionism and Pop art. De Wilde was assisted by Wim Beeren (born 1928), the head of the Department of Painting and Sculpture.

and Lueg, *Die 60er Jahre, Kölns Weg zur Kunstmetropole*, *op. cit.*, pp.525–526.

131 In Dutch, this expression designates a structure in which the screws are loose. In the figurative sense, it signifies an unstable situation.

132 *Op Losse Schroeven, Situaties en Cryptostructuren*, Stedelijk Museum, Amsterdam, 15 March–27 April 1969. Artists: Andre, Anselmo, Beuys, Boezem, Bollinger, Calzolari, De Maria, Dibbets, Van Elk, Ferrer, Flanagan, Heizer, Huebler, Icaro, Jenny, Kaks, Kounellis, Long, Merz, Morris, Nauman, Oppenheim, Panamarenko, Prini, Ruthenbeck, Ryman, Saret, Serra, Smithson, Sonnier, Viner, Weiner and Zorio. The catalogue of the Amsterdam show was one of the first publications to include a section of artists' works.

133 See, for instance: Carel Block, 'Letter from Holland', *Art International*, vol.3, no.5, May 1969, pp.51–53. However, the atmosphere remained hostile and Beeren eventually left the museum a year after the show to become a Lecturer at the University of Groningen.

134 Wim Beeren, ''Op Losse Schroeven', Pro Memoria, An exhibition at the Stedelijk Museum, 15.3-27.4.1969', in *'60–'80, Attitudes-Concepts-Images, A Selection from twenty years of visual arts* (exh. cat.), Stedelijk Museum, Amsterdam, 1982, p.55.

135 *When Attitudes Become Form (works, concepts, processes, situations, information)*, Kunsthalle, Bern, 22 March–27 April 1969. Artists: Andre, Anselmo, Artschwager, Bang, Bark, Barry, Beuys, Boetti, Bochner, Boezem, Bollinger, Buthe, Calzolari, Cotton,

The originality of the artworks presented at *Op Losse Schroeven* was largely misunderstood by the local audience. Many works had been specially produced; for example Dibbets's *Museumsokkel met 4 hoeken van 90°*, in which the corners of the museum building were dug out so as to make its 'base' appear. Although Beeren experienced a good deal of aggression, some of the press welcomed the fact that the show opened up the field of art.[133] Many of the participating artists wanted to organise a symposium as a sequel to the exhibition in order to explain themselves, but nothing came of it.[134]

When Attitudes Become Form (works, concepts, processes, situations, information) opened a week later, on 22 March 1969, at the Kunsthalle Bern.[135] The Kunsthalle had been directed by Harald Szeemann (1933–2005) since 1961. In 1960, he had completed his doctorate in Art History and this was his first institutional job. In Bern, he had given solo shows to artists such as Etienne Martin, Tom Doyle and Richard Paul Lohse.

Szeemann had the advantage of private funding from Philip Morris, or more precisely from Ruder & Finn Inc. (New York), the publicity agency of the tobacco firm.[136] This financial support[137] enabled him to travel widely in Europe and the United States in January and February 1969 to meet dealers, critics and artists.[138] Before Szeemann left, he had compiled a list of people he wanted to see. This list had been completed by Fischer in November 1968.[139] Szeemann and Fischer had known each other since the opening of the Düsseldorf gallery in October 1967. At that time, Szeemann had been installing a *Science-Fiction* exhibition at the Kunsthalle, Düsseldorf. Through Fischer, he had met artists such as Andre.[140]

When Attitudes Become Form was much more ambitious in scale and more daring with the choice of works than *Op Losse Schroeven*.[141] Not only was the budget bigger than Beeren's, but the Kunsthalle, as a small provincial institution, allowed Szeemann more freedom in programming than with Beeren at the Dutch national museum. The Stedelijk's Director De Wilde gave his permission for the show only after lengthy discussions.[142]

As in Amsterdam, a great number of works in the show directly impacted on the building and its surroundings. Heizer's *Bern Depression* partly destroyed the pavement around the museum, while Weiner's *A 36" × 36" removal to the lathing or support wall of plaster or wallboard from a wall*, was created on a wall.

Darboven, Dibbets, Van Elk, Ferrer, Flanagan, Glass, Haacke, Heizer, Hesse, Huebler, Icaro, Jacquet, Jenney, Kaltenbach, Kaplan, Kienholz, Klein, Kosuth, Kounellis, Kuehn, LeWitt, Lohaus, Long, Louw, McLean, De Maria, Medalla, Merz, Morris, Nauman, Oldenburg, Oppenheim, Panamarenko, Pascali, Pechter, Pistoletto, Prini, Raetz, Ruppersberg, Ruthenbeck, Ryman, Sandback, Saret, Sarkis, Schnyder, Serra, Smithson, Sonnier, Tuttle, Viner, Walther, Wegman, Weiner, Wiley and Zorio.

136 According to Lynda Morris, Philip Morris funded cultural activities at flash points in cities facing political unrest due to US involvement. The tobacco company is still actively funding Biennales in Cuba, Mexico, Turkey and Korea under the curatorship of Rosa Martinez, who had declared at a Tate conference in 2002 that she wanted to do a Biennale in Kabul. Morris in conversation with the author, *op. cit.* See also: Hubertus Butin, 'When Attitudes Become Form – Philip Morris Becomes Sponsor, Arts sponsorship in Europe against the background of developments in America', 2000, www.societyofcontrol.com/research/butin_engl.htm.

137 Philip Morris provided funding of $ 15,000 for the show and $ 10,000 for the catalogue. See: Harald Szeemann, 'Journal et carnets de voyage touchant aux préparatifs et aux retombées de l'exposition 'When Attitudes Become Form (works, concepts, processes, situations, information)' et à rien d'autre', *Les Cahiers du Musée national d'art moderne*, no.73, autumn 2000, p.8.

138 Szeemann's diary, describing the organisation of the Bern exhibition, was published in the catalogue of the Amsterdam show.

Conversely, some works existed only as information in the catalogue or as a poster in the space, such as Long's *A Walking Tour in the Bern Oberland*.

Jean-Christophe Ammann (born 1939)[143] wrote enthusiastically about this show:

> No doubt, Harald Szeemann has organised the most important show of the year. The consequences cannot yet be evaluated, but they should be enormous. What different progressive galleries in Europe, such as Konrad Fischer (Düsseldorf), Ricke and Zwirner (Cologne), Heiner Friedrich (Munich), Sperone (Turin), Wide White Space (Antwerp) and Sonnabend (Paris), have achieved until now with groundwork for the propagation of 'Land Art', 'Arte Povera' and 'Anti-Form' is here outstandingly united.[144]

However, the content of the exhibition outraged the Bern public. A couple of days after the opening, protesters placed a dunghill in front of the Kunsthalle's entrance. A month after the closing of the exhibition and probably under pressure from the city art committee, Szeemann resigned, leaving the museum in September 1969.[145]

Travelling shows

Op Losse Schroeven and *When Attitudes Become Form* were both travelling shows. That they toured simultaneously to museums in the Rhineland further underlines the importance of the region. The Amsterdam exhibition was presented at the Museum Folkwang in Essen (9 May–22 June 1969) under the title *Verborgene Strukturen* (Hidden Structures). The Bern show was presented at the Museum Haus Lange, Krefeld (10 May–15 June 1969). The Museum Haus Lange had been closed for several years for renovation; *Vorstellungen nehmen Form an* was the reopening show.[146]

When Attitudes Become Form was presented in a third venue, the Institute of Contemporary Arts (ICA) in London (28 September–27 October 1969). The show was curated by Charles Harrison (born 1942), who was assistant editor of *Studio International*. The ICA was offered *Attitudes* at the same time that Harrison had proposed to organise a group show of young British artists, featuring Flanagan,

See: Harald Szeemann, 'Reisebericht von den Vorbereitungen und nur von diesen für die Ausstellung 'When Attitudes Become Form (works, concepts, processes, situations, information)', in *Op Losse Schroeven, Situaties en Cryptostructuren* (exh. cat.), Stedelijk Museum, Amsterdam, 1969, unnumbered pages.

139 Szeemann, 'Journal et carnets de voyage', *Les Cahiers du Musée national d'art moderne*, *op. cit.*, p.11.

140 Harald Szeemann in conversation with the author, Maggia, 22 July 2003, audio-tape recording (Appendix 4.15).

141 Sixty-nine artists (127 works) were shown in Bern, whereas there were only 33 artists (34 works) in Amsterdam. All of the artists included in *Op Losse Schroeven* were also exhibited in *When Attitudes Become Form* (except Olle Kaks). More than 30 artists, including Darboven, Kosuth, LeWitt and Weiner, were only shown in Bern.

142 'Wim Beeren, Des chevilles carrées dans des trous ronds, Interview par Bart de Baere et Selma Klein Essink', *Art Press*, special issue no.17, 1996, p.135.

143 Jean-Christophe Ammann was Director of the Kunstmuseum in Lucerne from 1968 onwards. He previously worked for a couple of years as an assistant to Harald Szeemann at the Kunsthalle Bern.

144 Jean-Christophe Ammann, 'Schweizer Brief', *Art International*, vol.3, no.5, 20 May 1969, p.47 (author's translation).

145 Hans Rudolf Reust, *Aus dem Musée éclaté an dem Ort des Werks, Kunsthalle Bern 1969–1993*, Kunsthalle, Bern, 1993, p.22–24. Subsequently, Szeemann settled as a freelance curator; he also founded the Agentur für geistige Gastarbeit (Agency for Spiritual

Long, Louw, Victor Burgin and Bruce McLean.[147] Subsequently, it was decided to mix both shows, since Philip Morris's sponsorship was essential for the ICA to set up such a large-scale exhibition.[148] According to Harrison, the ICA accepted *Attitudes* mainly for financial reasons; he doubted that the director, Michael Kustow, whose background was in theatre, was aware of the kind of works included in the show.[149]

Harrison knew a number of the Conceptual artists included in *Attitudes* because he had been encouraged to attend Prospect 68 on behalf of *Studio International*.[150] It was agreed by Philip Morris that two American and three European artists would be flown over to London for the opening. It seems that the ICA were planning to fly over Andre and Morris.[151] Harrison remembers that he invited Smithson, who came over.[152] Other attendees included Dibbets, Van Elk, Richard Artschwager, Ruthenbeck and Arte Povera artists, including Anselmo and his assistant Giuseppe Penone.[153] Schum was invited to show his *Land Art* film for the duration of the exhibition.[154]

In addition to the fact that they presented Conceptual art on a large scale, *Op Losse Schroeven* and *When Attitudes Become Form* were also important because they were the first international Conceptual art touring exhibitions.To that extent, they acted as models for forthcoming shows. The publicity that the artists got from being included in such large-scale shows also encouraged dealers to organise exhibitions of their work in their spaces. This was particularly true at the time of the original showings in Amsterdam and Bern in March and April 1969.

As was the case with Documenta, Conceptual art dealer galleries took advantage of the presence of American artists in Europe. In March 1969, Wide White Space organised a show of *Young American Artists*, including Andre, LeWitt and Nauman.[155] During the same month, Sperone set up a one-man show of Mario Merz, followed in April by a solo show of Morris.[156] In April 1969, Sonnabend organised the first solo show of Merz in France.[157] Finally, also in April, Friedrich presented Heizer's *Munich Depression*.[158]

Lawrence Weiner

On 10 April 1969, Fischer held the debut European one-man show of Weiner (born 1942).[159] This was also the first time that the artist's statements had been

Guest Work). *Attitudes* did establish his reputation, however: he was appointed to direct Documenta 5 in 1972.

146 Paul Wember, 'Vorstellungen nehmen Form an', in *20 Jahre Museum Haus Lange, Eine Retrospektive der Ausstellungen 1955–1975* (exh. cat.), Kaiser Wilhelm Museum, Krefeld, 1976, p.88. The exhibition had a huge influence on the museum's programme. All the solo shows organised in 1969 were given to Conceptual artists presented during this exhibition: Franz Erhard Walther (June), Flanagan (September–October), Long (July 1969–July 1970), Fred Sandback (July–August), LeWitt (October–November) and Dibbets (December 1969–January 1970). The four last shows were arranged by Fischer. See: 'Konrad Fischer interviewed by Georg Jappe', *Studio International*, *op. cit.*, p.68.

147 Harrison had heard of *Op Losse Schroeven* and *When Attitudes Become Form* from Barry Flanagan. See: Charles Harrison, 'The late sixties in London and elsewhere', in *1965 to 1972 – When attitudes became form* (exh. cat.), Kettle's Yard Gallery, Cambridge, 1984, p.15, note 5. See also: Charles Harrison in conversation with the author, Banbury, 19 May 2003, audio-tape recording (Appendix 4.7).

148 The sponsor paid nearly half of the exhibition costs. The budget was established as follows: £5,743 for Philip Morris and £7,016 for the ICA. See: Document entitled 'Budget as at 18 August 1969', in Folder IV, 'When Attitudes Become Form', ICA Archive, Tate Library and Archive, London (hereafter TLAL). Lynda Morris remembers that Philip Morris cigarettes were distributed free at the opening. Morris in conversation with the author, *op. cit.*

exhibited in Europe. The show consisted of small cards with statements, such as 'The residue of a flare ignited upon a boundary' (1969) pinned on the wall.[160] In February 1969, LeWitt had sent Fischer some booklets of work by Weiner, Kosuth, Huebler and Barry, suggesting that he should exhibit these artists.[161] John Weber from the Dwan Gallery also proposed to Fischer that he should present a show of Weiner while the artist was over for *Op Losse Schroeven*:

> Larry Weiner will be in Amsterdam for Beeren's show at the Stedelijk. I asked him to contact you about a possible exhibition. He is a friend of mine and a very good artist that is being talked about a lot in New York now. He could do a show for you while he is in Europe if you have a space in your schedule.[162]

The artist remembers that they met in a bar in Amsterdam and that Fischer immediately invited him to show in his gallery.[163] This solo exhibition at Fischer's and the Bern and Amsterdam shows launched Weiner's career in Europe.[164] After the original showing in April 1969, he had solo shows at Wide White Space (June),[165] at Art & Project (September)[166] and at Sperone (December).[167] This demonstrates that the Conceptual network was well established by 1969. Conceptual dealer galleries were networking with each other and the first major museum shows were organised. Galleries that had previously focused on other kinds of art started to arrange exhibitions of Conceptual artists from 1969 onwards.

Yvon Lambert, Paris

Buren's second solo show in a progressive dealer gallery took place in May 1969 at Galerie Yvon Lambert, Paris (rue de l'Echaudé).[168] This exhibition did not present striped works or installations, but a series of ten black-and-white films.[169] They were screened on a 'scopitone', a sort of jukebox with a 16mm film component that could be found at the time in Parisian cafés. This exhibition marked the beginning of Lambert's interest in Conceptual art.

Lambert had taken part in Prospect 68 (showing César, Alain Jacquet, Robert

149 Harrison in conversation with the author, *op. cit.*

150 See: Charles Harrison, 'Düsseldorf commentary, Prospect '68 – an international showcase', *Studio International*, vol.176, no.905, November 1968, p.204. Harrison had heard about the event from Nigel Greenwood who was in Düsseldorf for the Axiom Gallery. Morris in conversation with the author, *op. cit.*

151 Report on Meeting between the ICA and Philip Morris dated 11 July 1969, and Letter from Ann Lauterbach, ICA, to Margot Slate, Philip Morris, New York, dated 31 July 1969, in Folder I, 'When Attitudes Become Form', ICA Archive, TLAL. Lauterbach was an American poet and her father was a friend of Peter Townsend's from China. Morris in conversation with the author, *op. cit.* Penone discussed this with Morris in Norwich in 1996.

152 Harrison in conversation with the author, *op. cit.*

153 Sue Davies, who was the ICA curator at the time, remembered that she had to take some Italian Arte Povera artists to Soho to buy materials to create their pieces. Sue Davis in an e-mail to the author, 4 March 2003.

154 Letter from Ann Lauterbach to Gerry Schum, Berlin, dated 14 July 1969, and Letter from Schum to Lauterbach dated 30 July 1969, in Folder I, 'When Attitudes Become Form', ICA Archive, TLAL. The *Land Art* film by Gerry Schum (1938–73) was first broadcast on the Sender Freies Berlin (SFB) on 15 March 1969. It included original contributions by Marinus Boezem, De Maria, Dibbets, Flanagan, Heizer, Long, Dennis Openheim and Smithson.

155 *Young American Artists: Andre, Artschwager, Bollinger, De Maria, Flavin, LeWitt, Nauman*, Wide White Space, Antwerp, 1–31 March 1969. This show was put together with pieces that belonged to Wide White Space, Konrad Fischer and Rolf Ricke. It coincided with the first trip of De Decker and Lohaus to New York. See: Aupetitallot, *Wide White Space*, *op. cit.*, pp.60–258.

156 *Mario Merz*, Galleria Gian Enzo Sperone, Turin, March 1969.

Malaval), where he had seen Buren's massive striped installation. From 1967 onwards, the dealer regularly visited Wide White Space, where Buren was given his first solo show in January–February 1969.[170] Following his two first exhibitions in Antwerp and Paris, Buren's debut German solo show was at Konrad Fischer in September 1969. This exhibition consisted of blue-and-white striped papers that were exhibited not only in the gallery, but also all over the city of Düsseldorf.[171]

Françoise Lambert, Milan

In June 1969, the Galleria Françoise Lambert in Milan (Via di Borgonuovo) was launched with an exhibition of Richard Serra.[172] Françoise Lambert, Yvon Lambert's ex-wife, had decided to open a dealer gallery after her divorce. She had met Serra during *When Attitudes Become Form* and was determined to open her gallery with a show of the American artist.[173] She soon took on other Conceptual artists (Long, Ryman, Lamelas).

A 379089, Antwerp

In July 1969, De Decker and Lohaus, together with the artists James Lee Byars and Marcel Broodthaers, the critics Jef Cornelis and Geert Bekaert, and the collectors Herman Daled, Isi Fiszman and Hubert Peeters, launched the alternative international art and cultural institute A 379089. Kasper König, who had just come back from New York, was the artistic coordinator. It was founded as a reaction to the lack of progressive and politically independent institutions in Belgium.[174] The first event organised by A 379089 was a breakfast with champagne to celebrate the landing on the moon of the American mission Apollo 11 on 20 July 1969.[175]

July–August–September 1969 and *557,087*

Between July and September 1969, Siegelaub organised an exhibition that took place simultaneously in 11 different locations all over the world. *July–August–September 1969* brought together European and American artists, who were

See: Minola, Mundici, Poli and Roberto, *Gian Enzo Sperone*, *op. cit.*, pp.134–138.

157 *Mario Merz*, Ileana Sonnabend, Paris, 22 April–June 1969.

158 *Michael Heizer, Munich Depression*, Galerie Heiner Friedrich, Munich, April 1969. See the list of shows organised by Heiner Friedrich, in Urbaschek, *Dia Art Foundation*, *op. cit.*, p.233.

159 *Lawrence Weiner*, Konrad Fischer, Düsseldorf, starting 10 April 1969. See: *Ausstellungen bei Konrad Fischer*, *op. cit.*, p.30. See also: Database 3, Section Lawrence Weiner (Appendix 1.3).

160 This work had been realised and the residues of the action exhibited in *Op Losse Schroeven*. It was acquired in 1970 from Fischer by Panza. See: Database 5 on the Panza Collection (Appendix 1.5).

161 Manuscript letter from LeWitt to Fischer dated 10 February [1969], in Korrespondenz mit Künstlern, 1969–1970, AKFGD.

162 Manuscript letter from Weber to Fischer dated 10 March 1969, in Galerie Korrespondenz 1967–69, AKFGD. Weber, however, never exhibited Weiner at the Dwan Gallery.

163 Daniel Birnbaum, 'Art and the Deal, Daniel Birnbaum on Konrad Fischer/Lueg', *Artforum*, February 2000, p.19.

164 See: Database 3, Section Lawrence Weiner (Appendix 1.3).

165 *Lawrence Weiner*, Wide White Space, Antwerp, 10–30 June 1969. See: Aupetitallot, *Wide White Space*, *op. cit.*, p.261. De Decker and Lohaus had met Weiner through Siegelaub during their first trip to New York in March 1969. During a dinner with Andre, they were the first to offer him a solo show in a European dealer gallery. In the end, this was not possible due to time constraints. Weiner subsequently had his first show at Fischer's. Weiner in conversation with the author, *op. cit.* See also: 'Interview Yves Aupetitallot, Lawrence Weiner', in Aupetitallot, *Wide White Space*, *op. cit.*, p.113.

166 'Lawrence Weiner, A translation from one language to another', *Art & Project Bulletin*, no.10, 1 September 1969. This show existed solely in the form of a bulletin. There was no exhibition of works in

invited to make a contribution to the exhibition in a location of their choice.[176] The only place where all the works could be seen together was in the catalogue.[177] Andre's contribution, for example, was to be seen at his solo show held at the Gemeentemuseum, The Hague from 23 August 1969.[178] Joseph Kosuth's contribution was a photograph, *Matter in General (Art as Idea as Idea)* (1968) held in the collection of the Eastern New Mexico University, Portales (New Mexico).

On 5 September 1969, the exhibition *557,087*, organised by Lippard at the Seattle Art Museum opened.[179] This was one of the first shows in America to present works by American Conceptualists, such as a wall drawing by LeWitt, alongside their European peers.[180] It was an indoor and outdoor exhibition that spread to a 50-mile radius around the city.

After solo shows in Germany (Fischer, Friedrich) and Belgium (Wide White Space), Andre held his first Italian solo exhibition at Gian Enzo Sperone, Turin, in September 1969.[181] This was his fourth gallery in Europe. The show, consisting of three long stripes of copper, tin and brass exhibited on the floor, had been proposed to Sperone by Andre's main dealer Fischer.[182]

Prospect 69 and the Cologne Kunstmarkt

Following the success of Prospect 68, Fischer and Strelow decided to organise a second event in 1969. Like the previous show, Prospect 69 was organised as an 'international preview of art from the world's galleries'; it was held at the Kunsthalle Düsseldorf from 30 September–12 October.[183] It appears from the record of expenses that the organisers travelled to London, Milan, Turin (Fischer)[184] and Paris (Strelow), as well as to New York (both) to prepare the show.[185]

The selection was again made by an international jury of seven. It included the private collectors José Luis de Castillejo (Bonn) and Visser (Bergeyk); the art critic Michel Claura (Paris); and the museum directors/curators Enno Develing (Gemeentemuseum, The Hague), Jasia Reichardt (ICA, London), Paul Wember (Kaiser Wilhelm Museum, Krefeld) and Harald Szeemann (at the time a freelance curator). This time, however, the jury selected the artists first. It was only after this choice had been made that the artists' dealer galleries were invited to

the gallery space. Stanley Brouwn's exhibition in May–June 1969 had introduced Art & Project to Conceptual artists. See: Cherix, 'Un entretien avec les éditeurs du Art & Project Bulletin (Février–Mars 2003)', in Press Release, *op.cit.*

167 *Lawrence Weiner*, Galleria Gian Enzo Sperone, Turin, 3–10 December 1969. See: Minola, Mundici, Poli and Roberto, *Gian Enzo Sperone*, *op. cit.*, p.149.

168 In 1961, Yvon Lambert launched his gallery in Saint-Paul de Vence, Southern France. A few years later, in 1966, he decided to move it to the 6th arrondissement in Paris, an area renowned for its numerous dealer galleries. He focused his programming on contemporary French artists such as Robert Malaval, Claude Gilli and André Cadere (all in 1966). See: 'Entretien avec Yvon Lambert', in *paris-art.com*, 28 January 2005. The archive of the Galerie Yvon Lambert is closed to the public. For a comprehensive outline of exhibitions of Conceptual artists at the gallery, see: Database 1, Section Yvon Lambert (Appendix 1.1). For an extensive overview of exhibitions organised by Yvon Lambert, see: Appendix 3.4.

169 *Daniel Buren, Interruption*, Galerie Yvon Lambert, Paris, May 1969. See: *Daniel Buren, Mot à Mot*, *op.cit.*, pp.F 14–F 15.

170 'Interview Yves Aupetitallot, Anny De Decker, Bernd Lohaus', in Aupetitallot, *Wide White Space*, *op. cit.*, pp.33–38.

171 Daniel Buren, Position – Proposition, Konrad Fischer, Düsseldorf, 30 September–12 October 1969. See: *Ausstellungen bei Konrad Fischer*, *op. cit.*, p.37. Although not officially invited, Buren had participated in *When Attitudes Become Form*, with an in-situ work that consisted of the pasting of striped posters in the streets of Bern, *Expositon personnelle sur les limites de la liberté de l'artiste vis-à-vis de la société*. This work belonged to the Belgian collector Herman Daled and it was he who suggested to Buren that he make it in Bern. See: Letter from Daled to Buren dated 17 March 1969, reproduced in *Daniel Buren, Mot à Mot*, *op. cit.*, p.A 04.

exhibit. The jurors had to vote from a short list of 57 international artists, and could pick a maximum of 27.[186] The artists who received at least three or four votes were selected and their primary dealer gallery was invited to exhibit their work. Barry, Huebler, Kosuth and Weiner, for example, got three to five votes each. As a result, their dealer Seth Siegelaub was invited. However, some galleries were still asked to participate even when their artist had received few votes. An example was Stanley Brouwn, who received just one vote and yet Art & Project, his gallery, was invited to participate.

In the end, 19 international dealer galleries were contacted, of which five, including Castelli and Pace, declined the invitation.[187] Half of the participating galleries were American, which was a major change from Prospect 68. The Conceptual dealer galleries who participated in 1968 did so again: Wide White Space, Yvon Lambert and Gian Enzo Sperone. Newcomers included Art & Project and Seth Siegelaub.[188] Dealer galleries did not always exhibit the artists for whom they had been selected. For instance, Wide White Space was shortlisted for Ben D'Armagnac, Ad Dekkers and Christo, but exhibited works by Lamelas and Beuys. Although the selection procedure was more restrictive than in the previous year, in that the organisers told the galleries which artists to exhibit, it seems that the dealers managed to get a certain freedom of choice. Several Conceptual artists were invited by the jury to exhibit at Prospect 69 independently of any dealer gallery. These included Darboven, Dibbets, LeWitt and Long.[189]

The opening of Prospect 69 drew many visitors.[190] Szeemann was invited to give a speech.[191] In his talk entitled 'Im Wendekreis des Prospects' (On the topic of Prospect), Szeemann emphasised the fact that in order to organise such shows, one no longer travelled to places, but to people one already knew, notably artists, dealers and museum directors, and that these people met not only during the day, but also in the evening in bars, with the intention of presenting tangible examples of the new art: letters, catalogues, exhibitions etc.[192] Szeemann was clearly referring to his own experience while preparing *Attitudes* and to the existence of an international network of Conceptual artists.

Except for specialist art magazines, the general press responded to the show

172 See: 'Elenco Mostre, Françoise Lambert Milano', Françoise Lambert Archive, Milan. This is the only document from Françoise Lambert's private archive that I was able to obtain. For a comprehensive outline of exhibitions of Conceptual artists at the gallery, see: Database 1, Section Françoise Lambert (Appendix 1.1). For an extensive overview of exhibitions organised by Françoise Lambert, see: Appendix 3.3.

173 Françoise Lambert in conversation with the author, Paris, 21 October 2004, manuscript notes. Exhibitions of Conceptual artists at Yvon Lambert in Paris were often followed by shows at Françoise Lambert in Milan and vice versa. For instance, Long had his first solo show in a gallery other than Fischer's at Yvon Lambert from 5–26 November 1969. At almost the same time, from 15 November to 12 December 1969, he had his first solo show in Italy at Françoise Lambert. See: Database 3, Section Richard Long (Appendix 1.3).

174 'Interview Yves Aupetitallot, Isi Fiszman', in Aupetitallot, *Wide White Space*, *op. cit.*, p.132.

175 De Decker in conversation with the author, *op. cit.* See also: Piet van Daalen, 'Uit de dossiers van A 379089 te Antwerpen', *Museumsjournaal*, vol.19, no.1, February 1974, p.21.

176 Siegelaub had been to Europe to see *When Attitudes Become Form* in Bern. See: Siegelaub in conversation with the author, *op. cit.* Fischer paid him a visit during a trip to New York in March–April 1969. See: Document entitled 'Konrad Fischer New York vom 25.3–9.4. 1969', in Galerie Korrespondenz 1967–69, AKFGD.

177 *July–August–September 1969*, in 11 different countries around the world, July–September 1969. Artists: Andre, Barry, Buren, Dibbets, Huebler, Kosuth, LeWitt, Long, N.E. Thing Co. Ltd., Smithson and Weiner. See: *July–August–September 1969* (exh. cat.), Seth Siegelaub, New York, 1969.

178 *Carl Andre*, Gemeentemuseum, The Hague, 23 August–5 October 1969.

with incomprehension. With the intention of communicating with a general audience, a public discussion was held at the Kunsthalle Düsseldorf at the end of Prospect 69. It included, among others, Szeemann, Ruhrberg, the journalist Willi Bongard and the artist Klaus Geldmacher.[193]

In the late 1960s, Prospect played an important part in the Conceptual art scene in Europe, presenting not only the artists as a progressive group, but also their dealer galleries. This innovative concept brought together art world specialists for shows of progressive contemporary art, principally Conceptual art, whilst also promoting the places where this art could be seen and purchased. Buren wrote retrospectively in 1973: 'Now what was Prospect, if not precisely, as its name indicates, the place where the result of the "prospecting" of "good" galleries was to be shown, in order to create tomorrow's market?'[194]

Fischer and Strelow, however, were concerned that their event should not compete again with the Cologne Kunstmarkt. The emphasis was placed on the exhibition and presentation of artworks rather than on the dealing aspect.[195] Furthermore, the organisers stressed Prospect's internationalism.[196] VPDK, on the other hand, had decided not to invite international dealer galleries to Cologne in 1969. The refusal to allow foreign dealers' stands indicated how threatened they felt by the competition.[197] Friedrich, now a member of VPDK, was the only dealer to present Conceptual artists (Andre, Darboven, LeWitt, Ryman). Perhaps as a sign of appeasement, VPDK decided to invite the main dealer in Conceptualism at the time and the instigator of the rival event, Konrad Fischer.[198]

Growth of European art fairs

With the appearance of art fairs in the late 1960s, the idea that art was merchandise just like any other goods had made its way into people's minds. Art fairs became places where one could find out about prices and the functioning of the art market. In 1969, other fairs appeared in Europe. The Association of Berlin Art Dealers, for instance, organised the Internationale Frühjahrsmesse (International Spring Fair). In Cologne, an alternative art fair entitled Neumarkt der

179 *557,087*, Seattle Art Museum, 5 September–5 October 1969. Artists: Acconci, Andre, Arnatt, Artschwager, Asher, Atkinson, Baldessari, Baldwin, Barry, Barthelme, Baxter, Beery, Bochner, Bollinger, Borofsky, Burgy, Buren, Castoro, Darboven, De Maria, Dibbets, Ferrer, Flanagan, Graham, Haacke, Heizer, Hesse, Huebler, Huot, Kaltenbach, Kawara, Kienholz, Kinmont, Kosuth, Kozlov, Latham, Le Va, LeWitt, Louw, Lundon, McLean, Morris, Nauman, N.Y. Graphic Workshop, Nikolaides, Oppenheim, Perreault, Piper, Rohm, Ruppersberg, Ryman, Ruscha, Sandback, Saret, Sawchuk, Serra, Sims, Smithson, Sonnier, Wall, Weiner and Wilson. The exhibition was shown under the modified title of *955,000* at the Vancouver Art Gallery, University of British Columbia, 13 January–8 February 1970. The exhibition was named after the total population of the city in which it was shown.

180 *Anti-Illusion: Procedures/Materials* organised for the Whitney Museum, New York by James Monte and Marcia Tucker (19 May–16 July 1969) only included works of American artists. Artists on show were Andre, Asher, Benglis, Bollinger, Duff, Ferrer, Fiore, Glass, Hesse, Jenney, Le Va, Lobe, Morris, Nauman, Reich, Rohm, Ryman, Serra, Shapiro, Snow, Sonnier and Tuttle.

181 *Carl Andre*, Galleria Gian Enzo Sperone, Turin, 29 September–October 1969. See: Database 3, Section Carl Andre (Appendix 1.3). See also: Minola, Mundici, Poli and Roberto, *Gian Enzo Sperone*, *op .cit.*, p.140.

182 *Ibid.*, p.39.

183 Prospect 69, Kunsthalle, Düsseldorf, 30 September–12 October 1969. Artists: Barry, Bernd and Hilla Becher, Benglis, Beuys, Boetti, Brouwn, Buren, Calzolari, Cooper, Darboven, Dibbets, Griffa, Gronen, Heizer, Hidalgo, Huebler, Kosuth, Kounellis, Lamelas, LeWitt, Long, Mattiacci, Marchetti, Marden, Ohlson, Oppenheim, Penone, Prentice, Prini, Raetz, Ross, Ruthenbeck, Ryman, Schnyder, Smithson, Toroni, Weiner and Wheeler.

Künste (New Market of the Arts) took place at the same time as the Kunstmarkt. This open-air event, organised by the bookseller and dealer Michael Siebrasse, presented all kinds of art productions.[199] It was a popular fair, supported by the city of Cologne, and seen as a counterpart to the elite and selective Kunstmarkt.

Konzeption/Conception

Op Losse Schroeven and *When Attitudes Become Form* had such an impact on the Conceptual art network that Fischer decided to organise a further Conceptual group exhibition. *Konzeption/Conception* was held at the Städtisches Museum in Leverkusen (near Düsseldorf) from 24 October to 23 November 1969.[200] It was a radical Conceptual art show because it did not include three-dimensional works, but showed documentation, instructions and artists' writings. Thus the event was subtitled 'Documentation of a Current Tendency'.[201] Broodthaers, for example, suggested that his participation be the letter of agreement he sent to the museum to participate in the show. Fischer had contacted Lippard and Siegelaub for their advice on putting together such a document-oriented exhibition.[202]

Konzeption/Conception was organised in a small provincial museum not particularly engaged with contemporary art. Surprisingly, when the Director, Rolf Wedewer, proposed the project to the city's cultural committee it was approved unanimously.[203] The collaboration between Wedewer and Fischer did not go well. At the end of the show, Fischer decided that he would never work again with the museum director. One of the main reasons for this was that some of the artists alleged that Wedewer did not send copies of the catalogue or return the works to the artists after the end of the show.[204] Consequently, Fischer suggested to his artists that they should refuse to show their work on other occasions in Leverkusen. This demonstrates the protective attitude of the dealer towards his artists. It also underlines Fischer's strategy of organising museum shows of his artists himself. He argued: 'I want to convey information, to show an artist's work; I couldn't care less where I do it. I have never put a notice advert in a paper. I'd rather do museum exhibitions which are linked with my name.'[205]

184 During his trip to New York, Fischer visited the following galleries as part of his preparation for Prospect 69: Dwan (John Weber), Castelli, Nicholas Wilder, Marilyn Fischbach, Donald Droll, Bykert Gallery (Klaus Kertess), John Gibson, Seth Siegelaub and Goldowsky Gallery (Dick Bellamy). In Milan, he visited Françoise Lambert. See: Document entitled 'Konrad Fischer New York vom 25.3–9.4. 1969', in Galerie Korrespondenz 1967–69, AKFGD. Fischer's London visit coincided with the installing of *When Attitudes Become Form* at the ICA in September 1969. Morris in conversation with the author, *op. cit.*

185 All in all, Prospect 69 cost about DM 27,300. See: Document entitled 'Aufstellung der Aufwendung und Unkosten für die Organisation von 'Prospect 69'' (list of spending and expenses for the organisation) dated 21 December 1969, in File IV 29371–138, AKDSD.

186 See: Documents entitled 'Wahlen' (votes) and 'Galerien, Zusagen' (galleries, confirmation), in File IV 29371–138, AKDSD. The documents are reproduced as Appendices 2.2.a and 2.2.b.

187 The Minami Gallery (Tokyo) was invited even though its artists had not been included on the shortlist. It seemed to have been eventually replaced by the Mickery Gallery (Loenersloot).

188 Siegelaub's contribution was the publication of an interview of his four artists in the exhibition catalogue.

189 These were all artists represented by Fischer. Although the Dwan gallery had been selected to exhibit Heizer and LeWitt, it ended up exhibiting works by Ross and Smithson. See: *Prospect 69, Katalog-Zeitung zur internationalen Vorschau auf die Kunst in den Galerien der Avantgarde* (exh. cat.), Städtische Kunsthalle Düsseldorf, 1969, cover page.

190 It was, however, decided not to organise a big free party as had been done the previous year. See: Letter from Jürgen Harten (assistant, Kunsthalle Düsseldorf) to Harald Szeemann dated 5 September 1969, in File IV 29367, AKDSD.

Joseph Kosuth

Konzeption/Conception included works by artists, such as Kosuth, who had never exhibited at Fischer's. Kosuth had been recommended to the dealer by LeWitt and Siegelaub. His first solo show in a Conceptual dealer gallery opened on 9 November 1969 at Gian Enzo Sperone, Turin.[206] A few days later, on 22 November, the artist's second one-man show opened at Art & Project, Amsterdam.[207] Since August 1969, Kosuth and Fischer had been in contact about a possible show in Düsseldorf, but the dealer postponed the date.[208] Finally, on 25 November 1969, Fischer wrote to the artist:

> The Leverkusen show is finished since yesterday. It will not travel ...
>
> I think it is not a good time to do a show with you now. There had been so much information about you in Europe last time: Amsterdam, Bern (2 times), Prospect, Leverkusen, Oxford, Art & Project. I think it is much better to wait some time. Perhaps you have the same feeling.[209]

Fischer later declared in an interview: 'When something gets recommended to me, and I have the feeling that I don't understand it – as with Kosuth's texts – then I leave it alone.'[210]

Dealers networking

On 11 November 1969, Ryman's second solo show opened with Konrad Fischer.[211] The exhibition consisted of 14 fibreglass paintings that Ryman made directly on the gallery walls. This was the first of a series of exhibitions of Ryman in Conceptual dealer galleries in Europe.[212] On 22 November an exhibition of the drawings and paintings by the artist opened at Heiner Friedrich, Munich.[213] In December 1969, Ryman had his first one-man exhibitions outside Germany with Yvon Lambert in Paris and with Françoise Lambert in Milan.[214]

The dealers shared Ryman's travelling costs. Naomi Spector, assistant to Marilyn Fischbach, wrote to Fischer in October 1969:

191 *Ibid.*

192 Szeemann's opening speech entitled 'Prospect, 30.09.69', in Box '1969 – Miscellaneous', in Harald Szeemann Archive, Maggia (hereafter HSAM).

193 See: 'Unmut über 'Prospect' konnte sich nicht entladen', *Rheinische Post*, 23 October 1969; 'Drei Stunden-Debatte', *Düsseldorfer Nachrichten*, 23 October 1969 in *Ibid.*

194 Daniel Buren, 'The function of an exhibition', *Studio International*, vol.186, no.961, December 1973, p.216.

195 Letter from Jürgen Harten to Otto van de Loo dated 20 May 1969, and Letter from Van de Loo to Harten dated 6 June 1969, in File IV 29367, AKDSD.

196 'Kunstmarkt Köln', Kunsthalle and Kunstverein, Cologne, 14 October–9 November 1969. In 1969, the Cologne Art Fair had between 35,000 and 40,000 visitors, and made a general turnover of DM 3.5 million. See: Statistics of the 1969 Kunstmarkt Köln, in CD-Rom, 'Kunstmarkt Köln '67', *Sediment*, *op. cit.*

197 Minutes of the organisation's annual meeting in Berlin dated 24 January 1969 (Mitgliederversammlung des Vereins progressiver deutscher Kunsthändler), in File A 72 IV 2, Zadik.

198 This occurred on the basis of a previous application made by Fischer. See: Letter from Van de Loo to Fischer dated 2 December 1968, in Galerie Korrespondenz 1967–69, AKFGD. Although Fischer was one of the organisers of Prospect, he did not participate in the event as an exhibitor.

199 See: 'Kunstmarkt Köln '67', *Sediment*, *op. cit.*, pp.39–41.

200 *Konzeption/Conception*, Städtisches Museum, Leverkusen, 24 October–23 November 1969. Artists: Arnatt, Baldessari, Barry, Baxter, H. and B. Becher, Bochner, Boetti, Broodthaers, Brouwn, Buren, Burgin, Burgy, Butler, Calzolari, Cotton, Darboven, Dibbets, Fulton, Gilbert and George, Graham, Huebler, Jackson, Kawara, Kosuth, Lamelas, LeWitt, McLean, Penone, Polke, Prini, Raetz,

> I am sending carbon copies of this letter to Heiner Friedrich, Françoise Lambert, Franz Dalem, Yvon Lambert and Galerie Sperone.
>
> Bob Ryman will arrive in Düsseldorf around the 1st [November] for your show. Then he will go to Stuttgart to see Domberger. He might stay there for several days to work on some prints. Then he'll go to Heiner in Munich, then to Françoise and Dalem in Milan. The last two shows will be with Sperone and Yvon Lambert.
>
> Bob will only need a few days to set up each exhibition, and the order listed above seems reasonably definite.[215]

On 26 November, a solo show of Dibbets's work opened at Art & Project, Amsterdam.[216] For this exhibition, the artist created a project that showed that he was well aware of the network that was developing at the time. The work consisted of four maps: Amsterdam, the Benelux, Europe and the world. The *Art & Project Bulletin* sent out on this occasion included a form to be posted back. A text on the back cover read: 'Send the right page of this bulletin (stamped) by return post to Art & Project. Each returned bulletin will be marked on the world map by a straight line from your home to Amsterdam.' The returned forms were collected and lines drawn on the appropriate map to indicate their journey. All in all, 196 responses were sent back to Amsterdam (Amsterdam: 57, Benelux: 51, Europe: 37, world: 34, bulletins received after the deadline: 17).[217] This work gives an accurate picture of the network of Conceptual art in 1969. Van Eelen, Dibbets, Develing, Martin and Mia Visser, Merz, Jürgen Harten, Maenz, Fischer, Siegelaub and LeWitt were among the many people who returned the forms.

Arte Povera, Conceptual, Actual or Impossible Art?

In the same year, 1969, a number of major publications and teaching courses on Conceptual art were launched. Germano Celant was the first art critic and curator to publish a book on the innovative contemporary art tendencies. *Arte Povera, Conceptual, Actual or Impossible Art?* was simultaneously published in English, German and Italian.[218] The book included an introductory text by Celant,

Ruppersberg, Ruscha, Sandback, Sladden, Smithson, Ulrichs, Venet, Weiner and Zaj.

201 Rolf Wedewer and Konrad Fischer, *Konzeption/Conception, Dokumentation einer heutigen Kunstrichtung, documentation of a to-day's tendency* (exh. cat.), Westdeutscher Verlag, Cologne and Opladen, 1969.

202 Letter from Fischer to Lippard dated 11 July 1969, and Letter from Siegelaub to Fischer dated 29 July 1969, in Galerie Korrespondenz 1967–69, AKFGD. In April 1969, Siegelaub contacted Fischer about the *July–August–September 1969* exhibition proposing to him that an artist's work be done in Düsseldorf. Subsequently, LeWitt made a piece in the city. See: Letter from Siegelaub to Fischer dated 15 April 1969, in Galerie Korrespondenz 1967–69, AKFGD.

203 Document entitled 'Vorlage für den Kulturausschuss' (presentation for the cultural committee), in File StALev 410.1302, Stadtarchiv, Leverkusen.

204 Letter from Huebler to Fischer dated 6 April 1970, Letter from Fischer to Huebler dated 15 April 1970, and Letter from Fischer to Huebler dated 2 June 1970, in Künstler Korrespondenz 1970–71, AKFGD.

205 'Konrad Fischer interviewed by Georg Jappe', *Studio International*, *op. cit.*, p.71.

206 'Joseph Kosuth', Galleria Gian Enzo Sperone, Turin, 9–16 November 1969. See: Minola, Mundici, Poli and Roberto, *Gian Enzo Sperone*, *op. cit.*, p.148. See also: Database 3, Section Joseph Kosuth (Appendix 1.3). In 1968, Kosuth received his first American one-man show at Leo Castelli, New York.

207 *Joseph Kosuth, Art as Idea as Idea*, Art & Project, Amsterdam, 22–30 November 1969. See: *Art & Project Bulletin*, no.14, 18 November 1969. In October 1969, the first part of Kosuth's essay 'Art after Philosophy' had been published in *Studio International*. See: Joseph Kosuth, 'Art after Philosophy', *Studio International*, vol. 178, no.915,

followed by photographs of artworks by American and European Conceptual artists and Arte Povera artists.[219] However, it was more a collection of photographs of artworks than a study of the movement.

Art & Language's teaching

In Europe, one of the most important teaching activities was the Art Theory course set up by Art & Language at Coventry College of Art in 1969.[220] The College was receptive to new ideas. As we have already seen, Barbara Reise, a key Minimal art and Conceptual art critic, was teaching at the College as a US visitor since 1968. The Art & Language group was founded in 1968 in Coventry by Terry Atkinson, Michael Baldwin, David Bainbridge (born in 1941) and Harold Hurell (born in 1940). They considered teaching as part of their art practice. The course was worked out as an alternative to studio work and was divided into five sections: Art Theory, Audio Visual, Epistemology, Romanticism and Technos. According to Art & Language, these divisions reflected the various aspects of art production.[221]

The group also edited and published *Art-Language, The Journal of Conceptual Art* from May 1969 onwards. The first issue included contributions not only by Art & Language members, but also by American Conceptualists: LeWitt's 'Sentences on Conceptual Art', Dan Graham's 'Poem-schema' and Weiner's 'Statements'.[222] With their teaching activities, the editing of the journal and writing within the group, Art & Language members developed the idea of an alternative art community as part of their wider politics.

Conceptual art teaching courses

Art & Language's teaching course paved the way for other institutions of higher education to establish contacts with the network of Conceptual artists. For instance, Roselee Goldberg, then a girlfriend of Celant, established an exhibition and artists' visiting programme at the Royal College of Art. Lynda Morris set up a similar programme for the Arts Association at the Slade School of Art (1974–76). As Student Coordinator, she organised lectures by art critics

October 1969, pp.134–137; vol.178, no.916, November 1969, pp.160–161; vol.178, n.917, December 1969, pp.212–213.

208 Letter from Fischer to Kosuth dated 26 August 1969, and Letter from Kosuth to Fischer dated 27 August 1969, in Korrespondenz mit Künstlern 1969–70, AKFGD.

209 Letter from Fischer to Kosuth dated 25 November 1969, Korrespondenz mit Künstlern 1969–70, AKFGD.

210 'Konrad Fischer interviewed by Georg Jappe', *Studio International*, *op. cit.*, p.70. Fischer later admitted to regretting this comment. Morris in conversation with the author, *op. cit.*

211 'Robert Ryman', Konrad Fischer, Düsseldorf, 11 November–12 December 1969. See: *Ausstellungen bei Konrad Fischer*, *op. cit.*, p.39.

212 See: Database 3, Section Robert Ryman (Appendix 1.3).

213 *Robert Ryman, Drawings and Paintings*, Galerie Heiner Friedrich, Munich, 21 November–20 December 1969.

214 *Robert Ryman*, Galerie Yvon Lambert, Paris, December 1969. *Robert Ryman*, Galleria Françoise Lambert, Milan, December 1969–January 1970.

215 Letter from Naomi Spector, assistant Fischbach Gallery New York, to Konrad Fischer dated 17 October 1969, in Galerie Korrespondenz 1967– [1969], AKFGD. In the end, however, Ryman did not exhibit at Sperone's.

216 *Jan Dibbets*, Art & Project, Amsterdam, 26 November–16 December 1969. See: *Art & Project Bulletin*, no.15, 26 November 1969.

217 Dibbets's project was published in *Studio International* in 1970 with a detailed list of the people who had sent back their bulletins. See: Jan Dibbets, 'Project for Art & Project', *Studio International*, vol.180, no. 924, July–August 1970, p.41–44.

218 Germano Celant, *Arte Povera, Conceptual, Actual or Impossible Art?*, Mazzotta, Milan, Studio Vista: London, Praeger: New York, Studio Wasmuth: Tübingen, 1969. Although the book is dated 1969, it appears to have been published a bit later. Morris in conversation

(including Barbara Reise, Peter Townsend and Clement Greenberg) and events by artists (Art & Language, Broodthaers, Buren, Flanagan, Lamelas, Graham, Cadere).[223] Moreover, the Slade arranged an artists' exchange programme with Stuart Brisley and the Hochschule für Bildende Künste in Hamburg, where Franz Erhard Walther was a professor of sculpture from 1971 onwards.

In North America, many Conceptual art exhibitions took place in the late 1960s in universities and colleges. One of the first teaching courses to be established was the 'Projects Class', launched in 1969 by the artist David Askevold (born 1940) at the Nova Scotia College of Art and Design, Halifax, Canada.[224] Askevold had originally been hired in 1968 as a sculpture teacher. However, in the fall of 1969, he organised a course that consisted of inviting Conceptual artists to submit a proposal for students to execute. They could either work directly with the students or send their proposal by mail or telephone.[225] The first visitors were the American artists Rex Lau and James Lee Byars, who arranged a week of performances and exhibitions. LeWitt later presented a list of works for the class to execute, including: '1) A work that uses the idea of error, 2) A work that uses the idea of incompleteness, 3) A work that uses the idea of infinity.'

Dibbets describes his activity at the College: 'It wasn't even teaching, I'd say. It was like I was young, they were young, and we were doing all sorts of things together.'[226] His proposed project consisted of the whole class making a trip from Halifax to Toronto by train. Every student had to think about themselves and record what they did during this very long journey. Dibbets's contribution was to have a student photograph him every hour, even during the night. At the end of the trip, all of the documents were exhibited together.

The College's exhibition space, the Anna Leonowens Gallery, was directed by Charlotte Townsend, the niece of Peter Townsend, editor of *Studio International*. The gallery hosted many shows of Conceptual artists, including Weiner and Kosuth in 1969. In 1972, NSCAD set up a university press to publish a series of books of source material on contemporary artists edited by Kasper König (*The Nova Scotia Series*).[227]

with the author, *op. cit.*

219 Artists featured in the book are: Andre, Anselmo, Barry, Beuys, Boetti, Boezem, Calzolari, De Maria, Dibbets, Fabro, Flanagan, Haacke, Heizer, Hesse, Huebler, Kaltenbach, Kosuth, Kounellis, Long, Merz, Morris, Nauman, Oppenheim, Paolini, Penone, Pistoletto, Prini, Ruthenbeck, Serra, Sonnier, Van Elk, Walther, Weiner and Zorio.

220 For a contemporary discussion of the Art & Language course at Coventry, see: Lynda Morris, *Art – Art Education – Education, Three titles for a discussion of fine art education*, unpublished MA thesis, Royal College of Art and Design, London, 1973, pp.47–54.

221 The course was increasingly criticised for producing texts rather than works. In 1971, Baldwin and Bainbridge, both on a part-time contract, were fired for advocating language as the main medium of their students' art practice. The course was thus abruptly terminated. Terry Atkinson, the only one to have a permanent contract, ran the course until 1973 for the already registered students and then eventually resigned. It was only after their teaching activities were terminated that Art & Language started to consider the art market as an alternative source of finance for the group. See: 'Some concerns in Fine Art Education', *Studio International*, vol.182, no.937, October 1971, pp.120–122. See also: Charles Harrison, 'Educating Artists', *Studio International*, vol.183, no.944, May 1972, pp.222–224.

222 *Art-Language, The Journal of Conceptual Art*, vol.1, no.1, May 1969.

223 See: 'Slade' File, in Lynda Morris Archive, Norwich (hereafter LMAN). In March 1976, Lynda Morris arranged for André Cadere to show his work in various London pubs popular with protagonists of the art world (Gilbert & George, Jack Wendler, Robert Self, Lynda Morris, Nigel Greenwood) or those related to galleries and museum (ICA, Lisson Gallery, Slade). See: *André Cadere, Histoire d'un travail*, Herbert-Gewad, Gent, 1982, no.35, unnumbered pages.

In the late 1960s and 1970s, many Conceptual artists taught in art colleges and universities. In Canada, Ian Baxter (N.E. Thing Co.) was teaching at the University of British Columbia and at Simon Fraser University in Vancouver.[228] Huebler taught at Bradford College (Massachusetts) from 1957 to 1973. He later taught at Harvard University, Cambridge (Massachusetts) from 1973 to 1975, before becoming Dean of Art at the California Institute of the Arts in Valencia, California (1976–1988). Baldessari (from 1970) and Michael Asher also taught at 'CalArts'.[229] At the University of California in Irvine, Helen Weiner, the partner of the artist Jack Goldstein, set up a comprehensive exhibition programme.[230]

In the late 1960s, teaching courses, as well as the publication of artists' writings and exhibition catalogues, further enlarged the Conceptual network. Publications became particularly relevant as Conceptual artists increasingly used instructions, texts and documentation as media.

224 The College was founded in 1967 in a remote area, far away from any art centre. Right from the beginning it was decided to compensate for the geographical isolation by making the college function as a gallery, print workshop, press and lecture centre for the arts. The young Canadian painter Garry Neil Kennedy (born 1935) became the first Head of NSCAD. He hired many artists to teach; these included Pat Kelly, Bill Nolan, Walter Ostrom and Frank Fox. For a contemporary insight into NSCAD teaching courses, see: Morris, *Art – Art Education – Education*, *op. cit.*, pp.58–60.

225 Most artists, however, would come to the college themselves. See: David Askevold, 'The Projects Class', in *Conceptual Art: The NSCAD Connection, 1967–1973* (exh. cat.), Nova Scotia College of Art and Design, Halifax, 1994. Artists participating in the Projects Class at the time were: Barry, Bochner, Byars, Dibbets, Graham, Huebler, Kosuth, Rex Lau, LeWitt, Lippard, N.E. Thing Co., Smithson, Weiner.

226 Dibbets in conversation with the author, *op. cit.*

227 See: *Proposals from Halifax: an exhibition of selected typescripts, flyers, posters, catalogues, books, mailers and postcards of a Conceptual nature produced from 1969 to 1999 by affiliates of the Nova Scotia College of Art and Design (NSCAD)* (exh. cat.), National Gallery of Canada, Ottawa, 2000.

228 Ian Baxter later taught at the Emily Carr Institute of Art and Design, York University, Toronto (1972–75) and at the School of Visual Arts, University of Windsor (since 1988).

229 The California Institute of the Arts opened in 1961 through the merger of the Chouinard Art Institute and the Los Angeles Conservatory of Music. It was the first degree-granting institution of higher learning in America to teach both the visual and performing arts. It was relocated to Valencia in 1971.

230 Helen Weiner later started Metro Pictures in New York.

231 The Ühl was Fischer's favourite bar. The Cream Cheese was launched in 1967 in the Düsseldorf Altstadt by Bim Reinert and

2.3 Conclusion

In 1968 and 1969, the international network of Conceptual artists developed in Europe. New dealer galleries were founded and existing galleries started to exhibit Conceptual artists. The set of connections established between the dealers led to the exchange of artists and to a series of exhibitions in the galleries. This meant that dealers shared artists' travelling costs. The notion of people moving around the network was very important.

The late 1960s also saw the organisation of group shows of Conceptual art in Europe. Thus artists working in a different field, but sharing common thinking and ideas (for instance, the Arte Povera artists), were able to develop links with Conceptualists. The organisation of mixed exhibitions meant that the network expanded into the public sector.

Conceptual art meeting places

The relatively restricted number of people involved in Conceptual art led to a small but dynamic support network. Dealers, curators, private collectors and critics had to stick together to move forward. Many people I interviewed highlighted the friendships that developed between the members of the network. In every city, there would be a few key individuals who would introduce people to each other. Discussions and meeting places such as the bars the Ühl and the Cream Cheese in Düsseldorf were important.[230] In New York, Max's Kansas City and the Spring Street Bar were focal points.[231]

Internationalism and equality (for example between America and Europe, or between men and women) were amongst the main characteristics of the community that developed around Conceptual art in Europe in the late 1960s. In the context of the postwar period, it was significant that Americans and Germans were sitting together and talking, including Jewish Americans.

In the early 1970s, the network further expanded. Most Conceptual artists had major solo shows in public institutions and several major mixed exhibitions

her husband. It was located in the same street as Fischer's gallery, Neubrückstraße. The interior design was conceived by Günther Uecker, Joseph Beuys and some of his students. The walls consisted of television screens. It was a 'multimedia action place' where slide projections and underground films were shown, where progressive bands such as Kraftwerk played, and where happenings took place. The Cream Cheese closed in 1977. See: Stephan von Wiese, 'Creamcheese – Eine Kneipe als Forum der Kunst', in *Brennpunkt Düsseldorf 1962–1987* (exh. cat.), Kunstmuseum, Düsseldorf, 1987, pp.120–121.

232 Max's Kansas City was a bar, restaurant and night club located on Park Avenue South, just off Union Square. It was launched in 1965 by Mickey Ruskin (1933–83), who was also an art collector. The place became an important socialising venue for the New York art world. For an extensive discussion, see: Yvonne Sewall-Ruskin, *High on rebellion: Inside the underground at Max's Kansas City 1965–1981*, Thunders Mouth Press, New York, 1998.

established the movement within the wider art world in Europe and in America. It was, however, precisely this settlement within that wider world that gradually led to the fragmentation of the original network.

Chapter 3

The international network and major exhibitions: 1970–72 and later

3.1 1970

In 1970, the network of Conceptual artists achieved a more international dimension. In each country, certain dealers assumed the role of the primary contact for Conceptualism. Dealer galleries established closer ties to ensure that their artists were represented all over Europe. It can be argued that 1970 marked the consolidation of the network.

Germany: Fischer and Friedrich; The Netherlands: Art & Project

Sol LeWitt, who had been one of the first American Conceptual artists to be exhibited in Europe in the late 1960s, had until then only been represented by German dealer galleries, Fischer and Friedrich.[1] In 1970, they were the two main Conceptual art dealers in Germany. On 2 January 1970, an Art & Project Bulletin by LeWitt was mailed out.[2] The show consisted of the mailing of the bulletin as no works were presented in the gallery space.[3] Since 1969, Art & Project had become the Dutch gallery for Conceptual Art, with shows by Weiner, Kosuth, Dibbets and Barry in that year.

Douglas Huebler

Nevertheless, there were other Conceptual artists still to have their first European solo shows. This was the case with Douglas Huebler, to whom Fischer gave a one-man exhibition in January 1970.[4] The artist's work had already been shown on several occasions in Europe: for instance at *Op Losse Schroeven* and *When*

1 See: Database 3, Section Sol LeWitt (Appendix 1.3).

2 'Sol LeWitt, Lines and Combinations of Lines', *Art & Project Bulletin*, no.18, 2 January 1970.

3 Sol LeWitt's subsequent shows at Art & Project would mostly take the form of a bulletin. See, for instance: 'Sol LeWitt, Ten Thousand Lines – Six Thousand Two Hundred and Fifty Lines', *Art & Project Bulletin*, no.32, 4 January 1971, and 'Sol LeWitt', *Art & Project Bulletin*, no.60, 25 September 1972.

4 *Douglas Huebler*, Konrad Fischer, Düsseldorf, 15–31 January 1970. See: *Ausstellungen bei Konrad Fischer*, *op. cit.*, p.41.

5 Letter from Douglas Huebler to Konrad Fischer dated 7 November 1969, in Korrespondenz mit Künstlern 1969–70, AKFGD.

6 Letter from Fischer to Huebler dated 16 November 1969, in Korrespondenz mit Künstlern 1969–70, AKFGD.

7 Letter from Huebler to Fischer dated 21 November 1969, in Korrespondenz mit Künstlern 1969–70, AKFGD. Robert Barry never showed at Konrad Fischer's, but his first show at Sperone's opened on 30 December 1969.

8 *Douglas Huebler, Oeuvres variables*, Galerie Yvon Lambert, Paris, 11–18 March 1970. See: Database 3, Section Douglas Huebler (Appendix 1.3).

9 *Douglas Huebler, Duration Piece*, Galleria Gian Enzo Sperone, Turin, 24 March–8 April 1970.

10 *Douglas Huebler, Location Piece No.8, Amsterdam, Holland*, Art & Project, Amsterdam, 25 April– 8 May 1970. See: *Art & Project Bulletin*, no.22, 17 April 1970.

Attitudes Become Form. The notion of 'primary dealer' was very important because negotiations for future shows or sales of the artist were made through this first contact. On this matter, correspondence between Huebler and Fischer is revealing. In November 1969, Huebler wrote to Fischer:

> I have just recently been able to sit with Seth Siegelaub and Robert Barry and know enough definite information to write this letter to you.
>
> I understand from Mr Siegelaub that you have agreed to exhibit my work for one week early in 1970 either before or after a similar week of showing Barry. I am very pleased that you are willing to do this. I also understand that you will be sharing the expenses with Gallery Sperone (where I will also show) for transportation ... etc. I should know from you more information concerning the arrangements and your expectations from a financial agreement. You should understand that I am not very experienced conducting 'business' so I put myself into your hands to tell me what these arrangements are.[5]

Fischer's reply openly addressed the question of the 'priority of showing' in Europe:

> I have a strange feeling about something, I have to ask you: You are going to do a show with Art & Project in Amsterdam, why did you not write it to me? What is the reason, that Art & Project is having the priority in showing you in Europe? I also think, that all galleries, doing a show with you, have to share the expenses. By the way, what are your expenses? May I hear from you what you think about all this?[6]

To Fischer's questions, Huebler answered:

> There were some things that I did not understand enough. I apologize for that. Certainly you are right. It is for you to have priority to show my work.
>
> I did not write to you about Art & Project because my letter had just left when I received one from Art & Project asking me to do something. I did not understand that they were a real gallery as it seemed that what they really were

11 Letter from Douglas Huebler to Konrad Fischer dated 20 February 1970, in Künstler Korrespondenz 1970–71, AKFGD. Giuseppe Panza owned 20 early pieces by Douglas Huebler. See: *Art of the Fifties, Sixties and Seventies, The Panza Collection*, *op. cit.*, pp.303–304.

12 *Bruce Nauman*, Konrad Fischer, Düsseldorf, 5 February–3 March 1970. See: *Ausstellungen bei Konrad Fischer*, *op. cit.*, p.42.

13 Letter from Nauman to Fischer dated 3 January 1970, in Korrespondenz mit Künstlern 1969–70, AKFGD.

14 Letter from Fischer to Nauman dated 19 January 1970, in Künstler Korrespondenz 1970–71, AKFGD.

15 Letter from Nauman to Fischer dated 1 April [1970], in Künstler Korrespondenz 1970–71, AKFGD. See: Database 5 on the Panza Collection (Appendix 1.5). See also: *Art of the Fifties, Sixties and Seventies, The Panza Collection*, *op. cit.*, p.308.

16 *Bruce Nauman*, Galleria Gian Enzo Sperone, Turin, 25 February–10 March 1970. See: Minola, Mundici, Poli and Roberto, *Gian Enzo Sperone*, *op. cit.*, p.158.

17 Minola, Mundici, Poli and Roberto, *Gian Enzo Sperone*, *op. cit.*, p.39.

18 See: Database 1, Section Gian Enzo Sperone (Appendix 1.1).

19 *Jan Dibbets – Shadows, Krefeld 69*, Galleria Françoise Lambert, Milan, 25 February–March 1970.

20 *Jan Dibbets*, Yvon Lambert, Paris, starting 19 February 1970. See: Database 3, Section Jan Dibbets (Appendix 1.3).

21 *Mario Merz*, Konrad Fischer, Düsseldorf, 7–31 March 1970.

doing was publishing their bulletin.

I will write to them and cancel my project.

I did, however, understand that you knew that both Barry and I will also be in Italy to do a show at Sperone and that he would be sharing our expenses with you.

Is that true?

It seems that expenses would be about $500 ... $350 for air fares to Europe and in Europe ... and about $150 to spend for 3 weeks to eat, etc.

If, perhaps, Art & Project is willing to share expenses then your feelings would be different. If you happen to speak with them you might learn that. But I don't think that they have money to do that so I am now not expecting to do anything there. Again may I say I am sorry about that. It is, as you know, difficult to arrange something from so far away and only by letter.[7]

Eventually, Huebler's exhibition took place at Fischer's in January 1970. It was followed by shows at Yvon Lambert (March)[8], at Gian Enzo Sperone (March–April)[9] and at Art & Project (April–May).[10] There was clearly a transfer of the artist from one Conceptual art dealer to the next. The sharing of expenses contributed towards establishing the network that linked the dealers to each other.

Huebler's naivety regarding the priority of showing and dealing arrangements may have been somewhat disingenuous. At the time, he was teaching at the Bradford Junior College (Massachusetts). In New York, he had been represented by Siegelaub since 1968 and he had also had a solo show with Eugenia Butler in Los Angeles in 1969. Correspondence with Fischer after the show reveals that he was well aware of the implications of dealing and collecting. On 10 February 1970, he wrote to Fischer that the collector Giuseppe Panza:

has become somebody very mysterious for me. He wanted, from Sperone, as much of my work as possible ... then when I came back I learned that he had written to Eugenia Butler in LA for work ... and bought from her, then wanted more work. No one in America has my work otherwise at this time. Now I hear that apparently he is in touch with you. Sperone wanted more work, and now

See: *Ausstellungen bei Konrad Fischer*, *op. cit.*, p.43.

22 Letter from Sonnabend to Fischer dated 12 May 1969, in Galerie Korrespondenz 1967–[1969], AKFGD.

23 See: Database 3, Section Mario Merz (Appendix 1.3). Later that year, in October 1970, Mario Merz would have his first solo show at Françoise Lambert, Milan.

24 *Marcel Broodthaers, MTL–DTH*, Galerie MTL, Brussels, 13 March–10 April 1970. See: Database 3, Section Marcel Broodthaers (Appendix 1.3).

25 For an extensive discussion of the work, see: Anne Rorimer, 'The Exhibition at the MTL Gallery in Brussels, March 13–April 10, 1970', *October*, no.42, Fall 1987, pp.101–125. The work was acquired in 1970 by the Belgian collector Isi Fiszman. See: *Ibid.*, p.102, note 3. See also: *Marcel Broodthaers, Cinéma* (exh. cat.), Fundació Antoni Tápies, Barcelona, 1997, pp.100–111.

26 The archive of the Galerie MTL is kept privately by the artist Lili Dujourie, Spillemaeckers's widow. In 1993, she gave numerous documents related to the gallery to the Archives de l'art contemporain en Belgique, Brussels (AACBB). This archive contains mostly invitation cards, posters, photographs and press cuttings, but no correspondence.

27 In 1965, Spillemaeckers had received shows at the Studio Callebert in Roeselare (January) and at the Toonzaal van papiergroothandel g.h. bührmann n.v. in Antwerp (November). In 1966, he was exhibited at the Galerie Egmont in Dendermonde Willebroek (January) and at the Museum voor Schone Kunsten,

> Eugenia Butler wants more. And Panza is the one who has begun to create pressure against the law of supply and demand. I am flattered by that but, naturally, it makes strange problems ... Like he almost owns me ... at least, very much of my 'early' work.[11]

The primary dealer was the one who took care of the interests of the artist and made arrangements for shows, even if they were held at other galleries. This was, for example, the case with Nauman's second solo show at Konrad Fischer.[12] Indeed, a month before the opening on 5 February 1970, Nauman sent instructions to the dealer, writing: 'Here are instructions for the piece which I described to you. If it is possible, I think you should go ahead and have the piece made and have the show without my presence, for I want to stay home and work for a while.'[13] Fischer replied that it would be no problem to have the piece, a diagonal wall covered with acoustic material, constructed, but that he regretted that the artist would not be able to come to Düsseldorf. He also asked him for drawings to sell.[14] It was again Panza who acquired the work on show, *Diagonal Sound Wall (Acoustic Wall)* (1969–70).[15]

Italy: Gian Enzo Sperone and Françoise Lambert

Soon after his show in Düsseldorf, Nauman had his first exhibition at the Galleria Sperone from 15 February to 10 March 1970.[16] Until then, the artist had been represented in Europe by both Fischer and Sonnabend. The Italian dealer had met Nauman during his first trip to New York in late 1969.[17] For his show in Turin, Nauman created an environment, *Audio/Tactile Separation Piece* (1970), consisting of walls fitted with sensors that reacted to physical contact and that transmitted it to loudspeakers.

This example shows how primary dealers arranged for secondary dealers to take on their artists. Moreover, it demonstrates that Sperone had developed as an important dealer for Conceptual art in Italy. By 1969, he had already shown several Conceptualists, including Andre, Kosuth and Weiner.[18] In Milan, Françoise Lambert also positioned herself in the network of Conceptual art, and nearly always worked in tandem with Yvon Lambert. For example, on 26 February, Jan Dibbets's first Italian solo show opened at the Galleria Françoise

Feestpaleis, Wapenplein, Oostende (September). See: 'Dossier noir collectif Fernand Spillemaeckers', in AACBB. He later invented a Conceptual artist named Léo Josefstein. Nowadays, this name is sometimes used by the Belgian artist Jacques Charlier.

28 Lili Dujourie in conversation with the author, Lovendegem, 27 October 2004, manuscript notes. And: Yves Gevaert in conversation with the author, Brussels, 28 October 2004, manuscript notes. Spillemaeckers edited a magazine *MTL Art Actuel* that included texts by artists and critics.

29 Jacques Charlier in conversation with the author, Liège, 13 May 2004, manuscript notes. During our conversation, Charlier showed me an empty can of the tomato base with an 'MTL' red, yellow and black logo.

30 Lili Dujourie in conversation with the author, *op. cit.*

31 For a complete list of shows organised at the MTL gallery, see an untitled document written by Spillemaeckers and kept in the archive of Jacques Charlier, Liège. An enhanced listing of MTL exhibitions is reproduced as Appendix 3.6. For a comprehensive outline of exhibitions of Conceptual artists at the gallery, see: Database 1, Section MTL (Appendix 1.1).

32 MTL did, however, show Broodthaers and Buren in 1970.

33 De Decker in conversation with the author, *op. cit.*

34 *Ibid.* (author's translation).

35 *Lawrence Weiner*, Galerie Yvon Lambert, Paris, 19–26 March 1970. In November–December 1970, Weiner had two further solo shows at Konrad Fischer and Gian Enzo Sperone. See: Database 3,

Lambert.[19] Only a week before, another one-man show of the artist had opened at Yvon Lambert, Paris.[20]

Mario Merz

In March 1970, Mario Merz's first solo show took place at Konrad Fischer.[21] His work had already been shown in Düsseldorf during Prospect 68, where he had been represented by Ileana Sonnabend. She contacted Fischer about a possible Merz show in Düsseldorf. Earlier, in May 1969, during the artist's first show in Paris, Sonnabend had written to Fischer: 'I remember your mention of your interest in Merz. Since I would like very much to show him in Germany, I would be delighted if you might consider arranging an exhibition for him. Do let me know what your thoughts are upon this matter.'[22] Fischer was Merz's third dealer, after Sperone in Italy and Sonnabend in France, and the first one in Germany.[23]

Belgium: Wide White Space and MTL

Marcel Broodthaers's first solo exhibition in a Conceptual art gallery other than Wide White Space also opened in March 1970.[24] This show marked the beginning of MTL's engagement with Conceptualism. The exhibition and work's title *MTL–DTH* refers to the name of the Brussels gallery and to the middle three letters of the artist's surname. The piece consisted of various documents related to earlier works (drawings and manuscripts, notably from his practice as a poet), a colour film and the exhibition catalogue.[25]

The Galerie MTL was opened by Fernand Spillemaeckers (1938–78) in 1969 (rue Armand Campenhout).[26] He came from a Flemish family and had attended the Académie des Beaux-Arts in Brussels. He had worked as an artist in the mid-1960s before deciding to launch a gallery.[27] His aim was to open a space to exhibit visually the artists that he was interested in theoretically: the philosophical and theoretical writings of Buren and Toroni, and of the critics Michel Claura and René Denizot.[28]

It is unclear where the name MTL came from. According to the artist Jacques Charlier, it derived from the name of a tomato base, 'Marie Thumas Louvain (triple concentré de tomates)', used by Lili Dujourie (born 1941) at the time.[29] Dujourie, the dealer's widow rejects that explanation, arguing that the letters

Section Lawrence Weiner (Appendix 1.3).

36 See: Database 1, Section Yvon Lambert (Appendix 1.1).

37 '18 Paris IV.70', Paris, April 1970. Artists: Barry, Broodthaers, Brouwn, Buren, Dibbets, Dijan, Gilbert & George, Guinochet, Huebler, Kawara, Lamelas, LeWitt, Long, Ruscha, Ryman, Toroni, Weiner and Wilson. The title of the exhibition refers to the number of artists, location and duration of the exhibition.

38 *January 5–31, 1969*, *March 1–31, 1969* and *July–August–September, 1969*.

39 *18 Paris IV.70* (exh. cat.), Michel Claura and Seth Siegelaub, Paris, 1970. See also: Michel Claura and René Denizot, '18 Paris IV.70', *Studio International*, vol.179, no.921, April 1970, p.179.

40 *Conceptual Art and Conceptual Aspects*, New York Cultural Art Center, New York, 10 April–25 August 1970. Artists: Art & Language, Barthelme, Barry, Baxter, Bochner, Buren, Burgy, Burn, Byars, Cutforth, Dibbets, Haacke, Huebler, Kaltenbach, Kawara, Kosuth, Kozlov, Nauman, Oppenheim, Piper, Ruscha, Venet, Wilson and Weiner. It is interesting to highlight that this was the first show to use the term 'Conceptual art' in its title.

41 Donald Karshan, 'The seventies: post-object art', *Studio International*, vol.180, no.925, September 1970, p.69.

42 Donald Karshan (ed.), *Conceptual Art and Conceptual Aspects* (exh. cat.), New York Cultural Art Center, New York, 1970. Buren's text had first been published in French in the exhibition catalogue of the *Konzeption/Conception* exhibition in Leverkusen. See: Daniel Buren, 'Mise en garde', in Wedewer and Fischer, *Konzeption/Conception*,

were chosen for no other reason than that they formed a pleasing combination.[30] The first exhibitions were dedicated to the Flemish artists Guy Mees and Yves de Smet.[31]

Now there were two dealer galleries for Conceptual art in Belgium: one in Brussels and one in Antwerp. Spillemaeckers took on artists, such as Dibbets, Darboven and Huebler, who were not represented by Wide White Space.[32] There was, however, a certain competition between the two galleries since there was only a small number of collectors.[33] Nevertheless, according to Anny De Decker, each dealer had his territory:

> In the beginning, I was alone as far as Belgium was concerned, then afterwards there was the MTL. But Fernand Spillemaeckers took on the artists I hadn't shown (Darboven, Huebler, Barry, etc.). So it wasn't a problem because we didn't have the same artists. Fischer was there for the Rhineland, Art & Project for Holland, etc. Basically we all covered big territories.

France: Yvon Lambert and Ileana Sonnabend

Weiner's first solo show in Paris opened at the Galerie Yvon Lambert on 19 March 1970.[35] Lambert had begun to establish himself as a major Conceptual art dealer in France. In 1969, he had exhibited Buren, Long and Ryman and in early 1970, he had already hosted solo shows of Huebler, Lamelas and Dibbets.[36] Lambert became, along with Sonnabend, the key contact in Paris for the Conceptual network.

18 Paris IV.70

In April 1970, the French art critic Michel Claura organised, in collaboration with Siegelaub, the exhibition *18 Paris IV.70*. The event took place on the rue Mouffetard in the 5th arrondissement.[37] The show was based on an original concept by Siegelaub, continuing the principles he had developed in 1969.[38] Twenty-two artists were invited to participate in the exhibition and to propose a project. All the projects received were then sent back to the artists who were asked to submit their final proposal. This could be a confirmation or modification of the original project, thus underlining the evolution of artistic concepts.

op. cit., unnumbered pages.

43 Gilbert Proesch (Italian) and George Pasmore (English) met in 1967 at Central St Martins College of Art and Design in London. In 1969, they started to execute performances, such as *The Meal*, in which they served David Hockney in front of an audience as a work of art. The same year, they also began to perform their famous 'Singing Sculpture', *Underneath the Arches*.

44 *Gilbert & George*, Konrad Fischer, Düsseldorf, 10 May–5 June 1970. See: *Ausstellungen bei Konrad Fischer*, *op. cit.*, p.46. Fischer gained a key reputation among young British artists because he was the first to show many of them: Long (1968), Fulton (June 1969), McLean (September 1969), Gilbert & George (May 1970). This was the second exhibition to take place in Fischer's new gallery space in the Andreastraße. The space had been inaugurated in April 1970 with an exhibition of Gerhard Richter.

45 Letter from Gilbert & George to Fischer dated April 1970, in Künstler Korrespondenz 1970–71, AKFGD.

46 Lynda Morris in conversation with the author.

47 'My name is Konrad Fischer. You will do somezing wiz me in Düsseldorf, eeh... ?, A conversation with Gilbert and George', in Kölle, *Die Kunst des Ausstellens*, *op. cit.*, p.261.

48 *Ibid.*, p.262.

49 'Interview with Nigel Greenwood', in Moseley, *Conception*, *op. cit.*, p.132.

50 The alternative *between* events were launched in February 1969 and took place at the Kunsthalle, Düsseldorf during the period

Sol LeWitt's participation was described as follows: 'I. On a wall (smooth and white if possible) a draftsman draws 500 yellow, 500 grey, 500 red and 500 blue lines, within an area of 1 square meter. All lines must be between 10 cm and 20 cm long and straight. / II. Delete the first project.'[39]

Conceptual Art and Conceptual Aspects

At the same time, Donald Karshan (1930–2003) organised a group show at the New York Cultural Art Center: *Conceptual Art and Conceptual Aspects*.[40] Karshan had previously worked for the Museum of Graphic Arts; he had also collected prints since the early 1960s. In 1970, he was founding Director of the New York Cultural Art Center. The exhibition, clearly influenced by Karshan's own artistic interest, consisted of mostly language-based works on paper. For him, Conceptual art was an 'area of serious art "investigations"'.[41] Thus the exhibition catalogue was a collection of artists' texts, such as Kosuth's 'Art after Philosophy' and Daniel Buren's 'Beware!'.[42]

Gilbert & George

Spring 1970 marked the launch of Gilbert & George (born 1943 and 1942 respectively) in the network of Conceptual art.[43] Their first solo show opened on 10 May 1970 at Konrad Fischer, Düsseldorf.[44] The exhibition consisted of charcoal on paper drawings, *Relaxing. From Walking, Viewing, Relaxing* (1970). The artists performed a 'Living Sculpture' during the opening.[45]

Fischer first met Gilbert & George at the opening of *When Attitudes Become Form* at the ICA, London, in September 1969.[46] The artists performed an informal 'Living Sculpture' at the opening; at the end of the evening Fischer asked them to show with him.[47] The dealer first arranged performances elsewhere in Germany to build their reputation before their show in Düsseldorf.[48] Gilbert & George performed the *Singing Sculpture* during Prospect 69 (September–October 1969), although not as part of the official programme.[49] Their work was also included in *Konzeption/Conception* in Leverkusen (October–November 1969) and in *between 4* at the Kunsthalle Düsseldorf (February 1970).[50] Thus Gilbert & George's work had already been presented in various contexts that associated them with Conceptual art before their first solo show with Fischer in Düsseldorf.

between two official exhibitions. See: Jürgen Harten (ed.), *25 Jahre Kunsthalle Düsseldorf*, Städtische Kunsthalle, Düsseldorf, 1992, unnumbered pages. See also the recent exhibition *between 1969–73 in der Kunsthalle Düsseldorf, Chronik einer Nicht-Ausstellung* at the Kunsthalle in Düsseldorf from 27 January to 9 April 2007.

51 See: Database 3, Section Gilbert & George (Appendix 1.3).

52 *Gilbert & George, Art Notes and Thoughts*, Art & Project, Amsterdam, 12–23 May 1970. See: *Art & Project Bulletin*, no.20, 1 March 1970. This bulletin was sent from Tokyo because Art & Project temporarily moved their activities to Japan from February to April 1970. Via their bulletin, the gallery functioned as easily in Tokyo as in Amsterdam.

53 *Gilbert & George, Underneath the Arches, Singing Sculpture*, Galerie Heiner Friedrich, Munich, 14 May 1970. See the list of shows organised by Heiner Friedrich, in Urbaschek, *Dia Art Foundation*, *op. cit.*, p.233.

54 Letter from Fischer to Gilbert & George dated 15 December 1969, in Korrespondenz mit Künstlern 1969–70, AKFGD.

55 *Idea Structures*, Camden Arts Centre, London, 24 June–19 July 1970. Artists: Arnatt, Burgin, Herring, Kosuth, Atkinson, Bainbridge, Baldwin and Hurrell.

56 Charles Harrison (ed.), *Idea Structures* (exh. cat.), Survey '70, Borough of Camden, London, 1970.

57 *Art-Language*, vol.1, no.2, February 1970 (contributions by Atkinson, Bainbridge, Baldwin, Barthelme, Brown-David, Burn, Hirons, Hurrell, Kosuth, McKenna, Ramsden and Thompson), and

A couple of days after the opening in Düsseldorf, a whole series of events by Gilbert & George were launched in key dealer galleries across Europe.[51] On 12 May, a solo show opened at Art & Project, consisting of drawings and a performance.[52] On 14 May, they made a performance at Heiner Friedrich, Munich.[53] Correspondence with the artists shows that Fischer tried to arrange performances in other German locations, for instance at the museum in Mönchengladbach and at René Block in Berlin.[54]

1970 Venice Biennale

The Venice Biennale took place during the summer of 1970. The protests of 1968 had led to a number of modifications: the Grand Prizes were abolished, and single and celebratory shows were replaced by more 'democratic' exhibitions arranged around themes such as 'Research and Planning' and 'Art in Society'. The sales office, considered to be an instrument of the commercialisation of art, was also eliminated.

Idea Structures

Also during that summer, a number of Conceptual group shows were held in Europe and in America. Charles Harrison organised *Idea Structures* (June–July 1970) for the London Borough of Camden's annual survey of developments in contemporary art.[55] The works on show were commissioned from the artists and the catalogue contained works by all of them.[56] This exhibition was entirely Anglo-Saxon, presenting British artists alongside the American artist Kosuth. At that time, Harrison was increasingly involved with Art & Language. Kosuth also became close to the group. In the second and third issues of *Art-Language*, published in February and June 1970, he was named American editor.[57]

Conceptual Art, Arte Povera, Land Art

At about the same time, Celant launched *Conceptual Art, Arte Povera, Land Art* at the Galleria Civica d'Arte Moderna in Turin.[58] This was one of the first major international shows in Italy, and the first one in Europe to include the term 'Conceptual art' in its title.[59] It presented an extensive survey of the innovative art tendencies of the day, including works and films by Nauman, Ryman, Merz and Darboven (*Index 00–99*).[60]

Art-Language, vol.1, no.3, June 1970 (contributions by Baldwin, Bihari, Burn, Cutforth, Howard and Ramsden).

58 *Conceptual Art, Arte Povera, Land Art*, Galleria Civica d'Arte Moderna, Turin, June–July 1970. Artists: Andre, Anselmo, Baldessari, Barry, Beuys, Bochner, Boetti, Calzolari, Christo, Darboven, De Maria, Dibbets, Fabro, Flavin, Fulton, Gilbert & George, Haacke, Heizer, Huebler, Kaltenbach, Kawara, Klein, Kosuth, Kounellis, LeWitt, Manzoni, Merz, Morris, Nauman, Oppenheim, Paolini, Pascali, Penone, Pistoletto, Prini, Ryman, Sandback, Serra, Smithson, Sonnier, Venet, Weiner and Zorio.

59 Germano Celant, *Conceptual Art, Arte Povera, Land Art* (exh. cat.), Galleria Civica d'Arte Moderna, Turin, 1970.

60 Previously, in May 1970, one of the first group shows to present Arte Povera outside Italy was held at the Kunstmuseum, Lucerne. *Processi di pensiero visuaolizzati, Junge italienische Avantgarde* (Visualised thinking processes, Young Italian avant-garde), Kunstmuseum, Lucerne, 30 May–5 July 1970. Artists: Anselmo, Boetti, Calzolari, Fabro, Griffa, Kounellis, Maini, Mattiacci, Merz, Paolini, Penone, Pistoletto, Prini, Salvo and Zorio. Most artists were represented by the Galleria Sperone, Turin.

61 In 1966, Kynaston McShine had organised the *Primary Structures* exhibition at the Jewish Museum, New York. He is now Associate Curator of painting and sculpture at MoMA.

62 In 1969, the Art Workers Coalition, including artists such

Information

On 2 July 1970, an exhibition arranged by Kynaston McShine opened at the Museum of Modern Art in New York.[61] *Information* took place in an atmosphere of the emerging critique of art institutions, notably by the Art Workers Coalition group.[62] It was the first large-scale international group show of Conceptual artists to be held in such a renowned US institution.[63] This exhibition was a report on new international art and also included theoretical architecture and design. The project had originally been proposed in spring 1969, and additional events were to take place around New York and in other countries.[64]

In his introductory text, McShine underlined the growing internationalisation and interconnectedness of the art world. He pointed out that exchange between artists was becoming increasingly straightforward due to technological improvements allowing the wide dissemination of information, and air travel.[65] Here, too, artists were invited to create their own contribution for the catalogue, which could be independent of or related to the work on show. Dibbets, for example, wanted to be represented by the museum's own typed questionnaire, which served as a disclosure of its hierarchical selection process.

Studio International: July–August 1970

In the summer of 1970, Seth Siegelaub was invited by Peter Townsend to arrange a magazine show in the July–August edition of *Studio International*.[66] Siegelaub invited six international art critics to each edit an eight-page section of the magazine, which they would make available to artists that interested them. The invited critics were Claura (France), Harrison (UK), Celant (Italy), Hans Strelow (Germany), Lippard and David Antin (USA).[67] Claura, for instance, made his entire section available to Daniel Buren, who filled the pages with his characteristic stripes. Thus the magazine issue was conceived by Siegelaub as an exhibition of works, just as he had previously arranged exhibitions in catalogues.

Richard Long, Mönchengladbach

At that time, two major solo shows of Long and LeWitt took place in European public institutions. After having shown Andre and Darboven, the museum in Mönchengladbach arranged a show of Long.[68] It was again Fischer who was the intermediary between Cladders and the artist.[69] The exhibition was created in

as Andre and Huebler, but also Lippard and Siegelaub, had demonstrated at the MoMA, demanding free admission and the inclusion of a broader field of artists. The AWC crystallised the claims of a newly politicised art public, which wanted a truly democratic public art and challenged the authority of art institutions. See: Lucy Lippard, 'The Art Workers Coalition: not a history', *Studio International*, vol.180, no.927, November 1970, pp.171–174.

63 *Information*, Museum of Modern Art, New York, 2 July–20 September 1970. Artists: Acconci, Andre, Armajani, Arnatt, Art-Language (Atkinson- Bainbridge- Baldwin), Artschwager, Art & Project (Bulletin 21 of Matsuzawa), Askevold, Baldessari, Barrio, Barry, Barthelme, Bernd and Hilla Becher, Beuys, Bochner, Brecht, Broegger, Brouwn, Buren, Burgin, Burgy, Burn and Ramsden, Byars, Carballa, Cook, Cutforth, D'Alessio, Darboven, De Maria, Dibbets, Ferguson, Ferrer, Flanagan, Group Frontera, Fulton, Gilbert & George, Giorno Poetry Systems, Graham, Haacke, Hardy, Heizer, Hollein, Huebler, Huot, Hutchinson, Jarden, Kaltenbach, Kawara, Kosuth, Kozlov, Latham, LeVa, LeWitt, Lippard, Long, McLean, Meirelles, Minujin, Morris, N.E. Thing Co. Ltd., Nauman, New York Graphic Workshop, Newspaper, Group Oho, Oiticica, Ono, Oppenheim, Panamarenko, Paolini, Pechter, Penone, Piper, Pistoletto, Prini, Puente, Raetz, Rainer, Rinke, Ruscha, Sanejouand, Sladden, Smithson, Sonnier, Sottsass Jr., Thygesen, Van Saun, Vaz, Venet, Wall, Weiner and Wilson.

situ and included two mud sculptures, a pine-needle piece and a wood sculpture.[70] The Städtisches Museum in Mönchengladbach became a milestone institution for progressive art in Germany.

Sol LeWitt, Gemeentemuseum, The Hague

Two years after the *Minimal Art* exhibition, Enno Develing arranged a solo show of LeWitt at the Gemeentemuseum in The Hague in July–August 1970.[71] It took place just after three one-man shows by the artist had been held in European dealer galleries: Yvon Lambert (4–27 June 1970), Gian Enzo Sperone (starting 12 June 1970) and Lisson Gallery (15 June–14 July 1970).[72]

Strategy: Get Arts

On 23 August 1970, an exhibition celebrating the Düsseldorf art scene, *Strategy: Get Arts*, opened at Edinburgh College of Art.[73] It was arranged by Richard Demarco (born 1930), together with the Kunsthalle Düsseldorf, for the Edinburgh International Festival.[74] Demarco had been to Düsseldorf in January 1970 because some of the artists he was showing in his gallery lived there (Günther Uecker, Heinz Mack).[75] Many of the German artists included, such as Beuys, were showing for the first time in Britain. A number of them came to Edinburgh to create pieces in situ. Blinky Palermo made a wall drawing, *Blau/Gelb/Weiss/Rot*, in the main stairwell of the college.[76]

Avalanche

In autumn 1970, Willoughby Sharp and Liza Béar published the first issue of the art magazine *Avalanche* in New York. It was a tribute to Conceptual artists and thus contributed to the movement. Conceived as an artists' magazine, its priority was to enable artists to communicate directly with the readers through interviews and artists' projects. There was no review section although it did contain adverts.[77] The first edition contained interviews with Andre and Dibbets.[78] It also included a biography and numerous illustrations of Long's work.[79] At the time, art magazines had the power to define and legitimise new developments in art.[80] Moreover, magazines were important to dealers because they enabled the works of their artists to enter the public domain.

64 Ken Allan, 'Understanding Information', in Corris, *Conceptual Art: Theory, Myth and Practice*, *op. cit.*, p.144.

65 *Information* (exh. cat.), The Museum of Modern Art, New York, Summer 1970, p.140. Lynda Morris remembered that McShine always stayed with Greenwood in London.

66 'July–August 1970', *Studio International*, vol.180, no.924, July–August 1970. Artists: Graham, Cohen, Baldessari, Serra, Antin, Lonidier, Nicolaidis, Sonnier (David Antin); Anselmo, Boetti, Calzolari, Merz, Penone, Prini, Pistoletto, Zorio (Germano Celant); Buren (Michel Claura); Arnatt, Atkinson- Bainbridge- Baldwin, Hurrell, Burgin, Flanagan, Kosuth, Latham, Louw (Charles Harrison); Barry, Kaltenbach, Weiner, Kawara, LeWitt, Huebler, N.E. Thing Co., Bartheleme (Lucy Lippard); Dibbets, Darboven (Hans Strelow). This edition was also published as a hardcover book.

67 David Antin (born 1932) is an American performance artist and poet. Since 1968, he has been Professor of Art at the University of California, San Diego. He is married to the artist Eleonor Antin.

68 *Richard Long, 4 Skulpturen (England, Germany, Africa, America, 1966–1970)*, Städtisches Museum, Mönchengladbach, 16 July–30 August 1970. This show took place after a solo show of the artist at Konrad Fischer (11 May–9 June 1970). See: Database 2, Section Städtisches Museum, Mönchengladbach (Appendix 1.2) and Database 3, Section Richard Long (Appendix 1.3).

69 Letter from Cladders to Long dated 27 January 1970, in File Ausstellungen: Panamarenko, Manzoni, Druckgraphik, Thorn Prikker, Hollein, Long, Brouwn, Etzold I und II, Neuerwerbungen

1970 Cologne and Basel art fairs

The members of the VPDK staged another Kunstmarkt in October 1970.[81] The invited dealers from the Conceptual art network were again Fischer and Friedrich. The Kunstmarkt confirmed itself as a popular event, visited by approximately 50,000 people. Again, only German dealers were represented. The turnover was between DM3.5 and 4 million.[82] Fischer made important sales of Conceptual artists, including Andre, Darboven, Dibbets, Huebler, LeWitt, Long and Weiner. Friedrich also sold works by Conceptualists such as Andre and Ryman.[83] The Cologne Art Fair demonstrated that there was a potential market for Conceptual art, even if it was on a small scale in comparison with movements such as Pop art.

For financial and organisational reasons, Prospect did not take place in 1970. The city of Basel, however, set up its first international art fair from 12 to 16 June 1970.[84] Ninety dealer galleries and 20 editors from America and several European countries presented an extensive panorama of the art of the twentieth century on the 6,000m^2 site. Art Basel would become the Cologne Kunstmarkt's most serious rival. The organising committee was made up of Swiss and foreign representatives of the art world (Ernst Beyeler, Franz Meyer, André Emmerich). Any international dealer gallery could participate, as no jury or restrictions were applied. Nevertheless, the participating dealer galleries did not exhibit many Conceptual artists, with the exception of Bruno Bischofberger, Zurich (LeWitt, Flavin, Judd).[85]

Art Basel rapidly imposed itself as one of the major fairs for American and European dealer galleries. Switzerland, which was outside the European Economic Community (EEC), did not have to apply EU taxes such as VAT. In addition, German-speaking countries such as Switzerland had the advantage of speaking English over other European countries and therefore had an easy connection to the US. This was particularly true in Germany since the country had been occupied by American and British troops in the postwar period.

VPDK had been aware of the setting up of an art fair in Basel in June of the same year, six months before the opening of the 1970 fair. It was agreed that all members should decide for themselves whether they wanted to participate.[86] Although Art Basel was, in terms of both geography and date, distant from the

1970, Graphik, Buren, Planke, Pop Graphik (Etzold III), ASMM.

70 The wood sculpture was a loan from Giuseppe Panza. See: Johannes Cladders in conversation with the author, Krefeld, 13 April 2005, audio-tape recording (Appendix 4.3). See also: Wischermann, *Johannes Cladders*, *op. cit.*, p.43. For his 1969 solo show at Fischer's, Long had covered the gallery floor with pine needles. For his 1970 show, he had made a mud floor piece. See: *Ausstellungen bei Konrad Fischer*, *op. cit.*, pp.34–47.

71 *Sol LeWitt*, Gemeentemuseum, The Hague, 25 July–30 August 1970.

72 This was the first exhibition of a Conceptual artist at the Lisson Gallery. From that moment on, Nicholas Logsdail became more and more involved in Conceptualism. See: Database 3, Section Sol LeWitt (Appendix 1.3).

73 *Strategy: Get Arts*, Edinburgh College of Art, Edinburgh, 23 August–13 September 1970. Artists: Alvermann, Bernd and Hilla Becher, Beuys, Böhmler, Brecht, Brüning, Christiansen, Döhl, Filliou, Gerstner, Graubner, Heerich, Iannone, Kagel, Klapheck, Knoebel, Kohlhöfer, Kriwet, Luther, Mack, Mommartz, Morgan, Palermo, Polke, Reusch, Richter, Rinke, Rot, Ruthenbeck, Spoerri, Thomkins, Uecker, Walther, Weseler and Wewerka.

74 In Edinburgh, Richard Demarco, who had previously worked as artistic director for the Traverse Gallery, launched his own space in 1966. The inaugural exhibition, *Contemporary Italian Art*, included works by Burri, Fontana, Kounellis and Manzoni. He gave solo shows to young British artists, including Rory McEwen, Ian Hamilton Finlay

Cologne event, it was seen as a threat. VPDK had to adapt to the situation. The competition with other events made them accept what they had originally rejected. They reconsidered inviting international galleries.[87]

Kunstkompass

From 1970 onwards, the Cologne-based culture and economics journalist Willi Bongard (1931–85) and Linde Rohr-Bongard published the Kunstkompass (Art Compass) in the German business magazine *Das Capital*.[88] This is a list of the top 100 international artists in the contemporary art market. It provides an empirical and indicative insight into the art market of the time, and reflects the critical and market interest that surrounded the artists of the 1960s and 1970s. To measure the artists' 'status', it took into account 'exhibitions of international standing; the most important museums; the most qualified literature'.[89] A points system for each exhibition in selected museums, temporary exhibition spaces and dealer galleries, for purchases by museums and for published articles, was devised. The sum of these points determined the position of the artist in the top-100 chart.[90]

The first 'Capital Kunstkompass', which was published in October 1970 at the time of the Kunstmarkt Cologne, considered artists of the 1960s.[91] For each artist, the compass also included the average price of a representative middle-sized artwork. The top ten comprised: Rauschenberg (5,515 points), Vasarely, Fontana, Johns, Oldenburg, Tinguely, Arman, Klein, Lichtenstein and Dine (3,080 points). Several Conceptual artists were also included in this first listing. LeWitt was at number 61 (1,315 points) with works valued up to DM30,000; Andre occupied the 62nd position (1,290 points) with works up to DM40,000; Nauman was placed 71st (1,240 points) and his pieces were valued between DM15,000 and DM30,000.

Robert Rauschenberg stayed at number one until 1979, when Beuys took over his position. Most of the Conceptual artists studied here entered the Kunstkompass between 1972 and 1974. In 1972 their ranking was: Dibbets (49), Huebler (55), Merz (62), Long (74), Gilbert & George (82), Kosuth (84) and Weiner (92). In 1973, Ryman (73) and Darboven (89). And in 1974, Broodthaers (80) and Buren (96) appeared on the list for the first time.[92]

and to the Australian painter Arthur Boyd.

75 'Strategy: Get Arts', History, *Palermo Restore*, at www.eca.ac.uk/palermo/index.htm.

76 For a recent survey of this exhibition, see the show *Strategy: Get Arts Revisited*, Scottish National Gallery of Modern Art, Edinburgh, 22 October 2005–8 January 2006.

77 At the time, the development of portable tape recorders encouraged art magazines to print interviews with artists.

78 Andre had a solo show at the Guggenheim Museum, New York, in September–October 1970. See: *Carl Andre* (1970), *op. cit.*

79 'Richard Long', *Avalanche*, no.1, Fall 1970, pp.18–47.

80 Furthermore, *Avalanche* was supported by Conceptual art dealers. Among the first pages of the Winter 1971 issue, one could find the following two-page advertisement: 'This advertising space has been paid for by Paul Maenz, Cologne, to support the work of *Avalanche*.' In the following issue (spring 1972), Gian Enzo Sperone gave publicity to the whole network of Conceptual art with an advertisement reading: 'Gian Enzo Sperone is in love with Art & Project, Leo Castelli, Konrad Fischer, Heiner Friedrich, Yvon Lambert, Paul Maenz, Franco Toselli, John Weber.' See: *Avalanche*, no.3, Winter 1971 and *Avalanche*, no.4, Spring 1972.

81 Kölner Kunstmarkt 70, Kunsthalle and Kunstverein, Cologne, 13–18 October 1970.

82 Statistics of the 1970 art fair, in CD-Rom, 'Kunstmarkt Köln '67', *Sediment*, *op. cit.*

83 *Art Memo – Internationaler Kunstbrief*, 27 October 1970, in File

Heiner Friedrich, Cologne

Heiner Friedrich, who had opened a gallery in Munich in 1965, launched a second space in Cologne in October 1970 at the time of the Kunstmarkt. His ex-wife Six Friedrich continued to manage the Munich space, together with Fred Jahn and Sabine Knust. Exhibitions in the two galleries were often linked. The Cologne gallery hosted the major exhibitions, while the Munich gallery showed complementary exhibitions of drawings and prints.[93] The opening exhibition in Cologne in October 1970 was dedicated to Gilbert & George (*Frozen into the Nature for your Art*).[94] The artists performed a Singing Sculpture *Underneath the Arches* at the opening, repeating it later in the Munich gallery.[95]

Friedrich opened his gallery in the Galeriehaus Köln 18–22 Lindenstraße. This building was the first to assemble seven dealers dedicated to contemporary art under one roof: Reinhardt Onnasch, Hans-Jürgen Müller, Hans Neuendorf, Rolf Ricke, M.E. Thelen, Dieter Wilbrand and Heiner Friedrich. In 1969, Fischer had also considered the possibility of joining it.[96] The model for such a concentration of dealer galleries in one place came from New York's 57th Street, where many art spaces were located. The grouping enabled the dealers to promote themselves more effectively. They organised common openings and in 1971 they also edited a small monthly magazine about their activities.[97]

Nigel Greenwood Inc. Ltd., London

In November 1970, a month after their show at Heiner Friedrich in Cologne, Gilbert & George had their first solo exhibition at Nigel Greenwood, London (Glebe Place).[98] Greenwood became their British dealer. This exhibition marked the debut of Greenwood's engagement with Conceptual art.[99] He described Gilbert & George's show:

> I first saw their *Singing Sculpture* at Prospect, the alternative art fair in Düsseldorf in 1969. I put it on in the gallery, but only for a week. The following week we showed the drawings 'To be with Art is all we ask', a big text piece with two drawings down the side, which all folded away into a laundry box. That was what was for sale. Gilbert & George named the price, £1,500 I think.[100]

A72 IV 2, Zadik.

84 See: *Internationale Kunstmesse, Salon international d'Art, International Art Fair* (exh. cat.), Basel, 1970.

85 At around this time, from 21 June–4 October 1970, the third edition of the 'Salon international des galeries-pilotes' in Lausanne was also held. It hosted stands of international dealer galleries such as, for example, Castelli, Sonnabend, Swart and Wide White Space. The first two editions of the art fair, founded by the Swiss art historian René Berger, were held in 1963 and 1966. See: Aupetitallot, *Wide White Space*, *op. cit.*, p.272.

86 Minutes of the Organisation's annual meeting in Cologne dated 13 February 1970 (Mitgliederversammlung des Vereins progressiver deutscher Kunsthändler), in File A72 IV 2, Zadik. From 1971 onwards, however, members and guests had to choose between their participation in the Cologne and Basel art fairs.

87 Minutes of a discussion between the members of the Organisation in Cologne dated 2 July 1970 (Diskussion der Mitglieder des Vereins), in File A72 IV 2, Zadik.

88 Willi Bongard previously worked as a journalist for newspapers and magazines such as *Die Zeit*, *Frankfurter Allgemeine Zeitung* and *Das Capital*. After Bongard's sudden death in a car crash in 1985, his wife Linde Rohr-Bongard, continued the publication of the Kunstkompass. It is still published today in the magazine *Das Capital* (www.capital.de).

89 'The magnificent 100', *Flash Art*, no.38, January 1973, p.17.

90 Among the considered institutions were the Städtisches

Greenwood, who had previously run the Axiom Gallery, opened his first gallery, Nigel Greenwood Inc. Ltd., in Chelsea, London, in 1969. He explained: 'It was called Nigel Greenwood Inc. Limited because I didn't want to be just "Limited" so I put in that sort of hiccup of "Inc." Also to please the Americans as American firms are Incorporated.'[101] Greenwood started his gallery by taking over some of the Axiom artists such as Malcolm Carder and John Walker. He also gave first shows to artists like Keith Milow and Terry Setch.[102] He considered himself more as an art 'enabler' than a dealer: '1967/68 were days of idealism ... "who needs galleries" ... "temples to consumerism or to capitalism". This was the time when we believed we could all do it everywhere.'[103]

Paul Maenz, Cologne

In late 1970, Paul Maenz opened his dealer gallery in Cologne near the Galeriehaus Lindenstraße. Until then, he had run an underground 'head shop' called Pudding Explosion, which he had opened with Peter Roehr in 1968 in Frankfurt.[104] It was a counter-culture meeting place for various cultural and political activities.[105] Maenz had already considered the possibility of opening a dealer gallery in December 1969. In a letter to Hans Haacke (born 1936), a German artist who had moved to New York, he explained:

> I'm gradually admitting that there is hardly any alternative for me but an occupation in art. The most effective and practical way certainly lies in one's own 'gallery'... The thing is to create a relatively flexible instrument that is suitable to present contemporary art and that is actually as unrestricted as possible, which means adequate for the presented things.[106]

Maenz's meeting with the music scientist and editor Gerd de Vries (born 1944) was a determining factor in his decision to open a gallery. They opened together the Galerie Paul Maenz, Cologne. Maenz himself admitted that there were few Conceptual artists without a dealer at the time he launched his own space: 'I was not an artist, that was clear, but I wanted to "be with the avant-garde". So it came to a gallery. For this it seemed to be really late, because there was only a handful of artists I was interested in; the cake I was attracted to was small.'[107]

Museum, Mönchengladbach, the Kunstmuseum, Basel and the Tate Gallery, London; exhibitions included Documenta and the Venice Biennale; dealer galleries considered were, among others, Castelli, Dwan, Schmela, Fischer, Axiom, Kasmin, Sperone, Denise René, Yvon Lambert, Art & Project, Swaart and Wide White Space. For a complete list, see: Willi Bongard, 'Capital Kunst Kompass', *Das Capital*, vol.9, no.11, October 1970, p.148. Bongard stated that 106 German and Swiss 'art experts' put together the reference list of institutions and publications, without mentioning precisely who they were.

91 *Ibid.*, pp.143–156. The 'Kunstkompass' lists from 1970 to 1977 are reproduced as Appendix 2.3.

92 All studied Conceptual artists, except Art & Language, were represented in the 'Kunstkompass' during the 1970s. For an overview of all the lists published from 1970 to 2000, see: Linde Rohr-Bongard (ed.), *Kunst = Kapital, Der Capital Kunstkompass von 1970 bis heute*, Salon Verlag, Cologne, 2001, pp.37–61.

93 A publishing house was founded in Munich for this purpose, Edition der Galerie Heiner Friedrich. See: 'Six Friedrich', *Kunstforum International*, *op. cit.*, p.248.

94 Gilbert & George, *Frozen into the Nature for your Art*, Galerie Heiner Friedrich, Cologne, October 1970. The photographic work *Frozen into the Nature for your Art* had previously been shown in June 1970 at Françoise Lambert in Milan. It was Fischer who contacted the artists and made the request for them to open Friedrich's Cologne space in October 1970. See: Letter from Fischer to Gilbert & George

It seems that Maenz saw Fischer's gallery as a model.[108] But, because Fischer and Friedrich already represented many Conceptual artists in Germany, he had to take on artists of a slightly different sensibility not already represented in the country.[109] Although the gallery was launched in 1970, it officially opened on 16 January 1971 with an exhibition of Haacke.[110] This was one of the artist's first solo shows. The second exhibition was Kosuth,[111] his first show in a German gallery; he had previously shown with Sperone and Art & Project.[112] Maenz focused on Conceptual artists using language and texts, such as Kosuth, Art & Language and Victor Burgin. However, he also took on others, including Roelof Louw and Arte Povera artists such as Giulio Paolini.

In the early 1970s, established dealer galleries also started to exhibit Conceptual art. Franco Toselli, who had opened his space in Milan in 1969, arranged showings of artists such as Bochner (1970), Buren (1971) and Weiner (1973). Similarly, Daniel Templon in Paris showed Conceptualists from 1970 onwards: Victor Burgin (1970), Mel Ramsden, Ian Burn and Art & Language (1970–71). In London, the Situation Gallery was launched by Robert Self and Anthony de Kerdral. It hosted shows of Bruce McLean, Hamish Fulton, Klaus Rinke (1972), Gilbert & George (*It Takes a Boy to Understand a Boy's Point Of View*, 1972) and Braco Dimitrijevic (1973).[113]

Conceptualism in art magazines

At that time, publications were becoming increasingly important, notably with the development of artists' books by dealers. Friedrich, Sperone, Greenwood and Yvon Lambert all began publishing around this time.[114] New art magazines, including *VH101* were also launched.[115] It was also noticeable that an increasing number of articles on Conceptual art were being published.[116] The German art magazine *Kunst* published a special edition dedicated to Conceptual art.[117] It was coordinated by Klaus Honnef (born 1939), who was responsible for the cultural section of the journal *Aachener Nachrichten*, and had also been exhibition organiser for the Gegenverker-Zentrum für aktuelle Kunst in Aachen, since 1968.[118]

By 1970, the network of Conceptual art in Europe was established. Key dealers appeared in a number of countries: Fischer and Friedrich in Germany, Art & Project in the Netherlands, Sperone and Françoise Lambert in Italy,

dated 15 September 1970, in Künstler Korrespondenz 1970–71, AKFGD.

95 See the list of shows organised by Heiner Friedrich, in Urbaschek, *Dia Art Foundation*, *op. cit.*, p.233.

96 Letter from the Grundstückgemeinschaft Vowinckel, Cologne (property community) to Fischer dated 25 November 1969, in Galerie Korrespondenz 1967–69, AKFGD.

97 See: *Galeriehaus Köln, Lindenstrasse 18–22*, no.1–9, March–December 1971. See also: Brigitte Jacobs, 'Galeriehaus Köln, ein Hauch von 57. Straße: Aus dem Zentralarchiv 17', *Frankfurter Allgemeine Zeitung*, 18 August 2001.

98 Gilbert & George, *To be with Art is all we ask*, Nigel Greenwood Inc. Ltd., London, November 1970.

99 In 1970, Greenwood also showed Barry and Tremlett. See: Database 1, Section Nigel Greenwood (Appendix 1.1).

100 'Interview Nigel Greenwood', in Moseley, *Conception*, *op. cit.*, p.132.

101 *Ibid.*, p.131.

102 For a comprehensive outline of exhibitions of Conceptual artists at the gallery, see: Database 1, Section Nigel Greenwood (Appendix 1.1). For an extensive overview of exhibitions organised by Greenwood, see: Appendix 3.2. The archive of Nigel Greenwood Inc. Ltd. is kept by the Tate Archive, London, but it is currently unavailable to researchers.

103 'Interview Nigel Greenwood', in Moseley, *Conception*, *op. cit.*, p.131.

Wide White Space and MTL in Belgium, Sonnabend and Yvon Lambert in France, Lisson and Nigel Greenwood in England. 1970 also saw the organisation of a number of important group shows in museums in Europe and in the United States. These exhibitions presented Conceptualism to a wider audience. Solo shows in museums remained rare, except in public institutions in the Netherlands (The Hague) and Germany (Mönchengladbach, Krefeld, Aachen). The network was to develop in this area during the next couple of years.

3.2 1971

Fischer, Sperone and Panza

Relations between Konrad Fischer and Gian Enzo Sperone developed in 1971. The Italian dealer was then occupying an increasingly important position in the Conceptual network. The connections between the two dealers strengthened because of the collector Giuseppe Panza (born 1923). Sperone had established a business relationship with Panza when he collected Pop art, via Leo Castelli and Ileana Sonnabend. When the collector moved on to Minimal and Conceptual art, Sperone wanted to remain closely associated with him. Likewise, Fischer wished to enter the Italian art market to ensure his percentage on sales by Sperone to Panza.

A joint show of Huebler that took place simultaneously at both galleries opened on 6 January 1971.[119] The exhibitions consisted of various documents (maps, photographs, notes) illustrating the artist hitchhiking from one gallery to the other, *Variable Works (in Progress), Düsseldorf, Germany – Turin, Italy* (1970). Documents of his journey to the north were exhibited with Fischer and those to the south with Sperone.

A couple of days later, on 8 January, a Conceptual group show arranged by Fischer and Sperone opened at the Addison Gallery of American Art in

104 Later in 1968, Peter Roehr died from cancer aged 24. Paul Maenz took over his estate and arranged the first exhibition of Roehr's work at the Städtisches Museum in Leverkusen in 1971.

105 'Lies mich, Baby. Hippie-Zubehör', *Der Spiegel*, vol.12, no.8, 19 February 1968, p.76.

106 Letter from Maenz to Haacke dated 19 December 1969, in File 1–2, Box 16, Series II, in Galerie Paul Maenz Köln Records, 1956–91, Accession no. 910066, Getty Research Institute, Los Angeles (hereafter GRILA) (author's translation). The archive of the Galerie Paul Maenz was acquired in 1991 by the Getty Research Institute, Los Angeles. See: www.getty.edu/research/tools/ special_collections/ maenz_m1.html/. See also: Gerda Wendermann, 'Paul Maenz – Galerist und Sammler der Avantgarde', in Hans Dickel (ed.), *Die Sammlung Paul Maenz, 1. Objekte, Bilder, Installationen, Neues Museum Weimar*, Hatje Cantz Verlag, Ostfildern, 1999, p.16.

107 'Paul Maenz', *Kunstforum International, op. cit.*, p.285 (author's translation).

108 *Ibid.* See also: Maenz, 'Before 1970', in *Paul Maenz Köln 1970–1975, op. cit.*, p.15.

109 This conception was acknowledged by Paul Maenz. See: Paul Maenz in a conversation with the author, Berlin, October 2004, manuscript questionnaire (Appendix 4.11).

110 *Hans Haacke*, Galerie Paul Maenz, Cologne, 16 January–13 February 1971. For a comprehensive outline of exhibitions of Conceptual artists at the gallery, see: Database 1, Section Paul Maenz (Appendix 1.1). For an overview of the exhibitions organised by Maenz, see: De Vries, *Paul Maenz Köln 1970–1980–1990, op. cit.*, pp.254–257. See also: Appendix 3.12.

111 'Joseph Kosuth', Galerie Paul Maenz, Cologne, 16 February–5 March 1971. See: *Joseph Kosuth, Zettel 1–3 (The 8th Investigation, Proposition 2)* (exh. cat.), Paul Maenz, Cologne, 1971.

112 See: Database 3, Section Joseph Kosuth (Appendix 1.3).

Andover (Massachusetts). *Formulation* reassembled works by European artists represented by both dealers.[120] The Addison Gallery was an institution devoted exclusively to American art. Huebler, who was then living and working in Bradford, Massachusetts, had held a one-person show there in 1970. Fischer was aware of this exhibition, and it is likely that it was Huebler who introduced the dealer to the museum staff.[121] *Formulation* was the first show of European Conceptual artists to be organised by European dealers in America.

Daniel Buren, Mönchengladbach

The first major museum showing of Daniel Buren was also organised in January 1971. The Städtisches Museum Mönchengladbach arranged a solo show that took place in 14 different locations all over Germany.[122] In every city, the artist realised one or several installations of striped papers in a different colour.[123] In the Mönchengladbach museum, the artist pasted blue-and-white striped papers on the lower part of the walls in the exhibition rooms.[124] In the Westfälischer Kunstverein in Münster, Buren's yellow-and-white striped papers were pasted in the foyer and the function rooms.[125] This first exhibition of a Conceptual artist in Münster coincided with Klaus Honnef's appointment as Director of the Kunstverein.[126]

***6th Guggenheim International Exhibition* and the New York art scene**

In February 1971, Buren found himself at the centre of a scandal developing at the Guggenheim Museum, New York. The *6th Guggenheim International Exhibition*, organised by Diane Waldman and Edward Fry, both associate curators, took place at that time.[127] The museum occasionally hosted international exhibitions of contemporary artists from all over the world as a review of the current state of art.[128] The 1971 event was dedicated mostly to Conceptual art. When Diane Waldman went over to Europe to prepare the show, she was influenced by Fischer.[129] Fischer himself believed that the *6th Guggenheim* gave his European artists the opportunity to 'be represented in a central position in New York'.[130]

At the time, surveys of contemporary art tendencies in Europe and the United

113 When the Situation Gallery closed in about 1975, Robert Self opened his own gallery in London, showing artists such as Baldessari, Burgin and Gilbert & George. He also opened a gallery in Newcastle upon Tyne.

114 See, for instance: Daniel Buren, *Limites Critiques*, Yvon Lambert, Paris, 1970; Mario Merz, *Fibonacci 1202*, Gian Enzo Sperone, Turin, 1970, and Lawrence Weiner, *Tracce/Traces*, Gian Enzo Sperone, Turin, 1970.

115 *VH101* was edited in Paris by Otto Hahn and Françoise Essellier from the spring of 1970 onwards. The first issue contained contributions on Andy Warhol and Martial Raysse, but also on Lamelas, Buren and Andre.

116 For example, in the autumn 1970 issue of *VH101*, the art critic Catherine Millet published an article entitled 'L'art Conceptuel comme sémiotique de l'art'. This issue also contained works and statements by Huebler, Kosuth and Weiner. See: *VH101*, no.3, Autumn 1970, p.3–21. One can also mention: Jack Burnham, 'Alice's Head: Reflections on Conceptual Art', *Artforum*, February 1970, pp.37–43. This also demonstrates that the term 'Conceptual Art' was imposing itself.

117 'Concept Art', *Kunst*, vol.10, no.38, 1970. The special issue included a text by Klaus Honnef, completed by a chronology of events, a bibliography, images of selected works and a transcript of a discussion between, among others, Brouwn, Dibbets, Fischer, Siegelaub and Harten.

118 In Aachen, Klaus Honnef had organised shows of Conceptual artists, such as Jan Dibbets in March–April 1970 and Weiner in May 1970.

119 *Douglas Huebler*, Konrad Fischer, Düsseldorf, 6–12 January 1971. See: *Ausstellungen bei Konrad Fischer*, *op. cit.*, p.59. *Douglas Huebler*, Galleria Gian Enzo Sperone, Turin, starting 6 January 1971. See: Minola, Mundici, Poli and Roberto, *Gian Enzo Sperone*,

States had underlined the international trend of Conceptual art. 'Although these international shows included US artists, for the first time in over a decade they were neither the majority nor the most dominant, but equal with other groups who shared a similar agenda.'[131] It seems that the Guggenheim was trying to find a middle ground between contrary attitudes that were developing at the time in the New York art world.[132] On the one hand, people such as Kynaston McShine (Jewish Museum, then MOMA) had opened up the *Information* show to international contemporary artists. On the other hand, critics like Hilton Kramer defended a conservative and traditional view of US art.[133]

Buren's contribution, *Peinture-Sculpture* (1971), consisted of two huge blue-and-white striped banners that were to be hung both outside and inside the museum building. On the inside, the work, 20 metres high and 10 metres wide, occupied the entire central space of the building. This installation not only questioned the nature of painting, but also, and principally, the politics of cultural institutions by obstructing this strategic space at the heart of a museum built by Frank Lloyd Wright in the 1950s, which was sometimes seen as a work of art itself.[134]

Alexander Alberro suggests that there were generational conflicts between the established American Minimal and Land art artists in the show and this young French artist.[135] Indeed, it was mainly Judd, Flavin, De Maria and Michael Heizer who wanted Buren's installation removed, arguing that it was disturbing their work by obstructing the rotunda. A counter-movement was launched by other artists with a petition expressing disapproval of the censorship of Buren.[136] The argument went so far that Andre decided to remove his works (*Joint*, 1968 and *Copper 'Ribbon' Piece*, 1969) from the show in support of Buren.[137]

In the end, the museum's Director, Thomas Messer, decided to withdraw Buren's work on the day of the opening. It seems, however, that it was not only the artists' protests, but also Buren's statements that motivated this decision. The day before the opening, he had declared to the *New York Times* that artists and museums in the traditional sense were obsolete, adding that the Guggenheim museum was killing every work of art because it was one itself.[138] The

op. cit., pp.178–179.

120 *Formulation*, Addison Gallery of American Art, Phillips Academy, Andover, Massachusetts, 8 January–14 February 1971. Artists: Atkinson, Boetti, Brouwn, Buren, Darboven, Dibbets, Fulton, Paolini, Penone and Salvo.

121 Letter from Huebler to Fischer dated 6 April 1970, and Letter from Fischer to Huebler dated 2 June 1970, in Künstler Korrespondenz 1970–71, AKFGD.

122 'Daniel Buren, Position/Proposition, Senkrechte farbige und weiße Streifen', Städtisches Museum, Mönchengladbach, 28 January–7 March 1971. See: Press release dated 5 March 1971, in File Ausstellungen: Panamarenko, Manzoni, Druckgraphik, Thorn Prikker, Hollein, Long, Brouwn, Etzold I und II, Neuerwerbungen 1970: Graphik, Buren, Planke, Pop Graphik (Etzold III) [1970–71], ASMM.

123 Locations: Städtisches Museum, Kaufhaus Heinemann and buses, Mönchengladbach (blue); Gegenverkehr-Zentrum für aktuelle Kunst, Aachen (violet); Interstil Schröder, Dortmund (grey); Museum Folkwang, Essen (red); Künstlersiedlung, Gelsenkirchen (orange); Kunsthaus, Hochschule für Bildende Künste and Beckmann-Möbel, Hamburg (red); Wohnbedarf Loeser, Hannover-Linden (pink); Kunsthalle, Cologne (violet); Die Einrichtung Schröer, Krefeld (yellow), Städtisches Museum, Leverkusen (red); Westfälischer Kunstverein, Landeshaus, Landeskreis and Stadthaus, Münster (yellow); Saaruferstrasse, Saarbrücken (yellow); Freizeitgarten der Zigarettenfabrik Jüldis, Saarlouis (grey); Staatsgalerie, Stuttgart (red). See: Undated letter from Cladders to all participants, reproduced in Wischermann, *Johannes Cladders*, *op. cit.*, pp.363–366. See also: Talk (Diskurs) from Cladders delivered during the opening of the exhibition, 28 January 1971, in File Ausstellungen Panamarenko, Manzoni, Druckgraphik, Thorn Prikker, Hollein, Long, Brouwn, Etzold I und II, Neuerwerbungen 1970: Graphik, Buren, Planke, Pop

museum's censorship of Buren's work appears to have been an act of damage control.[139]

The *6th Guggenheim International Exhibition*, the last in the series, was supposed to be followed by a solo show of Haacke, an artist who was then also producing works of art that were critical of cultural institutions. This exhibition was abruptly cancelled, and Edward Fry, the organiser of both the Guggenheim International and the Haacke show, was fired.[140] Haacke's exhibition was cancelled because of his work *Shapolsky et al. Manhattan Real Estate Holdings, A Real-Time Social System, as of May 1, 1971* (1971), which demonstrated that members of the Guggenheim's Board of Trustees had questionable New York slum real-estate empires. The show was cancelled with the excuse that it dealt with specific social situations not considered art.

The *6th Guggenheim International Exhibition* may have influenced New York dealers. After this show, Castelli took on Barry (April–May 1971), Huebler (May–June 1971) and Weiner (February 1971),[141] although only the latter had been included in the Guggenheim exhibition. Other artists represented by Castelli included Morris (since 1967), Nauman (1968), Judd (1969) and Flavin (1970). Thus in 1971, Castelli took on the group of Conceptual artists who had until then been represented by Siegelaub, who was soon to retire from the art world to concentrate on other projects including the history of textiles and Marxism.[142]

The Artists' Reserved Rights Transfer and Sale Agreement

At the same time, February 1971, Siegelaub developed, together with the lawyer Bob Projansky, The Artists' Reserved Rights Transfer and Sale Agreement.[143] This was a reproducible poster that could be photocopied and used as a legal document. It was an attempt to redress inequities between artists, dealers, collectors and museums, by protecting artists' economic rights and control over their work. This agreement, developed by one of the most eager defenders of progressive contemporary art tendencies, demonstrates that Conceptual art had become a business. It also reflects the sense that there was a need for certificates to authenticate ownership. Some artists, such as Long and Buren, incorporated

Graphik (Etzold III) [1970–71], ASMM.

124 Grasskamp, *Johannes Cladders, op. cit.*, p.48. From 7 February to 14 March 1970, an exhibition of the Etzold Collection took place simultaneously in the same rooms. See Buren's recollections in: *Documenta 5, Befragung der Realität, Bildwelten von Heute* (exh. cat.), Bertelsmann Verlag, Kassel, 1972, Chapter 17, p.31, A23.

125 Wischermann, *Johannes Cladders, op. cit.*, p.366.

126 For a comprehensive outline of exhibitions of Conceptual artists at this institution, see: Database 2, Section Kunstverein, Münster (Appendix 1.2).

127 *6th Guggenheim International Exhibition 1971*, The Solomon R. Guggenheim Museum, New York, 12 Feb–11 April 1971. Artists: Brazil: Dias; France: Buren; Germany: Darboven; Great Britain: Burgin, Long; Italy: Merz; Japan: Kawara, Takamatsu; The Netherlands: Dibbets; United States: Andre, De Maria, Flavin, Heizer, Judd, Kosuth, LeWitt, Morris, Nauman, Ryman, Serra and Weiner.

128 The 'Guggenheim International Exhibition' series began in 1956. The 5th event, *Sculpture from twenty nations*, which had taken place in 1967, had been dedicated to sculpture in the 1960s.

129 Morris in conversation with the author.

130 'Konrad Fischer interviewed by Georg Jappe', *Studio International*, *op. cit.*, p.70.

131 Alexander Alberro, 'The Turn of the Screw: Daniel Buren, Dan Flavin, and the Sixth Guggenheim International Exhibition', *October*, no.80, Spring 1997, p.66.

132 By deliberately looking to Europe, as in the 1920s and 1930s, the Guggenheim Museum took the opposite position to the US bias of the Whitney Museum of American Art, New York.

133 *Ibid.*, pp.66–67.

134 Earlier, in 1968, Buren had hung green-and-white stripes on walls as high as the building at the Kunsthalle in Düsseldorf for Prospect 68. See: *Daniel Buren, Mot à Mot, op. cit.*, pp.P10–P11.

certificates into their works.[144]

In Europe, numerous shows of Conceptual art were organised in dealer galleries in the first half of 1971. These were mostly group shows of Conceptual artists in secondary dealer galleries and first showings in supplementary dealer galleries of already exhibited artists. Sperone, in particular, seems to have taken the lead. The network of Conceptual artists was continuing to grow and tighten.

Lisson Gallery, London

In January, Nicholas Logsdail (born 1945) set up *Wall Show* at Lisson, presenting works by Conceptual artists LeWitt and Weiner, alongside British artists like Barry Flanagan, David Tremlett, John Latham and Roelof Louw.[145] This exhibition and the 1970 LeWitt exhibition, consolidated the dealer's engagement with Conceptual artists. In April 1967, Logsdail, then a student at the Slade School of Art in London, had launched an exhibition space in a building he owned in Lisson Street to show the work of some fellow art students.[146] The exhibition was relatively successful, and Logsdail decided to continue the activities and called the space the Lisson Gallery, showing young American and British artists such as Jene Highstein (1967) and Peter Schmidt (1968).[147]

In the same way, Françoise Lambert hosted two mixed exhibitions of Conceptual artists in February and March 1971, featuring among others Dibbets, Merz, Huebler and Nauman.[148] Unlike museums, most dealer galleries in the network had hosted solo shows of Conceptual artists before arranging mixed exhibitions from 1971 onwards.

Dealers networking

On 3 February 1971, the first solo show of Carl Andre at the Galerie Yvon Lambert in Paris opened.[149] This exhibition must have been organised with the help of Fischer, the artist's primary dealer, since the works shown in Paris had all been part of Andre's 1969 show in Düsseldorf (*Alloy Squares*).[150] Weiner's second solo show opened with Lambert in Paris at the same time, presenting artist's books (*10 works*).[151]

135 Alberro, 'The Turn of the Screw', *October*, *op. cit.*, pp.71–75.

136 See: Petition signed by Long, Serra, Merz, Ryman, Weiner, Darboven, LeWitt, Dibbets, Nauman and Dias, reproduced in *Daniel Buren, Mot à Mot*, *op. cit.*, pp.c24–c53. It is interesting to note that most of the artists who supported Buren were part of the network of Conceptual art.

137 See: 'Gurgles around the Guggenheim, Statements and comments by Daniel Buren, Diane Waldman, Thomas M. Messer, Hans Haacke', *Studio International*, vol.181, no.934, June 1971, pp.246–250. See also: 'Correspondence', *Studio International*, vol.81, no.935, July–August 1971, p.6.

138 Grace Glueck, 'Museum presents wide media range', *New York Times*, 10 February 1970, p.26. On this matter see also: Daniel Buren, 'Notes on Work in connection with the Place where it is installed', *Studio International*, vol.190, no.977, September 1975, p.175.

139 Alberro, 'The Turn of the Screw', *October*, *op. cit.*, p.83. Subsequently, photographs of Buren's work that was on show only for a few hours in the Guggenheim museum were published in an *Art & Project Bulletin*. See: 'Daniel Buren', *Art & Project Bulletin*, no.40, 2 June 1971. Censorship of his work can perhaps also be considered an inevitable consequence of Buren's strategy.

140 See: Barbara Reise, 'A tail of two exhibitions: The aborted Haacke and Robert Morris shows', *Studio International*, vol.182, no.935, July–August 1971, pp.30–34.

141 See: 'Exhibition Chronology', in Jakobson, *Leo Castelli*, *op. cit.*, pp.67–69.

142 In 1971, Siegelaub moved from New York to Paris. In the early 1970s, he founded the International Mass Media Research Centre at the International Institute of Social History in Amsterdam, which holds thousands of documents related to Marxism and mass media. He also founded the publishing house International General (New York) to publish books related to left-wing ideology and communication.

On 13 March 1971, Sperone launched his first solo show of Dibbets in his Turin gallery.[152] However, this was not the artist's first one-man exhibition in Northern Italy; he had shown in 1970 with Françoise Lambert in Milan.[153] In Turin, Dibbets exhibited a photographic series of 80 pictures on light and time, arranged in sequence along the walls. The pictures were all taken from a window of his Amsterdam house at predetermined intervals from dawn to dusk. Also exhibited were his *Perspective Corrections* (1968–69) and *Painting 1 + 2* (1970), two video editions realised with Gerry Schum.[154] A few weeks later, Fischer inaugurated a further solo show of Dibbets in Düsseldorf.[155] He exhibited works similar to those in Turin, namely 'shutter speed' and 'shadow' pieces taken in Fischer's gallery in 1969 and 1971. At the same time, an *Art & Project Bulletin* designed by Dibbets was also distributed.[156]

In April 1971, Sperone arranged the first solo show at his gallery of Richard Long.[157] In May 1971, Gilbert & George had their first show in Turin.[158] Both Long and Gilbert & George had previously exhibited in Italy with Françoise Lambert in 1969 and 1970 respectively. Sperone, however, became their representative from that moment on.[159] This shows the competition between two dealers in the same country, and also demonstrates how one dealer took the lead from another. At that time, Sperone and Fischer had strengthened their business relationship and Sperone's leading role in Conceptual art in Italy was a result of this.

Art & Language

Among the Conceptual art dealers, Sperone was the first Italian Conceptual gallery to give a solo show to Art & Language, in June–July 1971.[160] This coincided with the end of their teaching activities at Coventry College of Art. With Sperone, they exhibited *Maps* (1966–69), including *Map to not indicate* (1969) showing only the outlines of the states of Iowa and Kentucky. Just a few months before, in April–May 1971, they had held their first solo show, at Galerie Daniel Templon, Paris.[161] A few months later, Art & Language showed at Galleria Templon in Milan, a second space just opened by the Paris-based dealer. By the early 1970s, Northern Italy had developed as an important centre for contemporary art; this

143 Seth Siegelaub and Bob Projansky, 'The Artists' Reserved Rights Transfer and Sale Agreement', *Studio International*, vol.81, no.932, April 1971, pp.142–144 and pp.186–187. It was also published in the April issues of *Art News* and *Arts Canada*.

144 See: 'Avertissement/Documents devant accompagner toute œuvre en circulation, systématiquement utilisés par D.B. lors d'une transaction', *Daniel Buren, Mot à Mot*, *op. cit.*, pp.A50–A51.

145 *Wall Show*, Lisson Gallery, London, January 1971. Artists: Arnatt, Arrowsmith, Edmonds, Flanagan, Ginsborg, Hemsworth, Hilliard, Latham, Lew, LeWitt, Louw, Munro, Newman, Palermo, Rinke, Sirrs, Stezaker, Tremlett, Weiner and Wentworth. In June–July 1971, Sol LeWitt had his second solo show at the Lisson Gallery. It was originally planned that LeWitt should have solo shows at Yvon Lambert, Sperone and/or Françoise Lambert at that time, but it seems that these plans were replaced by a London showing. See: Manuscript letter from Sol LeWitt to Konrad Fischer dated 6 March [1970], in Künstler Korrespondenz 1970–71, AKFGD.

146 *Terence Ibbott, Derek Jarman, Paul Martin, Keith Milow, Paul Riley*, Lisson Gallery, London, 12 April–14 May 1967. See: 'Lisson Gallery – Exhibitions List (1967–99)', in Lisson Gallery Archive, London. Except for this document, the archive of the Lisson Gallery is closed to researchers.

147 Nicholas Logsdail in conversation with the author, London, 21 February 2005, audio-tape recording (Appendix 4.10). See also: Louisa Buck, 'Diary of a London dealer: Nicholas Logsdail', *The Art Newspaper*, no.131, December 2002, p.41. For a comprehensive outline of exhibitions of Conceptual artists at the gallery, see: Database 1, Section Lisson Gallery (Appendix 1.1). For an overview of all the exhibitions organised by Logsdail see: Appendix 3.5.

148 *Group show (Brouwn, Dibbets, Flavin, LeWitt, Merz, Nauman, Oppenheim, Ryman, Salvo)*, Galleria Françoise Lambert, Milan, February 1971. *Eight Proposals (Barry, Buren, Burgy, Dibbets, Huebler,*

was due not only to Arte Povera but also to Conceptual art.

In the late 1960s, the Rhineland had become a central area for progressive art in Europe. From the early 1970s, Northern Italy imposed itself as another centre of interest. To these two pivotal areas, one has to add the increasing importance of Belgium and the Netherlands, foremost through the activities of Dutch museums and Belgian galleries.

A number of solo shows of Conceptual artists were arranged by Flemish, Belgian and Dutch dealer galleries during the first half of 1971. Wide White Space held shows of Andre (April–May)[162] and Buren (May–June).[163] Coinciding with the end of Buren's show in Antwerp was the distribution of an *Art & Project Bulletin* by the artist.[164]

Sonsbeek 71

On 19 June 1971, the Netherlands launched the first major Conceptual group show of the year, Sonsbeek 71.[165] This outdoor event was arranged by a working committee headed by Wim Beeren in Arnhem, a city close to the German border.[166] It was the sixth in a series of international exhibitions of sculpture, but unlike the previous events it was not restricted to the Sonsbeek park, but took place all over the Netherlands.[167] Long, for instance, scratched his work *Celtic sign* in the dunes of the Northern coast (Waddeneilanden), while a photograph documenting the piece was exhibited in the Leens museum in Groningen.[168] Thus Sonsbeek 71 was not mounted as a sculpture exhibition, but as a show of artists in particular spaces.

In the park were works by mainly American, Dutch and German artists including Andre (*Light wine circuit*, 1971) and LeWitt (*Modular piece – 4 sections*, 1971). The works were created specifically for their location within the park. The show also included films (Nauman) and various publications, including concepts printed in newspapers and the catalogue by Weiner, Huebler, Merz, Darboven and others. A conference hall was set up where visitors could speak directly with each other or with members of the Sonsbeek staff.[169]

Sonsbeek 71 was held from June to August 1971. During that period, galleries

Kienholz, Hidetoshi, Nagasawa, Weiner), Galleria Françoise Lambert, Milan, 26 February–March 1971. See: Database 1, Section Françoise Lambert (Appendix 1.1).

149 *Carl Andre*, Galerie Yvon Lambert, 3 February–1 March 1971. See: Database 3, Section Carl Andre (Appendix 1.3).

150 *Carl Andre, Alloy Squares*, Konrad Fischer, Düsseldorf, 12 October–11 November 1969. See: *Ausstellungen bei Konrad Fischer, op. cit.*, p.38. Compare with: *Carl Andre, Sculptor 1996*, *op. cit.*, p.249.

151 *Lawrence Weiner, 10 works*, Galerie Yvon Lambert, 3–13 February 1971. See: Dieter Schwarz, *Lawrence Weiner, Books 1968–1989, Catalogue raisonné*, Verlag der Buchhandlung Walther König, Cologne and Editeur Le Nouveau Musée, Villeurbanne, 1989.

152 *Jan Dibbets*, Galleria Gian Enzo Sperone, Turin, 13–23 March 1971. See: Minola, Mundici, Poli and Roberto, *Gian Enzo Sperone, op. cit.*, pp.183–185.

153 See: Database 3, Section Jan Dibbets (Appendix 1.3).

154 See: Ulrike Groos, Barbara Hess and Ursula Wevers (eds), *Ready to Shoot, Fernsehgalerie Gerry Schum, videogalerie schum* (exh. cat.), Snoeck, Kunsthalle, Düsseldorf, 2003, pp.248–249. Just a month before, in February 1971, Gerry Schum's *Identification* (1970) had been screened at Sperone. See: Minola, Mundici, Poli and Roberto, *Gian Enzo Sperone, op. cit.*, p.180.

155 *Jan Dibbets*, Konrad Fischer Galerie, Düsseldorf, 6–22 April 1971. See: *Ausstellungen bei Konrad Fischer, op. cit.*, p.62.

156 'Jan Dibbets, A white wall', *Art & Project Bulletin*, no.36, 7 April 1971.

157 *Richard Long*, Galleria Gian Enzo Sperone, Turin, starting 13 April 1971. See: Minola, Mundici, Poli and Roberto, *Gian Enzo Sperone, op. cit.*, pp.188–189. Long had previously been shown in Italy by Françoise Lambert in Milan in 1969.

158 *There were two young men by Gilbert and George*, Galleria Gian Enzo Sperone, Turin, starting 28 May 1971. See: Minola, Mundici,

such as Art & Project showed artists who were part of this major international exhibition: Huebler (May–June),[170] Long (July–August)[171] and Yutaka Matsuzawa (August).

New York, 420 West Broadway and John Weber

September 1971 was marked by an important event in New York. Following the trend of 'gallery houses', Leo Castelli, Ileana Sonnabend, André Emmerich and John Weber opened new spaces in a building situated at 420 West Broadway (Soho). The inaugural exhibition of Castelli's second gallery was a group show presenting films by Morris, Nauman (*Art Makeup No.1, White*, 1967–68), Serra and Sonnier.[172] Sonnabend, who still had her Paris gallery, opened her New York space with the first American show of Gilbert & George.[173] During the 1960s, Emmerich had established himself as a key dealer of Colour Field painting (Robert Louis, Kenneth Noland) and his gallery had become a leading venue for colour abstraction and monumental sculpture (Anthony Caro).[174]

Weber decided to launch his own space after Dwan Gallery closed in June 1971.[175] He continued to show many artists whom Virginia Dwan had represented. The inaugural exhibition of the gallery presented LeWitt's metallic structures and wall drawings.[176] According to Weber, LeWitt was always the artist who sold best at the gallery.[177]

Also in September 1971, LeWitt had two solo shows in Europe, at Konrad Fischer (starting 3 September)[178] and at Art & Project (starting 7 September).[179] In Düsseldorf, LeWitt showed wall drawings, including *Straight yellow lines 40" (100 cm) long, on two walls. Left wall: vertical, right wall: horizontal* (1971). In Amsterdam, the artist showed folded papers.

In Another Moment and *At the Moment*

In September 1971, one of the rare Conceptual art shows in Eastern Europe took place. At the instigation of the artists Braco and Nena Dimitrijevic,[180] *In Another Moment* was organised at the new Gallery SKC (Studenski Kulturni Centar) in Belgrade, Yugoslavia.[181] It was based on an original concept as it comprised three

Poli and Roberto, *Gian Enzo Sperone*, *op. cit.*, pp.194–195. See also the 'Magazine Sculpture' of the same series published at the time by Gilbert & George in *Studio International*: 'Gilbert and George, There were two young men who did laugh', *Studio International*, vol.181, no.933, May 1971, pp.220–221.

159 See: Database 3, Section Jan Dibbets, Gilbert & George and Richard Long (Appendix 1.3). From 1972, Sperone would also take over the representation of Buren in Italy, although the artist had been shown by Françoise Lambert in 1970. See: Database 3, Section Daniel Buren (Appendix 1.3).

160 *Art & Language (Atkinson, Baldwin, Bainbridge, Hurrell)*, Galleria Gian Enzo Sperone, 22 June–5 July 1971. See: Minola, Mundici, Poli and Roberto, *Gian Enzo Sperone*, *op. cit.*, p.199. See also: Database 3, Section Art & Language (Appendix 1.3).

161 According to Michael Baldwin and Mel Ramsden, the Parisian art world was keen on the radical avant-garde at the time. There was a receptiveness to their work in France that they did not find in Anglo-Saxon countries. In France, the avant-garde artist was seen and accepted as an intellectual and a provocateur. Art & Language in conversation with the author, Banbury, 19 May 2003, manuscript notes.

162 *Carl Andre, Weathering Piece*, Wide White Space, Antwerp, 22 April–6 May 1971. See: Aupetitallot, *Wide White Space*, *op. cit.*, p.280. In June–July, Andre had a show at the Galerie Heiner Friedrich, Munich, and in July–August 1971 at Konrad Fischer, Düsseldorf. See: Database 3, Section Carl Andre (Appendix 1.3).

163 *Daniel Buren*, Wide White Space, Antwerp, 11 May–5 June 1971. See: Aupetitallot, *Wide White Space*, *op. cit.*, p.282. See also: Database 3, Section Daniel Buren (Appendix 1.3).

164 See: 'Daniel Buren', *Art & Project Bulletin*, *op. cit.*

165 Sonsbeek 71, Sonsbeek Park, Arnhem, 19 June–15 August 1971. Artists: Acconci, Ader, Andre, Armagnac, Artschwager, Baille, Bakker,

separate shows, each of five days duration. In April 1971, the Dimitrijevics had arranged the group exhibition *At the Moment* in Zagreb (Doorwayhall, Frankopanska) featuring Conceptual artists such as Buren, Huebler and Weiner.[182] Conceptualism was truly an international movement, with contacts not only between European and American artists, but also between Western and Eastern Europeans.[183]

Data

During that same month, September 1971, the first issue of a new Italian art magazine, *Data*, was published in Milan. The editor, Tommaso Trini, had previously worked as an art critic for *Domus*. In 1966–67, he had taken over the management of Sperone's second gallery in Milan.[184] The magazine was truly international: it was bilingual, with texts in Italian and English. The editorial committee included mostly Italian contributors such as Celant. However, there were also international members such as Claura and Klaus Honnef.[185] From the beginning, *Data* largely supported Conceptualism. The first issue comprised articles and interviews on Merz and Wilson, as well as texts by Buren, Claura and René Denizot. In addition, it included an important article by Celant on artists' books, 'Book as Artwork 1960/1970'.[186]

1971 Cologne Kunstmarkt and IKI

The Kunstmarkt in Cologne was held between 5 and 10 October 1971.[187] Because of the pressure from competing art fairs, notably the one in Basel, international dealer galleries, including several key Conceptual galleries, were invited to participate. In addition to Fischer and Friedrich, Castelli, Sonnabend, Sperone, Wide White Space and Videogalerie Gerry Schum also took part.[188] For the network of Conceptual dealer galleries this was an international and wide-ranging platform. However, the assessment of the fair by VPDK was not optimistic. The number of visitors (40,000) and the financial turnover (DM4 million) were no more impressive than the previous year's statistics.[189] VPDK welcomed the fact that they had managed to impose themselves over their rivals, but found

Beuys, Bladen, Boezem, Brouwn, Buren, Christo, Conrad, Darboven, De Maria, Dekkers, Dibbets, Van Elk, Engels, Enschede, ERG, Eykelboom, Flanagan, Fluxus, Gilbert & George, Frampton, Gehr, Graham, Grosvenor, Heizer, Huebler, ICW, Jacobs, Joepat, Judd, Kawara, Knoebel, Koetsier, Kraan, Kubelka, Landow, Lawder, LeWitt, Long, Mass Moving, Matsuzawa, Merz, Moore, Morris, Nauman, Nelson, Noord-Brabant, Oldenburg, Oppenheim, Kawara, Paik, Panamarenko, Philips, Prini, Rinke, Roehr, Rückriem, Ruscha, Sandback, Sanéjouand, Schippers, Serra, Sharits, Siegel, Smith, Schum, Shinkichi, Smithson, Snelson, Snow, Stuyf, Tajiri, Tenjo, Yokoyama, Visser, Volten, Vries, Wechgelaar, Weiner and Wieland.

166 Wim Beeren was at that point a Lecturer at the University of Groningen. Geert van Beijeren, one of the Directors of Art & Project, was one of the editors of the exhibition catalogue.

167 P. Sanders, 'Sonsbeek 71 – an adventure', in *Sonsbeek 71, Sonsbeek buiten de perken* (exh. cat.), Park Sonsbeek, Arnhem, 1971, vol.1, p.6.

168 Carel Blotkamp, 'Sculpture at Sonsbeek', *Studio International*, vol.183, no.936, September 1971, p.70.

169 A number of artists, critics and private collectors were intrigued by the issues raised by Sonsbeek 71 and initiated the foundation Sonsbeek Unlimited in September 1971 to enable artists to realise works that could not be hosted in traditional institutions and to present the public with art outside the usual museum context.

170 *Douglas Huebler, Variable Piece 1 (January 1971)*, Art & Project, Amsterdam, 22 May–11 June. See: *Art & Project Bulletin*, no.39, 19 May 1971.

171 *Richard Long, Reflections on the Little Pigeon River, Great Smoky Mountains, Tennessee* (1970), Art & Project, Amsterdam, 17 July–6 August 1971. See: *Art & Project Bulletin*, no.35, 22 March 1971. This was Long's first solo show at Art & Project.

172 *Works on Film (Morris, Nauman, Serra, Sonnier)*, Leo Castelli

that too many galleries made the event look like a supermarket.[190]

In the early 1970s, the concept of art fairs and the importance of a market position for dealers and artists had started to make their mark on the public consciousness. More and more people were interested in buying art. In 1971, the turnover of Art Basel was SFR 7 million.[191] Across Germany, numerous art fairs were founded at this time: Pro art 71 (Duisburg), Kunstmarkt (Göttingen), Art Information 71 (Kiel) and Erste freie Produzentenmesse (Munich).

But in 1971, the Cologne Kunstmarkt had to face a more serious local competitor. Michael Siebrasse and Ingo Kümmel (Neumarkt der Künste) initiated the Internationale Kunst und Informationsmesse (IKI, International Art and Information Fair) in Cologne, which took place at the same time.[192] Like Art Basel, the IKI was an open and democratic event and could therefore attract a wide range of dealer galleries.[193] However, apart from Bischofberger (LeWitt, Nauman), no dealer galleries represented Conceptual art at this fair.

Prospect 71

In October, the 1971 edition of Prospect focused, as before, on an 'international preview' of art in progressive dealer galleries.[194] Prospect 71 was subtitled 'Projection' and focused on film, video and slide projections; art media that had become increasingly important. It was the first event to focus entirely on technology and art. New criteria were applied to the selection process. It was the organisers themselves – Fischer and Strelow with Jürgen Harten (the new director of the Kunsthalle Düsseldorf) – who selected the works to be shown.[195] The invited galleries provided the selected works. These included Art & Project, Friedrich and Sperone.[196] Over 100 projections were shown in five project rooms. The popular event attracted 3,000 visitors during the first three days.[197] The exhibition travelled to the Louisiana Museum for Moderne Kunst in Humlebaek, Denmark (22 January–14 February 1972).[198]

Prospect 71 was a survey exhibition of new media art. It coincided with the opening on 8 October 1971 in Düsseldorf of Videogalerie Schum, the first dealer gallery to be exclusively dedicated to video art.[199] The inaugural exhibition was

Gallery, West Broadway, New York, 25 September–9 October 1971.

173 *Gilbert & George, The General Jungle + Underneath the Arches*, Ileana Sonnabend Gallery, New York, 25 September–October 1971. In early 1970, Sonnabend opened the Sonnabend Auxiliary Space in New York, presenting artists whom she was already showing in Paris. For instance, in April–May 1970, she arranged the first American solo show of Mario Merz.

174 André Emmerich (born 1924 in Germany) had immigrated to America in 1940, where he had opened his gallery in 1954.

175 The last exhibition at the Dwan Gallery, New York, was a group show featuring Anastasi, Arakawa, De Maria, Flavin, Heizer, LeWitt, Long, Ross, Ryman, Sandback, Smithson and Snelson (1–25 June 1971). See: Amy Baker Sandback, 'Virginia Dwan, l'aventure d'un marchand d'art', *artpress*, special issue fiac 90, no.151, October 1990, p.46. For a discussion of the closure of the Dwan Gallery, see: Virginia Dwan, interviewed by Charles Stuckey, Archives of American Art, Smithsonian Institute, Washington, May 1984, tape 10, p.5, in Suzaan Boettger, 'Behind the earth movers: the adventurous support of dealer Virginia Dwan allowed earthwork artists Michael Heizer, Walter De Maria, Robert Smithson and others to realize their pioneering projects – Patronage – Biography', *Art in America*, April 2004.

176 *Sol LeWitt, Structures and Wall Drawings*, John Weber Gallery, New York, 25 September–20 October 1971. See: Manuscript letter from LeWitt to Fischer dated 22 April 1971, Künstler Korrespondenz 1970–71, AKFGD.

177 Paul Taylor, 'John Weber', *Flash Art*, May–June 1986, p.66.

178 *Sol LeWitt*, Konrad Fischer, Düsseldorf, 3 September–1 October 1971. See: *Ausstellungen bei Konrad Fischer*, *op. cit.*, p.66. See also: Database 3, Section Sol LeWitt (Appendix 1.3).

179 *Sol LeWitt*, Art & Project, Amsterdam, 7 September–2 October 1971. See: *Art & Project Bulletin*, no.43, 1 September 1971. The

dedicated to videos by the German artist Ulrich Rückriem. Gerry Schum soon established contacts with Conceptual art galleries for the exclusive right to retail the videos he produced: Art & Project, MTL, Sperone and Jack Wendler.[200]

The end of the year saw a series of solo shows of Conceptual artists in European institutions. Conceptual artists were getting increasing attention from public museums and temporary exhibition spaces.[201] Moreover, these public showings were often linked to solo shows in the artists' main dealer galleries.

Hanne Darboven, Kunstverein, Münster

On 16 October 1971, a solo show of Hanne Darboven was launched at the Kunstverein Münster.[202] It had been organised in cooperation with the artist's principal dealer Fischer.[203] For one full year, 1 January–31 December 1971, Darboven's *Ein Jahrhundert in einem Jahr* (1970) was presented at Fischer's.[204] It was a huge work comprising 365 files of 100 pages each.[205] In Münster, the artist also exhibited a vast ensemble of drawings and writings, *Arbeit I / 1. Kapitel / [100 × 100] / –* and *Arbeit II / 1. Kapitel / [100 × 100] / –*.

Marcel Broodthaers, Mönchengladbach

On 21 October 1971, a solo show of Broodthaers was launched at the Städtisches Museum, Mönchengladbach.[206] The exhibition comprised of films, slide projections and objects, highlighting the trend launched by Project 71, as Cladders noted in his inaugural talk.[207] At the same time, Wide White Space presented works by Broodthaers owned by the gallery,[208] and in December 1971, the artist had his first one-man show in France with Yvon Lambert, presenting the film *Au delà de cette limite (vos billets ne sont plus valables)* (1971).[209]

Actualité d'un Bilan

Yvon Lambert gained influence in the network by affirming his support for Conceptual art. In October 1971, he arranged a survey exhibition of the activities of his gallery since it opened in 1966.[210] *Actualité d'un Bilan* (Current Assessment) was organised, in collaboration with Claura, as a strong statement by the dealer.

bulletin was folded into 48 rectangles.

180 Braco Dimitrijevic (born 1948) had studied at the University of Zagreb and continued his studies in 1971 at Saint Martins School of Art in London. In 1971, he had his first solo show at Lucio Amelio, Naples. In the early 1970s, he became internationally known for his *Casual Passer-by* works, in which he exhibited the gigantic photo portraits of unknown people on city facades and billboards, places usually reserved for pictures of dignitaries or publicity messages.

181 *In Another Moment*, Gallery SKC, Belgrade, 15–20 September, 22–27 September and 29 September–3 October 1971. Artists: Anselmo, Barry, Beuys, Brouwn, Buren, Burgin, Dibbets, Dimitrijevic, Flanagan, Grupa/E KOD, Grupa OHO, Huebler, Kirili, Kounellis, Lamelas, Latham, LeWitt, Trbuljak, Weiner and Wilson. The Belgrade Student Centre would subsequently become an internationally renowned and highly frequented exhibition site.

182 See: Nena Dimitrijevic in her text for the exhibition catalogue, *In Another Moment* (exh. cat.), Gallery SKC, Belgrade, 1971, unnumbered pages.

183 [Editor's note: Also important is Galeria Foksal in Warsaw who showed Robert Barry in 1973 and many other Conceptual artists subsequently. See: *Galeria Foksal 1966–1974*, Foksal, Warsaw 1974.]

184 Maria Christina Mundici, 'Torino 1963–1968', in Minola, Mundici, Poli and Roberto, *Gian Enzo Sperone*, *op. cit.*, pp.23–24.

185 See: Correspondence between Tommaso Trini and Klaus Honnef in June–July 1971, in File 802/367, Archive Kunstverein, Münster, Westfälisches Archivamt, Münster (hereafter AKMWAM).

186 See: Germano Celant, 'Book as Artwork 1960/1970', *Data*, vol.1, no.1, September 1971. Celant's article was later published in English in September 1972 as an exhibition catalogue at Nigel Greenwood Inc. Ltd. in London, in French in the autumn issue (no.9) of *VH 101* and in German in the 1974 (no.11) issue of *Interfunktionen*. The exhibition will be discussed in Chapter 3.3.

He declared: 'I wanted to organise this exhibition freely, without insisting on repeating the errors I might have made in the past, by simply asking myself the question ... whom I would still like to present today.'[211] As a result, the show included pieces by Conceptual artists, but none by the French artists whom he had exhibited in the early days of his gallery.

Gilbert & George, travelling museum show

In October 1971, the Stedelijk Museum in Amsterdam held an exhibition of Gilbert & George.[212] This was the first individual show that the institution had dedicated to a Conceptual artist.[213] The event, *The Paintings (with Us in Nature)*, was a travelling exhibition. It had originally been set up by Konrad Fischer for the Whitechapel Art Gallery, London (July 1971) and for the Kunstverein, Düsseldorf (September–October 1971).[214] Rini Dippel, curator of Painting and Sculpture at the Stedelijk Museum, had been at the opening of the show in London and had immediately made contact with the artists and with Fischer, wishing to take the show.[215] The exhibition continued to travel in Europe, first to the Koninklijk Palais voor Schone Kunsten, Antwerp (February–March 1972) and then to the Kunstmuseum, Lucerne (May–June 1972).[216] There were also discussions about taking the show to the Kunstverein in Münster, but this project did not materialise.[217]

Gilbert & George's exhibition was shown in the majority of the countries in the Conceptual network: Britain (July 1971), Germany (September–October 1971), the Netherlands (October–November 1971), Belgium (February–March 1972) and Switzerland (May–June 1972). This shows how the network established itself in public institutions at the time. At the same time, the principal dealers of the artists in these countries organised shows in their galleries: Nigel Greenwood (November–December 1971), Art & Project (December 1971–January 1972) and Konrad Fischer (January 1972).[218]

Jan Dibbets, Stedelijk Van Abbemuseum, Eindhoven

On 3 December 1971, Dibbets's first solo show in a public institution opened at

187 Kölner Kunstmarkt, Kunsthalle and Kunstverein, Cologne, 5–10 October 1971.

188 See: *KKM '71, Kölner Kunst Markt, Cologne Art Fair, Cologne Foire d'Art* (exh. cat.), Verein Deutscher Kunsthändler, Cologne, 1971.

189 Statistics of the 1971 art fair, in CD-Rom, 'Kunstmarkt Köln '67', *Sediment, op. cit.*

190 Minutes of the Organisation's annual meeting in Cologne dated 8 December 1971 (Mitgliederversammlung des Vereins progressiver deutscher Kunsthändler), in File A72 IV 3, Zadik.

191 Volker Rattemeyer and Renate Penzinger, 'Das Kunstkarussell des Jahres 1971', in *20 Jahre Kunstmarkt 1967–1986*, *op. cit.*, unnumbered pages.

192 'Internationale Kunst- und Informationsmesse 1971', Belgisches Haus and Volkshochschule, Cologne, 5–10 October 1971. See: Brigitte Jacobs, 'Entstehungsgeschichte und Gründungsumstände der Kunstmesse IKI in Düsseldorf 1968–1972', *Sediment*, Zadik, Bonn, no.3, 1998, pp.89–96.

193 In 1971, the IKI presented 66 dealer galleries, and the Cologne art fair 34. See: *Internationale Kunst- und Informationsmesse 1971* (exh. cat.), Belgisches Haus, Volkshochschule, Cologne, 1971.

194 Prospect 71 – *Projection*, Kunsthalle, Düsseldorf, 8–17 October 1971. Artists: Acconci, Ader, Baldessari, Barry, Bernd and Hilla Becher, Ben, Beuys, Böhmler, Boltanski, Breakwell, Brehmer, Broegger, Broodthaers, Brouwn, Burgin, Chamberlain, Close, Cutforth, Darboven, De Maria, Dibbets, Dominicis, Van Elk, Flanagan, Fox, Frampton, Fried, Fulton, Gilbert & George, Graham, Graves, Haacke, Hall, Hamilton, Heizer, Hilliard, Hödicke, Huot, Jaffee, Knoebel, Kriwet, Lamelas, Latham, Le Va, Levine, McLean, Merz, Morgan, Morris, Nauman, Oldenburg, Oppenheim, Penck, Pirelli, Polk, Polke, Reutersward, Richter, Rinke, Roehr, Ross, Rückriem, Salvo, Serra, Smithson, Snow, Sonnier, Stembera, Tremlett, Uecker, Vostell,

the Stedelijk Van Abbemuseum in Eindhoven.[219] The event was set up under the directorship of Jan Leering (1934–2005), who had been director of the museum since 1963. Four recent pieces were exhibited: *Dutch Mountains* (1971), *Horizons* (1971), *Shortest Day* (1970) and *Diagonals* (1971). From 27 November to 18 December 1971, Art & Project presented a solo show of the artist, featuring his film *Louverdrape*.[220] In December 1971, the Galerie MTL arranged Dibbets's first show in Brussels.[221]

Richard Long, MOMA, Oxford

Long also received his first museum show in late 1971. On 9 December, a solo exhibition was launched at the Museum of Modern Art (MOMA) in Oxford.[222] It was arranged by Peter Ibsen, the Director of the museum since 1970,[223] and was the first showing of a work realised by tramping footprints in local red clay. It was intended to be the artist's first one-man show in England, but was immediately preceded by an exhibition at the Whitechapel Art Gallery, London (9–21 November 1971).[224]

Jack Wendler, London

A new dealer gallery focusing on Conceptual art opened in London in late 1971. The American businessman and private collector Jack Wendler launched his space on 30 December 1971 with the first exhibition of Weiner in London.[225] Wendler had come to England with substantial financial means and many New York contacts. He was a friend of Nick Wilder, Lippard and Siegelaub.[226] He was perceived as a competitor by Logsdail,[227] and Greenwood did not know if he was a customer or a competitor.[228] In London, Wendler quickly became an important figure in the art world. He was important socially as he organised parties and dinners at his home after openings where one met many people.[229]

Wendler's gallery consisted of the second floor of a terraced house in North Gower Street. His shows were exhibitions of single works by Conceptual artists. Wendler did not need to sell these works to keep his business going. In fact he purchased most of the works himself; he was a collector as well as a dealer.

Walther, Warhol, Wegman and Weiner.

195 Hans Strelow opened his gallery in Düsseldorf at around this time. He concentrated on abstract painting.

196 Dealer galleries: APG (London), Art Intermedia (Cologne), Art & Project (Amsterdam), L'Attico (Rome), Block (Berlin), British Arts Council (Cologne), Bykert (New York), Castelli (New York), Cooper (New York), Fischer (Düsseldorf), Flowers (London), Friedrich (Cologne), De Gestlo (Hamburg), Gemini G.E.L. (Los Angeles), Gibson (New York), Jysk (Copenhagen), Lisson (London), Maenz (Cologne), Marconi (Milan), Mayer (Düsseldorf), Palley (New York/San Francisco), Ricke (Cologne), Schmela (Düsseldorf), Schum (Düsseldorf), Situation (London), Skulima (Berlin), Sonnabend (Paris), Sperone (Turin), Templon (Paris), Thelen (Cologne), Weber (New York), Werner (Cologne) and Wide White Space (Antwerp).

197 See: 'In drei Tagen über 3000 Besucher', *Rheinische Post*, 14 October 1971, and 'In drei Tagen 3000 Besucher bei 'Prospect'', *Neue Rhein-Zeitung*, 14 October 1969. See also: Georg Jappe, 'Projection: the new trend at Prospect 71', *Studio International*, vol.182, no.939, December 1971, pp.258–261.

198 See the document entitled 'Prospect 71 – Projection', in Box 'Prospect 71', ASKDD. See also: 'Materialabholung, 1971', in File IV 31523, AKDSD.

199 Ulrike Groos, 'Beginn, Umfeld und Ende der Videogalerie Schum in Düsseldorf', in Groos, Hess and Wevers, *Ready to Shoot*, *op. cit.*, p.223.

200 See: 'Video-Informationen', brochure of the Videogalerie Schum dated March 1972, reproduced in *Ibid.*, p.303.

201 As we will see in Chapter 5.2., many of these solo shows were linked with purchases for the permanent collections of public institutions.

202 *Hanne Darboven*, Kunstverein, Münster, 16 October–14 November 1971.

Art Aktuell

By 1971, the Conceptual network was well established in dealer galleries and in public institutions. From that moment on, it also had its own international guide in the form of a bi-monthly art information letter, *Art Aktuell*, edited by Willi Bongard, who had also edited the 'Kunstkompass' since 1970. *Art Aktuell* was a small publication (four pages) subtitled 'Confidential information about the International Art Scene'. It included articles on artists, dealers and museum staff, current and upcoming exhibitions and fairs, and auctions and museum acquisitions.[230] Each issue was a limited edition; there were 500 signed and numbered copies, which were only available through subscription.[231]

3.3 1972

By 1972, Fischer and Sperone held key positions in the international network of Conceptual art. Heiner Friedrich in South Germany, Art & Project in the Netherlands and Yvon Lambert in Paris were also strong protagonists. From 1972 onwards, Spillemaeckers in Brussels and Wendler in London occupied increasingly important positions in the European network. Their programming was entirely dedicated to European and American Conceptual artists.

MTL, Brussels

During the first two years of MTL's existence, from circa 1969 to 1970, Spillemaeckers established a programme that included younger Belgian and Conceptual artists several of whom were also being shown at Wide White Space. These included Broodthaers (March–April 1970), Buren (June–July 1970) and Charlier (September 1970).[232]

From late 1971, the MTL gallery found its own group of Conceptual artists. Spillemaeckers concentrated on cerebral and language-based art. He arranged

203 Honnef in conversation with the author, *op. cit.*

204 Editor's note: The exhibition took place in the Andreastrasse space that Fischer had opened with a Richter show in April 1970. On Kawara's *One Million Years* was shown in the space 14 October–10 November 1971.

205 See: *Ausstellungen bei Konrad Fischer*, *op. cit.*, p.58. See also: Database 3, Section Hanne Darboven (Appendix 1.3).

206 *Marcel Broodthaers, Film als Objekt, Objekt als Film*, Städtisches Museum, Mönchengladbach, 21 October–7 November 1971. See: *Marcel Broodthaers, Cinéma*, *op. cit.*, pp.190–193.

207 Wischermann, *Johannes Cladders*, *op. cit.*, p.375. See also: Frank Lubbers, Anna Hakken and Maria Gilissen (eds), *Marcel Broodthaers, Projection* (exh. cat.), Stedelijk Van Abbemuseum, Eindhoven, 1992, pp.50–62.

208 *Marcel Broodthaers, Figures anciennes et modernes*, Wide White Space, Antwerp, 27 September–27 October 1971. See: Aupetitallot, *Wide White Space*, *op. cit.*, p.283.

209 *Marcel Broodthaers, Au delà de cette limite (vos billets ne sont plus valables)*, Galerie Yvon Lambert, Paris, starting 15 December 1971. The same exhibition was taken over by Françoise Lambert, Milan from 14 April to 5 May 1972. See: Database 3, Section Marcel Broodthaers (Appendix 1.3).

210 *Actualité d'un Bilan*, Galerie Yvon Lambert, Paris, 29 October–5 December 1971. Artists: Andre, Arakawa, Askevold, Barry, Beckley, Broodthaers, Buren, Christo, Darboven, Dezeuze, Dibbets, Fulton, Huebler, Jacquet, Kawara, Kienholz, Lamelas, LeWitt, Long, Mangold, Marden, Oppenheim, Renouf, Ristori, Ryman, Salvo, Sandback, Toroni, Tuttle, Twombly and Weiner.

211 *Yvon Lambert, Actualité d'un Bilan, Paris 1972* (exh. cat.), Galerie Yvon Lambert, Paris, 1972, unnumbered pages (author's translation).

212 *Gilbert & George, The Paintings (with Us in Nature)*, Stedelijk

inaugural solo shows of many artists in Belgium, including Stanley Brouwn (26 November–14 December 1971), Dibbets (18 December 1971–15 January 1972), Wilson (21–23 January 1972),[233] Darboven (1–29 February 1972), Barry (7–20 March 1972) and Huebler (22 March–22 April 1972).[234] Thus from this time onwards, MTL represented a wide-ranging group of Conceptual artists in Belgium, independent of Wide White Space.[235] This programming demonstrates connections with the principal dealers of these artists, namely Art & Project and Fischer. That the latter helped to set up Spillemaeckers's programming, is suggested in a letter he wrote to Weiner in November 1971:

> There is a gallery in Brussels called MTL owned by Mr. Spillemaeckers. He starts a new programme now beginning with Stanley Brouwn, J. Dibbets, Hanne, Barry, Doug Huebler, and I want to ask whether you are interested to do something there in spring ...
>
> P.S. If you find an interesting artist, please inform me.[236]

In the end, Weiner decided to stay with his first dealer gallery, Wide White Space, where he had first exhibited in 1969. In 1972, he had solo shows at Konrad Fischer (April), Art & Project (April–May 1972) and Wide White Space (June).[237]

London: Jack Wendler, the Lisson Gallery and Nigel Greenwood

In London, Wendler's gallery was a modest yet important space for Conceptual artists. In the first few months of 1972, he arranged the first British show of Buren (February 1972), Dibbets (25 February–9 March), Wilson (March 1972), Huebler (April 1972), Merz (2–16 May 1972), Darboven (May–June 1972) and Broodthaers (December 1972).[238] Until then, the Lisson Gallery had presented the work of LeWitt (1970–71), while Greenwood had shown Gilbert & George, David Tremlett (both in 1970) and Ed Ruscha (1971).[239] However, in 1972, Logsdail became more and more involved with Conceptualism. He concentrated on American artists, showing Graham (February), Andre (May)[240] and Barry (December).

Museum, Amsterdam, 28 October–28 November 1971.

213 See: Database 2, Section Stedelijk Museum, Amsterdam (Appendix 1.2).

214 Since 1964, the Whitechapel Art Gallery had been directed by Mark Glazebrook with assistance from Jennie Stein (Acting Director from 1971 to 1974). The Director of the Kunstverein, Düsseldorf since 1961 had been Karl-Heinz Hering. Gilbert & George acknowledge the dealer's help in getting important museum showings. See: 'My name is Konrad Fischer. You will do somezing wiz me in Düsseldorf, eeh ...? A discussion with Gilbert and George', in Kölle, *Die Kunst des Ausstellen*, *op. cit.*, p.263.

215 See: Letter from Edy de Wilde to Karl-Heinz Hering dated 20 August 1971, and Letter from De Wilde to Gilbert & George c/o Konrad Fischer dated 1 September 1971, in Box 145, Tentoonstellingen 1971, Archive Stedelijk Museum, Amsterdam (hereafter ASMA).

216 'Gilbert & George, The Paintings (with Us in Nature)', Kunstmuseum, Lucerne, 10 May–25 June 1971. In Lucerne, 1,120 visitors came to see the exhibition. See: *Jahresbericht 1972*, Kunstgesellschaft Luzern, Lucerne, May 1973, unnumbered pages.

217 See: Letter from De Wilde to Klaus Honnef dated 6 Januar 1972, in Box 145, Tentoonstellingen 1971, ASMA.

218 *Gilbert & George, The Ten Pieces*, Nigel Greenwood Inc. Ltd., London, 29 November–December 1971; *Gilbert & George, New Photo-Pieces*, Art & Project, Amsterdam, 22 December 1971–21 January 1972; *Gilbert & George, Christmas of 1971*, Konrad Fischer, Düsseldorf, starting 3 January 1972. See: Database 3, Section Gilbert & George (Appendix 1.3).

219 *Jan Dibbets*, Stedelijk Van Abbemuseum, Eindhoven, 3 December 1971–16 January 1972. See: Database 2, Section Van Abbemuseum, Eindhoven (Appendix 1.2). See also: Database 3, Section Jan Dibbets (Appendix 1.3).

220 *Jan Dibbets, Louverdrape*, Art & Project, Amsterdam,

'Konzept'–Kunst

In March and April 1972, the Kunstmuseum Basel hosted a group show of Conceptual Art, *'Konzept'–Kunst*; curated by Fischer.[241] In December 1971, he wrote to several artists, including Huebler:

> The Kunstmuseum Basel wants to do a so called Concept Art exhibition. I was asked to arrange this show, and I like very much to do it, for the Kunstmuseum in Basel is a very important place. Also it is the first time that this museum is going to do a group show of contemporary artists. Of course it will not be a very large show; I thought of 10 or 12 artists as there are Barry, Bochner, Darboven, Huebler, On Kawara, Kosuth, Weiner... For this there is plenty of space: one floor of the museum. The exhibition will start on the 18th of March, going til the 30th of April 72 (pretty soon).
>
> There will be a catalogue with a biblio- and biography and a text by Klaus Honnef.
>
> I would like very much to show an older and a new work of yours and also all publications you did.
>
> Please write me what you suggest to show there and also what publications you did and the publisher.
>
> Again I want to mention that this show can be very important, for the Kunstmuseum Basel is a very serious place.
>
> Please answer me soon. All the best and Okey Dokey,
> yours Konrad Fischer
> P.S. If you have an idea for the title for this show, please tell me.[242]

Artists' books and publications constituted an important part of the exhibitions. Erika Fischer (born 1950), Konrad's sister, who had worked at the gallery since 1970, contacted dealers who were also publishers, including Art & Project, Castelli, Yvon Lambert, Spillemaeckers and Sperone.[243] The catalogue consisted of original contributions by the artists. The exhibition *'Konzept'–Kunst* focused on works that resulted from 'trains of thought' (*Gedankengänge*),[244] conceptual

27 November–18 December 1971. See: *Art & Project Bulletin*, no.46, 23 November 1971.

221 *Jan Dibbets, Venetian Blinds*, Galerie MTL, Brussels, 18 December 1971–15 January 1972.

222 *Richard Long, Mud Spiral*, Museum of Modern Art, Oxford, 9–23 December 1971.

223 The MOMA had been created in 1965 by the local architect Trevor Green and its main patron was the Arts Council. In 1970, the Arts Council grant was £6,000 a year. See: Lynda Morris, 'The Museum of Modern Art in Oxford 1965–1975', *Studio International*, vol.190, no.978, November–December 1975, p.238.

224 Long would have his first American solo exhibition at the MOMA, New York, in the 'Project' series, from 14 March to 17 April 1972.

225 *Lawrence Weiner, And/or: green as well as blue as well as red*, Jack Wendler, London, 30 December–6 January 1971. For a comprehensive outline of exhibitions of Conceptual artists at the gallery, see: Database 1, Section Jack Wendler (Appendix 1.1). For an overview of all the exhibitions organised by Wendler, see: Appendix 3.8. The archive of Wendler's gallery is private.

226 Lynda Morris, 'Norwich July 2001', in Moseley, *Conception*, *op. cit.*, pp.143–144. Jack Wendler had been at college with the Los Angeles-based dealer Nick Wilder. He was the son of cinema director Billy Wilder.

227 Logsdail in conversation with the author, *op. cit.*

228 Morris in conversation with the author.

229 *Ibid.*

230 For a comprehensive set of *Art Aktuell* issues, see: Box SK 153, Zadik.

231 From 1973 onwards, *Art Aktuell* was also obtainable in English. See: 'Art Aktuell', *Avalanche*, no.8, November 1973, p.62.

232 See: Database 1, Section MTL, and Section Wide White Space

processes and ideas. Huebler exhibited *Variable Piece: 70 (In Progress)* (November 1971) and *Location Piece #14 Global Proposal* (July 1969).

Books on Conceptual art

At the time of the exhibition in Basel, on 23 March 1972, Fischer presented an extensive study of Conceptual art written by Klaus Honnef in Düsseldorf.[245] In 1970, Honnef had been contacted by Alexander Schleber, the German representative of the Phaidon publishing house in Cologne, who asked him to write the book.[246] *Concept Art* was published in autumn 1971, and was at the same time an exhibition.[247] The last part of the publication was conceived as an exhibition and comprised of specially realised projects by 14 Conceptual artists, including Darboven, Dibbets, Huebler and Wilson.[248] In March and April 1972, the book was 'exhibited' at the Kunstverein in Münster. *Das Konzept ist die Form* (The Concept is the Form) was a show combining the presentation of Honnef's book alongside documentary material of the artworks in display cabinets.[249]

In 1972, a series of in-depth theoretical studies of Conceptualism were published, including books by Ursula Meyer,[250] Ermanno Migliorini,[251] Grégoire Müller[252] and Gregory Battcock.[253] While Meyer's book was a collection of images, documents and statements on Conceptual art, Migliorini's publication was a critical anthology, analysing and describing Conceptual works. Müller's study was a comprehensive analysis of the work of a number of Minimal, Land and Conceptual artists, in which he tried to explain why and how Conceptual artists came to create a new type of art. Both Müller and Honnef claimed that Conceptualism modified the art market and the design of exhibitions, thus bringing about a new group of dealers and museum curators.[254] Battcock assembled texts by prominent critics and artists, including Dore Ashton, Jack Burnham, Lippard and Kosuth.

In 1971–72, no less than five books on Conceptual art were published in Europe (Cologne, London, Florence) and in America (New York). They were available in German, Italian and English. These publications demonstrate that Conceptualism was now seen as an established art movement.[255]

(Appendix 1.1). See also: Database 3, Section Broodthaers and Buren (Appendix 1.3).

233 In Europe, Fischer was the first to show the work of Ian Wilson (born 1940) in November 1970. At very nearly the same time, Art & Project presented the artist's work in one of their bulletins. See: *Ausstellungen bei Konrad Fischer*, *op. cit.*, p.54, and *Art & Project Bulletin*, no.30, 30 November 1970.

234 See: Database 3, Section Dibbets, Darboven and Huebler (Appendix 1.3). At the same time, Darboven also had a solo show presenting *Ein Jahrhundert* at Heiner Friedrich, Cologne (14 January–13 February 1972).

235 De Decker and Lohaus focused on a different group. These included Broodthaers, Buren, Andre and Weiner, but also Lamelas, Edward Kienholz, Beuys, Christo and Panamarenko.

236 Letter from Fischer to Weiner dated 21 November 1971, in Künstler Korrespondenz 1970–71, AKFGD.

237 *Lawrence Weiner*, Konrad Fischer, Düsseldorf, April 1972. See: *Ausstellungen bei Konrad Fischer*, *op. cit.*, p.77. *Lawrence Weiner*, Art & Project, Amsterdam, 11 April–12 May 1972. See: *Art & Project Bulletin*, no.53, 18 April 1972. 'Lawrence Weiner, Contributions to newspapers: Gazet van Antwerpen, International Herald Tribune', Wide White Space, 24–25 June 1972. See: Aupetitallot, *Wide White Space*, *op. cit.*, p.294. See also: Database 3, Section Lawrence Weiner (Appendix 1.3).

238 See: Database 1, Section Jack Wendler (Appendix 1.1). See also: Database 3, Section Buren, Dibbets, Huebler, Merz, Darboven and Broodthaers (Appendix 1.3). During that time, Yvon Lambert also hosted solo shows of Dibbets (starting 3 February 1972) and Huebler (16–31 March 1972) in Paris.

239 See: Database 1, Section Lisson Gallery and Nigel Greenwood (Appendix 1.1).

240 At the same moment, Fischer also hosted a solo show of Andre

Marcel Broodthaers

Broodthaers, who had been shown at the Wide White Space (since 1966), MTL (1970) and Yvon Lambert (1970), was now also exhibiting in Italy at Françoise Lambert (April–May 1972), in Germany at Heiner Friedrich (May 1972) and Michael Werner, in England at Jack Wendler (December 1972) and in the Netherlands at Art & Project (March 1973).[256] During that period, Broodthaers also had shows at the MTL gallery (May–June 1972) and at Wide White Space (June 1972).[257] In addition, in May 1972, the *Département des Aigles, Section des Figures (Der Adler vom Oligozän bis Heute)* (Eagle Department, Figures Section, the Eagle from the Oligocene to Today) of his Musée d'art Moderne was inaugurated at the Städtische Kunsthalle in Düsseldorf.[258] This was the first presentation of an artist's museum in a public cultural institution.[259]

Broodthaers had founded his *Musée d'art Moderne* in September 1968, in reaction to the political unrest of the period and to denounce the lack of interest in contemporary art in Belgian museums. The Département des Aigles referred to military rigour.[260] The first section of his museum, the *Section XIXe siècle* (Nineteenth-century section) had been inaugurated in September 1968 in his house in Brussels.[261] In February 1970, this section was reinstalled at the Kunsthalle Düsseldorf, when Broodthaers was invited by Jürgen Harten to participate in the 'between' project series.[262]

Sol LeWitt and Douglas Huebler, Oxford

In England, LeWitt and Huebler had their first museum shows at the Museum of Modern Art in Oxford in April–May 1972, when the museum was directed by Peter Ibsen.[263] This exhibition of two American artists took place after a series of events dedicated to British Conceptualists, including Gilbert & George (1970), Flanagan (October–November 1971), Long (December 1971) and Fulton (April 1972).[264] It also occurred at the same time as Huebler's first London solo show at Jack Wendler and his show at Konrad Fischer.[265] Both exhibitions presented *Variable Pieces*.

(May 1972) in Düsseldorf.

241 *'Konzept'-Kunst*, Kunstmuseum, Basel, 18 March–23 April 1972. Artists: Art & Language, Baldessari, Barry, Bochner, Brouwn, Buren, Burgin, Darboven, Dibbets, Gilbert & George, Haacke, Huebler, Kawara and Weiner.

242 Letter from Fischer to Huebler of 30 December 1971, in Künstler Korrespondenz 1970–71, AKFGD. Fischer sent similar letters to Kosuth (28 December 1971), Kawara and Weiner (both 30 December 1971).

243 See the letters from Erika Fischer to Art & Project (7 February 1972), Galleria Sperone (7 February 1972), Yvon Lambert (24 February 1972), Leo Castelli (25 February 1972) and Fernand Spillemaeckers (25 February 1972), in Allgemeine Korrespondenz 1972–73, AKFGD.

244 Zdenek Felix, 'Zur Ausstellung', in *'Konzept'- Kunst* (exh. cat.), Kunstmuseum, Basel, 1972, unnumbered pages.

245 See: Letter from Klaus Honnef to Paul Maenz dated 20 March 1972, in File 802 / 369, AKMWAM.

246 Honnef in conversation with the author, *op. cit.* See also: Letter from Alexander Schleber to Klaus Honnef dated 15 December 1970, in File 802/366, AKMWAM.

247 Honnef, *Concept Art*, *op. cit.*

248 Artists: Barry, Brouwn, Buren, Darboven, Dibbets, Gilbert & George, Huebler, Kawara, Kosuth, LeWitt, Prini, Weiner and Wilson. Honnef contacted the artists in 1970 about this project. See, for instance: Letter from Klaus Honnef to Hanne Darboven dated 16 January 1970, and Letter from Honnef to Ian Wilson dated 22 December 1970, in File 802/366, AKMWAM.

249 Honnef in conversation with the author, *op. cit. Das Konzept ist die Form*, Kunstverein, Münster, 25 March–April 1972.

250 Meyer, *Conceptual Art*, *op. cit.* Artists: Acconci, Atkinson, Atkinson-Bainbridge-Baldwin-Hurrell, Bainbridge, Baldessari, Barry, Barthelme, Battcock, Becher, Bochner, Buren, Burgin, Burgy, Burn,

De Europa

After the show they had set up in Andover (Massachusetts) in January 1971, Sperone and Fischer organised a second exhibition of European Conceptual artists at the John Weber Gallery, New York in April–May 1972. Fischer and Weber had known each other since the late 1960s, when Weber directed the Dwan Gallery. *De Europa* (Of Europe) included work by artists represented by both dealers, such as Salvo and Zorio, Darboven and Long.[266] Subsequently, Weber hosted solo shows of several European artists, including Anselmo (October–November 1972), Boetti (March 1973) and Buren (October–November 1973).

In June 1972, Buren had his first solo show at the Sperone Gallery in Turin.[267] The exhibition consisted of a large length of red-and-white striped fabric, hung between two buildings in the courtyard of the gallery. At the same time, he had a solo show at Wide White Space.[268] This was the artist's third exhibition (earlier ones had been held in 1969 and 1971). It was organised on the same principle, but this time, white-and-yellow striped papers were pasted in the gallery space, symmetrically, on either side of the door.

1972 Venice Biennale

On 11 June 1972, the 36th Venice Biennale opened.[269] For the first time, it had a general theme, 'Work or Behaviour'. The work of several Conceptual artists was presented. Dibbets exhibited in the Dutch Pavilion, and it established his international reputation.[270] The German pavilion hosted a solo show of Richter's *48 Portraits*, while Merz's work was shown in the Italian pavilion alongside that of Germano Olivotto and Bacari.[271]

On 15 June 1972, Art & Language's first show in Germany opened at Galerie Paul Maenz.[272] The artists had met Maenz through Templon.[273] After Sperone (June–July 1971), this was the artists' second show in a dealer gallery.[274] The exhibited work *Documenta Memorandum (Indexing)* (1972) referred to the huge *Index 001* installation that the group exhibited at Documenta 5, which opened a couple of weeks later.[275] This was a cross-referential index system consisting of

Burn-Ramsden, Castoro, Cutforth, Dibbets, Fernbach-Flarsheim, Graham, Haacke, Huebler, Kaltenbach, Kawara, Kirili, Kosuth, Kozlov, LeWitt, Merz, Morris, Nauman, N.E. Thing Co. (Ian Baxter), Oppenheim, Perrreault, Piper, Ramsden, Ruscha, Venet, Weiner and Wilson. Meyer was born in 1915 in Hanover. From 1968, she was Associate Professor of Sculpture at Leham College, City University of New York.

251 Ermanno Migliorini, *Conceptual Art*, Il Fiorino, Florence, 1972. Artists: Atkinson, Bainbridge, Barry, Barthelme, Buren, Burn, Cutforth, Huebler, Hurrell, Kosuth, LeWitt, Ramsden and Weiner. Migliorini was a Milan-based art historian.

252 Grégoire Müller, *The New Avantgarde, Issues for the Art of the Seventies*, Pall Mall Press, London, 1972. Artists: Andre, Beuys, De Maria, Flavin, Heizer, LeWitt, Merz, Morris, Nauman, Serra, Sonnier and Smithson. Müller was a Swiss art critic and the editor of *Art* Magazine. He had written one of the texts for the *When Attitudes Become Form* catalogue. See: Grégoire Müller, 'Diversité, abundance...', in Szeemann, *When Attitudes Become Form*, *op. cit.*, unnumbered pages.

253 Gregory Battcock (ed.), *Idea Art, A Critical Anthology*, Dutton, New York, 1973. Critics: Dore Ashton, Gregory Battcock, Jonathan Benthall, Cheryl Bernstein, Jack Burnham, Joseph Kosuth, Lucy Lippard, Ursula Meyer, John Perreault, Arthur Rose, Harold Rosenberg, Seth Siegelaub, Robert Hughes and documentation on Conceptual art by Weiner, Buren, Bochner and LeWitt. Battcock was an American artist, critic and teacher.

254 Honnef, *Concept Art*, *op. cit.*, pp.53–55; Müller, *The New Avantgarde*, *op. cit.*, pp.4–5.

255 At the time, various documents and photographs from Szeemann's archive were also published. See: *Dokumente zur aktuellen Kunst 1967–1970, Material aus dem Archiv Szeemann, Texte von Georg Jappe, Aurel Schmidt und Harald Szeemann*, Kunstkreis AG,

350 separate texts organised into various systems and exhibited in eight filing cabinets. The index challenged the viewers' ability to make sense of it according to habitual means of classification, and questioned the relations between compatibility, incompatibly and the lack of relational value.

Documenta 5

On 30 June 1972, Documenta 5 was launched.[276] It had been organised under the supervision of Szeemann, who had been nominated general secretary in 1970.[277] The working committee comprised of Jean-Christophe Ammann, Arnold Bode and Szeemann. The event was arranged under the general theme of 'Befragung der Realität, Bildwelten von Heute' (Questioning Reality, Image Worlds of Today). It not only presented works of art, but also other kinds of 'social iconography', including posters, comics, pornography and banknotes, questioning the relationship between art and society.[278] Furthermore, this Documenta was conceived by Szeemann as a 'Hundred Day Event'. It included many performances and happenings. Beuys, for instance, opened his Bureau for Direct Democracy during the time of the exhibition and tirelessly debated political and social issues with all comers.[279]

Documenta 5 included a section dedicated to Conceptual art. Szeemann was not particularly fond of Conceptualism, but included it as an important contemporary art tendency. A report of July 1971 about the preparation of the event shows that it was Wim Beeren who had first been thought of as an organiser of this section.[280] Finally, however, Szeemann contacted Klaus Honnef, asking him to curate a Conceptual art section. Honnef did not feel like organising such a show himself and he suggested that he collaborate with Fischer. For Honnef, Fischer was the key person for Conceptualism.[281] Szeemann had originally contacted Honnef rather than Fischer because he preferred to work with museum people rather than dealers, who he did not consider to be objective.[282]

Fischer's recommendation for a section on *Minimal Art, Structuralism, Land Art, Concept Art* was officially accepted in October 1971.[283] Honnef and Fischer had a budget of DM 100,000 at their disposal to prepare their section, funding

Lucerne, 1972. It comprised of various documents related to Conceptual art, including invitation cards, photographs, reproductions of exhibition catalogues and press cuttings.

256 Marcel Broodthaers, *Au-delà de cette limite (vos billets ne sont plus valables)*, Françoise Lambert, Milan, 19 April–5 May 1972. *Marcel Broodthaers, Zeichnungen, Dias, Filme*, Heiner Friedrich, Munich, 6–25 May 1972. *Marcel Broodthaers*, Nigel Greenwood Inc. Ltd, London, 1–22 December 1972. Marcel Broodthaers, *Rétrospective (October 1963–March 1973)*, Art & Project, Amsterdam, March 1973. See: Database 3, Section Marcel Broodthaers (Appendix 1.3).

257 *Marcel Broodthaers, Tractatus Logico-Catalogicus*, Galerie MTL, Brussels, 15 May–17 June 1972. *Marcel Broodthaers, Editions Le Corbeau et le Renard* (1967–1972), Wide White Space, Antwerp, 17–30 June 1972.

258 *Marcel Broodthaers, Musée d'art Moderne, Département des Aigles, Section des Figures (Der Adler vom Oligozän bis Heute)*, Kunsthalle, Düsseldorf, 16 May–9 July 1972.

259 Jürgen Harten, 'L'aigle de l'Oligocène à nos jours, Düsseldorf 1972, Musée d'Art Moderne Département des Aigles, Section des Figures', in Klüser and Hegewisch, *L'Art de l'Exposition*, *op. cit.*, p.383.

260 *Ibid.*, p.384.

261 Marcel Broodthaers also inaugurated a *Section Littéraire* in his Brussels house (1968), a *Section XVIIe Siècle* at A379089 in Antwerp (1969), a *Section Cinéma* at the Nurgplatz in Düsseldorf (1971), a *Section Finance* at the Galerie Michael Werner, Cologne (1971) and a *Section Publicité* at Documenta 5 in Kassel in 1972. After this show, he closed his museum permanently.

262 *between 4 (Becher, Broodthaers, Castoro, Cotton, Dürr, Gilbert & George, Morgan, Stüttgen, Ulrichs, Weh, Polke, Kohlhöfer)*, Kunsthalle, Düsseldorf, 14–15 February 1970.

263 *Douglas Huebler/Sol LeWitt*, Museum of Modern Art, Oxford, 28 April–27 May 1972.

that allowed them to travel to New York.[284] The Conceptual art section was entitled 'Idee+Idee/Licht' (Idea+Idea/Light) and included about 25 European and American artists.[285] Many, but not all of them were represented by Fischer; the exceptions included Art & Language and Richard Serra. Honnef wrote the introductory text for the exhibition catalogue. He was positioning himself as one of the main theorists of Conceptual art.[286] Documenta 5 also included performances and video projections by numerous Conceptual artists, including Gilbert & George, Merz and Nauman.[287]

In addition to Honnef and Fischer, other central characters of the Conceptual art network took part in the organisation of Documenta 5. Ammann organised a section dedicated to 'Realismus' (Realism), presenting the work of artists such as Artschwager, McLean and Richter.[288] Cladders, together with Szeemann, arranged a section on the theme of 'Individuelle Mythologien' (Individual Mythologies),[289] including Broodthaers, Alighiero Boetti and Ed Ruscha.[290] Another section presented artists' museums, including the final section of Broodthaers's *Musée d'art moderne (Section Publicité)*[291] and Claes Oldenburg's *Mouse Museum*.[292] Kasper König had originally contacted Szeemann, asking him if he would be interested in showing Oldenburg's work. Szeemann was very enthusiastic, and was glad that König, who was still living in New York, could take care of all the necessary arrangements.[293]

Documenta 5 was visited by 220,000 people.[294] Consequently, it gave extensive publicity to the exhibited artists. A number of works included in the show were sold for a sum of about DM 130,000.[295] Some Cologne dealers, notably Rudolf Zwirner, rented a space in Kassel to exhibit their artists during the time of Documenta to protest against their exclusion.[296] The success of the 1972 Documenta gave the go-ahead to public institutions to show and acquire Conceptual works.[297] It was this phenomenon that marked for many protagonists of the network the official institutional acceptance of Conceptualism.[298]

A number of dealers organised shows in their galleries of Conceptual artists who were part of Documenta 5 to take advantage of the publicity. In Germany, Maenz launched an exhibition of Art & Language (June–July), while Fischer

264 See: Database 2, Section MOMA, Oxford (Database 1.2).

265 *Douglas Huebler, Variable Pieces: 15, 16, 17, 18, 19*, Jack Wendler, London, April 1972. *Douglas Huebler*, Konrad Fischer, Düsseldorf, 13 April–4 May 1972. See: Database 3, Section Douglas Huebler (Appendix 1.3). See also: *Ausstellungen bei Konrad Fischer*, *op. cit.*, p.76.

266 *De Europa*, John Weber Gallery, New York, 29 April–24 May 1972. Artists: Anselmo, Art & Language, Boetti, Buren, Darboven, Dibbets, Fulton, Long, Merz, Paolini, Ruthenbeck, Salvo and Zorio.

267 *Daniel Buren, Invito a leggere come indicazione di quello che c'è da vedere (Peinture suspendue)*, Galleria Gian Enzo Sperone, Turin, starting 12 June 1972. See: Minola, Mundici, Poli and Roberto, *Gian Enzo Sperone, op. cit.*, pp.208–209. See also: *Daniel Buren, Mot à Mot, op. cit.*, p.T 36.

268 *Daniel Buren*, Wide White Space, Antwerp, 2–15 June 1972. See: Aupetitallot, *Wide White Space, op. cit.*, pp.202–292.

269 *36 Biennale di Venezia: Esposizione Internationale d'Art*, Venice, 11 June–1 October 1972. Artists: Dibbets (Holland); Hollein, Oberhuber, Oswald (Austria); Alechinsky (Belgium); Boltansky, Le Gac, Titus-Carmel, Girardi, Fernandez, Viseux (France); Olivotto, Merz, Bacari (Italy); Gilliam, Sonnier, Davies, Estes, Nutt, Arbus (USA); Richter (Germany); Schum (Italian Pavillion); Tucker, Walker (UK); Thanako (Japan); Redinger, Iskovitz (Canada); Botero (Columbia); Lam (Cuba); Makowsky (Poland); Lohse (Switzerland).

270 On the occasion of his contribution to the Venice Biennale, Dibbets designed an *Art & Project Bulletin*. See: *Art & Project Bulletin*, no.56, 12 June 1972.

271 See: *36 Biennale di Venezia: Esposizione Internationale d'Art* (exh. cat.), Ente Autonomo 'La Biennale di Venezia', Venice, 1972.

272 *The Art & Language Institute, Documenta Memorandum (Indexing)*, Galerie Paul Maenz, Cologne, 15 June–1 July 1972. Artists: Atkinson, Bainbridge, Burn, Baldwin, Harrison, Hurrell,

hosted a show of LeWitt (September–October). In Belgium, Wide White Space showed Buren and Weiner (both in June), while MTL also organised a show of LeWitt (July–September).[299] Yvon Lambert presented Long (May), and Sperone exhibited Buren (June). In England, Wendler showed Merz (May) and Darboven (May–June).[300]

The New Art

Another major show of contemporary art tendencies, *The New Art*, was launched in London at the Hayward Gallery around the time of Documenta 5. Opening on 17 August 1972,[301] it was organised for the Arts Council of Great Britain by Anne Seymour, who had recently been appointed Assistant Curator of contemporary art at the Tate Gallery. She was assisted by Nicholas Serota (born 1947), a regional Art Officer at the Arts Council, who became the Director of the Museum of Modern Art in Oxford the following year.

Seymour wrote in the exhibition catalogue that 'Britain is a quiet place to work, but New York, Düsseldorf, Paris and Turin are where [the artists] sell and display their ideas.'[302] The show had a narrow point of view in comparison to other shows organised in Europe at the time, since it only presented works by British artists, but it offered an extensive overview of the Conceptual artists in the UK.[303] It brought together renowned British Conceptualists (Art & Language, Long, Gilbert & George), with less well-known London-based artists. But it was important enough for prominent dealers to come over for the opening: Castelli, Sonnabend, Fischer, Schum and Van Ravesteijn all attended.[304]

The Book as Art Work 1960–1972

In September 1972, Nigel Greenwood Inc. Ltd. presented an extensive exhibition on artists' books, *The Book as Art Work 1960–1972*.[305] This exhibition was inspired by an article on artists' books from 1960 to 1970 by Celant in the first issue of *Data* magazine, September 1971.[306] The show was organised by Lynda Morris (who had started the bookshop at the ICA and was then Greenwood's gallery assistant) in negotiation with Celant, who believed that the article would inspire

Kosuth and Ramsden. See: De Vries, *Paul Maenz Köln 1970–1980–1990*, *op. cit.*, p.38. See also: *Art & Language, Documenta Memorandum (Indexing)/Alternate Map for Documenta (Based on Citation A)* (exh. cat.), The Art & Language Institute/Paul Maenz, Cologne, 1972.

273 Art & Language in conversation with the author, *op. cit.*

274 See: Database 3, Section Art & Language (Appendix 1.3).

275 According to Harrison, the *Index* was purchased by Bruno Bischofberger. See: Harrison in conversation with the author, *op. cit.*

276 Documenta 5, Museum Fridericianum and Neue Galerie, Kassel, 30 June–8 October 1972.

277 This was a different procedure from that of Documenta 4 in 1968, where a committee of about 20 people was responsible for the organisation.

278 On this, see: Jürgen Harten, ''Documenta 5' at Kassel', *Studio International*, vol.184, no.946, July–August 1972, p.3.

279 Beuys had founded his Bureau for Direct Democracy in 1969. It was installed in an office next to Fischer's Andreastrasse gallery in the Düsseldorf Altstadt. It is said that Fischer paid the rent. 'It was good for business to have Beuys next door.' See: Lynda Morris, 'Recollection: Joseph Beuys', *Art Monthly*, no.284, March 2005, pp.42–43.

280 Report dated 14 July 1971 entitled 'Zwischenbericht über die Vorbereitung d5', in Box 2–d5, HSAM.

281 Honnef in conversation with the author, *op. cit.*, and Szeemann in conversation with the author, *op. cit.* Szeemann suggested that it was Honnef who asked to collaborate with Fischer. Honnef, however, recalled that he had the choice of curating the show alone or together with Fischer and that he decided to go for the second option.

282 Szeemann in conversation with the author, *op. cit.*

283 Letter from Szeemann to Fischer dated 18 October 1971, in Allgemeine Korrespondenz 1972–73, AKFGD.

284 See: Contract of Honnef and Fischer for Documenta 5,

an important exhibition.[307] Celant's original list was enhanced from 75 to around 250 titles by Morris.[308] Greenwood, Fischer, Hans Jörg Meyer, Barbara Reise and Art & Language helped her to concentrate her additions to Conceptual artists' books.[309] She designed the installation of the exhibition and described it as 'a single shelf running round the room with the rare books behind Perspex. There was a second lower shelf where we put spare copies of the books that could be looked at and that were for sale.'[310]

At the time, artists' books were becoming increasingly important to many dealers, such as Greenwood, Lambert, Maenz and Friedrich, who also became publishers. Later that year, the Stedelijk Museum set up an exhibition of artists' books from its collection, including publications by Conceptual artists such as Barry and Weiner.[311]

Cologne and Düsseldorf Kunstmarkts

Faced with the rivalry of the Basel and IKI Kunstmarkts, VPDK felt that the Cologne Kunstmarkt had to evolve and adapt if it was to continue. Several ways of boosting the Kunstmarkt were considered, from a move to Cologne's commercial exhibition centre, to disbanding and forming an association with the IKI.[312] The Cologne Kunstmarkt started on 3 October 1972, opening up, unexpectedly, to international dealer galleries and to Conceptual art dealers in particular.[313] The Conceptual art dealers who had already had a stand the previous year (Fischer, Friedrich, Sperone, Wide White Space, Sonnabend and Castelli), were now joined by Art & Project, Paul Maenz and John Weber.[314] But faced with a greater choice of art fairs, visitors dropped to 30,000 and the fair's turnover remained at DM4.5 million.[315]

After long negotiations with the cities of Cologne and Düsseldorf about its future location, the IKI accepted the latter's offer. The rival fair moved from Cologne to the nearby city, thus reinforcing the competition between the two cities. The IKI took place from 6 to 11 October 1972 in Düsseldorf's Messegelände (Exhibition Centre), where there was plenty of space.[316] This new location asserted artworks as an economic benefit, since all kinds of merchandise

included in a Letter from Gerald Just to Fischer dated 10 January 1972, in Allgemeine Korrespondenz 1972–73, AKFGD. See also: Honnef in conversation with the author, *op. cit.*

285 'Idee'. Artists: Agnetti, Art & Language (Kosuth), Baldessari, Barry, Bernhard and Hilla Becher, Bochner, Brouwn, Buren, Darboven, Dibbets, LeWitt, Long, Merz, Nauman, Panamarenko, Rinke, Rockburne, Rückriem, Ruthenbeck, Serra, Weiner and Zorio; 'Idee/Licht', Artists: Alexander, Asher, Cooper, Deutsch, Moses and Wudi. See: *Documenta 5*, *op. cit.*, section 1, pp.42–45 and section 17, pp.1–82.

286 See: Klaus Honnef, 'Einführung', in *Ibid.*, section 17, pp.1–9. See also: Letter from Honnef to Fischer dated 6 April 1972, in File 802/367, AKMWAM.

287 *Videos*, Artists: Acconci, Baldessari, Beuys, Boetti, Brouwn, Brus, Buren, Dibbets, De Dominicis, Gilbert & George, Long, Merz, Nauman, Oppenheim, Rinke, Roehr, Rückriem, Ruthenbeck, Sonnier and Wegman. See: *Documenta 5*, *op. cit.*, section 1, p.35.

288 *Ibid.*, section 1, p.13 and section 15, pp.1–2.

289 *Ibid.*, section 1, pp.29–34, section 16, pp.1–5.

290 *Individuelle Mythologien*, Artists: Boetti, Boltanski, Brecht, Broodthaers, Brus, Cornell, Fernie, Filliou, Graves, Harloff, Herbin, Insley, Jensen, LeGac, Martin, Melani, Nitsch, Page, Paolini, Penck, Polke, Rainer, Ruscha, Samaras, Thek, Watts, Westermann, Wiley and Young.

291 See: Maria Gilissen and Benjamin H.D. Buchloh (eds), *Marcel Broodthaers, Section Publicité du Musée d'art Moderne, Département des Aigles* (exh. cat.), Marian Goodman Gallery, New York, 1995.

292 *Documenta 5*, *op. cit.*, section 1, p.9. 'Museen von Künstlern', Artists: Broodthaers, Distel, Duchamp, Oldenburg and Ben.

293 Szeemann in conversation with the author, *op. cit.*

294 Schneckenburger, *Documenta*, *op. cit.*, p.111.

295 Document entitled 'Stand der documenta 5-Verkäufe' dated

were regularly presented in the exhibition centre. No less than 191 exhibitors participated in the 1972 IKI. Bischofberger and Friedrich were again the dealers who exhibited some Conceptual artists (Broodthaers, LeWitt, Kosuth).[317] The success of the IKI in Düsseldorf was overwhelming, with 35,000 visitors and an income of DM 14 million.[318]

Jan Dibbets, Stedelijk Museum, Amsterdam

In October 1972, a major solo show of Dibbets opened at the Stedelijk Museum, Amsterdam.[319] After his December 1971 show in Eindhoven, this was his second one-man show in a Dutch museum.[320] Seventy-nine works from the late 1960s up to 1972 were exhibited. The Conceptual network was extensively used to set up the show. Artworks, advice on the organisation of the exhibition and information for the catalogue were sought from private collectors such as Herman and Henriette van Eelen, the Vissers and Panza, and dealers such as Spillemaeckers, Fischer, Wendler, Yvon Lambert, Sperone and Art & Project.[321] Dibbets had a solo show at the MTL gallery in Brussels at the same time.[322]

Douglas Huebler, Münster

In December 1972, a solo show of Huebler opened at the Kunstverein in Münster.[323] It comprised about 30 works from the late 1960s to 1972, including *Site Sculpture, Project Windham* (1968). It seems that the show was conceived by Honnef, negotiating directly with the artist, because the pieces were sent to Münster from America by Huebler.[324]

Paris art world

The Paris art world developed significantly at this time. In December 1972, Daniel Templon co-founded, with his partner Catherine Millet (born 1948), the magazine *Art Press*, which became an important theoretical forum for contemporary art. The magazine not only focused on art, but on all expressions of avant-garde culture and progressive ideas. A militant and intellectual publication for the French intelligentsia, *Art Press* had close links with Philippe Sollers's

4 September 1972, in Box 10-d5, HSAM.

296 Szeemann in conversation with the author, *op. cit.*

297 This was notably the case for the Tate Gallery, as we will see in Chapter 5.4.

298 See, for instance, De Decker's comments, in 'Interview Yves Aupetitallot, Anny De Decker, Bernd Lohaus', in Aupetitallot, *Wide White Space*, *op. cit.*, pp.66–67. See also: Honnef in conversation with the author, *op. cit.*

299 This was LeWitt's first solo show at MTL. *Sol LeWitt, Wall Drawings*, Galerie MTL, Brussels, 5 July–26 September 1972. Simultaneously, LeWitt had a solo show presenting wall drawings at Konrad Fischer (September–October 1972) and an *Art & Project Bulletin* mailing (*Art & Project Bulletin*, no.60, 25 September 1972). See: Database 3, Section Sol LeWitt (Appendix 1.3).

300 See: Database 1, Section Fischer, Maenz, Wide White Space, MTL, Yvon Lambert, Gian Enzo Sperone and Wendler (Appendix 1.1).

301 *The New Art*, Hayward Gallery, London, 17 August–24 September 1972. Artists: Arnatt, Art & Language, Burgin, Craig-Martin, Dye, Flanagan, Fulton, Gilbert & George, Hilliard, Long, Milow, Newman, Stezaker and Tremlett.

302 *The New Art* (exh. cat.), Hayward Gallery and the Arts Council of Great Britain, London, 1972, p.5. See also: Rudi H. Fuchs, 'More on The New Art', *Studio International*, vol.184, no.949, November 1972, pp.194–195.

303 For a discussion of Anne Seymour's choice of artists, see: William Wood, 'Still You Ask for More: Demand, Display and 'The New Art'', in Newman and Bird, *Rewriting Conceptual Art*, *op. cit.*, pp.66–87.

304 Morris, 'Norwich November 2000', in Moseley, *Conception*, *op. cit.*, p.141. She also recalls Schum was in London at the time of the opening to prepare new videos with Gilbert & George. The works were presented in September 1972 at Nigel Greenwood's gallery

literature magazine *Tel Quel* and defended sexual liberty and Marxist ideology.[325] The first issue contained the publication in French of Kosuth's 'Art after Philosophy', marking the beginning of the French intellectuals' interest in art theory.[326]

A new gallery opened in Paris. The space, which changed its name for every exhibition (Galerie 1, Galerie 2, etc.), was launched by Anka Ptaszkowska, who had previously worked at the Galerie Foksal in Warsaw.[327] She was close to a group of French artists and theorists, including Buren, Toroni, Claura, Denizot and Sers. Ptaszkowska was befriended by De Decker and Lohaus, whom she met at the 3e Salon International des Galeries Pilotes in Lausanne in 1970.[328] She exhibited artists such as Jacques Charlier and André Cadere (March–April 1973), Peter Downsbrough (May 1973) and Bernd Lohaus (December 1973).

Gian Enzo Sperone & Konrad Fischer, Rome

In December 1972, Fischer and Sperone took a further step in their collaboration by launching a joint gallery in Rome. Gian Enzo Sperone & Konrad Fischer opened with a Gilbert & George exhibition on 7 December 1972 (Piazza Ss. Apostoli).[329] A series of charcoal drawings were shown and the artists performed a 'Living Sculpture' at the opening in front of 'a public of Turin and Rome artists and collectors'.[330] In September–October 1972, Gilbert & George had two solo shows (at Nigel Greenwood and at MTL), at which they presented their new videos.[331] In late 1972, they had two further exhibitions at Nigel Greenwood (photographic works) and at Art & Project, Amsterdam.[332]

Sperone wanted to open a gallery in the Italian capital in order to widen his circle of collectors and to avoid an identification of his gallery with the Turin art scene.[333] He also wanted to have a space for Conceptual art in a city in which other galleries such as the Galleria La Tartaruga, L'Attico (Fabio Sargentini) and Salita were increasingly showing artists of this type.[334] Sperone had talked to Fischer about his project for some time. He finally managed to convince the German dealer to join him in this gallery during the 1972 Cologne Art Fair.

The second show organised at the common gallery was a solo show of Kosuth,

(*Gordon's Makes Us Drunk, In the Bush, A Portrait of the Artists as Young Men*). See: Groos, Hess and Wevers, *Ready to Shoot*, *op. cit.*, pp.280–285.

305 *The Book as Art Work 1960–1972*, Nigel Greenwood Inc. Ltd., 20 September–14 October 1972. Artists: Acconci, Agnetti, Andre, Anselmo, Art & Language, Atkinson, Ayo, Bainbridge, Baldessari, Baldwin, Barry, Baruchello, Becher, Ben, Beuys, Blackwell, Blake, Bochner, Boshier, Boyle, Brecht, Bremer, Brogger, Broodthaers, Brouwn, Buren, Burgin, Burgy, Burn, Byars, Cage, Carlin, Castillejo, Chiari, Christo, Collins, Corner, Costa, Crane, Croce, Cunningham, Cutforth, Darboven, De Maria, Dibbets, Fabbris, Fahlstrom, Ferguson, Filliou, Fisher, Fluxus, Flynt, Forti, Fulton, Gilbert & George, Giorno, D. Graham, R. Graham, Greco, Gregory, Hamilton, Harrison, Harvey, Hemsworth, Hidalgo, Higgins, Huebler, Hurrell, Iannone, Jackson, Jennings, Johnson, Kaltenbach, Kahn, Kaprow, Knowles, Kosuth, Lamelas, La Monte Young, Lang, Latham, Lewis, Lole, Long, LeWitt, Maclow, Maloney, Manzoni, Marcelle, Marchetti, Maxfield, McLean, Merz, Morris, Nauman, N.E. Thing Co., Oldenburg, Ono, Oppenheim, Paik, Paolini, Paolozzi, Patterson, Penone, Phillips, Pilkington, Pistoletto, Prini, Ramsden, Riley, Roehr, Rot, Rothenberg, Ruppersberg, Ruscha, Rushton, Safro, Smith, Sonnier, Spiller, Spoerri, Staeck, Stezaker, Tacha, Titus-Carmel, Tuttle, Vautier, Van Elk, Venet, Vostell, Walther, Warhol, Watts, Weiner, Williams, Wolff and Zazeela. In November–December 1971, Lamelas had already organised an exhibition as an artist's book for the Greenwood gallery, *Publication (Arnatt, Barry, Brouwn, Buren, Burgin, Claura, Gilbert & George, Latham, Lippard, Maloney, Reise, Weiner).*

306 Celant, 'Book as Artwork 1960/1970', *Data*, *op. cit.*

307 Morris in conversation with the author.

308 See: Germano Celant (ed.), *The Book as Art Work 1960–1972* (exh. cat.), Nigel Greenwood Inc. Ltd, London, 1972, pp.32–47.

309 See: Morris, 'Norwich July 2000', in Moseley, *Conception*,

an artist represented by Sperone since 1969.[335] It opened on 21 December 1972. This exhibition presenting the 'Second Proposition' of the artist's *9th Investigation*, was a direct continuation of the 'First Proposition', presented shortly before at Leo Castelli, New York (4–25 November 1972).

The programme of the Rome gallery focused on the key artists of both galleries, with an emphasis on Conceptual art and Arte Povera.[336] The third show of the gallery presented works by artists from both galleries, including Andre and Long, Anselmo and Art & Language.[337]

Major Conceptual art group exhibitions and solo shows were organised all over the continent, in temporary exhibition spaces and in museums, including Mönchengladbach, Münster, The Hague, Amsterdam, Eindhoven, Lucerne and Oxford. The network of Conceptual art had expanded to include the public sector.

3.4 From 1973 onwards

From 1973, the dealers' network developed further, bringing about the opening of new and existing gallery branches. The Belgian, Italian and Swiss markets all expanded significantly. At the same time, shared dealer galleries were launched; dealers were forced to join ranks due to the financial consequence of the oil crisis. Indeed, in 1973, the first oil crisis engendered a rate of inflation that had repercussions for all Western economies and for the art market.[338]

Belgian art world

In early 1973, several Belgian dealer galleries opened Le Bailli, small 'shop windows' in a covered passage between the Avenue Louise and the Rue du Bailli in Brussels, incorporating MTL, Wide White Space and Galerie D. They were later joined by Paul Maenz, Galerie Oppenheim and Plus Kern. Anny De Decker recalls:

op. cit., p.141.

310 *Ibid.*

311 'Kunst als Boek', Stedelijk Museum, Amsterdam, 16 December–7 January 1972.

312 Minutes of the Organisation's extraordinary meeting in Cologne dated 6 September 1972 (außerordentliche Mitgliederversammlung des Vereins progressiver deutscher Kunsthändler), in File A72 IV 3, Zadik.

313 '6. Kölner Kunstmarkt 1972, Cologne Art Fair 1972, Cologne Foire d'Art 1972', Kunsthalle and Kunstverein, Cologne, 3–8 October 1972.

314 See: *6. Kölner Kunstmarkt 1972* (exh. cat.), Cologne, 1972, unnumbered pages.

315 Statistics of the 1972 art fair, in CD-Rom, 'Kunstmarkt Köln '67', *Sediment*, *op. cit.*

316 IKI, Internationaler Markt für aktuelle Kunst 1972, Neues Messegelände, Düsseldorf, 6–11 Oktober 1972.

317 *IKI, Internationaler Markt für aktuelle Kunst 1972, Düsseldorf* (exh. cat.), Düsseldorf, 1972, unnumbered pages.

318 Brigitte Jacobs, 'Im Spannungsfeld zwischen Kunstelite und Populärkultur. Der Kölner Kunstmarkt und seine Gegen- und Konkurrenzveranstaltungen in der Medienkritik', *Sediment*, Zadik, Cologne, no.6, 2003, p.34. See also: 'Die Kunst im Olympiajahr 1972', in Rattemeyer and Penzinger, *20 Jahre Kunstmarkt 1967–1986*, *op. cit.*, unnumbered pages.

319 *Jan Dibbets*, Stedelijk Museum, Amsterdam, 18 November–14 January 1973. The show did not travel, although the Walker Art Center, Minneapolis, for example, was interested. See: Letter from Edy de Wilde to Martin Friedman, Walker Art Center, Minneapolis, dated 1 September 1972, in Box 153, Tentoonstellingen 1972, ASMA.

320 See: Database 3, Section Jan Dibbets (Appendix 1.3).

321 See: Correspondence kept in Box 153, Tentoonstellingen 1972,

> It was Spillemaeckers who told me there were two of them in that gallery and that they did openings together. He asked us if we'd like to join them. I told myself that if they were doing things together, I had to be there; otherwise, I'd be forgotten ... So I hired a space, then Paul Maenz came along a few months afterwards and also the Plus Kern gallery and the Galerie Oppenheim (Dadaism and Russian Constructivism) ... I took part in Le Bailli, but basically I lost a huge amount of energy in it. It didn't really bring much to the gallery. I sold a few pieces, but I would have sold them in Antwerp anyway. But I'd convinced myself I had to be there, because everything happens in Brussels and no one comes to Antwerp.[339]

Le Bailli created a dynamic around contemporary art in Brussels and attracted many people because the openings took place at the same time. The rear wall of the passage was rented by the private collector Herman Daled and made available to Buren. He used it for a work of striped papers that was produced in a different colour for each show.[340]

In Antwerp, MTL and Art & Project also opened a shared dealer gallery in September 1973, Art & Project/MTL (Mechelsesteenweg) to create more business opportunities. Antwerp was chosen because it was conveniently situated between Belgium and Holland, and private collectors in both countries were important.[341] The common space hosted solo shows of artists from the two galleries, such as LeWitt and Gilbert & George.[342]

Palais des Beaux-Arts, Brussels

In the 1960s and 1970s, Belgian public institutions were not that involved with international contemporary art. The main problem was the dependence of national museums on the government and the lack of financial subsidy. The institutions' budgets were minimal, which led to a preference for national art.[343] Very few institutions bought international works of art, except the Association of the Museum of Contemporary Art in Gent, which opened in 1975.[344]

In 1973–74, the Palais des Beaux-Arts in Brussels hosted some of the first museum exhibitions of Conceptual artists in Belgium. This happened mainly through the instigation of Yves Gevaert, the assistant to the Director Jan van Lerberghe since 1968. Although Van Lerberghe was rather traditional in his way

ASMA.

322 *Jan Dibbets*, Galerie MTL, Brussels, 18 October 1972–14 January 1973.

323 *Douglas Huebler*, Kunstverein, Münster, 17 December 1972–28 January 1973.

324 Letter from Huebler to Honnef dated 30 September 1972, and Letter from Honnef to Huebler dated 11 October 1972, in File 802/368, AKMWAM. See also: *Douglas Huebler* (exh. cat.), Westfälischer Kunstverein, Münster, 1972, unnumbered pages.

325 See: Annick Colonna-Césari, 'Art Press 30 ans après', *L'Express*, 15 December 2002.

326 Joseph Kosuth, 'Art after Philosophy', *Art Press*, no.1, December 1972–January 1973.

327 See: 'Anka Ptaszkowska', *Ohm, Un petit journal de l'art contemporain*, L'école régionale des beaux-arts Caen la mer, Caen, no.22, February 2004. The avant-garde Galerie Foksal had been founded in 1966 by the critics Wieslaw Borowski, Mariusz Tchorek and Anka Ptaszkowska.

328 De Decker in conversation with the author, *op. cit.* See: *3e Salon international des Galeries-Pilotes* (brochure), Lausanne, 1970, in File 'Fonds divers: Documentation presse WWS, Anvers', AACBB.

329 *A New Sculpture by Gilbert & George*, Gian Enzo Sperone & Konrad Fischer, Rome, starting 7 December 1972. See: Minola, Mundici, Poli and Roberto, *Gian Enzo Sperone*, *op. cit.*, pp.46–216. For an overview of the exhibitions of Conceptual artists organised at Sperone & Fischer in Rome, see: Database 1, Section Gian Enzo

of directing the museum, he was curious about contemporary art. Thus he sent Gevaert to make reports on the *Minimal Art* exhibition in The Hague in 1968 and on Broodthaers's solo show at the Kunsthalle Düsseldorf in 1972. When Van Lerberghe was fired in 1973 due to the theft of a painting, there was an administrative vacuum that Gevaert filled until the arrival of the new Director, Karel Geirlandt, in 1974.[345]

The first event that Gevaert arranged was a show of Belgian artists: *Marcel Broodthaers, Jacques Charlier, Jef Geys, Bernd Lohaus, Guy Mees, Panamarenko, Maurice Roquet* in May–June 1973.[346] The artists were invited to realise site-specific works in relation to a particular wall rather than a whole room. Broodthaers's work, *Miroir d'Epoque Regency* (1973), a convex mirror in a gilded wood frame, was acquired by the Friends of the Museum of Gent.[347]

In January–February 1974, the Palais des Beaux-Arts hosted a major Conceptual art group show, presenting works by Andre, Broodthaers, Buren, Burgin, Gilbert & George, On Kawara, Long and Richter.[348] Every artist chose a room and realised a work in situ and a work for the catalogue. Broodthaers' *Jardin d'Hiver* (1974), an installation based on a winter garden and a museum of natural history, occupied a whole room.[349] The show was accompanied by conferences and talks, notably by Buren, Burgin and Andre.

Following these two group shows, Gevaert worked on several solo shows of Conceptual artists in 1974, including Ryman, Darboven, LeWitt and Broodthaers.[350] In autumn 1974, Karel Geirlandt was appointed the new Director of the Palais des Beaux-Arts. Geirlandt's appointment meant that Gevaert no longer determined the exhibition programme on his own.[351]

However, in 1975, Gevaert arranged an exhibition of both Charlier and Kawara.[352] Charlier's show was a room full of photographs of the openings of the main art events in Belgium and neighbouring countries in 1974, such as LeWitt's opening at the Stedelijk Museum Amsterdam and the Cologne Kunstmarkt.[353] The catalogue was a collection of photographs taken by Charlier at his own opening. It includes photographs of art world people – Fischer, Benjamin Buchloh, Annick and Anton Herbert, Lynda Morris, Cadere and Peter Downsbrough – looking at photographs of themselves at various openings.[354] Charlier stated that he wanted to show how the art world of the time functioned.[355]

Sperone, exhibitions followed by (R) (Appendix 1.1).

330 *Ibid.*, p.51.

331 *Gilbert & George, Videos*, Nigel Greenwood Inc. Ltd., London, starting 27 September 1972. *Gilbert & George, Videos*, Galerie MTL, Brussels, October 1972. This was the artists' first exhibition in Brussels.

332 *The Morning Before the Morning After*, Nigel Greenwood Inc. Ltd., London, 20 November–December 1972. *Gilbert & George*, Art & Project, Amsterdam, Winter 1972. See: *Art & Project Bulletin*, no.66, 1972. See also: Database 3, Section Gilbert & George (Appendix 1.3).

333 Minola, Mundici, Poli and Roberto, *Gian Enzo Sperone*, *op. cit.*, pp.49–50.

334 On this, see: Daniela Lancioni (ed.), *Roma in mostra 1970–1979, Materiali per la documentazione di mostre azioni performance dibatti* (exh. cat.), Palazzo delle Esposizioni, Rome; Edizioni Joyce and Co., Rome, 1995.

335 *Joseph Kosuth, The 9th Investigation, Proposition 2*, Gian Enzo Sperone & Konrad Fischer, Rome, starting 21 December 1972. See: Minola, Mundici, Poli and Roberto, *Gian Enzo Sperone*, *op. cit.*, p.218.

336 The announcement card comprised a list with the following artists: Andre, Anselmo, Art & Language, Baldessari, Barry, Becher, Boetti, Buren, Darboven, Dibbets, Flavin, Fulton, Gilbert & George, Griffa, Huebler, Judd, LeWitt, Long, Kawara, Kosuth, Marden, Merz, Nauman, Paolini, Penone, Pisani, Pistoletto, Ruthenbeck, Richter, Ryman, Salvo, Twombly, Zorio, Wegman and Weiner. See: *Ibid.*, p.214.

337 Group Show: Andre, Anselmo, Art & Language, Barry, Boetti,

Deurle 11/7/73

In March 1973, Spillemaeckers, together with De Decker and Maenz, decided to arrange a public discussion between artists in conjunction with a related exhibition at which these artists (and others) could present their work. The symposium, 'L'art et son contexte culturel' (Art and its cultural context) was held at La Cambre, a school of art, design and architecture in Brussels from 1–3 July 1973.[356] Conceptual artists such as Andre, Art & Language, Broodthaers, Buren, Cadere, Haacke, LeWitt, Toroni and Weiner took part. It was intended that the symposium should be complemented by an exhibition and a publication of artists' texts.

An exhibition of Conceptual artists, including those who had taken part in the congress, was set up at the Museum Dhont-Dhaenens in Deurle.[357] It was intended that the show would include a LeWitt wall drawing, an installation by Buren and objects by Broodthaers.[358] However, due to organisational problems the exhibition was cancelled just before the opening.[359] Subsequently, Spillemaeckers decided to present the documentation, texts and artworks that existed in printed form in black folders on tables in one room of the museum.[360] A *Barre de bois rond* (Round Bar of Wood) by Cadere was the only physical artwork to be exhibited.

Spillemaeckers also had the artists' texts published in a booklet.[361] A controversy over the legitimacy of this publication broke out between Spillemaeckers on one side, and De Decker and Maenz on the other. There were also tensions between Buren and Cadere, who had not been officially invited. Buren did not want Cadere to take part in the show, since he was irritated by Cadere exhibiting his *Round Bar of Wood* uninvited in other artists' shows.[362]

Italian art world

In Italy, two new dealer galleries that included Conceptual artists in their programme opened in 1973. Massimo Minini launched a gallery Banco in Brescia (Lombardy), showing Conceptual and Arte Povera artists (Buren, Burgin, Clemente, Salvo). In the south of the country, Marilena Bonomo started her space in Bari (Puglia), exhibiting artists such as LeWitt and Boetti.

Buren, Darboven, Dibbets, Fulton, Gilbert & George, Huebler, Kosuth, LeWitt, Long, Nauman, Paolini, Penone, Pisani, Ryman, Weiner, Gian Enzo Sperone & Konrad Fischer, Rome, starting 1 February 1973. See: *Ibid.*, p.492. The collaboration between Sperone and Fischer in Rome ended in Autumn 1974.

338 In October 1973, the ongoing Yom Kippur War, opposing Israel to Syria and Egypt, pushed the Organisation of Arab Petroleum Exporting Countries (OPEC) to use petrol as a weapon. They decided to limit their exports to the countries supporting Israel, i.e. the United States and its allies in Western Europe. Moreover, OPEC members agreed to use their influence on the world price-setting mechanism for oil to quadruple oil prices. Due to the dependence of the industrialised world on OPEC oil, these price increases were dramatically inflationary to the economies of the targeted countries and provoked a crisis climate. The industrial countries, already weakened by the inflation, were forced to reduce their economic activities. A severe recession came about, which resulted in an increase in unemployment, a fall in consumption and inflation.

339 De Decker in conversation with the author, *op. cit.* (author's translation).

340 Aupetitallot, *Wide White Space*, *op. cit.*, p.307.

341 Dujourie in conversation with the author, *op. cit.*

342 For an overview of the exhibitions organised at Art & Project/MTL, see: Appendix 3.6 b. See also: 'Art & Project', *Flash Art*, no.54–55, May 1975, p.2.

343 Karel J. Geirlandt, 'Museums, collectors, policies', *Studio*

Contemporanea

In November 1973, the Italian critic and curator Achille Bonito Oliva (born 1939) arranged the first group show in Italy with an international perspective in an underground garage in Rome. *Contemporanea* traced the developments in art since the 1950s, presenting Conceptualism in the continuity of previous international art movements.[363] *Contemporanea* included works by European and American artists, such as Merz and Beuys, George Segal and Donald Judd. The show was part of the Incontri Internazionali d'Arte (International Art Meetings) in Rome,[364] which involved cinema, theatre, architecture and a section dedicated to artists' books and records curated by Yvon Lambert and Michel Claura. This international show was a great success, attracting more than 100,000 visitors.[365]

Public discussions on the state of the contemporary art world were held in Italy at this time. In April 1975, a debate on the European and American art worlds, particularly aspects of the market and collections, was held at the Centro Informazione Alternativa degli Incontri Internatzionali. Participants included Bonito Oliva, Maurizio Calvesi, Filiberto Menna, Carlo Arturo Quintavalle and Tommaso Trini.[366]

Swiss art world

In Switzerland, the second half of the 1970s was marked by the increasing importance of Art Basel. It grew to be a mammoth event, with 270 exhibitors in 1973 presenting some 2,000 artists.[367] But the unlimited number of exhibitors and the continuous growth of the fair was increasingly criticised. Many believed that the situation was spiralling out of control, with too many fairs all over Europe.[368] This backfired on the dealers themselves, since many collectors only came to the fairs once a year, and no longer took the time to visit individual galleries. In some countries such as Germany, due to inflation, monetary restrictions slowed down the availability of cash, consequently reducing the turnover of most art fairs.[369]

Art Basel had the advantage of being outside the European Community. In 1976–77, the Swiss Parliament decided not to tax the transaction of works of art on the basis of turnover, but on the difference between cost and profit. This had immediate repercussions in the market and favoured Swiss dealers.[370]

International, vol.188, no.970, October 1974, p.115.

344 The Association of the Museum of Contemporary Art in Gent was founded in 1957 under the initiative of Karel Geirlandt. Its ambition was to put together a collection of international contemporary art for a future museum. The Gent museum opened in 1975 under the directorship of Jan Hot. It was the first institution in Belgium to be dedicated to contemporary art.

345 Gevaert in conversation with the author, *op. cit.*

346 *Marcel Broodthaers, Jacques Charlier, Jef Geys, Bernd Lohaus, Guy Mees, Panamarenko, Maurice Roquet*, Palais des Beaux-Arts, Brussels, 25 May–24 June 1973. The show toured to MOMA, Oxford from 30 June to 4 August 1974.

347 Gevaert in conversation with the author, op. cit. See also: Michael Baudson and Yves Gevaert, 'Aspects of the Avant-Garde in Belgium', *Studio International*, vol.188, no.970, October 1974, pp.142–143.

348 *Carl Andre, Marcel Broodthaers, Daniel Buren, Victor Burgin, Gilbert & George, On Kawara, Richard Long and Gerhard Richter*, Palais des Beaux-Arts, Brussels, 9 January–3 February 1974. See: *Carl Andre, Marcel Broodthaers, Daniel Buren, Victor Burgin, Gilbert & George, On Kawara, Richard Long and Gerhard Richter* (exh. cat.), Palais des Beaux-Arts, Brussels, 1974. See: Barbara Reise, ''Incredible' Belgium: Impressions', *Studio International*, vol.188, no.970, October 1974, pp.117–118.

349 According to Yves Gevaert, Broodthaers refused to allow Buren to use the ceiling of his room. He also put a red carpet at the entry to

In the second half of the 1970s, several new dealer galleries opened in Switzerland. Ileana Sonnabend opened a branch in Geneva (rue Etienne Dumont) in April 1974. The inaugural exhibition was dedicated to Robert Rauschenberg and the gallery programme focused on Pop artists. It closed down a year later in March 1975.

One can also mention Johannes Gachnang (1939–2005) and his work at the Kunsthalle Bern, which he directed from 1974 onwards. He organised exhibitions of Andre (1975), Judd (1976) and Long (1977).

Rolf Preisig

Except for a few shows at Bruno Bischofberger in Zürich, Conceptual artists were not really represented by dealer galleries in Switzerland. On 23 November 1973, Rolf Preisig opened a gallery in Basel (Wettsteinallee) with a show of Stanley Brouwn.[371] Preisig had previously worked in advertising. In October 1967, he moved from Basel to Düsseldorf to work for the GGK advertising company (Gerstner, Gredinger und Kutter). He arrived in Düsseldorf at the time when Fischer was launching his gallery. He befriended the dealer and later married Alfred Schmela's gallery assistant.[372]

Preisig was completely won over by Conceptual artists. He collected a few pieces before finally deciding to open his own space to show these artists in Switzerland. He explained: 'I wondered whether to go to Basel or to Zurich. As at that time the Basel Kunstmuseum was simply better – directed by the legendary Franz Meyer – and the Basel Kunsthalle was an interesting place too, I decided for Basel.'[373] As Willi Bongard highlighted in *Art Aktuell*, most of the artists that Preisig took on were represented by Fischer.[374] But Preisig clarified that there were neither contracts nor financial dependence.[375] Nevertheless, Preisig and Fischer worked closely together and even had a common stand at Art Basel in 1975 and again in 1976.

French art world

From 1973, Conceptualism was increasingly exhibited in France. The 7th Paris Biennale included a 'Concept' section organised by Nathalie Aubergé, Catherine Millet and Alfred Pacquement.[376] This included the work of European and

prevent Andre from further expanding his floor piece. There were negotiations for the purchase of the work by the museum in Gent that did not materialise. Gevaert in conversation with the author, *op. cit.*

350 'Robert Ryman' (1974), 'Hanne Darboven and Sol LeWitt' (16 May–16 June 1974) and 'Marcel Broodthaers, Catalogue/Catalogus' (27 September – 3 November 1974), Palais des Beaux-Arts, Brussels.

351 In 1976, Gevaert was dismissed. He then became a librarian, specialising in early twentieth-century books and later also a publisher of artists' books. See: *Books, Prints, Objects published by Yves Gevaert* (exh. cat.), Van Abbemuseum, Eindhoven, 1992.

352 *Vernissage des Expositions, Jacques Charlier, On Kawara*, Palais des Beaux-Arts, Brussels, 7 January–21 February 1975. On Kawara's show, presenting his 1973 'Date Paintings', was previously shown at the Kunsthalle, Bern, where it had been conceived by Kasper König and Johannes Gachnang.

353 The photographed events were the *4e foire d'art actuel, Knokke, Projekt, Köln, Sol LeWitt, Darboven, Finlande, Palais des Beaux-Arts, Brussels, Réception chez les Daled, Vernissage Sol LeWitt, Amsterdam, Fête Karel Geirlandt, Klapheck Palais des Beaux-Arts, Brussels, Vernissage Triennale 3, Brugge, Broodthaers, Palais des Beaux-Arts, Brussels*, IKI, Düsseldorf and Kunstmarkt, Köln. See: Jacques Charlier, *Dans les règles de l'art* (exh. cat.), Editions Lebeer Hossmann, Brussels, 1983, p.81.

354 *Vernissage des Expositions J. Charlier, On Kawara* (exh. cat.), Société des expositions du Palais des Beaux-Arts, Brussels, 1975.

355 Jacques Charlier in conversation with the author, Luxembourg,

American Conceptual artists, many of whom were represented by Templon: Art & Language, Barry, Darboven, Dimitrijevic, Kosuth, Christine Kozlov, Lamelas, Ramsden and Bernar Venet.

16 Place Vendôme

In 1973, there was a revival of interest in painting in Europe. In Paris, in June–July, Michel Claura and René Denizot organised *16 Place Vendôme, Paris, Mai–Juin 1973 (exposition de peinture réunissant certains peintres qui mettraient la peinture en question)* (exhibition of painting bringing together painters that supposedly question painting).[377] The exhibition was also shown by the Städtisches Museum in Mönchengladbach (November–December 1973),[378] the Kaiser Wilhelm Museum, Krefeld (January–February 1974) and at the Internationaal Cultureel Centrum (ICC), Antwerp (9 March–7 April 1974), directed by Florent Bex.

Michel and Liliane Durand-Dessert

Until the mid-1970s, Yvon Lambert was the central dealer for Conceptual art in Paris. Nevertheless Ileana Sonnabend (from 1968), Daniel Templon (from 1970) and Anka Ptaszkowska (from 1972) also exhibited Conceptual artists.

In October 1975, Michel and Liliane Durand-Dessert launched a dealer gallery in Paris (rue de Montmorency) with an exhibition of sculpture by the German artist Ulrich Rückriem.[379] They exhibited many Conceptual artists, for example, Kosuth (January–February 1976), Darboven (May 1976), Tremlett (June–July 1976), Charlton (February–April 1977), Wilson (May 1977) and Anselmo (April–June 1978).[380] Their exhibition programme was modelled on that of Fischer.[381] Fischer and Wide White Space were the dealer galleries that interested them the most, but they were also in contact with Maenz and Friedrich.[382]

In the early 1970s, the Durand-Desserts had started to collect contemporary art. Liliane was then a professor of French literature, while Michel worked in the advertising industry. They also acted as editors for *Multiplicata* and published artists' books by French artists such as Boltanski, LeGac and Buren, and European artists like Acconci and Broodthaers, all of whom they would later represent in their gallery.

5 October 2005, digital recording (Appendix 4.2).

356 *L'art et son contexte culturel*, La Cambre, Brussels, 1–3 July 1973. La Cambre was founded by Henri van de Velde in 1926.

357 *Deurle 11/7/73*, Museum Dhont-Dhaenens, Deurle, 11 July–8 August 1974. Artists: Andre, Baldessari, Barry, Broodthaers, Burgin, Burn, Ramsden, Cadere, Graham, Huebler, Kosuth, LeWitt, Ryman, Romeu, Weiner, Wilson. *Deurle 11/7/73* was restaged from 18 January to 29 February 2004 at the Museum Dhont-Dhaenens. It was accompanied by a symposium bringing together Jacques Charlier, Edith Doove, Anton Herbert, Roger Matthys, Johan Pas and Johan van Steenkiste. See: 'Deurle 11/7/73', in *MDD Jaarcatalogus 2004*, Museum Dhont-Dhaenens, Deurle, 2004, pp.4–17.

358 Johan van Steenkiste, 'Verslag debat Deurle 11/7/73 – op zoek naar het Geheugen van de Kunst in de Jaren Zeventig', leaflet, Museum Dhont-Dhaenens, Deurle, 2004.

359 However, the invitations had already been sent out and some people had not been told that the show was cancelled. Thus Annick and Anton Herbert went to the cancelled opening, where they got to know Fernand Spillemaeckers. Annick and Anton Herbert in conversation with the author, *op. cit.*

360 Already in 1970, Fernand Spillemaeckers had organised an exhibition of texts by philosophers, critics and artists in the Café Celbeton in Dendermonde (Barthes, Derrida, Athusser, Claura, Denizot, Buren). The texts were exhibited in the café; they had also been recorded on tape.

361 *Deurle 11/7/73* (exh. cat.), Galerie MTL, Brussels, 1973.

In the late 1970s, the opening of the Centre George Pompidou in Paris in 1977, under the directorship of Pontus Hulten, was an important event.[383] The museum had several Conceptual works in its permanent collection, such as Kosuth's *One and Three Chairs* (1965) and Gilbert & George's *Le Bar no.1* (1972), both acquired by the French state in 1974 and 1975 respectively.[384]

German art world

From 1973, the German art world organised a number of major group shows of Conceptual artists.

Cologne Art Fair and IKI

In September–October 1973, the Cologne and Düsseldorf Kunstmarkts took place at the same time.[385] VPDK wanted to renew the Cologne Kunstmarkt to compete with other events. It became possible for members to participate in other fairs on the condition that they showed completely different work. The focus of the Kunstmarkt remained international, thereby continuing to deny IKI's earlier claim to uniqueness among German fairs. Each German dealer was in charge of one or several international guests. For instance, in 1973, Fischer invited Sperone, Maenz invited Art & Project and Yvon Lambert, and the Galerie Reckermann invited John Weber.[386]

VPDK developed its catalogue, adding texts by several dealers to the listing of the galleries.[387] It also founded a prize awarded to members of the international art world for their work in the service of contemporary art.[388] These changes, however, did not manage to boost the Kunstmarkt. It comprised about 100 stalls, but the number of visitors did not grow significantly (30,000) and its turnover dropped to DM2.5 million.[389] In comparison, the IKI had 300 stalls and its turnover was DM14 million.[390]

A major event that occurred in October 1973 was that the VPDK became part of the Europäische Kunsthändlervereinigung (EK, European Art Dealers' Association). This new association was founded in Zurich by German and Swiss dealers: Bischofberger, Brusberg, Emmerich, Huber, Neuendorf, Stünke and Zwirner.[391] By creating this European association, they wanted to win over international dealer galleries. Moreover, the association was a support structure

362 De Decker in conversation with the author, *op. cit.* See: 'Controversy on Bruxelles, Letters and Answers', *Flash Art*, no.43, December 1973–January 1974, p.6, and 'Deurle', *Flash Art*, no.44–45, February–May 1974, p.32.

363 'Contemporanea', Parking of the Villa Borghese, Rome, 30 November 1973–28 February 1974. Artists: Acconci, Agnetti, Andre, Anselmo, Arman, Art & Language, Baldessari, Barry, Baumgarten, Becher, Beuys, Bochner, Boetti, Buren, Burgin, Brecht, Broodthaers, Cane, Castellani, Chiari, Christo, Darboven, De Dominicis, De Maria, Dibbets, Dine, Fabro, Festa, Filliou, Flavin, Fulton, Gilbert & George, Griffa, Haacke, Hamilton, Heizer, Huebler, Johns, Judd, Kaprow, Kounellis, Kawara, Kelly, Klein, Kosuth, LeWitt, Lichtenstein, Long, Lo Savio, Lüthi, Maciunas, Mangold, Manzoni, Marden, Martin, Merz, Morris, Nauman, Newman, Noland, Oldenburg, Opalka, Palermo, Paolini, Pascali, Pisani, Pistoletto, Prini, Rauschenberg, Reinhardt, Richter, Rokburne, Rosenquist, Rotella, Ryman, Schifano, Segal, Serra, Simonetti, Sonnier, Spoerri, Stella, Tinguely, Tuttle, Twombly, Vautier, Vostell, Warhol, Watts, Weiner, Whitman and Ian Wilson.

364 The Incontri Internazionali d'Arte was a cultural association created and directed by Graziella Lonardi with the contribution of Bonito Oliva. See: *Contemporanea* (exh. cat.), Incontri Internationali d'Arte, Centro Di, Rome, 1973.

365 Achille Bonito Oliva, 'Contemporanea', in Hegewisch and Klüser, *L'art de l'exposition*, *op. cit.*, p.409.

366 'Europa-America', *Art Dimension*, no.2, April–June 1975, pp.3–28.

providing assistance in case of theft, information on customs and tax, and advice on legal matters. Its aim was to ease the organisation of art fairs and to organise its own event that could possibly replace the Cologne Kunstmarkt.[392]

Prospect 73

Leading the trend of a renewed interest in painting, Prospect 73 was dedicated to painters and subtitled 'Malers Painters Peintres'.[393] The aim was not to provide a 'preview' of the latest developments in art, but to propose a survey of painting from the last 15 years, including canvases by Roy Lichtenstein and Ellsworth Kelly. The intention to trace a continuity from Abstract Expressionism to Pop art to Minimal painting was reinforced by the first European screening of Emile de Antonio's film *Painters Painting, The New York Art Scene 1940–1970* (1972), which included interviews with artists such as De Kooning, Johns, Stella and Warhol.

Thus Prospect 73 presented a panorama of modern and contemporary paintings and not the current tendencies. The event received much criticism.[394] Both Rosetta Brooks and Georg Jappe suggested that this renewed interest in painting was provoked mainly by dealers' interests.[395] Indeed, Prospect 73 took place at the same time as the Cologne Art Fair and the IKI Düsseldorf, clearly positioning the event within the art market.[396] Moreover, by 'going back' to painting, Prospect seemed to lose sight of its idealistic origin, and became just 'one prospectus among others'.[397]

However, the aim of the organisers of Prospect 73 (Fischer, Harten, Strelow and Evelyn Weiss) was to introduce Minimal painting to a European audience. Until 1973, Minimal painting was little shown in Europe, unlike sculpture, which was introduced through artists' writings (Judd, LeWitt, Morris). For instance, Yvon Lambert did not show Mangold and Marden until 1973. The same year, Nigel Greenwood exhibited Alan Charlton for the first time. Fischer had already shown Marden in 1971 and Charlton in 1972, but he did not exhibit Mangold until 1974.[398] Lynda Morris argues that there was a distorted chronology of Minimalism in Europe due to the political unrest at Venice and Documenta in 1968 as a consequence of the Vietnam War.[399]

Furthermore it seems that the interest that Giuseppe Panza showed in Minimal painting from 1973 was an important factor for dealers.[400] At Prospect 73,

367 'Exklusiv – Interview mit dem Direktor des Kunstmuseums Basel, Dr. Franz Meyer', *Art Aktuell*, June 1973, unnumbered pages.
368 During the 1970s, more art fairs were founded, such as the Foire internationale d'art contemporain (FIAC) in Paris and the 1ier Salon international d'Art actuel in Brussels from 8–15 April 1974, which included 200 exhibitors from 15 countries.
369 Georg Jappe, 'Art fairs – vanity fairs?', *Studio International*, vol.186, no.961, December 1973, p.245.
370 'Research in Art and Public Institutions: The Dutch Case', *Flash Art*, May–June 1977, pp.14–16.
371 *Stanley Brouwn*, Galerie Rolf Preisig, Basel, 23 November–22 December 1973. For an overview of the exhibitions of Conceptual artists organised at the gallery, see: Database 1, Section Rolf Preisig (Appendix 1.1). For a listing of all the exhibitions organised by Preisig, see: Appendix 3.7.
372 Rolf Preisig in conversation with the author, Zurich, 27 October 2005, digital recording (Appendix 4.12).
373 *Ibid.* (author's translation).
374 'Rolf Preisig', *Art Aktuell*, vol. 3, no.22, 30 November 1973, p.4.
375 Preisig in conversation with the author, *op. cit.* See also: Martin Kunz, 'Der Galerist Rolf Preisig – Ein Porträt eines leisen Bahnbrechers, Er inszeniert gegen den Strich: cool', *National-Zeitung Basel*, no.404, 28 December 1976, p.25.
376 7e Biennale de Paris, Parc Floral de Vincennes, Paris, 24 September–1 November 1973.
377 *16 Place Vendôme, Paris, Mai–Juin 1973 (exposition de peinture*

several Conceptual art dealers exhibited Minimal painting, such as Fischer (Charlton, Marden, Mangold, Ryman, Richter), Friedrich (Georg Baselitz, Imi Knoebel, Palermo), Lambert (Renouf), Sperone (Giorgio Griffa) and Weber (Mangold).[401]

Projekt '74

In the summer of 1974, several Cologne institutions collaborated on a vast exhibition *Projekt '74, Aspekte internationaler Kunst am Anfang der 70er Jahre* (Aspects of Art at the Beginning of the 1970s).[402] This blockbuster was arranged by the Wallraf-Richartz Museum to celebrate its 150th anniversary. Most works were commissioned for the show.

Of 'Documenta proportions',[403] *Projekt '74* was criticised as an all encompassing event with no clear direction. It appeared to be yet another exhibition among many aiming to present a panorama of the current avant-garde. Its selection criterion was confusing, artificially mixing artists of different generations and interests in six different sections: 'Time', 'Perception', 'Formal Systems', 'Conceptual Systems', 'Video' and 'Performance'. Maenz was the leading force behind the organisation of the show.[404] Brooks complained that 'Conceptualism [had] denied its own principles' and that 'the avant-garde mentality [had] got a little bored with dematerialization'.[405] As had happened at Prospect 73, Conceptualism seemed to be tailing off. Lynda Morris offered the following summary in 1973:

> The question in most minds was the future of the big gang bang shows. There still remain unresolved money problems from Documenta 5. The Venice Biennale sank earlier this year. Contemporanea, the Roman extravaganza, froze all enthusiasm in an underground garage. The last Prospect set the seal of confusion on everyone's mind.[406]

Prospect/Retrospect

The retrospective tendency was reinforced with Prospect 76, the final show planned in the series.[407] *Prospect/Retrospect, Europa 1946–1976* was a survey exhibition of art in Europe from the postwar period to the present.[408] It documented

réunissant certains peintres qui mettraient la peinture en question), private apartment, Paris, June–July 1973. Artists: Buren, Charlton, Griffa, Lohaus, Marden, Martin, Ryman, Palermo and Toroni.

378 *Eine Malerei-Ausstellung mit Malern, die die Malerei in Frage stellen könnten*, Städtisches Museum, Mönchengladbach, 15 November–23 December 1973. See: Michel Claura and Rene Denizot, *Eine Malerei-Ausstellung mit Malern, die die Malerei in Frage stellen könnten* (exh. cat.), Städtisches Museum, Mönchengladbach, 1973. See also: Wischermann, *Johannes Cladders, op. cit.*, pp.196–199. However, it was not exactly the same show as works had to be lent from other sources, such as Konrad Fischer. See: Letter from Michel Claura to Konrad Fischer dated 3 October 1973, in File Ausstellungen: Programm Zufall System, Sieben Räume, Rückriem, Weiner, Eine Malerei Ausst., Koptische Stoffe, Jansen-Winkeln, Albers, Caumont, Mack, Richter, Dimitrijevic, Parasol Press, Dieckmann, Neugebauer [1973–75], ASMM.

379 *Ulrich Rückriem*, Galerie Durand-Dessert, Paris, 14 October–15 November 1975.

380 For an overview of the exhibitions organised by Michel and Liliane Durand-Dessert, see: *L'art au Futur antérieur, L'engagement d'une galerie, Liliane et Michel Durand-Dessert, 1975/2004* (exh. cat.), Musée de Grenoble; Actes Sud, Arles, 2004, no.1–222.

381 Guy Tosatto, 'Entretien avec Liliane et Michel Durand-Dessert', in *Ibid.*, p.14. It is said that Michel and Liliane Durand-Dessert had established business links with Konrad Fischer. Fischer recommended they contacted Morris when they went to London to research

what had happened in the visual arts over the last 30 years, and what remained significant for 1976 and for the future. Importantly, the show combined the history of art in Europe with the reception of US art in Europe.[409] The catalogue comprised a historical and chronological overview of key exhibitions that had been organised in European dealer galleries and museums. Fischer was critical of the exhibition and catalogue, saying it was for children.[410] The choice of exhibitions was seen as rather subjective, and Fischer and Strelow were accused of rewriting art history in accordance with their dealing interests.[411]

Skulptur Ausstellung in Münster and Documenta 6

With a similar intention, Klaus Bussmann and Kasper König set up an exhibition of abstract sculpture from the early twentieth century up to the present throughout the city of Münster in 1977.[412] *Skulptur Ausstellung in Münster* is a series that occurs every ten years. Bussmann was responsible for the 'historic' sculptures, while König was in charge of commissioned works by contemporary artists. The works of Oldenburg (*Giant Pool Balls*) and Judd (*Untitled*) were taken over permanently by the city. *Skulptur Ausstellung in Münster* took place at the same time as Documenta 6 in Kassel organised by the German art historian Manfred Schneckenburger.[413] The latter show had a strong emphasis on video, film and drawing.

British art world

From 1973, the British art world became increasingly involved in the international Conceptual network. Logsdail organised some of the first shows of Conceptual artists in London.[414] In December 1972–January 1973, the Lisson Gallery hosted Ryman's first British solo show. On 23 January 1973, Long's first solo show in a dealer gallery in the UK opened.[415] Logsdail recalls:

> I think my first contact with Richard Long was in 1968 or 1969. He was already quite close to Konrad. Konrad didn't really want him to show in London. I sensed that there was this kind of battle going on, where he was referring to Konrad and Konrad would say 'You don't need a London gallery, you have me!' Konrad was very like that he wanted to be the number one person for the

artists. Morris in conversation with the author.

382 *Ibid.*, pp.14–15. In London, Lynda Morris gave them key addresses and arranged studio visits on the request of Konrad Fischer. Morris in conversation with the author.

383 Pontus Hulten (1924–2006) had previously been the first Director of the Moderna Museet in Stockholm (1959–73), for which he established one of the first collections of contemporary art in Europe.

384 See: *XXe/MNAM/Collections, Une histoire matérielle*, Musée national d'art moderne; Editions du Centre Georges Pompidou, Paris, 1999, unnumbered pages. The museum does not provide access to information on the provenance of its artworks.

385 7. Kölner Kunstmarkt, Kunsthalle and Kunstverein, Cologne, 29 September–6 October 1973. IKI, 3. internationaler Markt für aktuelle Kunst, Messegelände, Düsseldorf, 29 September–7 October 1973.

386 Minutes of the Organisation's meeting in Grenzach dated 18 June 1973 (Mitgliederversammlung des Vereins progressiver deutscher Kunsthändler), in File A72 IV 3, Zadik.

387 Manfred Schneckenburger wrote a rather critical article about the Conceptual art market. See: Manfred Schneckenburger, 'Wer kauft die (fast) unsichtbare Kunst?', in *7. Kölner Kunstmarkt, 29.9–6.10.73*, Cologne, 1973, pp.28–29.

388 The 1973 winner of the award was Willem Sandberg for his work at the Stedelijk Museum, Amsterdam.

389 Statistics of the 1973 art fair, in CD-Rom, 'Kunstmarkt

artists, especially in the early days. He maintained relationships with the artists he represented and the artists would always refer to him before doing anything. Konrad turned it a little bit into a joke: 'Maybe you should show with Nigel, maybe you should show with Jack, maybe you should show with Nicholas.' So in fact, he was playing a little bit of a game. It was a kind of strange humour, it was like turning something quite serious into humour and thereby creating confusion ...

I paved the way and he kept coming to the gallery. He kept sending me postcards. This is Richard's way of saying, 'I'm paying attention to you. Don't forget me, I'm here.' What convinced Richard to do a show is that we'd started to do little artists' books. Nobody was doing artists' books. So we did a book together, which unfortunately we were all terribly amateur about as we did not have enough experience in making books. The printing wasn't very good and Richard wasn't happy with it. So we had it reprinted and it was to his liking.[416]

Later that year, in October 1973, the Lisson Gallery hosted the first show solely dedicated to Art & Language in Britain.[417] After Templon in Paris and Milan, Sperone in Turin and Rome, and Maenz in Cologne and Brussels, this was the group's third dealer in Europe.[418] The show 'consisted of statements in red ink pasted poster-like to the wall, typescripts, and material on microfiche.'[419]

Record as Artwork and *Strata*

After the *Book as Artwork* show in 1972, Celant organised *Record as Artwork* for the Royal College of Art, London, in November 1973.[420] The show presented a selection of records from the period 1959–73, from Yves Klein to Lawrence Weiner.[421] The show travelled to the Galleria Françoise Lambert, Milan, in December 1973, and to the Galerie Rolf Ricke, Cologne, in 1974. In 1977–78, Celant curated the show for several American and Canadian museums under the title *The Record as Artwork: from futurism to conceptual art*.[422]

From 14 January to 1 February 1974, the Royal College of Art Galleries hosted an exhibition entitled *Strata* with paintings, drawings and prints by Marden, Agnes Martin, Ryman, Twombly and Kelly.[423] This show was organised by Lynda Morris, who was invited by Roselee Goldberg to 'arrange a show around "Cool

Köln '67', *Sediment*, *op. cit.*

390 Rosetta Brooks, 'Prospect', *Studio International*, vol.186, no.959, November 1973, p.194.

391 Minutes of the Organisation's members meeting in Bad Soden dated 20–21 January 1973 (Mitglieder-versammlung des Vereins progressiver deutscher Kunsthändler), in File A72 IV 3, Zadik. See also: Jappe, 'Art fairs–vanity fairs?', *Studio International*, *op. cit.*, p.244.

392 See: *Ibid.*

393 Prospect 73, *Malers, Painters, Peintres*, Städtische Kunsthalle, Düsseldorf, 28 September–7 October 1973. Artists: Baer, Baselitz, Battaglia, Berghuis, Baldessari, Baselitz, Broodthaers, Cane, Charlton, Diao, Dutterer, Erben, Gertsch, Gilbert & George, Girke, Graubner, Green, Griffs, Hucleux, Humphrey, Kelly, Klapheck, Knoebel, Kosuth, Lichtenstein, Lüpertz, Mangold, Marden, Novros, Owen, Olitski, Palermo, Penck, Polke, Poons, Renouf, Richter, Ryman, Schonzeit, Tadeusz, Twombly, Verheyen, Verna, Weiner, Zenuik, Zucker.

394 See, for instance: Giancarlo Politi, 'Prospect '73, Which painting', *Flash Art*, no.43, December 1973–January 1974, p.5.

395 Brooks, 'Prospect', *Studio International*, *op. cit.*, p.194. And: Georg Jappe, 'Gemalt, dass sich die Balken biegen', *Frankfurter Allgemeine Zeitung*, 1 October 1973.

396 Introduction to *Prospect 73, Malers, Painters, Peintres* (exh. cat.), Städtische Kunsthalle Düsseldorf, 1973, unnumbered pages.

397 Buren, 'The function of an exhibition', *Studio International*, *op. cit.*, p.216.

Painting" or "back to order" art'.[424] This was a further example of the back-to-painting tendency that was emerging at this time.

Conceptual artists' museum shows

By 1973, most Conceptual artists had had solo exhibitions exhibitions in several public institutions across Europe: Broodthaers (Mönchengladbach, Düsseldorf), Buren (Mönchengladbach, Münster, Oxford), Darboven (Mönchengladbach, Münster), Dibbets (Eindhoven, Amsterdam), Gilbert & George (Amsterdam, Lucerne), Long (Mönchengladbach, Oxford), Andre (Mönchengladbach), Huebler (Oxford, Münster) and LeWitt (Oxford).

The majority of European museums had by this point organised exhibitions of Conceptual artists.[425] The Museum of Modern Art Oxford and the Stedelijk Van Abbemuseum in Eindhoven became increasingly important for the international Conceptual network. This was mainly due to the arrival of new directors in these institutions. There was also the opening of the Ludwig Museum in Cologne in 1976. The Kunstverein Münster, which had been important for Conceptual art in the early days, became less and less vital. This was mainly due to Honnef's departure for the development of the new Rheinisches Landesmuseum in Bonn from 1975.[426]

The Museum of Modern Art, Oxford

In Britain, the Museum of Modern Art in Oxford (MOMA) was the institution most engaged with Conceptualism. From March to May 1973, Ibsen arranged several shows of Conceptual artists. On 31 March a solo exhibition of Buren was held.[427] Wendler helped to organise this show, which consisted of six striped banners hung from the vaulted ceiling of the upper gallery. At the same time, the artist's work was presented in a show at Wendler's London gallery.[428]

On 28 April, two shows, one of LeWitt, the other of Huebler, were launched simultaneously at MOMA Oxford.[429] Logsdail arranged LeWitt's exhibition of wall drawings. At the same time, a solo show of wall drawings and metal structures was held at the Lisson Gallery.[430] Huebler's small retrospective was based on an exhibition organised by Honnef at the Kunstverein Münster in December 1972 to January 1973.[431]

398 See: Database 3.2 (Nigel Greenwood), Database 3.4 (Yvon Lambert) and *Ausstellungen bei Konrad Fischer*, *op. cit.*, pp.339–346.

399 Morris, 'Introduction to the Conference 'New Research into Conceptualism in Europe'', *New Research into Conceptualism in Europe*, *op. cit.*, unnumbered pages.

400 *Ibid.* Giuseppe Panza bought nearly all of the works from the Alan Charlton exhibition at Konrad Fischer in October–November 1972. See: 'The art world now is a very different place. A conversation with Alan Charlton', in Kölle, *Die Kunst des Ausstellen*, *op. cit.*, p.268.

401 Galleries: Bykert (New York), Cuningham Ward (New York) Konrad Fischer (Düsseldorf), Heiner Friedrich (Cologne), Galerie de Gestlo (Hamburg), Nancy Hoffman Gallery (New York), Annely Juda Fine Art (London), Yvon Lambert (Paris), Mikro Galerie (Berlin), Rolf Ricke (Cologne), Alfred Schmela (Düsseldorf), Gian Enzo Sperone (Turin), Hans Strelow (Düsseldorf), Pyramid Galleries (Washington), Daniel Templon (Paris), Toselli (Milan), John Weber Gallery (New York) and Michael Werner (Cologne).

402 *Projekt '74, Kunst bleibt Kunst, Aspekte internationaler Kunst am Anfang der 70er Jahre*, Wallraf-Richartz Museum, Kunsthalle Köln, Kunst- und Museumsbibliothek, Kölnischer Kunstverein, Cologne, 6 July–8 September 1974. Artists included: Acconci, Andre, Anselmo, Arakawa, Art & Language, Asher, Baldessari, Barry, Bell, Beuys, Bochner, Boltanski, Boyle, Broodthaers, Buren, Burgin, Darboven, Dekkers, De Maria, Dibbets, Dye, Fabro, Fulton, Gilbert & George, Graham, Haacke, Harrison, Heerich, Heizer, Hilliard, Huebler, Kosuth, Lamelas, LeVa, LeWitt, Long, Merz, McLean, Mochetti,

The links between the private and public sector were well established in the international network. In the early 1970s, Oxford was one of a network of major galleries in English towns, such as the Arnolfini in Bristol, the Ikon in Birmingham, the Midland Group in Nottingham and the Bluecoat in Liverpool. Its growing success was facilitated by an annual Arts Council grant, which was increased to £10,000 in 1972–73, subsequently to £12,500 in 1973–74.[432]

In July 1973, Nicholas Serota was appointed director of MOMA Oxford. For Serota, the museum in Mönchengladbach and its director, Johannes Cladders, acted as a model in terms of initiative and imagination. He explains:

> What I saw was a very small institution close to large cities, Düsseldorf and Cologne, where an individual had, by inviting the right artists, created a programme that had an internal coherence and which, through the involvement of the artists, had resulted in some memorable exhibitions. He'd also given the artists the opportunity to do something that they hadn't previously done. Cladders seemed to me, from 1966–67, to be one of the people who'd done this most strongly.[433]

Serota placed MOMA Oxford in the network of Conceptual artists through collaborations. In 1973, the Huebler show travelled there from the Kunstverein Münster. The following year, in 1974, the Darboven and *Charlier, Lohaus, Mees, Panamarenko, Roquet, Vansnick* shows were both brought over from the Palais des Beaux-Arts in Brussels, where they had been organised by Yves Gevaert.[434] Serota also presented the work of the young British artists, whom he had worked with on *The New Art* show in 1972 at the Hayward Gallery with Anne Seymour. Among those who had shows at MOMA were Fulton (1972–73), Flanagan, Tremlett (1974), Charlton, McLean and Art & Language (1975).

Under Serota's directorship, from 1973 to 1976, MOMA gained an international reputation. It became a landmark institution in the network of Conceptual artists. By 1975, the visitors at the museum had increased from 100 a week to 150 a day.[435]

Morris, Nauman, Oppenheim, Paolini, Penone, Polke, Rainer, Richter, Rückriem, Rinke, Serra, Stezaker, Weiner and Zorio.

403 Rosetta Brooks, 'Projekt '74', *Flash Art*, no.48–49, October–November 1974, p.15.

404 *Ibid.* See also: Lynda Morris, 'Projekt '74', *Studio International*, vol.188, no.969, September 1974, p.7.

405 *Ibid.*, p.8.

406 *Ibid.* However, smaller Conceptual art shows were also questioned. For example, in January–February 1974, Honnef had contributed to the setting-up of an exhibition of Conceptual artists at the Kunstverein Braunschweig. It lasted only three weeks and was considered incomplete. *Concept Art*, Kunstverein Braunschweig, 25 January–17 February 1974. Artists: Barry, Brouwn, Buren, Darboven, Dibbets, Gilbert & George, Huebler, On Kawara, Kosuth, LeWitt, Prini, Weiner and Wilson. See: *Concept Art* (exh. cat.), Kunstverein Braunschweig, 1974, unnumbered pages. See also: 'Conceptual Art', *Flash Art*, February–May 1974, p.62.

407 'Wie können wir die interessantesten Künstler in Düsseldorf zeigen ohne Geld zu haben? Ein Gespräch mit Hans Strelow', in Kölle, *Die Kunst des Ausstellen*, *op. cit.*, p.235.

408 *Prospect/Retrospect, Europa 1946–1976*, Kunsthalle, Düsseldorf, 20–31 October 1976.

409 Benjamin H.D. Buchloh, 'Avant-Propos zu Re(tro)spect', in Jürgen Harten (ed.), *Prospect/Retrospect, Europa 1946–1976* (exh. cat.), Kunsthalle, Düsseldorf, 1976, p.6.

410 Morris in conversation with the author.

411 Wieland Schmied, 'Kunsthändler als Historiker', *Frankfurter Allgemeine Zeitung*, 27 October 1976. This was one of the last exhibitions that Fischer curated in a public institution.

412 Skulptur Ausstellung in Münster, *Die Entwicklung der abstrakten Skulptur im 20. Jahrhundert und die autonome Skulptur der Gegenwart*, Münster, 3 July–13 November 1977. Artists: Archipenko,

Stedelijk Van Abbemuseum, Eindhoven

Another institution that became increasingly important from 1973 onwards was the Stedelijk Van Abbemuseum in Eindhoven. The museum started to show a real commitment towards Conceptualism following the appointment of Rudi Fuchs as Director in 1975. Before his appointment, Fuchs had been a Lecturer at the Art History Institute of Leiden; he had also worked as an art critic for several newspapers. For him, there were two important factors that led to his decision to focus the museum's programming on Conceptualism: the existence of a support network and the consciousness of the historical importance of Conceptualism:

> ... they were the same group of people, the same galleries, the same bars, the same occasions where you met most of them, in Düsseldorf, in Basel, in Brussels, in Paris, in London. We travelled quite a lot at the time. There were small shows, mostly in galleries, that we went to. Düsseldorf was close by, it was an hour by car from Eindhoven. Brussels was close, Amsterdam too ...
>
> To continue collecting in Eindhoven, after Judd or Andre or Stella, it seemed the logical thing to go to Conceptual art. There was a strong feeling, which I still have, that it was a very decisive movement in art, because of the redefinition of many things ...
>
> I compare it with the moment in Florence in the early fifteenth century when the Renaissance began. It was profound and also so simple. The entire conception of art, everywhere, was changed. We saw this happen with Conceptual art. I was thinking at the time, probably quite consciously, that we should collect it, because it was going to be very important.[436]

Fuchs believed it was important to work in parallel on exhibitions and on purchases. In 1975, the overall budget of the museum was £500,000. Ten per cent of it was allocated to exhibitions.[437] The series of solo shows by Conceptual artists organised during the second half of the 1970s included LeWitt and Wilson (1975), Weiner, Buren (1976), Graham, Barry (1977), Kosuth, Long and Andre (1978).[438] Fuchs explains:

Arp, Bill, Boccioni, Brancusi, Calder, Caro, Chillida, Duchamp-Villon, Fontana, Freundlich, Gabo, Giacometti, Gonzàles, Graesel, Hermanns, Kobro, Kricke, Lardera, Laurens, Lipschitz, Moholy-Nagy, Moore, Pevsner, Picasso, Prager, Rabinowitch, Man Ray, Reineking, Rodin, Rodchenko, Schlemmer, Scott, Smith, Spagnulo, Steiner, Stenberg, Di Suvero, Tatlin, Di Teana, Tucker, Uhlmann and Vantongerloo; Andre, Asher, Beuys, Judd, Long, Nauman, Oldenburg, Rückriem and Serra.

413 Documenta 6, Fridericianum, Kassel, 26 June–2 October 1977.

414 In London, one can also mention the Robert Self Gallery, which opened in 1976–77.

415 *Richard Long*, Lisson Gallery, London, 23 January–24 February 1973. See: Database 3, Section Richard Long (Appendix 1.3). From 15 March to 12 April 1973, Long also had his first show at Wide White Space in Antwerp. See: Aupetitallot, *Wide White Space*, *op. cit.*, p.303.

416 Logsdail in conversation with the author, *op. cit.*

417 'Art & Language', Lisson Gallery, London, 16 October–10 November 1973.

418 See: Database 3, Section Art & Language (Appendix 1.3). See also: Michael Baldwin, Charles Harrison, Mel Ramsden, *Art & Language in practice, Illustrated Handbook* (exh. cat.), Fundacio Antoni Tàpies, Barcelona, 1999, p.291.

419 John Walker, 'Review, Art-Language at the Lisson Gallery, 16 October–10 November', *Studio International*, vol.186, no.961, December 1973, p.248.

420 'Record as Artwork', Royal College of Art, London, November 1973.

421 'Record as Artwork', *Flash Art*, no.43, December 1973–January 1974, p.6.

422 'The Record as Artwork: from futurism to conceptual art', Fort Worth Art Museum, Fort Worth, Texas, 4 December 1977–15 January 1978; Moore College of Art Gallery, Philadelphia, Pennsylvania, 3

> I've always found that when you're collecting with a focused interest, making an exhibition is the best way to check things out. It's the best way to find out how certain things work, what it could be. You put it to the test in a sense. And of course, I thought it was important to make all those things more public.[439]

European dealers in America

From 1973 onwards, there were also increasing links and exchanges between the European and American art worlds.

In early 1973, Castelli started to exhibit European Conceptual artists, with Dibbets (February 1973) and Darboven (April–May 1973). The dealer explained his views on Conceptual art:

> It is an international scene. I come back to that. It is for the first time. While you probably will find the Europeans different from, even in this very abstract medium, different from the Americans, there is a difference in the way of expressing themselves. But still for the moment at least, I'm experimenting with that. I think that it is a movement that for the first time actually has an international flavour. All these American artists – Conceptual artists like Kosuth and Lawrence Weiner and so on – spend a lot of time in Europe. They travel around. So there's a lot of bridging, of communication, among all these artists constantly ... Because I think that this was a movement and was clearly international, I wanted to see what the whole range of it was. Therefore, I had to start including Europeans; because my presentation of this case – of whatever you call them, Conceptual artists – seemed to be less strong if I limited myself just to the local crowd.[440]

It was at this time that Sperone opened a space in New York (Green Street) with a group show featuring Judd, Kosuth and LeWitt.[441] It seems that this was more an exhibition space than a dealer gallery; it enabled him to have a foot in the American art world.[442] The display rarely changed, showing mostly works of European artists such as Anselmo (November 1974), Penone and Braco Dimitrijevic (both May 1975).

In Los Angeles, Françoise Lambert and Claire Copley, the daughter of the

February–8 March 1978; Musée d'art contemporain, Montreal, Quebec, 7 September–22 October 1978.

423 *An exhibition called Strata with paintings, drawings and prints by Marden/Martin/Ryman/Twombly and Kelly*, Royal College of Art, London, 1974.

424 Letter from Roselee Goldberg to Lynda Morris dated 2 November 1973, in LMAN. The Agnes Martin work travelled to the Scottish National Gallery of Modern Art, Edinburgh.

425 For an overview of exhibitions of Conceptual artists in European institutions, see: Database 2 (Appendix 1.2).

426 In 1975, Honnef was replaced by Herbert Molderings as Director of the Kunstverein, Münster.

427 *Daniel Buren, Sanction of the Museum*, Museum of Modern Art, Oxford, 31 March–15 April 1973.

428 *Daniel Buren, Manipulation*, Jack Wendler, London, 9–30 March 1973. See: Database 3, Section Daniel Buren (Appendix 1.3). See also: *Daniel Buren, Mot à Mot, op. cit.*, pp.F18–F19.

429 *Sol LeWitt* and *Douglas Huebler*, Museum of Modern Art, Oxford, 28 April–27 May 1973. See: Database 2, Section MOMA, Oxford (Appendix 1.2).

430 *Sol LeWitt, Wall Drawings and Structures*, Lisson Gallery, London, 3–31 May 1973. See: Database 3, Section Sol LeWitt (Appendix 1.3).

431 *Douglas Huebler*, Kunstverein, Münster, 17 December 1972–28 January 1973.

432 Morris, 'The Museum of Modern Art in Oxford 1965–1975',

American artist William Copley, opened a gallery together in 1973 (La Cienega Blvd).[443] The Françoise Lambert & Claire Copley Gallery started with an exhibition of drawings by William Wegman (October 1973). The artists shown were international, with a focus on Californian artists (Ed Ruscha, David Lamelas, Allan Ruppersberg).[444]

The German collector and art dealer Reinhard Onnasch, who had a gallery in Cologne, launched a second space in New York (Spring Street) also in 1973.[445] The opening exhibition in September 1973 was Gerhard Richter's first solo show in America.[446] It was organised through Fischer who travelled to New York with Richter to attend the opening at Onnasch's expense.[447] A few months later, in May 1974, René Block launched a gallery in New York (West Broadway) with a performance by Beuys, *I like America and America likes me*, and a group exhibition of European artists, including Brouwn, Palermo and Polke.[448] Onnasch and Block both wanted to promote their German artists on the American art market.

In late 1973, another German, Heiner Friedrich launched a gallery in New York. The inaugural exhibition in his space in Wooster Street in Spring 1974 was dedicated to De Maria.[449] He did not exhibit his German artists. Instead, he focused on projects with American artists, particularly those who were not represented by other New York dealers (La Monte Young, Marian Zazeela, Fred Sandback). The exhibitions lasted for three months, and no real advertising or mailing was carried out. Thus Friedrich was seen in New York more as an art enabler and merchant than a dealer.[450]

Friedrich focused his attention on the establishment of an art foundation dedicated to Land art.[451] Heiner Friedrich Inc. was run by the young art historian Helen Winkler. Friedrich and Winkler, together with the lawyer Gerald Ordover, launched the Dia Art Foundation in 1974.[452] Its function was to enable the large-scale artistic projects that might not otherwise be realised. The scale of Land art works was beyond the means of individual collectors and outside the domain of art museums. The Foundation was created to fill this gap. From 1975, the support of Philippa de Menil, the daughter of the art patron and heir to the Schlumberger oil fortune, Dominique de Menil and who later became Friedrich's wife, allowed Dia to realise large-scale and site-specific pieces, such as De Maria's *Lightning Field* (1977, New Mexico).

Studio International, *op. cit.*, pp.238–239.

433 Nicholas Serota in conversation with the author, London, 24 January 2005, audio-tape recording (Appendix 1.13).

434 For an overview of the exhibitions organised by the MOMA, Oxford, see: Database 2, Section MOMA, Oxford.

435 Morris, 'The Museum of Modern Art in Oxford 1965–1975', *Studio International*, *op. cit.*, p.241.

436 Fuchs in conversation with the author, *op. cit.*

437 Morris, 'The Museum of Modern Art in Oxford 1965–1975', *Studio International*, *op. cit.*, p.240.

438 See: Database 2, Section Van Abbemuseum, Eindhoven.

439 Fuchs in conversation with the author, *op. cit.*

440 'Interview with Leo Castelli, conducted by Paul Cummings', Archives of American Art, Smithsonian Institute, Washington, 14 May 1969–8 June 1973, at www.aaa.si.edu/collections/digitalcollections/oralhistoriesonline/.

441 *Judd, Kosuth, LeWitt*, Gian Enzo Sperone, New York, starting December 1972. See: Minola, Mundici, Poli and Roberto, *Gian Enzo Sperone*, *op. cit.*, p.215.

442 *Ibid.*, p.491.

443 See: 'Françoise Lambert & Claire Copley Gallery', *Artforum*, October 1973, p.24. See also: 'Françoise Lambert & Claire Copley Gallery', *Flash Art*, no.42, October–November 1973, p.2.

444 Initially, Françoise Lambert wanted to open a shared gallery with Yvon Lambert in New York. Lambert in conversation with the author, *op. cit.*

In 1973–75, a number of European dealers launched spaces in America. Most of these were in New York, although there were also some in Los Angeles. An article published at the time by Thomas B. Hess, entitled 'The Germans are coming! The Germans are coming!'[453] shows that the war and the military occupation of Germany by the US was still in people's minds, and that their presence in New York was resented.

In 1975, Sperone and Fischer joined Angela Westwater to launch a dealer gallery in New York (Greene Street).[454] The Sperone-Westwater-Fischer Gallery opened with an exhibition of Andre in October 1975.[455] The three had met in 1971 and 1972 in Europe, where Westwater had travelled to visit the leading contemporary art galleries and to meet European artists with her partner Carl Andre. They joined forces in order to cope with the economic recession brought on by the oil crisis.[456] As in Rome, the New York gallery exhibited artists from all three dealers. However, a number of other artists, including many Americans, were also shown (Fulton, Michael Singer, Graham).[457]

Thus the dealers' network of Conceptual artists was well-established in Europe, and had also expanded to America.

Art magazines, Books and PhDs

From 1973 onwards, there was a burgeoning of art magazines. In New York, the free avant-garde publication *Art-Rite* was produced by Edit deAk, Walter Robinson and Joshua Cohn from 1973 to 1978. Between 1974 and 1976, the American part of Art & Language (Kosuth, Corris, Ramsden, Kozlov) published *The Fox*.[458]

Audio Arts, a quarterly magazine in the form of audiotapes was launched in 1973 in London by Barry Barker and Bill Furlong. The magazine presented the latest art developments via artists' statements, theoretical discussions and interviews. For instance, the second issue of the second volume was devoted to Andre's public lecture on his poems shown at MOMA Oxford in June–July 1975.[459] Listeners were able to follow the artist as he moved around the exhibition, describing the works and their references.[460]

Art magazines contributed to the support structure around Conceptual art and were important enough to become the topic of travelling exhibitions.

445 Reinhard Onnasch opened his gallery in Berlin in 1968, before moving to Cologne's Lindenstraße in 1970. His programme was based on artists such as Arman and Christo, Beuys and Richter, Kienholz and Warhol.

446 *Gerhard Richter, Paintings 1962–1973*, Gallery Reinhard Onnasch, New York, 15 September–15 November 1973. See: 'Gerhard Richter', *Artforum*, September 1973, p.94. See also: 'Interview', in Bernhard Kerber, *Bestände Onnasch* (exh. cat.), Neues Museum Weserburg, Bremen, 1992, pp.5–7.

447 Morris in conversation with the author.

448 *Joseph Beuys, I like America and America likes me* (23–26 May 1973) and 'First exhibition: Beuys, Brehmer, Brouwn, Hödicke, Palermo, Polke, Richter, Ruthenbeck' (starting 29 May 1973), René Block Gallery, New York.

449 *Walter De Maria*, Heiner Friedrich Inc., New York, Spring 1974. See the list of shows organised by Friedrich, in Urbaschek, *Dia Art Foundation*, *op. cit.*, p.233.

450 *Ibid.*, pp.96–97. Heiner Friedrich Inc. started to appear as a dealer gallery when the Dia Art Foundation moved to other premises in 1976. In 1977, the gallery moved to West Broadway, in the same area as the Castelli, Sonnabend and Weber galleries.

451 *Ibid.*, p.97.

452 *Ibid.*, pp.16–19. As Friedrich decided to stay permanently in the USA, Thordis Moeller took over the management of the Cologne gallery in 1974.

453 Thomas B. Hess, 'The Germans are coming! The Germans are

In 1973, a show entitled *Avalanche, die Entwicklung einer Avantgarde-Zeitschrift* (The Development of an Avant-garde magazine) was shown in different Kunstvereins across Germany (Cologne, Hanover, Münster, Frankfurt). It contained issues of the magazine, drawings, layout sheets, correspondence and audio interviews.[461] In 1976, the magazine *Artforum* was the subject of a satirical exhibition organised by Nicholas Wegner at The Gallery, London.[462]

As John A. Walker wrote in 1976 in an issue of *Studio International* entirely dedicated to art magazines:

> 'The Art Press': an exhibition on the history of art periodicals at the Victoria & Albert Museum ... an international conference on the art periodical at Sussex University in April 1976 and another at Bologna the following month ... a surge of new art magazines in recent years... a spate of articles on the new magazines in established art journals ... a display featuring *Artforum* at The Gallery, London ... a whole issue of *Studio International* devoted to the subject of art magazines. There is no doubt that at the moment there is an unprecedented interest in the art magazine.[463]

Conceptual art continued to be a subject of critical and academic interest. Gregory Battcock,[464] Gerd de Vries,[465] Ernst-Otto Erhard[466] and Celant[467] all published books on Conceptual art at this time. In 1973, Lippard published *Six Years: The Dematerialization of the Art Object from 1966 to 1972*, a wide-ranging documentation of facts and events, as well as an overview of the chronological development of Conceptualism.[468]

In the late 1970s, Conceptual art became a subject of academic research. Two PhDs were written on the art developments of the time. Robert C. Morgan submitted a thesis entitled *The role of documentation in Conceptual art: an aesthetic inquiry* at New York University in 1978.[469] He analysed the role of photo-documentation in Conceptual art and the possibilities of phenomenological reception of artworks. He attempted to do so through a specific form of presentation of the 1970s.[470]

In Europe, also in 1978, Francis Smets submitted a thesis linked with Conceptualism at the Catholic University of Louvain. Its title was: *A reading of*

coming!', *New York Magazine*, June 1974, p.54.

454 Angela Westwater had previously been *Artforum*'s advertising manager. She was Andre's partner at the time. Morris in conversation with the author.

455 *Carl Andre*, Sperone-Westwater-Fischer Gallery, New York, starting 4 October 1975. See: Minola, Mundici, Poli and Roberto, *Gian Enzo Sperone, op. cit.*, p.493. See also: *Carl Andre, Sculptor 1996, op. cit.*, p.255. And: Roberta Smith, 'Review', *Artforum*, vol.14, no.5, January 1976, pp.61–62.

456 Minola, Mundici, Poli and Roberto, *Gian Enzo Sperone, op. cit.*, p.49.

457 For an overview of the exhibitions organised by the Sperone, Westwater and Fischer Gallery, see: *Ibid.*, pp.493–494. In autumn 1982, after a Long exhibition, Fischer decided to leave the collaboration with Westwater and Sperone in New York, because he could not identify with the figurative art of the Neuen Wilden that was exhibited in the gallery. See: 'Konrad Fischer', *Kunstforum International, op. cit.*, pp.280–281.

458 See: Alexander Alberro, 'One Year under the mast: Alexander Alberro on *The Fox* – history of periodical devoted to art-related practice', *Artforum*, June 2003.

459 *Carl Andre – Poems, 1958–1974*, MOMA, Oxford, 8 June–20 July 1975. See: Lynda Morris, 'Carl Andre Poems 1958–1974', *Studio International*, vol.190, no.977, September–October 1975, pp.160–161.

460 See: 'Carl Andre', *Audio Arts*, vol.2, no.2, 1975. There was also the *Aspen* multimedia magazine, published by Phyllis Johnson in

the discourse of Pop art and Conceptual art about the ready-mades of Duchamp as a contribution to the study of the late Capitalism.[471] Smets tried to demonstrate that ideology is present in all texts written by artists and critics. Through this research about reception and language philosophy, he considered contemporary art as an ideology-breaking act of defiance.

Closing of primary dealer galleries

In the mid-1970s, just when Conceptual art was being shown by a growing number of galleries and museums and was being more extensively written about, a number of primary dealer galleries closed down. This was a result of the economic recession that followed the first oil crisis. Wendler shut his gallery in July 1974 but made a final exhibition of Merz in the space under *Studio International* in West Central Street.[472] The collaboration between Sperone and Fischer in Rome ended in autumn 1974, although Sperone continued to run the gallery on his own.[473] Art & Project/MTL in Antwerp was taken over and Le Bailli in Brussels closed in December 1974.[474]

In 1975, Spillemaeckers went bankrupt and looked for someone to take over the gallery.[475] After having made contact with the Galerie Vega in Liège, he finally sold MTL to Gilbert Goes, who continued the initial programme of the gallery to show Conceptual artists.[476] The first show organised by Goes in April 1975 was dedicated to André Cadere.[477] He went on to exhibit artists such as Gilbert & George (May–June 1975), Huebler (September–October 1975) and Broodthaers (December 1975).[478] Subsequently, Spillemaeckers moved to Ostende, but he did not leave the art world. In 1978, he published, together with the artist Marc Poirier and the private collector André Goeminne, a book on Belgian art from the late 1960s to the late 1970s.[479]

Wide White Space closed down in June 1976 after an exhibition of Long.[480] The decision was motivated by a mixture of disillusionment and exhaustion. Moreover De Decker recalls that, due to the arrival of new secondary dealers, they had to start fighting for the artists who they had been the first to show: 'For me, that wasn't why I'd opened a gallery. I felt it was a contradiction in terms to have

New York from 1965 to 1971. This three-dimensional magazine contained an assortment of booklets, reproductions, broadsheets and recordings on plastic discs in a box. The double issue no.5–6 published in Autumn 1967 was devoted to Minimal and Conceptual art. The issue, designed and edited by Brian O'Doherty, contained 28 numbered items, including an essay by Roland Barthes ('The Death of the Author'), a phonograph recording of Feldman and Cage, and the description of an installation at the Dwan Gallery by Sol LeWitt (*Serial Project #1*, 1967).

461 Manuscript letter from Willoughby Sharp to Klaus Honnef dated 30 November 1971, in File 802 / 368, AKMWAM. More recently, the magazine's history was explored in an exhibition organised by Lisa Le Feuvre at the Chelsea College of Art and Design, London in June–July 2005: *Avalanche 1970–1976*.

462 John A. Walker, 'Internal Memorandum', *Studio International*, vol.192, no.983, September–October 1976, p.113. See also: Amy Newman, *Challenging Art: Artforum 1962–1974*, Soho, New York, 2000.

463 Walker, 'Internal Memorandum', *Studio International*, *op. cit.*, p.113.

464 Battcock, *Idea Art*, *op. cit.*

465 Gerd de Vries (ed.), *Über Kunst, Künstlertexte zum veränderten Kunstverständnis nach 1965/On art, artists's writings on the changed notion of art after 1965*, Verlag DuMont Schauberg, Cologne, 1974.

466 Ernst-Otto Erhard, *Pop, Kitsch, Concept-Art, Aufsäte zur Gegenwärtigen Situation der Kunst*, Otto Maier-Verlag, Ravensburg, 1974.

467 Germano Celant, *Pre-cronistoria, 1966–69: Minimal art, Pittura sistemica, Arte povera, Land art, Conceptual art, Body art, Arte ambientale e nuovi media*, Centro DI, Florence, 1976.

468 Lippard, *Six Years*, *op. cit.*

469 Robert C. Morgan, *The role of documentation in Conceptual art: an aesthetic inquiry*, unpublished PhD, Dept. of Art, New York University, New York, 1978.

to fight tooth and nail, because my idea had been to show artists who weren't having exhibitions anywhere else.'[481] Wide White Space hosted a last exhibition of Weiner in May–June 1977, after which the gallery closed.[482]

A little later, in 1978, Friedrich's Munich gallery, which was directed by his former wife, changed its name to Galerie + Edition Sigrid Friedrich und Sabine Knust.[483] In 1980, the Cologne gallery, which had been run by Thordis Moeller since 1974, closed.[484] Preisig closed his gallery in 1979. Here too, it was the financial situation that led to its closure.[485]

470 Later, Robert C. Morgan published several books on Conceptual art, including: *Art into ideas, Essays on Conceptual art*, Cambridge University Press, Cambridge, 1996.

471 Francis Smets, *Een lectuur van discursus van Pop art en Conceptual art over de ready-mades van Duchamp als bijdrage tot de studie van de ideologie in het laatkapitalisme*, unpublished PhD, Catholic University of Louvain, Belgium, 1978.

472 'Mario Merz, It is possible to have a space with tables for 88 people as it is possible to have a space with tables for no one, Tables from drawings of Mario Merz (Fibonacci tables)', Jack Wendler, London, 14 June–5 July 1974. See: 'Jack Wendler Gallery', *Flash Art*, October–November 1974, p.37.

473 Minola, Mundici, Poli and Roberto, *Gian Enzo Sperone*, *op. cit.*, p.491.

474 The Art & Project/MTL gallery in Antwerp was taken over by Marian Verstraeten. See: 'MTL, Antwerp', *Flash Art*, no.60–61, December 1975–February 1976, p.6.

475 According to Jacques Charlier, Spillemaeckers wanted to sell the MTL gallery for 3.5 Million Belgian Francs. Charlier in conversation with the author, Liège, *op. cit.*

476 'MTL, Brussels', *Flash Art*, no.66–67, July–August 1976, p.2.

477 *André Cadere, noir, blanc, jaune, orange, rouge, violet, bleu, vert*, MTL, Brussels, 16–30 April 1975.

478 See: Database 1, Section MTL.

479 Fernand Spillemaeckers (ed.), *Ooidonk 1978: Belgische kunst 1969–1977*, Brussels, 1978. Later that year, Fernand Spillemaeckers died in a car crash. See: Bernard Marcelis, 'Ils savaient ce qu'ils voulaient', *+–0*, no.23, 24 October 1978, pp.4–5.

480 *Richard Long, Driftwood*, Wide White Space, Antwerp, 25 May–10 June 1976. See: Aupetitallot, *Wide White Space*, *op. cit.*, p.337.

481 'Interview Yves Aupetitallot, Anny De Decker, Bernd Lohaus', in *Ibid.*, p.67.

3.5 Conclusion

From 1973, the international network of Conceptual artists became increasingly institutionalised. Conceptualism was shown in big group exhibitions and in a large number of solo shows in museums all over Europe. Dealers joined forces to open shared gallery spaces; some opened second spaces in America. In addition, several secondary dealer galleries opened and took over the now established Conceptual artists, including Rolf Preisig and Michel and Liliane Durand-Dessert. A number of public talks and conferences were organised, and several books and academic studies were published at the time.

However, from 1974, a certain downturn can be perceived. Many galleries closed. The economic recession that resulted from the oil crisis was largely responsible for this situation. The renewed interest in painting also contributed to the downfall of the original network of Conceptual artists. But as the network developed, the public was increasingly confronted with Conceptual works of art. From the early 1970s, Conceptualism was largely exhibited in temporary exhibition spaces and in museums. Whereas dealers seemed to have had to deal with mockery,[487] the public appears to have been more receptive in public institutions.[488] The mid-1970s marked the high point of interest from European museums, who were purchasing for public collections of Conceptual art. This aspect will be studied in Part II.

482 *A work of Lawrence Weiner presented within the context of an installation*, Wide White Space, Antwerp, 4 May–5 June 1977. See: *Ibid.*, p.338.
483 'Six Friedrich', *Kunstforum International*, *op. cit.*, pp.248–249.
484 Urbaschek, *Dia Art Foundation*, *op. cit.*, p.91.
485 Preisig in conversation with the author, *op. cit.*
486 Both De Decker and Françoise Lambert remember visitors to the galleries mocking the exhibits. De Decker and Lambert in conversation with the author, *op. cit.*
487 Serota in conversation with the author, *op. cit.* See also: About 20 sheets with reactions of visitors to *When Attitudes Become Form* at the ICA in London in 1969, in Folder II, 'When Attitudes Become Form', ICA Archive, TLAL.

Part II: Dealing structure

Historical background

Having studied the development of the Conceptual network, it is important to examine the development of private and public collections in Northern Europe from the late 1960s to the late 1970s. Sales were the highest step in the development of the careers of Conceptual artists. Furthermore, sales to museums appear to have been much more important than originally thought at the beginning of the research.

Many of the ideas this research addresses cannot be understood without an appreciation of how contemporary public collections evolved. The idea of a museum collecting contemporary art derived from the activity of American private collectors at the beginning of the twentieth century that culminated in the founding of the Museum of Modern Art in New York. From the 1920s onwards, prominent art patrons saw how modern art could contribute to America's cultural image. Modern art museums and foundations were created both to provide the country with significant cultural institutions and to instruct the public. Three Europeans dominate the development of collecting in the US: Joseph Duveen, Roger Fry and Marcel Duchamp.

The Museum of Modern Art, New York

In the late 1920s, three progressive patrons of modern art, Lillie P. Bliss,[1] Mary Quinn Sullivan and Abby Aldrich Rockefeller[2] came together in New York. Their aim was twofold: to create one of the most important museums of art of the twentieth century, and to encourage people to enjoy and understand progressive works. As a result, the Museum of Modern Art was founded in 1929 as an artistic and educational institutionand a Board of Trustees was elected.

1 Lillie P. Bliss was close to the painter Arthur B. Davies. Her collection originated at the *Armory Show* (1913) where she bought works by Odilon Redon and Paul Cézanne.

2 Abby Aldrich Rockefeller had gone to Europe in 1894 and discovered European contemporary art.

In 1929, Alfred H. Barr Jr. (1902–81), then a teacher of modern art at Princeton University, was invited to become the founding director of MoMA in New York.[3] Barr's aim was 'to educate the public as well as the artists of the 1930s'.[4] He organised *Modern Architecture: International Exhibition* (1932), *Machine Art* (1934), *Cubism and Abstract Art* (1936) and *Fantastic Art, Dada, Surrealism* (1937), and modern art movements were revealed in his chart, *Development of Abstract Art* (1936).[5]

From 1933 to 1941, Barr also developed a diagram of the ideal permanent collection for MoMA, starting from 1875 (Paul Cézanne, Vincent Van Gogh) and going up to 1950 (School of Paris, United States and Mexico).[6] Barr divided the collection into various departments, which included for the first time disciplines such as design, photography and architecture (1932). The public success was overwhelming and the museum was forced to relocate three times in ten years to larger premises, arriving in 1939 in a new modern building on West 53rd Street. In 1949, René d'Harnoncourt was named Director of MoMA, while Barr concentrated on developing the permanent collections. The latter's long-standing relationships with collectors led to numerous donations by people such as Sidney Janis, Peggy Guggenheim and Katherine Dreier.[7]

Along with the artists Marcel Duchamp and Man Ray, the artist and collector Katherine Dreier (1877–1952) created the Société Anonyme Inc. in 1920, for the study and promotion of international modern art.[8] At the time, Duchamp acted as a dealer in America, he advised not only Dreier, but also Walter Arensberg on their collections of modern art. Dreier, Duchamp and Man Ray assembled a collection of over 1,000 international modernist works of art.

In 1930, the Whitney Studio Club, founded in 1914 by Gertrude Vanderbilt Whitney (1875–1942), became the Whitney Museum of American Art, an institution dedicated to American vanguard artists. From 1936, the painter and art advisor Hilla Rebay organised a series of travelling exhibitions derived from the modern art collection of Solomon R. Guggenheim (1861–1949). The Solomon R. Guggenheim Foundation, created in 1937, opened the Guggenheim Museum in 1952.

In 1896, Carnegie founded a Museum of Art in Pittsburgh. In 1922, the Barnes Foundation was established in Philadelphia by Dr Arthur C. Barnes to

3 Sybil Gordon Kantor, *Alfred H. Barr, Jr., and the Intellectual Origins of the Museum of Modern Art*, The MIT Press, Cambridge, Mass. and London, England, 2002, p.189.
4 *Ibid.*, p.314.
5 See: *Ibid.*, p.23.
6 See: *Torpedo moving through time*, in *Ibid.*, p.367.
7 *Ibid.*, p.371.
8 See: William Clark, 'Katherine Dreier and the Société Anonyme', *Variant*, vol.2, no.14, Winter 2001, pp.4–7.

promote the advancement of education and the appreciation of fine arts. Parts of Arthur Jerome Eddy's collection of contemporary art, notably his works by Wassily Kandinsky, were integrated into the Chicago Art Institute in 1931. Likewise, the Louise and Walter Arensberg Collection (400 paintings, sculptures and drawings, including numerous works by Marcel Duchamp) became a prominent part of the Philadelphia Museum of Modern Art in 1950.[9]

This brief outline shows that in the 1920s and the 1940s, American museums of modern art developed as private institutions. This was quite different from Europe, where museums were mostly public. This situation was largely due to the fact that the promotion of the arts in the USA relied on private funding, since the American constitution contained no requirement for the State to take any specific responsibility for the cultural sector.[10] American museums were directed by Boards of Trustees formed by industrialists and businessmen. MOMA, New York, is a clear example of an institution dominated by a wealthy patron-family, the Rockefellers.[11]

The activities of people such as Duveen, Fry and Duchamp testify to early contacts and exchanges between Europe and the United States. The immigration to America of contemporary European artists seeking refuge following the outbreak of the Second World War would deepen the transatlantic relationships. After 1933 and during the war, European museums and private collections had been despoiled, works of art confiscated, sold, lost or destroyed and artists persecuted. In the postwar period, the whole cultural arena needed rebuilding and the artistic void needed to be filled.

In the 1950s, the attention of the European art world was directed towards the US. During this decade, the European art world adopted their idea of the freedom of the artist from the US. European private collectors such as Peter Ludwig and Giuseppe Panza started to collect American art. Museum directors used MOMA as a model for museums dedicated to modern art. People such as Willem Sandberg at the Stedelijk Museum in Amsterdam and Franz Meyer at the Kunstmuseum in Basel started to acquire contemporary art for their permanent collections.

In the late 1960s, European private collectors were the first to respond to Conceptual art and to collect such works early on. Most museums, however, did

9 One could also mention Cone (Baltimore), John Spaulding (Boston), as well as the painter and collector Albert E. Gallatin, who, in 1927, opened the Gallery of Living Art at New York University with his private collection of international abstract art as a centrepiece. In 1943, Gallatin donated his collection of more then 160 works to the Philadelphia Museum of Art (Picasso, Léger, Miró, Arp). See: Gail Stavitsky, 'The A.E. Gallatin Collection: An Early Adventure in Modern Art', *Bulletin of the Philadelphia Museum of Art*, no.89, 1994, pp. 3–47.

10 Butin, 'When Attitudes Become Form – Philip Morris Becomes Sponsor', *op. cit.*

11 On this matter, see: Cockcroft, 'Abstract Expressionism, Weapon of the Cold War', *Artforum*, *op. cit.*, p.39.

not collect Conceptualism before the early 1970s. Some countries were more dynamic than others. Consequently, for the purposes of this research, the analysis of purchases of Conceptual art by private collectors and European museums is organised geographically.

Chapter 4

Purchases of Conceptual art by private collectors

In Northern Europe, in the late 1960s and 1970s, about a dozen private collectors showed an interest in Conceptual art. Most of them were to be found in Germany and in the Flemish-speaking countries, the Netherlands and Belgium. Some of the biggest private collectors had started to acquire art in the 1950s or 1960s, which meant that only part of their collections were dedicated to Conceptual art. Others began their collections with Minimalism. If one considers their long-term intentions and their different ways of establishing their collections, two major tendencies emerge. A few kept their collections private; others wanted them in the public domain. It is possible to get access to detailed information about private collections that are now part of a public institution, while the content of personal collections can only be viewed in temporary exhibitions. Consequently, this chapter focuses on the Visser Collection at the Kröller-Müller Museum, Otterlo and on the Panza Collection at the Guggenheim Museum, New York.[12]

4.1. West Germany

After the Second World War, collecting art in Germany was mainly the privilege of wealthy industrialists and bankers. From the late 1960s, the middle-class began to buy works of art. Among the collectors of Conceptual art were doctors, scientists, restorers and lawyers. Due to the presence of many dealer galleries

12 Purchases of Conceptual artworks from dealer galleries and private collectors remain unclear as both are very discreet about the subject. There is no correspondence or documentation about sales to private collectors in dealer gallery archives, at least not in accessible files. [Editor's note: The Paul Maenz papers at the Getty Museum in Los Angeles are an exception.]

and museums, the Rhineland was a central region for German private collectors. There were, of course, collectors in other German regions, like Hesse and Bavaria. However, during the 1960s and 1970s, most collectors were living in North Rhine-Westphalia. One can mention for instance the collections of Cremer (Dortmund), Hack (Cologne), Schniewind (Neviges), Forberg and Beck (both in Düsseldorf). These collectors were mostly interested in Constructivism, German Expressionism, the École de Paris and Pop art.[13]

No more than a handful of private collectors bought contemporary art as a matter of conscious aesthetic conviction. However, a number of contemporary German artists built up personal collections, by exchanging works; these included Gotthard Graubner (Saxony), Konrad Klapheck and Günther Uecker (both in Düsseldorf). Several Conceptual art dealers, including Paul Maenz and Heiner Friedrich, purchased works from their own stock for their private collection. The purchase of works by dealers was often a condition set by the artist when making a show at a gallery. Other dealers, such as Reinhard Onnasch, had first been private collectors.[14]

In Germany, the Museumsverein (Museums Association) played an important part in setting up private collections. By paying a subscription, members, which included numerous German and international private collectors,[15] supported the activities of an institution. In return, each year the museum offered their members an edition of an artwork, such as an etching, a lithograph or a small bronze sculpture, at a special price. The works were by artists who had recently exhibited in the museum. These works were cheaper than on the official art market and were only available to German and international private collectors who were members of the 'Museumsverein'.[16]

Peter Ludwig

In the 1960s and 1970s, Peter Ludwig (1925–96), a chocolate manufacturer based in Aachen, was one of the biggest German private collectors. The scope of his collection ranged from medieval artefacts to the most recent art tendencies. In the 1960s, Ludwig and his wife Irene were important collectors of Pop art (Lichtenstein, Warhol). It is said that they discovered the work of Pop artists in 1966 in New York by visiting the galleries of Sydney Janis, Richard Bellamy

13 Christian Herchenröder, 'Collectors', *Studio International*, vol.183, no.941, February 1972, p.86.

14 See: Emese Doehler et al., *Neues Museum Weimar, Die Sammlung von Paul Maenz*, Hatje Kantz Verlag, Cologne, 2001. See also: Kerber, *Bestände Onnasch*, *op. cit.*

15 Johannes Cladders in conversation with the author, *op. cit.*

16 *Ibid.*

and Leo Castelli.[17]

Conceptual art was not widely represented in Ludwig's collection in the late 1960s and 1970s, mainly because he was not convinced of the merit of that kind of radical art. Nevertheless, in order to have examples of the art of the day, he acquired several pieces by artists such as Andre (*Lock Series (Köln Steel Lock)*, 1967) and Darboven (*1.10.71–31.10.71*, 1971).[18] Ludwig's collecting was unusual because he was not only putting together a private holding of works, but also buying to enrich museums' collections. He clearly wanted to make his collection accessible to a wide audience.

Over the years, the Ludwigs set up numerous foundations and arranged donations and long-term loans.[19] However, most of these did not relate to Conceptual art, except for the 1976 donation that launched the Museum Ludwig in Cologne.[20] The Ludwigs' private collection was exhibited many times in temporary exhibitions across Europe. While many shows focused on Photorealism and Pop art,[21] an exhibition entitled *Conceptual art and Hyperrealism, Ludwig Collection* was presented at the Musée d'Art moderne de la Ville de Paris in1974.[22] This was one of the rare shows of the Ludwig Collection to include works by Conceptualists such as Andre, Heizer, Kosuth and Long.

The way in which the Ludwigs organised their private collection was also unusual. They adopted a museum-like method of managing their acquisitions. Although their 'empire' had an educational motive, the numerous foundations, museums and loans were run like companies. The collection was 'closed', which means that the works were not resold or exchanged. They often purchased works according to the needs of the museums. That Ludwig collected Minimal and Conceptual artworks without conviction highlights the fact that he had subjected himself to a type of acquisition obligation. This also shows the extent of the Ludwigs' influence on institutions across Europe since the 1960s.

Karl Ströher

Karl Ströher (1890–1977) was another prominent German collector. He came from Darmstadt, where he worked as a businessman in the family company Wella. Unlike Ludwig, he only purchased contemporary works from the 1960s and 1970s. He started to collect contemporary art in the mid-1960s. From then

17 Hans van der Meyden, 'Peter and Irene Ludwig', *Apollo*, June 1989, vol. 129, no.328, p.400. For an account of the Ludwig's Pop Art collection, see: Gert von der Osten (ed.), *Kunst der sechziger Jahre (Sammlung Ludwig), Hundert Werke im Wallraf-Richartz-Museum*, Wallraf-Richartz-Museum, Cologne, 1969.

18 Reiner Speck, *Peter Ludwig Sammler*, Insel Verlag, Frankfurt/Main, 1986, p.118.

19 For an exhaustive report on the Ludwig foundations, donations and permanent loans, see: *ibid.*, pp.187–190.

20 Conceptual artworks in the collection of the Museum Ludwig will be discussed in Chapter 5.1.

21 One can mention the exhibition *Photo-Realism, paintings, sculpture and prints from the Ludwig Collection and others* held at the Serpentine Gallery, London, in 1973, and also *A decade of great American Art, the Ludwig collection* organised at the Kunstmuseum, Lucerne, the same year.

22 *Art Conceptuel et Hyperréalisme: Collection Ludwig*, ARC/Musée d'Art moderne de la Ville de Paris, 31 January–10 March 1974.

on, he had close relationships with Franz Dahlem, who became his adviser, and Heiner Friedrich.[23] Over one-third of the artworks in Ströher's collection were acquired between 1966 and 1973 at the Galerie Friedrich in Munich (Andre, Flavin, De Maria, Judd).[24] Between 1968 and 1970, Ströher and Friedrich often travelled together to visit artists' studios in the United States. According to Dahlem, no German collector prior to Ströher had acquired complete sets of an artist's works at once.[25]

In autumn 1967, Ströher made an important addition to his collection. He purchased the entire Joseph Beuys exhibition organised by Johannes Cladders at the Städtisches Museum in Mönchengladbach (about 140 artworks).[26] Friedrich and Dahlem seem to have played an important role in setting up this deal. It shows the extensive financial means that the collector had at his disposal; being able to purchase many works at once meant that he could amass a large collection in a limited period of time – over the course of about a decade (1966–77). Furthermore, it underlines the task Ströher had set himself, namely to be a patron of the arts. Indeed, the sale of the 'Block Beuys' gave the artist financial stability for many years.[27] A year later, in 1968, the acquisition of Leon Kraushar's collection of Pop art from the United States (Oldenburg, Lichtenstein, Warhol) became a significant counterbalance to this German art collection.[28] The dealers Hans-Jürgen Müller, Friedrich and Dahlem, who had owned a gallery in Darmstadt since 1967, convinced Ströher to make this acquisition.[29]

Ströher's collection was 'open', meaning that he resold certain works to buy others. The focal points of the collection were Beuys and Warhol. In the late 1960s, he also collected works by European and American Conceptual artists such as Reiner Ruthenbeck, Ryman and LeWitt (*Double Cubes*, 1969).[30] In 1969, the entire private collection was exhibited in museums in Berlin and Düsseldorf.[31] After the show, in 1970, the Sammlung Ströher was put on long-term loan to the Landesmuseum Darmstadt (Hesse). Ströher's long-standing aim had been to exhibit and donate his whole collection to a public museum.[32] After his death in 1977, his heirs sold nearly the complete art collection to the Museum für moderne Kunst (MMK, Museum of Modern Art) in Frankfurt.[33]

Ströher's collection was put together mainly on the advice of Heiner

23 Urbaschek, *Dia Art Foundation*, *op. cit.*, p.76. See also: 'Franz Dahlem', *Kunstforum International*, *op. cit.*, p.244.

24 *Museum für Moderne Kunst und Sammlung Ströher*, Museum für Moderne Kunst, Frankfurt/Main, 1991, pp.86–88

25 Franz Dahlem quoted in Urbaschek, *Dia Art Foundation*, *op. cit.*, p.85.

26 Grasskamp, *Johannes Cladders*, *op. cit.*, p.39.

27 Urbaschek, *Dia Art Foundation*, *op. cit.*, pp.80–82.

28 The American insurance broker Leon Kraushar died suddenly in 1967 at the age of 54. His collection of about 200 paintings, sculptures and drawings from American Pop artists was sold by his widow to Karl Ströher.

29 Katharina Schmidt and Philip Ursprung (eds), *White Fire, Flying Man, Amerikanische Kunst 1959–1999 in Basel, Werke aus der Öffentlichen Kunstsammlung Basel und der Emanuel Hoffmann-Stiftung* (exh. cat.), Museum für Gegenwartskunst, Basel, 1999, p.11.

30 See: Manuscript letter from Sol LeWitt to Konrad Fischer dated 23 January 1969, in Korrespondenz mit Künstlern 1969–70, AKFGD.

31 See: *Sammlung 1968 Karl Ströher* (exh. cat.), Deutsche Gesellschaft für bildende Kunst, Kunstverein and Nationalgalerie der Staatlichen Museen preußischer Kulturbesitz in der Neuen Nationalgalerie, Berlin and Städtischen Kunsthalle, Düsseldorf, 1969.

32 Urbaschek, *Dia Art Foundation*, *op. cit.*, p.85.

33 The Karl Ströher collection was used as a base for the MMK, Frankfurt, which was founded in 1981. The museum opened in 1991 under the directorship of Jean-Christophe Ammann, former Director

Friedrich. In 1969, the art critic Klaus Honnef remarked that the collection was 'acutely subject to dealing interests'.[34]

Reiner Speck

At this time, there were several other contemporary art collectors. The Cologne-based physician Dr Reiner Speck was a significant patron. He started to assemble works by Beuys in the mid-1960s and has since expanded his collection to include many contemporary artists. He owns works by Conceptual artists such as Broodthaers, Merz, Nauman and Andre (*Venus Ellipse*, 1978). In the early 1970s, Speck's collection was seen as particularly pragmatic and free of any decorative or investment considerations.[35] One of its main focuses is contemporary German art, with artists such as Arnulf Rainer, Martin Kippenberger and Günther Förg.[36] Since 2002, part of the Sammlung Speck has been on permanent loan to the K21 Kunstsammlung Nordrhein-Westfalen in Düsseldorf.[37]

Wolfgang Hahn

Wolfgang Hahn (1924–87) was the Head of the Restoration Department of the Wallraf-Richartz-Museum in Cologne. He collected mostly Fluxus and Nouveau Réaliste works (Arman, Hains). Hahn also acquired works by Conceptual artists such as Weiner, Andre (*36 hot-rolled steel plates*, 1968) and Nauman (*Lead with ridge piece*, 1969).[38] In 1968, his collection was presented in an exhibition at the Cologne museum.[39] A decade later, in 1978, the Sammlung Hahn was acquired by the Austrian State for the Museum für Moderne Kunst (Museum of Modern Art) in Vienna (400 pieces from the art of the 1960s and 1970s).[40]

Jost Herbig, Wolfgang Hock and other collectors

Other private collections of Minimal and Conceptual art of significance are those of the Munich-based chemist Dr Jost Herbig (1938–95) and of the Krefeld-based banker Wolfgang Hock. Herbig's collection focuses on Minimal and Conceptual artists, such as Buren, Nauman and Huebler (*Variable Piece no. 11*, 1970–71). It was exhibited in 1973 at the Lehnbachhaus in Munich.[41] In 1975, Herbig put his collection on long-time loan to the Neue Galerie, Kassel.[42]

of the Kunstmuseum Luzern in the 1970s. For an exhaustive description of the Ströher collection's history, see: Katrin Sauerländer (ed.), *Karl Ströher. Eine Sammlungsgeschichte*, Zusammenarbeit mit dem Museum für Moderne Kunst, Revolver – Archiv für aktuelle Kunst, Frankfurt/Main, 2005.

34 Klaus Honnef quoted in Urbaschek, *Dia Art Foundation*, *op. cit.*, p.85 (author's translation).

35 Herchenröder, 'Collectors', *Studio International*, *op. cit.*, p.86.

36 For an account of Reiner Speck's collection, see: *Sammlung Speck* (exh. cat.), Museum Ludwig, Cologne, 1996.

37 See: *Blinde wehrte Euch! Arbeiten aus der Sammlung Speck* (exh. cat.), K21 Kunstsammlung Nordrhein-Westfalen, Düsseldorf, 2004.

38 See: Letter from Konrad Fischer to Bruce Nauman dated 20 January 1969, in Korrespondenz mit Künstlern 1969–70 and Letter from Erika Fischer to Wolfgang Hahn dated 6 December 1972, in Allgemeine Korrespondenz 1972–73, AKFGD.

39 See: *Sammlung Hahn, Zeitgenössische Kunst* (exh. cat.), Wallraf-Richartz-Museum, Cologne, 1968.

40 See: *Sammlung Hahn* (exh. cat.), Museum für Moderne Kunst, Vienna, 1979.

41 See: *Bilder–Objekte–Filme–Konzepte: Sammlung Herbig* (exh. cat.), Städtische Galerie im Lehnbachhaus, Munich, 1973.

42 In the late 1990s however, the Herbig collection was sold at auction at Christie's. The Neue Galerie in Kassel only managed to acquire the works by Joseph Beuys.

Hock started his collection about 1967, and was a good client of Fischer.[43] Conceptual artists in his collection include Gilbert & George, LeWitt and Weiner. The collections of Herbig and Hock both remain in the private realm and are therefore less well-known.[44] The collections of Helga and Walther Lauffs (Krefeld), of Burda, a women's magazine publisher in Munich (Hubert Burda Media), and of an anonymous collector who owned a private museum in the islands of the Rhine at Rhein-Duisburg are also notable.[45]

During the 1960s and 1970s, there were numerous private collectors in West Germany. About half a dozen were particularly keen on Contemporary art, including Conceptual art. Some collectors, like Ströher and Hahn, eventually stopped buying. Others, such as Ludwig and Speck, have continued to add to their collections. It appears that prominent German private collectors acted consciously as patrons of the arts. In the late 1960s and 1970s, most collections were shown in temporary exhibitions across Europe. Private collectors also arranged for their artworks to be integrated into the collections of public institutions. Their motive was to enrich public museum collections. This contributed to the tendency, begun in the postwar period, of re-establishing German museum collections that had been damaged and despoiled. Through this cultural generosity, private collectors could also acquire a certain prestige as their names became associated with museums that achieved an international reputation. There were also social benefits such as private views and dinners, and travel to foreign cities, which brought them into contact with like-minded friends.

4.2. Belgium

Belgium has a long-standing tradition of art collecting. The Flemish population, in particular, had a habit of purchasing original canvases. After the war, most private collectors were in Brussels. The French-speaking part of the country had an affinity with France, where many well-known artists lived in the first half of the twentieth century. Important collections of works by international and

43 See: Willi Bongard, 'Willy [sic] Bongard Sammlerporträt: Dr. Wolfgang Hock', *Kunstforum International*, September 1973, vol. 4, no.5, pp.49–51. See also: Letter from Konrad Fischer to Gilbert & George dated 15 September 1970, in Künstler Korrespondenz 1970–71, AKFGD.

44 There are several other private collectors who were interested in Conceptualism, but who remained very discreet, for instance: Dr. Hermann Kern, one of the founders of the Kunstraum in Munich (1973), Christophe and Catharina Sattler (Munich) and Dr. Franz Schwarz (Hüttenberg). Collectors such as Anna and Josef Froehlich (Stuttgart) and Friedrich Erwin Rentschler (Laupheim) did not start to acquire artworks before the late 1970s and early 1980s. The latter was an important collector of Galerie Paul Maenz, Cologne. Maenz in a conversation with the author, *op. cit.*

45 Lynda Morris in conversation with the author, and Marlis Grüterich in a letter to the author, 28 September 2005.

46 Geirlandt, 'Museums, Collectors, Policies', *Studio International*, *op. cit.*, p.115.

47 Many Belgian private collectors took part in the exhibition *Chambres d'Amis* (Guest Bedrooms) organised by Jan Hoet in 1986 in Gent. Fifty inhabitants of the city made their houses and apartments available for artists to use as exhibition spaces. For example, Buren created a complementary installation in the home of Annick and Anton Herbert and in the Museum van Hedendaagse Kunst (*Le Décor et son double*). See: Jan Hoet, 'Chambres d'Amis Gand 1986', in Klüser and Hegewich, *L'Art de l'Exposition*, *op. cit.*, pp.413–423.

Belgian artists such as Picasso, Léger, Delvaux and Magritte were assembled by collectors such as Fernand Graindorge (Liège), Philippe Dotremont and J.B. Urvater (both in Brussels).

From the late 1960s, more people from the Flemish part of the country started to collect modern art.[46] This was a period when the Walloon steel industry was falling apart, stimulating an economic downturn in the region. At the same time, the diamond industry was flourishing in Antwerp. The Rhineland was becoming increasingly significant for contemporary art. Flemish people spoke German and felt comfortable going to museums and dealer galleries in Germany. Belgian private collectors, who began to buy art in the late 1960s and early 1970s focussed on the contemporary. Another characteristic of most Belgian private collections at the time was that they remained concealed. For instance, Betty Barman, Carlo van den Bosch (both in Antwerp), Dr Roger Matthys (Deurle), Dr Hubert Peeters (Bruges) and André Goeminne (Gent) were discreet about their art collections.[47]

Roger Matthys

Dr Roger Matthys was a psychiatrist living in Deurle (near Gent). Pop art was the main focus of his collection. However, he was interested in contemporary art; he was the Chairman of the Association for the Museum of Contemporary Art in Gent, founded in 1957 as a Contemporary Art Society.[48] Conceptual art found its way into his collection.[49] He acquired works by Andre (*Copper-Steel Alloy Square*, 1969),[50] LeWitt (*Wall Drawing #115*, 1971),[51] Dibbets (*1971 Panorama*, 1971)[52] and Gilbert & George.[53] In late 1975 and early 1976, an exhibition of drawings by contemporary artists in Flemish private collections was organised by Yves de Smet at the International Cultural Center (ICC), Antwerp, then directed by Florent Bex. Some of the drawings in Matthys's collection were included in the show.[54]

Hubert Peeters

The Bruges-based Dr Hubert Peeters was particularly interested in Pop art and Hyperrealism. The artists most represented in his collection were Lichtenstein, Oldenburg and Warhol. He acquired his Pop works from the Sonnabend Gallery.[55] Works by Stella, Morris and Judd were also to be found in his collection.

48 'Interventie Roger Matthijs', *MDD Jaarcatalogus 2004*, *op. cit.*, p.8.

49 For an installation shot of Dr. Matthys's art collection, see: Geirlandt, 'Museums, Collectors, Policies', *Studio International*, *op. cit.*, p.116. One can clearly recognise structures by LeWitt and floor sculptures by Andre.

50 *Carl Andre, Sculpture 1958–1974* (exh. cat.), Kunsthalle, Bern, 1975, p.43.

51 Suzanna Singer (ed.), *Sol LeWitt, Wall Drawings 1968–1984* (exh. cat.), Stedelijk Museum, Amsterdam; Van Abbemuseum, Eindhoven; Wadsworth Atheneum, Hartford CT, 1984, p.169. See also: Gary Garrels (ed.), *Sol LeWitt, A retrospective* (exh. cat.), San Francisco Museum of Modern Art, San Francisco, 2002, p.405. The mention of the 'Collection of Dr. and Mrs. R. Matthys, Deurle, Belgium' in this recent catalogue shows that the collection still exists.

52 *Jan Dibbets* (exh. cat.), Stedelijk Museum, Amsterdam, 1972, unnumbered pages.

53 Lynda Morris remembered visiting Matthys's house about 1975 and seeing one of Gilbert & George's *The rude writing* pictures. Morris in conversation with the author, *op. cit.*

54 See: 'Contemporary drawings', *Flash Art*, December 1975–February 1976, no.60–61, p.11.

55 'Interview Yves Aupetitallot, Anny De Decker, Bernd Lohaus', in Aupetitallot, *Wide White Space*, *op. cit.*, p.35. See also: De Decker in conversation with the author, *op. cit.*

At the beginning of the 1970s, he had acquired early works by Broodthaers, such as *Nuages* (1966) and *Fémur de Belge* (1967).

In 1968, Peeters was one of the members of the selection committee of Prospect.[56] The following year he participated in the foundation of the alternative exhibition space A 379089 (Antwerp).[57] Even if Peeters did not really collect the art of the 1970s, he showed an interest in it. He was in contact with Wide White Space, although he does not seem to have bought from them.[58] Peeters was one of the Belgian collectors to exhibit his works publicly, first in 1968 in Eindhoven and Gent, then in 1972 in Münster.[59]

André Goeminne

Another Flemish collector worth mentioning is André Goeminne. He lived in Nazareth Bell (Gent) and his business was as a food wholesaler.[60] Works of Conceptual artists such as Nauman (*Hologram Serie*), Andre (*6-Part Sort*, 1972; *Fourteenth Copper Cardinal*, 1974) and Weiner (*... And then relegated to another gender*) were in his collection. [62] Some drawings from Goeminne's collection were shown, together with works on paper from other private collections, at the ICC in Antwerp in 1975–76.[63]

Sylvain Perlstein

The Antwerp-based diamond merchant Sylvain Perlstein started to collect Conceptual art in the early 1970s. At the time, he travelled regularly to New York for professional reasons. He got to know people like LeWitt, Andre and Barry, since they frequented the same clubs and restaurants. His collection started with drawings that were given to him by the artists. Perlstein was interested in light and he collected pieces by Flavin, Nauman, Buren and the Bechers.

Perlstein remains discreet on the subject of the dealers he visited during the 1970s. It is likely that he bought from Wide White Space because he lived in Antwerp.[64] He also went to auction houses. In 1974, for example, he bought a small date painting by On Kawara at Sotheby's in London.[65] Later, Dada and Surrealism became another focus of the collection. He slowed down his purchasing activities in the late 1980s and his collection remains entirely private.

56 *Prospect '68*, *op. cit.*, p.1.

57 See: Chapter 2.2.

58 Anny De Decker recalls him visiting the gallery and states that he did not think that their artists were as good as the American Pop artists.

59 *Three blind mice*, *op. cit.*, 1968. *Everbody knows, Sammlung Dr. Hubert and Marie-Thérèse Peeters, Brügge* (exh. cat.), Landesmuseum, Münster, 1972.

60 It is said that Goeminne has sold his private collection to a European institution.

61 *Carl Andre* (exh. cat.), Gemeentemuseum, Den Haag; Stedelijk Van Abbemuseum, Eindhoven, 1987, p.62.

62 Marja Bloem (ed.), *Lawrence Weiner, Works from the beginning of the sixties towards the end of the eighties*, Stedelijk Museum, Amsterdam, 1988, p.28.

63 'Contemporary drawings', *Flash Art*, *op. cit.*, p.11.

64 During our conversation, Perlstein mentioned Wide White Space several times without clearly saying that he bought there.

65 *Sale of Contemporary Art 1945–1974*, Sotheby's & Co., London, Part 1, 4 December, Part 2, 6 December 1974, no.30. See manuscript information written in the sales catalogue held at Sotheby's Library, London.

He is currently working on an inventory of his collection, which may result in an exhibition and a publication.[66]

Isi Fiszman

From the mid-1960s, the diamond merchant, printer and publisher Isi Fiszman (Antwerp) was one of the key supporters of Wide White Space. He did not consider himself a collector of artworks, but rather a supporter of the gallery and the artists.[67] He was sometimes referred to as the 'Conceptual Collector', because of his interest in establishing a relationship with the artist, rather than in the possession of works. He was close to many artists, including Andre, Beuys and Broodthaers. He also acquired works by Panamarenko, Bernd Lohaus and Paul Joostens.[68] Fiszman largely financed the alternative exhibition space A 379089 in Antwerp run by Kasper König, in which Peeters was also involved.

From the early 1970s, Fiszman became politically engaged. He sold some of his artworks to finance political publications such as *Le Point* and *Pour*.[69] During her stay in Belgium in 1974, the American critic Barbara Reise visited the offices of *Pour*, describing it ironically as 'that smugly "Marxist"-leftist newspaper for the "people" published by the diamond-millionaire Issy [sic] Fiszman'.[70] Fiszman's collection remains private. He continues to support Conceptual artists to this day.[71]

Herman Daled

Conceptual art is the focal point of the private collection of Herman Daled (Brussels). Dr Daled and his first wife Nicole Verstraeten were important collectors from the late 1960s onwards. He now lives in the only house in Brussels designed by Henry van de Velde, the Hotel Wolfors. Daled came from a collector's family in Bruges; to him, purchasing artworks was natural.[72] In 1967, after Daled purchased one of his works, Broodthaers became a close friend. Through him he got to know many Conceptual artists. He owns works by Long (*On this Hillside*, 1972), Huebler (*Duration Piece #12*, 1970), Wilson (*Discussion, 23 January 1972*, 1972) and Weiner (*Middle of the Road*, 1970).[73] Fischer and Wendler were among the dealers from whom he purchased.

66 Sylvain Perlstein in conversation with the author, Paris, 20 October 2004, audio-tape recording.

67 'Interview Yves Aupetitallot, Isi Fiszman', in Aupetitallot, *Wide White Space*, *op. cit.*, p.130.

68 *Ibid.*, pp.227–269.

69 *Ibid.*, p.132.

70 Reise, '"Incredible" Belgium: Impressions', *Studio International*, *op. cit.*, p.118.

71 During my stay in Düsseldorf in April 2005, I met Isi Fiszman at the Konrad Fischer Galerie. He had come especially from Antwerp to see a new Hanne Darboven exhibition (*Sunrise / Sunset*, 1984).

72 'Interview with Herman Daled', in Moseley, *Conception*, *op. cit.*, p.119.

73 Anny De Decker recalled that Herman Daled 'had writing pads printed with works by Weiner which he had purchased so that every visitor could tear off a sheet and take it home'. See: *The Collection Visser at the Kröller-Müller Museum*, Stichting Kröller-Müller Museum, Otterlo, 2000, p.26. For more examples of Conceptual artworks in Daled's collection, see: Héman, Poot and Visser, *Conceptual art in the Netherlands and Belgium 1965–1975*, *op. cit.*, pp.185–194.

Although Daled has a very large private collection, he does not live surrounded by works of art. 'It appears as if the radical position of certain artists has been just as radically translated into a very specific relationship with art', wrote Hripsimé Visser of Daled's attitude.[75] Some works are hung for a short period of time, others remain wrapped. Furthermore, Daled only acquires 'easily manageable' works by living artists. This excludes huge installations and large formats. Most of his collection is on loan to museums. Despite its importance a complete overview of the Daled collection has never been shown in a temporary exhibition and no catalogue has ever been published.

Annick and Anton Herbert

In the 1960s, the Gent-based collectors Annick and Anton Herbert collected Flemish Expressionism. Again, Anton Herbert was following the practice of his father, who had extensively collected such works.[78] The turning point in their thinking about art occurred in the early 1970s as a result of contact with Spillemaeckers and Fischer, whom they met in the summer of 1973 at the cancelled opening of the *Deurle 11/7/73* exhibition at the Museum Dhont-Dhaenens. Herbert recalls the start of their collecting activities:

> This didn't happen from one day to the next. There was a long preparatory period of discussions, a 'battle of words' with Spillemaeckers, with Fischer and with the artists. We wanted to know exactly what we were dealing with. We wanted to test the ground. For us, it was a fast-track training. In three or four months, we'd completely changed our way of seeing, which had been fairly bourgeois and local. Let's say we'd been passively prepared by the spirit of 1968. We had a particular attraction to this new world.[79]

The Herberts started to collect Conceptual artworks in about 1973. Their first acquisition was a set of drawings by LeWitt. It included *Lines, not straight, from the top and the left side*, realised on 6 July 1972 in Brussels. This work was made for the artist's solo show at the MTL gallery *Sol LeWitt, Wall drawings* (5 July–26 September 1972). Annick Herbert describes their first acquisition:

74 'Interview with Herman Daled', in Moseley, *Conception*, *op. cit.*, p.120.

75 Hripsimé Visser, 'Conceptuele Kunst 1965–1975', *Bulletin Stedelijk Museum Amsterdam*, vol.15, no.3, April 2002, p.4.

76 *Ibid.*

77 In 2004 at the Maison Rouge – Fondation Antoine de Galbert in Paris, the exhibition 'L'intime, le collectionneur derrière la porte' reconstructed one room of private collector's homes. Daled only exhibited a list of artworks. Since 2005, Daled has been the Chairman of the Wiels Center for Contemporary art in Brussels.

78 Jan Debbaut quoted in *L'Architecte est absent – Works from the collection of Annick and Anton Herbert, Répertoire* (exh. cat.), Stedelijk Van Abbemuseum, Eindhoven, 1984–85, p.18. For an overview of the private collection of Tony Herbert, Anton Herbert's father, see: *De Verzameling Tony Herbert* (exh. cat.), Stedelijk Van Abbemuseum, Eindhoven, 1999.

79 Annick and Anton Herbert in conversation with the author, *op. cit.* (author's translation).

> The very first work we bought were some drawings by Sol LeWitt, four small drawings as a group. It was the first timid commitment we made. They're magnificent! That was at MTL when they were in Antwerp with Art and Project. We did that one week and then the next we already started buying something else. That left its mark on me.[81]

Andre's floor sculpture *64 Lead Square* (1969) was another of the early acquisitions.[82] A wood sculpture *Henge on 3 Right Thresholds* (1971) exhibited in July–August 1971 at Konrad Fischer, entered the Herberts' collection in May 1975.[83] From 1976, this work was put on permanent loan to the Stedelijk Van Abbemuseum in Eindhoven.[84]

Annick and Anton Herbert bought mostly from dealer galleries or at art fairs such as the Cologne Kunstmarkt. However, contact with the artist was essential: 'First of all you had to be in perfect harmony with the artist. You had to know him and have at least three or four serious discussions with him to see if it held water or not.'[85] Collecting was like an engagement with the artists,[86] and an engagement with those challenging conventional values and established systems. Anton Herbert explains:

> As we started to collect in 1973, we had to show our colours. The purchase of a text by Lawrence Weiner, a discussion by Ian Wilson or a striped fabric by Daniel Buren constituted a declaration. One was announcing one's convictions and one's vision with a certain fanaticism ... We were preoccupied in an obsessive manner with our generation; nothing else existed. We could do nothing else but collect.[87]

Although the Herberts went to most art fairs, they did not travel to buy works. For them, art fairs were places where galleries presented their artists. They bought from dealer galleries, but as Annick Herbert points out:

> But we didn't go to buy an object for the collection. It was the culmination of a discussion, after a long preparation. It was a whole ritual ... We went to see

80 *Many coloured objects placed side by side to form a row of many coloured objects, Works from the collection of Annick and Anton Herbert, Programme* (exh. cat.) Casino Luxembourg-Forum d'art contemporain, Luxembourg, 2000, p.171.

81 Annick and Anton Herbert in conversation with the author, *op. cit.* (author's translation).

82 Jan Debbaut, 'Subjectivité, partialité, independence, qualité, flexibilité', in *Many coloured objects*, *op. cit.*, p.21. Andre's floor sculpture was first exhibited at the Dwan Gallery, New York, in April–May 1969. See: *Carl Andre, Sculptor 1996*, *op. cit.*, p.245.

83 Anton Herbert in an e-mail to the author, 12 May 2006. See: *Ausstellungen bei Konrad Fischer*, *op. cit.*, p.65. See also: *Many coloured objects*, *op. cit.*, pp.190–191. No correspondence or documentation regarding the Gent collectors is kept in the archive of the Konrad Fischer Galerie, Düsseldorf.

84 See: Database 1.6, Section Stedelijk Van Abbemuseum, Eindhoven. It is said that at the time, Anton Herbert was a member of the Board of Trustees of the Van Abbemuseum.

85 Annick and Anton Herbert in conversation with the author, *op. cit.*

86 For instance, in 1982, four years after André Cadere's death in 1978, the Herberts published a book which had been conceived by the artist in the late 1970s. See: *André Cadere, Histoire d'un travail*, *op. cit.*

87 Oscar Van Den Boogaard, 'Discussion with Annick and Anton Herbert', *A-Priori*, no.1, 1999. (author's translation).

> what new things the artist was showing. It was a meeting place for the artist. Then we came back home and the next day talked together about all these works. We took our time.[88]

From the early 1970s, the couple travelled regularly to New York. They always went first to Leo Castelli's to see what was happening there. They had great respect for the dealer whom they saw as an 'old guru'. Further, 'You received a kind of consecration from him, even as a collector. For many people, Castelli's name was like a guarantee of quality. Sonnabend too, but Castelli most of all.'[89] On Fischer's advice they went to Castelli's gallery particularly to see and buy pieces by Nauman, who became extremely important to them at that time. Angela Westwater (of the Sperone-Westwater-Fischer Gallery) was another dealer to sell artworks to the Herberts, including Nauman's *White Breathing* (1976) in 1978.[90]

From the early 1970s, Annick and Anton Herbert were becoming increasingly important collectors. In Belgium, there was a sort of 'challenge' between them and Herman Daled. Anton Herbert remembers that, at the time, 'Daled came to Gent to take a look at those collectors who were starting to move in. He was already collecting actively many years before us and wanted to hang on to his territory.'[91] Nevertheless, the Herberts and Daled had completely different attitudes towards Conceptualism. Unlike Daled, the Gent collectors did not hesitate to purchase very large and difficult installations like Kounellis's rather dangerous *Fuochi* (1971) or the large *6765* (1976) by Mario Merz.[92]

The Herberts' home has been arranged according to the needs of their collection. Since the early 1980s, the collectors have lived surrounded by their artworks in an old industrial building, a 'private museum', spread over three floors, on an overall surface of 2,000 m^2.[93] At this time, the Herberts also started to collect a younger generation of artists (Jan Vercruysse, Franz West).

Their collection has been exhibited on three occasions in European museums. In 1984–85, it was shown for the first time in an exhibition entitled *L'Architecte est absent, Works from the collection of Annick and Anton Herbert, Répertoire* at the Stedelijk Van Abbemuseum, Eindhoven.[94] A second showing, entitled *programme* took place in 2000 at the Casino Luxembourg – Forum d'art contemporain.[95] A third showing was presented in 2006 at the MACBA Barcelona

88 Annick and Anton Herbert in conversation with the author, *op. cit.* (author's translation).

89 *Ibid.* (author's translation).

90 *Many coloured objects*, *op. cit.*, pp.160–161. See also: *L'Architecte est absent*, *op. cit.*, p.28.

91 Annick and Anton Herbert in conversation with the author, *op. cit.* (author's translation).'

92 See: *L'Architecte est absent*, *op. cit.*, pp.41–76.

93 For recent installation shots of the Herbert collection, see: Bernard Marcelis, 'Forcer l'utopie/Utopia the Only Option', in 'Paroles de Collectionneurs', *Art Press*, supplement to no.305, October 2004, pp.12–13. On the occasion of my first visit to Gent on 19 April 2003, the Herberts took me on a tour of their 'private museum'.

94 'L'Architecte est absent, Works from the collection of Annick and Anton Herbert, Répertoire', Stedelijk Van Abbemuseum, Eindhoven, 23 November 1984–6 January 1985.

95 *Many coloured objects placed side by side to form a row of many coloured objects, Works form the collection of Annick and Anton Herbert, Programme*, Casino Luxembourg – Forum d'art contemporain, Luxembourg, 29 October 1999–11 February 2000. The exhibition catalogue is dedicated to Fernand Spillemaeckers and Konrad Fischer.

and at the Kunsthaus Graz.[96] The exhibition title *Works and Documents from the Herbert Collection, Inventaire* implies that they have put an end to their art collecting. They now focus on collecting archival material and documents of the period. They plan to announce the formation of a Foundation in Autumn 2008.

In the late 1960s and 1970s, Flemish cultural identity and the artworld became closely linked. The identity of this group of private collectors was important because it reflected the tensions between the Walloon and Flemish in Belgium. The country has been divided since the 1960s, with part of the population looking towards the Netherlands for cultural affinities, the other to France.[98] The Belgian artist Jacques Charlier suggests that the difference in attitude towards Conceptualism between the Belgians, and the Flemish and Dutch was influenced by opposing religious cultures. The Belgian Catholics, who had a long-lasting tradition of figurative painting going back to Rubens, were receptive to Pop art and Nouveau Réalisme. The Dutch Calvinists, who rejected representations of Biblical figures, were much more comfortable with an abstract and meditative art.[99] Rudi Fuchs echoes this view that abstract and theoretical art have always been largely accepted in the Netherlands.[100]

In Belgium, the intensity of private collecting activities seemed to form a sort of counterbalance to the lack of contemporary art in museums. Belgian museums were very fond of Pop art and were less receptive to Conceptual art. Unlike their German counterparts, Belgian collectors were not inclined to make donations to national museums, as they knew 'the works [would] be relegated to store, or to out-of-date rooms deserted by the public, for an indefinite time'.[101] Indeed, all Belgian private collections remained private at the time. However, the collectors pooled their efforts in various ways. Through the Association for the Museum of Contemporary Art in Gent, a number of private collectors contributed to the purchase of works that would constitute the core of a public collection of contemporary art. Belgian collectors also provided the money that Conceptual artists needed to realise specific projects. In return, the artists would give a number of works to the collectors to share between themselves.[102]

96 'Public Space/Two Audiences, Works and Documents from the Herbert Collection, Inventaire', Museu d'art contemporani de Barcelona, 8 February–1 May 2006; Kunsthaus, Graz, 10 June–3 September 2006.

97 [Editor's note: They have added works by John Baldessari in recent years.]

98 In Belgium, a linguistic border was set up in 1962, along with the partition of the Ministry of Education and Cultural Affairs. In 1977, under Léo Tindeman's government, the Pacte d'Egmont divided the country into three parts: Flanders, Wallonia and Brussels.

99 Charlier in conversation with the author, Luxembourg, *op. cit.*

100 Fuchs in conversation with the author, *op. cit.*

101 Geirlandt, 'Museums, Collectors, Policies', *Studio International*, *op. cit.*, p.116.

102 Perlstein in conversation with the author, *op. cit.* One can also mention the exhibition *Vom Pop zum Konzept, Kunst unserer Zeit in Belgischen Privatsammlungen* (From Pop to Concept, Art of Our Time in Belgian Private Collections) organised at the Neue Galerie-Sammlung Ludwig in 1975.

4.3. The Netherlands

As in Belgium, there was a long-standing tradition of private collecting in the Netherlands. The State encouraged private collecting by providing subsidies on purchases of artworks valued at less than *f*3,000 ($1,050), in the form of a 20 per cent cut of the original price. But no tax reductions were given on the acquisition of larger works.[103] Most collectors focused on post-1945 artists. In the 1950s, many Dutch people started to collect pieces by Realists and members of the Cobra group. There were, for instance, the collections of De Jong (Hengelo), Sijmons (Amsterdam), Tiessen (Hilversum), De Groot (Groningen), Piet Sanders (Schiedam), Van Achterbergh (Amstelveen) and Van der Wal (Ouderkerk). Additionally, Piers (Amsterdam), Kuilman (Schiedam) and Groenendijk (Amsterdam) mostly bought works by Dutch artists. Maarten and Reina van Bommel-van Dam opened a museum in 1971 in Venlo to host their collection of modern Dutch art.

In the early 1970s, the collection of Tromp Meesters was added to the holdings of the Museum Van Bommel-Van Dam. It included pieces by Conceptual artists such as Dibbets, Dekkers and Van Elk. Wijnand and Annette Wildenberg (Amstelveen) collected Dutch artists such as Pieter Engels and Theo Niermeijer, but also Conceptual artists such as Gilbert & George, Ruthenbeck and Van Elk. In the late 1960s and 1970s, Dutch artists were also collecting Conceptual art. Dibbets, for instance, always spent about ten per cent of his earnings on contemporary art.[104]

Frits and Agnes Becht

One of the largest private collections was put together by Frits and Agnes Becht (Hilversum). Frits Becht was interested in contemporary art and was involved in planning the exhibition programme at the art gallery De Posthoorn in The Hague. They also provided financial support for contemporary art events such as Sonsbeek 71.[105] The scope of their 'closed' collection was large, including Cobra, Pop art, Nouveau Réalisme, contemporary Dutch art (Van Elk) and Conceptual art: Gilbert & George (*Postcard Sculpture*, 1972; *Conception and Nothing but The*

103 Geert van Beijeren, 'Note on private collections in the Netherlands', *Studio International*, May 1973, vol. 185, no.955, pp.233–235. See also: Oxenaar, 'On art and museum policies in the Netherlands', *Studio International*, *op. cit.*, p.205.

104 Dibbets in conversation with the author, *op. cit.* During my visit to his home in Amsterdam, Dibbets showed me some of the works in his private collection, such as Andre and Ryman.

105 See: *Sonsbeek 71*, Part 1, *op. cit.*, p.17.

Best, 1970), Andre (*Aluminium Piece, 21 units*, 1967), Long (*Untitled*, 1972) and Schum (*Land Art*, 1969). Part of the Becht collection was shown publicly in 1968 at the Stedelijk Van Abbemuseum, Eindhoven, and in 1984 at the Stedelijk Museum, Amsterdam.[106]

Herman and Henriëtte van Eelen

Herman and Henriëtte van Eelen (Amsterdam) formed a small but coherent private collection. He was the first Dutch male model; she was a speech therapist. The Van Eelens started by collecting works by Cobra artists (Reinier Lucassen, Karel Appel). In the late 1960s, Lucassen introduced them to Dibbets, and they were among the first collectors to buy his work (*Twee dozen*, 1966).[107] Dibbets in turn introduced them to many Conceptual artists and also to Fischer. They purchased numerous works through the Düsseldorf dealer, including Long's *Rectangle of Sticks* (1968)[108] and Ryman's *Orrin* (1967). For many years, this was the only piece by the American artist in the Netherlands. They purchased the painting from Fischer after he had visited the artist during a trip to New York in 1969.[109]

Fischer was influential in the constitution of the Van Eelen collection. Herman van Eelen remembers several sales that occurred through the Düsseldorf dealer:

> Professionally, I was an actor, so I travelled to several places in Europe. I'd always go back home via Düsseldorf. I'd go to the gallery and Konrad would say: 'I have another piece for you.' I'd reply: 'But Konrad, I have no money.' He'd respond: 'Am I talking about money? You need this piece. You have to have it.' One day, I went there and told Konrad: 'I have to put this work down, I can't pay.' It was two drawings by Bruce Nauman [*Untitled (Design for a space)*,1971, *Untitled (Positive and Negative)*, 1971] ... Yes, this is what Konrad would do. He'd say: 'Now you have a Robert Ryman, you have a Nauman ...' Then I'd ask him: 'Who else do I need in my collection?' He'd reply: 'Richard Long.' He explained and we finally bought the work before actually seeing it. [*Rectangle of Sticks*, 1968].[110]

106 See: *Three blind mice*, *op. cit.*, and *Collectie Becht: Beeldende Kunst Uit De Verzameling Van Agnes En Frits Becht/The Becht Collection: Visual Art from the Agnes and Frits Becht Collection* (exh. cat.), Uitgeverij Reflex, Utrecht; Stedelijk Museum, Amsterdam, 1984.

107 Visser, 'Conceptuele kunst 1965–1975', *Bulletin Stedelijk Museum Amsterdam*, *op. cit.*, p.4.

108 See: Héman, Poot and Visser, *Conceptual art in the Netherlands and Belgium*, *op. cit.*, p.165.

109 Herman and Henriëtte van Eelen in conversation with the author, *op. cit.*

110 *Ibid.*

The Van Eelens also bought at Art & Project and from De Decker. Herman van Eelen sums up the situation: 'That was the circuit: there was Art & Project, Konrad Fischer – maybe he was a bit more important than the others – and Anny De Decker. That was also the circuit of the artists.'[111]

The Van Eelens mostly bought small and early pieces by Conceptual artists. They wanted to buy artworks that could be put in their house, as they lived surrounded by art. Other works in their collection include Broodthaers (*La Signature Série 1*, 1969), Darboven (*Ohne Titel*, 1971), Huebler (*Location Piece No. 8*, 1969–1970) and Weiner (*A turbulence within a body of water*, 1969).[112] The now famous *Project for Art & Project* (1969), realised for Dibbets's solo show at Art & Project in November–December 1969, and published in the Siegelaub special issue of *Studio International* (July–August 1970), is also part of the Van Eelen collection.

Additionally, the Van Eelens supported Conceptual artists' exhibitions in the Netherlands. In 1971, they sponsored the realisation of Daniel Buren's work at Sonsbeek 71.[113] In 1972, their collection was shown, together with that of Mia and Martin Visser, in the exhibition *Conceptual Art of Two Private Collections* in Utrecht.[114] The Herman and Henriëtte van Eelen collection is relatively small (35 works), but it is important enough to interest Dutch museums. They are currently negotiating its sale with the Kröller-Müller Museum, Otterlo.[115]

Martin and Mia Visser

Martin and Mia Visser were important Dutch private collectors. Martin Visser came from an artistic background: his father was the painter Arie Visser and his brother was the artist Carel Visser. He himself was a furniture designer. Mia Visser was actively engaged in the art world, working for the Galerie Seriaal, Amsterdam. In the 1950s, whilst they were still living in Amsterdam, the Vissers started their collection with Cobra works.

At the end of the decade, they moved into a mid-1950s Rietveld house in Bergeyk (Eindhoven) in the south of the Netherlands. They put their Cobra works in deposit, since they felt they would be inappropriate in the modern architecture of their new home. They eventually sold these works when they became interested in Nouveau Réalisme artists such as Piero Manzoni and Lucio Fontana, Arman and Christo. They bought some of these pieces at Wide White

111 *Ibid.*

112 This statement was acquired from the artist in exchange for a plane ticket from Europe to New York. See: *ibid.*

113 See: *Sonsbeek 71*, *op. cit.*, p.17.

114 *Conceptual Art from two private collections* (exh. cat.), Utrechtse Kring, Neudeflat, Utrecht, 5–26 March 1972.

115 For an overview of the Conceptual artworks in the Van Eelen collection, see the document: 'Kröller-Müller Museum, gegevensoverzicht, total aantal werken: 35', in Herman and Henriëtte van Eelen Archive, Amsterdam.

Space in Antwerp, which was close to Bergeyk.[116] The Vissers became close friends with De Decker and Lohaus.

In the late 1960s, the Vissers discovered Conceptual artists. They gradually sold most of their Nouveau Réalisme works to start a new collection. They got to know Fischer via Kasper König[117] and were among the first collectors of the Düsseldorf dealer following his inaugural exhibition of Andre in 1967:

> Martin and Mia Visser were immediately convinced by *Altstadt Rectangle*, the floor-filling sculpture that Carl Andre exhibited at Konrad Fischer in October 1967. At the opening they invited the artist to make a work especially for their house ... Instead of a wall-to-wall floor piece, in Bergeyk it was a modest rug [*Square piece (for Mia and Martin Visser)*, 1967]. Martin and Mia Visser were a little disappointed with the result: 'I found it so marvellous at Konrad Fischer's, but so small here', Martin Visser reminisces.[118]

Martin Visser remembers that they had close links with four galleries at the time. 'In the first place there was Galerie Schmela (Alfred and Monika Schmela) in Düsseldorf and the Wide White Space. Next, one has to mention the galleries of Michael Werner in Cologne and Konrad Fischer in Düsseldorf. We went to Germany and Belgium nearly every week.'[119]

The Vissers also commissioned works. For instance, in January 1969, in the Dartmoor region of England, Long realised a photographic work in collaboration with Gerry Schum, *Seven Views of a Sculpture Made for Martin and Mia Visser of Bergeyk, Holland*.[120] In 1972, the Vissers bought a piece of woodland near their home for Long to execute the slate work *Sculpture* (1972) there.[121] In February 1969, Buren made an installation of green-and-white stripes in their house.[122] The collectors let Buren choose the space and he decided on the main wall in the library.[123] The deal was arranged through Wide White Space. In 1972, their Conceptual art collection was so extensive that the Vissers had a large semi-circular extension built by Aldo van Eyck in which to keep some of the works. They also put up two prefabricated sheds in an industrial park to display more works.[124]

In the late 1960s, the Vissers were very active in the Conceptual network. They got to know Buren at Prospect 68 in Düsseldorf, where Martin Visser was

116 'Interview Yves Aupetitallot, Anny De Decker, Bernd Lohaus', in Aupetitallot, *Wide White Space*, *op. cit.*, pp.32–124.

117 'Two-women show as good as solo show, Ein Gespräch mit Kasper König', in Kölle, *Die Kunst des Ausstellen*, *op. cit.*, p.242.

118 *The Collection Visser at the Kröller-Müller Museum*, *op. cit.*, unnumbered pages.

119 'Interview Yves Aupetitallot, Martin Visser', in Aupetitallot, *Wide White Space*, *op. cit.*, p.123.

120 *Sculpture by Richard Long, made for Martin & Mia Visser, Bergeijk*, publication no.9, sponsored by Martin and Mia Visser, Bereijk, published by Fernsehgalerie Gerry Schum, Cologne, 1969.

121 Van Beijeren, 'Notes on private collections in the Netherlands', *Studio International*, *op. cit.*, p.233. This work was co-owned by one of Martin Visser's brothers, Geertjan Visser (Antwerp), with whom the Vissers built up a separate collection of mostly larger and more expensive Conceptual pieces.

122 'Interview Yves Aupetitallot, Anny De Decker, Bernd Lohaus', Aupetitallot, *Wide White Space*, *op. cit.*, pp.55–125.

123 According to Carel Blotkamp, Martin Visser feels more enthusiastic about works that are obstacles in his house, as a sort of challenge to his own job as a functional furniture designer. See: *The Collection Visser at the Kröller-Müller Museum*, *op. cit.*, p.20.

124 For installation shots of the Visser's home and sheds, see: *Ibid.*, pp.14–22.

on the selection committee.[125] He continued to assume this responsibility at Prospect 69.[126] In 1969, he also contributed to the setting up of the alternative art institute A 379089 in Antwerp. In 1971, the Dutch collectors were sponsors of Sonsbeek 71.[127] And from the late 1960s onwards, Mia Visser was the assistant of Dick van der Net at Edition Bergeyk.[128]

In the late 1960s and 1970s, the Visser collection was shown publicly several times. In 1968 (Eindhoven) and 1972 (Utrecht), it was presented together with other private collections.[129] In 1976, drawings from the Mia and Martin Visser and Gertjaan Visser collections were exhibited at the Kunstmuseum Basel, then directed by Franz Meyer.[130]

From the late 1970s, Martin Visser donated and sold part of the Conceptual collection to the Kröller-Müller Museum in Otterlo. The first gifts and sales were made in 1977, the year of Mia Visser's death. Later, Visser got married again, to Joek van der Heijden, with whom he started to collect new German art. As he had done previously, he sold Conceptual artworks to start this new collection. Visser remarked on this process:

> 'When you take your works of art to a museum, it is like sending your children off to an orphanage', Carl Andre once wrote to us. Such a bond, as between parents and children, has never existed between art and ourselves. We always saw this relationship as temporary in the sense that we were allowed to look after it for a while. And the better the work of art, the more aloof it was. This is how we felt about it.[131]

The Visser Collection at the Kröller-Müller Museum, Otterlo

Between the late 1970s and 2001, 125 works of the Conceptual artists studied here purchased by the Vissers between the late 1960s and the late 1970s were integrated into the Kröller-Müller Museum's permanent collection. Although this represents only part of the Visser Collection of Conceptual art, it gives an instructive insight into the collectors' purchasing procedure.[132]

Of the 125 works, 101 were purchased between 1967 and 1976.[133] Most works were originally purchased by the collectors from Konrad Fischer, Düsseldorf (45). Artists were the source for 49 of the works, the collectors receiving 34 as gifts,

125 *Prospect '68*, *op. cit.*, p.1. See also: Chapter 2.1.

126 *Prospect '69*, *op. cit.*, p.1. See also: Chapter 2.2.

127 *Sonsbeek 71*, *op. cit.*, p.17.

128 See for instance: Letter from Edition Bergeyk to Prospect 68, Kunsthalle Düsseldorf, dated 16 September 1969, signed by Mia Visser and Dick van der Net, about the manufacture of steel works by Bruce Nauman, in File IV 29371-138, AKDSD.

129 *Three blind mice*, *op. cit.*, and *Conceptual Art from two private collections*, *op. cit.*

130 *Zeichnen/Bezeichnen: Zeichnungen aus der Sammlung Mia und Martin Visser, Bergeijk, mit Beiträgen aus der Sammlung Geert Jan Visser, Antwerpen* (exh. cat.), Kunstmuseum Basel, 1976.

131 'Interview Yves Aupetitallot, Martin Visser', in Aupetitallot, *Wide White Space*, *op. cit.*, p.124.

132 The comprehensive catalogues of the Visser Collection at the Kröller-Müller Museum contain many details on the acquisition of the works, the artworks themselves, and information on the provenance and date of purchase by the collectors. They also record the circumstances and date on which the pieces were acquired by the museum. See: *The Collection Visser at the Kröller-Müller Museum*, *op. cit.*, and *The Collection Visser at the Kröller-Müller Museum, Supplement*, Stichting Kröller-Müller Museum, Otterlo, 2001. For an overview of the Visser Collection at the Kröller-Müller Museum, Otterlo, see: Database 4 (Appendix 1.4).

133 See: Database 4 (Appendix 1.4).

while 15 were purchased. Wide White Space (6) and Art & Project (7, including one with MTL) were other important sources. Among additional dealers were the Galerie Seriaal (2), John Weber (2), Michael Werner (1), Rolf Ricke (1), Rolf Preisig (1), Durand-Dessert (1), the Lisson Gallery (1) and Nigel Greenwood (1). Five works were purchased from Dick van der Net. The provenance of three works remains unknown. We clearly see that, except for the artist themselves, Fischer was the main source. The studied Conceptual artists most represented in the Visser Collection now in the Kröller-Müller Museum are Sol LeWitt (40), Carl Andre (20) and Bruce Nauman (16), many of which are working drawings.

4.4. Great Britain, France, Switzerland, Italy

Compared with West Germany, Belgium and the Netherlands, countries such as Great Britain, France, Switzerland and Italy had fewer Conceptual art collectors.

Great Britain

Several private collectors bought Conceptual art without amassing comprehensive collections in Britain. The publisher Hugh Pilkington purchased pieces from the early 1970s. The American painter Princess Sylvia Guirey (a decendent of Hugo von Hofmannsthal) bought drawings and small works by Brice Marden, Keith Milow and Gilbert & George from Nigel Greenwood.[134] Patricia Rawlings (now Baroness Rawlings), a Conservative Party European politician, backed Greenwood. She enabled him to put on an Ed Ruscha exhibition in 1973 by buying two works.[135]

Peter Palumbo and Max Gordon

In the 1970s, the major property developer Peter Palumbo (now Lord) was an important private collector. He collected Pop art (Rauschenberg, Johns) and owned buildings by prominent architects, such as Mies van der Rohe, Frank Lloyd Wright and Le Corbusier.[136] He possessed many buildings in Cork Street,

134 Morris in conversation with the author.

135 At the time, Rawlings lived in Turner's studio on the Cheyne Walk on the border of the River Thames in London and was a friend of Princess Margaret. Morris in conversation with the author.

136 In 1972, Palumbo bought Mies van der Rohe's Farnsworth House in Plano, Illinois, to which he added the designer's furniture. Since 1986, he has also owned Kentuck Knob, a private house built by Wright in Chalk Hill, Pennsylvania, and Le Corbusier's Maisons Jaoul in Neuilly-sur-Seine, France. Information from Lynda Morris. See: 'Lord Palumbo', *The Tatler*, vol. 290, no.9, September 1995, p.149.

London, in which dealer galleries were established in the 1970s. He backed Nigel Greenwood's Barry Le Va exhibition set up in 1971 in an underground garage. Palumbo is a powerful member of the London art scene. In 1978, he briefly became Chairman of the Tate Gallery; he was also Chairman of the Whitechapel Art Gallery during Nicholas Serota's Directorship.[137]

The architect Max Gordon, who lived in Belgravia Square in London, collected the works of artists such as Brice Marden. He was an active member of the Contemporary Art Society (CAS), which contributed works in order to increase the representation of contemporary British artists in British museums. Gordon also had connections with the Museum of Modern Art in New York. When Kynaston McShine (MOMA) and John Coplans (*Artforum*) came over to London, he organised artworld parties.[139] Max Gordon was close to the artist Keith Milow, who exhibited at the Kasmin Gallery and later at Nigel Greenwood.

Ted and Alan Power

Ted Power was a businessman working for Murphy Radios in Cambridge. He collected mainly Abstract Expressionism and owned important works such as Barnett Newman's *Uriel* (1955). He was also involved in the Contemporary Art Society. In the early 1970s, he was one of the Trustees of the Tate Gallery, London.[140] Moreover, Power was interested in Conceptual art. Greenwood, who was one of his dealers, considered him as 'mentally a very young collector'.[141] He sold him some of the small-edition pieces *Speeches* by Gilbert & George. Power bought numerous works by Judd and LeWitt from the Lisson Gallery.[142] Ted Power's son, Alan, also acquired Conceptual artworks, such as Long's *Walking a Line in Peru* (1972) and *Three Stone Circles*.[143]

Conceptual art dealers such as Greenwood and Wendler also established collections at the time.[144] The latter had a comprehensive collection of Conceptual art, since he had already collected in the US through Sieglaub before opening a gallery in London. British Conceptual artists themselves, for instance, Charlton, Long and Gilbert & George, also put together art collections by exchanging works.

137 Later, Palumbo became the Chairman of the Tate Gallery's Foundation (1986–87) and the Chairman of the Arts Council of Great Britain (1988–93) at the time of the development of the rules for the introduction of the National Lottery Funding. He is currently the Chairman of the Serpentine Gallery and a Trustee of the National History Museum. A backer of the Conservative Party, he used to be a polo teammate of Prince Charles.

138 Max Gordon's brother, the property developer David Gordon, was a Kasmin collector.

139 Morris in conversation with the author.

140 See: 'The Tate Gallery: acquisitions, exhibitions, trustees, future developments', *Studio International*, vol.185, no.954, April 1973, p.188.

141 'Interview with Nigel Greenwood', in Moseley, *Conception*, *op. cit.*, p.131.

142 Logsdail in conversation with the author, *op. cit.*

143 See: Letter from Konrad Fischer to Alan Power dated 22 August 1972, in Allgemeine Korrespondenz 1972–73, AKFGD.

144 The content of the Greenwood gallery was sold at auction in 1992. See: *The Contents of the Nigel Greenwood Gallery, Sold by Order of the Creditors*, Sotheby's, London, 15 October 1992.

France

In the late 1960s and 1970s, Conceptual art did not make a huge impact in France. The lack of a real engagement on the part of the art world with Conceptual artists did not stimulate private collecting. Roger Mazarguil (Paris) was one of the rare collectors of Conceptual works. He owned pieces by Wilson (*The Roger Mazarguil, Daniel Buren and Ian Wilson discussion of February 23, 1970*, 1970), Buren and Weiner. He was one of the first clients of the Galerie Durand-Dessert, Paris.[145] Other collectors included Françoise and Jean-Philippe Billarant (Buren, *Sans Titre*, 1972; Toroni, Downsbrough, Weiner),[146] Jacques and Myriam Salomon, Jean Brolly and Vicky Rémy (Saint-Tropez). The latter donated her collection of over 700 works by artists such as Robert Filliou and Art & Language (*Secret Painting*, 1967–68) to the Musée d'art Moderne in Saint-Étienne (1992).[147]

Some French dealers put together private collections of the works of the artists they were representing. Yvon Lambert, for instance, owned many pieces by such artists as Cadere (*Barre de bois rond formée de segments de bois point*, 1977), Long (*Sculpture at Yvon Lambert, Paris, 1969*, 1969), Ryman (*Untitled*, 1975) and Weiner (*Down and out, out and down, down and out, out and down*, 1971).[148] The dealers Liliane and Michel Durand-Dessert also acquired pieces by their artists, Darboven (*Variante 58*, 1975) and Tremlett (*Staring at the Sky and Watching the Way They Dart and Fly*, 1977).[149] The art merchant Ghislain Mollet-Viéville (Paris) put together a collection of Conceptual art from the late 1960s onwards. Part of this is now held by the MAMCO, Geneva (Cadere's *Barre de bois rond*, 1976; Andre's *Ten steel row*, 1967; LeWitt's *Wall drawing #43*, 1970).[150]

Switzerland

There were not many Swiss private collectors interested in Conceptual art during the 1970s. The Basel-based dealer Rolf Preisig mentioned a dentist named Oettli, from Wettingen, who regularly bought from his gallery in the 1970s (Rückriem, Fulton, Richter).[151]

Urs Raussmüller

Central to private art collecting in Switzerland was the artist and architect Urs Raussmüller. From the late 1970s onwards, he advised the Migros supermarket

145 Guy Tosatto, 'Entretien Liliane et Michel Durand-Dessert', in *L'art au Futur antérieur*, *op. cit.*, p.17.

146 See: *De concert, Oeuvres d'une collection privée* (exh. cat.), Frac des Pays de la Loire, Carquefou, 2002.

147 See: *Collection Vicky Rémy* (exh. cat.), Musée d'art moderne, Saint-Étienne, 2005.

148 In 2000, a private museum to host the Collection Lambert, opened at the Hôtel de Caumont in Avignon, Southern France. See: *Rendez-vous, Collection Lambert*, Actes Sud, Arles, 2000.

149 In 2004, the collection of Liliane and Michel Durand-Dessert was exhibited at the Musée de Grenoble. See: *L'art au Futur antérieur*, *op. cit.* In October 2005, a large part of their private collection was sold at auction at Sotheby's, Paris.

150 For an overview of the Mollet-Viéville collection, see: *GMV, Agent d'Art* (exh. cat.), École régionale des Beaux-Arts Georges Pompidou, Dunkerque, 1986.

151 Preisig in conversation with the author, *op. cit.*

company, which had begun collecting contemporary art (Dibbets, Darboven, Andre).[152] Between 1978 and 1981, Raussmüller launched, together with the Migros-Genossenschafts-Bund (MGB), the Halle für Internationale neue Kunst (InK) in Zürich.[153] The InK supported the production of large works and organised exhibitions of Swiss and international contemporary art (Ryman, Merz, Weiner, Long) and later acquired some of the works.

From 1974, Raussmüller also formed, for several important Swiss industrialists of the Cosmorex company, the renowned Sammlung Crex (a collection of contemporary art) in Zurich.[154] Numerous works of the Crex Collection found their way into the Hallen für neue Kunst.[155] This private museum was founded in 1984 by Raussmüller in a former textile factory on the Rhine in Schaffhausen. Artworks from Raussmüller's own collection, together with long-term loans from fellow Swiss collectors and artists turned this institution into an impressive venue for Conceptual art.[156] Major pieces by artists such as Long (*Lightning Fire Wood Circle*), Merz, Nauman, Ryman and Weiner (*Iron Steel and Glass strewn underfoot upon a Path from Place to Place*) have been installed in the museum. Urs Raussmüller was one of Fischer's main collectors.

Italy

As in France, the Italian art market suffered from a lack of dealer galleries and museums interested in Conceptual art during the 1960s and 1970s. There were a number of smaller private collectors, such as Frua de Angeli (Milan), Pier Luigi Pero (Turin), Marco Brignone, (Turin), Giorgio Franchetti (Rome), Corrado Levi (Turin), Alberto Mazzoni, Ennio Brion (both in Milan) and Carlo Catelani (Modena). Catelani (who died in 1996) was a dealer and an important Minimal and Conceptual art collector (LeWitt, Ryman, Flavin, Morris). He was a good friend of the dealer Massimo Minini, Brescia, and of Giancarlo Politi (*Flash Art*).[158]

Egidio Marzona and Angelo Baldassare

Egidio Marzona, who founded a publishing company in the mid-1970s in Milan, began collecting Conceptual art in the late 1960s. He acquired works from Konrad Fischer, Heiner Friedrich and Rolf Ricke.[159] Hundreds of works by artists

152 In 1996, the Migros Museum für Gegenwartskunst was founded in Zürich.

153 Christel Sauer, 'InK – die Halle für internationale neue Kunst', *Du*, April 1980, pp.6–11. See also: *InK. Halle für internationale neue Kunst*. Information, InK, Halle für internationale neue Kunst, Zürich, 1978.

154 Works from the Crex Collection were shown in an exhibition organised at the Stedelijk Van Abbemuseum, Eindhoven in 1978. Since 1993, the Crex Collection has been on view at the Kammgarnareals, Schaffhausen. See: 'Das Projekt Kammgarn ist eine einmalige Chance für die Region', *Wochen-Express*, 3 February 1993, pp.6–9.

155 See: Kira van Lil, *Kurzführer Hallen für neue Kunst*, Hallen für neue Kunst, Schaffhausen, 1999.

156 Among Swiss collectors participating in the Schaffhausen project were the bank director Robert Strebel, the lawyer Hans B. Wyss and the collector Michael Liebelt. This situation of privately and collectively owned artworks led, however, to several misunderstandings and legal actions. See: Elfie Kreis, 'Wem gehört das Kapital? Besitzrechtstreit um Beuys-Installation in den Hallen für neue Kunst Schaffhausen', *Informationsdienst KUNST*, no.325, 28 April 2005, pp.6–10.

157 'Konrad Fischer', *Kunstforum International*, *op. cit.*, pp.281.

158 Massimo Minini in an e-mail to the author, 21 February 2006. Carlo Catelani sold large parts of his Conceptual collection at Sotheby's, London, in the 1970s. See: *Sale of Contemporary Art 1945–*

such as Buren and Merz, Andre and Kosuth were part of his collection.[160] According to Françoise Lambert, who ran a dealer gallery in Milan from 1969 onwards, the two main Italian private collectors of Conceptual art at the time were Angelo Baldassare (Bari) and Giuseppe Panza (Varese).[161] Baldassare is very discreet about his collection, which he keeps private.

Giuseppe Panza

Count Giuseppe Panza di Biumo (born 1923) was a Milan businessman, working in the family business of real estate development and industrial alcohol manufacture. The extensive financial means he had at his disposal after he came into his inheritance in the mid-1950s allowed him to gather, together with his wife Giovanna, one of the biggest collections of postwar art in Europe. In the 1950s, Panza started his collection with Nouveau Réalisme (Tàpies, Fautrier) and Pop art (Rauschenberg, Lichtenstein). From the early 1960s onwards, he was in regular contact with American dealer galleries (Castelli, Sonnabend) and the Galleria Gian Enzo Sperone, Turin, who all represented Pop artists.[162]

Panza's first encounter with Conceptual art occurred at *When Attitudes Become Form*, organised in 1969 by Harald Szeemann at the Kunsthalle Bern. In autumn 1970, he went to New York and tried in vain to get in touch with Seth Siegelaub. Finally, he bought his first pieces by Huebler and Weiner from Sperone.[163] In 1973, Panza explained his acquisition methods:

> I don't buy from artists but always from dealers. I don't like discussing prices with them, nor making my choice in their presence. I've never bought anything during the big international events ... Some merchants have a determining role; without their work of preliminary selection and attentive, intelligent and sensible research into the complex and disconcerting world of artists who experiment with new ways of expression and new ideas, it would be very difficult for me to discern the most important personalities. For example, it is thanks to Leo Castelli and Dick Bellamy that I could acquire, in 1962, numerous Pop works; and it is thanks to Sperone and Fischer that I acquired Conceptualists in 69 and 70.[164]

1974, Sotheby & Co, London, Part 1, 3 April 1974, Part 2, 4 April 1974; *Sale of Contemporary Art 1945–1974* (December), *op. cit.*; *Sale of Contemporary Art 1945–1976*, Sotheby's, London, 2 December 1976; *Sale of Contemporary Art 1945–1977*, Sotheby's, London, 30 June 1977. These sales took place against a background of a ban on foreign transactions in Italy due to the first oil crisis.

159 'Joachim Kreibohm im Gespräch mit Egidio Marzona', *Artist Kunstmagazin*, February 1994, no.20, pp.12–15.

160 In 2002, the Marzona Collection was purchased by the Nationalgalerie Hamburger Bahnhof Museum für Gegenwartskunst in Berlin. See: *The Marzona Collection*, Hatje Cantz, Ostfildern, 2002. [Editor's note: In 1993, Edition Marzona Bielefeld published *Ausstellungen bei Konrad Fischer Düsseldorf Oktober 1967–Oktober 1992*.]

161 Françoise Lambert in conversation with the author, *op. cit.*

162 *Art of the Fifties, Sixties and Seventies, The Panza Collection*, *op. cit.*, pp.28–41.

163 'Un grand collectionneur européen d'art américain: Giuseppe Panza', *XXe siècle*, vol.35, no.41, December 1973, p.126.

164 *Ibid.*, p.126 (author's translation).

As an illustration, Huebler's *Site Sculpture Project, Duration Piece #9, Berkeley, California – Hull, Massachusetts* (1969) was part of the Bern show (March–April 1969). In the exhibition catalogue it was cited as being part of the collection of the artist.[165] A year later, in March 1970, the piece was exhibited in a solo show of the artist at Sperone's.[166] Huebler's *Duration Piece #9* is part of the catalogue of works in the Panza Collection.[167] Similarly, the statement *Beside itself* (1970) was exhibited at Weiner's solo show at Sperone's in December 1970. The work is also mentioned in the catalogue of the Panza Collection.[168] We know from Panza that he bought his first Conceptual pieces after *Attitudes* at Sperone's, and can therefore deduce that he purchased these two works from Sperone in Turin.

If we compare the pieces exhibited in Weiner's solo show at Konrad Fischer in April 1969, with the early works of the artist in the Panza Collection, we see that three works match: *The residue of a flare ignited upon a boundary*, *One Kilogram of lacquer poured upon a floor* and *1000 German Marks worth medium bulk material transferred from one country to another*.[169] The first of these works is now part of the collection of the Guggenheim Museum, New York. From the research I have undertaken on the Panza Collection held at this museum, it emerges that Weiner's statement was purchased in 1970 from Fischer.[170]

In 1968–69, Panza acquired over 40 works by Nauman, among others, from Castelli.[171] A year later, in 1970, he bought many paintings by Ryman, notably from Friedrich. He explained:

> When Ryman showed at the Lambert Gallery in Milan in '69, suddenly I realised how beautiful this radical way of painting was, how strong this way of conceiving art was. I decided to buy all the Ryman paintings available in Europe and America. At this time Ryman had several shows in Europe, but he sold almost nothing. So it was possible to buy about 20 paintings in just a few months, which was all Ryman's production over several years.[172]

The Italian collector also visited and purchased works at the Cologne Kunstmarkt from the late 1960s onwards.[173] In 1972, Panza visited the art fair at which each dealer gallery presented one artist on its stand. Fischer exhibited recent work by Dibbets, notably *Daylight* and *Horizon* pieces.[174] Panza purchased

165 Harald Szeemann (ed.), *When Attitudes Become Form* (exh. cat.), Kunsthalle Bern, 1969, work no.38.

166 Minola, Mundici, Poli and Roberto, *Gian Enzo Sperone*, *op. cit.*, p.161.

167 *Art of the Fifties, Sixties and Seventies, The Panza Collection*, *op. cit.*, p.303.

168 Minola, Mundici, Poli and Roberto, *Gian Enzo Sperone*, *op. cit.*, p.177. See also: *Art of the Fifties, Sixties and Seventies, The Panza Collection*, *op. cit.*, p.312.

169 *Ausstellungen bei Konrad Fischer*, *op. cit.*, p.30. See also: *Art of the Fifties, Sixties and Seventies, The Panza Collection*, *op. cit.*, p.312.

170 For this transatlantic research, I am indebted to the help of Sharon Newfeld from the Archive of the Solomon R. Guggenheim Museum, New York. (E-mails in February–March 2004.)

171 *Art of the Fifties, Sixties and Seventies, The Panza Collection*, *op. cit.*, pp.48–50.

172 *Ibid.*, pp.45–49.

173 Letter from Konrad Fischer to Giuseppe Panza dated 9 November 1969, in Galerie Korrespondenz 1967–69, AKFGD.

174 *6. Kölner Kunstmarkt 1972*, *op. cit.*, unnumbered pages.

175 Lynda Morris remembered the sale taking place, in conversation with the author. See also: *Art of the Fifties, Sixties and Seventies, The Panza Collection*, *op. cit.*, p.302

176 Between 1956 and 1976, Panza spent about $1.5 million to acquire 600 works of art, spending no more than $10,000 on any one piece. See: *Ibid.*, pp.32–59.

several works by Dibbets on this occasion.[175]

Panza collected Conceptual art from 1969 until 1976, when the Italian economic downturn and the resulting slow-down of his business forced him to stop.[17] During that period, he not only acquired hundreds of Conceptual artworks, but also commissioned artists to realise works and installations in his Italian home. He lived in the large Villa Menafoglio Litta Panza, Biumo Superiore, in Varese near Milan. Even as early as December 1968, Buren executed the in-situ *White and Green Papers Collage, Varese*.[177] Around 1972, due to a need to increase available space, the stables were transformed into small exhibition spaces. Installations of Conceptual artists such as Flavin and Graham were installed in the stables, as well as in the main body of the house.[178]

Panza also actively participated in the art world with writings, conferences, exhibitions and loans. He wrote extensively on artists, museums and cultural legislation in numerous publications (*Gran Bazar*, *Data*, *Cimaise*, *Il Sole: 24 Ore*, *La Stampa*).[179] Among other cultural responsibilities, he was on the Advisory Council of the DIA Art Foundation, New York, founded by Friedrich in 1974.[180] From 1975 onwards, Panza was involved in the Edinburgh Art Festival activities organised by the Scottish dealer Richard Demarco.[181] In the early 1980s, he became a Founding Trustee of the Museum of Contemporary Art (MOCA), Los Angeles.[182]

During the 1970s, Panza tried to place parts of his collection as long-term loans in various museums in Europe. He was particularly motivated to do this after the Italian government enacted legislation concerning cultural patrimony laws. In 1972, he offered part of his collection on long-term loan to the Stedelijk Museum.[183] However, this proposal was turned down by the museum, possibly because of the collector's demands regarding the quality of the rooms in which his works would be permanently exhibited.[184]

Two years later, in 1974, Panza made an offer of a 15-year loan to the new Städtisches Museum, Mönchengladbach, due for completion in 1979.[185] Johannes Cladders, the museum's Director, showed great interest. Cladders and Panza signed a contract, which agreed deadlines for the delivery of the new building and the availability of the collection.[186] A couple of years later it became apparent that both parties would be unable to honour the terms of the contract.

177 *Ibid.*, p.278. See also: *Daniel Buren, Mot à Mot*, *op. cit.*, p.A32.

178 Today, only a few installations by Conceptual artists remain in their original settings (Flavin, Irwin and Turrell). During my visit to the villa during the summer of 2003, there were mainly works of contemporary Italian and American artists on view (Ettore Spalletti, Vittorio Tavernari, David Simpson, Ford Beckman). See: *The Panza Collection, Villa Menafoglio Litta Panza – Varese*, FAI, Skira, Milan, 2002.

179 See: Series III, in Inventory of the Giuseppe Panza Papers, 1956–90, GRILA. (Accession no. 940004, www.getty.edu/research/tools/ special_ collections/panza_ m1.html) Panza's archive was acquired in 1995 by the Getty Research Institute, Los Angeles.

180 See: Dia Art Foundation Annual Report 1975, in Urbaschek, *Dia Art Foundation*, *op. cit.*, p.252.

181 See: Series VI, Box 235–4, 242–3, in Inventory of the Giuseppe Panza Papers, 1956–90, GRILA.

182 See: Series IV, Boxes 198+202, in *Ibid.*

183 Manuscript letter from Panza to De Wilde dated 20 December 1972, in Box 153, Tentoonstellingen (1972), ASMA.

184 Letter from De Wilde to Panza dated 8 January 1973, in Box 153, Tentoonstellingen 1972, ASMA.

185 'Mönchengladbach', *Flash Art*, no.46–47, June 1974, p.73. See also: Series I, Box 58–1, in Inventory of the Giuseppe Panza Papers, 1956–90, GRILA.

186 Johannes Cladders in conversation with the author, *op. cit.*

The building works took longer than originally planned (the construction was not completed until 1982), while Panza encountered legal problems in the form of new Italian laws on exportation.[187] Werner Schmalenbach, from the Museum of North Rhine Westphalia, Düsseldorf, heard of Cladder's difficulties in delivering a new building on time, and tried to take over the contract. But Cladders would only agree to transfer the contract to him in return for half of the Düsseldorf museum's collection of works by Paul Klee (about 60 pieces); Schmalenbach refused.[188]

In 1974, Panza approached the Kunstmuseum in Basel, with an offer of a 15-year loan of his Conceptual works on condition that it would be housed in a suitable building.[189] Between 1974 and 1979, numerous written correspondences between Panza, Franz Meyer, Jean-Christophe Ammann and Maja Sacher bear witness to the intense negotiations.[190] However, the Museum für Gegenwartskunst (Museum for Contemporary Art), which opened in 1980, and which housed the contemporary collection of works from the 1960s and 1970s of the Kunstmuseum and of the Emmanuel-Hoffmann-Stiftung, was already full. The museum in Basel did not want to separate the private collection from its main building, which was too small to house all of the works. As a compromise, the museum hosted an eight-month exhibition of the Panza Collection from November 1980 until June 1981.[191]

The Panza Collection at the Guggenheim Museum, New York

A substantial part of Panza's Conceptual art collection (250 pieces) was finally acquired in 1990 by the Guggenheim Museum, New York.[192] In 1991, 150 supplementary works were donated by the collector. Of these 400 works, 111 were from the Conceptual artists studied here: Darboven (3), Long (10), Andre (13), Huebler (9), LeWitt (6), Nauman (32), Ryman (24) and Weiner (16). Half of the works of the Conceptual artists studied here that are in Panza's collection, are now kept by the New York institution (111 of 207).[193]

Of the Panza collection now held at the Guggenheim Museum in New York,[194] most Conceptual works came from Fischer (16), Castelli (12), Sperone (11) and Weber (10). Other pieces came from Yvon Lambert (6), Sperone-Westwater-Fischer (4), Sonnabend (4), Friedrich (2), Françoise Lambert (2), the Ace Gallery

187 In 1976, the Italian government passed new laws regarding estates abroad. These forbade Italians from keeping property abroad. Unfortunately, they did not recognise that cultural activities and long-term loans of artworks were not exempt. Panza had to decide to either sell the portions of his collection that were on loan abroad and bring the money back to Italy, or to bring the works back. But due to the new legislation, he was reported to the criminal court in Rome. He was finally found not guilty.

188 Cladders in conversation with the author, *op. cit.*

189 Schmidt and Ursprung, *White Fire, Flying Man*, *op. cit.*, p.48.

190 See: Series I, Box 11–1 and 11–2, in Inventory of the Giuseppe Panza Papers, 1956–90, GRILA. Many drawings testify to the care and attention that Panza devoted to the installation of the works.

191 Franz Meyer (ed.), *Minimal und Conceptual Art aus der Sammlung Panza* (exh. cat.), Museum für Gegenwartskunst, Basel, 1981.

192 A large part of the Giuseppe Panza collection is now kept by American institutions. In 1984, Panza sold over 80 works of Abstract Expressionism and Pop Art to the MOCA, Los Angeles. In 1994, he made a donation of 79 supplementary works by contemporary Californian artists. In 1996, Panza donated his villa in Varese and 140 works to the Fondo per l'Ambiente Italiano (FAI). The villa has been open to the public since 1999. See: *The Panza Collection, Villa Menafoglio Litta Panza – Varese*, *op. cit.*, p.30.

193 For a comprehensive list of works in the Panza Collection, see: *Art of the Fifties, Sixties and Seventies, The Panza Collection*, *op. cit.*, pp.299–313.

(2), the artists (2) and the Lisson Gallery (1). Five works have an unknown provenance. There is a balance between works acquired from European and American dealer galleries. We have seen that, because of his collection of Pop art, Panza had been in contact with American dealer galleries since the early 1960s. Living in Italy, he was naturally in touch with Sperone and later also with Françoise Lambert. Moreover, he had contacts with several other dealers, including Marilena Bonomo and Richard Demarco.[195]

Panza bought several pieces from certain periods of an artist's production. In Database 4, we see that most works by Andre in the Panza collection were produced either between 1966 and 1969 or between 1974 and 1975. Panza acquired most Conceptual artworks between 1970 and 1974 (51).[196] The Conceptual artists most strongly represented in the Panza Collection at the Guggenheim are Nauman (32), Ryman (23), Weiner (16) and Andre (13).

4.5. Conclusion

In the late 1960s and 1970s in Western Europe, a number of private collectors acquired Conceptual works. The core of private collecting was situated in Germany, Belgium and the Netherlands, although important private collectors could also be found in other countries. The most visible private collections of Conceptual art were Annick and Anton Herbert, Mia and Martin Visser and Giuseppe Panza.

Within the art world, private collectors were the first to react to the new tendency of Conceptual art, and to support the artists and the dealers. From the late 1960s, Konrad Fischer was one of the dealers to play an important part in the development of private collections (Herbert, Visser, Van Eelen). He did not feel comfortable in discussing art purely in terms of sales. He wanted collectors to believe in what he was proposing to them.[197] According to Daniel Birnbaum, Fischer could be stubborn if he did not like the attitude of potential buyers:

194 A list of Conceptual works in the Panza Collection at the Guggenheim Museum in New York, including information on acquisition dates and provenances, was given to me by the museum. Unfortunately, not all files are available and part of the records could not be checked. The database on the Panza collection (Database 5, Appendix 1.5) comprises only artworks for which all the information was available (77 works).

195 See: Correspondences, lists of purchases and payment receipts, in Series VI, Box 242, Files 1–10, in Inventory of the Giuseppe Panza Papers, 1956–90, GRILA.

196 See: Database 5, Section Carl Andre (Appendix 1.5).

197 Jocks, 'Einseitig muss man sein, damit etwas weitergeht', *Kunstforum*, *op. cit.*, p.403.

> The gallerist's unorthodox unwillingness to sell, and at times even to communicate, no doubt confused and alienated some. If potential clients wanted to buy for the wrong reasons, Fischer would pretend that there was nothing for sale or even feign an inability to hear what they were saying.[198]

Private collectors paved the way for the entry of Conceptual artists into museum collections, acting as a sort of value confirmation of Conceptualism. Some private collectors influenced public collections in European museums; examples include Annick and Anton Herbert and the Stedelijk Van Abbemuseum, Eindhoven and Martin Visser and the museum in Rotterdam. We have also seen that some collectors transferred part or the whole of their collections to public institutions, while others founded their own museums.

One aspect that should be underlined is that dealers offered works at different prices to collectors than to museums because they bought more works more rapidly.[199] Private collectors would expect a substantial discount on prices.[200] However, sales to museum were official and public, they established market prices. Anny De Decker states that she tended to give better prices to museums because these sales were more prestigious for artists.[201] A number of dealers gave between 10 per cent and 12 per cent discount on sales to museums (Nigel Greenwood, Lisson Gallery), but at the height of the currency crisis this could go up to 40 per cent (Gian Enzo Sperone).[202]

During the 1970s, European museums put together large public collections of Conceptual art. Public institutions' collections have a historical and educational goal, which leads to the acquisition of representative works. Museum directors often bought works from exhibitions organised in their institutions; sometimes, these works were made especially for the occasion. This aspect will be discussed in the next chapter.

198 Birnbaum, 'Art and the Deal, Daniel Birnbaum on Konrad Fischer/Lueg', *Artforum*, *op. cit.*, p.17. This is also Dibbets's opinion. See: 'Trinken und lachen, ja. Aber nicht über Kunst reden. Ein Gespräch mit Jan Dibbets', in Kölle, *Die Kunst des Ausstellens*, *op. cit.*, p.258.

199 Annick and Anton Herbert in conversation with the author, *op. cit.*

200 Morris in conversation with the author.

201 De Decker in conversation with the author, *op. cit.*

202 See: Chapter 5, pp.268–269. See also: Letter received by De Wilde from Sperone on 25 October 1971, in 1972 Acquisition File, ASMA.

Chapter 5

Purchases of Conceptual art by European museums

From the late 1960s onwards, a number of public institutions across Europe started to acquire Conceptual art. The museum directors and curators committed to Conceptualism established their acquisitions policy. Their role was central in the development of public collections. The relationship between temporary exhibitions and purchases, as well as the prices of the artworks, will be discussed. The collecting policies of the different museums are studied from the artists' or dealer galleries' point of view, depending on which was most significant. The general discussion will be followed by an in-depth study of the purchasing policy of the Tate Gallery, London.[1]

5. 1. Germany

Städtisches Museum, Mönchengladbach

The Städtisches Museum in Mönchengladbach was directed by Johannes Cladders from 1967 to 1985. During the studied period, he was responsible for the constitution of the permanent collection.[2] We have seen that the museum was a small city-owned provincial institution and it was public money that was used to acquire Conceptual works. The museum's committee (Museumsvorstand) acted as a consultant concerning purchases. At the time, the committee included people such as Karl Heinemann and Rolf Hoffmann, who had nothing to do with art professionally, but were private collectors.[3] Some pur-

1 Although I have researched several museums' archives (Mönchengladbach, Cologne, Basel, Amsterdam, London), I found that the Tate Gallery is the only museum to keep extensive publicly accessible acquisition files.

2 For an overview of the Conceptual art collection put together by the museum during the 1970s, see: Database 6, Section Städtisches Museum Mönchengladbach (Appendix 1.6). The inventory catalogue of the Städtisches Museum Mönchengladbach, edited in 1981, provided information on the works included in the permanent collection. See: Sabine Kimpel-Fehlemann (ed.), *Städtisches Museum Abteiberg Mönchengladbach, Bestandskatalog, Gemälde, Skulpturen, Aquarelle, Zeichnungen* (2 vols.), Städtisches Museum Abteiberg, Mönchengladbach, 1981. The catalogue gives the title, date and media of the works, and significantly the date of purchase and the inventory number. Working on the inventory catalogue allowed me to identify my own record of 29 Conceptual works purchased between 1967 and 1980. The provenance of the works was provided by the senior curator of the museum. See: Letter from Hannelore Kersting to the author, 30 August 2004. During my stay in Mönchengladbach in April 2005, I was able to double-check these figures myself. The archive files of the period include documents concerning essentially the organisation of exhibitions and correspondence with artists and other museums. Some papers relate to purchases of works of art included in the museum's shows. Johannes Cladders, the Director of the museum during the period under review, explained that at the time it was 'deals with handshake'. Cladders in conversation with the

chases were supported financially by the state, North Rhine Westphalia. The Museumsverein (Museums Society) also purchased several artworks for donation to the collection.

The Städtisches Museum began to buy Conceptual works very early. In 1969, two major floor pieces by Andre, *8001 Mönchengladbach Square* and *8002 Mönchengladbach Square*, entered the permanent collection. These were among the six floor pieces especially produced for and exhibited at the artist's first solo show in a European museum organised in October–December 1968 in Mönchengladbach.[4] This show was set up with the help of Fischer, who had been Andre's main European dealer since 1967.[5] The two works, with their certificate drawings, were purchased from the Galerie Alfred Schmela in Düsseldorf. Schmela and Fischer were close. Fischer-Lueg had been one of Schmela's artists, and Schmela had wanted him to set up a second gallery for young artists.[6] This friendly relationship between the two men provides an explanation as to why works of an artist represented by Fischer were acquired from Schmela. The financial support received for this purchase from the state of North Rhine Westphalia should be highlighted. It shows that, from the 1960s, public institutions were buying Conceptual artworks with official support.

Another artist to be included early in the collection of the museum was Hanne Darboven. She held her first exhibition in Mönchengladbach in February–April 1969.[7] This show had been set up with the support of her main dealer Fischer.[8] The show included the work *6 Filme nach 6 Büchern über 1968*, which was an ensemble of 'six films after six books about 1968'. It was decided to film the artist's books because the museum space was too small to present the large paper installations.[9] The work was donated by the artist to the museum after the show, possibly because it had been made especially for the Mönchengladbach museum.

The early Conceptual art exhibitions organised at the museum in Mönchengladbach clearly show how a dealer influenced the programme. Fischer believed that museum exhibitions that were linked with his name were particularly effective for an artist's promotion.[10] It was Fischer again who arranged for a show of Long to be held in Mönchengladbach in July–August 1970.[11] The exhibition included *4 Sculptures (England, Germany, Africa, America, 1966–1970)*. A year later,

author, *op. cit.*

3 *Ibid.* See also: *Sammlung Heinemann* (exh. cat.), Städtisches Museum, Mönchengladbach, 1982.

4 'Carl Andre', Städtisches Museum, Mönchengladbach, 18 October–15 December 1968.

5 The help of Konrad Fischer, Düsseldorf and the Dwan Gallery, New York, are both acknowledged in the exhibition catalogue. See: *Carl Andre* (1968), *op. cit.*

6 See: Ruhrberg, *Alfred Schmela*, *op. cit.*, pp.49–57. See also: 'Konrad Fischer interviewed by Georg Jappe', *Studio International*, *op. cit.*, p.68.

7 'Hanne Darboven, Ausstellung mit 6 Filmprojektoren nach 6 Büchern über 1968', Städtisches Museum, Mönchengladbach, 25 February–7 April 1969.

8 Again, Fischer's help was acknowledged in the catalogue. See: *Hanne Darboven* (exh. cat.), Städtisches Museum, Mönchengladbach, 1968. Darboven had her first European solo show at Konrad Fischer in December 1967.

9 Wischermann, *Johannes Cladders*, *op. cit.*, pp.39–40.

10 'Konrad Fischer interviewed by Georg Jappe', *Studio International*, *op. cit.*, p.71.

11 *Richard Long, 4 Skulpturen (England, Germany, Africa, America, 1966–1970)*, Städtisches Museum, Mönchengladbach, 16 July–30 August 1970. See: Letter from Cladders to Long dated 27 January 1970, in File Ausstellungen: Panamarenko, Manzoni, Druckgraphik, Thorn Prikker, Hollein, Long, Brouwn, Etzold I und II,

the set of photographs *Four Weeks Documentation: Evidence from July 26–August 26 Africa 1969* (1969) was acquired directly from the artist.

These early examples of Andre, Darboven and Long highlight the links between temporary exhibitions, in-situ installations and purchases for the permanent collection. Many Conceptual artists designed their own exhibitions and created the works accordingly. A number of pieces made especially for shows in Mönchengladbach entered the museum's collection. For his solo exhibition in 1975, Buren realised an in-situ work called *Von da an/A partir de là* (From here on).[12] He covered every wall of the museum with blue-and-white stripes, leaving blank the spots where works had previously hung. The work was acquired for the museum following an agreement with the artist. A letter from Cladders to Buren of November 1975 suggests that the museum's budget had run out. Acquiring Buren's installation was a way to get around paying Buren's expenses and fee.[13]

However, if temporary exhibitions were often followed by purchases, it was not always the pieces included in the shows that were acquired. For example, Broodthaers's show in October–November 1971 was followed by a purchase in 1972. Cladders, a friend of the artist, recalled spontaneously purchasing the work *Théorie des Figures* (1970–71) during a visit to his studio in Düsseldorf in 1972.[14] In 1980, Cladders visited a plaster manufacturer near Liège with the artist Benjamin Katz. This industrialist intended to sell works by Broodthaers from his personal collection. Cladders wanted to buy two mural installations, *Untitled* and *Narcisse* (both 1966). There was no money left in the museum's acquisition fund, so Cladders asked the Museumsverein to make the purchases.[15]

Most artists represented in the permanent collection of the Mönchengladbach museum had a solo show in the museum during the late 1960s and 1970s: Andre (1968), Darboven (1969), Long (1970), Broodthaers (1971), Buren (1971, 1975), Weiner (1973). The other artists, except for Merz, were represented in shows presenting recently purchased artworks: Huebler (1975), LeWitt (1975) and Nauman (1976).[16]

It can be seen from Database 6, on museum purchases, that except for the pieces that were purchased in relation to temporary exhibitions, half of the works acquired were working drawings (14 out of 29). For instance, by 1980, no major wall drawing or sculpture by LeWitt was acquired; the five works by

Neuerwerbungen 1970: Graphik, Buren, Planke, Pop Graphik (Etzold III) [1970–71], ASMM. Long had his first solo show at Konrad Fischer's in September 1968.

12 *Daniel Buren, Senkrechte farbige und weisse Streifen, Position-Proposition*, Städtisches Museum, Mönchengladbach, 28 January–7 March 1971.

13 Letter from Cladders to Buren dated 26 November 1975, in File Abgeschl. Ausstellungen: Brouwershaven, Fischer, Buren, Bestandsausstellung, Lissitzky, Nauen (IHK), Kunst am Bau, Plakate (Krefeld), Hafner, Räume, Smithson [1975–76], ASMM.

14 Grasskamp, *Johannes Cladders, op. cit.*, p.45.

15 Cladders in conversation with the author, *op. cit.*

16 For an overview of the exhibitions of Conceptual artists at the museum, see: Database 3, section Städtisches Museum, Mönchengladbach (Appendix 1.3). Cladders explained that the absence of a Mario Merz show was due to a lack of money and time. See: *Ibid.*

the artist in the permanent collection were all drawings.

In 1975, the museum acquired Nauman's *Forced Perspective #2*, a large 64-part sculpture (300 × 935 cm). From December 1975 to January 1976, the work was shown in a solo exhibition at Konrad Fischer.[17] This sculpture was purchased with its certificate drawing from the Düsseldorf gallery at the time of the show. The transaction shows that the museum in Mönchengladbach could afford to purchase major Conceptual artworks independently of temporary exhibitions.[18]

Recently acquired artworks from the permanent collection were presented in annual temporary exhibitions entitled *Beleg* (Instance). Major Conceptual pieces in the collection were important enough to be included in those exhibitions from 1975 onwards. In 1976, *6 Räume* (6 Rooms) presented one work by six artists in six separate rooms (Andre, Broodthaers, Buren, Nauman, Richter and Rückriem).[19]

Perhaps the most interesting fact that emerges from Database 6 is that half of the artworks (14 out of 29) were purchased from Fischer.

The exhibition programme and origins of the purchases suggest that there were close links between Cladders and Fischer. Although Cladders acknowledges Fischer's help in providing the original contact with Conceptual artists such as Andre[20] and although he recognised that he was an interesting dealer,[21] he seems intentionally to minimise Fischer's influence. Indeed, if we exclude the Conceptual artworks purchased from Fischer and those that were either purchased or donated by the artists,[22] the only other dealer galleries from which the museum purchased at the time were Alfred Schmela (but we have seen his links to Fischer), René Block, Berlin, and Thomas Borgmann, Cologne. However, those two galleries only sold pieces to the museum in 1980, when the original network of Conceptual art had changed.

Cladders underplays Fischer's influence by always mentioning him in relation to other dealers, such as De Decker, Werner, Friedrich and especially Maenz. However, none of Maenz's artists, such as Kosuth or Art & Language, were exhibited or collected by the museum. According to Cladders, Fischer and Maenz made attempts early on to place works in museums, a motivation which he was sympathetic to as he believes that a public institution 'ennobles' a work

17 *Bruce Nauman, Forced Perspective/Open Mind/Equal Mind/ Parallel Mind (Allegory and Symbolism)*, Konrad Fischer, Düsseldorf, 16 December 1975–24 January 1976. See: *Ausstellungen bei Konrad Fischer*, *op. cit.*, p.124.

18 The same observation can be made about Huebler. *Alternative Piece 3 North Paris, France* (1970) was acquired in 1972 from Konrad Fischer, where it had been exhibited in April–May 1972. *Douglas Huebler*, Konrad Fischer, Düsseldorf, 13 April–4 May 1972. See: *Ausstellungen bei Konrad Fischer*, *op. cit.*, p.76.

19 *6 Räume (Andre, Broodthaers, Buren, Nauman, Richter, Rückriem)*, Städtisches Museum, Mönchengladbach, 29 August–3 October 1976. See: *6 Raüme* (exh. cat.), Städtisches Museum, Mönchengladbach, 1976.

20 Grasskamp, *Johannes Cladders*, *op. cit.*, p.41.

21 Cladders in conversation with the author, *op. cit.*

22 The artists themselves played a significant part in getting their work in the museum's collection. Broodthaers, Buren, Long, Darboven and Weiner, all artists represented by Fischer, sold or donated their works themselves to the institution.

of art. But in order to maintain his independence, he claims that the exhibitions were led by his interest in the artists.[23]

Cladders saw these dealer galleries as supplementary opportunities to discover what artists were doing at that moment, and not as sites at which he could be introduced for the first time to their works.[24] However, regarding the museum's exhibition programme, especially in the late 1960s, Fischer's influence and his ability to get hold of the work of artists such as Andre, Darboven and Long cannot be doubted. Moreover, Cladders affirms that the museum in Mönchengladbach had a certain reputation and that led artists to be interested to get in contact. He was often asked how he got to know the artists and explains that it wasn't very difficult: they came to see him and not the other way round.[25]

In some cases, of course, the original contact between the artist and the museum Director was direct, as for example with Weiner. Weiner and Cladders agreed to plan an exhibition after meeting at Documenta 5 in the summer of 1972.[26] But in order to prepare the show, Weiner asked Cladders to contact Fischer to arrange a meeting, showing the artist's reliance on his main dealer.[27] Furthermore, Weiner's solo show in Mönchengladbach held in October–November 1973 and entitled *8 Works*, included *1) Down a Hatch, 2) Up a Tree, 3) Around a Town* (1973).[28] Cladders acquired these statements, which had previously been shown in April 1972 in Düsseldorf, from Fischer for the permanent collection.[29]

Cladders also had friendly and supportive contacts with Wide White Space in Antwerp. Referring to his relationship with De Decker and Lohaus, Cladders said: 'I could always count on support, if needed, although never in the form of financial assistance. Nor did the gallery profit financially from the museum. The museum's budget, as it were, was never sufficient for any acquisitions worth mentioning.'[30] Cladders' affirmation reinforces my own findings: I could find no trace of any commercial transaction between the museum in Mönchengladbach and Wide White Space in the 1970s.

Even if the museum's acquisition budget was restricted, it was still large enough for the museum to acquire a number of Conceptual works. In 1967, the annual acquisition budget was of DM 70,000.[31] Cladders got around these financial limitations by concentrating the collection on contemporary works. At the

23 Cladders in conversation with the author, *op. cit.*

24 *Ibid.*

25 *Ibid.*

26 Letter from Lawrence Weiner to Johannes Cladders dated 14 July 1972, in File Ausstellungen: Programm Zufall System, Sieben Räume, Rückriem, Weiner, Eine Malerei Ausst., Koptische Stoffe, Jansen-Winkeln, Albers, Caumont, Mack, Richter, Dimitrijevic, Parasol Press, Dieckmann, Neugebauer [1973–75], ASMM.

27 Letter from Weiner to Cladders dated 4 June 1973, in File Ausstellungen: Programm Zufall System, Sieben Räume, Rückriem, Weiner, Eine Malerei Ausst., Koptische Stoffe, Jansen-Winkeln, Albers, Caumont, Mack, Richter, Dimitrijevic, Parasol Press, Dieckmann, Neugebauer [1973–75], ASMM.

28 *8 Arbeiten von Lawrence Weiner*, Städtisches Museum, Mönchengladbach, 4 October–4 November 1973.

29 *Lawrence Weiner*, Konrad Fischer, Düsseldorf, April 1972. See: *Ausstellungen bei Konrad Fischer*, *op. cit.*, p.77.

30 'Interview Yves Aupetitallot, Johannes Cladders', in Aupetitallot, *Wide White Space*, *op. cit.*, p.139.

31 Grüterich, 'Mönchengladbach', *Studio International*, *op. cit.*, p.28.

time, Conceptual works were relatively inexpensive in comparison to other modern art movements. Cladders explained his strategy:

> In such a museum, I can only succeed if I put together a collection from the present situation onwards – a situation that I live directly, assess immediately, with all the risks implied in the current assessment, in the speculation, that some things – and I don't mean material values – that these works will remain significant for the development of art in the long run. I've always told my art committee in Mönchengladbach: the little money, that you put at my disposal for purchases – which I can cope with if I buy in the immediate present – if ten per cent of that work outlives our present time, then I have, from the point of view of the money, paid for the whole museum and everything around it. Because someday the work will be worth millions, and all expenses will be compensated for.[32]

Cladders' purchasing strategy was built upon the speculative belief that contemporary works would gain intellectual and financial value in the future. Instead of acquiring works by already recognised artists, which he could not have afforded, he took the risk of investing in contemporaries in whom he believed. He was well aware that he was spending the taxpayers' money, and he saw it as a moral obligation to buy only works that he could square with his own conscience.[33] As Marlis Grüterich underlined at the time: 'This was not done to further the accumulation of accepted art history, but to present landmarks in the latest art developments.'[34] In Germany, the Städtisches Museum was seen as a milestone institution for progressive art. The temporary exhibitions programme and the acquisition strategy are testimony to this attitude. Further, they show how a dealer can influence a public institution, and the links between temporary exhibitions and acquisitions.

Museum Ludwig, Cologne

The case of the Museum Ludwig is unusual because it is based on a private collection. We have seen that Peter Ludwig did not believe in the future of Conceptual art, but he included some works in his collection because they

32 Grasskamp, *Johannes Cladders*, *op. cit.*, pp.88–89 (author's translation).

33 *Ibid.*, p.90.

34 Grüterich, 'Mönchengladbach', *Studio International*, *op. cit.*, p.28.

were representatives of their times.[35] This attitude reflects his desire to act in the public interest by collecting for a public museum. In 1976, Peter and Irene Ludwig donated part of their collection (nearly 300 works) to the city of Cologne. The Ludwig Collection and the collection of twentieth-century art of the Wallraf-Richartz Museum were combined to create the Museum Ludwig. Nearly all of the Conceptual artworks that entered the museum's collection were from the Ludwig donation of ten items.[36]

From Database 6 we see that the Ludwigs purchased works of American Conceptualists directly from American dealer galleries. They were great Pop art collectors and therefore already collaborating with American dealers. The purchases of works by Andre and Nauman are representative of the Ludwigs' attitude. Andre's work *Lock Series (Köln Steel Lock)* (1967), a 36-part sculpture with its certificate drawing, was acquired in 1969 from the Dwan Gallery, New York. This sculpture was exhibited in 1968 at the *Minimal Art* exhibition organised at the Gemeentemuseum in Den Haag.[37] The Ludwigs might have seen Andre's work on that occasion. In 1970, Ludwig acquired a second work by Andre from Dwan, *Timber Piece (Well)* (1964–70). This work was included in Andre's first American solo show in a museum, held in 1970 at the Guggenheim Museum in New York.[38] The works the collectors acquired from Andre were key works included in important shows.

The purchase of Bruce Nauman's *Westerman's Ear* (1967–68) is representative of Peter and Irene Ludwig's plan to collect for public museums. The Los Angeles dealer Eugenia Butler contacted Wolfgang Becker, the Director of the Neue Galerie–Sammlung Ludwig in Aachen, in January 1971 to propose that he acquire the work for $6,000.[39] Becker and Ludwig knew each other well: the collector had been associated with the institution since 1970. It is likely that Becker spoke with the collector about Butler's proposition. Finally, Ludwig decided to purchase the work in 1971.

Rudolf Zwirner was a significant dealer in the Rhine region, and an adviser to Ludwig.[40] In 1968, he sold a sculpture by LeWitt, *3 Part Set 789 (B)* (1968), to the Ludwigs. In January–February 1968, the work had been exhibited at Konrad Fischer, in LeWitt's first European solo show.[41] As Zwirner was one of Ludwig's dealers, it is probable that he had purchased the work from Fischer and resold it

35 Speck, *Peter Ludwig Sammler*, *op. cit.*, p.118.

36 The catalogues of holdings provide information on the date the artworks entered the museum, but not always on the original provenance, nor the date of purchase by the Ludwigs. See: Siegfried Gohr (ed.), *Museum Ludwig Köln, Gemälde, Skulpturen, Environments vom Expressionismus bis zur Gegenwart, Bestandskatalog*, Prestel Verlag, Munich, 1986. See also: *Bestandsverzeichnis der Zeichnungen, Graphische Sammlung Museum Ludwig*, Museum Ludwig, Cologne, 1986. In Cologne, the artwork files held by the Documentation Department of the Museum Ludwig were useful for complementing the missing data. However, some more facts, especially regarding the drawings, had to be investigated via the Ludwig Stiftung in Aachen. Eventually, I came to the conclusion that ten Conceptual artworks had been integrated into the Museum Ludwig by 1980. See: Database 6, Section Museum Ludwig, Cologne.

37 *Minimal Art*, Gemeentemuseum, The Hague, 23 March–26 May 1968. See: *Minimal Art*, *op. cit.*

38 See: *Carl Andre* (exh. cat.), Guggenheim Museum, New York, 1970.

39 Letter from Eugenia Butler to Wolfgang Becker dated 19 January 1971, in Bruce Nauman Files, Documentation Department, Museum Ludwig, Cologne.

40 Reiner Speck mentions Rudolf Zwirner and Rolf Ricke as some of Ludwig's dealers and advisers. See: Speck, *Peter Ludwig Sammler*, *op. cit.*, pp.118–119.

41 'Sol LeWitt', Konrad Fischer, Düsseldorf, 6 January–3 February

to Ludwig.[42] Zwirner also sold two sets of drawings by Darboven to the Ludwigs in 1973: *00–99/100 à 19 = 19×42 No/2K–61 K* (1970) and *1.10.71–31.10.71* (1971). A third set of 596 drawings, *24 Songs: A Form 1974* (1974) was donated by the artist to the Museum Ludwig in 1976.[43]

The two works by Kosuth that were added to the collection of the Ludwig Museum by 1980 were both purchased from another Cologne dealer, Paul Maenz. *Frame – One and Three* (1965) was purchased in 1973 by Ludwig.[44] Maenz asked Ludwig to sponsor a Kosuth show at the gallery, but the collector refused.[45] The second work, a photographic blow-up, entered the collection of the Ludwig Museum in a different way. *Titled (art as idea as idea (definition 'Abstract'))* (1967) was purchased in 1972 by Gert von der Osten, Director of the Wallraf-Richartz Museum.

Most Conceptual artworks in the collection of the Museum Ludwig in Cologne originated from the Ludwig donation in 1976. However, there were also gifts by artists and works that had originally been in the twentieth-century art section of the Wallraf-Richartz Museum. Although Ludwig was not particularly convinced by Conceptualism, he referred to several German and American dealers, who recommended which artists to acquire (Zwirner, Maenz, Dwan, Butler).

5.2. Switzerland

Kunstmuseum, Basel

During the 1960s and 1970s, the permanent collection of the Kunstmuseum Basel was composed of two different collections: its own and that of the Emanuel Hoffmann-Stiftung. The foundation has been hosted by the museum on permanent loan since 1941.[46] Both collections have to be taken into account if one wants to gain a complete picture of the situation during the period. Conceptual works did not enter the collection of the Kunstmuseum Basel before the 1970s. 49 Conceptual pieces were acquired for the permanent collection during that period; three quarters of these (36 out of the 49) were by American artists.[47]

1968. See: *Ausstellungen bei Konrad Fischer, op. cit.*, p.16.

42 At the time, Konrad Fischer declared: 'More than 50 per cent of what I sell goes to other galleries.' See: 'Konrad Fischer interviewed by Georg Jappe', *Studio International, op. cit.*, p.71.

43 The same year, the 'B' version of this work had been donated by the artist to the Städtisches Museum, Mönchengladbach.

44 In 1973, works by Kosuth were presented in March–April at the Paul Maenz Gallery in Brussels, and in April–May in an early Conceptual art group exhibition at the Maenz Gallery in Cologne. 'Joseph Kosuth, Art as Idea as Idea, 1967/68', Galerie Paul Maenz, Brussels, 17 March–19 April 1973; 'Einige wesentliche Beispiele früher Konzeptueller Kunst analytischen Charakters', Galerie Paul Maenz, Cologne, 10 April–12 May 1973. See: De Vries, *Paul Maenz Köln 1970–1980–1990, op. cit.*, pp.41–43.

45 See: Series I (General Correspondence), Part 2, Box 8, Folder 10, Inventory of the Galerie Paul Maenz Köln, 1956–91, GRILA.

46 The Emanuel Hoffmann-Stiftung was founded in 1933 in Basel by the young widow Maja Hoffmann (later Maja Sacher) in memory of her husband's commitment to contemporary art. The foundation collects works by artists who develop new forms of art production.

47 See: Database 6, Section Kunstmuseum, Basel (Appendix 1.6). Defining the scope of Conceptual works purchased until the late 1970s was achieved through an analysis of the Jahresberichte (yearly accounts) of the museum. See: Franz Meyer, 'Die Sammlungspolitik des Kunstmuseums im Bereiche von Malerei und Skulptur, 1968–1977', *Öffentliche Kunstsammlung Basel, Jahresbericht 1977*, Basel,

In the postwar period, the exhibition programme and purchasing policy of the museum had shown a commitment to American art.[48] Franz Meyer was the Director of the Kunstmuseum Basel from 1962 to 1980. He explained the acquisition policy of the museum in the 1970s:

> It was mainly works by American artists that were acquired. This was based on the conviction that, in the art period 1950–1970, the essential art performances refer to them, and that one should concentrate first on these American 'originals' and less on their European echoes in establishing a consequent exhibition policy.[49]

Meyer's curatorial assistants were Carlo Huber (1963–70) and later Zdenek Felix (1970–76). Huber had received a stipend from the Museum of Modern Art to stay for six months in New York from October 1969. He came back to Basel with numerous ideas and contacts, thus influencing the programme of the museum.[50] The acquisitions of the Kunstmuseum Basel (*Öffentliche Kunstsammlung Basel*, Public Art Collection Basel) were determined by a purchasing commission.[51] The Director of the museum had a consulting position.

The merit of this large collection of Conceptual art gathered during the 1970s is that it comprised key works of the major phases of the artists. The case of LeWitt exemplifies this: the five works that entered the collection at the time were two drawings, one modular cube, one wall structure and one wall drawing. The latter three works were acquired in different ways. *Large Modular Cube* (1969) came from the Emanuel Hoffmann-Foundation, but it was originally purchased from Fischer in 1970. *Wall Structure 5 4 3 2 1* (1966–73) was obtained in 1975 from the Rolf Preisig Gallery. However, in an article published during Art Basel in 1975, the critic Maria Netter pointed out that the work was purchased from Fischer for DM 20,000.[52] Preisig and Fischer shared a stand at the 6th Art Basel.[53] This highlights the teamwork between the two dealers and might imply some financial arrangement. Finally, the third work by LeWitt, *Circle, Grids, Arcs from four Corners and Sides* (1973), was a gift from the artist in 1977 in memory of Carlo Huber.

The Director Franz Meyer was persistent and if he could not convince the

1977, pp.38–52. The exhibition catalogue focusing on American art in the collections of the museum and the Emanuel Hoffmann-Foundation was also useful in compiling this data. See: Schmidt and Ursprung, *White Fire, Flying Man, op. cit.* The annual reports provide an exhaustive chronological list of acquisitions, but do not include information on the provenance of the works. This data was difficult to obtain, but in the end the Director's assistant and the assistant of the Print Department made it available, Katrin Steffen during a phone call to the author on 22 November 2004, and Franziska Heuss in a letter to the author dated 7 November 2005. I am also grateful for the advice and assistance of Mira Preisig, the daughter of the former dealer Rolf Preisig and the manager of the Friends of the Basel museum. The foundation's catalogue, which mentions the date of acquisition and the provenance of each work, was also used. See: *Emanuel Hoffmann-Stiftung Basel*, Wiese Verlag, Basel, 1991.

48 In the postwar period, under the directorship of Arnold Rudlinger, the Kunsthalle Basel had been one of the European institutions to host shows of contemporary American artists organised by the International Council of the Museum of Modern Art, New York (*Die neue Amerikanische Malerei*, 1958).

49 Meyer, 'Die Sammlungspolitik des Kunstmuseums', *Öffentliche Kunstsammlung Basel, op. cit.*, p.45 (author's translation).

50 Schmidt and Ursprung, *White Fire, Flying Man, op. cit.*, pp.12–49.

51 In 1970, the members of the purchasing commission were: Frank Vischer (president), Martin H. Burckhardt, Karl Bernhard, Walter Bodmer, Hermann Fillitz, Dorothea Herzog-Christ, Carl

museum committee to purchase a piece, he would buy it with his own money and transfer it later to the public collection. For instance, Andre's 100-part sculpture *10 × 10 Altstadt Square* (1967) was first acquired by Meyer himself from Friedrich at Art Basel in 1970.[54] The work was put on permanent loan at the museum. Four years later, in 1974, the sculpture entered the museum's collection, with financial support from the City of Basel. This process highlights the fact that the Director was not making a personal donation, but was finding a way to secure a work for the museum. Meyer did donate a drawing by Broodthaers in 1975 (*Jardin d'Hiver I*, 1974).

Heiner Friedrich was one of the dealers to have close links to the Kunstmuseum Basel. In December 1969, he helped to put together a *Minimal Art* exhibition, presenting works by Judd, Andre, Flavin and Ryman.[55] Meyer acknowledged that Friedrich was an important mediator in Germany and later in America.[56] A number of works were acquired from him by the museum in the first half of the 1970s. There were, for example, a collection of films by Broodthaers acquired in 1974–75, several films by Nauman purchased in 1973, as well as a major painting by Ryman (*Aacon*, 1968) obtained in 1971.[57]

There were also important connections between Basel and Düsseldorf. In March–April 1972, Fischer organised a major group show of Conceptual artists at the Kunstmuseum, *'Konzept'-Kunst*.[58] Meyer declared: 'Most important in Germany at the time was Konrad Fischer in Düsseldorf, a gallery that covered nearly the whole spectrum of my interest.'[59] The dealer sold only three works directly to the museum: Darboven's *Grosse Zeichnung (3/11/7/5/9)* (1967, Emanuel Hoffmann-Foundation) and *Ein Jahr 1974* (1974) in 1974,[60] and *Large Modular Cube* (1969) by LeWitt in 1970 (Emanuel Hoffmann-Foundation).

In Switzerland, Rolf Preisig in Basel and Bruno Bischofberger in Zurich were significant dealers working with the Kunstmuseum. Bischofberger, who was at the time an established dealer in Zurich, provided two major works by Nauman: *Storage Capsule for the Right Rear Quarter of my Body* (1966), purchased by the museum at Art Basel in 1971, and *The true artist helps the world by revealing its mystic truths (Window or Wall Sign)* (1967), acquired in 1978. Bischofberger was mainly a secondary dealer of Conceptual art, meaning that he would acquire works from other dealers and resell them to his clients.[61] The two works by

Maurice Jacottet, Adolf Jann, Lenz Klotz, Aja Petzold-Müller and Peter G. Staechelin.

52 Maria Netter, 'Mit aller Konsequenz auf die Moderne ausgerichtet, Zur Einkaufspolitik des Baseler Kunstmuseums', *Handelsblatt*, 12–13 September 1975, p.16.

53 See: *Die Internationale Kunstmesse, Art 6 '75* (exh. cat.), Basel, 1975, unnumbered pages.

54 Schmidt and Ursprung, *White Fire, Flying Man*, *op. cit.*, p.48. The title of the work suggests that it had originally been manufactured for Andre's first European solo show at Fischer's gallery in 1967. It is likely that Friedrich purchased the piece from Fischer. See: *Ausstellungen bei Konrad Fischer*, *op. cit.*, p.13.

55 *Minimal Art (Judd, Andre, Flavin, Ryman)*, Kunstmuseum, Basel, December 1969–January 1970. Most works in the exhibition were lent by Heiner Friedrich and by the artists. See: Schmidt and Ursprung, *White Fire, Flying Man*, *op. cit.*, p.25.

56 *Ibid.*, p.49.

57 In October–November 1974, Broodthaers had a solo show at the Kunstmuseum Basel. In June–July 1971, Ryman had a solo show at the Galerie Friedrich in Cologne. *Aacon* had been exhibited at Ryman's first European solo show in October–November 1968 at Friedrich, Munich.

58 *'Konzept'-Kunst*, Kunstmuseum, Basel, 18 March–23 April 1972. See: *'Konzept'-Kunst*, *op. cit.*

59 Schmidt and Ursprung, *White Fire, Flying Man*, *op. cit.*, p.49 (author's translation).

Nauman that he sold to the Basel museum are early pieces, which he possibly purchased from Castelli or Fischer, the artist's main American and European dealers respectively.

Some works now in the permanent collection of the Kunstmuseum Basel were acquired from temporary exhibitions in other Swiss institutions. In 1977, there was a solo show of Long at the Kunsthalle in Bern, where the Emanuel Hoffmann-Stiftung acquired the large *Stone Line* (1977, 900 × 200 cm).[62] Because there seems to have been no intermediary, one can suppose that the work was acquired directly from the artist. In June–August 1975, the Kunsthalle in Basel organised a solo show of Robert Ryman.[63] The museum purchased the exhibited painting *Singer I* (1975) for $30,000 from the John Weber Gallery, New York,[64] with support from the Max Geldner-Stiftung.[65]

Several artworks were bought directly in America. These included Andre's *Cedar Piece* (1959–64) in 1976 from John Weber, New York. Nauman's *Henry Moore bound to fail, Back view* (1967–70) was purchased at Sotheby's, New York, in 1974 (Emanuel Hoffmann-Foundation) and *Two Models for Underground Tunnels, No 1–Horizontal, No 2–Vertical* (1978) were acquired in 1978 from Ace Gallery, Venice (California). A collection of 16 early drawings (1966–67) by Nauman was acquired from Richard Bellamy, New York, in 1973 (Emanuel Hoffmann-Foundation).

A major advantage enjoyed by the Kunstmuseum Basel was that its purchase procedure was supported by a couple of important foundations. Almost three quarters of the Conceptual artworks (35 of the 49) in the collection were a deposit of the Emanuel Hoffmann-Foundation. The Max Geldner-Foundation supported the purchase of works by Darboven and Ryman. In addition, the Karl August Burckhardt-Koechlin-Fonds purchased and donated two drawings by LeWitt (*Arcs from four sides & four corners* and *Grid and Arcs from two opposite sides*, 1972).[66] Marlis Grüterich pointed out that 'the museum in Basel was the first ever public collection of works of art bought by private citizens'.[67]

Prominent European private collectors also showed an interest in the museum. In 1971 and 1973, the Ludwigs put numerous Pop art works from their collection on permanent loan. As we have seen, Panza proposed in 1974 to place a large amount of his collection of Minimal and Conceptual art on permanent

60 In November–December 1974, Darboven had a solo show at the Kunstmuseum Basel. The acquired drawing installation was part of this exhibition. *Hanne Darboven, Ein Monat, ein Jahrhundert, Werke von 1968 bis 1974*, Kunstmuseum, Basel, 9 November–29 December 1974.

61 Morris in conversation with the author.

62 *Richard Long*, Kunsthalle Bern, 15 July–7 August 1977.

63 *Robert Ryman*, Kunsthalle Basel, June–August 1975.

64 See: Netter, 'Mit aller Konsequenz auf die Moderne ausgerichtet.', *Handelsblatt, op. cit.*, p.16. In November 1975, Weber organised a show of recent prints and paintings by Ryman. *Robert Ryman, Paintings and Prints*, John Weber Gallery, New York, 1–26 November 1975.

65 The Swiss collector Max Geldner created the foundation in 1948 to support purchases of the Kunstmuseum Basel. In 1958, he donated his collection of mainly Flemish painting of the sixteenth and seventeenth century and modern Swiss art to the museum.

66 The Karl August Burckhardt-Koechlin-Fonds buys drawings for the Kupferstichkabinett on the recommendation of the curator. At the time, it was Dr Dieter Koepplin. The fund was founded in 1961 by Martin Burckhardt in memory of his father, the architect Karl August Burckhardt (1879–1960). The collection of twentieth century drawings is on deposit at the Print Department of the museum in Basel.

67 Marlis Grüterich, 'Switzerland', *Studio International*, vol.190, no.977, September–October 1975, p.159.

loan in Basel, a proposition that was never to materialise. Artists donated works to build and enhance the collection, notably Darboven with a huge drawing installation, *Ein Monat, August 1968* (1968), in 1976.[68] During the period studied, the Kunstmuseum Basel received five Conceptual pieces as gifts.

We can therefore see that the works from the Emanuel Hoffmann-Foundation (35) and the gifts (5) constitute the core of the Kunstmuseum Basel's permanent collection (40 works out of 49). Nauman is the best represented, with 20 works, including films and drawings. Overall, film and drawing are well represented in the collection (9 and 22 works respectively). The exhibition policy further reflected an interest in drawings, which was stimulated by the existence of a *Kupferstichkabinett* (Drawings and Prints Department).[69]

Kunstmuseum, Lucerne

Jean-Christophe Ammann directed the Kunstmuseum Lucerne from 1968 to 1977. He had previously been Harald Szeemann's assistant at the Kunsthalle in Bern. In 1972, he organised the Photorealism section at Documenta 5. Ammann was convinced by Conceptualism and secured Castelli's organisational and financial support for the exhibition programme.[70] The museum had a comprehensive commitment to Conceptual shows, exhibiting Gilbert & George (1972), Kosuth (1973), Art & Language and Buren (1974), Darboven and Dibbets (1975).[71]

However, the museum's purchasing policy was minimal.[72] From the artists studied, only one work – a set of drawings by Darboven – entered the museum's permanent collection between 1967 and 1980, and this work was donated by the artist. It seems that the small budget led to the lack of purchases. At the end of 1977 the annual purchase budget was SFR 16,000 (about $7,000).[73] In the collection policy (Sammlungsleitbild) the aims of the permanent collection were stated as follows: 'The collecting activity is oriented towards the past and present of the institution and of the art of the canton of Lucerne and not towards the model of the reconstruction of an art historical development.'[74] Consequently, it comes as no surprise that the one Conceptual work in the collection was exhibited in a major show at the Kunstmuseum in 1975. Darboven had donated a collection of 126 drawings, *Atta Troll (I–VIII, 1117)* (1975). Here too, the artist's generosity enabled her works to enter a public collection.

68 This work was included in Darboven's solo show at the museum in 1974. See: *Hanne Darboven, Ein Monat, Ein Jahr, Ein Jahrhundert, Arbeiten von 1968 bis 1974* (exh. cat.), Kunstmuseum, Basel, 1974, p.20.

69 See: *Diagrams & Drawings, Carl Andre, Christo, De Maria, Mark di Suvero, Dan Flavin, Michael Heizer, Don Judd, Sol LeWitt, Robert Morris, Bruce Nauman, Claes Oldenburg, Richard Serra, Robert Smithson* (exh. cat.), Kunstmuseum Basel, 1973. See also: *Zeichnen/Bezeichnen, op. cit.*

70 Jean-Christophe Ammann in conversation with the author, Frankfurt/Main, 4 October 2004, written questionnaire (Appendix 4.1).

71 See: Database 3, Section Kunstmuseum, Lucerne (Appendix 1.3).

72 See: Database 6, Section Kunstmuseum, Lucerne (Appendix 1.6). In the 1970s, the museum's yearly reports included figures and descriptions about visitors, temporary exhibitions, sales and purchases. Several of those reports provided the data about purchases of Conceptual works at the time. See: *Jahresbericht 1972, op. cit.*; *Jahresbericht 1973*, Kunstgesellschaft, Lucerne, April 1974; *Jahresbericht 1974*, Kunstgesellschaft, Lucerne, June 1975. The curators of the museum provided information on the provenance of the Conceptual art pieces. Cornelia Dietschi and Christoph Lichtin in e-mails to the author, January and September 2004.

73 Ammann in conversation with the author, *op. cit.*

74 'Sammlungsziele', *Sammlungsleitbild*, Kunstmuseum Lucerne, undated, unnumbered pages (author's translation).

5.3. The Netherlands

Stedelijk Museum, Amsterdam

The Stedelijk Museum is run by the city of Amsterdam, but also acts as the national museum of modern art. From the postwar period until the early 1960s, the museum was directed by Willem Sandberg. Through his commitment to the American avant-garde, the museum gained international renown. From 1963 to 1985, Edy de Wilde was the museum's Director. From 1965 to 1970, he was assisted by Wim Beeren, Head of the Department of Painting and Sculpture. Ad Peterson and Rini Dippel assisted him in the early 1970s. Geert van Beijeren, the partner of Adriaan van Ravesteijn from Art & Project worked at the Stedelijk Museum, first as a librarian, then as a curator in the Department of Painting and Sculpture from 1973.

The budgets of Dutch museums rose annually from the 1950s onwards. The resources were provided either by the cities or by the government. Dutch museums always had a commitment to collecting avant-garde works. In 1973, a public study revealed that nearly half of the Stedelijk's budget between 1966 and 1971 was used to buy works by American artists. Further, it showed that most of the money went to American dealer galleries.[75] This had certain repercussions for Dutch museums' policies. In the 1970s, the State itself, independently of museums, purchased Dutch contemporary art. Those collections were shown nationally and internationally in exhibitions organised by the Netherlands Art Foundation.[76] In addition, a certain percentage of the public museums' budgets had to be spent on the purchase of Dutch contemporary art.[77]

In the late 1960s and 1970s, the Stedelijk Museum was the institution that most actively collected Conceptual art (62 works).[78] The museum showed a real commitment to amassing a coherent set of works by a large number of Conceptual artists. The temporary exhibitions programme paralleled the Stedelijk's purchasing policy.[79] From the late 1960s, the Director and the curators showed an interest in the latest art developments, and were exhibiting and collecting Conceptual art. In 1969, De Wilde and Beeren initiated the organisation of *Op Losse Schroeven*, one of the first group exhibitions in Europe to present a wide

75 Liesbeth Brandt Corstius, 'Holland', *Studio International*, March 1974, vol. 187, no.964, p.4.

76 Oxenaar, 'On art and museum policies in the Netherlands', *Studio International*, *op. cit.*, p.204.

77 Jan Dibbets in conversation with the author, *op. cit.*

78 See: Database 6, Section Stedelijk Museum, Amsterdam (Appendix 1.6). The catalogue of acquisitions of the Stedelijk Museum provided information on the Conceptual works in the collection, as well as the purchasing date and provenance of each work. See: Joop M. Joosten (ed.), *20 Years of Art Collecting. Acquisitions Stedelijk Museum Amsterdam 1969–1984. Painting and Sculpture*, Stedelijk Museum, Amsterdam, 1984. A wide range of documentation about the artworks, including invoices and, in some cases, extensive correspondence, was found by researching the inventory cards of the works, the acquisition files and the annual purchasing records held in the Registrar's Department and in the archive of the museum.

I am indebted to the support of Maurice Rummens, Head of the Research and Documentation Department, who sent me copies of a large number of inventory cards (January 2004). It is interesting to note that on certain documents, the purchasing price was literally cut out of the paper or covered with a thick black pen. See for example: Invoice from Robert Ryman, New York, dated 8 January 1973, for the acquisition of *VII* (1969), in 1972 Acquisition File, ASMA.

79 See: Database 3, Section Stedelijk Museum, Amsterdam (Appendix 1.3).

panorama of Conceptualism.[80] The first Conceptual artworks to enter the museum's collection came from that exhibition. These were Mario Merz's assemblage with neon *Città irreale* (1968) and Bruce Nauman's neon *My name as though it was written on the surface of the moon* (1968). Ileana Sonnabend, Paris, who had represented both artists since 1968–69, lent the works for the show.[81] They were both purchased in 1969 from the Paris-based dealer, for *f*3,240 and *f*7,200 respectively.[82]

The Stedelijk Museum did not buy further Conceptual artworks until two years later. In December 1971, the museum acquired Dibbets's *Perspective Correction – My Studio II* (1968) and Douglas Huebler's *Alternative piece no.4 (s)* (1970) from the Galleria Sperone, Turin.[83] Shortly afterwards, in January 1972, Kosuth's *Five fives (to Donald Judd)* (1965) was acquired. Correspondence between De Wilde and Sperone between July and October 1971 reveals that the curator visited the dealer gallery in the summer. During this meeting, Sperone offered the curator a number of works by his artists at about 50 per cent of the selling price. De Wilde enquired about a more precise proposition.[84] In October 1971, Sperone made the following offer:

> Hereby is my proposition concerning a series of works at particular conditions: I have indicated in red the real sale prices, which besides are old (I hope to be able to verify it personally with you in Amsterdam). The work of Kosuth in neon is in three copies: one is owned by Panza, the second by you, the third is in Switzerland. (Sonnabend has nothing to do with Kosuth).

Dibbets, '*Perspective correction*' 1969 on canvas	1100	*1500* [red]
Weiner, to choose	700	*1000*
Barry, idem	1000	*1500*
Huebler, idem	1000	*1500*
Boetti, idem	700	*1400*
Kosuth, *Neon (From one to twenty-five)*	2000	*3500*
Zorio, to choose	700	*1400*
Fulton, idem (small)	150	*250*
Fulton, idem (large size)	600	*1000*

80 See: Chapter 2.2.
81 *Op Losse Schroeven*, *op. cit.*, artist no.21.
82 Letter from Sonnabed to De Wilde dated 20 June 1969, and Invoice from the Sonnabend Gallery dated 18 November 1969, in 1969 Acquisition File, ASMA.
83 Huebler's *Alternative Piece no.4 (s)* (1970) was exhibited simultaneously in January 1971 at Konrad Fischer and at Gian Enzo Sperone. The original project of the work was to document the artist's trip from Düsseldorf to Turin. See: Minola, Mundici, Poli and Roberto, *Gian Enzo Sperone*, *op. cit.*, pp.178–179.
84 Letter from De Wilde to Sperone dated 28 July 1971, and Letter from De Wilde to Sperone dated 5 October 1971, in 1972 Acquisition File, ASMA.

Anselmo, idem		750	*1500*
	Dollars	8540	*14300*

> Calculating Fulton large size.
> For Kosuth there is 700 Dollars more for the material.
> The percentage of reduction is 40%, as you can see. If you are interested, we can agree on the choice of works and the payment which we should make quickly.[85]

De Wilde replied rapidly in a letter dated 5 November 1971:

> I am very interested by your proposition. From now, I accept it with pleasure concerning:
> Dibbets – *Perspective correction*, 1969
> Kosuth, *Neon (From one to twenty-five)*
> As you also know, I had already decided to buy these two works:
> Zorio – to choose
> Anselmo – to choose
> As to Weiner, Barry, Huebler, Boetti and Fulton, I would like to have more information.[86]

De Wilde and Sperone met in Turin a month later, on 7 December 1971. Three weeks after the meeting, De Wilde confirmed in writing the deal they had agreed on:

> You will send me by plane the following works:
> 1. Dibbets *Perspective Correction*, purchased for the price of $1,100
> 2. Huebler *Alternative piece no.4* $1,000
> 3. Kosuth *Five fives (to Donald Judd)* $2,000 + $700 (for the material)
> These works are offered to me in your letter of the month of November 1971 with the indication of prices ...
> I was very pleased by my visit to your gallery which realises amazing work on the European level.[87]

85 Letter received by De Wilde from Sperone on 25 October 1971, in 1972 Acquisition File, ASMA (author's translation).
86 Letter from De Wilde to Sperone dated 5 November 1971, in 1972 Acquisition File, ASMA (author's translation).
87 Letter from De Wilde to Sperone dated 26 December 1971, in 1972 Acquisition File, ASMA (author's translation).

The works were finally received by the Stedelijk Museum in March 1972.[88] In a letter to De Wilde dated 15 June 1972, the dealer mentioned again the three works for which the museum would pay him a total amount of $4,100, a price that excluded the manufacturing costs of the Kosuth piece. Sperone added that he would travel to Amsterdam in July and that he would like to pick up the money himself.[89]

The range of Conceptual artists whose works were collected in the early 1970s shows the intention of the museum to form a comprehensive collection of Conceptual art. Works from nearly all of the artists in the collection were purchased at that time (Darboven, Dibbets, Gilbert & George, Long, etc). 1972–73 marked the peak of Conceptual art acquisitions for the Amsterdam museum. During these two years, no less than 28 works were acquired, including comprehensive sets of works by Dibbets and Ryman. This period also marks the launch of a series of major solo exhibitions of Conceptual artists.

The first major exhibition of Conceptual artists was a Gilbert & George show held in October–November 1971, *The Paintings (With Us in Nature)*.[90] Following the show, the Stedelijk Museum acquired *16 part photo piece* (1971) and a film *Gordon's Makes Us Drunk* (1972). Art & Project sold both pieces to the museum in 1972 for *f*7,500 and *f*2,118 respectively.[91]

From November 1972 to January 1973, the Stedelijk Museum presented an extensive solo show of Dibbets.[92] In 1972 and 1973, the museum acquired nine works by Dibbets, eight photographic pieces and one film. Unique photo-collages cost between *f*10,000 (*Louverdrape Horizontal*, 1971) and *f*20,000 (*Film: White table*, 1972).[93] Most works were acquired from Art & Project, the artist's Dutch dealer gallery since 1969.

However, since his first German solo show in Düsseldorf in August 1968, Fischer had been Dibbets's main European dealer.[94] Dibbets himself declared: 'For me the gallery was Fischer.'[95] Thus, there must have been arrangements between Art & Project and Fischer, possibly about the Amsterdam gallery getting the deals with Dutch institutions. Fischer did, however, also sell to the museum, thus affirming his position as Dibbets's first dealer. In 1972, the Vincent van Gogh Stichting purchased for donation an early photographic work, *Perspective correction-diagonal/crossed/diagonal* (1968), from the Düsseldorf dealer.[96] The

88 Letter from De Wilde to M. Barile, the person in charge of the Arts Department at the Turin-based transportation company Zúst Ambrosetti, dated 13 March 1972, in 1972 Acquisition File, ASMA.

89 Letter from Sperone to De Wilde dated 15 June 1972, in 1972 Acquisition File, ASMA. Sperone's desire to collect the money personally stems from the specific economic conditions prevailing in Italy at the time. There was a financial crisis, and it was prohibited to bring in or take out large amounts of money from the country. Lynda Morris in conversation.

90 Gilbert & George, *The Paintings (With Us in Nature)*, Stedelijk Museum, Amsterdam, 28 October–28 November 1971.

91 Invoice (Rekening) from Art & Project dated 9 February 1972, and Invoice from Art & Project dated 3 November 1972, in 1972 Acquisition File, ASMA. In December 1971–January 1972, Art & Project set up an exhibition of the artists presenting *New Photo-Pieces*. See: *Art & Project Bulletin*, no.47, 28 December 1971.

92 See: *Jan Dibbets, op. cit.*, 1972.

93 1972 Annual Purchasing Record, in Registrar's Dept., ASMA.

94 Jan Dibbets, Rasenrolle, Holzbündel, Wasserpfütze, Konrad Fischer, Düsseldorf, 15 August–17 September 1969. See: *Ausstellungen bei Konrad Fischer, op. cit.*, p.22.

95 Jan Dibbets in conversation with the author, *op. cit.*

96 The Vincent van Gogh Stichting was originally set up in 1960 to administrate and build a museum for the art collection of Vincent Willem van Gogh (the artist's nephew). The Vincent van Gogh Museum in Amsterdam opened its doors in 1973. The Foundation

work was originally purchased for the sum of DM20,000 (*f*20,000).[97]

From December 1973 to January 1974, the Stedelijk Museum hosted a solo exhibition of Long, another of Fischer's artists.[98] Here too, the museum acquired a number of pieces at the time of the show. The three photographic pieces purchased in 1973 had previously been shown in key exhibitions in which Fischer had an influence on the organisation. *Guggenheim Piece* (1971) was part of the *6th Guggenheim International Exhibition* in February–April 1971 in New York.[99] *A Rolling Stone, Resting places along a journey* (1973) had been shown at Long's solo show at Fischer's in May–June 1973.[100] Finally, *Zig-zag. Städtisches Museum Mönchengladbach* (1970) had been made for Long's solo show at the German museum in September 1970.[101] The first two works were acquired for *f*31,888, and the last one for *f*9,092.[102]

One of the best-represented artists in the Stedelijk Museum's collection was Ryman (eight works). Even before the artist's solo show at the museum in February–March 1974,[103] several major paintings had been purchased, mainly from Fischer and Weber. De Wilde acquired the first work during a visit to the artist's studio in New York in 1971.[104] *VII* (1969), a group of seven paintings, was sold by Ryman through Fischer for *f*30,000.[105] The work was kept at Fischer's and transported from Düsseldorf to Amsterdam, where it arrived in July 1972.[106]

It was during his 1971 trip to New York that De Wilde conceived of the idea to organise a Ryman exhibition in Amsterdam. After his return to Europe, in November 1971, he contacted John Weber, the artist's main American dealer at the time, writing: 'In my opinion it would be of importance, also for Ryman, to have his first works hung in a European museum.'[107]

Ryman's solo show took place in early 1974. The Stedelijk Museum bought three pieces included in the exhibition, *Classico 3* (1968) and two *Untitled* works on aluminium (1973). All three paintings were acquired from Fischer between December 1973 and January 1974.[108] The first painting had been exhibited at Ryman's first European solo show in Düsseldorf in November–December 1968.[109] It was bought for *f*50,026.[110] The *Untitled* pieces had also been shown at Fischer's in a solo show in November–December 1973. One work, consisting of five paintings, was bought for *f*50,340, the other for *f*29,227.[112]

From November 1974 to January 1975, an exhibition of prints by LeWitt was

also supported the setting up of other Dutch museums' collections.

97 Acceptance of gift (Aanvaarden schenkingen), Excerpt from the report of the Mayor and the Council members of Amsterdam dated 16 September 1972, in 1972 Acquisition File, ASMA. See also: Inventory card of the work, in Registrar's Dept., ASMA.

98 *Richard Long, Sculptures, Video Pieces*, Stedelijk Museum, Amsterdam, 7 December 1973–27 January 1974.

99 *6th Guggenheim International Exhibition*, Solomon R. Guggenheim Museum, New York, 12 February–11 April 1971. See: *6th Guggenheim International Exhibition 1971* (exh. cat.), The Solomon R. Guggenheim Museum, New York, 1971, unnumbered pages.

100 *Richard Long, A Rolling Stone*, Konrad Fischer, Düsseldorf, 29 May–25 June 1973. See: *Ausstellungen bei Konrad Fischer*, *op. cit.*, p.92.

101 *Richard Long, 4 Skulpturen (England, Germany, Africa, America, 1966–70)*, Städtisches Museum, Mönchengladbach, 16 July–30 August 1970. See: *Richard Long* (exh. cat.), Städtisches Museum, Mönchengaldbach, 1970.

102 Invoice from Fischer dated 6 July 1975, and Invoice from Sperone dated 30 May 1973, in 1973 Acquisition File, ASMA. See also: 1973 Annual Purchasing Record, in Registrar's Dept., ASMA.

103 *Robert Ryman, Paintings: Survey from 1958 until now*, Stedelijk Museum, Amsterdam, 1 February–24 March 1974.

104 Letter from Edy de Wilde to Robert Ryman dated 15 September 1972, in Box 160, Tentoonstellingen 1974, ASMA.

105 Letter from De Wilde to Mr. Wethouder, Head of Cultural

set up through the original input of Robert Feldman, the founder of Parasol Press in New York.[113] This survey of the artist's complete etchings, presented with some silkscreens and lithographs from 1970 to 1975, travelled to the Kunsthalle Basel, then directed by Carlo Huber (former assistant at the Kunstmuseum Basel).[114] Although no works were acquired from this exhibition, a number of drawings had been purchased in 1970–72. For example, *Fold* (1972) was acquired for *f*320 from Art & Project, where an exhibition of paper works had been organised in 1971.[115]

In January 1975, Darboven's Basel exhibition travelled to Amsterdam. The show, presenting a survey of the artist's work from 1968 to 1974, transferred from the Kunstmuseum Basel, where it was organised by the director Franz Meyer.[116] The Stedelijk had already acquired two sets of drawings by Darboven in 1972 and 1973. After the exhibition, the artist donated a vast drawing installation to the museum, *24 Gesänge. B Form* (1974).[117] The work of 120 drawings was shipped from Leo Castelli, New York, where it had been exhibited in a solo show of the artist in November 1974.[118] In New York, the piece was valued at $40,000 (*f*147,200).[119] De Wilde saw this gift as a sign of Darboven's sympathy with the Stedelijk Museum.[120] In November 1976, the drawing installation was exhibited in the permanent display.[121]

Buren had a solo show at the Stedelijk Museum in April–June 1976.[122] This exhibition, entitled *Hier/Ici* (Here), was connected to other shows organised at the same time in other Dutch museums: the Van Abbemuseum in Eindhoven (then directed by Rudi Fuchs) and the Kröller-Müller Museum in Otterlo. The show presented a number of in-situ installations. However, it was not until 1983 that one of these works was acquired by the museum (*Kaleidoscope, un travail in situ*).[123]

The survey of temporary exhibitions of Conceptual artists at the Stedelijk Museum, from the late 1960s to the late 1970s, reveals clear links between exhibitions and purchasing policy. Works by all the artists who had solo shows were acquired at the time (Gilbert & George, Dibbets, Long, Ryman, LeWitt, Darboven, Buren).[124]

A characteristic that emerges from Database 6 on museum purchases is that the Stedelijk Museum acquired many more films and videos compared with

Affairs of Amsterdam Town Hall, dated 21 July 1972, and Invoice from Ryman dated 8 January 1973, in 1972 Acquisition File, ASMA.

106 Transportation form 'Buiten collectie' dated 4 May 1972, in 1972 Acquisition File, ASMA.

107 Letter from Edy de Wilde to John Weber dated 14 November 1971, in Box 160, Tentoonstellingen 1974, ASMA.

108 Letter from Van Beijeren to Ryman dated 28 March 1974, in Box 160, Tentoonstellingen 1974, ASMA. See also: Inventory cards of the works, in Registrar's Dept., ASMA.

109 *Robert Ryman*, Konrad Fischer, Düsseldorf, 21 November–17 December 1968. See: *Ausstellungen bei Konrad Fischer, op. cit.*, p.25.

110 1974 Annual Purchasing Record, in Registrar's Dept., ASMA.

111 *Robert Ryman*, Konrad Fischer, Düsseldorf, November 1973. See: *Ausstellungen bei Konrad Fischer, op. cit.*, p.99

112 Invoice from Fischer dated 22 March 1974, in 1973 Purchasing File, and 1974 Annual Purchasing Record, in Registrar's Dept., ASMA.

113 *Sol LeWitt, Prints*, Stedelijk Museum, Amsterdam, 29 November 1974–26 January 1975. See: Manuscript letter from Sol LeWitt to Loenen Martinet, curator Stedelijk Museum, dated 11 February 1974, in Box 162, Tentoonstellingen 1974, ASMA.

114 Letter from Ad Petersen to Carlo Huber dated 9 June 1975, in Box 162, Tentoonstellingen 1974, ASMA.

115 Invoice from Art & Project dated 23 August 1972, in 1972 Acquisition File, ASMA. Sol LeWitt, Art & Project, Amsterdam, 7 September–2 October 1971. See: Art and Project Bulletin, no.43, 1 September 1971.

other European institutions (15 pieces). Schum produced a large number of these films and videos. Other acquisitions in 1972 included Dibbets's *4 Diagonals* (1970) and Gilbert & George's *Gordon's Makes Us Drunk* (1972, limited edition of 25) from Art & Project. There was a difference in price depending on the amount in an edition. Thus Dibbets's video cost *f*800, while Gilbert & George's cost *f*2,118.[125]

From December 1979 to January 1980, a memorial retrospective of Gerry Schum's work was organised at the Stedelijk Museum, Amsterdam.[126] At that time, a collection of videos originally edited by the Videogalerie Schum was purchased by the museum. Works by artists such as Gilbert & George, Merz and Weiner were acquired from Projektion Ursula Wevers, Cologne.[127] In addition, new tape copies of some films acquired in the early 1970s, like Dibbets's *4 Diagonals* (1970), were provided by Wevers.[128]

In 1979, the Stedelijk Museum acquired a set of seven films by Nauman from Castelli-Sonnabend Tapes & Films, Inc., New York, for a sum of *f*2,840.[129] The Castelli-Sonnabend Tapes & Films, Inc. had been founded in 1975 by Castelli and Sonnabend in New York. Wevers established links with the New York organisation. They agreed to collaborate on supporting films by a number of artists, including Nauman and Keith Sonnier.[130]

With 62 Conceptual artworks, including only five drawings, the Stedelijk Museum established one of the strongest collections of Conceptual art in Europe at the time. Perhaps as a result of the purchasing policy imposed on Dutch museums during the 1970s, the Conceptual artist most represented was Dibbets (19 works). Nauman (10) and Ryman (8) were also well represented.

In the late 1960s and 1970s, the dealer galleries to sell the most to the museum were Art & Project (18) and Konrad Fischer (12). But we have seen that Fischer was the main dealer of many artists, and that there was probably an arrangement with the Amsterdam gallery. A number of works were also acquired from American dealers, with 16 works purchased from Ileana Sonnabend, John Weber, Sydney Janis, Sperone-Westwater-Fischer and Leo Castelli.

The presence of Sydney Janis as a dealer selling a painting by Ryman (*Monitor*, 1978) in 1979 is characteristic of the late appearance of secondary dealers into the Conceptual network. This shows that in the late 1970s existing dealer

116 *Hanne Darboven, Ein Monat, ein Jahr, ein Jahrhundert, Arbeiten von 1968 bis 1974*, Stedelijk Museum, Amsterdam, 10 January–2 March 1975. See: Letter from De Wilde to Meyer dated 12 November 1974, in Box 165, Tentoonstellingen 1975, ASMA.

117 Letter from De Wilde to Darboven dated 5 April 1976, in 1976 Gift File, ASMA. In 1976, Darboven also donated the 'A' version of this work to the Ludwig Museum, Cologne.

118 *Hanne Darboven, 24 Songs*, Leo Castelli Gallery, New York, 16–30 November 1974. See: Jakobson, *Leo Castelli, Gentle Snapshots, op. cit.*, p.71.

119 Letter from De Wilde to Mr Wethouder dated 26 July 1976, in 1976 Gift File, ASMA.

120 Letter from De Wilde to Darboven dated 23 July 1976, in 1976 Acquisition File, ASMA.

121 Inventory card of the work, Registrar's Dept., ASMA. See also: Letter from De Wilde to Darboven dated 5 April 1976, in 1976 Acquisition File, ASMA.

122 *Daniel Buren, Hier/Ici*, Stedelijk Museum, Amsterdam, 30 April–7 June 1976.

123 See: Inventory card of the work, Registrar's Dept., ASMA.

124 Further Conceptual artists to be given solo shows at the Stedelijk Museum included Brouwn (1971, 1973), Ruthenbeck (1972), Fulton (1973), Barry, Van Elk (1974), Baldessari (1975), Ruscha (1976) and Morris (1977).

125 Invoice from Art & Project dated 8 March 1972, and Invoice from Art & Project dated 3 November 1972, in 1972 Acquisition File,

galleries took on Conceptual artists to update their profile. The same observation can be made in the case of Nauman. After sales by Sonnabend and Castelli, it was yet another secondary dealer gallery, Schellman & Klüser, Munich, that sold the film *Clear vision* (1973) to the museum in 1980.

The Stedelijk's Conceptual art acquisition budget

The Stedelijk Museum did not profit from many gifts, but had the financial means to form a large collection. It appears, on reviewing the figures in Database 7 on Conceptual art prices,[131] that it was the more 'traditional' art forms that remained the most expensive. Sculpture (Andre, Long) and painting (Ryman) reached sums of *f*23,000 up to *f*150,000. Quite expensive too were Darboven's drawing installations (*f*147,200) and Dibbets's photo-collages (*f*22,000–26,000). Other art media ranged from *f*250 to *f*10,000: neon pieces (*f*6,400–7,900), drawings (*f*1,200), photographs (*f*7,000–10,000), videos (*f*250–2,500).

Throughout its history, the Stedelijk Museum had integrated contemporary art into its permanent collection. The vast collection of Conceptual works that it acquired from 1967 to 1980 results from this policy. The wide range of sources from which it purchased also contributed to the richness of the museum's permanent collection. All major Conceptual art galleries active at that time contributed to the collection in one way or another. The extent of the collection cannot only be explained by this openness. The Stedelijk had a much larger acquisition budget at its disposal than other European institutions.[132]

The acquisition fund of the museum was increased annually from the late 1960s until 1976. In 1977, it was reduced by about ten per cent. It was, however, augmented again in 1978 by approximately 25 per cent. In 1979, the budget was halved, but a year later increased by 40 per cent, bringing it back to the level it had been in 1972–73. Later it seems to have been drastically reduced again.

Between 1969 and 1980, the total purchasing budget of the museum was *f*10,825,100. During that period, the amount spent by the museum on acquiring works of the Conceptual artists studied was approximately *f*1,061,330.[133]
In about ten years, the Museum spent roughly ten per cent of its budget on acquiring works of the Conceptual artists studied.[134]

ASMA. A brochure published in March 1972 by the Vidogalerie Schum indicates that several dealer galleries across Europe, among others Art & Project, exclusively presented and sold its productions. See: Groos, Hess and Wevers, *Ready to Shoot*, *op. cit.*, p.303.

126 Dorine Mignot (ed.), *Gerry Schum* (exh. cat.), Stedelijk Museum, Amsterdam, 1979.

127 Invoice from Projection Ursula Wevers dated 22 July 1978, in 1978 Acquisition File, ASMA. On Schum's death in 1973, his widow took over the promoting of the tapes produced by the Videogalerie under the name Projektion Ursula Wevers.

128 Inventory card of the works, Registrar's Dept., ASMA.

129 Invoice from Castelli-Sonnabend Tapes & Films dated 4 April 1979, in 1979 Acquisition File, and 1979 Annual purchasing record, Registrar's Dept., ASMA.

130 Groos, Hess and Wevers, *Ready to Shoot*, *op. cit.*, p.43. See also: Victor Ancona, 'Video art: Castelli-Sonnabend, a gallery geared to new art forms', *Videography*, 2 January 1977, pp.41–43.

131 Database 7 on prices of Conceptual art (Appendix 1.7) details the individual prices of each work. For the sake of coherence, the Dutch Guilder (*f*) was chosen as the reference currency. Numerous original invoices of artworks indicate the acquisition price in other foreign currencies. This information is indicated in brackets. Cross-referencing of the information of the annual purchasing records and of the invoices allowed for an estimation of the exchange rates. The exact rate between Dutch Guilders and other European currencies, as well as its fluctuations during the 1970s is difficult to establish.

Stedelijk Van Abbemuseum, Eindhoven

The Stedelijk Van Abbemuseum, founded by a tobacco industrialist in 1936, was run by the city of Eindhoven. After the Second World War, under the direction of Edy de Wilde, the museum became known for its exhibitions and collection of modern art.[135] From 1963 to 1973, Jan Leering was the Director of the museum. He continued its policy of collecting the avant-garde of the day. Under his directorship, only one Conceptual piece entered the collection: *The shortest day at the Van Abbemuseum* (1970), a series of photographs by Dibbets, purchased in 1971 from Art & Project, Amsterdam. The work was exhibited at the artist's solo show at the museum in December 1971 to January 1972.[136] As the photographic work was directly linked to the museum, it was no surprise that it was added to the permanent collection. In 1974, the Van Abbemuseum had no director. Still, a box with books by Buren entitled *Passage* (1974) was purchased at that time from the Gallery Seriaal, Amsterdam.

In 1975, Rudi Fuchs (born 1942) became the Director of the museum, a position he retained until 1988. His appointment was not trouble-free as he had to face the opposition of members of staff. This went so far that contemporary Dutch artists such as Dibbets and Van Elk launched a countermovement to support his candidature.[137] It seems that this controversy was provoked by two opposing views on the function of a museum. From 1968–69, Leering had changed his programme from a connoisseur-oriented policy towards an engagement with social and educational functions. Rather than continuing the social principles of his predecessor, Fuchs adopted Leering's earlier programme of showing and collecting contemporary art. The main criticism of Fuchs was that, by setting up an 'insider' specialist conceptual programme, he was not making the current art accessible to a larger public.[138]

It was under Fuchs's direction that a comprehensive collection of Conceptual works was put together. In 1975, the overall budget of the museum was £500,000.[139] When one considers the purchases that Fuchs made, the acquisition fund must have formed a substantial part of that sum. He also believed that in order to turn this small provincial museum into an interesting and special institution it had to focus on the avant-garde. 'You could have a first-grade programme with something new, never seen before.'[140] Fuchs also had the

However, by comparing two entries, it was possible to ascertain an approximate exchange rate between US Dollars and Dutch Guilders, and between German Deutschmarks and Dutch Guilders. The price calculations in the database are based on the following exchange rates: in 1971: \$1=*f*3,19 / 1973: \$1=*f* 2,6 / 1976: \$1=*f*3,68 / 1979: \$1=*f*2. In 1975: DM1=*f*1,04 / 1977: DM1=*f*1,05. During the late 1960s and 1970s, the sale of artworks was not excluded from taxation in the Netherlands. The Dutch equivalent of VAT (Value Added Tax) is the 'btw' (belasting toegevoegde waarde). At that time, it represented 4% of the price of goods. The tax was only clearly marked on invoices by Dutch dealer galleries, Art & Project and the Galerie Seriaal. See for instance: Invoice from Art & Project dated 12 August 1976 for Jan Dibbets's *Monet's dream study* (1975) (*f*15,000 + 4% btw (*f*600) = *f*15,600), in 1976 Acquisition File, ASMA.

132 During the late 1960s and 1970s, the annual purchasing budget of the institution was established as follows: 1967: no report / 1968: no report / 1969: *f*770,000 / 1970: *f*820,000 / 1971: *f*850,000 / 1972: *f*900,000 / 1973: *f*900,000 / 1974: *f*942,500 estimate (*f*935,000 spent) / 1975: *f*1,037,900 estimate (*f*1,173,400 spent) / 1976: *f*1,073,000 estimate (*f* 1,178,500 spent) / 1977: *f*924,000 / 1978: *f*1,145,700 / 1979: *f*553,000 / 1980: *f*909,000. See: Verslagen der bedrijven, diensten en commissies van Amsterdam. 35 Gemeentemusea (Annual report Stedelijk Museum), Amsterdam, 1967–80, in Registrar's Dept., ASMA.

133 See: Database 7, Section Stedelijk Museum, Amterdam.

134 If we take an average of the turbulent exchange rate between

advantage of an absolute freedom in leading the museum. Although he had to submit his choices to the Trustees, their role was more to check the amount paid rather than the work itself.[141] He was also aided by the fact that among his most important Trustees were Rudolf Oxenaar (Director of the Kröller-Müller Museum, Otterlo) and the collectors Martin Visser and Anton Herbert, people who had already been won over by Conceptualism. Furthermore, Fuchs believed that it was important to link purchases with exhibitions.

By 1980, the museum in Eindhoven had established one of the biggest collections of Conceptual art in Europe. No fewer than 51 works had been acquired at that point.[142] An interesting aspect of this collection is that the museum acquired works from artists that were not collected elsewhere. For instance, it was the only institution to organise yearly discussions with Wilson from 1975 onwards. Five *Discussions* entered the permanent collection between 1976 and 1980. All works were purchased directly from the artist. The acquisition of such extreme works showed the daring attitude of Fuchs towards the most up-to-date art of the period.

The Van Abbemuseum was one of those rare institutions (along with the museum of Mönchengladbach) to acquire statements by Weiner. The American artist was the Conceptual artist most represented in the collection (16 works, comprising six statements and ten films). In 1975, three statements from Weiner's solo show at Konrad Fischer's were purchased by the museum: *On a smooth*, *In the rough* and *On a rough* (all from 1975).[143] Two other statements were purchased in the same year from Castelli, the artist's American dealer. They were two versions of *Up (on) in the air. Down (on) in the ground. Being within the context of (a) reaction* (1975). Weiner's films were also collected in Eindhoven. Indeed, the ten films were purchased mainly from Castelli-Sonnabend Tapes & Films in 1976 and 1978. A solo show of Weiner's films was put together at the museum in February 1979.[144]

The museum in Eindhoven was the institution to acquire the most works by Kosuth. One work was purchased directly from the artist: a painting on glass, *One and Nine a Description* (1965) in 1979. In 1977, the museum bought *Art as Idea as Idea (First Investigation)* (1968) from Paul Maenz, Cologne. In 1978, Kosuth's work was presented in a solo show in Eindhoven.[145]

the Dutch Guilders and the US Dollar in the 1970s ($1 = *f*2,86) it gives us a purchasing budget of $3,785,000. The amount spent on Conceptual works was thus $371,094.

135 Oxenaar, 'On art and museum policies in the Netherlands', *Studio International*, *op. cit.*, p.205.

136 *Jan Dibbets*, Stedelijk Van Abbemuseum, Eindhoven, 3 December 1971–16 January 1972.

137 Brandt Corstius, 'Holland', *Studio International*, *op. cit.*, p.135.

138 Cor Blok, 'Holland, A change of atmosphere at the Van Abbe Museum', *Studio International*, January–February 1977, vol. 193, no.985, pp.30–31.

139 Morris, 'The Museum of Modern Art in Oxford 1965–1975', *Studio International*, *op. cit.*, p.240.

140 Fuchs in conversation with the author, *op. cit.*

141 *Ibid.*

142 The collection catalogue was used to compile some of the data. See: Jan Debbaut and Monique Verhulst (eds), *A Companion to Modern and Contemporary Art, Van Abbemuseum*, Van Abbemuseum and NAi Publishers, Eindhoven, 2003. Records of the provenance of the artworks were compiled mainly from information provided by the Assistant Curator Margo van de Wiel and the librarians of the museum Diana Franssen and Marleen Gijsenin: e-mails to the author between August 2003 and January 2004. See: Database 6 (Appendix 1.6).

143 *Lawrence Weiner, 3 Works in Relation to a Place*, Konrad Fischer, Düsseldorf, 28 January–20 February 1975. See: *Ausstellungen bei*

Another characteristic revealed by the study of the Van Abbemuseum's database was its contacts with private collectors. In 1978, the collector Martin Visser sold LeWitt's *Wall Drawing no.265* (1975) to the museum. On two occasions, in 1968 and 1970, part of the Vissers' collection was shown at the museum.[146] The proximity of Eindhoven and Bergeyk, where the private collector lived, facilitated contacts. The museum was also in touch with the collectors Annick and Anton Herbert. In 1976, the Herberts put a wood sculpture by Andre on permanent loan to the museum, *Henge on 3 right Thresholds* (1971). As we have seen, Herbert and Visser were Trustees of the museum. In 1977, *Wood Circle* by Long (1977) was placed on permanent loan by another private collector, Mrs A. Korevaar-Visser from The Hague. The Van Abbemuseum benefited from the interest and support of several private collectors in setting up its own collection.

Sol LeWitt was among the Conceptual artists most collected (5 works). In 1975, the museum acquired three drawings from Art & Project, and in 1977 a *Wall Structure* (1972) from Fischer. The German dealer sold many works to the Van Abbemuseum. For instance, he sold a major sculpture by Andre, *Twenty-Fifth Steel Cardinal* (1974) and one by Nauman, *Driven Man, Driven Snow* (1976) in 1976 and 1977 respectively. Between 1975 and 1980, works by Darboven (*Konstruktion 21 × 21 – Zahlen: 1, 3, 5, 7. (+ 5) = 21*, 1968), Gilbert & George (*Are you angry or are you boring?*, 1977), and Merz (*Igloo Nero*, 1967–79) were acquired for the museum through Fischer.[147]

Most of Dibbets' works held by the Van Abbemuseum entered the permanent collection through Art & Project. Five photographic works were purchased between 1971 and 1979. In 1980, *Colorstudy C1, C2, C3, C4* (1980) came into the collection through Fischer. In 1980, the museum also organised a solo show of the Dutch artist.[148]

The case of Long highlights links between dealers and the diverse provenances of works in the museum's collection. In 1976, the first of his works, *Crossing two rivers* (1974), was purchased from Art & Project. In 1975, the photographs had been exhibited in a solo exhibition at Art & Project.[149] *Sixty Stones* (1975), a large 60-part sculpture, was acquired in 1977 from Fischer. We have already seen that *Wood Circle* (1977) was lent by Mrs A. Korevaar-Visser in 1977. Preisig provided *Peeting Place* (1977), a work that might have been exhibited in

Konrad Fischer, *op. cit.*, p.115.

144 *Lawrence Weiner, Video*, Stedelijk Van Abbemuseum, Eindhoven, 18–25 February 1979.

145 *Joseph Kosuth, Tekst-Kontekst*, Stedelijk Van Abbemuseum, Eindhoven, 1978.

146 *Three blind mice, The collectors Visser (Bergeijk, Antwerpen), Peeters (Bruges) and Becht (Hilversum)* in 1968 and *Summer exhibition with guest: Martin Visser (furniture) and Aldo van den Nieuwelaar (lights)* in 1970.

147 Andre's work had been exhibited in a solo show at Fischer's in 1974, and Gilbert & George's work in 1977. *Carl Andre*, Konrad Fischer, Düsseldorf, 21 June–20 July 1974. *Gilbert & George, The Dirty Words*, Konrad Fischer, Düsseldorf, 26 November–23 December 1977. See: *Ausstellungen bei Konrad Fischer*, *op. cit.*, pp.107–147.

148 *Jan Dibbets*, Stedelijk Van Abbemuseum, Eindhoven, 3 December 1970–16 January 1971.

149 *Richard Long, River Avon Driftwood, Crossing Two Rivers/Minnesota/Wiltshire*, Art & Project, Amsterdam, 18 March–15 April 1975. See: *Art & Project Bulletin*, no.89, 18 March 1975.

Basel in May–June 1977 during a solo show of the artist.[150] The Rolf Preisig gallery, Basel, sold several other works to Eindhoven. For instance, in 1977 one piece consisting of photographs and stickers by Huebler, *Variable Piece #111, London* (1974), and one white painting by Ryman, *Untitled* (1974).

The Van Abbemuseum in Eindhoven was the only institution to purchase from Wide White Space. Broodthaers's *Série de neuf tableaux* (1972) was purchased in 1975 from the Antwerp-based gallery. In 1977, Buren's painting *Peinture sur toile* (1977) was acquired. It is interesting to note that both works were sold at a moment in time when the gallery was about to or had already closed down. This shows that Wide White Space continued to be commercially active even after its closure in 1976.

It appears from Database 6 that the Stedelijk Van Abbemuseum's purchasing policy included a strong commitment towards Conceptual art. This commitment was largely orchestrated by Fuchs from 1975 onwards. He had the advantage of access to a budget that was sufficient to set up a comprehensive purchasing and temporary-exhibitions programme focusing on Conceptual art. His risky choices, notably with Wilson and Weiner, demonstrate that he could acquire whatever works he wanted.

It appears that the museum purchased works from a variety of sources and did not hesitate to buy from international galleries. Indeed, of the museum's 51 Conceptual works, most were purchased from Fischer (11), Art & Project (9) and Castelli-Sonnabend Tapes & Films (9). Fuchs himself thought that Fischer and Spillemaeckers were the most important dealers at the time.[151] The most collected Conceptual artists were Weiner (16), Dibbets (6), LeWitt (5) and Wilson (5). Nearly half of the Conceptual works (23 of the 51) in the permanent collection were acquired during Fuchs's first two years at the Van Abbemuseum, 1975 to 1977.

150 *Richard Long*, Rolf Preisig, Basel, 17 May–21 June 1977.

151 Fuchs in conversation with the author, *op. cit.* Moreover, Fuchs and Fischer were good friends.

5.4. Great Britain

Tate Gallery, London

After the Second World War, Britain was slow to adopt the American concept of a museum dedicated to modern art. There was a continuity of traditions in the British museum system because the country had not been occupied and museums had not been despoiled during the War. Work was mainly acquired through legacies and living artists were not shown until the late 1930s. Although the Tate Gallery became independent from the National Gallery in 1954,[152] it had been allocated an independent purchasing fund from the government to set up a collection in 1946.[153]

From the mid-1950s to the mid-1960s, the Tate Gallery was looking to gain an international role. In April–June 1964, the exhibition *Painting and Sculpture of a Decade, 1954–1964* was organised by the Calouste Gulbenkian Foundation for the Tate.[154] It was the first exhibition in Britain to show an international collection of modern art. This allowed for the formation of a permanent collection that was divided into three sections: the historic British collection, the British national collection and the international collection.

From 1964 through the 1970s, Sir Norman Reid was the Director.[155] Reid's daughter was married to the British hard-edge painter Robyn Denny. In the 1960s, Denny was showing at the Kasmin Gallery, which dealt with British and American art. Through his family, Reid had connections with the American art world. During Reid's Directorship, many gifts were made to the Tate through the American Federation of Arts (AFA).[156] These connections provided contacts with American dealers such as Leo Castelli. One major change that Reid undertook when he became the Director was to establish a Department of Modern Art. This had two main functions: to establish both a national British collection and an international collection of modern art.

In the early 1970s, several young curators were appointed to run the Department of Modern Art: Ronald Alley (Keeper), Richard Morphet and Anne Seymour (both Assistant Keepers). From 1972, they were joined by two research assistants (Penelope Marcus and Christopher Johnstone). This shows the extent

152 The National Gallery of British Art, as the Tate Gallery was originally named, had been a national art museum since 1897.

153 *The Tate Gallery 1976–1978, Illustrated Catalogue of Acquisitions*, The Tate Gallery, London, 1979, p.7.

154 See: *Painting and Sculpture of a Decade, 1954–1964* (exh. cat.), Calouste Gulbenkian Foundation and Tate Gallery, London, 1964. This exhibition travelled to Basel, Amsterdam and Humlebaek, Denmark.

155 Reid had previously been the right-hand man of Sir John Rothenstein, the Tate's Director since 1938. He had trained as an artist and was a friend of many artists who would donate works to the Tate (e.g. Barbara Hepworth, Henry Moore, Ben Nicholson).

156 The American Federation of Arts was founded in 1909 in New York with the aim to initiate art exhibitions and to provide educational and professional programs in museums in the US and abroad. The Museum Donor Programme facilitated donations by American collectors to museums.

to which the Department had expanded in a relatively short time. Alley, Morphet and Seymour were concerned with art developments of the day. Their interest was shared by Michael Compton, the keeper of the Department of Exhibitions and Education from 1970.[157] These people initiated the purchase of Conceptual works of art for the permanent collection. Nicolas Serota, the Director of the Tate Gallery since 1988, explains that Reid:

> appointed some younger curators, Michael Compton (who later became Keeper of Exhibitions), Richard Morphet and Anne Seymour (who later became Anne d'Offay). Those three people made recommendations for acquisitions. It was at a time when Norman Reid was rather successful in persuading the government to give the Tate quite large additional sums for purchasing. In the context of those large additional sums, it was possible for the Tate to buy Conceptual art, giving a certain licence to these younger curators, while actually spending very little money. What Reid did was to respond to the proposals made by some young curators, by spending a limited amount of money to reflect what was happening now.[158]

The purchase of all works to be included in the permanent collection had to be agreed by the Board of Trustees.[159] Proposals were either put forward by the Trustees themselves or suggested by the Director. Every proposal was discussed and deliberated during meetings of the Board. From the mid-1960s, Reid modified the procedure, which he felt did not allow for a coherent build-up of a national collection. The Trustees were no longer able to initiate a recommendation, but had to refer it to the Director first. Further, the Director had the limited autonomy to buy individual works spontaneously, when either geographical distance or time factors meant that it was not feasible to consult the Board. The modified purchasing process, which gave the Director more control over the acquisition policy, also allowed the curators to propose contemporary works. Under Reid's Directorship, it was mainly staff members who initiated purchases.[160]

It appears from a discussion published in April 1973 in *Studio International* between Richard Cork, Norman Reid and the curatorial staff, including the

157 *The Tate Gallery 1970–72*, published by order of the Trustees, London, 1972, pp.216–217.

158 Serota in conversation with the author, *op. cit.*

159 For example, in 1970–72, the Board of Trustees included: Sir Robert Sainsbury (Chairman), Sebastian de Ferranti, Andrew Forge (until 1971), Lord Harlech (from 1971), Dame Barbara Hepworth, Howard Hodgkin, Geoffrey Jellicoe, Niall MacDermont, Stewart Mason, John Piper and the private collector Ted Power.

160 At the time, a red book was established at the Tate, briefing staff members on the correct conduct between curators and dealers. This led Seymour eventually to resign because she had married dealer Anthony d'Offay.

Keepers of the Modern Collection, that two directions were adopted for acquisitions: filling gaps in the early modern period and setting up a contemporary collection. Ronald Alley pointed out that the Tate had the responsibility of amassing a representative collection of twentieth-century international art, since it was the only institution in Britain to present such works publicly.[161]

Even under these circumstances, the Tate's purchasing policy did not allow for direct and spontaneous purchases. Proposals had to be submitted to the Director and to the Trustees, which implied a long procedure and the compiling of detailed dossiers. The staff had to work from photographs or drawings because many works were located in continental Europe or in America, and because some works had to be commissioned before being made, so the process was further prolonged. This implies that the Board had to make some purchases based on documents alone.[162]

Reid's predecessors had not acquired contemporary artworks for the permanent collection. The founding of a Department of Modern Art and the appointment of younger curators was a first step towards collecting the art of the day. To the question of how he responded to modern art proposals, Reid replied:

> As far as I'm concerned, it's judged on each particular case. I've always tried to take the view that in order for me to be able to persuade the Trustees, I must myself be convinced. And therefore I listen very carefully to what the younger members of staff say; and in fact I think they have argued with great effect. We have bought a number of things which perhaps left to myself I would not have done.[163]

Exhibitions such as *When Attitudes Become Form* (London, September–October 1969) and the *6th Guggenheim International* (New York, February–April 1971) influenced the Tate. In June–October 1972, *Documenta 5* acted as a justification for the museum to start collecting Conceptual art. Ronald Alley visited the exhibition to see what was going on in the contemporary art scene.[164] In early 1973, he announced that he had asked Anne Seymour and Richard Morphet to establish a list of Conceptual or 'post-object' artists that they thought should be represented in the collection. He requested a list of available works for

161 'The Tate Gallery', *Studio International*, *op. cit.*, pp.182–185.
162 See, for example, the extensive correspondence about the purchase of Sol LeWitt's *Six Geometric Figures* (1980) in 1980, in Tate Acquisition File (TG 4/2/626/2), TLAL.
163 'The Tate Gallery', *Studio International*, *op. cit.*, p.182.
164 Morris had dinner with Alley in Kassel on the closing weekend of Documenta 5. Morris in conversation with the author.

discussion. Seymour explained: 'In terms of inhibiting the purchase, the problem in the present situation is that we have left it too long, and we've got landed with having to deal with 25 people at once, rather than taking them one at a time as they came up.'[165] Morphet added: 'The list we're concentrating on at the moment is far from exhaustive: It's just to make a big impact in this field.'[166]

Several letters written at the time between the Keepers of the Modern Collection and dealers relate to this list. In November 1972, a number of key international dealer galleries were contacted and asked about representative works for sale. This was three months after *The New Art* exhibition organised by Seymour for the Arts Council at the Hayward Gallery, London, in August–September 1972. The show presented an overview of the latest art developments in Britain, including Art & Language, Gilbert & George and Long. Through this exhibition, Seymour had contact with some of the most influential dealers in Europe and America.[167] Seymour was brought up in Cologne, where her father worked for the British Council in the postwar years. Seymour was therefore responsible for writing to German dealers, including Fischer.

In a letter dated 21 November 1972 from Seymour to Fischer, the curator wrote that the Tate was looking to acquire works of several British and international artists, including Art & Language, Darboven, Dibbets, Gilbert & George, LeWitt, Long, Nauman, Tremlett and Weiner. In his response, dated 13 December, Fischer provided a list of available works for purchase by the Tate Gallery:

Hanne Darboven, *One Century*, 1971, $30,000
Hanne Darboven, *No 1–No 42*, 1971, $3,000
On Kawara, *One Million Years*, 1970–71, $6,000
Sol LeWitt, *Double Open Modular Cube, Off Half*, 1970, $7,500
Bruce Nauman, *Corridor with reflected image*, 1971, $6,000
Bruce Nauman, *Wall with 2 Fans*, 1970, $6,000
Robert Ryman, *Untitled Painting*, 1963, $11,000
David Tremlett, *The Spring Recordings*, 1972, $1,500
Lawrence Weiner, *5-part piece*, 1970, $4,000

165 'The Tate Gallery', *Studio International*, *op. cit.*, p.186.
166 *Ibid.*
167 Seymour and Serota had negotiated loans for *The New Art* show via dealers.

He wrote:

> I have as well a big choice of major Sol LeWitt – sculptures. One of them will be offered to you by Yvon Lambert (Paris). I think, the one I offer to you, is the best one for the Tate Gallery situation – not too large and not too small. A new work of Jan Dibbets will be offered to you by my friends from Art & Project (Amsterdam).
>
> I would be delighted, if the Tate could decide to buy some of these pieces of younger artists. If not – never mind! In that case, could you please send back to me the offers as soon as possible.[168]

At the same time, Morphet, an expert on Pop art, contacted American dealers.[169] On 22 November 1972, he wrote to John Weber, enquiring about Conceptual artists' works for sale. In a response of 2 December 1972, Weber proposed a series of works available for sale: LeWitt wall drawings ($4,000 each, regardless of size) and large metal pieces (1965–66, $12,000), a Long walk work (1970, $2,500), a Dibbets photo-work (1971, $2,500) and Darboven photographs (1972, $2,500 each).[170]

In a letter dated 5 December 1972 addressed to Anne Seymour, the assistant of Sperone in Turin, Anne Tuteur, listed:

> 1) Art & Language, *On Normal Law*, 1966–67, 1,800 $
> 2) Art & Language, *Physical Properties*, 1966–67, 1,800 $
> 3) Hanne Darboven, *Untitled*, 1968, 2,000 $
> 4) Jan Dibbets, *The sound of 25 kilometres...*, 1969, 2,500 $
> 5) Jan Dibbets, *Perspective Correction*, 1968, 8,000 $
> 6) Jan Dibbets, one big work, 5,500 $
> 7) Hamish Fulton, several small works, 300 £ each + England, four set, 1,000 $
> 8) Sol LeWitt, *Low Modular Floor Structure*, 1966, 14,000 $
> 9) Sol LeWitt, *Cube–Cube*, 1966, 11,000 $
> 10) Sol LeWitt, *Lines one centimetre long drawn at random using four colors and their combinations ...*, 1970, 6,500 $
> 11) Richard Long, *Zig Zag Piece*, 1970, 2,500 $

168 Letter from Seymour to Fischer dated 21 November 1972, and Letter from Fischer to Seymour dated 13 December 1972, in Tate Acquisition File (TG 4/2/768/1), TLAL.

169 In 1970, Morphet had organised exhibitions of Andy Warhol and Richard Hamilton at the Tate Gallery.

170 Letter from Morphet to Weber dated 22 November 1972, and Letter from Weber to Morphet dated 2 December 1972, in Tate Acquisition File (TG 4 PC2/10/1), TLAL.

12) Robert Morris, *36 inches*, 1963–1972, 4,500 $
13) Robert Morris, idem
14) Robert Morris, idem
15) Lawrence Weiner, *Mobile before relegation ... before relegation*, 1972, 1,500 $
16) Lawrence Weiner, *Dulled after mutilation ... after mutilation*, 1972, 1,500 $
17) Lawrence Weiner, *Being rolled during incarceration ... during incarceration*, 1972, 1,500 $
18) Richard Serra, *Untitled*, 1967, 8,000 $[171]

This correspondence with Fischer, Weber and Sperone shows clearly that by 1972 the Keepers of the Modern Collection were actively engaged in developing a contemporary collection in which Conceptual art had a large place. Documenta 5 and *The New Art* had influenced the Tate to start collecting Contemporary art. The exhibitions influenced the choice of Conceptual artists and works. The list requested by Alley must have included the artists mentioned in the letters. British contemporary artists to be looked at were Art & Language, Fulton, Gilbert & George, Long and Tremlett.[172] The international artists were Darboven, Dibbets, Kawara, LeWitt, Morris, Nauman, Serra, Ryman and Weiner.[173]

Between 1970 and 1980, the Tate Gallery bought 37 Conceptual works.[174] Conceptual art purchases had been discussed by the curators since 1970.[175] A tentative start was initiated in 1971 with the acquisition of two sets of lithographs by LeWitt, *Sixteen lithographs in color* (1970–71) and a set of five lithographs in black and white, *Entitled* (1971), both purchased from the Lisson Gallery, London, where they had been exhibited in June–July 1971.[176]

1972 marks the beginning of acquisitions of major Conceptual works with pieces by Andre and Gilbert & George. Two sculptures by Andre entered the Tate collection via the American dealer John Weber.[177] *Ladder No.2*, also called *Last Ladder* (1959) was an early wooden sculpture purchased from the artist through Weber. *Entitled* or *Equivalent VIII* (1966) was first exhibited at the artist's solo show at the Tibor de Nagy Gallery, New York, in March 1966. The work was destroyed soon after the show. Originally made in limestone, it was recreated in 1969 with 120 firebricks.[178] This floor piece would trigger the 'Tate bricks scandal' in 1976.[179]

171 Letter from Anne Tuteur, Gian Enzo Sperone Gallery, to Seymour dated 5 December 1972, in Tate Acquisition File (TG 4 PC 2/10/1), TLAL.

172 All these artists were part of *The New Art* show. See: *The New Art*, *op. cit.*, p.3.

173 Most of these artists were included in the *Idee/Idee Licht* section of Documenta 5, organised by Fischer and Honnef. See: *Documenta 5*, *op. cit.*, section 17.

174 The database on the Tate Gallery was constructed largely by researching the museum's reports and catalogues of acquisitions. See: *The Tate Gallery, Acquisitions 1968–69*, Tate Gallery, London, 1969; *The Tate Gallery 1970–72*, *op. cit.*; *The Tate Gallery 1972–74, Biennial Report and Illustrated Catalogue of Acquisitions*, published by order of the Trustees, London, 1975; *The Tate Gallery 1974–76, Illustrated Catalogue of Acquisitions*, The Tate Gallery, London, 1978; *The Tate Gallery 1976–1978*, *op. cit.*; *The Tate Gallery, Illustrated Catalogue of Acquisitions 1978–80*, The Tate Gallery, London, 1981. These biennial publications, now suspended, give many physical details on the artworks, even the provenance and the year of purchase. Supplementary information about the circumstances of the sales (correspondence, invoices) was obtained from the comprehensive Tate Acquisition Files (Public Records Series) held at the Tate Library and Archive in London. (However, the Tate Gallery Acquisition Files are subject to a 30-year closure. Thus, only material up to 1976 could be publicly accessed by the researcher. To obtain information on the price and provenance of the works acquired between 1977 and 1980, I

The other important acquisition of Conceptual works of art in 1972 was a group of works by Gilbert & George. In this case, it was the Director of the Tate himself who purchased the work of his own volition. In a letter to the Trustees and Chairman of the Tate dated 18 November 1972, Reid explained:

> The Chairman has asked me to let you know that I have purchased a photo-piece by Gilbert & George from their current exhibition at the Nigel Greenwood Gallery, 41 Sloane Square, London SW1.
>
> I have bought [the piece] for the Gallery under the authority delegated to me by the Trustees. The piece is unique and the price was £1,300.
>
> At the same time I purchased a set of three video tapes made by Gilbert & George for the price of £650. These videos are issued in a series of 25 copies and in my view they contain the essence of one aspect of what Gilbert & George have been doing, so that to have these video tapes will be extremely valuable, both from the point of view of our visitors and for the archive as well.[180]

The photo-piece in question, *Balls: The Evening before the Morning after, Drinking Sculpture* (1972), consisted of 114 black and white photographs mounted between glass and card. The three videos are *In the Bush*, *Gordon's Makes us Drunk* and *A Portrait of the Artists as young Men*. All three 'sculptures on video tape' were edited and editioned by the Videogalerie Schum, Düsseldorf, in 1972.[181] Gilbert & George's solo show with Nigel Greenwood gallery opened on 20 November 1972.[182] As we have seen, Reid's letter is dated 18 November 1972. This shows that he acquired the works before the opening, thus underlining his enthusiasm and will to secure the works. Gilbert & George installed the show themselves the weekend before the opening.[183]

In 1973, works by some of those on the list of contemporary artists began to appear in the collection. One of the Nauman pieces and the work by Tremlett proposed to the museum by Fischer were purchased by the Tate. Nauman's *Corridor with Mirror and White Lights*, also known as *Corridor with Reflected Image*, was originally produced for the artist's solo exhibition at Konrad Fischer in March–April 1971.[184] Tremlett's *Spring Recordings*, 81 audio tapes, was also exhibited at Fischer's gallery in October–November 1972, after having been

had to submit a demand to the Freedom of Information Group of the Tate Gallery. Subsequently, Ben Newman, Head of Legal, sent me copies of various documents. I am grateful to Lisa Cole from the Gallery Records Department for her assistance in researching the Public Records of the Tate Gallery.) The Tate Acquisition Files are organised by artists; the works are then listed chronologically within each artist's entry. The catalogue of the Tate Collection available online was also useful in compiling a complete list.

175 'The Tate Gallery', *Studio International*, *op. cit.*, p.185.

176 See: *The Tate Gallery 1970–72*, *op. cit.*, pp.137–138.

177 A list held in the Tate's Acquisition File records eight sculptures by Andre that were of interest to the museum. Five works were proposed by Weber, one by Fischer, one by Yvon Lambert and another by Templon. See: Tate Acquisition File (TG 4/2/17/1), TLAL.

178 *Carl Andre*, Tibor de Nagy Gallery, New York, March 1966. See: *Carl Andre, Sculptor 1996*, *op. cit.*, p.241.

179 This scandal will be studied at the end of this chapter. In 1979, Weber offered a drawing of *Equivalent VIII* to the Tate. The offer was declined by Reid in a letter to the dealer dated 23 February 1979. See: Tate Acquisition File (TG 4/2/17/1), TLAL.

180 Letter from Reid to the Trustees and Chairman of the Tate dated 18 November 1972, in Tate Acquisition File (TG 4/2/382/1), TLAL. See also: 'The Tate Gallery', *Studio International*, *op. cit.*, p.185.

181 See: Groos, Hess and Wevers, *Ready to Shoot*, *op. cit.*, pp.280–285.

182 Gilbert & George, *The Evening before The Morning after*, Nigel

shown at Documenta 5.[185]

The circumstances of the purchases in 1972 from Fischer shows in detail the length of the purchasing procedure of the Tate. We have seen that Seymour contacted Fischer in November 1972, and that the dealer made proposals the following month. In a letter to Fischer on 6 February 1973, Seymour wrote that the museum was interested in getting more details and confirmation of the prices of three works: Darboven's *No 1–No 42* (1971), Nauman's *Corridor* (1971) and Tremlett's *Spring Recordings* (1972). About two weeks later, on 17 February 1973, the German dealer provided the information.[186]

In a letter of 20 March 1973, Seymour put in writing the discussion she had had with Fischer on the phone the day before:

> 1) I was delighted to hear that Jan Dibbets has offered us a *Dutch Mountain* piece from his collection to replace the work from Art & Project which fell through ...
>
> 2) At their meeting last Thursday the Trustees considered the acquisition of David Tremlett's *Spring Recordings*, 1972, and I am very happy to report that they agreed to purchase this work at the price at which you offered it: $1,500 ...
>
> 3) The Hanne Darboven drawings *No 1–No 42* arrived safely just before the Trustees meeting. However when the acquisition of this work was discussed in principle by a subcommittee shortly before the Board Meeting, I am sorry to say it was decided not to bring this work up at the full meeting of Trustees ...
>
> 4) With regard to the Bruce Nauman *Corridor*, this was considered by the same purchasing subcommittee as being somewhat outside the scope of the group of works, which included the *Spring Recordings*, due to be brought before the Trustees. It was therefore proposed that *Corridor* should be considered on its own at a subsequent meeting.[187]

The deal that Fischer had arranged with Art & Project regarding a new work by Dibbets collapsed. He got around the problem by having the artist propose a work to the museum. Correspondence between 22 and 31 March 1973 concerned confirmation of prices for Dibbets's *Panorama Dutch Mountains 12 × 15° Sea II A* (1971), a series of colour photographs on paper.[188] In a letter to Seymour

Greenwood Inc. Ltd., London, 20 November–December 1972.

183 Morris in conversation with the author.

184 *Bruce Nauman*, Konrad Fischer, Düsseldorf, 5 March–1 April 1971. See: *Ausstellungen bei Konrad Fischer*, *op. cit.*, p.61

185 *Konrad Fischer*, Düsseldorf, 20 October–17 November 1972. See: *Ausstellungen bei Konrad Fischer*, *op. cit.*, p.83.

186 Letter from Seymour to Fischer dated 6 February 1973, and Letter from Fischer to Seymour dated 17 February 1973, in Tate Acquisition File (TG 4/2/768/1), TLAL.

187 Letter from Seymour to Fischer dated 20 March 1973, in Tate Acquisition File (TG 4 PC 2/10/1), TLAL.

188 Letter of Seymour to Fischer dated 22 March 1973, and Letter from Fischer to Seymour dated 31 March 1973, in Tate Acquisition File (TG 4 PC 2/10/1), TLAL.

189 Letter from Fischer to Seymour dated 7 April 1973, in Tate Acquisition File (TG 4 PC 2/10/1), TLAL.

190 Undated explanation file put together by Seymour for the Trustees, in Tate Acquisition File (TG 4/2/768/1), TLAL.

191 Letter from Seymour to Fischer dated 19 April 1973, Tate Acquisition File (TG 4/2/768/1), TLAL. It is not stated in the correspondence whether Nauman agreed to widen the corridor or if Fischer managed to convince the Trustees to leave the work unchanged. The original dimensions of the piece, as constructed in 1971 in Düsseldorf were 370 × 30.5 x 800 cm. The dimensions of the Tate's work, as mentioned in the catalogue of the 1972–74 acquisitions are 305 × 17.8 × 1220 cm (approx. 120 × 7 × 480 ft). See: *Ausstellungen bei*

dated 7 April 1973, Fischer confirmed that he had sent the Dibbets piece to the Tate for the Trustees meeting and gave extensive information on the Nauman piece. He also added, obviously disappointed by the museum's refusal: 'It would be very good if the Tate Gallery would also own a piece by Hanne Darboven sometime.'[189]

Seymour prepared a file on each work to be considered by the Board of Trustees on 18 April 1973.[190] On 19 April, she wrote to Fischer informing him that the Board had agreed to acquire *Panorama Dutch Mountains* by Dibbets and that they were also interested in Nauman's *Corridor*. However, they were worried that the narrowness of the work might provoke claustrophobia among spectators. They wondered if it would be possible to ask the artist to widen it.[191] In May 1973, there followed a letter from Fischer containing an explanations and drawings of the work.[192] The proposal for the work was presented to the Trustees at their meeting on 21 June 1973. Seymour wrote to Fischer on 27 June 1973 to advise him that the Trustees had agreed to purchase *Corridor*.[193] In August 1973, the artist sent drawings, notes and written instructions to the Tate to help them construct the installation.[194] An invoice of $6,000 was sent by Fischer to the museum on 26 October 1973. A stamp and Alley's signature confirm that the money was transferred to the artist through Fischer on 12 November 1973.[195]

While the Dibbets piece was acquired relatively quickly by the Board of Trustees, the procedure for the Nauman installation was longer. Considering that Seymour first contacted Fischer in a letter dated 21 November 1972 and that the work was finally bought on 12 November 1973, we can see that it took the Tate exactly one year to acquire this large piece.[196]

The acquisition of Dibbets's *Perspective Corrections* (1968) shows that the museum was sometimes confronted with tough dealing procedures. We have seen that Sperone offered the work in December 1972 for $8,000. On 6 February 1973, Seymour wrote to the dealer, informing him that the museum was interested in the acquisition of the piece.[197] About a week later, on 15 February 1973, Sperone replied that the work was still available, adding: 'However the selling price at the present time has changed due to the 10 per cent devaluation of the US dollar, and is 8,800 $.'[198] On 13 March 1973, the dealer set out further conditions for the sale:

Konrad Fischer, op. cit., p.61. See also: *The Tate Gallery 1972–74, op. cit.*, pp.217–218.

192 Letter from Fischer to Seymour dated 25 May 1973, and undated notes and drawings by Fischer, in Tate Acquisition File (TG 4/2/768/1), TLAL.

193 Letter from Seymour to Fischer dated 27 June 1973, in Tate Acquisition File (TG 4/2/768/1), TLAL.

194 Documents dated August 1973 sent by Nauman to the Tate, in Tate Acquisition File (TG 4/2/768/1), TLAL.

195 Invoice from Fischer dated 26 October 1973, in Tate Acquisition File (TG 4/2/768/1), TLAL.

196 This example also shows that the Trustees met on a monthly basis: about mid-March for Tremlett, mid-April for Dibbets and mid-June for Nauman.

197 Letter from Seymour to Sperone dated 6 February 1973, in Tate Acquisition File (TG 4/2/10/1), TLAL.

198 Letter from Sperone to Seymour dated 15 February 1973, in Tate Acquisition File (TG 4/2/10/1), TLAL.

> Upon eventual acquisition of Jan Dibbets, *Perspective Correction*, 1968, I wish to let you know my usual arrangements which I suggest that we use in this case as well:
>
> 1) For shipment purposes the work should be declared as four photographs on canvas, total value 200 £, for customs declaration, and declared as a value of 8,800 $ for insurance. Whether or not the work is bought by you, I cannot agree to pay even one way shipment for the work, as I have already paid for its shipment from Amsterdam to Torino.
>
> 2) In what concerns the payment for the work, I will come personally to collect the money, ... for bureaucratic reasons.[199]

The Trustees agreed to acquire *Perspective Correction* on 16 March 1973. A few days later, Seymour wrote to Sperone:

> At your insistence we are prepared to pay the costs of bringing Jan Dibbets' *Perspective Correction* from Turin to London. The work will have full insurance cover as you request by Government Indemnity. We should be glad, however, if you will make arrangements for Customs declaration, etc., and I should also like to point out that an invoice signed by you should be sent with the work, since the Customs Officers here will refuse to release the work without this document.[200]

About a month later, on 18 April 1973, internal correspondence at the Tate between Seymour and the Director shows that the museum was not satisfied with the way in which the deal was concluded. Seymour wrote:

> You asked if we paid the price asked for this piece ($8,800 – £3681 approx.) without demur.
>
> The answer is that no objection was made and I wrote to Gian Enzo Sperone on March 16th to say that the Trustees had agreed to purchase the work at the price stated, subject of course to its being inspected and found to be in good condition.
>
> We have not actually paid for it yet and I still need to write to Sperone

199 Letter from Sperone to Seymour dated 13 March 1973, in Tate Acquisition File (TG 4/2/10/1), TLAL. This demonstrates Sperone's habit of collecting money himself in foreign countries.

200 Letter from Seymour to Sperone dated 16 March 1973, and Letter from Seymour to Sperone dated 20 March 1973, in Tate Acquisition File (TG 4/2/10/1), TLAL.

> confirming that we have found it to be satisfactory.
>
> My feeling is that though we could start a wrangle at this stage Sperone might withdraw the work and make us pay the transport costs back to Turin.
>
> However it might be worth trying to get the $800 knocked off in view of its stretcherless condition.
>
> I agree entirely about being tough in the future. All these deals are getting hopelessly complicated.[201]

Reid replied on the same day: 'I am torn between wishing to conclude and irritation at what seems decidedly off hand treatment. Are we (?) to be doing more business with Sperone?'[202] In the end, the piece was purchased for the higher price of $8,800. This deal shows that Sperone was tough in business, and that the museum did not appreciate such an approach. Moreover, Seymour seems to have taken the side of the dealer over her employer.

In 1973, the Tate Gallery bought three works by Long. The acquisition procedure for these pieces was rather different. On 3 February 1970, the artist himself had contacted Alley, writing:

> I would like very much to propose that I make a sculpture for your gallery. I am sure this would prove a worthwhile and exciting enterprise, and of course I will be pleased to discuss fully my proposals.
>
> I am English, and my references for this are the Konrad Fischer Gallery in Düsseldorf, and the Dwan Gallery in New York.[203]

Although Alley responded in a letter dated 14 April 1970, stating that they would consider the matter, nothing happened in concrete terms until late 1972.[204]

Long's first solo show in a commercial gallery in Britain took place in January–February 1973 at the Lisson Gallery.[205] Fischer, who was the artist's first and main dealer, had agreed that Long be represented by the Lisson in London.[206] An invoice dated 30 January 1973 shows that on that occasion the Tate purchased its first work by the artist for £1,000: *A Hundred Mile Walk* (1972).[207] This work had previously been exhibited in *The New Art* show in 1972.[208]

201 Manuscript letter from Seymour to Reid dated 18 April 1973, in Tate Acquisition File (TG 4/2/10/1), TLAL.

202 *Ibid.*

203 Letter from Long to Alley dated 3 February 1970, in Tate Acquisition File (TG 4/2/641/1), TLAL.

204 Letter from Alley to Long dated 14 April 1970, in Tate Acquisition File (TG 4/2/641/1), TLAL.

205 *Richard Long*, Lisson Gallery, London, 23 January–24 February 1973. Two solo shows of Long had been organised in 1971 at the Whitechapel Art Gallery in London and at the MOMA in Oxford. See: Database 3, Section Richard Long (Appendix 1.3).

206 However, Logsdail underlined how protective Fischer was of Long and that he was reluctant to have him represented by a London gallery. See: Logsdail in conversation with the author, *op. cit.*

207 Invoice from the Lisson Gallery dated 30 January 1973, in Tate Acquisition File (TG 4/2/641/1), TLAL.

208 See: *The New Art*, *op. cit.*, pp.48–49.

At about the same time as Seymour and Morphet launched their enquiries to dealer galleries in November 1972, they also contacted Long directly about the purchase of works for the Tate Collection.[209] In a letter of 19 March 1973 addressed to the artist, Seymour states that the Trustees had agreed to purchase a floor piece specially made for the Tate.[210] Six months later, in a letter dated 1 October 1973, Seymour asked Long when he could come to install the piece in the galleries. The work in question was *Circle of Sticks* (1973), a 671 cm diameter (approximately 22 feet, 4 inches) circle composed of 76 wooden sticks.[211] Although it seems that the purchase was originally made independently of any commercial gallery, a letter from Seymour to Fischer, dated 10 October 1973 states:

> Yesterday Richard Long came to the Tate and put up the piece which he has specifically designed for us ... Richard tells me that he has spoken to you about the piece and that he wishes it to be sold through your gallery. I am therefore writing to ask you if you would be so kind as to send us an invoice by Express Post for the piece ... I do not know what Richard has said to you about the price of the work. When I spoke to him yesterday he appeared to have placed the matter entirely in your hands ... In November 1972 Richard agreed in principle to make an installation piece for us at a price of £1,000.[212]

Even though the dealer confirmed the price in a cable on 17 October 1973, it seems that the work was presented once again to the Trustees.[213] The cause might have been that the work was bought from the artist, but via his dealer. In a letter from Seymour to Fischer, dated 22 October 1973, the curator writes that the Trustees had agreed to purchase *Circle of Sticks* for £1,000.[214] An invoice for the work was sent to the Tate by Fischer on 26 October 1973. However, it appears from a letter addressed to Long by Seymour on 5 November 1973 that the money was paid directly into the artist's bank account.[215]

This example shows the complexity of sales agreements at the time. Fischer had been Long's main dealer since 1968. In January–February 1973, he agreed to the Lisson Gallery showing the artist in London. The deal for *Circle of Sticks* was originally agreed on by the Tate directly with the artist and the purchase was

209 Letter from Seymour to Long dated 23 November 1972, in Tate Acquisition File (TG 4/2/641/1), TLAL.
210 Letter from Seymour to Long dated 19 March 1973, in Tate Acquisition File (TG 4/2/641/1), TLAL.
211 Letter from Seymour to Long dated 1 October 1973, in Tate Acquisition File (TG 4/2/641/1), TLAL.
212 Letter from Seymour to Fischer dated 10 October 1973, in Tate Acquisition File (TG 4/2/641/1), TLAL.
213 Cable from Fischer to Seymour dated 17 October 1973, in Tate Acquisition File (TG 4/2/641/1), TLAL.
214 Letter from Seymour to Fischer dated 22 October 1973, in Tate Acquisition File (TG 4/2/641/1), TLAL.
215 Invoice from Fischer dated 26 October 1973, and Letter from Long to Seymour dated 5 November 1973, in Tate Acquisition File (TG 4/2/641/1), TLAL.

confirmed in March 1973. However, when it came to payment in October 1973, Long referred to Fischer and not to Logsdail, the Lisson's Director.

International Conceptual artists found dealer galleries to represent them in Britain. It was foremost the Lisson Gallery that acted as a mediator between artists and the Tate. We have seen that two lithographs by LeWitt were purchased by the Tate from the Lisson Gallery in 1971. Wall drawings by the artist had been exhibited at the *Wall Show* in January 1971.[216] We have also seen that in his letter of December 1972, Weber proposed wall drawings to the Tate.[217] In May 1973, the Lisson organised a show entitled *Sol LeWitt, Wall Drawings and Structures*.[218] As what the Tate was looking for at the time was available in London for the same price, it seems logical that the Tate went for the most direct solution. The piece *Wall Drawing, Four Basic Colors (black, yellow, red and blue) and all combinations* (1970) was purchased in March 1973 from the Lisson Gallery.[219]

We have also seen two major sculptures by Andre had been acquired for the permanent collection in 1971. Already possessing a wood and a brick piece, the museum decided to purchase a metal sculpture, *144 Magnesium Plates* (1969) in 1973. Between 1969 and 1973, the piece changed hands many times. It was originally created for Andre's solo show at the Dwan Gallery, New York, in April–May 1969.[220] The piece was then with the Ace Gallery, Los Angeles, where it was purchased by Mr and Mrs Thomas G. Terbell, Jr (Pasadena, California). It was transferred to Europe when the Los Angeles Comsky Gallery sold it to the Galerie Onnasch in Cologne. From there, the floor sculpture came into the hands of Heiner Friedrich, Cologne. Finally, in July 1973, the piece was purchased by the Tate from Friedrich, through the Lisson Gallery for DM99,000 (£16,528.55).[221] Here too, Logsdail's gallery played the role of intermediary.[222]

The last work of the Conceptual artists studied to have entered the Tate's permanent collection in 1973 was a site-specific sculpture project by Huebler. Mr and Mrs Joshua A. Gollin from New York donated *Site Sculpture Project, Windham College Pentagon, Putney, Vermont* (1968). The work was offered to the Tate via the American Federation of Arts (AFA).[223] The circumstances are highlighted in a letter of 7 December 1973 that Reid wrote to Joshua A. Gollin:

216 *Wall Show (Arnatt, Arrowsmith, Edmonds, Flanagan, Ginsborg, Hemsworth, Hilliard, Latham, Lew, LeWitt, Louw, Munro, Newman, Palermo, Rinke, Sirrs, Stezaker, Tremlett, Weiner, Wentworth)*, Lisson Gallery, London, January 1971.

217 Letter from Weber to Morphet dated December 1972, *op. cit.*

218 *Sol LeWitt, Wall Drawings and Structures*, Lisson Gallery, London, 3–31 May 1973.

219 Invoice from the Lisson Gallery dated 28 March 1973, in Tate Acquisition File (TG 4/2/626/1), TLAL.

220 'Carl Andre', Dwan Gallery, New York, 26 April–21 May 1969. See: *Carl Andre, Sculptor 1996*, *op. cit.*, p.245.

221 Invoice from the Lisson Gallery dated 17 July 1973, in Tate Acquisition File (TG 4/2/17/1), TLAL

222 See: *The Tate Gallery 1972–74*, *op. cit.*, p.75. See also: Ronald Alley, *Catalogue of The Tate Gallery's Collection of Modern Art, other than works by British artists*, Tate Gallery and Sotheby Parke Bernet, London, 1981, p.14.

223 The AFA served as a channel for the donation of works by American artists to international museums.

> I have chosen a work by Douglas Huebler to buy with the money which you kindly made available to the Tate Gallery.
>
> Douglas Huebler is one of the younger American artists whom we have been hoping to represent in this collection for some time, and I am delighted that your gift will make this possible. The name of the work is *Site Sculpture Project, Windham College Pentagon, Putney, Vermont*.
>
> The work is priced at $4,000 and is owned by the Leo Castelli Gallery at 420 West Broadway, to whom I am also sending a copy of this letter in the hope that this will simplify matters for you.
>
> As I think I told you, the American Federation of Art (Director: Wilder Green) have kindly acted on our behalf in the past in connection with gifts from American donors so that benefactors can obtain a tax benefit. As soon as I hear from you I will inform Wilder Green of the impending gift as I know that time is important.[224]

In October 1968, the Windham College in Putney, Vermont, had hosted a one-day exhibition of Huebler, at which the artist had presented a site-sculpture project, *The Windham Piece*.[225] From June to September 1973, the work was exhibited during the summer show at the Leo Castelli Gallery in New York.[226] It might have been on that occasion that Norman Reid saw the work, and decided to choose it for the gift made available to the Tate by Gollin through the AFA.[227]

In 1974, the museum acquired a second work by Huebler, *Variable Piece No. 44* (1971), part of a series of 47. 'This is the work in a large edition, in which ownership of each example is documented by the owner sticking in his own photograph each year, and exchanging photographs with adjacent owners.'[228] Thus, it was the owner's responsibility to complete the work. As the work was sold by the artist to the Tate (for $100, £42.20), Huebler appeared as the owner until 1974.[229] For the Tate, the owner was the current Chairman of the Trustees.[230] The work preceding it in the series was owned by Sperone's brother-in-law Gian Piero Bona, and the work following it belonged to the artist.

Also in 1974, the Tate Gallery acquired a work from another American artist whose work entered the permanent collection for the first time, Joseph Kosuth. The installation *Clock (One and Five) English/Latin Version* (1965) was purchased

224 Letter from Norman Reid to Joshua A. Gollin dated 7 December 1973, in Tate Acquisition File (TG 4 10/1 Douglas Huebler), TLAL.

225 *Douglas Huebler, The Windham Piece*, Windham College, Putney, Vermont, 23 October 1968. See: Lippard, *Six Years*, *op. cit.*, p.57.

226 *Group Show: Darboven, Dibbets, Flavin, Huebler, Kosuth, Nauman, Rauschenberg, Stella, Waldman*, Leo Castelli Gallery, New York, 3 June– 15 September 1973. See: *The Tate Gallery 1972–74*, *op. cit.*, p.175.

227 One should underline here the Tate's increasing importance to US artists, galleries and government. As we have seen above, after the war, the American administration sponsored shows of American artists in Europe. At the time, Switzerland, Germany and the Netherlands were seen as a front against the East. The last country to fall under the US influence was Britain, because it had less direct need of US assistance during and following the war. An interesting example is the 1969 *When Attitudes Become Form* exhibition. It was shown in Switzerland (Bern), Germany (Krefeld) and finally England (London) and was sponsored by the American tobacco manufacturer Philip Morris.

228 Note about Huebler's *Variable Piece No. 44*, in Tate Acquisition File (TG 4 10/4 390/4), TLAL.

229 Telegram from Huebler to Morphet dated 14 May 1974, in Tate Acquisition File (TG 4 10/4 390/4), TLAL.

from the artist through Nigel Greenwood. On 21 July 1973, the Board of Trustees discussed the acquisition of the work during their meeting. It is revealed in a letter addressed by Greenwood to Reid on 25 July 1973 that the Board required a large discount on the proposed price:

> Anne Seymour has spoken to me regarding your proposal to buy the work by Kosuth which went before your Trustees last week. I would love to say yes to £1,300 since I feel it is a very good work by Kosuth and one which should be a museum piece since it states so explicitly many current attitudes within art today. However, if I were to sell it to you at that price, then I would end up making a loss.
>
> I have bought the piece from Leo Castelli for $4,000 (less 23%) and I reoffered it to you for the same price as it would sell in New York i.e. $4,000 (£1580). You may say that the Tate could buy direct from New York and get a discount of 10% but in fact I kept that 10% to cover my own expenses:
>
> i. transport of work = £80
>
> ii. Phone calls/gallery work = £30
>
> iii. Duty paid on item = £ 130 – which will not be reimbursed for at least three months.
>
> I do not think 10% unreasonable to cover these various charges, all of which you might have been involved in if the Tate had bought direct. Added to this is the fact that the clock piece is unique and if I had not been in New York at the precise moment it was shown, it would not be available.
>
> Should you now buy the works for £1,300 (inc VAT etc.) then you will see that I would receive exactly £35 profit to cover transport etc. added to which the Government would also ask for £130 VAT from me. I hope you do not think a clear profit of £200 unreasonable on an item valued at £1,600, especially since our normal gallery commission on works shown in the Gallery is 40%.
>
> I fully realise your problems regarding the purchase of contemporary works which still appear 'avant-garde' to your Trustees and I am only too willing to do all I can to assist since of course it is in my interest to help you build up the finest collection of modern work in this country.[231]

230 Sir Robert Sainsbury and Sir Alan Bullock, as both were in the office for half a year in 1973.

231 Letter from Greenwood to Reid dated 25 July 1973, in Tate Acquisition File (TG 4/2/582/1), TLAL. This letter suggests that the dealer knew that the museum wanted to acquire a work by Kosuth, an artist who at the time had no dealer in London.

About a year later, an invoice dated 25 June 1974 shows that Greenwood again offered the work to the Tate for the same sum, $4,000 (£1,835). A stamp made on the paper shows that approval for payment for the work was granted on 8 July 1974.[232] This example demonstrates again the potential length of the Tate's acquisition procedure (one year).

We have seen that the Tate had already acquired two sets of lithographs and one wall drawing by LeWitt in 1971 and 1973 respectively. A note entitled 'Sol LeWitt, Further Representation in the collection', dated late November 1973, demonstrates that the museum was interested in purchasing a large open modular cube by the artist.[233] Thus the Tate wanted to complete the representation of the artist. Numerous black-and-white photographs received by the museum at the time show that Fischer, Yvon Lambert, Sperone, Weber, Dwan and Bischofberger all proposed modular cubes.[234]

In an advice note dated 18 December 1973 from Logsdail to Morphet, the dealer offered LeWitt's *Two Open Modular Cubes/Half-Off* (1970) for purchase for $5,000.[235] The work had previously been exhibited in October–November 1972 at the artist's solo show at the Kunsthalle in Bern.[236] The Keepers of the Modern Collection decided to put this work forward to the Trustees. This example further shows that the choice was made for a work owned by a London dealer gallery. However, it is difficult to say if the decision was taken for practical reasons or because of the quality of the work, or both. On their meeting of 18 April 1974, the Trustees agreed to purchase the piece for the permanent collection.[237]

The Director of the museum had limited power to acquire works on his own initiative when geographical distance and time factors were an issue. In April 1974, during a trip to New York, Reid bought a collage-print by Dibbets, *Collage* (1973), for $315 (£132.39).[238] The work was editioned and acquired from Castelli Graphics, which was run by Marian Goodman.[239] The collage-print was composed of invitation cards printed for the artist's exhibition at the Leo Castelli Gallery in February–March 1973.[240]

In 1975, the Tate purchased works by an artist who was not yet represented in the permanent collection, Broodthaers. The artist was living in England at the time and was represented by Jack Wendler since 1972. In April–June 1975,

232 Invoice from Greenwood dated 25 June 1974, in Tate Acquisition File (TG 4/2/582/1), TLAL.

233 Note on LeWitt dated late November 1973, in Tate Acquisition File (TG 4/2/626/1), TLAL.

234 See: About a dozen black and white photographs of Sol LeWitt modular cubes received from Fischer, Lambert, Sperone, Weber, Dwan, Bischofberger, in Tate Acquisition File (TG 4/2/626/1), TLAL.

235 Advice note from Logsdail to Morphet dated 18 December 1973, in Tate Acquisition File (TG 4/2/626/1), TLAL. Weber made a similar offer to the Tate. In a letter dated 29 March 1974, Alley turned it down, stating that they were already considering a modular cube from the Lisson Gallery. See: Letter from Ronald Alley to John Weber dated 29 March 1974, in Tate Acquisition File (TG 4/2/626/1), TLAL.

236 *Sol LeWitt*, Kunsthalle, Bern, 7 October–17 November 1972. See: *Sol LeWitt* (exh. cat.), Kunsthalle, Bern, 1972, unnumbered pages.

237 Letter from Seymour to Logsdail dated 18 April 1974, in Tate Acquisition File (TG 4/2/626/1), TLAL.

238 Letter from Sue Aylwin, Tate Gallery, to Leo Castelli dated 7 June 1977, and Undated invoice from Castelli, in Tate Acquisition File (TG 10/4/390/4), TLAL.

239 Marian Goodman, who set up her own gallery in New York in 1977, has become an important dealer for Conceptual art.

240 *Jan Dibbets*, Leo Castelli Gallery, New York, 10 February–3 March 1973. A twin collage-print was made by the artist for the Galleria Sperone, Turin. See: *Tate Gallery 1974–1976*, *op. cit.*, p.87. See also: Minola, Mundici, Poli and Roberto, *Gian Enzo Sperone*,

a major solo show of Broodthaers was organised at the Museum of Modern Art in Oxford.[241] It appears that Reid visited the exhibition and decided to propose several works for acquisition. In a letter to Morphet dated 27 May 1975, Nicholas Serota, the Director of MOMA, wrote:

> Following your Director's visit and our telephone conversation, I am arranging to deliver the three works by Marcel Broodthaers to the Tate on Tuesday 3rd June ... The three works are (my titles for identification): 1. 'Casserole of Mussels', 2. 'Ingres photopiece', 3. '9 part work on the subject of painting', 1973 and exhibited in (conceived for?) Prospect '73 (Maler), October 1973 ... Should the Tate decide to acquire one of these works, or wish to negotiate with Broodthaers, I think this might best be done through us.[242]

Correspondence between Seymour, Alley and Serota in May and June 1975 reveals that the Trustees considered the works during their meeting on 19 June 1975.[243] The minutes confirm that the Trustees agreed to acquire two of the three presented works: *Casserole et Moules Fermées* (1964) and *Mademoiselle Rivière and Monsieur Bertin* (1975).[244] On 20 June 1975, Seymour wrote to the artist officially confirming the purchases.[245] An invoice dated 5 July 1975 shows that the pieces were purchased from the artist through MOMA, for £2,300 and £850 respectively.[246] Serota recalls: 'The works were sold through Oxford but I don't think the Museum took a percentage. We just acted as an agent.'[247]

The following year, in 1976, the Tate intended to extend the representation of Long in the collection. In a note dated 27 November 1975, entitled 'Richard Long, Further representation', Morphet wrote:

> In early October, Anne and I reviewed with Richard Long his career so far, with a view to establishing the principal gaps in his representation here as we saw them. He clearly understood that our view was not necessarily the view of the Gallery. In any transactions, he would like us to deal with him direct, unless (as is the case with some works) it is a question of a work which a dealer already owns. He specifically does not regard the Lisson Gallery as his agent.
>
> Richard Long has only ever made one print as such. The Tate owns a copy

op. cit., p.227.

241 *Marcel Broodthaers, Le privilège de l'art*, MOMA, Oxford, 26 April–1 June 1975. In July 1975, Barry Barker organised a solo show of Broodthaers at the ICA in London. *Décor: A Conquest by Marcel Broodthaers*, ICA, London, 11 June–6 July 1975.

242 Letter from Serota to Morphet dated 27 May 1975, in Tate Acquisition File (TG 4 10/1 Marcel Broodthaers), TLAL.

243 Letter from Seymour to Serota dated 29 May 1975, and Letter from Morphet to Serota dated 20 June 1975, in Tate Acquisition File (TG 4 10/1 Marcel Broodthaers), TLAL.

244 Minutes of the Board of Trustees meeting dated 19 June 1975, in Tate Acquisition File (TG 4 10/1 Marcel Broodthaers), TLAL.

245 Letter from Seymour to Broodthaers dated 20 June 1975, in Tate Acquisition File (TG 4 10/1 Marcel Broodthaers), TLAL.

246 Invoice from the Museum of Modern Art, Oxford dated 5 July 1975, in Tate Acquisition File (TG 4 10/1 Marcel Broodthaers), TLAL.

247 Serota in conversation with the author, op. cit.

> (bought for a nominal sum from the museum in Mönchengladbach). Apart from this, the saleable works he has produced fall into two categories only: Unique works, consisting of: (a) framed works, to be hung on the wall, (b) sculptures ...
>
> 'Public freehold' works: In producing these very straightforward (in form) visual evidences of work undertaken by him in the landscape, Long never intended that each should be unique.[248]

Morphet then lists nine works by the artists that he proposed should be considered by the Board of Trustees for acquisition.

On 23 January 1976, Morphet sent a letter to the artist, informing him about possible works to be bought by the Tate, notably *Ben Nevis Hitch-Hike* (1967) and *Sixty stone zig-zag sculpture*.[249] In a letter received on 30 January 1976 by Morphet, Long advised on pieces that he thought would be appropriate for the museum's collection. He suggested *Ben Nevis Hitch-Hike* and a new work, *River Avon Driftwood*, instead of *Sixty stone*, which was already being considered for purchase by the Stedelijk Van Abbemuseum.[250] On 6 February 1976, Morphet wrote to Long informing him that they agreed with his recommendations.[251]

In June 1976, Reid wrote to the Trustees, saying that he wanted to propose at their next meeting the purchase of a group of works by Long, 'which would allow us to show at least one Conceptual artist in some depth'.[252] As the minutes of the meeting of 15 July 1976 show, eight works by Long were discussed and purchased at once.[253] They were two major floor sculptures, *119 Stones* (1976) and *River Avon Driftwood* (1976), and two framed works, *Ben Nevis Hitch-Hike* (1967, also known as *Untitled*) and *Cerne Abbas Walk* (1975). During their meeting, the Trustees also decided to acquire four 'public freehold' pieces. These are multiple works mostly made of photographs, cards and text: *Turf Circle* (1966), *Turf Sculpture* (1967), *A Line made by Walking* (1967) and *England* (1968).[254] The status of a 'public freehold' work is ambiguous because it is a straightforward visual documentation of a work made directly in nature by Long.[255]

Following the Trustees' decision, Seymour wrote on 23 July 1976: 'Richard has now said that he wants the deal to be done through the Lisson Gallery (that is for the four major works). The public freehold works are still to be purchased

248 Note from Morphet dated 27 November 1975, in Tate Acquisition File (TG 4/2/641/1), TLAL.

249 Letter from Morphet to Long dated 23 January 1976, in Tate Acquisition File (TG 4/2/641/1), TLAL.

250 Letter from Long received by Morphet on 30 January 1976, in Tate Acquisition File (TG 4/2/641/2), TLAL. As we have seen above, *Sixty Stone* (1975) was indeed purchased by the Van Abbemuseum, Eindhoven in 1977.

251 Letter from Morphet to Long dated 6 February 1976, in Tate Acquisition File (TG 4/2/641/1), TLAL.

252 Letter from Reid to Howard Hodgkin, Trustee, dated 28 June 1976, in Tate Acquisition File (TG 4/2/641/2), TLAL.

253 Minutes of the Board of Trustees dated 15 July 1976, in Tate Acquisition File (TG 4/2/641/2), TLAL.

254 Joy Sleeman, from the Slade School of Art, discussed in a recent conference the particularity of public freehold works that are 'independent of ownership'. See: Joy Sleeman, 'Land Art – The Movie – Moving Pictures', *New Research into Conceptualism in Europe*, *op. cit.*, unnumbered pages.

255 In the 1970s, the Tate did not have a Department of Photography. The pieces by Long, which were seen as Conceptual works with photography rather then photographs in themselves, were integrated into the permanent collection. The public freehold works, however, which are multiple works made of photographs, were held by the archive of the museum. They were seen as a documentation of works rather than works in themselves. Consequently, these works

direct from Long.'[256] It is interesting that the artist asked for this sale to be arranged through the Lisson Gallery, since three years before he had asked the museum to deal with Fischer. An invoice from the Lisson dated 24 July 1976 shows that the two floor sculptures and the two framed works were purchased from the artist through the gallery (for a total of £8,640). An invoice from Long dated 22 July 1976 shows that the four 'public freehold' works were purchased directly from the artist (for £200).[257] In the case of Long, we can clearly see the Tate's desire to fully represent all the techniques used by one major British Conceptual artist.

In February 1976, Andre's *Equivalent VIII* (1966) engendered the 'Tate bricks scandal'. Although the *Sunday Times* published the first article on the matter, it was the *Daily Mirror*'s front page coverage the following day that provoked public outrage.[258] This scandal, which focused on the value of the work, had a major impact on the Tate's purchasing policy.[259] From 1977 onwards, there was a drastic reduction of Conceptual art purchases.

The 'Tate bricks scandal' has to be placed in the overall political context of the time. In 1974, there had been a change of government; two consecutive Labour Prime Ministers, Harold Wilson (1974–76) and James Callaghan (1976–79), had succeeded Edward Heath (Conservative Party). At the time, England was facing long-term economic difficulties. Since 1975, Margaret Thatcher had been the leader of the Conservatives. As leader of the opposition, she started her 'war' against the waste of money in public services. It seems that she was looking for public examples.[260]

In 1977, the only Conceptual works to enter the Tate Gallery's permanent collection were works on paper. Several drawings by Andre were donated to the museum. Angela Westwater, who was Andre's girlfriend and, since 1975, had been the associate of Sperone and Fischer in the Sperone-Westwater-Fischer Gallery in New York, made the original contact. In a letter dated 27 January 1977, she wrote to Morphet that a friend of hers would like to donate a group of works on paper by Andre to a public institution. She further stated that her friend had thought of the Tate because Andre appreciated the commitment it had shown towards his work.[261] It appears from a note of 15 June 1977 from Morphet to Reid that it was Andre himself who had selected the museum.[262] Westwater had acted

were not included in the catalogue of acquisitions published by the museum at the time. See: *The Tate Gallery 1976–1978*, *op. cit.*, pp.107–109.

256 Note from Seymour dated 23 July 1976, in Tate Acquisition File (TG 4/2/641/2), TLAL.

257 Invoice from the Lisson Gallery dated 24 July 1976, and Invoice from Long dated 22 July 1976, in Tate Acquisition File (TG 4/2/641/2), TLAL.

258 Colin Simpson, 'The Tate drops a costly brick', Business News section, *Sunday Times*, 15 February 1976, and Philip Mellor, 'Whichever way you look at Britain's latest work of art ... What a load of rubbish', *Daily Mirror*, 16 February 1976.

259 In his article, Colin Simpson (*Sunday Times*) mentioned that Andre originally priced the work at $12,000. On 16 February 1976, Philip Mellor (*Daily Mirror*) wrote that he believed that the work was priced at £4,000. David Pallister wrote in *The Times* on 17 February 1976 that 'unconfirmed estimates range from £4,000 to £6,000'. See: David Pallister, 'The hot bricks floor the Tate', *The Times*, 17 February 1976. In fact, an invoice from Weber dated 25 April 1972 shows that the work was sold for $6,000 (about £2,300), half the price reported by the press. See: Tate Acquisition File (TG 4/2/17/1), TLAL.

260 This was also a period when the Conservative Party started to employ public consultants and publicity agencies. Saatchi & Saatchi managed their campaign 'Getting London out of the Red' and later also 'Labour isn't Working' (1979). According to Morris, the first campaign was influenced by Gilbert & George's *Angry Pictures*. Morris

as a sort of intermediary between Andre's friend, the American artist David Novros, and the American Federation of Arts. Indeed, the works were presented by Novros through the Museum Donor Programme of the AFA.[263]

Among a group of works on paper by Andre presented by Novros were four drawings and diagrams for installations and works. In addition, the original manuscript for Andre's article 'Line Work' (*Arts Magazine*, May 1967) and two texts related to it were included. The latter were considered to be more appropriate to the museum's archive. An undated note from the AFA to the Tate about the shipping of the works mentions '4 drawings (2 framed)/13 sheets writings and notes by Carl Andre' (total value $9,300).[264] The four drawings had come into the possession of Novros through an exchange of works with Andre. They were: *Diagram of 'Reef'* (1967), *Drawing for 'The Perfect Painting'* (1967), *Rotor Reflector Review* (1967) and *Diagram for Installation of Magnet Pieces 1966, at Tibor de Nagy Gallery, New York* (1966).[265]

In July 1977, a series of prints by Broodthaers was purchased from Greenwood for £1,127.52. One of these, *La Soupe de Daguerre* (1974), had been transformed into a collage by the artist, so as to turn it into a unique work. It cost £315, twice as much as the other works on paper.[266]

In 1978 and 1979, no Conceptual artworks were acquired by the Trustees for the Tate's permanent collection. In 1980, a major change took place when Alan Bowness was appointed the new Director.[267] Under his directorship, the American art collection was strengthened.

LeWitt's representation in particular was reinforced. A wall drawing and a modular cube were already part of the permanent collection. In 1980, a wall structure and a second wall drawing enhanced the artist's representation. The works were purchased from the Lisson Gallery, which confirmed Logsdail as the artist's dealer in London. In a letter to Bowness dated 21 April 1980, Logsdail proposed several structures and wall drawings to the Tate at the Director's request.[268] A month later, in a letter dated 14 May 1980, Logsdail gave extensive details and prices of several pieces that the museum was interested in acquiring, including *Untitled* (1965–67) and *Six geometric Figures drawn on a black wall with white lines approximately 1½" apart'* (1980).[269] The acquisition of the early geometric structure *Untitled* was agreed to by the Trustees during their meeting

in conversation with the author.

261 Letter from Angela Westwater to Richard Morphet dated 27 January 1977, in Tate Acquisition File (TG 4/2/17/1), TLAL.

262 Note from Morphet to Reid dated 15 June 1977, in Tate Acquisition File (TG 4/2/17/1), TLAL.

263 See: Four forms entitled 'American Federation of Art, Museum donor programme' signed by David Novros, in Tate Acquisition File (TG 4/2/17/1), TLAL.

264 Undated letter from the American Federation of Arts to the Tate, in Tate Acquisition File (TG 4/2/17/1), TLAL.

265 *The Tate Gallery 1976–1978, op. cit.*, pp.27–28.

266 Invoice from the Nigel Greenwood Inc. Ltd. dated 14 July 1977, Freedom of Information Request, TLAL.

267 Alan Bowness previously worked as an art critic and art historian. He was married to one of the twin daughters of Barbara Hepworth and Ben Nicholson. He had been one of the organisers of *Decade 54–64*.

268 Letter from Logsdail to Bowness dated 21 April 1980, in Tate Acquisition File (TG 4/2/626/2), TLAL.

269 Letter from Logsdail to Bowness dated 14 May 1980, in Tate Acquisition File (TG 4/2/626/2), TLAL.

on 29 May 1980 ($13,500, £6,637).[270] The purchase of the wall drawing was approved during their July 1980 meeting ($31,050, £13,274).[271]

The provenance of the metal wall structure *Untitled* (1965–67) was complex. A wooden version had been exhibited in May 1965 at the artist's first solo show at New York's Daniels Gallery, directed by Dan Graham and David Herbert.[272] The metal version was originally exhibited in Düsseldorf during Prospect 68, where LeWitt's work was presented by the Dwan Gallery. The work is believed to have been acquired by a German collector.[273] It reappeared at a sale of contemporary art at Sotheby's London in December 1979. The work was estimated at £3,000–£4,000, but as the bidding did not exceed £1,800, it was withdrawn from sale.[274] In 1980, the Lisson Gallery bought the piece from a private collection and resold it to the Tate.

The wall drawing *Six Geometric Figures* was re-entitled *On Four black walls, white vertical parallel lines, and in the centre of the walls, eight geometric figures (including cross, ×.) within which are white horizontal parallel lines. The vertical lines do not enter the figures* (1980). The work was originally installed in May 1980 at the Lisson Gallery in a group show (Buren, LeWitt, Long, Sandback). The piece comprised six figures executed on three walls.[275] Shortly after its purchase in May 1980, the work was installed at the Tate under the supervision of LeWitt. The artist decided to add two further figures to the sequence since there was more space available.[276]

A further work by Broodthaers, who was already represented in the permanent collection with three pieces, was also acquired in 1980. *Je retourne à la Matière, Je retrouve la Tradition des primitifs, Peinture à l'oeuf* (1966), a box with various objects, was purchased from the Galerie Isy Brachot, Brussels.[277] In April–May 1980, a solo show of Broodthaers was organised at the Tate.[278] He was the first Conceptual artist to have a solo exhibition at the museum.

In 1980, Long became the best-represented Conceptual artist (11 works) in the Tate's collection when Anthony d'Offay donated a floor piece to the museum. In 1979, d'Offay, who was a dealer in early twentieth-century British Art, had opened a new gallery for Conceptual art in London. It was rumoured that Fischer had a 10 per cent stake in the gallery, in return for allowing artists, such as Long (Lisson) and Gilbert & George (Greenwood/Lisson), to show at d'Offay's new

270 Minutes of the Board of Trustees Meeting dated 29 May 1980, in Tate Acquisition File (TG 4/2/626/2), TLAL.

271 Letter from Bowness to Logsdail dated 30 June 1980, and Invoice from the Lisson Gallery dated 17 July 1980, in Tate Acquisition File (TG 4/2/626/2), TLAL. One should underline here the difference in prices between a metal geometric structure and a wall drawing.

272 *Sol LeWitt*, Daniels Gallery, New York, 4–29 May 1965.

273 *The Tate Gallery 1980–82: Illustrated Catalogue of Acquisitions*, The Tate Gallery, London, 1984, p.167.

274 *Sale of Modern and Contemporary Art 1945–1979*, Sotheby's, London, 5 December 1979, no.348. See: handwritten information in the sales catalogue held by the Sotheby's Library, London.

275 See: Three black and white photographs from the exhibition at the Lisson Gallery, in Tate Acquisition File (TG 4/2/626/2), TLAL.

276 *The Tate Gallery 1980–82*, *op. cit.*, pp.167–168.

277 Invoice from Isy Brachot dated 30 May 1980, Freedom of Information Request, TLAL.

278 *Marcel Broodthaers*, Tate Gallery, London, 16 April–26 May 1980. See: *Marcel Broodthaers* (exh. cat.), The Tate Gallery, London, 1980.

venue. The opening of the gallery followed d'Offay's marriage to Anne Seymour. Due to the potential for conflicts of interest arising from her marriage to an art dealer, Seymour had to leave the Tate. She brought her expertise in Conceptual art and museum purchases to the dealer gallery, which had previously specialised in Bloomsbury artists and Japanese prints.

The first exhibition of Long at the Anthony d'Offay Gallery took place in March–April 1979.[279] At that time, d'Offay had contacted the Tate to offer recent slate and stone circles for consideration.[280] According to a confidential note from Morphet to Reid dated 8 May 1979, the Tate refused the offer because Long was already well represented in the collection. D'Offay was very disappointed by this refusal, particularly because Long wanted to be represented in the collection by a recent work. D'Offay apparently rang Morphet shortly afterwards, asking him not to discuss his offer or the Tate's refusal with Long, since he would like to make a gift instead. It seems that the dealer intended to tell the artist that the museum was interested in purchasing a recent floor piece, but that he wanted to donate it.[281] D'Offay's attitude demonstrates that he wished to impose his role as Long's new main London dealer. The work put forward was the large *Slate Circle* (1979), 260 cm in diameter (approximately 8 feet 8 inches), made from 214 pieces. On 19 May 1979, Reid wrote to the dealer that his 'offer was put to the Trustees formally at their meeting yesterday, and was very warmly received'.[282]

A Tate Gallery 'In Form' dated 31 December 1979 shows, the work arrived at the museum in January 1980, six months after the Trustees' approval.[283] In November–December 1979, Long's *Slate Circle* had been exhibited at the MOMA Oxford in a solo show.[284] This may explain the late arrival of the work.

The Tate's Conceptual art exhibition programme

During the 1970s, the Tate Gallery was one of the few European museums actively to engage with Conceptualism. In contrast with other institutions, its purchasing strategy was not paralleled by its temporary exhibition policy, although Michael Compton, the Keeper of the Department of Exhibitions and Education, was supportive of the latest artistic developments. At the time, he commented: 'I certainly agree that more and more of this kind of show should happen in London, and I personally think the Tate should do more and more of these

279 *Richard Long, The River Avon*, Anthony d'Offay Gallery, London, 15 March–12 April 1979.

280 Letter from d'Offay to the Tate Gallery dated 23 April 1979, in Tate Acquisition File (TG 4/2/641/2), TLAL.

281 Note from Morphet to Reid dated 8 May 1979, in Tate Acquisition File (TG 4/2/641/2), TLAL.

282 Letter from Reid to d'Offay dated 18 May 1979, in Tate Acquisition File (TG 4/2/641/2), TLAL.

283 Tate Gallery In-Form dated 31 December 1979 filled out by Richard Morphet, in Tate Acquisition File (TG 4/2/641/2), TLAL.

284 Richard Long, MOMA, Oxford, 11 November–23 December 1979. See: *The Tate Gallery, Illustrated Catalogue of Acquisitions 1978–80*, *op. cit.*, p.112. By then, MOMA Oxford was directed by David Elliott. In 1976, Serota became the Director of the Whitechapel Art Gallery, London, following the resignation of Jasia Reichardt.

shows. But I don't necessarily think that the Tate is *the* place to do the shows.'[285]

The only contemporary artist to have a major exhibition at the Tate during the 1970s was Broodthaers (posthumously). In February 1977, there was a screening of his films entitled *The Battle of Waterloo (and other films)* and, in April–May 1980, Long's work was presented in a group exhibition entitled: *Archive Display 1979–1980: Artists International Association, Richard Long, Paul Nash, Tom Phillips.*[286] Serota, the Director of the Tate from 1988 to the present day, explains:

> ... in 1970 the Tate took on, for the first time, responsibility for organising its own exhibitions in a serious way. Before that, most exhibitions that took place at the Tate were organised by the Arts Council. In 1968, the Arts Council opened the Hayward Gallery and thereafter made their exhibitions there. When the Tate started its own programme of exhibitions, they were testing the water. They felt that they had a number of responsibilities. They wanted to show classic British art and classic modern art, in which the collection wasn't strong enough. Then there was a small space in the programme to show contemporary art. They interpreted that obligation to show contemporary art by showing artists who were aged between 50 and 60, rather than between 30 and 40. They saw that younger artists were shown more readily by the Whitechapel Gallery, by the new Serpentine Gallery or by the ICA. That's where they thought these artists should be shown. There were exceptions with the Robert Morris exhibition in 1971 and in 1972, when they had a cancellation of an exhibition. Michael Compton made a show called *Seven Exhibitions* with Michael Craig-Martin, Bruce McLean, Joseph Beuys, David Tremlett, etc. Most of the exhibition was shown in the Duveen Galleries. It was an important manifestation.[287]

However, from early 1974, the newly acquired Minimal and Conceptual artworks were put on show in the permanent display. In January 1974, *Studio International* published the following note:

> The Tate Gallery will be opening two rooms of recently acquired 'Conceptual

285 'The Tate Gallery', *Studio International*, *op. cit.*, p.188.

286 We have seen above that the Tate did not collect photography as such, and thus did not have a Photography Department. Morris recalls that at the time a gift of photographs by Paul Nash was made to the Tate, but that the works were stored in the archive. Morris in conversation with the author.

287 Serota in conversation with the author, *op. cit.*

> art' in late January. The work will be shown in four phases, each lasting two months. The first will be of work which the public will be acquainted with: three floor pieces by Carl Andre, sculptures by Robert Morris and Don Judd, Carel Visser and a wall drawing by Sol LeWitt.[288]

The floor pieces by Andre were those acquired in 1972 and 1973: *Ladder No. 2 (Last Ladder)* (1959), *Untitled (Equivalent VIII)* (1966) and *144 Magnesium Plates* (1969). LeWitt's work was *Wall Drawing, Four Basic Colors (black, yellow, red and blue) and all combinations* (1970), acquired in 1973.[289] But in a letter to the artist dated 16 January 1974, Morphet wrote that the intention was for the work to be shown at a new acquisitions display of Minimal and Conceptual art in January 1974, but that there were difficulties with the costs of the execution and also about finding an appropriate place.[290] A further note published in *Studio International* in December 1974 revealed that the public exhibition of the work was still uncertain about a year later: 'The Tate Gallery's Sol LeWitt Wall Drawing will go on view in January [1975] provided the Ministry of Works have the room prepared on time.'[291] However, a postcard sent by the artist to Seymour, Morphet and Alley in July 1976 points out that the work still had not been realised.[292] In a letter to the artist on 26 August 1976, Morphet explained the situation as follows:

> As you know, the staff of the Modern Collection have been consistently anxious to see your wall drawing executed here at the earliest opportunity ever since it was acquired. We have been frustrated by a combination of lack of space approved for this work and lack of money approved for the purpose of paying people to execute it.
>
> Our new rear extension opens approximately in July 1977, with a two-phase exhibition of works in the permanent collection, larger than we have ever been able to put out on. Phase I will probably be devoted to work c.1875–c.1950. Between now and the opening of Phase II (at roughly Christmas 1977), virtually no work of recent years by anyone will be shown from the permanent collection, except one [creamed] room of easily-hung post-1950 works the public especially demand to see (Bacon, Pollock, Hockney, etc.). It is the very

288 'Review, News and Notes', *Studio International*, vol.187, no.962, January 1974, p.35.
289 Andre's *Equivalent VIII* was on public display until March 1976 when, in the context of the 'Tate bricks scandal', an exasperated visitor sprayed it with paint.
290 Letter from Morphet to LeWitt dated 16 January 1974, in Tate Acquisition File (TG 4/2/626/1), TLAL.
291 'Review', *Studio International*, vol.188, no.972, December 1974, p.R3.

strong wish of the Modern Collection staff that your wall drawing appear in Phase II of the Inaugural display and we are continuing to press for funds, etc., to permit this.[293]

However, it was not until November 1978 that the museum made contact with artists to execute the wall drawing. A manuscript paper entitled 'Sol LeWitt wall drawing' shows that Joe Watanabe and Susan Courteney finally executed the work in April 1979.[294] All in all, it took the Tate six years to put on public display the wall drawing it had acquired in 1973. A major reason was that the new rear extension of the museum (known as the North-East Quadrant) was not opened until May 1979.

In May 1974, Reid wrote a note to Seymour informing her that Nauman's *Corridor with Reflected Image* (1971) was to be presented in Phase III of the Conceptual Acquisitions in July 1974.[295] Huebler's *Variable Piece #44* (1971), purchased in 1974, was to be included in July 1974 in a display of new Conceptual art acquisitions at the Tate entitled *Aspect of Self-Awareness*.[296]

From 1974 onwards, the Tate publicly showed the Conceptual works acquired for its permanent collection. It appears that there were changing displays put together in January and July 1974 and probably also sometime between those dates. In 1979, the opening of the rear extension led to a new public display of work in the permanent collection. Phase II of the display included post-1950 works, among them Conceptual works, such as the LeWitt.

In the late 1960s and 1970s, the Tate was slow in responding to the new aesthetic ideas. It did not really start to collect Conceptual art until 1972–73. However, it emerges that the museum was one of the public institutions to collect the most. This was facilitated by the appointment of the Keepers of the Modern Collection, and by an open-minded Director and, as we will see, by a large purchasing budget. Greenwood remembered that at the time 'one was always frankly embarrassed, when people mentioned the old Tate'.[297] This statement shows that the museum was not able to display to full advantage the many contemporary artworks it collected possibly because it did not organise a comprehensive programme of temporary exhibitions of Conceptual artists.

The museum purchased mainly 'physical' artworks. It acquired a photo-piece

292 Postcard from LeWitt to Seymour, Morphet and Alley dated 10 July 1976, in Tate Acquisition File (TG 4/2/626/2), TLAL.

293 Letter from Morphet to LeWitt dated 26 August 1976, in Tate Acquisition File (TG 4/2/626/2), TLAL.

294 Letter from Ruth Rattenbury, Assistant Keeper, Dept. of Exhibitions and Education, to John Blake dated 24 November 1978, and Manuscript paper entitled 'Sol LeWitt wall drawing' dated April 1979, in Tate Acquisition File (TG 4/2/626/2), TLAL. Joe Watanabe and Susan Courteney were artists whom LeWitt regularly engaged to execute his wall drawings. They were paid £189 each for the execution of the work. Given that they were paid £27 per day, one can conclude that it took them seven days to realise this drawing on four walls. The museum also engaged Sharon Kivland as a supplementary help for two and a half days. She was paid £15 per day, which makes a total of £37.50 paid to her. For the overall execution of the wall drawing, the Tate paid a total amount of £415.50. See: *The Tate Gallery 1980–82*, *op. cit.*, pp.167–168. See also: Manuscript paper entitled 'Sol LeWitt wall drawing', in Tate Acquisition File (TG 4/2/626/2), TLAL.

295 Note from Reid to Seymour dated 13 May 1974, in Tate Acquisition File (TG 4/2/768/1), TLAL.

296 Manuscript note, in Tate Acquisition File (TG 4/390/4), TLAL.

297 'Interview with Nigel Greenwood', in Moseley, *Conception*, *op. cit.*, p.133.

and videos by Gilbert & George, but declined the offer the artists made in 1969 to perform their *Living Sculpture*.[298] In 1972, the Tate presented *King for a Day* by Bruce McLean and hosted lectures by Beuys. But 'Conceptual' or 'dematerialised' works, such as Weiner's 'Statements' and Wilson's 'Discussions', did not find their way into the permanent collection.[299]

The Tate's Conceptual art acquisition budget

From 1967 to 1980, the Tate acquired 37 works by Conceptual artists on which this study focuses. The artists most represented were Richard Long (11) and Carl Andre (7). In 1972 and 1973, the Keepers of the Modern Collection enriched the Tate collection with 14 Conceptual works. In 1976–77, 13 pieces entered the collection. Database 6 on the Tate's purchases shows that most Conceptual works were bought directly from the artists (17 works out of 37). The dealer galleries to sell the most to the Tate were Nigel Greenwood (5), the Lisson Gallery (3) and Konrad Fischer (3, including 2 through artists). Six works were received as gifts.

We have seen that dealers gave ten to 12 per cent reductions on sales to the Stedelijk Museum. The same percentage was offered by Logsdail and Greenwood on sales to the Tate. For instance, in 1972, Greenwood gave a ten per cent reduction on the purchase of a group of works by Gilbert & George, including *Balls: The Evening before the Morning After, Drinking Sculpture* (1972).[300] Long's *A Hundred Mile Walk* (1971–72) acquired in 1973 and LeWitt's wall drawing *On Four black walls ...* (1980) purchased in 1980 from the Lisson Gallery, were also offered at a reduction of ten per cent.[301]

In the 1970s, the VAT seems to have been about ten per cent for pieces sold by foreign dealers and about eight per cent for artworks sold by British dealers. For example, Long's *Circle of Sticks* (1973) was sold by the artist through Fischer. The invoice shows that ten per cent VAT was added to the original price.[302] In 1976, *119 Stones* (1976) was sold by Long through the Lisson Gallery with VAT of eight per cent.[302] In 1980, the VAT had increased to 15 per cent.[303] LeWitt's *On Four black walls...* (1980) was purchased with an addition of 15 per cent VAT.[304]

Fluctuations in prices due to exchange rates are exemplified by the purchase of Nauman's *Corridor with Mirror and White Lights* (1971).[305] In a letter to

298 Letter from Gilbert & George to the Tate Gallery dated 1969, in Tate Acquisition File (TG 4/2/382/1), TLAL.

299 The Department of Prints was only founded in 1975.

300 Invoices no.1197 (£750 – £ 5 = £675) and no.1198 (£1,300 – £130 = £1,170) from Nigel Greenwood each dated 4 December 1972, in Tate Acquisition File (TG 4/2/382/1), TLAL.

301 Invoice from the Lisson Gallery dated 30 January 1973 (£1,000 – 10% = £900), in Tate Acquisition File (TG 4/2/641/1), TLAL, and: Invoice from the Lisson Gallery dated 17 July 1980 ($30,000 – 10% = $27,000), in Tate Acquisition File (TG 4/2/626/2), TLAL.

302 Invoice from Fischer dated 26 October 1973 (£1,000 + 10% VAT = £ 1,100), in Tate Acquisition File (TG 4/2/641/1), TLAL.

303 Invoice from the Lisson Gallery dated 24 July 1976 (£2,000 + 8% VAT = £ 2,160), in Tate Acquisition File (TG 4/2/641/2), TLAL.

304 Invoice from the Lisson Gallery dated 17 July 1980 ($30,000 – 10% discount + 15% VAT = $31,050), in Tate Acquisition File (TG 4/2/626/2), TLAL.

305 Many invoices in the Tate Acquisition File give the price of artworks in Deutschmarks, US Dollars and British Pounds. By comparing two entries, it was possible to ascertain an approximate exchange rate between those currencies. The figures in Database 7 on Prices of Conceptual art (Appendix 1.7) are based on the following exchange rates: in 1972: $1=£0.38 / 1973: $1=£0.40 / 1974: $1=£0.45 / 1980: $1=£0.49. In 1973: DM1=£0.15 / 1977: DM1=*f*1.05.

Seymour dated 13 December 1972, Fischer offered the piece for $6,000 (£2,419).[306] On 27 June 1973, she contacted the dealer, informing him that the purchase of the work had been agreed by the Trustees, concluding: 'I have however, been instructed to ask you whether you would be prepared to let us have a ten per cent discount, as is customary.'[307]

On 17 July 1973, Fischer sent a new invoice in which the work was priced in Deutschmarks instead of US Dollars. The dealer explained in an accompanying letter:

> Concerning the invoice: I offered the piece to you December 13, 1972 on the price of $6,000. The rate of exchange of dollars at that date was 1 US$ = DM3.20. The price of the piece relates to this rate. That's the reason, I have to write out the invoice in DM: 6.000 $ × 3.20 = DM19,200, less 10% for the Tate Gallery. I hope all this sounds understandable to you.[308]

Through this manoeuvre the dealer tried to turn the exchange rate to his favour. If the piece was priced in Deutschmarks, the final price was calculated as follows: DM19,200 (£3,327) – 10% = DM17,280 (£3,010). Whereas if the piece was priced in US Dollars, it was cheaper: $6,000 [£2,374]. This was pointed out by Seymour in a letter to Fischer dated 27 July 1973:

> We were disturbed to find in your letter of 17 July that you are now quoting us a price in DM for the Nauman *Corridor* ...
>
> We do of course realise that the exchange rate has gone against you, but would like to point out that if it had gone against us, we should no doubt have held to the original figure in the currency named.
>
> We should very much like to get this problem sorted out as soon as possible.[309]

Finally, the dealer sent a new invoice on 26 October 1973 in which the price was fixed at $6,000.[310]

During the 1970s, the Tate had the advantage of an important acquisition budget. However, we have seen above that Reid mentioned in 1973 that it was

306 Letter from Fischer to Seymour dated 13 December 1972, in Tate Acquisition File (TG 4/2/768/1), TLAL.
307 Letter from Seymour to Fischer dated 27 June 1973, in Tate Acquisition File (TG 4/2/768/1), TLAL.
308 Invoice from Fischer dated 17 July 1973, in Tate Acquisition File (TG 4/2/768/1), TLAL.
309 Letter from Seymour to Fischer dated 27 July 1973, in Tate Acquisition File (TG 4/2/768/1), TLAL.
310 Invoice from Fischer dated 26 October 1973, in Tate Acquisition File (TG 4/2/768/1), TLAL.

difficult to convince the government to give the Tate additional sums for purchases. Furthermore, as Alley added: 'We find it terribly difficult to raise extra money from private sources, with the exception of the Friends.'[311] At the time, there was no tradition of company sponsorship. One should add that between 1973 and 1975, the attendances at the museum dropped from 1,200,000 visitors to less than 900,000 a year.[312]

From 1970 to 1974, the museum had an annual budget of £530,000 (about $1,325,000). It was increased substantially for the 1974–76 period, rising to £835,000 (about $2,087,500). For the 1976–78 period, it was further increased to £1,140,000. Lastly for 1978–80, the grant-in-aid was raised by 80 per cent to £2,915,972. During the 1970s, the Tate's annual purchasing fund was doubled in 1975 (from £265,000 to £570,000) and even tripled in 1978 (from £570,000 to £1,665,000).[313]

Between 1970 and 1980, the total acquisition budget of the Tate Gallery was approximately £6,093,869. Database 7 on prices of Conceptual art reveals that during this period, the museum spent approximately £82,803.17 on Conceptual works, representing 13 per cent of the public institution's budget.[314]

5.5. Conclusion

Public Conceptual art collections

The study of Conceptual art collections in Northern European museums from the late 1960s to the 1970s reveals that 238 works by the studied Conceptual artists were purchased (105 by European artists and 133 by US artists).[315] The European artists most intensively collected were Dibbets (29), Long (27) and Darboven (14). The American artists whose work was the most purchased were Nauman (41), LeWitt (23), Andre (21) and Weiner (21).

The European museums to have put together comprehensive collections of Conceptual art between 1967 and 1980 were the Stedelijk Museum (62) and the Stedelijk Van Abbemuseum (51). The Tate (37) and the Städtisches Museum

311 'The Tate Gallery', *Studio International*, *op.cit.*, p.182. The Contemporary Art Society (CAS), which has existed since 1910, donates works of British artists to British museums. There was also the American Friends of the Tate Gallery.

312 Morris, 'The Museum of Modern Art in Oxford 1965–1975', *Studio International*, *op. cit.*, p.241.

313 The Tate's grant-in-aid was established as follows: 1970–72: grant-in-aid £530,000 + gifts: £7,458 [1970–71: £265,000 + 1971–71: £265,000] / 1972–74: grant-in-aid £530,000 + gifts: £80,198 + special grant: £45,000 [1971–72: £265,000 + 1973–74: £265,000] / 1974–76: grant-in-aid £835,000 + gifts: £10,241 [1974–75: £265,000 + 1975–76: £570,000] / 1976–78: grant-in-aid £1,140,000 [1976–77: £570,000 + 1977–78: £570,000] / 1978–80: estimated grant-in-aid £2,915,972 [1978–79: £1,655,000 + 1979–80: £1,260,972]. See: *The Tate Gallery 1970–72*, *op. cit.*, p.269; *The Tate Gallery 1972–74*, *op. cit.*, p.269; *The Tate Gallery 1974–76*, *op. cit.*, p.97. For the acquisition budget in 1977–80, see: Public record files for Grant-in-aid (TG 17/1/1/4 1973–87), TLAL. See also: *The Tate Gallery 1976–1978*, *op. cit.*, p.7.

314 If we take an average of the exchange rate between the US Dollar and the British Pound in the 1970s ($1 = £0.43) we have a purchasing budget of $2,620,363.67. The amount spent on Conceptual works of art was $35,605.36.

315 See: Database 6 (Appendix 1.6).

Mönchengladbach (29) were also actively collecting Conceptual works. Most artworks were purchased between 1972 and 1977 (161).

Konrad Fischer (37) and Art & Project (28) were the European dealers who sold the most works to museums at the time. One has to keep in mind the arrangements set up between the dealers. We have seen the links between Fischer and Art & Project, Preisig, Logsdail and d'Offay. Thus, Fischer's influence on sales of Conceptual works to museums must have been widespread. Database 6 shows that all other European dealers sold between six (Sperone) and one work. The most successful American dealers during the period were Castelli and Sonnabend (28 works between them) and John Weber (6). Overall, European dealers sold 112 works and US dealers 36 works. The artists themselves sold 33 pieces. Loans, deposits, gifts and sales by private collectors make up the remaining 57 works.

Museum budgets and prices for Conceptual art

After having analysed the prices of Conceptual works of art purchased by the Stedelijk Museum and the Tate (Database 7), it is necessary to compare the data of the two institutions. For clarification purposes, the figures have been converted to US Dollars in order to compare the two museums. In the 1970s, both museums spent about the same percentage of their acquisition budgets on Conceptual art: 10 per cent for the Stedelijk and 13 per cent for the Tate. However, the Amsterdam museum, in real terms, had a larger purchasing fund ($3,785,000) than London ($2,620,000).

If one looks at the prices paid by both museums, one can conclude that large installations could be acquired for $30,000–50,000; sculptures and paintings for $2,500–50,000; neon pieces for $2,200–2,700; photographs for $2,500–7,900, and photo-collages from $4,800–9,000. Drawings were cheaper, about $400–1,100. Videos were affordable, with prices ranging from $90–870. As sales to museums were public, it was these deals that set the official value of Conceptual artists' works.

It is interesting to balance prices of Conceptual artworks with other goods at the time. In the late 1960s and early 1970s, a return flight from Germany (Munich, Düsseldorf) to New York cost about DM 1,400 (£210).[316] During the

316 See: Letter from Fischer to Friedrich dated 8 May 1968, Letter from Fischer to Friedrich dated 29 January 1968, and Manuscript letter from Fischer to Bischofberger from 1968, in Galerie Korrespondenz 1967–69, AKFGD. See also: Letter from Reisebüro J. Hartmann, Düsseldorf, to Fischer dated 24 November 1972, in Allgemeine Korrespondenz 1972–73, AKFGD.

same period, domestic flights in Germany (Düsseldorf to Munich, Berlin to Düsseldorf), and short distance flights in Europe (Brussels to Copenhagen) cost about DM250 (£37.50).[317] For working two days a week for Nigel Greenwood in 1971, Lynda Morris earned £15.[318] Michael Corris remembers seeing advertisements for jobs in London at the time that paid £25 a week.[319]

The findings of Database 6 on museum purchases allows us to determine the efficiency of certain strategies developed by Conceptual art dealers. Fischer seems to have been the most adept at establishing an alternative network for Conceptual art. He managed to network successfully with other dealers, thus allowing his artists to exhibit all over Europe. We have seen how secondary dealers, such as Bischofberger and Janis, took on board Conceptual artists to update the profile of their galleries. Further, from the late 1970s onwards, new dealers, such as d'Offay, represented Conceptual artists already established by other dealers. This shows that by the end of the 1970s, Fischer and other original dealers had lost control over the network they had established. Some of the orginial galleries, such as Wendler (1974), Wide White Space (1976) and Preisig (1979), had closed down. It also appears from the database that the impact of several dealers, such as Maenz and Wide White Space, was minimal. Other dealers, like MTL, are absent from sales to museums.[320]

In comparison with other art movements, Conceptual works were inexpensive at the time. Museum directors such as Cladders and Fuchs believed that the value of Conceptual pieces would increase with time, and that they were a good investment for a museum's permanent collection.[321] Nevertheless, it also appears that it took museums a long time to make the decision to acquire or even to pay for certain works. According to De Decker, at the end of the 1970s, some museums took up to a year to pay for a work.[322]

After having considered the private collections and the setting up of the collections of public museums in Europe between the late 1960s and late 1970s, one could look at the secondary markets of Conceptual art. A separate study of the market in prints and editions, and the role of auction houses, would contribute to an even more extensive view of the art market at the time.

317 See: Manuscript letter from Fischer to Friedrich from about February–March 1968, and Letter from Fischer to Friedrich dated 29 January 1968, in Galerie Korrespondenz 1967–[1969], AKFGD. See also: Letter from Mr Buchloh, Skandinavian Airlines System, Düsseldorf, to Fischer dated 2 March 1972, in Allgemeine Korrespondenz 1972–73, AKFGD.

318 Morris in conversation with the author.

319 Michael Corris in conversation with the author, London, Tate Modern, Symposium *Open Systems: Rethinking Art c.1970*, 16–19 September 2005, manuscript notes.

320 This does not mean, however, that these galleries were absent from the art market. Spillemaeckers, for instance, spontaneously proposed a work by Dibbets to the Tate in March 1973, but the offer was declined. See: Letter from Spillemaeckers to Seymour dated 19 March 1973, and Letter from Seymour to Spillemaeckers dated 2 April 1973, in Tate Acquisition File (TG PC2/10/1), TLAL.)

321 Cladders and Fuchs in conversation with the author, *op. cit.*

322 De Decker in conversation with the author, *op. cit.*

Part II: Conclusion

The study of the dealing structure of the international network of Conceptual artists makes apparent that from the late 1960s onwards important private and public collections were being established in Europe. Private collectors played an important part in the dealing structure: with them came the first recognition that Conceptual art was 'collectable'. They often acted as patrons rather than collectors. They paved the way for Conceptualism's entrance into national museums. Gifts, long-term loans and activities as trustees further enabled collectors to influence museums.

The attitude adopted by public institutions depended on the directorship. Some, such as Rudi Fuchs in Eindhoven, turned their museums into specialist Conceptual art institutions. But in certain museums such as the Tate, the acquisition procedure involved obtaining approval from a Board of Trustees, which sometimes led to processes that were long and complex. In institutions, temporary exhibitions played an important part in relation to sales, since they were often linked. The role played by dealers in the developing the exhibition programme and permanent collections of museums was crucial, for example Fischer at the Städtisches Museum in Mönchengladbach.

Through these public deals, gallerists and museum curators established the prices for Conceptual art. However, there was an opacity surrounding the Conceptual art market that still exists today. The difficulty in getting hold of the information on museum purchasing prices and budgets proves this. As the analysis of the Stedelijk and the Tate demonstrates, only a small percentage of the institutions' budget was spent on Conceptual art.

One should also highlight the attitude of Conceptual artists towards sales. From the correspondence between Fischer and several artists, it appears that some (for example LeWitt) could be very direct with the dealer. Others, Andre for instance, were rather shy.[323] At the time, only a few artists were able to live from their art: many had to teach to survive financially.[324] Some artists (a notable example is Darboven) also made donations to museums.

By studying the network of Conceptual artists set up by young dealers in the late 1960s and 1970s in Europe, one discovers more about public art collections. New knowledge regarding the relationship between dealers and curators and the

323 See: LeWitt and Andre early correspondence, in Korrespondenz mit Künstlern 1969–70, AKFGD.

324 See: 'Interview with Daniel Buren', in Moseley, *Conception*, *op. cit.*, p.117.

importance of temporary exhibitions becomes clearer if one looks at the chronology and the provenance of the acquired works. It is also important to note that many primary dealers, such as Fischer, Logsdail, Spillemaeckers and Lohaus had been trained as artists. Lynda Morris has suggested that Duchamp's role as a dealer in New York was important for Fischer.

The first dealer gallery to show an artist became the key person in the Conceptual network. Fischer held the most power until 1977 when his collaborative ventures with Sperone-Westwater and d'Offay were confused by collectors' enthusiasm for the new painting. Fischer's authority was mainly due to the connections he had established with other dealers in most European countries. The careers and status of the artists represented by Fischer seem to have developed more quickly than those represented by other dealers like Maenz and Templon (Kosuth, Art & Language). After 1977, powerful secondary dealers came in, and merged the primary network of Conceptual art with 'a new spirit in (Expressionist) painting'.

Conclusion

This research uniquely approaches Conceptual art in Europe from the economic rather than the more common theoretical perspective. The dissemination and distribution of Conceptual art are at its centre. The study reflects the internationalisation of an art movement and the way in which the careers of artists were guided and shaped by their dealers. It illustrates that, in the early phase of Conceptual art, these dealers were the centre of power as artists and curators became more widely known through association. The relationship between dealers and curators was crucial in establishing the value of Conceptual art and the public market and the shaping of public collections. Conceptual art histories tend to underplay the crucial role of the dealer,[1] which has virtually disappeared in accounts of the period written in the 1990s. Curators are generally presented as having occupied the central position in the setting up of museum collections. One of the aims of this book was to redress this balance, bringing attention to the network.

This international network was a network of cities rather than countries. Moreover, it was a league of small provincial cities that became key players. An important idea was that of increasing equality between America and Europe in the 1960s. The innovative working methods of young artists were encouraged by young dealers. The most important of these were working with artists rather than with objects, working with in situ productions and working outside the gallery space. These working methods came out of the artworks themselves. These practices were progressively taken over by curators and directors of public institutions. Thus, the new approaches were originally created by artists and art dealers, not by museums or critics. Dealers appear as being the centre of power

1 Fischer occupies an ambiguous position. On one hand, many protagonists play down his importance in the Conceptual network; on the other hand, people like to be linked with him because of his prestige. Typical of this attitude is, for example, Cladders. Cladders in conversation with the author, *op. cit.*

in this early phase of the Conceptual art network.

This study represents the development of a model of investigation that can be applied to all subsequent art movements, as many of the key dealers and artists have remained active through the 1980s and 1990s to the present day. Presenting research in the form of databases is a type of enquiry that can be applied to uncover connections in other art movements. The appendices can be used as an encyclopaedic tool for further research on Conceptualism and for curatorial studies.

In the 1970s, some Conceptual artists were highly conscious of the network and used it as the subject of their works. They focused their attention on dealer galleries, thus highlighting their role as the centre of power. In December 1970, Robert Barry initiated a project linking some of Europe's progressive dealer galleries. *Some places to which we can come, and for a while 'be free to think about what we are going to do' (Marcuse)* (1970–71) was an exhibition that took place successively at Sperone, San Fedele (Milan), Art & Project, Yvon Lambert and Paul Maenz between December 1970 and April 1971. In 1972, Barry initiated *Invitation Piece* (1972–73) consisting of eight invitation cards sent in rotation by Conceptual art dealer galleries (Maenz, Art & Project, Wendler, Castelli, Lambert, MTL, Tosselli, Sperone). Each dealer invited the recipient to a show of the artist in another gallery: Paul Maenz sent an invitation to a Robert Barry exhibition at Art & Project, Art & Project sent an invitation to a show at Jack Wendler, etc.[2]

Between 1969 and 1975, Jacques Charlier produced a series of caricatures that give an insight into the art world of the period.[3] They reveal something about the personalities and positions of the network's protagonists, although they were not always welcomed by their targets.[4] The documentary photographs that Charlier took at the time are also of primary importance for gaining an insight into the network: they document openings of key exhibitions and fairs in 1974.[5]

André Cadere (1934–78) was another artist who critiqued the network. Although he exhibited in some Conceptual dealer galleries (MTL in November 1973, Sperone in October 1975), his work enabled him to step out of the network. His signature piece was a round bar of wood, which he carried around with him (*Presentation of the work*). Because it was portable, he was able to present it officially or unofficially in galleries and museums or any other public spaces.

2 Robert Barry's *Invitation Piece* is part of the private collection of Annick and Anton Herbert. See: *L'Architecte est absent*, *op. cit.*, pp.70–71. One can also mention Dibbets' *Project for Art & Project* (1969) and Jacques Charlier's *Vernissage des Expositions* (1975). See: Chapters 2.2. and 3.4.

3 For an overview of all the caricatures, see: *Articides Follies, J. Charlier, 1969–75*, Daled & Gevaert, Brussels, 1975.

4 Charlier in conversation with the author, Luxembourg, *op. cit.*

5 See: Chapter 3.4. for a discussion of these photographs.

6 'André Cadere, tape recorded interview in London with Lynda Morris March 1976', unpublished document, in LMAN. [Editor's note: Published in: Karola Grässlin, Astrid Ihle, Fabrice Hergott, Alexander von Grevenstein, Lynda Morris, *André Cadere: Peinture Sans Fin*, Walther König, Cologne, 2008.]

7 I had occasion to discuss my research topic with peers during conferences I gave across Europe. For example: 'Okey Dokey – The "hidden" knowledge of art collections', conference paper given at the Symposium *Does art know? Collection and Knowledge in Discourse*, Kunsthaus Graz, Austria, 9–10 June 2006; 'Sculpture inside out: The Tate Gallery's collecting in the 1970s', conference paper given at the symposium in response to the exhibition *Open Systems: Rethinking Art c. 1970*, Tate Modern, London, 16–19 September 2005; 'Gerry Schum and the Conceptual art Network, 1968–1973', conference paper given at the *New Research into Conceptualism in Europe* symposium, Norwich School of Art and Design, 25 February 2005.

8 One drawing shows Fischer walking and smoking. His shadow is

Cadere declared: 'A gallery is a structure of power, so my work has a kind of critical attitude against the power. So it is possible to look at what is the power from the position of the work.'[6]

This study, and particularly the databases, has emphasised the extensive Conceptual art collections set up by European museums in the late 1960s and 1970s. Konrad Fischer appears to have had the central role in the network: the artists most collected were represented by him. This demonstrates the efficiency of his working and dealing methods and his ability as a promoter.[7] Some people were concerned by Fischer's power, however Charlier, who produced a number of caricatures presenting him as a formidable dealer,[8] described him as being highly authoritarian.[9] The artist Gerhard Richter wrote to Buchloh in the late 1970s: 'I feel uncomfortable about Konrad's increasing importance and monopoly ... I am angry that Konrad, like many other politicians, has so much power and prevents any moving forward.'[10] Richter wrote this letter when he was deciding to leave Fischer's gallery. He showed with the powerful dealers Anthony d'Offay in London, Sperone in Turin and Marian Goodman in New York, in the 1980s.[11]

If one looks closely at the chronology of acquisitions and at the provenance of the artworks, one finds a good deal of new information about dealing practices established at the time. Italy had draconian foreign exchange rules.[12] Moreover, there must have been a number of deals in which payments were made in cash, which left no trace of either monetary transactions or customs details. The importance of Rolf Preisig's Swiss gallery gave the network a base outside the EU. One can also point to the disagreement involving Darboven and Fischer in 1975–76.[13] The opaque relationships between dealers and curators sometimes provoked public outrage, as in the 'Tate bricks scandal' of 1976. These cases continue to occur today, although not always with Conceptual works. In the late 1980s, Fuchs got into trouble for purchasing a large work by Nauman at a high price from Fischer for the collection of the Haags Gemeentemuseum.[14]

Both dealers and museum curators tend to be discreet about money, and about the relationships between each other. This has arisen in part because of museum rules established in the nineteenth century, when museums collected

that of Napoleon with an eagle on his shoulder. The other caricature is a set of drawings showing the evolution of Fischer from a young artist to a powerful dealer. The last drawing shows him sitting on a throne with a sceptre in his hand. See: *Articides Follies*, *op. cit.*, unnumbered pages.

9 Charlier in conversation with the author, Luxembourg, *op. cit.*

10 Richter in a letter to Benjamin H.D. Buchloh dated 3 February 1979, cited in: Dietmar Elger, *Gerhard Richter, Maler*, Dumont, Cologne, 2002, p.298 (author's translation).

11 See: Minola, Mundici, Poli and Roberto, *Gian Enzo Sperone*, *op. cit.*, p.499.

12 See: Chapter 5.3.

13 The last exhibition of Darboven at Konrad Fischer took place in June 1975. It is said that she left the gallery over tax issues. See: *Ausstellungen bei Konrad Fischer*, *op. cit.*, p.107. See also: 'Konrad Fischer', *Kunstforum International*, *op. cit.*, p.281.

14 Fuchs was the director of the Gemeentemuseum in The Hague from 1987 to 1993. See: Kerstin Schweighöfer, 'Der Fuchs im Hühnerstall hatte zu grossen Appetit und Lust aufs Reisen: Rudi Fuchs hinterlässt in Den Haag Millionen-Schulden', *Art: das Kunstmagazin*, no.5, May 1993, p.139. See also: *Ausstellungen bei Konrad Fischer*, *op. cit.*, pp.258–271.

the work of dead artists or artists at the end of their career, or through the gift of legacies from private collectors and artists' estates. From the 1960s onwards, the interest in Conceptualism meant a move towards young artists still building their careers, with works passing from the studio to the museum in a matter of years or days. But the rules have never been fully established. This situation has created distortion between what is accepted common practice and the official rules.

This study has highlighted the need for a new openness based on factual studies of the post-1967 art market, the dealer galleries and public institutions, as well as accountability of public money. There is a need to map out correct approaches in terms of curatorial ethics. Training and educational courses for curators should examine these issues more fully, because the art world is now more public.

This concerns foremost the education of curators. The ethics of the profession should be based on knowledge of artists and the dealing network. Consequently, this research will be of particular interest for curatorial training courses.[15] An analysis of the complete European Conceptual art network was not possible because of the chronological and artistic boundaries that had to be set at the beginning of the research. However, this study gives a revealing and accurate insight into the European art world of the late 1960s and 1970s. Additional research in dealer gallery archives would have been useful to gain a broader perspective on the dealing network. The concealment or private nature of many archives did not permit these supplementary investigations at the time. These two points, however, demonstrate the potential for future investigations of the network of Conceptual art.[16]

15 There are, for example, the Curatorial Training Programme at the De Appel Foundation in Amsterdam, the MA in Curating Contemporary Art at the Royal College of Art in London and the curatorial studies programme at Goldsmiths, University of London.

16 For example, the Art & Project archive held at the Netherlands Institute for Art History in The Hague is now available to researchers. The Getty Research Institute holds the Paul Maenz and Giuseppe Panza Papers. The Smithsonian Institute retains, among others, the Carl Andre and Lucy Lippard Papers. One can also mention the Center for Curatorial Studies at the Bard College, Annandale-on-Hudson, which holds the Dwan Gallery Archive.

Jacques Charlier

Vernissage des Expositions, photographs, 1974–75

Selected photographs originally exhibited at the Palais des Beaux-Arts, Brussels, 1975

René Block
Cologne Kunstmarkt, 1974

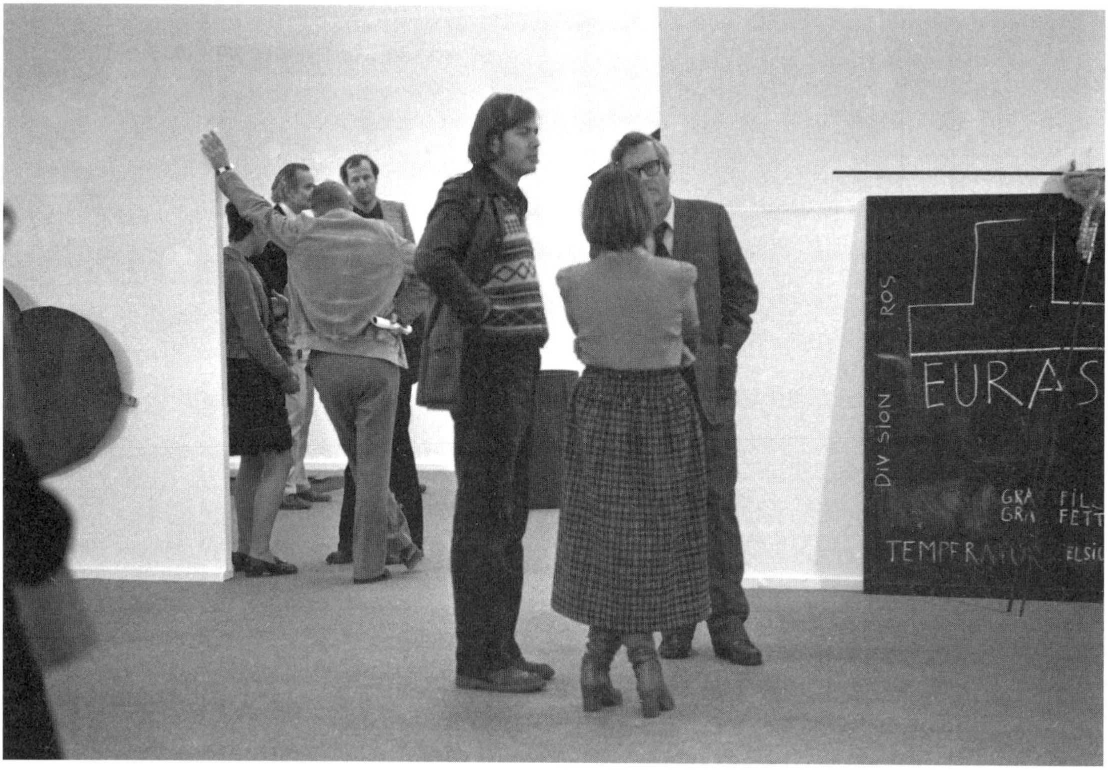

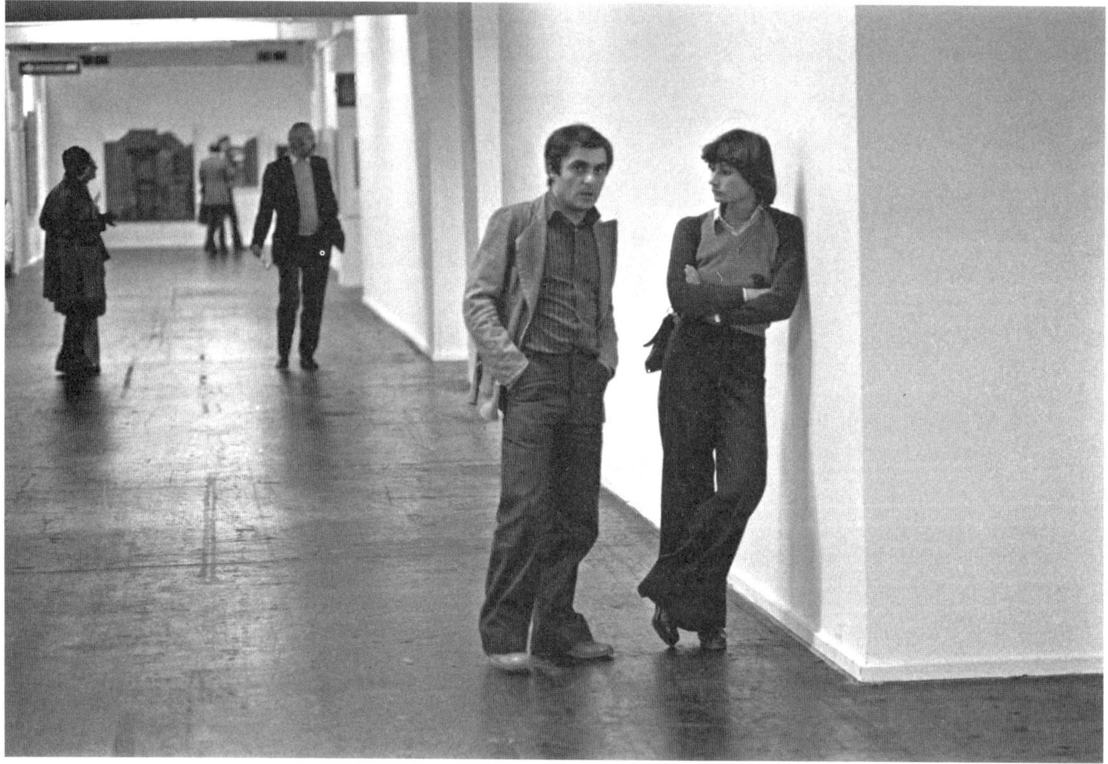

Giancarlo Politi, Catherine Millet
Cologne Kunstmarkt, 1974

Jacques Charlier, Manette Repriels, Bernard Marcelis, Nigel Greenwood
Cologne Kunstmarkt, 1974

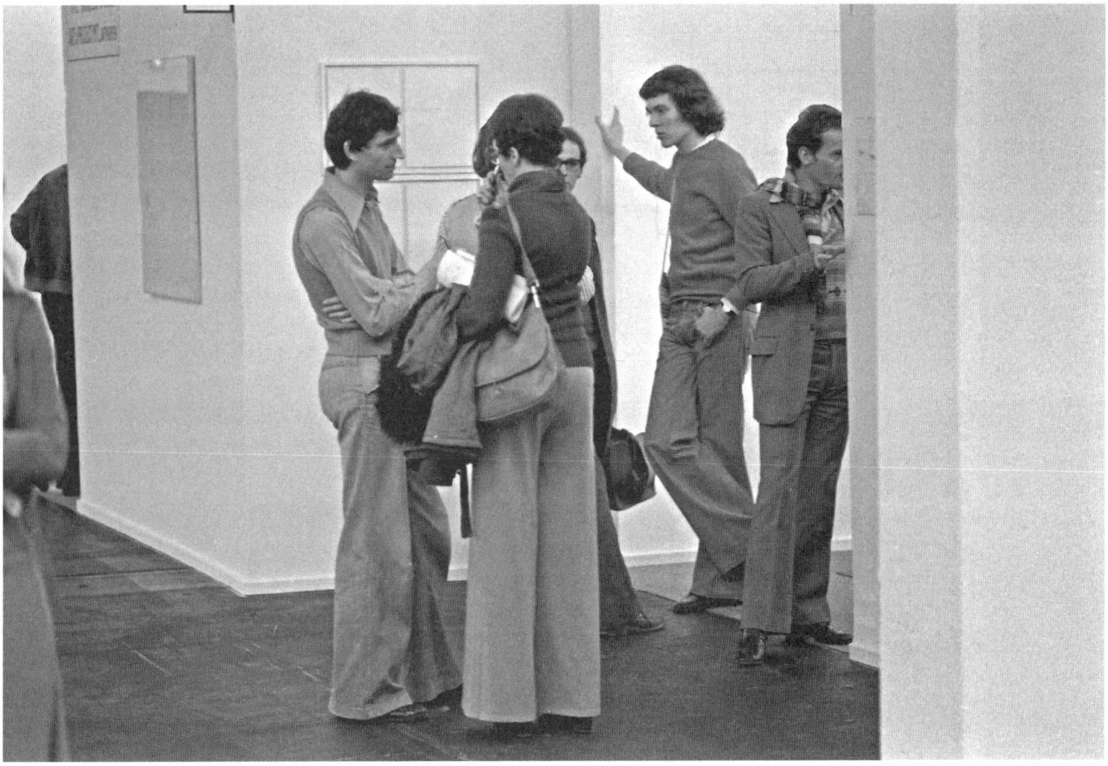

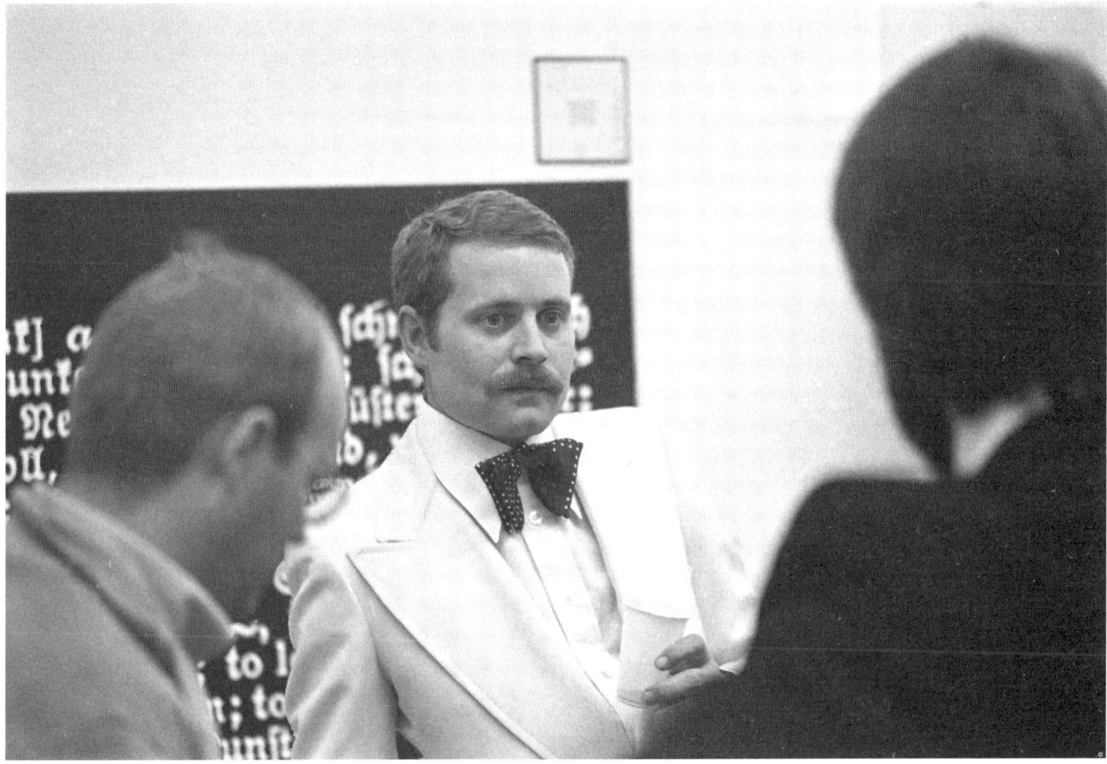

Paul Maenz
Cologne Kunstmarkt, 1974

John Gibson, Dan Graham
Cologne Kunstmarkt, 1974

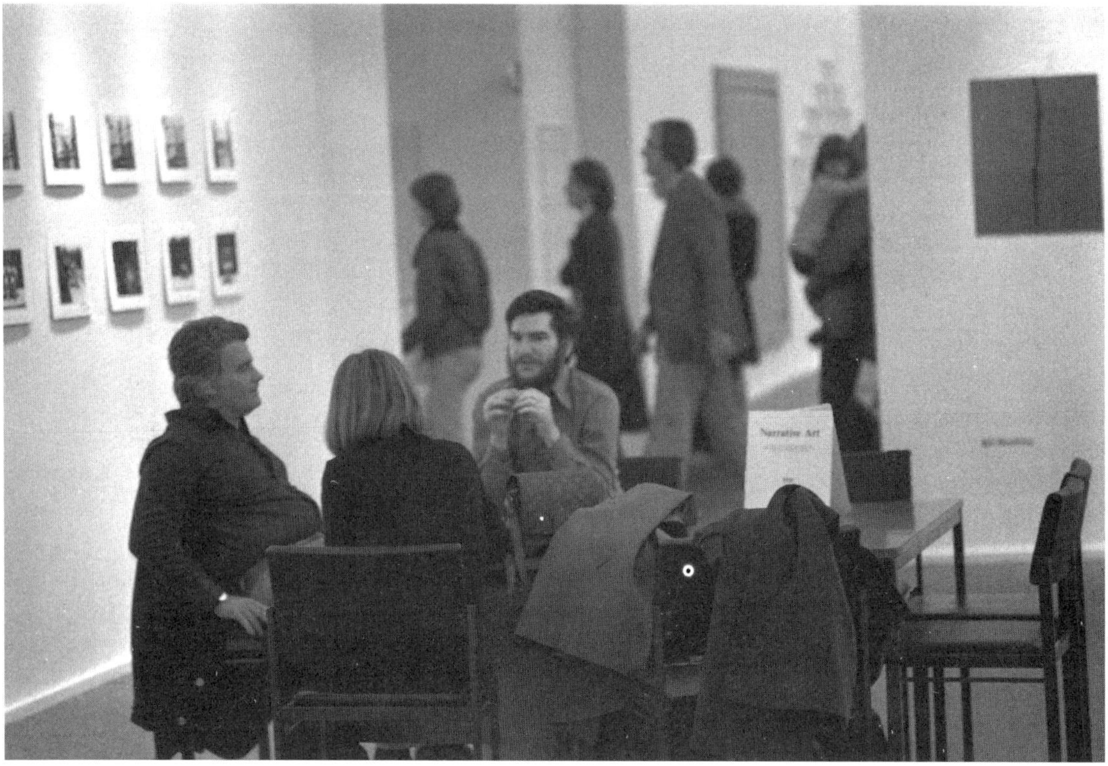

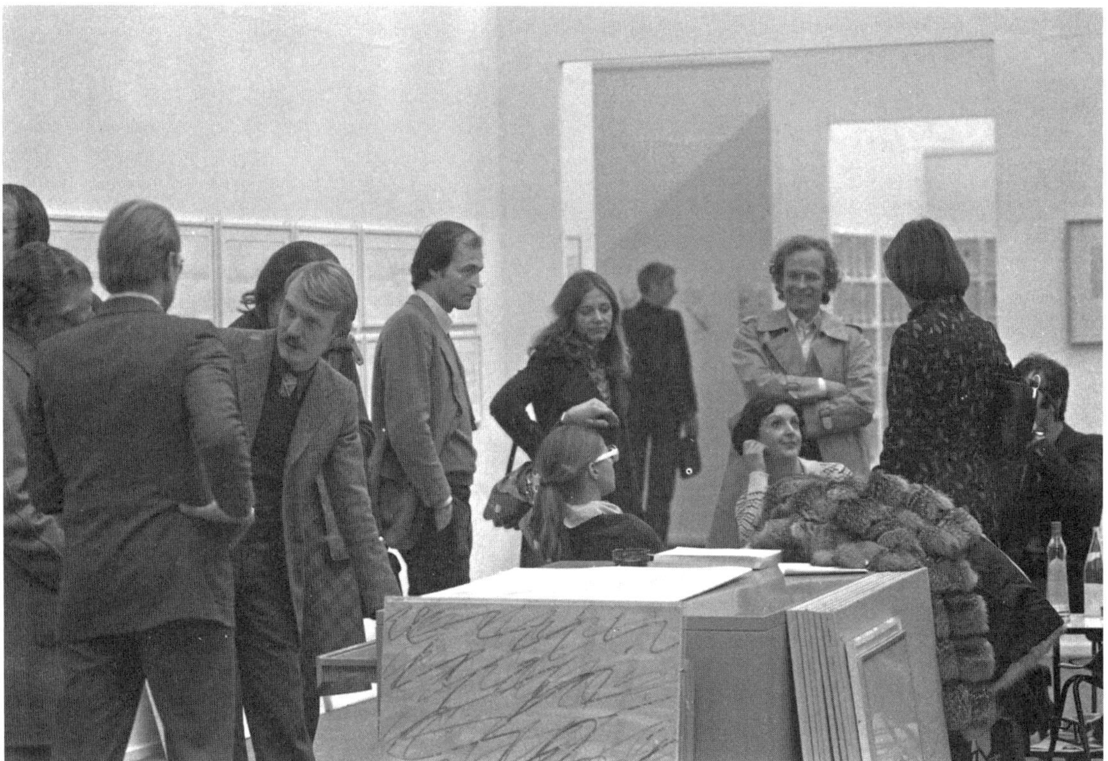

Heiner Friedrich, Thordis Moeller, Six Friedrich
Cologne Kunstmarkt, 1974

Stéphane Rona, Charlotte Moorman
Cologne Kunstmarkt, 1974

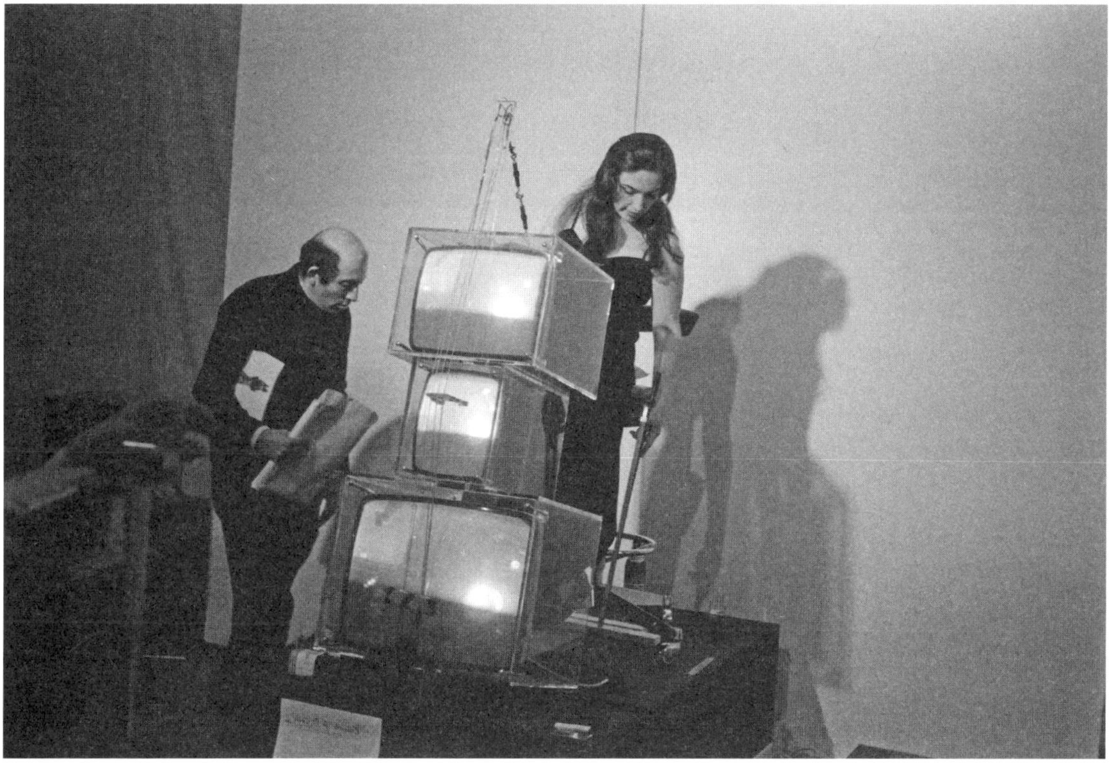

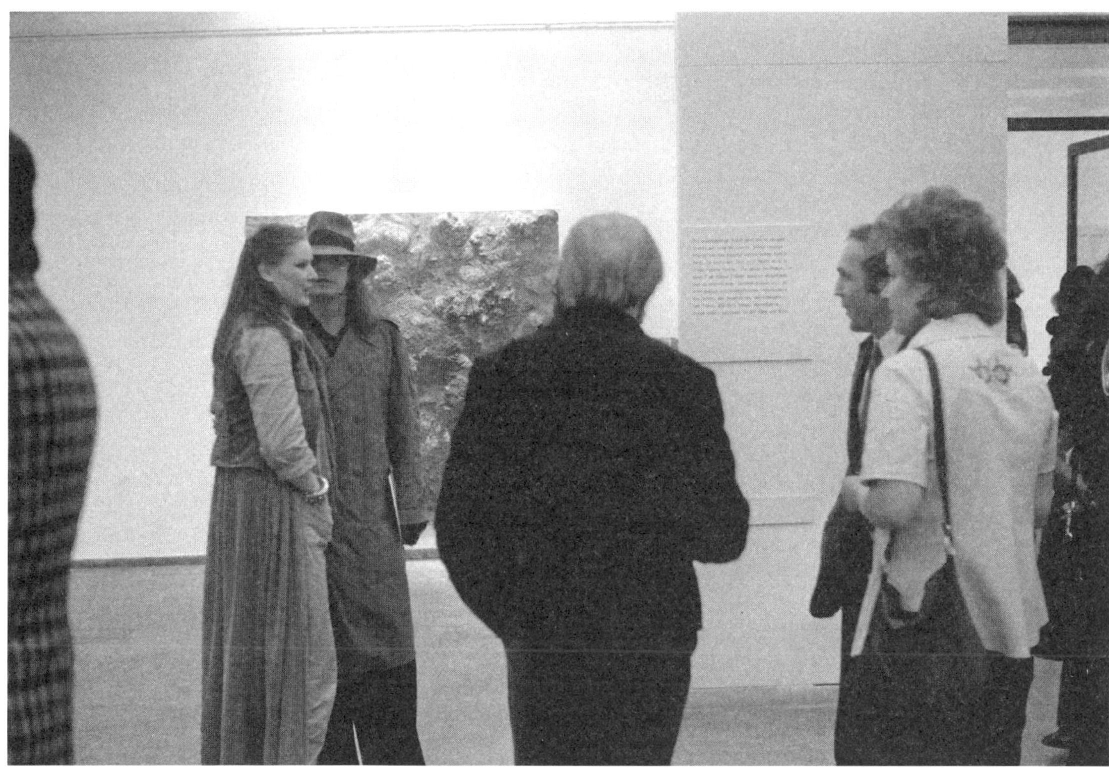

Katharina Sieverding, James Lee Byars
Cologne Kunstmarkt, 1974

Marcel Broodthaers
Konrad Klapheck, Palais des Beaux-Arts, Brussels, 1974

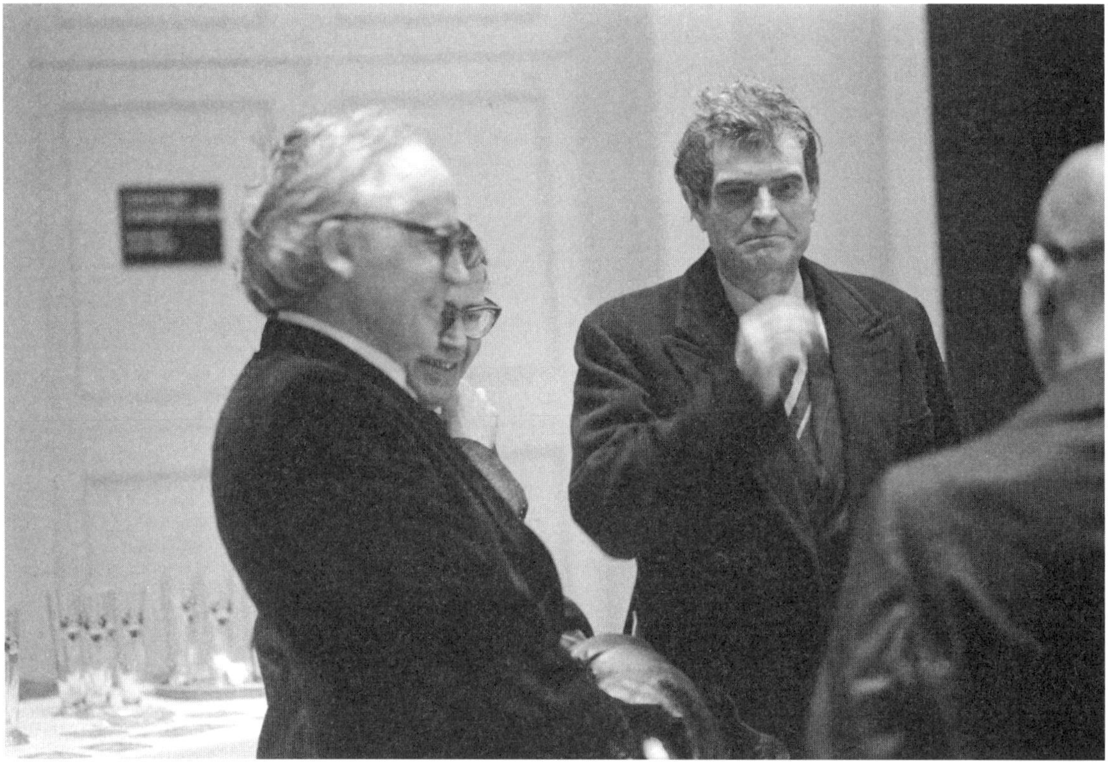

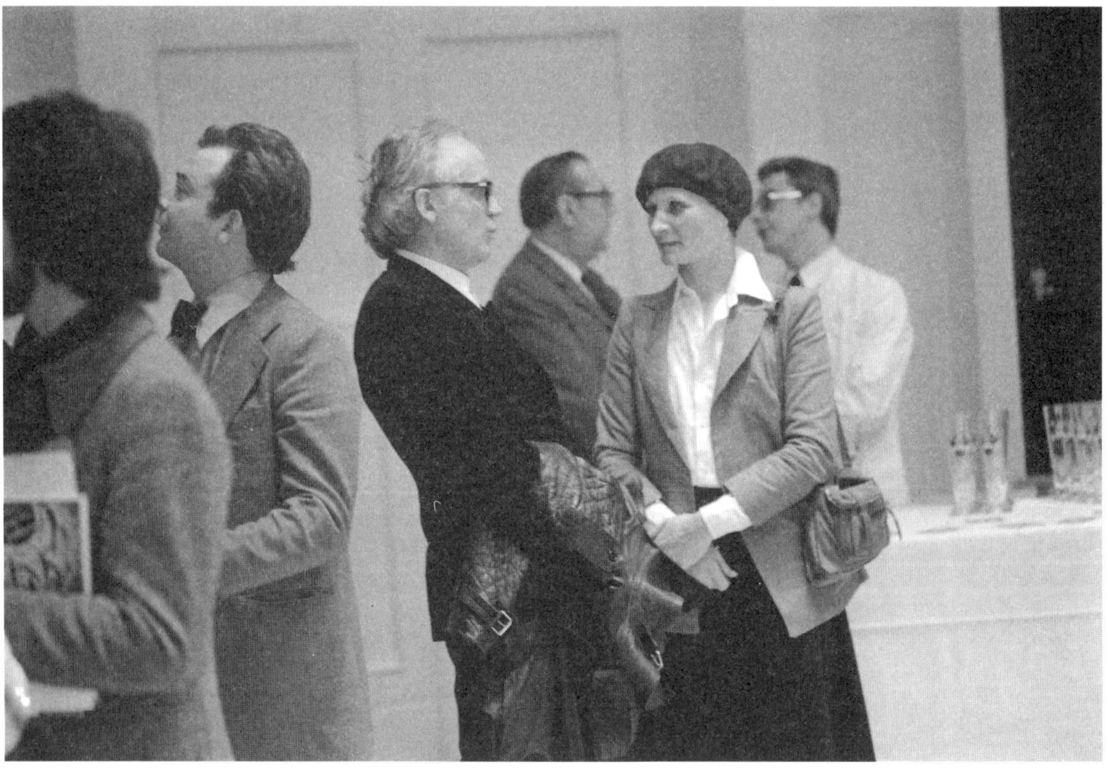

Maria Gilissen-Broodthaers
Konrad Klapheck, Palais des Beaux-Arts, Brussels, 1974

Sylvain Perlstein, Lili Dujourie, Yves Gevaert, Annick Herbert, Isi Fiszman
Palais des Beaux-Arts, Brussels, 1974

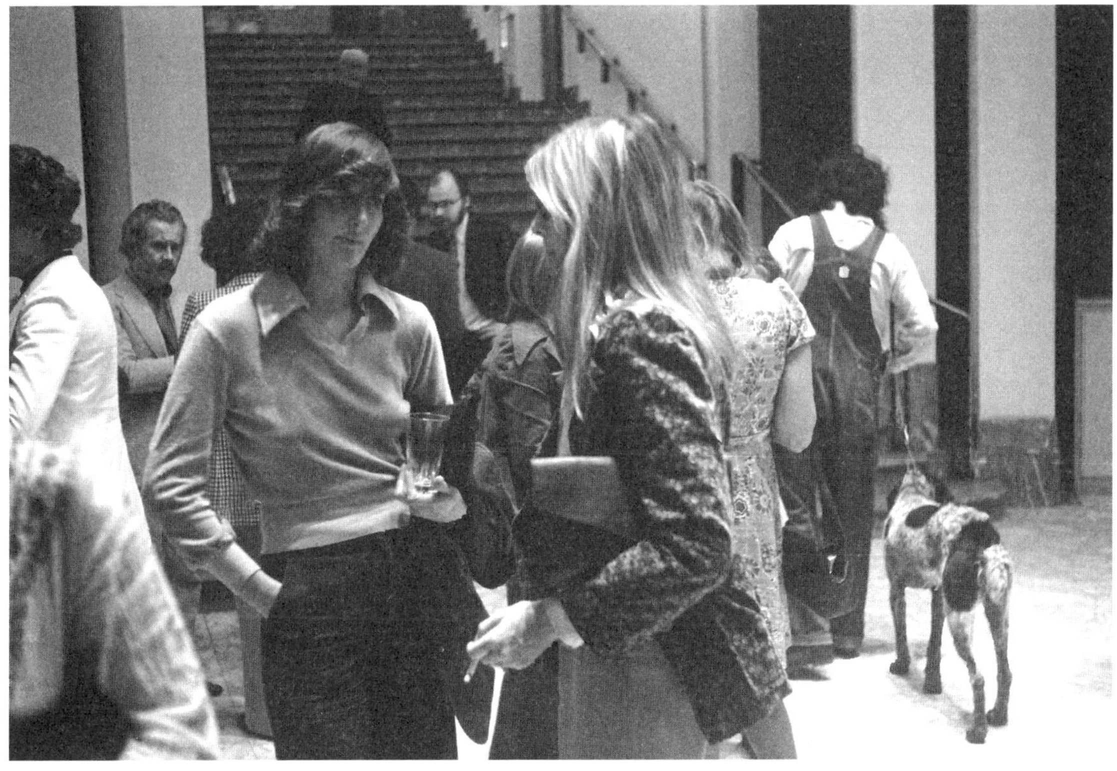

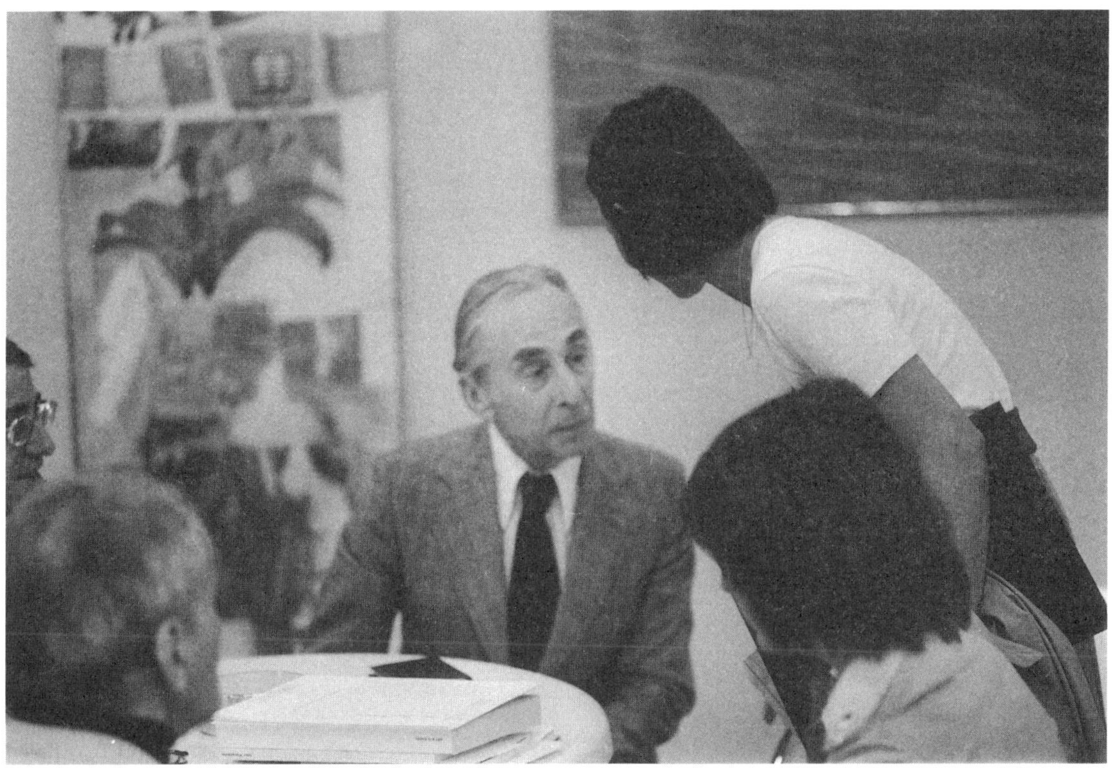

Leo Castelli

Annick Herbert, André Cadere, Anton Herbert
Marcel Broodthaers – Dan Van Severen, Palais des Beaux Art, Brussels, 1974

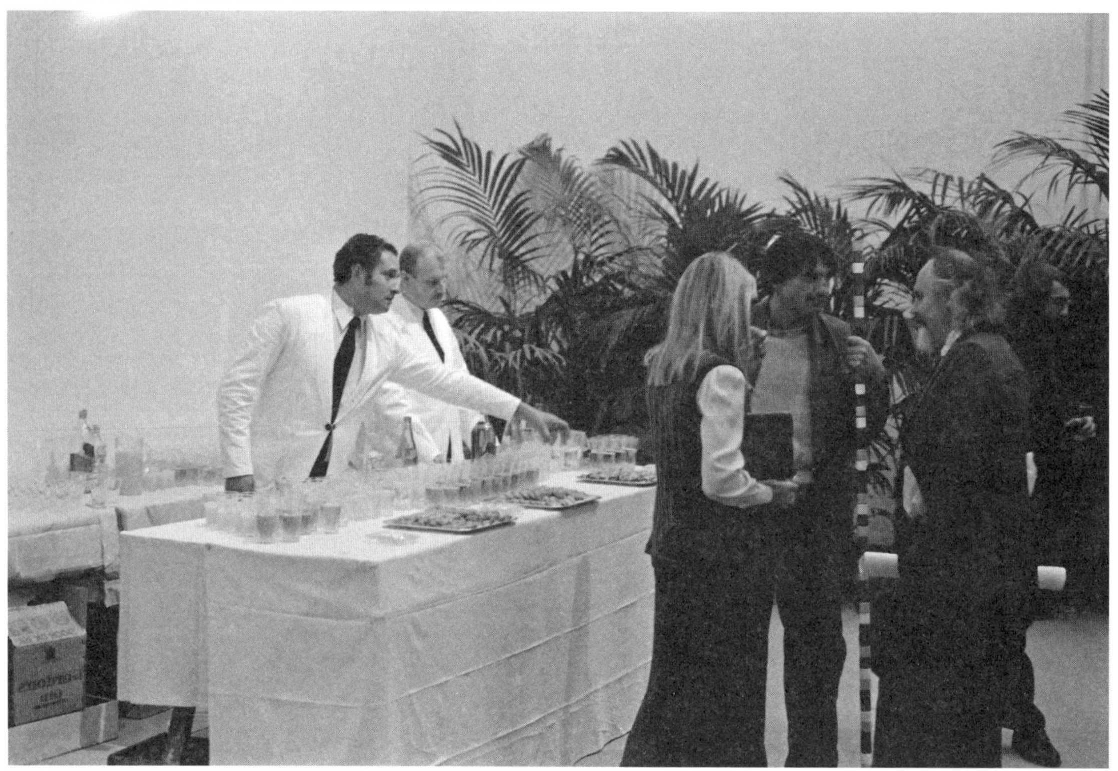

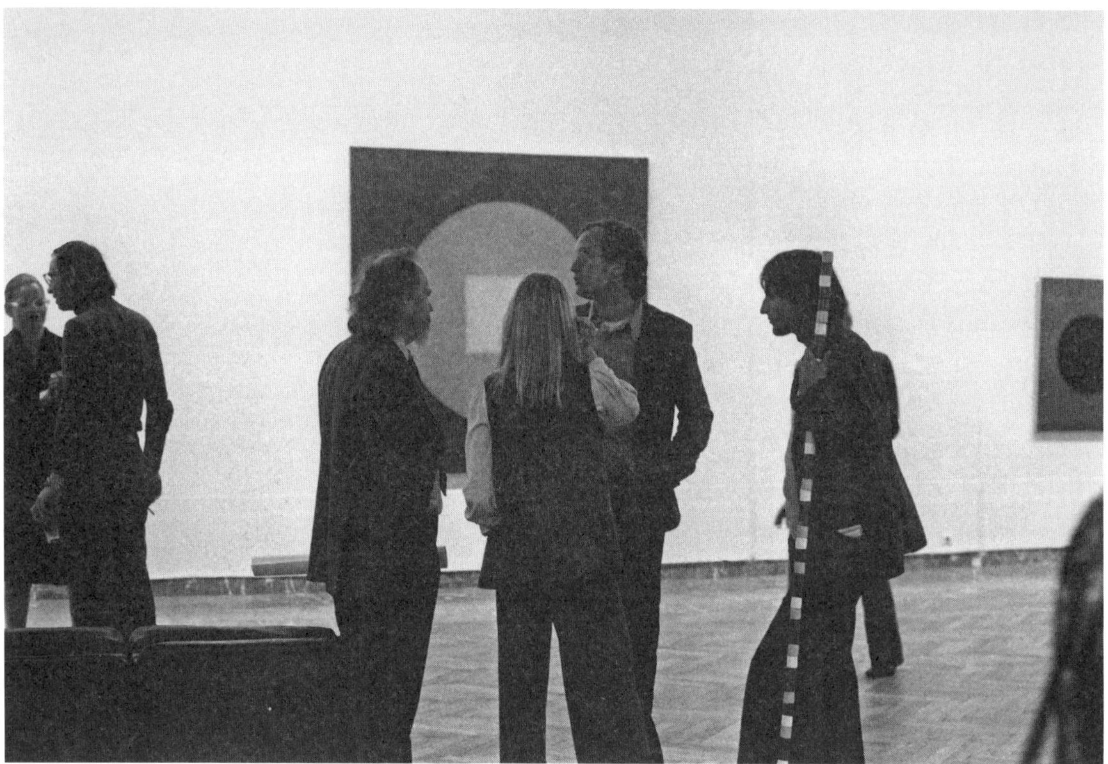

Thordis Moeller, Konrad Fischer, Anton Herbert, Annick Herbert, Fernand Spillemaeckers, André Cadere
Marcel Broodthaers – Dan Van Severen, Palais des Beaux Art, Brussels, 1974

Konrad Fischer, Rudolf Zwirner
Projekt '74 – Kunst Bleibt Kunst, Kunsthalle, Cologne, 1974

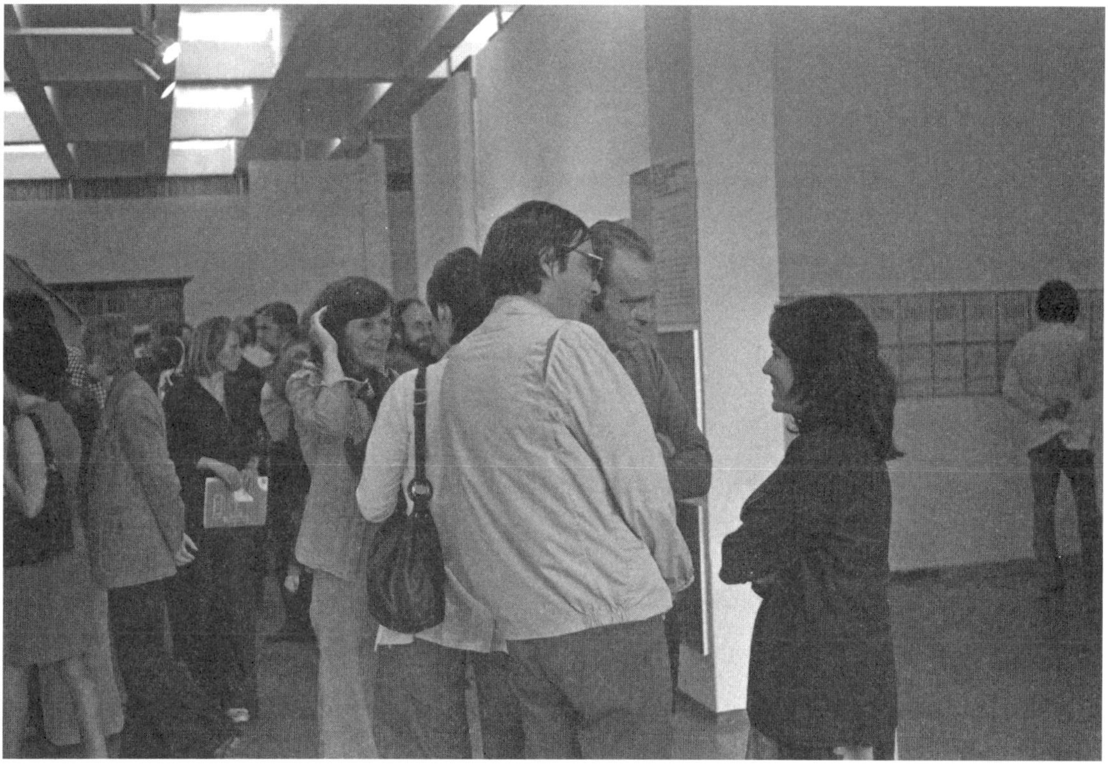

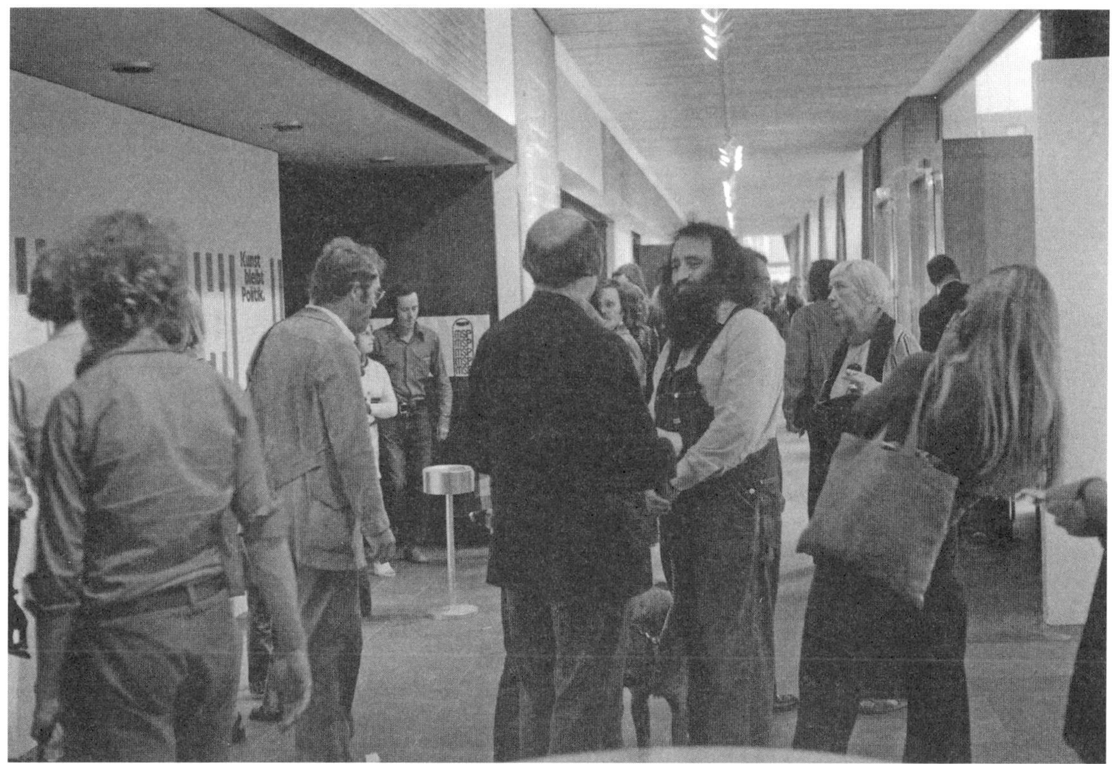

Bernd Becher, Isi Fiszman
Projekt '74 – Kunst Bleibt Kunst, Kunsthalle, Cologne, 1974

Daniel Buren, Benjamin Buchloh (Buren installing Hans Haacke)
Projekt '74 – Kunst Bleibt Kunst, Kunsthalle, Cologne, 1974

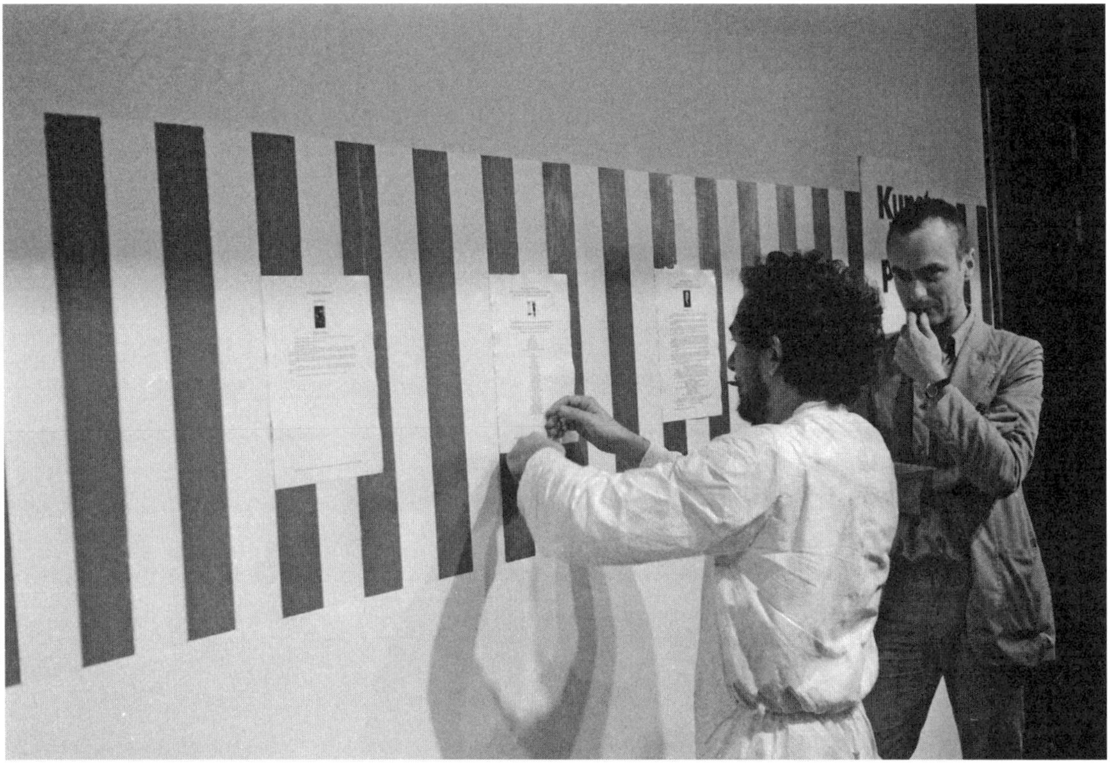

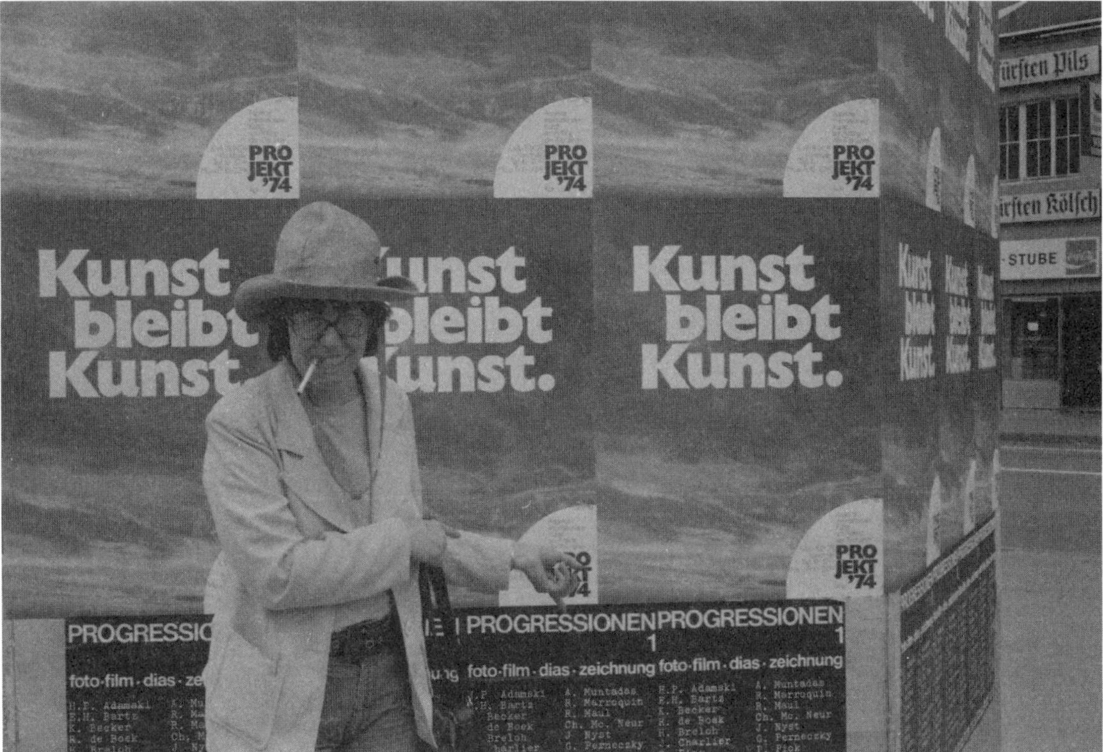

Barbara Reise
Projekt '74 – Kunst Bleibt Kunst, Kunsthalle, Cologne, 1974

Ileana Sonnabend, Antonio Homem
Projekt '74 – Kunst Bleibt Kunst, Kunsthalle, Cologne, 1974

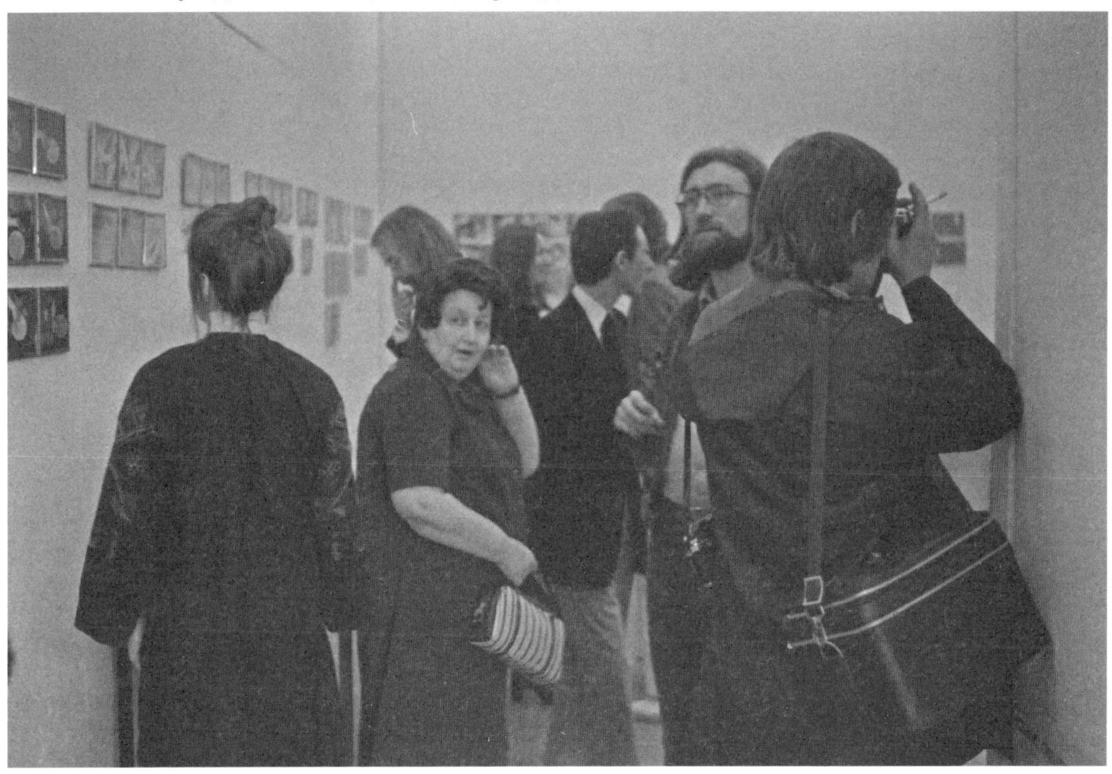

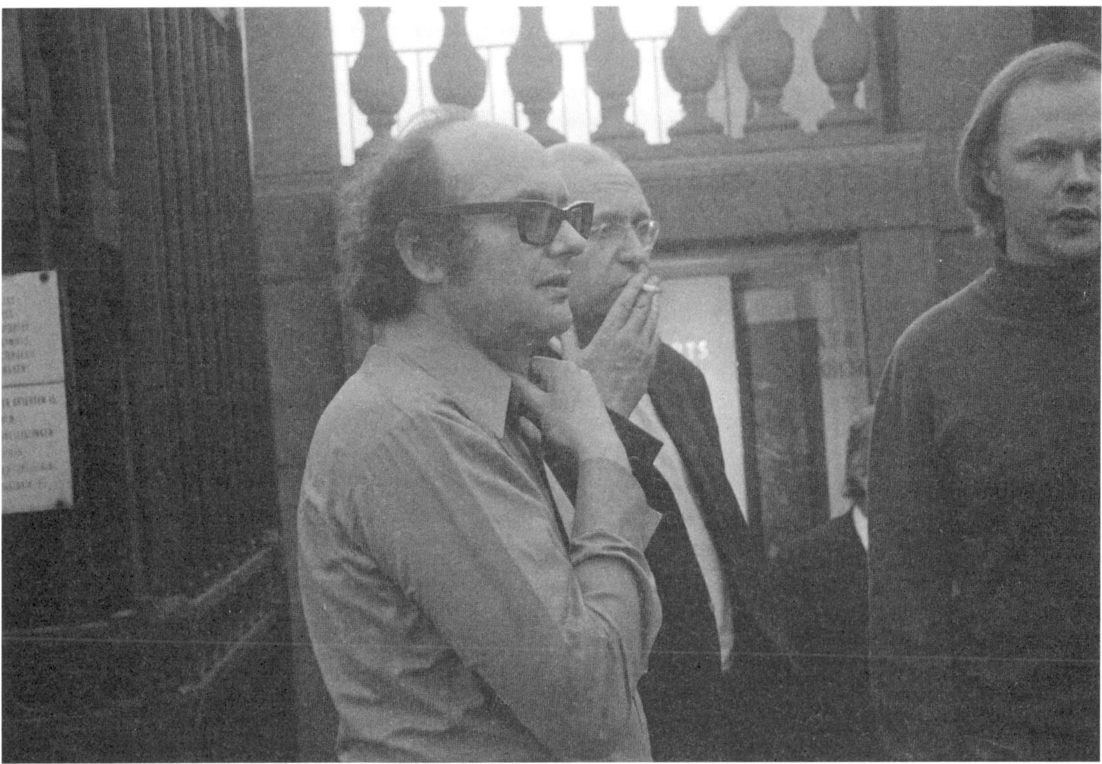

Sol LeWitt, Bernd Becher, Nicholas Logsdail
Palais des Beaux-Arts, Brussels, 1974

Bram Bogaert and his wife, Adriaan van Ravesteijn, Nicole Daled
Darboven – LeWitt – Finlande, Palais des Beaux-Arts, Brussels, 1974

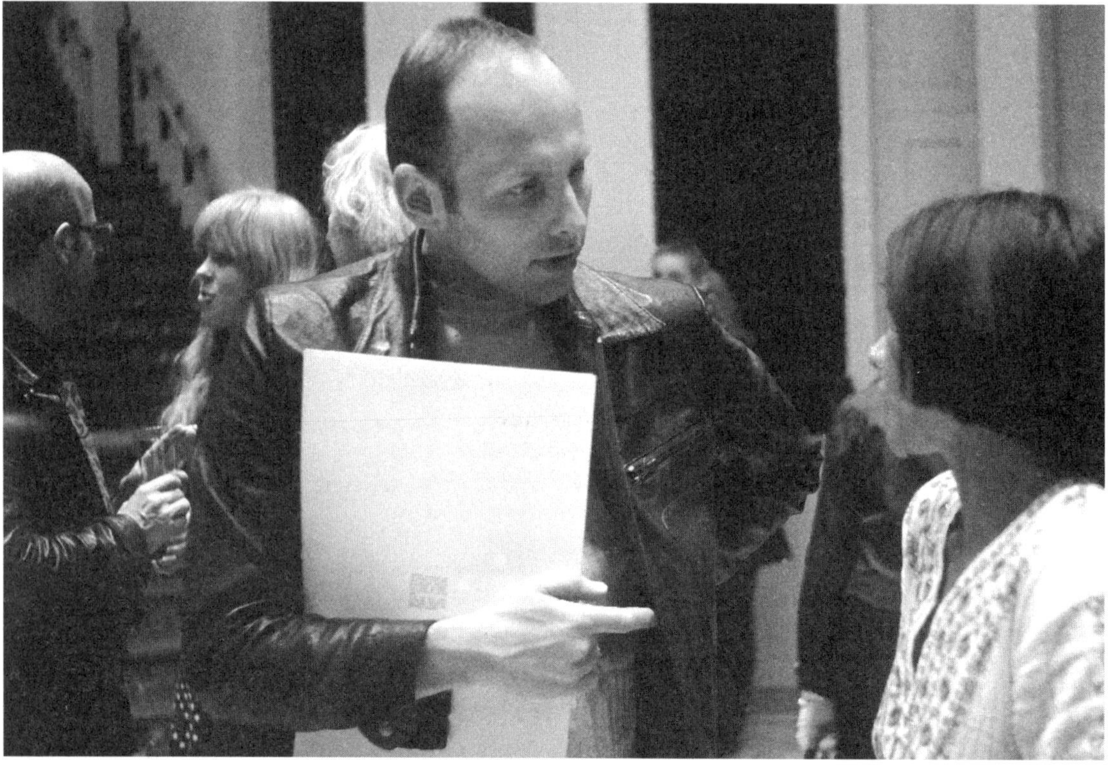

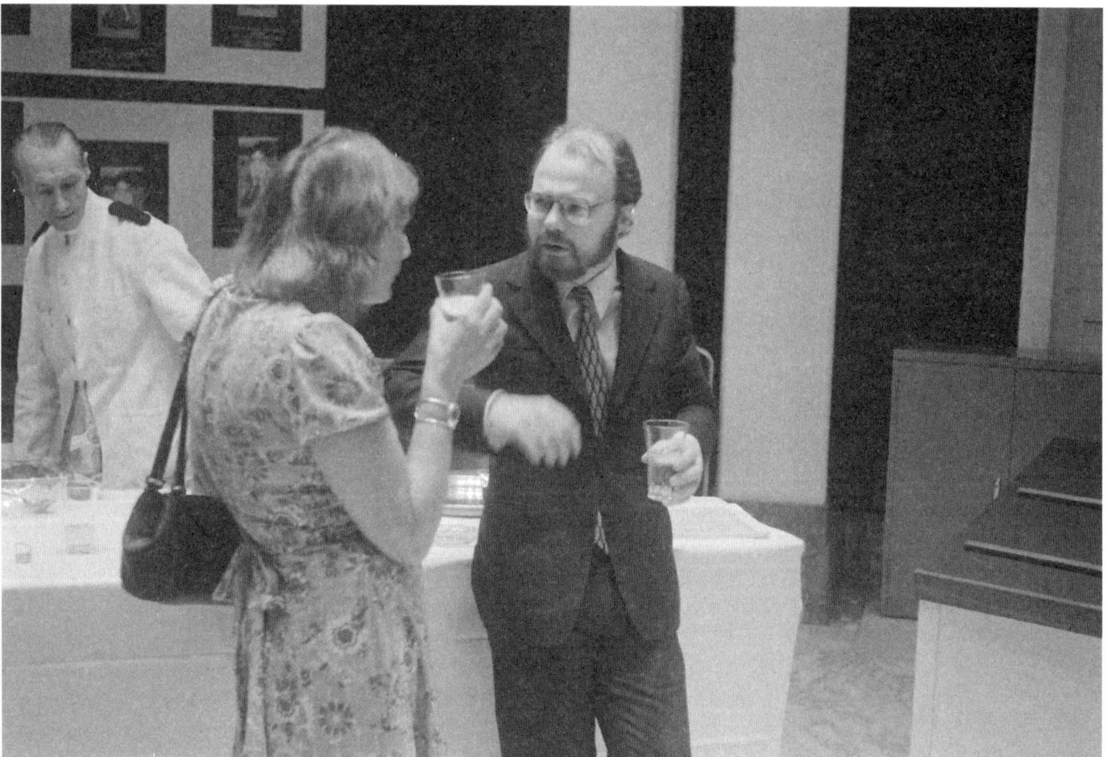

Yves Gevaert
Darboven – LeWitt – Finlande, Palais des Beaux-Arts, Brussels, 1974

Sol LeWitt
Sol LeWitt, Stedelijk Museum, Amsterdam, 1974

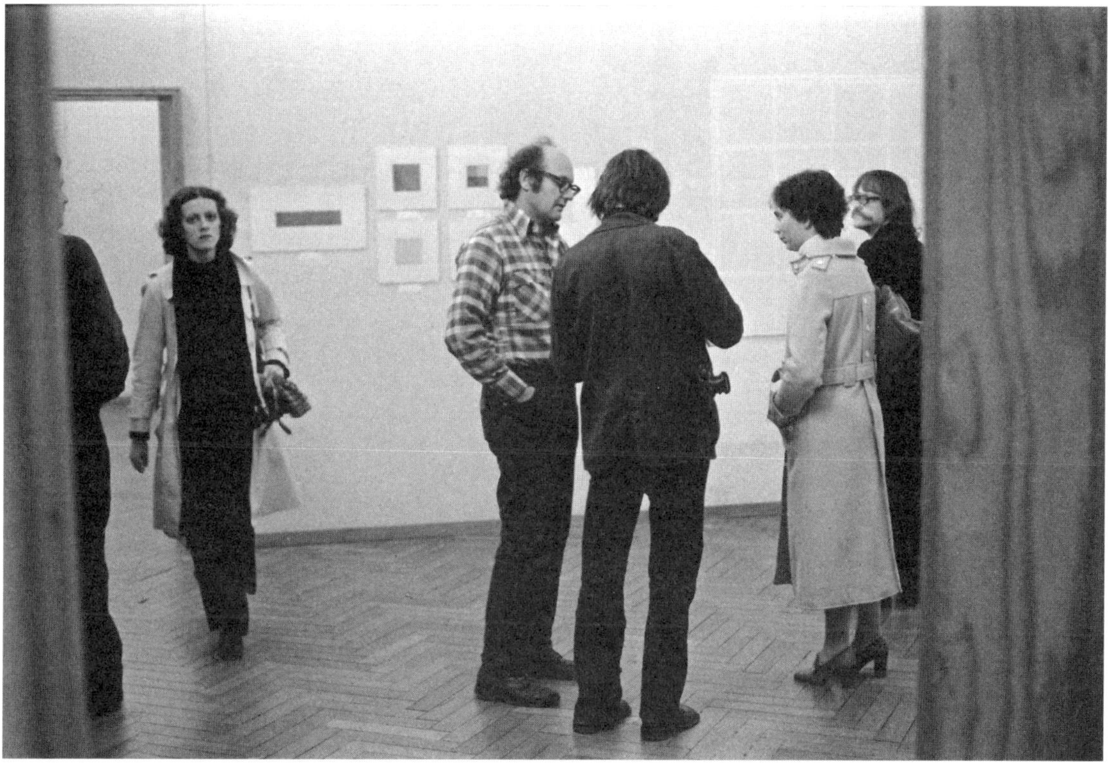

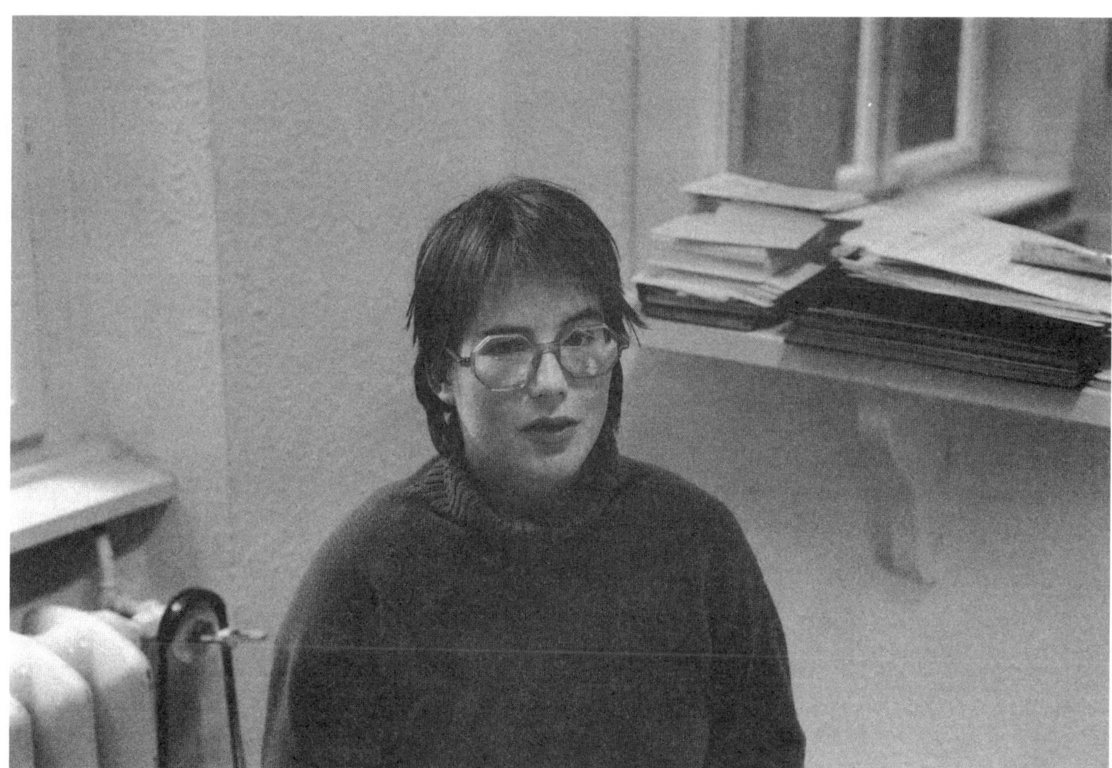

Erika Fischer

Konrad Fischer, Benjamin Buchloh, Anny De Decker
Palais des Beaux-Arts, Brussels, 1975

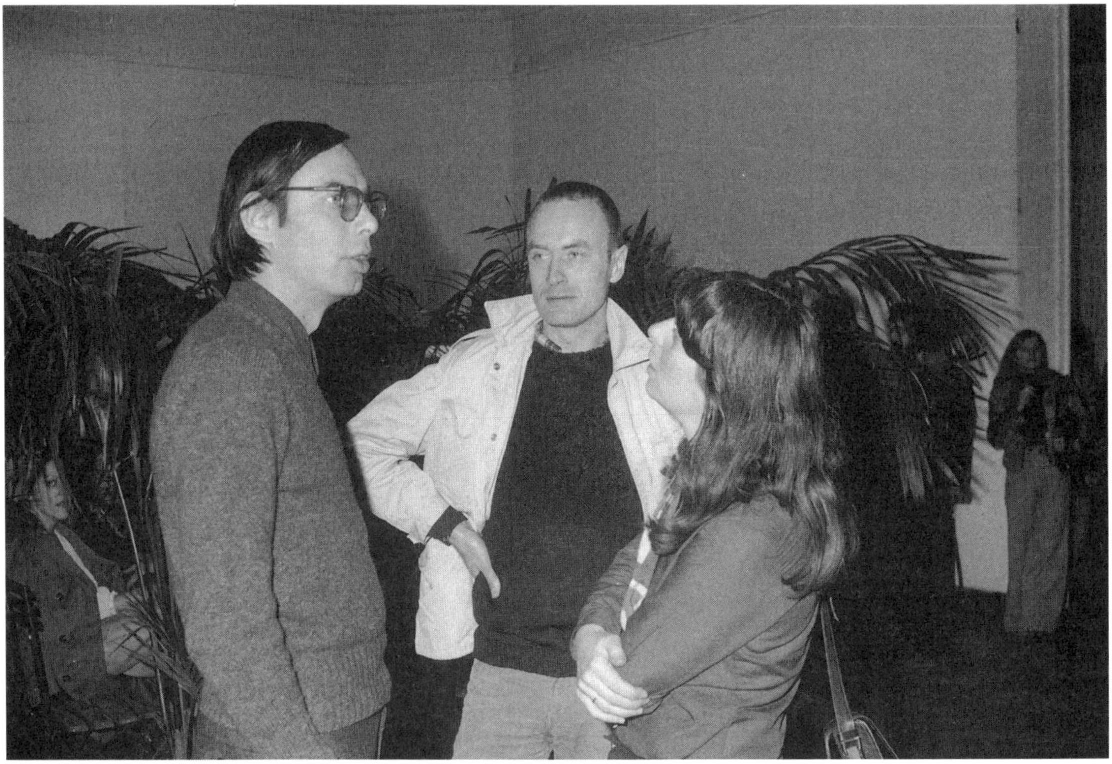

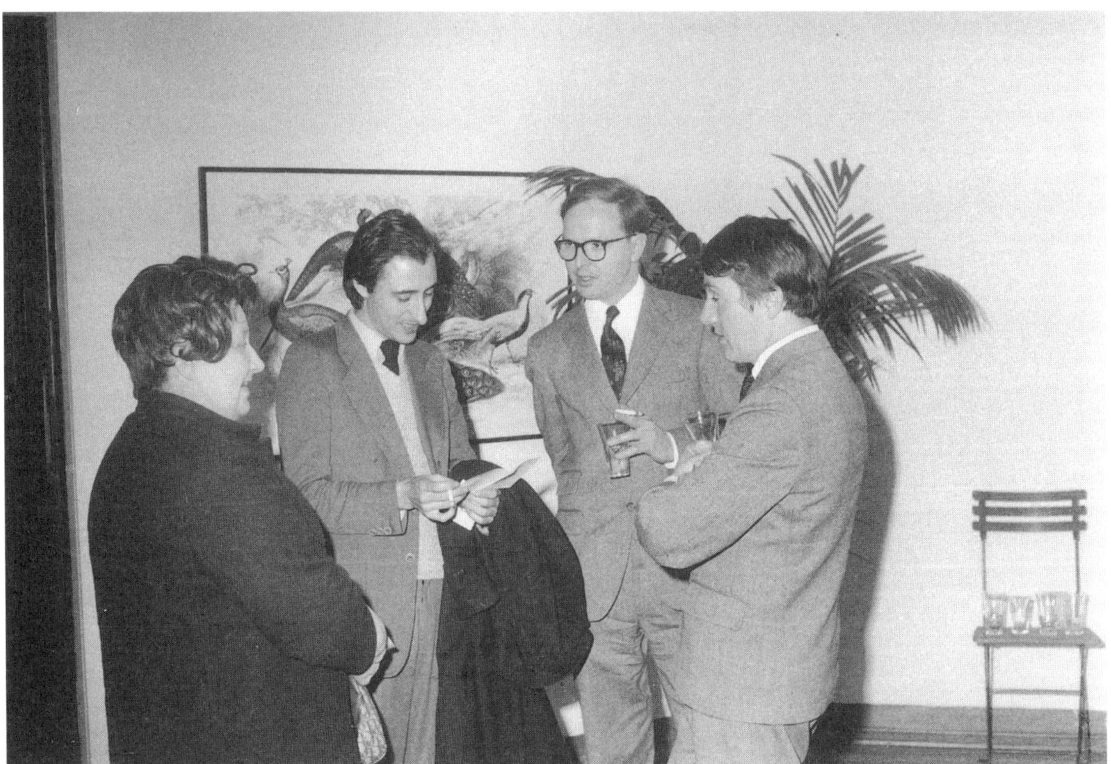

Ileana Sonnabend, Antonio Homem, George and Gilbert
Palais des Beaux-Arts, Brussels, 1975

Fernand Spillemaeckers
On Kawara – Jacques Charlier, Palais des Beaux-Arts, Brussels, 1975

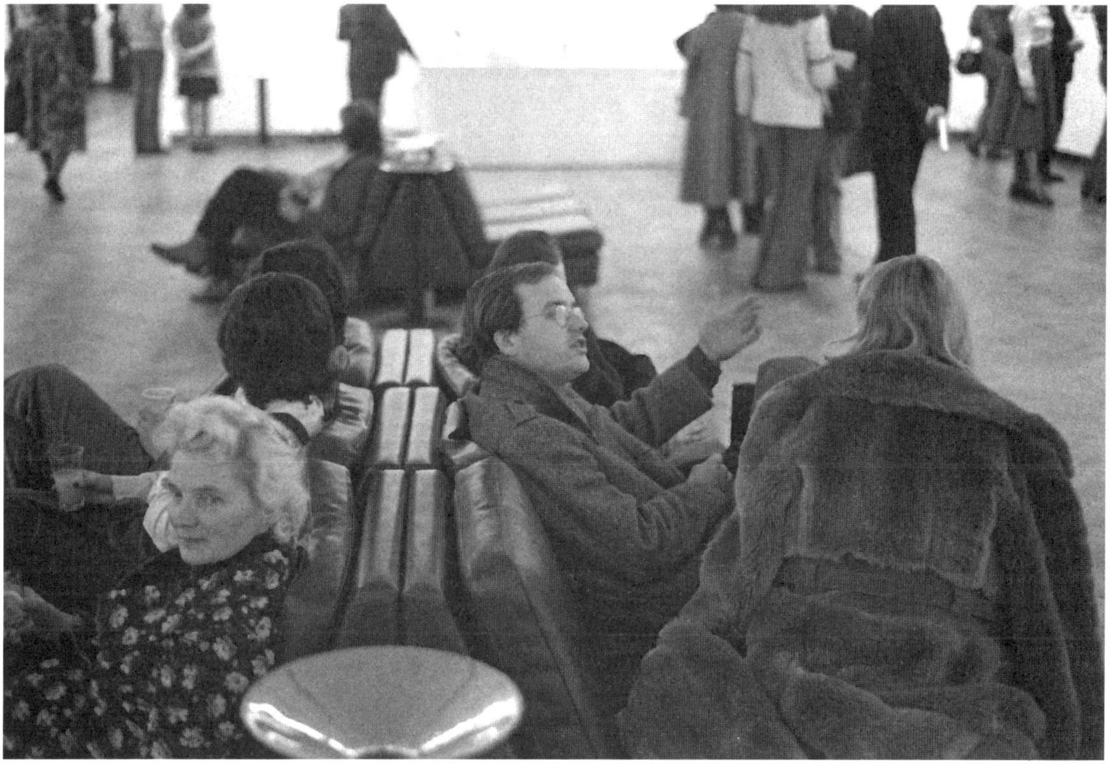

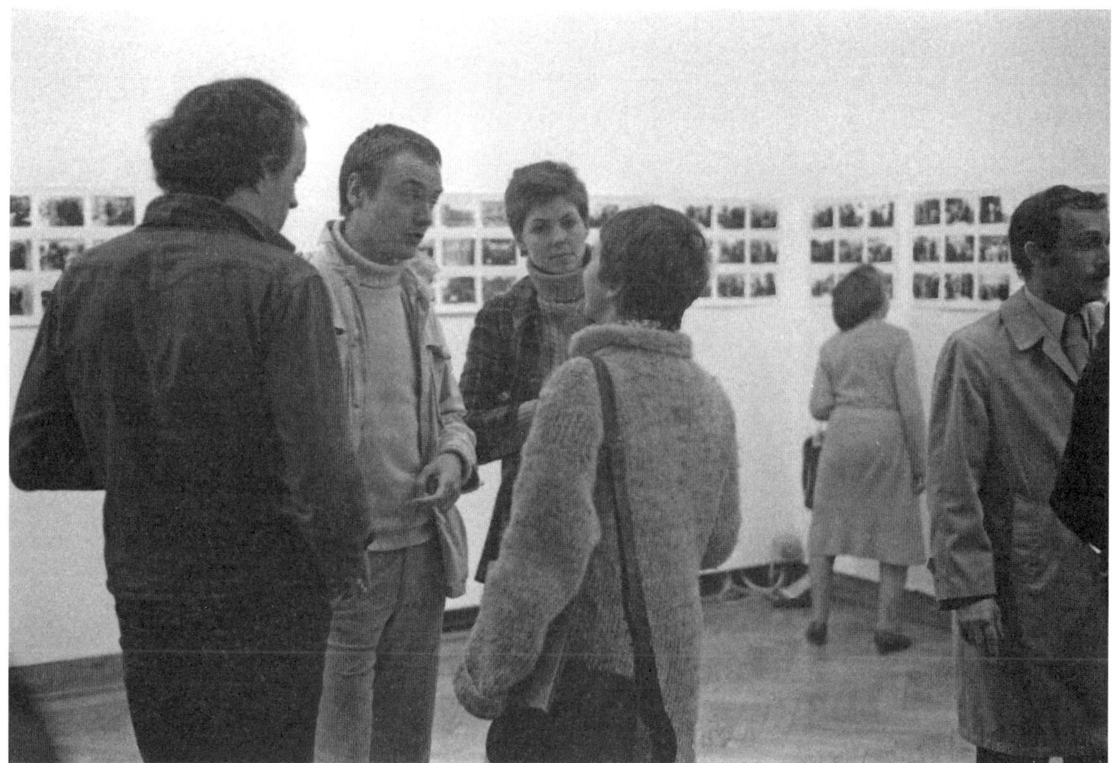

Peter Downsbrough, Benjamin Buchloh, Isa Genzken, Anka Ptaszkowska
On Kawara – Jacques Charlier, Palais des Beaux-Arts, Brussels, 1975

Lynda Morris, Anton Herbert, Peter Downsbrough, Jacques Charlier
On Kawara – Jacques Charlier, Palais des Beaux-Arts, Brussels, 1975

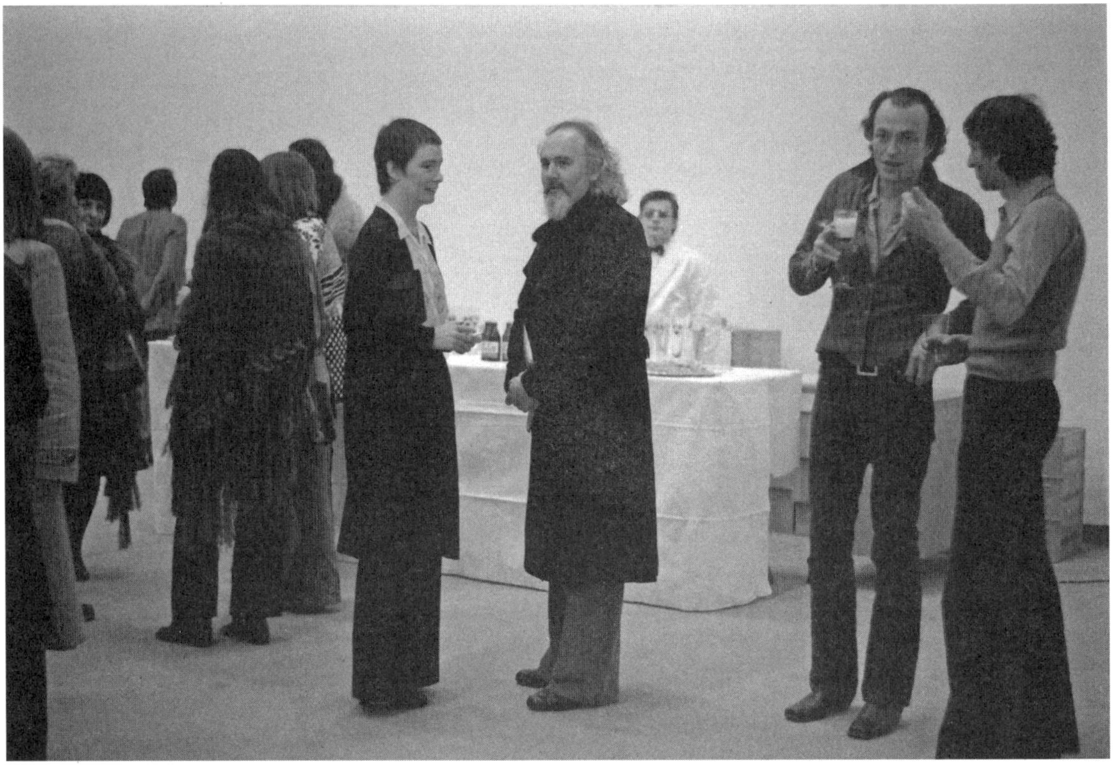

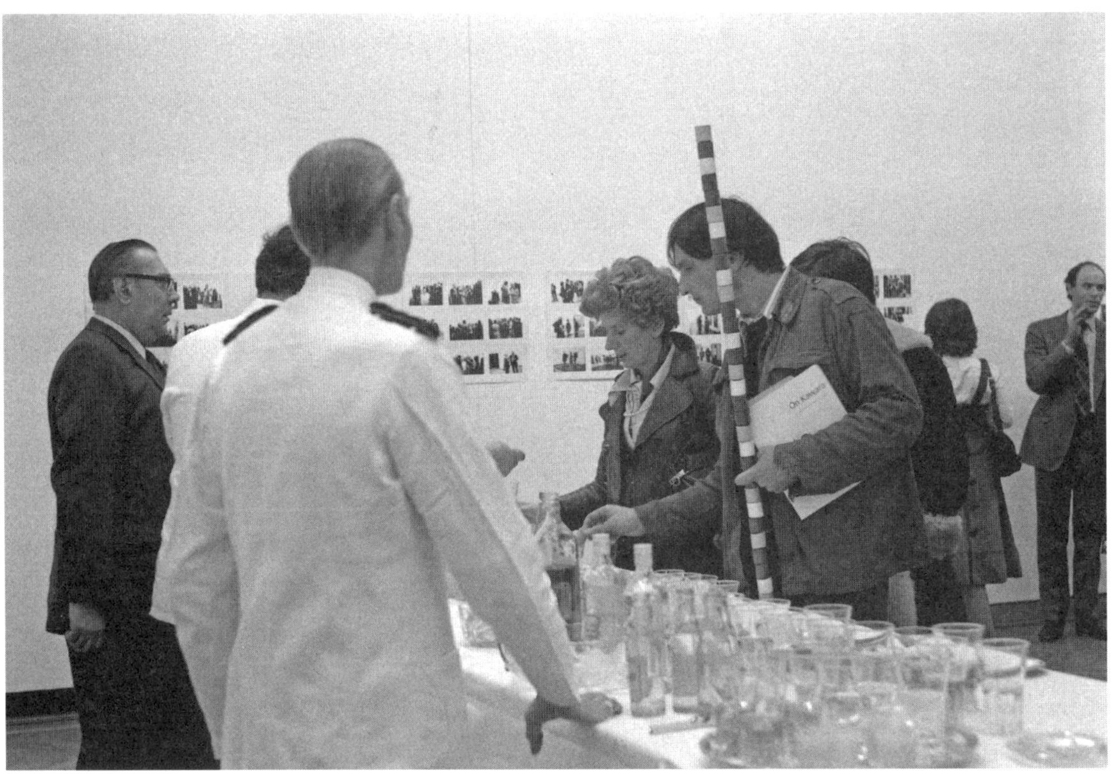

André Cadere
On Kawara – Jacques Charlier, Palais des Beaux-Arts, Brussels, 1975

Annick Herbert, André Goeminne and wife, Konrad Fischer, Anton Herbert, Karel Geirlandt
On Kawara – Jacques Charlier, Palais des Beaux-Arts, Brussels, 1975

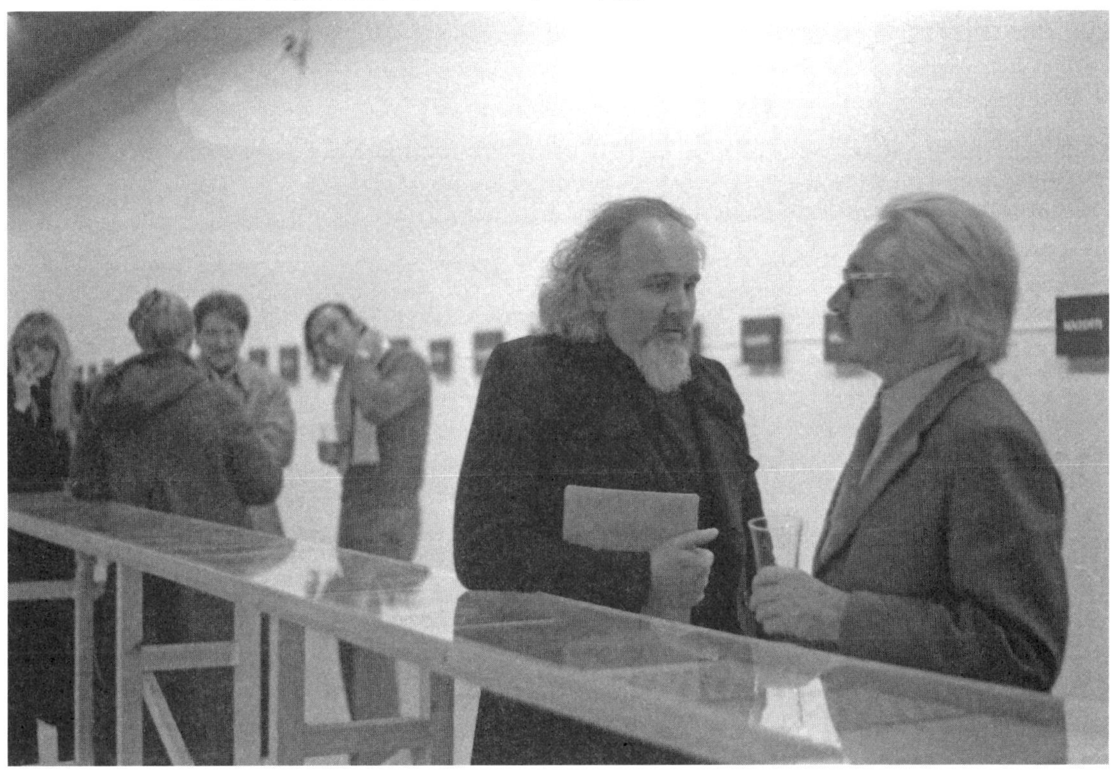

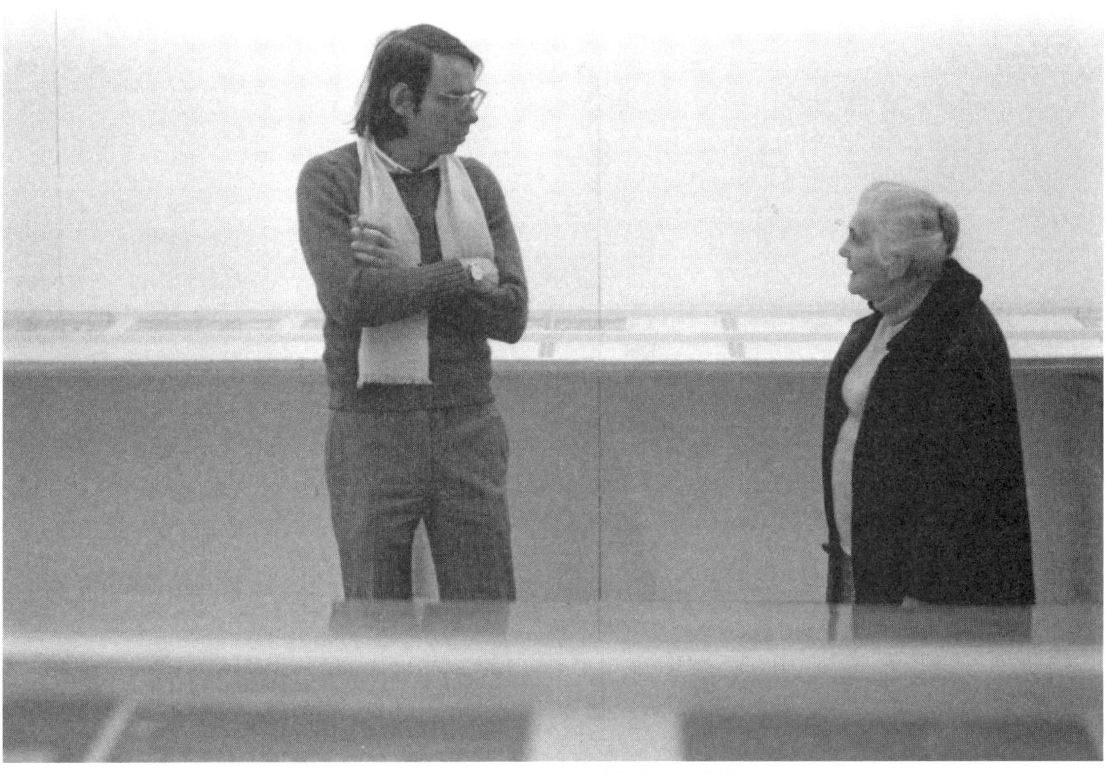

Konrad Fischer, Elisabeth Rona
On Kawara – Jacques Charlier, Palais des Beaux-Arts, Brussels, 1975

Joseph Kosuth

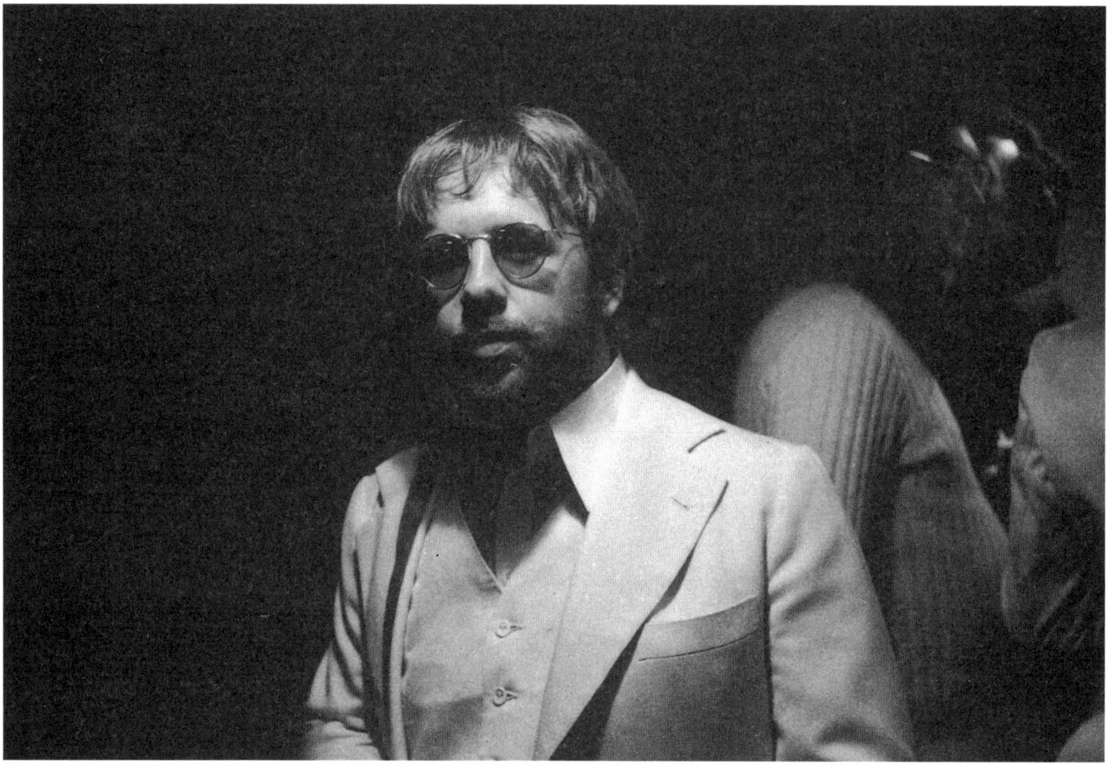

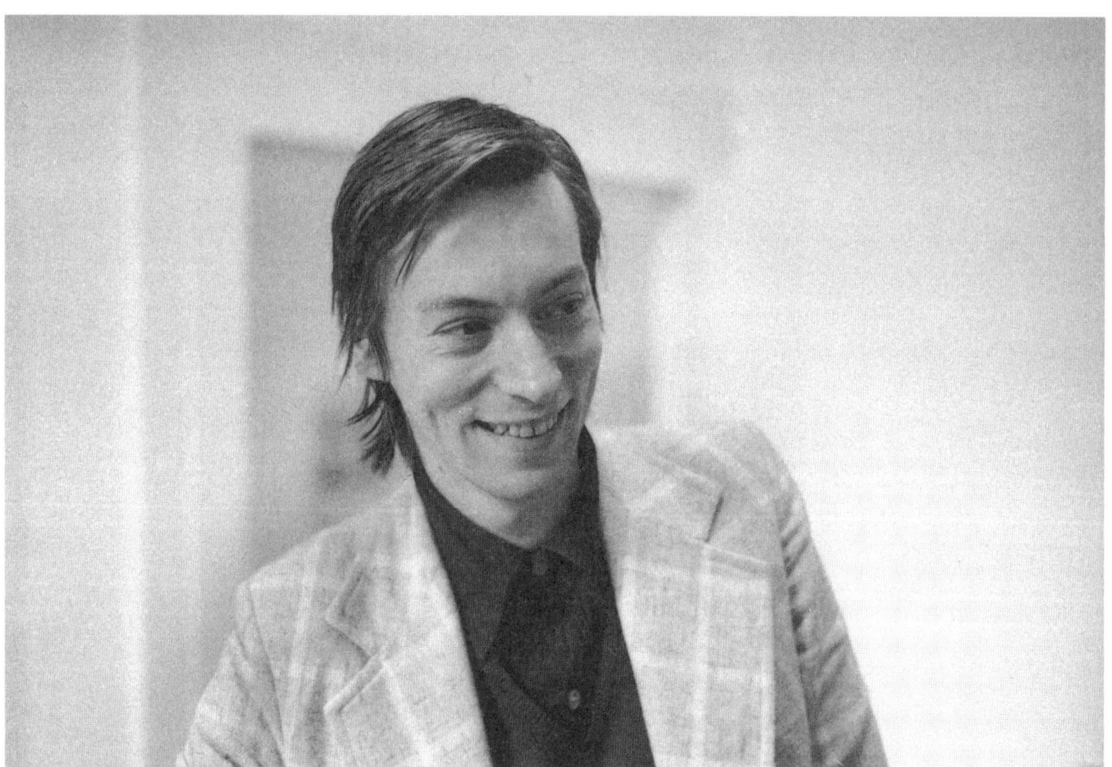

Barry Barker

Michael Werner

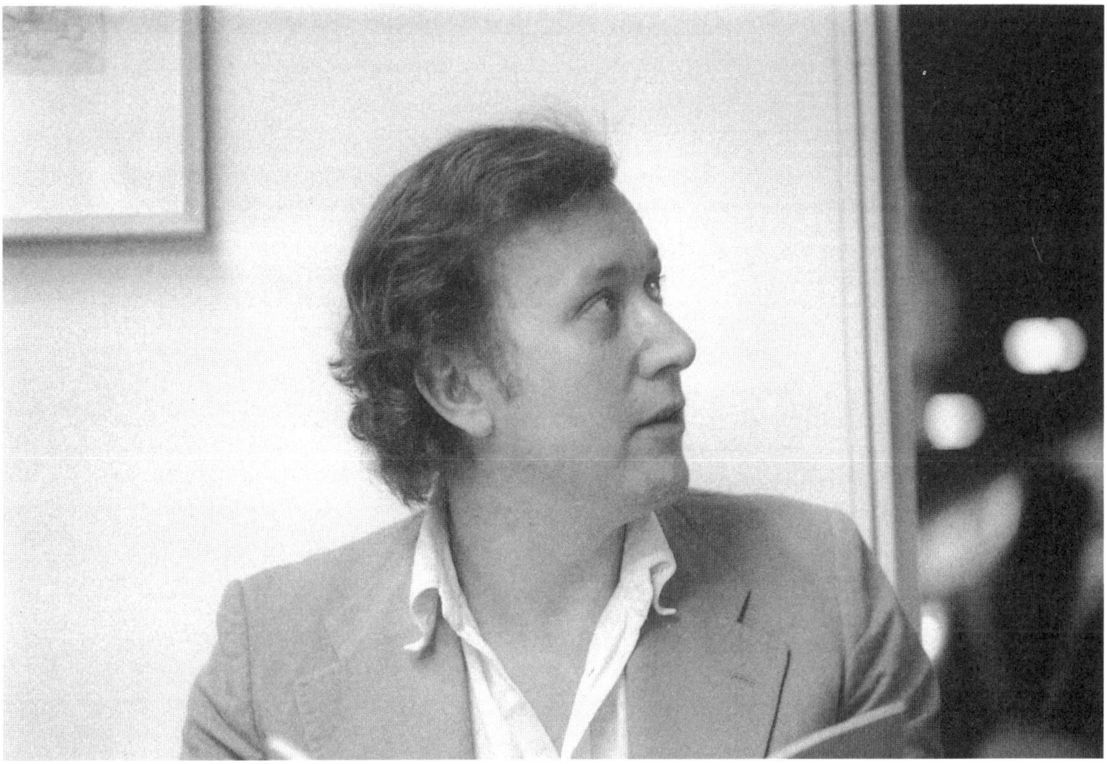

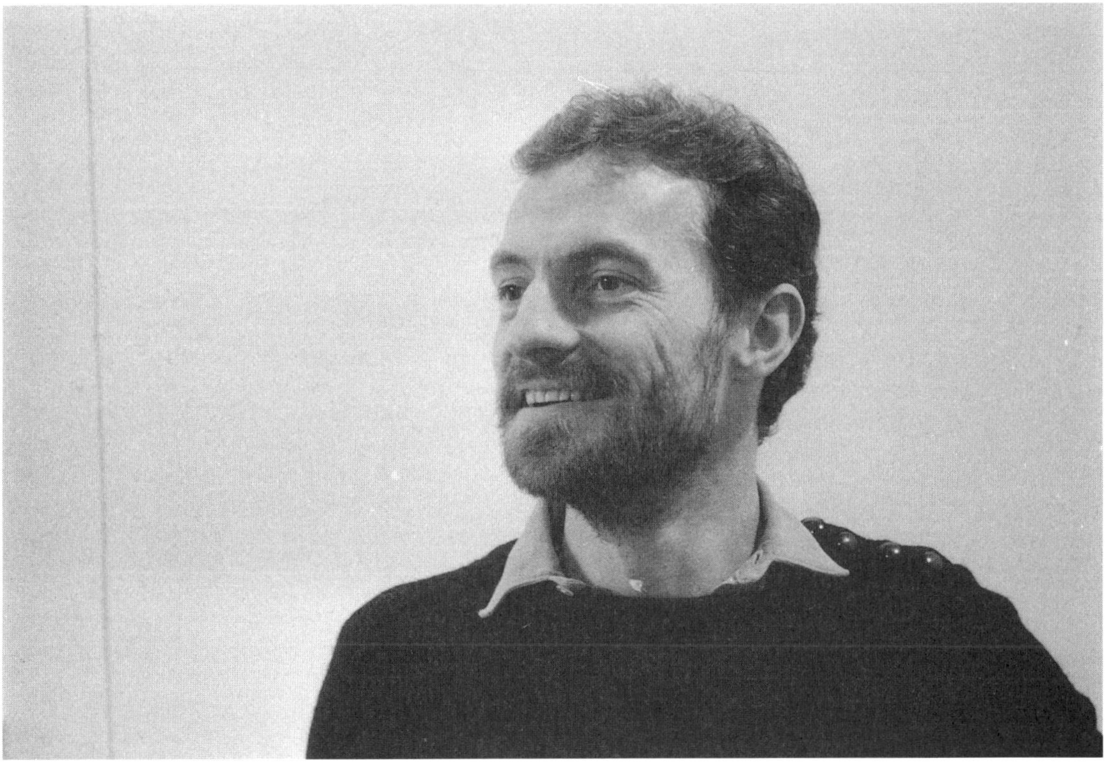

Nigel Greenwood

Panamarenko

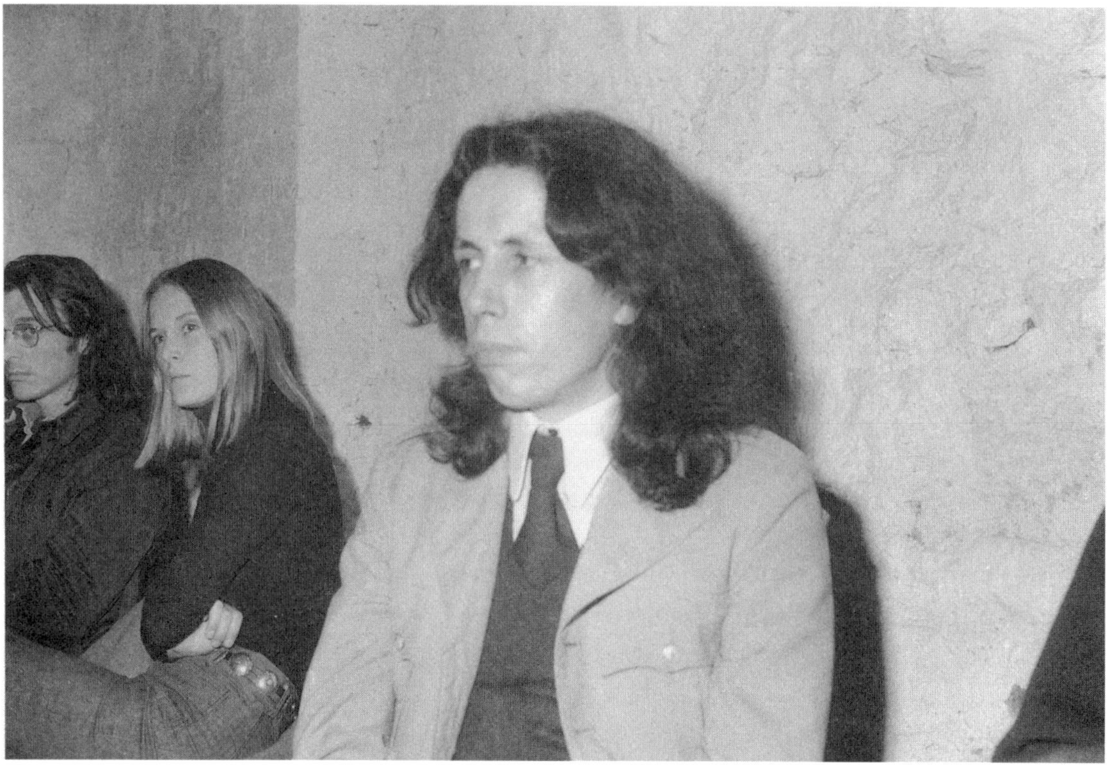

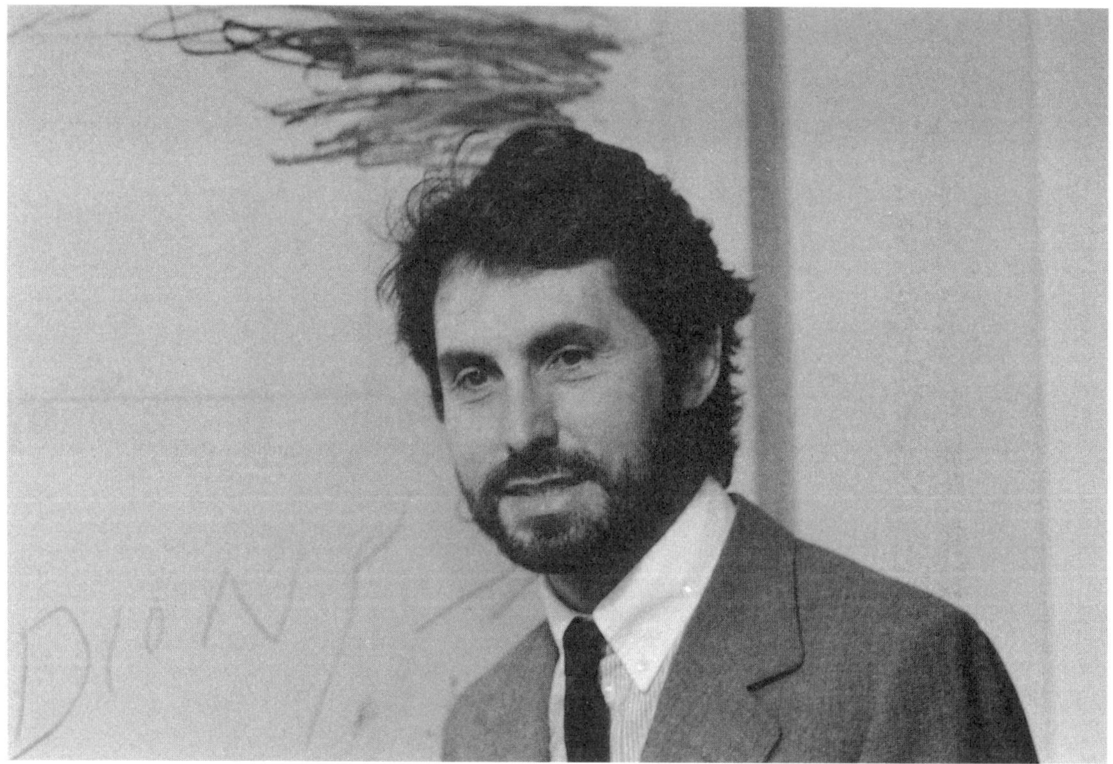

Gian Enzo Sperone

Caroline Tisdall, Jean-Claude Garot, Joseph Beuys

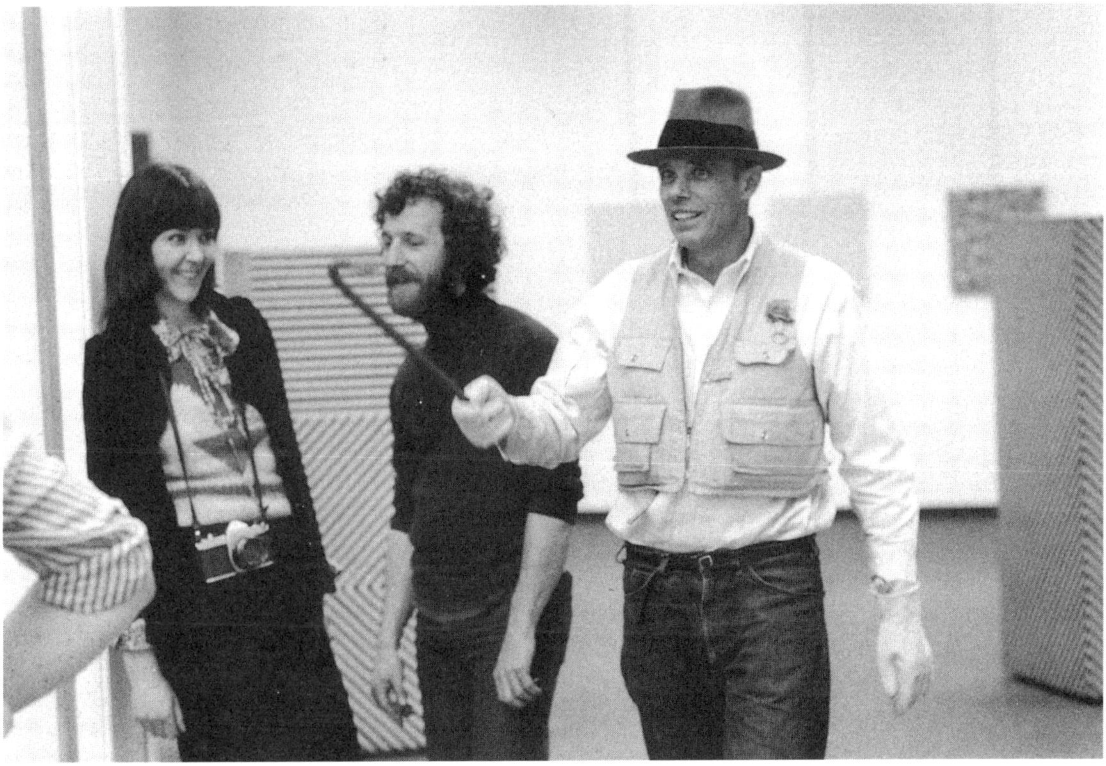

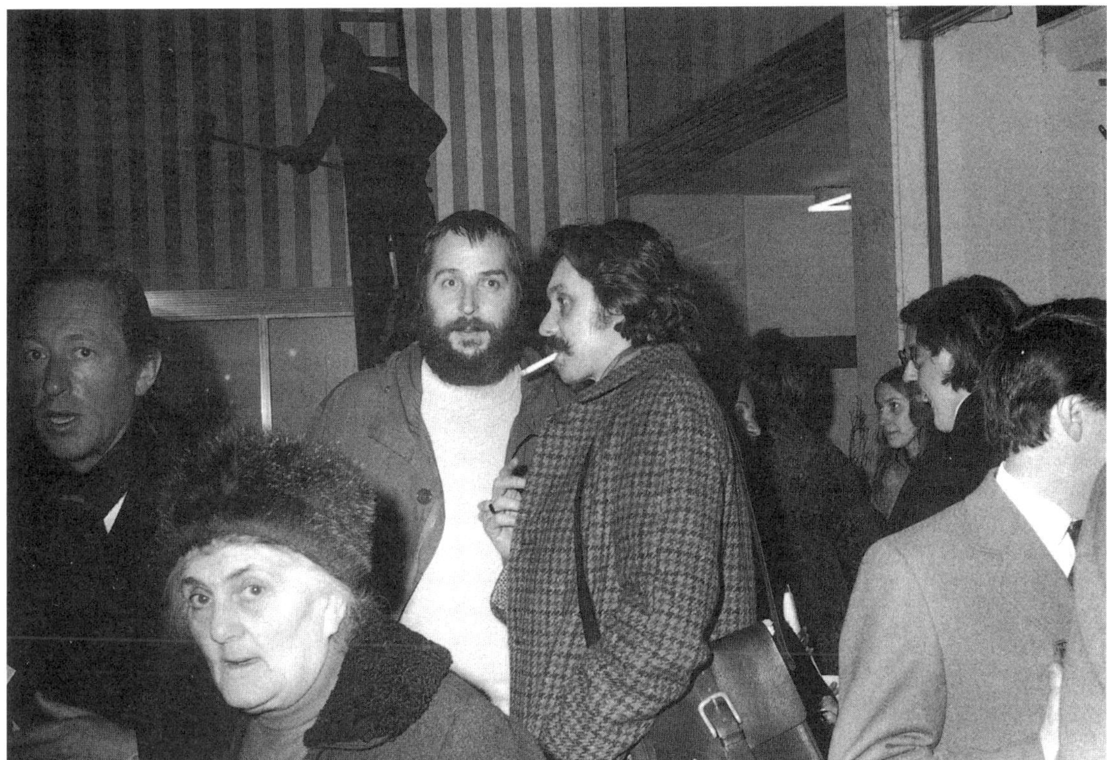

Elisabeth Rona, Daniel Buren, Niele Toroni, René Denizot, Gilbert & George

Appendices

Notes on databases

DATABASE 1.1: **Exhibitions in Dealer Galleries, 1967–77**
This is a double entry database. Dealer galleries are classified horizontally by countries and artists are classified vertically in alphabetical order, with the European artists first, then the American artists. For each artist, exhibitions in each dealer gallery are listed chronologically, with the earliest first. This classification allows the viewing of all the exhibitions of Conceptual artists organised at each dealer gallery (reading vertically), but also the viewing of all the exhibitions an artist had at the various dealer galleries (reading horizontally).

DATABASE 1.2: **Exhibitions in temporary exhibition spaces and museums, 1967–77**
This is organised according to the same principle as Database 1.1.

DATABASE 1.3: **Exhibitions of Conceptual artists in dealer galleries and public institutions, 1967–77**
This is a chronological listing, organised alphabetically by European and American artists. It lists solo exhibitions and group (*g*) exhibitions for each artist in chronological order, giving a sense of the development of artists' careers.

Appendix 1: Databases

Database 1

Exhibitions in dealer galleries, 1967–77 (European artists)

	Konrad Fischer Düsseldorf, Rome, New York	**Paul Maenz** Cologne, Brussels	**Heiner Friedrich** Munich, Cologne, New York	**Gian Enzo Sperone** Turin, Rome, Milan, New York	**Françoise Lambert** Milan	**Yvon Lambert** Paris	**Ileana Sonnaben[d]** Paris
Art & Language		15.06–01.07.72		22.06–05.07.71			
		13.01–07.02.73		01.02–[ ].73 (R)(*g*)			
		17.02–02.03.73 (B)		12.10–[ ].73			
		10.04–12.05.73					
		11.09–20.11.73					
		23.09–17.11.73					
		05.02–08.03.74 (B)					
		04.07–27.07.74					
		04.09–30.09.76 (*g*)					
Marcel Broodthaers	(1978)		06.05–25.05.72		19.04–05.05.72	29.10–05.12.71 (*g*)	
			12.74		01.73	15.12–[ ].71	
						10.72	
						14.06–20.06.73	
						06.11.73	
Daniel Buren	30.09–12.10.69	31.01–14.02.76		12.06–[ ].72	07.70	05.69	
	31.01–14.02.76	04.09–30.09.76 (*g*)		01.02–[ ].73 (R)(*g*)	02.71 (*g*)	02.12.70–05.01.71	
		01.03–26.03.77		14.11–[ ].73 (R)(*g*)	26.02–[ ].03.71 (*g*)	29.10–05.12.71 (*g*)	
				20.11–[ ].74	06.04–16.04.72 (*g*)	[ ]–10.11.73	
				14.12–[ ].74 (R)(*g*)			
				06.05–[ ].75 (R)(*g*)			
Hanne Darboven	05.12–[ ].67	04.09–30.09.76 (*g*)	1969 (*g*)	14.11–[ ].70		[ ]–18.05.73	
	22.10–15.11.68		03.06–17.06.69	01.02–[ ].73 (R)(*g*)			
	03.07–30.07.70		1971 (*g*)	15.05–[ ].74			
	01.01–31.12.71		14.01–13.02.72 (C)	06.05–[ ].75 (R)(*g*)			
	10.06–[ ].75			18.11–[ ].75 (R)(*g*)			
				22.12–[ ].75 (*g*)			
Jan Dibbets	15.08–17.09.68	04.09–30.09.76 (*g*)		13.03–23.03.71	26.02–[ ].03.70	19.02–[ ].70	
	06.04–22.04.71			01.02–[ ].73 (R)(*g*)	02.71 (*g*)	29.10–05.12.71 (*g*)	
	16.03–15.04.73			06.04–[ ].73 (R)	02–03.71 (*g*)	03.02–[ ].72	
	19.10–16.11.74			14.11–[ ].73 (R)(*g*)	06.04–16.04.72 (*g*)	11.74	
	12.02–10.03.77			15.02–[ ].74		12.05–[ ].77	
				22.12–[ ].75 (*g*)			
				29.04–[ ].76 (R)			
Gilbert & George	10.05–05.06.70		14.05.70	28.05–[ ].71	06.70		Autumn 73
	03.01–[ ].72		09 or 12.70 (*g*)	07.12–[ ].72 (R)			13.03–[ ].75
	17.03–17.04.74		10.70 (C)	01.02–[ ].73 (R)(*g*)			
	02–03.76			27.06–[ ].73			
	26.11–23.12.77			14.11–[ ].73 (R)(*g*)			
				14.09–[ ].74 (R)			
				06.05–[ ].75 (R)(*g*)			
				08.11–29.11.75 (NY)			
				10.76 (M)(*g*)			
				23.02–[ ].77 (R)(p)			
Richard Long	21.09–18.10.68		09.71 (C)(*g*)	13.04–[ ].71	15.11–01.12.69	05.11–26.11.69	
	05.07–01.08.69			01.72	06.71 (*g*)	29.10–05.12.71 (*g*)	
	11.05–09.06.70			16.03–[ ].76 (R)		03.05–[ ].72	
	29.05–25.06.73			04.12.76–08.01.77 (NY)		24.04–20.05.75	
	20.12.74–19.01.75			16.02–[ ].77 (R)(*g*)		03–04.76	
	15.05–11.06.76						
Mario Merz	07.03–31.03.70			19.01–[ ].68	01.10–03.11.70		22.04–[ ].06.69
	11.11–7.11.76			03.69	02.71 (*g*)		
				22.05–[ ].69 (*g*)			
				29.10–[ ].69 (*g*)			
				27.03–[ ].71			
				12.04–[ ].72			
				18.11–[ ].75 (R)(*g*)			
				22.12–[ ].75 (*g*)			
				20.02–[ ].76 (R)			
				07.04–[ ].76			
				14.04–[ ].76 (R)(*g*)			
				10.76 (M)(*g*)			
				16.02–[ ].77 (R)(*g*)			

g: group show; t: text; p: performance; mg: mailing
A: Antwerp; B: Brussels; C: Cologne; LB: Le Bailli, Brussels; M: Milan; NY: New York; R: Rome

Wide White Space Antwerp, Brussels	MTL Brussels, Antwerp	Art & Project Amsterdam, Antwerp	Nigel Greenwood London	Jack Wendler London	Lisson Gallery London	Rolf Preisig Basel	Collaborations Fischer/Sperone classified under Sperone; MTL/Art & Project under MTL
	15.03–29.03.75 17.06–10.07.76				16.10–10.11.73 01.74 02.75 08.02–05.03.77 (*g*)		*Maenz, Sperone, MTL, *Lisson
26.05–26.06.66 30.01–16.02.67 (*g*) 19.06–30.06.67 (*g*) 22.09–10.11.67 (*g*) 05.01–07.02.68 (*g*) 07.03–31.03.68 16.10–14.11.68 (*g*) 02.12–20.12.69 29.09–31.10.70 (*g*) 04.12–23.12.70 (*g*) 27.09–27.10.71 21.03–15.04.72 (*g*) 17.06–30.06.72 13.01–28.01.73 19.09–03.10.74 25.09–03.10.74 (B) 08.01–01.02.75 (*g*)	13.03–10.04.70 18.05–17.06.72 20.03–[ ].73 27.09–24.10.74 04.12–20.12.75 04.12.75–10.01.76	03.73	01.10.75–31.01.76 05.04–14.05.77	01–22.12.72		19–24.06.74 (*g*) 15.11–20.12.74	Friedrich, F. Lambert, *Y. Lambert, *Wide White Space, *MTL, *Art & Project, Greenwood, Wendler
17.01–06.02.69 11.05–05.06.71 02.06–15.06.72 22.06–28.07.73 23.04–[ ].06.74	13.06–01.07.70 01–02.75 (*g*) 03.11–29.11.75	06–07.70 (t) 02.06.71 (mg) 09.11.71 (mg) 03.74 18.04.76 (mg) 07–09.76 (*g*)	23.11–06.12.71 (*g*)	02.72 09–30.03.73	02.03–03.04.76	22.02–23.03.74 19–24.06.74 (*g*) 14.01–08.02.75 07–31.12.76	Fischer, Maenz, *Sperone, F. Lambert, *Y. Lambert, *Wide White Space, MTL, *Art & Project, Greenwood, Wendler, Lisson
	01.02–29.02.72 Winter 72 22.05.73 (LB) 12.03–06.04.74 (A) 26.03–06.04.74	24.10–13.11.70 16.12.72–09.01.73 12.03–23.03.74 06.01–24.01.76 07–09.76 (*g*)		23.05–06.06.72		19–24.06.74 (*g*)	*Fischer, Maenz, Friedrich, *Sperone, F. Lambert, *Y. Lambert, Wide White Space, *MTL, *Art & Project, *Lisson
	18.12.71–15.01.72 17.10.72 17.10–[ ].73 02.12.74–04.01.75 (A) 07.02–27.02.75	22.07.69 (mg) 26.11–16.12.69 07.04.71 (mg) 27.11–18.12.71 12.06.72 (mg) 1973 10.74 11.02–01.03.75 07–09.76 (*g*)		25.02–09.03.72 12.73		29.03–27.04.74 19–24.06.74 (*g*)	*Fischer, Friedrich, *Sperone, F. Lambert, Y. Lambert, Wide White Space
	10.72 17.03–[ ].73 (*g*) 02.74 (A) 30.05–25.06.75 1977 (p) 16.02.77 (B)	12.05–23.05.70 22.12.71–21.01.72 Winter 72 1974 07–09.76 (*g*) 01.11–26.11.77	11.70 23.11–06.12.71 (*g*) 29.11–12.71 04.07–[ ].72 27.09–[ ].72 20.11–12.72 16–21.07.73 05.06–05.07.74 06.01–[ ].77				Fischer, *Friedrich, Sperone, *F. Lambert, Y. Lambert, MTL, Art & Project, Lisson
15.03–12.04.73 15.04–16.05.75 25.05–10.06.76	17.03–[ ].73 (*g*)	17.07–06.08.71 1973 1974 18.03–15.04.75 1976 07–09.76 (*g*) 08.02–05.03.77			23.01–24.02.73 01–30.11.74 24–26.06.76 08.02–05.03.77 (*g*) 21.05–18.06.77	19–24.06.74 (*g*) 12.06–12.07.75 17.05–21.06.77	*Fischer, *Sperone, F. Lambert, *Y. Lambert, *Wide White Space, MTL, *Art & Project, Greenwood, Wendler, Lisson
	17.02–10.03.73 (LB/*g*)	20.01–10.03.73 (*g*)		02–16.05.72 02.74 14.06–05.07.74			

Exhibitions in dealer galleries, 1967–77 (American artists)

	Konrad Fischer Düsseldorf, Rome, New York	**Paul Maenz** Cologne, Brussels	**Heiner Friedrich** Munich, Cologne, New York	**Gian Enzo Sperone** Turin, Rome, Milan, New York	**Françoise Lambert** Milan	**Yvon Lambert** Paris	**Ileana Sonnabend** Paris
Carl Andre	21.10–28.11.67	04.09–30.09.76 (*g*)	13.02–08.03.68 (*g*)	29.09–[ ].69		03.02–01.03.71	
	12.10–11.11.69		16.03–18.04.68	01.02–[ ].73 (R)(*g*)		29.10–05.12.71 (*g*)	
	12.07–12.08.71		06–07.71	04.12–[ ].73		16.09–13.10.76	
	05.72		20.07–29.08.71 (C)(*g*)	02.75			
	01.06–28.06.73		04.12–20.12.76 (NY/*g*)	06.05–[ ].75 (R)(*g*)			
	21.06–20.07.74			20.09–[ ].75 (R)			
	26.06–31.07.76			04.10–01.11.75 (NY)			
				22.12–[ ].75 (*g*)			
				12.03–02.04.77 (NY/*g*)			
				04.05–28.05.77 (NY)			
				22.11–[ ].77 (R)			
Douglas Huebler	15.01–31.01.70			24.03–08.04.70	26.02–[ ].03.71 (*g*)	11.03–18.03.70	
	06.01–21.01.71			06.01–[ ].71	02.75	29.10–05.12.71 (*g*)	
	13.04–04.05.72			01.02–[ ].73 (R)(*g*)		16.03–31.03.72	
	05.09–26.09.74			21.03–[ ].73 (R)		10.74	
				14.11–[ ].73 (R)(*g*)			
				10.04–[ ].74			
				06.05–[ ].75 (R)(*g*)			
				18.11–[ ].75 (R)(*g*)			
				22.12–[ ].75 (*g*)			
				22.04–08.05.76 (NY)			
Joseph Kosuth		16.02–05.03.71		09.11–16.11.69			
		17.03–19.04.73 (B)		04.07–18.07.70			
		10.04–12.05.73 (*g*)		21.12–[ ].72 (R)			
		04.07–27.07.74 (*g*)		12.72 (NY)(*g*)			
		04.09–30.09.76 (*g*)		01.02–[ ].73 (R)(*g*)			
				28.11–[ ].74 (R)			
				06.05–[ ].75 (R)(*g*)			
				18.11–[ ].75 (R)(*g*)			
				22.12–[ ].75 (*g*)			
				16.02–[ ].77 (R)(*g*)			
Sol LeWitt	06.01–03.02.68	04.09–30.09.76 (*g*)	1968	12.06–[ ].70	02.71 (*g*)	04.06–27.06.70	
	22.04–16.05.69		13.02–08.03.68 (*g*)	12.72 (NY)(*g*)		09.70 (*g*)	
	03.09–01.10.71		09.70	01.02–[ ].73 (R)(*g*)		29.10–05.12.71 (*g*)	
	09–10.72		04.12–20.12.76 (NY/*g*)	12.06–[ ].74		09.01–[ ].73	
	07.05–07.06.75			23.09–[ ].75		03.74	
	12.03–01.04.77			18.11–[ ].75 (R)(*g*)			
				22.12–[ ].75 (*g*)			
				10.06–[ ].76 (R)			
				12.03–[ ].77 (NY)(*g*)			
Bruce Nauman	10.07–08.08.68		1971 (C)(*g*)	25.02–10.03.70	02.71 (*g*)	09.70 (*g*)	25.11–15.12.68
	05.02–03.03.70			01.02–[ ].73 (R)(*g*)	06.12.71–05.01.72		02.12–[ ].69
	05.03–01.04.71			18.11–[ ].75 (R)(*g*)	26.02–30.03.74 (*g*)		02.03–[ ].71
	04.02–06.03.74			30.10–27.11.76 (NY)			1974
	16.12.75–24.01.76						
Robert Ryman	21.11–17.12.68		13.02–08.03.68 (*g*)	01.02–[ ].73 (R)(*g*)	12.69–01.70	12.69	
	11.11 12.12.69		10–11.68	03.05–[ ].77 (R)	02.71 (*g*)	09.70 (*g*)	
	11.73		21.11–20.12.69		06.71 (*g*)	29.10–05.12.71 (*g*)	
			26.06–27.07.71 (C)		06.04–16.04.72 (*g*)		
			1972 (C)(*g*)				
			06.72				
			09–10.72 (C)				
Lawrence Weiner	10.04–[ ].69			03.12–10.12.69	26.02–[ ].03.71 (*g*)	19.03–26.03.70	
	25.11–11.12.70			14.12–22.12.70	9.11–14.11.72	03.02–13.02.71	
	04.72			01.02–[ ].73 (R)(*g*)		29.10–05.12.71 (*g*)	
	28.01–20.02.75			29.11–[ ].73 (*g*)		1972	
	27.04–13.05.77			30.11–[ ].73		12.09–26.09.74	
				26.04–[ ].75		1977	

g: group show; t: text; p: performance; mg: mailing
A: Antwerp; B: Brussels; C: Cologne; LB: Le Bailli, Brussels; M: Milan; NY: New York; R: Rome

Wide White Space Antwerp, Brussels	MTL Brussels, Antwerp	Art & Project Amsterdam, Antwerp	Nigel Greenwood London	Jack Wendler London	Lisson Gallery London	Rolf Preisig Basel	Collaborations Fischer/Sperone classified under Sperone; MTL/Art & Project under MTL
03.05–25.05.68 01.03–31.03.69 (*g*) 19.09–16.10.69 29.09–31.10.70 (*g*) 22.04–06.05.71 08.01–04.02.74 (B) 10.01–04.02.74	Winter 73 (*g*)	07.01–[ ].75 07–09.76 (*g*)			09.05–[ ].72 08.06–31.07.74 06–07.75	19–24.06.74 (*g*) 10–20.06.76 (*g*)	*Fischer, Maenz, *Friedrich, *Sperone, Y. Lambert, *Wide White Space, MTL, Art & Project, Lisson
	22.03–22.04.72 09.04–09.05.74 16.09–04.10.75 03.12–24.12.75	25.04–08.05.70 22.05–11.06.71 27.06.72 (mg) 15.08–[ ].73 07–09.76 (*g*)		04.72 13.04–18.05.73 1974		19–24.06.74 (*g*) 15.11–20.12.74	*Fischer, *Sperone, F. Lambert, Y. Lambert, *MTL, *Art & Project, Wendler
	1975 25.02–20.03.76 (*g*) 18.05–15.06.77 (*g*)	22.11–30.11.69					*Maenz, *Sperone, MTL, Art & Project
01.03–31.03.69 (*g*)	05.07–26.09.72 early 73 03.09–[ ].73 13.11–08.12.73 (A) 16.05–09.06.74 19.11–15.12.76	02.01.70 (mg) 04.01.71 (mg) 07.09–02.10.71 25.09.72 04.03–15.03.75 07–09.76 (*g*)			15.06–14.07.70 01.71 (*g*) 06–07.71 03–31.05.73 04–05.74 12.03–09.04.77	19–24.06.74 (*g*) 18.10–22.11.75	*Fischer, Maenz, Friedrich, *Sperone, F. Lambert, *Y. Lambert, Wide White Space, *MTL, *Art & Project, *Lisson
01.03–31.03.69 (*g*) 08.03–11.04.74 08.01–01.02.75 (*g*)			(1980)			19–24.06.74 (*g*)	*Fischer, Friedrich, *Sperone, F. Lambert, Y. Lambert, Wide White Space
	01–02.75 *g* 27.02–[ ].1975 (LB/*g*)	28.09–[ ].73			05.12.72–20.01.73 03.12.74–18.01.75 (*g*	19–24.06.74 (*g*) 10–20.06.76 (*g*)	Fischer, *Friedrich, Sperone, *F. Lambert, Y. Lambert, MTL, Art & Project, Lisson
20.06–30.06.69 24.06–25.06.72 06.73 27.11–22.12.73 (B) 04.05–05.06.77		01.09.69 (mg) 22.04–12.05.72 08.05.72 (mg) 11.12–21.12.73 07–09.76 (*g*)	23.11–06.12.71 (*g*)	30.12.71–06.01.72 17–30.09.73 25.09–16.10.73	01.71 (*g*)	10.05–08.06.74 19–24.06.74 (*g*) 28.11–23.12.75	*Fischer, *Sperone, F. Lambert, *Y. Lambert, *Wide White Space, MTL, *Art & Project, Greenwood, Wendler, Lisson

Exhibitions in temporary exhibition spaces and museums, 1967–77

	Städtisches Museum, Mönchengladbach	Kunstverein, Münster	Ludwig Museum, Cologne	Kunsthalle, Düsseldorf	Kunstmuseum, Basel	Kunstmuseum, Lucerne	Stedelijk Museum, Amsterdam
Art & Language					18.03–23.04.72 (*g*)	27.01–24.02.74	
Marcel Broodthaers	21.10–07.11.71 1976 (*g*)			20–29.09.68 (*g*) 14–15.02.70 (*g*) 09.10–18.11.70 (*g*) 15–17.06.71 (*g*) 08–17.10.71 (*g*) 16.05–09.07.72 02–06.05.73 (*g*) 28.09–07.10.73 (*g*)	05.10–03.11.74		
Daniel Buren	28.01–07.03.71 15.11–23.12.73 (*g*) 21.11–14.12.75 1976 (*g*)	01.71 25.03–[ ].72 (*g*)		20–29.09.68 (*g*) 30.09–12.10.69 (*g*)	18.03–23.04.72 (*g*)	29.09–03.11.74 1975	30.04–07.06.76
Hanne Darboven	25.02–07.04.69 22.06–16.07.75 (*g*)	16.10–14.11.71 25.03–[ ].72 (*g*)	27.09–31.10.76	30.09–12.10.69 (*g*) 08–17.10.71 (*g*)	18.03–23.04.72 (*g*) 09.11–29.12.74	11.05–22.06.75	10.01–02.03.75
Jan Dibbets		25.03–[ ].72 (*g*)		30.09–12.10.69 (*g*) 08–17.10.71 (*g*)	18.03–23.04.72 (*g*)	28.09–09.11.75	1967 (*g*) 15.03–27.04.69 (*g* 17.11.72–14.01.7
Gilbert & George		25.03–[ ].72 (*g*) 30.08–29.09.75 (*g*)		14–15.02.70 (*g*) 08–17.10.71 (*g*) 28.09–07.10.73 (*g*)	18.03–23.04.72 (*g*)	1971 (p) 20.05–25.06.72	03–04.69 p 28.10–28.11.71 10–11.03.77
Richard Long	16.07–30.08.70 22.06–16.07.75 (*g*)			30.09–12.10.69 (*g*)			15.03–27.04.69 (*g* 07.12.73–27.01.7
Mario Merz				20–29.09.68 (*g*) 08–17.10.71 (*g*)		30.05–05.07.70 (*g*) 16.03–20.04.75 (*g*)	15.03–27.04.69 (*g*
Carl Andre	18.10–15.12.68 1976 (*g*)			20–29.09.68 (*g*) 17.01–23.02.69 (*g*) 09.10–18.11.70 (*g*)	12.69–01.70 (*g*) 20.01–04.03.73 (*g*)		15.03–27.04.69 (*g*
Douglas Huebler	22.06–16.07.75 (*g*)	25.03–[ ].72 (*g*) 17.12.72–28.01.73		30.09–12.10.69 (*g*)	18.03–23.04.72 (*g*)		15.03–27.04.69
Joseph Kosuth		25.03–[ ].72 (*g*) 10.11–09.12.73		30.09–12.10.69 (*g*) 28.09–07.10.73 (*g*)		20.05–24.06.73	
Sol LeWitt	14.03–20.04.75 (*g*) 22.06–16.07.75 (*g*)	25.03–[ ].72 (*g*) 1975 (*g*)		20–29.09.68 (*g*) 17.01–23.02.69 (*g*) 30.09–12.10.69 (*g*)	20.01–04.03.73 (*g*)		29.11.74–26.01.7
Bruce Nauman	1976 (*g*)			20–29.09.68 (*g*) 08–17.10.71 (*g*) 28.08–23.09.73	20.01–04.03.73 (*g*) Spring 75 07.02–04.04.76 (*g*)	16.03–20.04.75 (*g*)	15.03–27.04.69 (*g* 30.04–06.06.71 (*g*
Robert Ryman	15.11–23.12.73 (*g*)	12.05–16.06.74 30.03–28.04.74 (*g*)		30.09–12.10.69 (*g*) 28.09–07.10.73 (*g*)	12.69–01.70 (*g*)		15.03–27.04.69 (*g* 01.02–24.03.74 25.05–22.06.75 (*g*
Lawrence Weiner	04.10–04.11.73 22.06–16.07.75 (*g*)	25.03–[ ].72 (*g*) 15.09–14.10.73		30.09–12.10.69 (*g*) 08–17.10.71 (*g*) 28.09–07.10.73 (*g*)	18.03–23.04.72 (*g*)		15.03–27.04.69 (*g* 16.12.72–07.01.7
Total exhibitions	19	17	1	37	16	11	21

Van Abbemuseum, Eindhoven	Palais des Beaux-Arts, Brussels	MOMA, Oxford	Tate Gallery, London	Total exhibitions
		21.09–26.10.75		3
968 (*g*)	25.05–24.06.73 (*g*)	26.04–01.06.75	09.01–18.02.77	17
	09.01–03.02.74 (*g*)			
	27.09–03.11.74			
nd 04–01.06.76	09.01–03.02.74 (*g*)	31.03–15.04.73		15
968 (*g*)	16.05–16.06.74 (*g*)	30.06–04.08.74		14
3.12.71–16.01.72		06.03–09.04.77		10
	09.01–03.02.74 (*g*)	1970 (p)		13
	09.01–03.02.74 (*g*)	09.12–23.12.71		7
				5
968 (*g*)				
	09.01–03.02.74 (*g*)	27.01–14.03.74 (*g*)	24.04–01.06.69 (*g*)	13
		08.06–20.07.75		
		11.01–08.02.76 (*g*)		
		28.04–27.05.72 (*g*)		8
		28.04–27.05.73		
				5
975	16.05–16.06.74 (*g*)	28.04–27.05.72 (*g*)	24.04–01.06.69 (*g*)	15
		28.04–27.05.73		
		27.01–14.03.74 (*g*)		
		11.01–08.02.76 (*g*)		
969 (*g*)				12
2.10–25.11.73				
	1974			10
2.03–26.04.76				11
[illegible]	10	16	3	

Exhibitions of Conceptual artists in dealer galleries and public institutions, 1967–77

	Serielle Formationen + 19:45–21:55 Frankfurt: Univ. + Galerie Loehr, 22.05–30.06.67 + 09.09.67	**Minimal Art** Gemeentemuseum, The Hague; 23.03–26.05.68	**Op Losse Schroeven** Amsterdam, Essen; 15.03–27.04.69	**When Attitudes Become Form** Bern, Krefeld, London; 22.03–27.04.69	**Konzeption/Conception** Leverkusen: Museum; 24.10–23.11.69	**Idea Structures** London: Camden Arts Centre; 24.06–19.07.70
Art & Language						•
Marcel Broodthaers					•	
Daniel Buren					•	
Hanne Darboven				•	•	
Jan Dibbets	SF + 19:45–21:55		•	•	•	
Gilbert & George					•	
Richard Long	19:45–21:55		•	•		
Mario Merz			•	•		
Carl Andre	SF	•	•	•		
Douglas Huebler			•	•	•	
Joseph Kosuth				•	•	•
Sol LeWitt	SF	•		•	•	
Bruce Nauman			•	•		
Robert Ryman			•	•		
Lawrence Weiner			•	•	•	

	Contemporanea Rome: Villa Borghese 30.11.73–28.02.74	**Projekt '74** Cologne: KH, KV, W-R. Mus.; 06.07–08.09.74	**Prospect/Retrospect** Düsseldorf: Kunsthalle; 20–31.10.76	**Anti-Illusion: Procedures/ Materials** New York: Whitney; 19.05–16.07.69	**Conceptual Art and Conceptual Aspects** New York: Cultural Center; 10.04–25.08.70	**Information** New York: MoMA; 02.07–20.09.70
Art & Language	• (Analitica)	• (Systems)	•		•	•
Marcel Broodthaers	• (Sintetica)	• (Time)	•			
Daniel Buren	• (Analitica)	• (Time)	•		•	•
Hanne Darboven	• (Analitica)	• (Time)	•			•
Jan Dibbets	• (Analitica)	• (Formsysteme)	•		•	•
Gilbert & George	• (Sintetica)	• (Time)	•			•
Richard Long	• (Analitica)		•			•
Mario Merz	• (Processuale)	•	•			
Carl Andre	• (Analitica)	(Withdrew)	•	•		•
Douglas Huebler	• (Analitica)	(Withdrew)	•		•	•
Joseph Kosuth	• (Analitica)	• (Time)	•		•	•
Sol LeWitt	• (Analitica)	(Withdrew)	•			•
Bruce Nauman	• (Processuale)	• (Perception)	•	•	•	•
Robert Ryman	• (Analitica)		•	•		
Lawrence Weiner	• (Analitica)	• (Systems)	•		•	•

Conceptual Art, Arte Povera, Land Art | Turin: Galleria civica d'arte m.; 07–08.70	**July–August–September 1969** London, *Studio International*; 07–08.69	**Sonsbeek 71** Arnhem; 19.06–15.08.71	**'Konzept'-Kunst** Basel: Kunstmuseum; 18.03–23.04.72	**Documenta 5** Kassel; 30.06–08.10.72	**The New Art** London: Hayward Gallery; 17.08–24.09.72	
			•	• (Idee/Licht)	•	**Art & Language**
				• (artist's mus.)		**Marcel Broodthaers**
	•	•	•	• (Idee/Licht)		**Daniel Buren**
•	•	•	•	• (Idee/Licht)		**Hanne Darboven**
•	•	•	•	• (Idee/Licht)		**Jan Dibbets**
•		•	•	• (Indiv. Myth.)	•	**Gilbert & George**
		•		• (Idee/Licht)	•	**Richard Long**
•	•	•		• (Indiv. Myth.)		**Mario Merz**
•		•				**Carl Andre**
•	•	•	•	• (Idee/Licht)		**Douglas Huebler**
•	•			• (Idee/Licht)		**Joseph Kosuth**
•	•	•		• (Idee/Licht)		**Sol LeWitt**
•		•		• (Idee/Licht)		**Bruce Nauman**
•				• (Idee/Licht)		**Robert Ryman**
•	•	•	•	• (Idee/Licht)		**Lawrence Weiner**

Guggenheim International Exhibition New York: Guggenheim; 12.02–11.04.71	**De Europa** New York: John Weber Gallery; 29.04–24.05.72	
	•	**Art & Language**
		Marcel Broodthaers
•	•	**Daniel Buren**
•	•	**Hanne Darboven**
•	•	**Jan Dibbets**
		Gilbert & George
•	•	**Richard Long**
•	•	**Mario Merz**
•		**Carl Andre**
		Douglas Huebler
•		**Joseph Kosuth**
•		**Sol LeWitt**
•		**Bruce Nauman**
•		**Robert Ryman**
•		**Lawrence Weiner**

Chronological list of exhibitions of Conceptual artists in dealer galleries and public institutions

ARTIST	DATE	EXHIBITION TITLE	LOCATION	CITY
Art & Language	22.06–05.07.71	**Art & Language Press**	Gian Enzo Sperone	Turin
	18.03–23.04.72	**'Konzept'-Kunst** *(g)*	Kunstmuseum	Basel
	15.06–01.07.72	**The Art & Language Institute, Documenta Memorandum (Indexing)**	Paul Maenz	Cologne
	13.01–07.02.73	**The Art & Language Institute**	Paul Maenz	Cologne
	01.02–[ ].73	**Group show**	Sperone/Fischer	Rome
	17.02–02.03.73	**Art & Language**	Paul Maenz	Brussels
	10.04–12.05.73	**Einige wesentliche Beispiele früher Konzeptueller Kunst analytischen Characters** *(g)*	Paul Maenz	Cologne
	11.09–20.11.73	**Art & Language (Pilkington, Ruschton)**	Paul Maenz	Cologne
	23.09–17.11.73	**Art & Language (Burn, Ramsden)**	Paul Maenz	Cologne
	12.10–[ ].73	**Art & Language**	Gian Enzo Sperone	Turin
	16.10–10.11.73	**Art & Language**	Lisson Gallery	London
	14.11–[ ].73	**Group show**	Sperone/Fischer	Rome
	01.74	**Art & Language**	Lisson Gallery	London
	27.01–24.02.74	**Art and Language, Proceedings**	Kunstmuseum	Lucerne
	05.02–08.03.74	**Art and Language**	Paul Maenz	Brussels
	04.07–27.07.74	**13 Projekt '74** *(g)*	Paul Maenz	Cologne
	02.75	**Art & Language**	Lisson Gallery	London
	15.03–29.03.75	**Art & Language**	MTL	Brussels
	21.09–26.10.75	**Art & Language, 1966–75**	MOMA	Oxford
	17.06–10.07.76	**Art & Language, A Critique of Virtue without Terror, Choruses from a Musical Comedy**	MTL	Brussels
	04.09–30.09.76	**Pläne/Zeichnungen/Diagramme** *(g)*	Paul Maenz	Cologne
	08.02–05.03.77	**Group show**	Lisson Gallery	London
Marcel Broodthaers	26.05–26.06.66	**Moules Œufs Frites Pots Charbon**	Wide White Space	Antwerp
	30.01–16.02.67	**Accrochage** *(g)*	Wide White Space	Antwerp
	19.06–30.06.67	**Group show**	Wide White Space	Antwerp
	22.09–10.11.67	**Group show**	Wide White Space	Antwerp
	1968	**Three Blind Mice** *(g)*	Van Abbemuseum	Eindhoven
	05.01–07.02.68	**Group show**	Wide White Space	Antwerp
	07.03–31.03.68	**Le Corbeau et le Renard**	Wide White Space	Antwerp
	20–29.09.68	**Prospect 68** *(g)*	Kunsthalle	Düsseldorf
	16.10–14.11.68	**Group show**	Wide White Space	Antwerp
	02.12–20.12.69	**Marcel Broodthaers à la Deblioudebliou/S, Exposition littéraire autour de Mallarmé**	Wide White Space	Antwerp
	14–15.02.70	**between 4** *(g)*	Kunsthalle	Düsseldorf
	13.03–10.04.70	**Marcel Broodthaers, MTL–DTH**	MTL	Brussels
	29.09–31.10.70	**Accrochage** *(g)*	Wide White Space	Antwerp
	09.10–18.11.70	**between 5** *(g)*	Kunsthalle	Düsseldorf
	04.12–23.12.70	**Multiples en grafische werken** *(g)*	Wide White Space	Antwerp
	15–17.06.71	**between 6** *(g)*	Kunsthalle	Düsseldorf
	27.09–27.10.71	**Figures anciennes et modernes**	Wide White Space	Antwerp
	08–17.10.71	**Prospect 71 – Projection** *(g)*	Kunsthalle	Düsseldorf
	21.10–07.11.71	**Marcel Broodthaers, Film als Objekt/Objekt als Film**	Museum	Mönchengladbach
	29.10–05.12.71	**Actualité d'un bilan** *(g)*	Yvon Lambert	Paris
	15.12–[ ].71	**Au delà de cette limite vos billets ne sont plus valables**	Yvon Lambert	Paris
	21.03–15.04.72	**Group show**	Wide White Space	Antwerp
	19.04–05.05.72	**Au delà de cette limite vos billets ne sont plus valables**	Françoise Lambert	Milan
	06.05–25.05.72	**Marcel Broodthaers, Zeichnungen, Dias, Filme**	Heiner Friedrich	Munich
	16.05–09.07.72	**Musée d'Art moderne, Département des Aigles, Section des Figures**	Kunsthalle	Düsseldorf
	18.05–17.06.72	**Marcel Broodthaers, Tractatus Logico-Catalogicus**	MTL	Brussels
	17.06–30.06.72	**Editions Le Corbeau et le Renard (1967–72)**	Wide White Space	Antwerp
	10.72	**Ecrire, Peindre, Parler, Copier, Fumer, Boire, Traduire**	Yvon Lambert	Paris
	01–22.12.72	**Marcel Broodthaers**	Jack Wendler	London

ARTIST	DATE	EXHIBITION TITLE	LOCATION	CITY
	01.73	**Fumer-Boire-Copier-Parler-Écrire-Peindre-Filmer**	Françoise Lambert	Milan
	13.01-28.01.73	**Fig.1 Programme**	Wide White Space	Antwerp
	03.73	**Rétrospective (October 1963-March 1973)**	Art & Project	Amsterdam
	20.03-[ ].73	**Marcel Broodthaers, Petrus Paulus Rubens**	MTL	Brussels
	25.05-24.06.73	**Broodthaers, Charlier, Geys, Lohaus, Mees, Panamarenko, Roquet** (*g*)	Pal. des Beaux-Arts	Brussels
	02-06.05.1973	**between 7** (*g*)	Kunsthalle	Düsseldorf
	14.06-20.06.73	**A, B, C - Paysage d'Automne**	Yvon Lambert	Paris
	28.09-07.10.73	**Prospect 73 - Malers Painters Peintres** (*g*)	Kunsthalle	Düsseldorf
	06.11.73	**Deux films de Marcel Broodthaers**	Yvon Lambert	Paris
	09.01-03.02.74	**Andre, Broodthaers, Buren, Burgin, Gilbert & George, Kawara, Long, Richter** (*g*)	Pal. des Beaux-Arts	Brussels
	19.09-03.10.74	**Ne dites pas que je ne l'ai pas dit, Le Perroquet**	Wide White Space	Antwerp
	25.09-03.10.74	**Marcel Broodthaers**	Wide White Space	Brussels
	27.09-24.10.74	**Marcel Broodthaers, 5 séries de 9 tableaux dont une reste la propriété de l'artiste (Série Culture Internationale)**	MTL	Brussels
	27.09-03.11.74	**Marcel Broodthaers, Catalogue-Catalogus**	Pal. des Beaux-Arts	Brussels
	05.10-03.11.74	**Éloge du Sujet, Filme, Dias, Objekte, Bilder**	Kunstmuseum	Basel
	12.74	**Die Lorelei**	Heiner Friedrich	Munich
	08.01-01.02.75	**Drawings** (*g*)	Wide White Space	Antwerp
	26.04-01.06.75	**Le privilège de l'art**	MOMA	Oxford
	01.10.75-31.01.76	**Marcel Broodthaers, Ceci Cela ou Rien**	Nigel Greenwood	London
	04.12-20.12.75	**Marcel Broodthaers, Les Poissons - De Vissen**	MTL	Brussels
	1976	**Räume** (*g*)	Museum	Mönchengladbach
	04.12.75-10.01.76	**La Conquête de l'Espace (Atlas à l'usage des artistes et des militaires)** (with Lebeer Hossmann, Brussels)	MTL	Brussels
	05.04-14.05.77	**The Complete Editions on Paper and Books**	Nigel Greenwood	London
Daniel Buren	20-29.09.68	**Prospect 68** (*g*)	Kunsthalle	Düsseldorf
	17.01-06.02.69	**Daniel Buren**	Wide White Space	Antwerp
	05.69	**Daniel Buren, Interruption (films)**	Yvon Lambert	Paris
	30.09-12.10.69	**Position-Proposition**	Konrad Fischer	Düsseldorf
	30.09-12.10.69	**Prospect 69** (*g*)	Kunsthalle	Düsseldorf
	06-07.70	**Daniel Buren** (t)	Art & Project	Amsterdam
	13.06-01.07.70	**Daniel Buren, A partir de/Vanaf**	MTL	Brussels
	07.70	**Daniel Buren**	Françoise Lambert	Milan
	02.12.70-05.01.71	**Daniel Buren**	Yvon Lambert	Paris
	01.71	**Daniel Buren**	Kunstverein	Münster
	28.01-07.03.71	**Position-Proposition, Senkrechte farbige und weisse Streifen**	Museum	Mönchengladbach
	02.71	**Group show**	Françoise Lambert	Milan
	26.02-[ ].03.71	**Eight Proposals** (*g*)	Françoise Lambert	Milan
	11.05-05.06.71	**Daniel Buren**	Wide White Space	Antwerp
	02.06.71	**Daniel Buren** (mg)	Art & Project	Amsterdam
	29.10-05.12.71	**Actualité d'un bilan** (*g*)	Yvon Lambert	Paris
	09.11.71	**A Private Collector (works of Daniel Buren)** (mg)	Art & Project	Amsterdam
	02.72	**Daniel Buren**	Jack Wendler	London
	18.03-23.04.72	**'Konzept'-Kunst** (*g*)	Kunstmuseum	Basel
	25.03-[ ].72	**Das Konzept ist die Form** (*g*)	Kunstverein	Münster
	06.04-16.04.72	**Group Show**	Françoise Lambert	Milan
	02.06-15.06.72	**Daniel Buren**	Wide White Space	Antwerp
	12.06-[ ].72	**Invito a leggere come indicazione di quello che c'è da vedere (Peinture suspendue)**	Gian Enzo Sperone	Turin

ARTIST	DATE	EXHIBITION TITLE	LOCATION	CITY
Daniel Buren	01.02–[ ].73	**Group show**	Sperone/Fischer	Rome
	09–30.03.73	**Daniel Buren, Manipulation**	Jack Wendler	London
	31.03–15.04.73	**Daniel Buren – Sanction of the Museum**	MOMA	Oxford
	22.06–28.07.73	**Daniel Buren**	Wide White Space	Antwerp
	[ ]–10.11.73	**Daniel Buren**	Yvon Lambert	Paris
	14.11–[ ].73	**Group show**	Sperone/Fischer	Rome
	15.11–23.12.73	**Eine Malerei Ausstellung** (*g*)	Museum	Mönchengladbach
	09.01–03.02.74	**Andre, Broodthaers, Buren, Burgin, Gilbert & George, Kawara, Long, Richter** (*g*)	Pal. des Beaux-Arts	Brussels
	22.02–03.03.74	**Daniel Buren: Triptyque, division I**	Rolf Preisig	Basel
	03.74	**Daniel Buren, Transparency**	Art & Project	Amsterdam
	04–13.03.74	**Daniel Buren: Triptyque, division II**	Rolf Preisig	Basel
	14–18.08.74	**Daniel Buren: Triptyque, division III**	Rolf Preisig	Basel
	23.04–[ ].06.74	**Daniel Buren**	Wide White Space	Antwerp
	19–24.06.74	**Eine Ausstellung zur ART 5'74**	Rolf Preisig	Basel
	29.09–03.11.74	**Daniel Buren**	Kunstmuseum	Lucerne
	20.11–[ ].74	**Suite n.1 nello spazio dato**	Gian Enzo Sperone	Turin
	14.12–[ ].74	**Suite n.2 nello spazio dato**	Sperone/Fischer	Rome
	1975	**Eparpillé-Rassemblé**	Kunstmuseum	Lucerne
	01–02.75	**Daniel Buren, Robert Ryman, Ian Wilson** (*g*)	MTL	Brussels
	14.01–08.02.75	**D'un éspace à l'autre/Von Raum zu Raum**	Rolf Preisig	Basel
	16.03–20.04.75	**Daniel Buren**	Kunstmuseum	Basel
	06.05–[ ].75	**Group show**	Gian Enzo Sperone	Rome
	03.11–29.11.75	**Daniel Buren, Morceler, Traverser, Limiter**	MTL	Brussels
	21.11–14.12.75	**Daniel Buren: Von da an..., Zweite Folge: von da an...**	Museum	Mönchengladbach
	1976	**Räume** (*g*)	Museum	Mönchengladbach
	31.01–14.02.76	**Vice Versa**	Konrad Fischer (with Maenz, Cologne)	Düsseldorf
	31.01–14.02.76	**Vice Versa**	Paul Maenz (with Fischer, Düsseldorf)	Cologne
	02.03–03.04.76	**Daniel Buren**	Lisson Gallery	London
	18.04.76	**Daniel Buren** (mg)	Art & Project	Amsterdam
	end 04–01.06.76	**Discordance-Cohérence: Ailleurs-Elders: travaux effectués in situ au Van Abbemuseum**	Van Abbemuseum	Eindhoven
	30.04–07.06.76	**Daniel Buren, Hier/Ici (Kaleidoscope, un travail in situ)**	Stedelijk Museum	Amsterdam
	07–09.76	**Summer group show**	Art & Project	Amsterdam
	04.09–30.09.76	**Pläne/Zeichnungen/Diagramme** (*g*)	Paul Maenz	Cologne
	07–31.12.76	**Daniel Buren, Exercises**	Rolf Preisig	Basel
	01.03–26.03.77	**Daniel Buren**	Paul Maenz	Cologne
Hanne Darboven	05.12–[ ].67	**Konstruktionen**	Konrad Fischer	Düsseldorf
	1968	**Three Blind Mice** (*g*)	Van Abbemuseum	Eindhoven
	22.10–15.11.68	**Hanne Darboven**	Konrad Fischer	Düsseldorf
	1969	**Group show**	Heiner Friedrich	Munich
	25.02–07.04.69	**Ausstellung mit 6 Filmprojektoren nach 6 Büchern über 1968**	Museum	Mönchengladbach
	03.06–17.06.69	**1968 + Ein Jahrhundert**	Heiner Friedrich	Munich
	30.09–12.10.69	**Prospect 69** (*g*)	Kunsthalle	Düsseldorf
	03.07–30.07.70	**Das Jahr 1970**	Konrad Fischer	Düsseldorf
	24.10–13.11.70	**00/366–1, 99/365–100 (100 books from 00–99)**	Art & Project	Amsterdam
	14.11–[ ].70	**Hanne Darboven (drawings)**	Gian Enzo Sperone	Turin
	1971	**Group show**	Heiner Friedrich	Munich
	01.01–31.12.71	**Ein Jahrhundert in einem Jahr**	Konrad Fischer	Düsseldorf
	08–17.10.71	**Prospect 71 – Projection** (*g*)	Kunsthalle	Düsseldorf
	16.10–14.11.71	**Hanne Darboven**	Kunstverein	Münster
	29.10–05.12.71	**Actualité d'un bilan** (*g*)	Yvon Lambert	Paris
	14.01–13.02.72	**Ein Jahrhundert**	Heiner Friedrich	Cologne
	01.02–29.02.72	**Hanne Darboven**	MTL	Brussels
	18.03–23.04.72	**'Konzept'-Kunst** (*g*)	Kunstmuseum	Basel
	25.03–[ ].72	**Das Konzept ist die Form** (*g*)	Kunstverein	Münster
	23.05–06.06.72	**Hanne Darboven**	Jack Wendler	London
	Winter 72	**Hanne Darboven**	MTL	Brussels
	16.12.72–09.01.73	**Hanne Darboven**	Art & Project	Amsterdam
	01.02–[ ].73	**Group show**	Sperone/Fischer	Rome
	[ ]–18.05.73	**Hanne Darboven**	Yvon Lambert	Paris
	22.05.73 (LB)	**Hanne Darboven**	MTL	Brussels

ARTIST	DATE	EXHIBITION TITLE	LOCATION	CITY
	12.03–06.04.74	**Hanne Darboven**	MTL/Art & Project	Antwerp
	12.03–23.03.74	**Hanne Darboven, '73, 1973; '74, 1974**	Art & Project	Amsterdam
	26.03–06.04.74	**Hanne Darboven, '73, 1973; '74, 1974**	MTL	Brussels
	15.05–[ ].74	**Hanne Darboven**	Gian Enzo Sperone	Turin
	16.05–16.06.74	**Hanne Darboven and Sol LeWitt** (*g*)	Pal. des Beaux-Arts	Brussels
	19–24.06.74	**Eine Ausstellung zur ART 5'74**	Rolf Preisig	Basel
	30.06–04.08.74	**Hanne Darboven**	MOMA	Oxford
	09.11–29.12.74	**Ein Monat, ein Jahrhundert, Werke von 1968 bis 1974**	Kunstmuseum	Basel
	10.01–02.03.75	**Een maand, een jaar, een eeuw, Werken van 1968 tot en met 1974**	Stedelijk Museum	Amsterdam
	06.05–[ ].75	**Group show**	Gian Enzo Sperone	Rome
	11.05–22.06.75	**Hanne Darboven**	Kunstmuseum	Lucerne
	10.06–[ ].75	**Hanne Darboven**	Konrad Fischer	Düsseldorf
	22.06–16.07.75	**Auswahl** (*g*)	Museum	Mönchengladbach
	18.11–[ ].75	**Group show**	Gian Enzo Sperone	Rome
	22.12–[ ].75	**Group show**	Gian Enzo Sperone	Turin
	06.01–24.01.76	**Hanne Darboven**	Art & Project	Amsterdam
	07–09.76	**Summer Group show**	Art & Project	Amsterdam
	04.09–30.09.76	**Pläne/Zeichnungen/Diagramme** (*g*)	Paul Maenz	Cologne
	27.09–31.10.76	**Hanne Darboven**	Wallraf-Richartz Museum	Cologne
Jan Dibbets	[ ].67	**Signalement 67** (*g*)	Stedelijk Museum	Amsterdam
	15.08–17.09.68	**Rasenrolle, Holzbündel, Wasserpfütze**	Konrad Fischer	Düsseldorf
	15.03–27.04.69	**Op Losse Schroeven, Situaties en Cryptostructuren** (*g*)	Stedelijk Museum	Amsterdam
	22.07.69	**Drawings, Jan Dibbets and Bernd Lohaus** (*g*) (mg)	Art & Project	Amsterdam
	30.09–12.10.69	**Prospect 69** (*g*)	Kunsthalle	Düsseldorf
	26.11–16.12.69	**Jan Dibbets**	Art & Project	Amsterdam
	19.02–[ ].70	**Jan Dibbets**	Yvon Lambert	Paris
	26.02–[ ].03.70	**Jan Dibbets – Shadows, Krefeld '69**	Françoise Lambert	Milan
	02.71	**Group show**	Françoise Lambert	Milan
	02–03.71	**Eight proposals** (*g*)	Françoise Lambert	Milan
	13.03–23.03.71	**Jan Dibbets, Painting 1 + 2 (Videogalerie Schum)**	Gian Enzo Sperone	Turin
	06.04–22.04.71	**Jan Dibbets**	Konrad Fischer	Düsseldorf
	07.04.71	**Jan Dibbets, A white wall** (mg)	Art & Project	Amsterdam
	08–17.10.71	**Prospect 71 – Projection** (*g*)	Kunsthalle	Düsseldorf
	29.10–05.12.71	**Actualité d'un bilan** (*g*)	Yvon Lambert	Paris
	27.11–18.12.71	**Jan Dibbets, Louverdrape** (film)	Art & Project	Amsterdam
	03.12.71–16.01.72	**Four Pieces: 1. Dutch Mountains, 1971; 2. Horizons, 1971; 3. Shortest Day, 1970; 4. Diagonals, 1971**	Van Abbemuseum	Eindhoven
	18.12.71–15.01.72	**Jan Dibbets, Venetian Blinds**	MTL	Brussels
	03.02–[ ].72	**Jan Dibbets**	Yvon Lambert	Paris
	25.02–09.03.72	**Jan Dibbets**	Jack Wendler	London
	18.03–23.04.72	**'Konzept'-Kunst** (*g*)	Kunstmuseum	Basel
	25.03–[ ].72	**Das Konzept ist die Form** (*g*)	Kunstverein	Münster
	06.04–16.04.72	**Group show**	Françoise Lambert	Milan
	12.06.72	**Jan Dibbets (Venice Biennale)** (mg)	Art & Project	Amsterdam
	17.11.72–14.01.73	**Jan Dibbets**	Stedelijk Museum	Amsterdam
	18.11.72–14.01.73	**Jan Dibbets**	MTL	Brussels
	1973	**Jan Dibbets**	Art & Project	Amsterdam
	01.02–[ ].73	**Group show**	Sperone/Fischer	Rome
	16.03–15.04.73	**Jan Dibbets**	Konrad Fischer	Düsseldorf
	06.04–[ ].73	**Jan Dibbets**	Sperone/Fischer	Rome
	17.10–[ ].73	**Jan Dibbets**	MTL	Brussels
	14.11–[ ].73	**Group show**	Sperone/Fischer	Rome
	12.73	**Jan Dibbets**	Jack Wendler	London
	15.02–[ ].74	**Jan Dibbets, Constructions of Land and Sea**	Gian Enzo Sperone	Turin
	10.74	**Jan Dibbets**	Art & Project	Amsterdam
	19.10–16.11.74	**Jan Dibbets**	Konrad Fischer	Düsseldorf
	11.74	**Jan Dibbets, Comète**	Yvon Lambert	Paris
	02.12.74–04.01.75	**Jan Dibbets**	MTL/Art & Project	Antwerp
	07.02–27.02.75	**Jan Dibbets, Autumn Strucutres**	MTL	Brussels
	11.02–01.03.75	**Jan Dibbets**	Art & Project	Amsterdam
	28.09–09.22.75	**Jan Dibbets, Autumn Melody**	Kunstmuseum	Lucerne
	22.12–[ ].75	**Group show**	Gian Enzo Sperone	Turin
	29.04–[ ].76	**Jan Dibbets**	Gian Enzo Sperone	Rome
	07–09.76	**Summer group show**	Art & Project	Amsterdam
	04.09–30.09.76	**Pläne/Zeichnungen/Diagramme** (*g*)	Paul Maenz	Cologne
	12.02–10.03.77	**Color Studies 1976**	Konrad Fischer	Düsseldorf
	06.03–09.04.77	**Jan Dibbets**	MOMA	Oxford
	12.05–[ ].77	**Jan Dibbets**	Yvon Lambert	Paris

ARTIST	DATE	EXHIBITION TITLE	LOCATION	CITY
Gilbert & George	03-04.69	**Pose Sculpture** (p)	Stedelijk Museum	Amsterdam
	1970	**Lecture Sculpture** (p)	MOMA	Oxford
	14-15.02.70	**between 4** (*g*)	Kunsthalle	Düsseldorf
	10.05-05.06.70	**Gilbert & George**	Konrad Fischer	Düsseldorf
	12.05-23.05.70	**Art Notes and Thoughts (Drawings)**	Art & Project	Amsterdam
	14.05.70	**Underneath the Arches, Singing Sculpture** (p)	Heiner Friedrich	Munich
	07.70	**Frozen into the Nature for Your Art**	Françoise Lambert	Milan
	09 or 12[ ].70	**Drawings** (*g*)	Heiner Friedrich	Munich
	10.70	**Underneath the Arches, Singing Sculpture** (p)	Heiner Friedrich	Cologne
	10.70	**Frozen into the Nature for Your Art**	Heiner Friedrich	Cologne
	mid-11.70	**Gilbert & George, To be with art is all we ask**	Nigel Greenwood	London
	[ ].71	**Underneath the Arches** (p)	Kunstmuseum	Lucerne
	28.05-[ ].71	**There were two men by Gilbert & George**	Gian Enzo Sperone	Turin
	08-17.10.71	**Prospect 71 – Projection** (*g*)	Kunsthalle	Düsseldorf
	28.10-28.11.71	**Gilbert & George, The Paintings (With Us in Nature)**	Stedelijk Museum	Amsterdam
	29.11-12.71	**Gilbert & George, The Ten Pieces**	Nigel Greenwood	London
	22.12.71-21.01.72	**New Photo-Pieces**	Art & Project	Amsterdam
	03.01-[ ].72	**Christmas of 1971**	Konrad Fischer	Düsseldorf
	18.03-23.04.72	**'Konzept'-Kunst** (*g*)	Kunstmuseum	Basel
		Das Konzept ist die Form (*g*)		
	25.03-[ ].72	**The Singing Sculpture, The Paintings**	Kunstverein	Münster
	20.05-25.06.72	**(With us in Nature)** (taken over from Amsterdam)	Kunstmuseum	Lucerne
	04.07-[ ].72	**Gilbert & George, Book**	Nigel Greenwood	London
	27.09-[ ].72	**Gilbert & George, Videos**	Nigel Greenwood	London
	10.72	**Gilbert & George, Videos**	MTL	Brussels
	07.12-[ ].72	**A New Sculpture by Gilbert & George**	Sperone/Fischer	Rome
	20.11-12.72	**The Evening before the Morning after**	Nigel Greenwood	London
	Winter 72	**Gilbert & George**	Art & Project	Amsterdam
	17.03-[ ].73	**Gilbert & George, Long, Fulton** (*g*)	MTL	Brussels
	01.02-[ ].73	**Group show**	Sperone/Fischer	Rome
	27.06-[ ].73	**Gilbert & George, New Decorative Works**	Gian Enzo Sperone	Turin
	16-21.07.73	**Gilbert & George, Recycling Drunk**	Nigel Greenwood	London
	Autumn 73	**Gilbert & George, Any Port in a Storm**	Ileana Sonnabend	Paris
	28.09-07.10.73	**Prospect 73 – Malers Painters Peintres** (*g*)	Kunsthalle	Düsseldorf
	14.11-[ ].73	**Group show**	Sperone/Fischer	Rome
	1974	**Gilbert & George, The Tuileries**	Art & Project	Amsterdam
	09.01-03.02.74	**Andre, Broodthaers, Buren, Burgin, Gilbert & George, Kawara, Long, Richter** (*g*)	Pal. des Beaux-Arts	Brussels
	02.74	**Gilbert & George**	MTL/Art & Project	Antwerp
	17.03-17.04.74	**Gilbert & George, Human Bondage**	Konrad Fischer	Düsseldorf
	05.06-05.07.74	**Gilbert & George, Dark Shadow**	Nigel Greenwood	London
	14.09-[ ].74	**Gilbert & George, Cherry Blossom, No. 10 Sculpture**	Sperone/Fischer	Rome
	13.03-[ ].75	**Gilbert & George, Bloody Life**	Ileana Sonnabend	Paris
	06.05-[ ].75	**Group show**	Gian Enzo Sperone	Rome
	30.05-25.06.75	**Gilbert & George, Bad Thoughts**	MTL	Brussels
	30.08-29.09.75	**Medium Fotography** (*g*)	Kunstverein	Münster
	08.11-29.11.75	**Gilbert & George**	Sper/Westw/Fischer	New York
	02-03.76	**Die rote Skulptur** (p)	Konrad Fischer	Düsseldorf
	07-09.76	**Summer Group show**	Art & Project	Amsterdam
	10.76	**Group show**	Ghiringhelli-Sperone	Milan
	1977	**The Red Sculpture** (p)	MTL	Brussels
	06.01-[ ].77	**Presentation of Dark Shadow by Gilbert & George**	Nigel Greenwood	London
	16.02.77	**Presentation of Dark Shadow, a new book by Gilbert & George**	MTL	Brussels
	23.02-[ ].77	**The Red Sculpture di Gilbert & George** (p)	Gian Enzo Sperone	Rome
	01.11-26.11.77	**New Photo-Pieces**	Art & Project	Amsterdam
	10-11.03.77	**The Red Sculpture** (p)	Stedelijk Museum	Amsterdam
	26.11-23.12.77	**The Dirty Words**	Konrad Fischer	Düsseldorf

ARTIST	DATE	EXHIBITION TITLE	LOCATION	CITY
Richard Long	21.09–18.10.68	**Richard Long**	Konrad Fischer	Düsseldorf
	15.03–27.04.69	**Op Losse Schroeven, Situaties en Cryptostructuren** (*g*)	Stedelijk Museum	Amsterdam
	05.07–01–08.69	**Richard Long**	Konrad Fischer	Düsseldorf
	30.09–12.10.69	**Prospect 69** (*g*)	Kunsthalle	Düsseldorf
	05.11–26.11.69	**Richard Long**	Yvon Lambert	Paris
	15.11–01.12.69	**A sculpture by Richard Long**	Françoise Lambert	Milan
	11.05–09.06.70	**Richard Long**	Konrad Fischer	Düsseldorf
	16.07–30.08.70	**4 Skulpturen (England, Germany, Africa, America, 1966–70)**	Museum	Mönchengladbach
	13.04–[ ].71	**Richard Long**	Gian Enzo Sperone	Turin
	06.71	**Group show**	Fr. Lambert	Milan
	17.07–06.08.71	**Reflections on the Little Pigeon River, Great Smoky Mountains, Tennessee (1970)**	Art & Project	Amsterdam
	09.71	**Soziologisches Experiement** (*g*)	Heiner Friedrich	Cologne
	29.10–05.12.71	**Actualité d'un bilan** (*g*)	Yvon Lambert	Paris
	09.12–23.12.71	**Richard Long, Mud Spiral**	MOMA	Oxford
	01.72	**Richard Long, A Hundred Mile Walk**	Gian Enzo Sperone	Turin
	03.05–[ ].72	**Richard Long, Look the Ground in the Eye**	Yvon Lambert	Paris
	1973	**Richard Long**	Art & Project	Amsterdam
	23.01–24.02.73	**Richard Long**	Lisson Gallery	London
	15.03–12.04.73	**Richard Long**	Wide White Space	Antwerp
	17.03–[ ].73	**Gilbert & George, Long, Fulton** (*g*)	MTL	Brussels
	29.05–25.06.73	**A Rolling Stone**	Konrad Fischer	Düsseldorf
	07.12.73–27.01.74	**Richard Long, Sculptures, Photo-Pieces**	Stedelijk Museum	Amsterdam
	1974	**Richard Long, Circle in the Andes**	Art & Project	Amsterdam
	09.01–03.02.74	**Andre, Broodthaers, Buren, Burgin, Gilbert & George, Kawara, Long, Richter** (*g*)	Pal. des Beaux-Arts	Brussels
	19–24.06.74	**Eine Ausstellung zur ART 5'74**	Rolf Preisig	Basel
	01–30.11.74	**Richard Long**	Lisson Gallery	London
	20.12.74–19.01.75	**River Avon Driftwood**	Konrad Fischer	Düsseldorf
	18.03–15.04.75	**River Avon Driftwood, Crossing Two Rivers/Minnesota/Wiltshire**	Art & Project	Amsterdam
	15.04–16.05.75	**Driftwood**	Wide White Space	Antwerp
	24.04–20.05.75	**Richard Long**	Yvon Lambert	Paris
	12.06–12.07.75	**Richard Long**	Rolf Preisig	Basel
	22.06–16.07.75	**Auswahl** (*g*)	Museum	Mönchengladbach
	1976	**Richard Long, A Line in the Himalayas**	Art & Project	Amsterdam
	03–04.76	**Richard Long**	Yvon Lambert	Paris
	16.03–[ ].76	**Richard Long**	Gian Enzo Sperone	Rome
	15.05–11.06.76	**River Avon Driftwood**	Konrad Fischer	Düsseldorf
	25.05–10.06.76	**Driftwood**	Wide White Space	Antwerp
	24–26.06.76	**Richard Long, Stones**	Lisson Gallery	London
	07–09.76	**Summer Group show**	Art & Project	Amsterdam
	04.12–76–08.01.77	**Richard Long**	Sper/Westw/Fischer	New York
	08.02–05.03.77	**Richard Long, Two Stone Lines**	Art & Project	Amsterdam
	08.02–05.03.77	**Group show**	Lisson Gallery	London
	16.02–[ ].77	**Group show**	Gian Enzo Sperone	Rome
	17.05–21.06.77	**Richard Long, Meeting Place**	Rolf Preisig	Basel
	21.05–18.06.77	**Richard Long**	Lisson Gallery	London
Mario Merz	19.01–[ ].68	**Mario Merz**	Gian Enzo Sperone	Turin
	20–29.09.68	**Prospect 68** (*g*)	Kunsthalle	Düsseldorf
	03.69	**Mario Merz**	Gian Enzo Sperone	Turin
	15.03–27.04.69	**Op Losse Schroeven, Situaties en Cryptostructuren** (*g*)	Stedelijk Museum	Amsterdam
	22.04–[ ].06.69	**Mario Merz**	Ileana Sonnabend	Paris
	22.05–[ ].69	**Disegni progetti** (*g*)	Gian Enzo Sperone	Turin
	29.10–[ ].69	**Group show**	Gian Enzo Sperone	Turin
	01.10–03.11.70	**Mario Merz, Sciopero generale azione politica relativa proclamata relativamente all'arte**	Françoise Lambert	Milan
	07.03–31.03.70	**Mario Merz**	Konrad Fischer	Düsseldorf
	30.05–05.07.70	**Processi di pensiero visuaolizzati, Giovane avanguardia italiana** (*g*)	Kunstmuseum	Lucerne
	01.10–03.11.70	**Sciopero generale azione politica relativa proclamata relativamente all'arte**	Françoise Lambert	Milan
	02.71	**Group show**	Françoise Lambert	Milan
	27.03–[ ].71	**Mario Merz**	Gian Enzo Sperone	Turin
	08–17.10.71	**Prospect 71 – Projection** (*g*)	Kunsthalle	Düsseldorf

ARTIST	DATE	EXHIBITION TITLE	LOCATION	CITY
Mario Merz	12.04–[ ].72	**Torino, ristorante della Spada, da 1 a 55 persone**	Gian Enzo Sperone	Turin
	02–16.05.72	**Mario Merz, A real sum is a sum of people**	Jack Wendler	London
	20.01–10.03.73	**8 Italians** *(g)*	Art & Project	Amsterdam
	17.02–10.03.73	**8 Italians** *(g)*	MTL	Brussels
	02.74	**Mario Merz**	Jack Wendler	London
	14.06–05.07.74	**Tables of drawings from Mario Merz (Fibonacci tables)**	Jack Wendler	London
	16.03–20.04.75	**Spiralen und Progressionen** (•)	Kunstmuseum	Lucerne
	18.11–[ ].75	**Group show**	Gian Enzo Sperone	Rome
	22.12–[ ].75	**Group show**	Gian Enzo Sperone	Turin
	20.02–[ ].76	**Mario Merz**	Gian Enzo Sperone	Rome
	07.04–[ ].76	**Mario Merz**	Gian Enzo Sperone	Turin
	14.04–[ ].76	**Group show**	Gian Enzo Sperone	Rome
	10.76	**Group show**	Ghiringhelli-Sperone	Milan
	11.11–17.11.76	**La Natura è l'Arte del Numero**	Konrad Fischer	Düsseldorf
	16.02–[ ].77	**Group show**	Gian Enzo Sperone	Rome
Carl Andre	21.10–28.11.67	**Carl Andre**	Konrad Fischer	Düsseldorf
	1968	**Three Blind Mice** *(g)*	Van Abbemuseum	Eindhoven
	13.02–08.03.68	**Group show**	Heiner Friedrich	Munich
	16.03–18.04.68	**22 Steel Row**	Heiner Friedrich	Munich
	03.05–25.05.68	**Carl Andre, Clastic**	Wide White Space	Antwerp
	20–29.09.68	**Prospect 68** *(g)*	Kunsthalle	Düsseldorf
	18.10–15.12.68	**Carl Andre**	Museum	Mönchengladbach
	17.01–23.02.69	**Minimal Art** *(g)*	Kunsthalle	Düsseldorf
	01.03–31.03.69	**Young American Artists** *(g)*	Wide White Space	Antwerp
	15.03–27.04.69	**Op Losse Schroeven, Situaties en Cryptostructuren** *(g)*	Stedelijk Museum	Amsterdam
	24.04–01.06.69	**The Art of the Real, USA 1948–68** *(g)*	Tate Gallery	London
	19.09–16.10.69	**Carl Andre**	Wide White Space	Antwerp
	29.09–[ ].69	**Carl Andre**	Gian Enzo Sperone	Turin
	12.10–11.11.69	**Alloy Squares**	Konrad Fischer	Düsseldorf
	12.69–01.70	**Minimal Art** *(g)*	Kunstmuseum	Basel
	29.09–31.10.70	**Accrochage** *(g)*	Wide White Space	Antwerp
	09.10–18.11.70	**between 5** *(g)*	Kunsthalle	Düsseldorf
	03.02–01.03.71	**Carl Andre**	Yvon Lambert	Paris
	22.04–06.05.71	**Weathering Piece**	Wide White Space	Antwerp
	06–07.71	**39 Part Retrograde Invention**	Heiner Friedrich	Munich
	12.07–12.08.71	**Four Meditations on the Year 1960**	Konrad Fischer	Düsseldorf
	20.07–29.08.71	**Group show**	Heiner Friedrich	Cologne
	29.10–05.12.71	**Actualité d'un bilan** *(g)*	Yvon Lambert	Paris
	05.72	**Small Floor Pieces**	Konrad Fischer	Düsseldorf
	09.05–[ ].72	**Carl Andre, Sorts**	Lisson Gallery	London
	01.02–[ ].73	**Group show**	Sperone/Fischer	Rome
	01.06–28.06.73	**Dipoles Al–Cu–Fe**	Konrad Fischer	Düsseldorf
	04.12–[ ].73	**Carl Andre. Copper Cardinals**	Gian Enzo Sperone	Turin
	Winter 73	**Flavin, Andre, Judd** *(g)*	MTL	Brussels
	1974	**Carl Andre**	Kunstmuseum	Basel
	08.01–04.02.74	**Carl Andre**	Wide White Space	Brussels
	09.01–03.02.74	**Andre, Broodthaers, Buren, Burgin, Gilbert & George, Kawara, Long, Richter** *(g)*	Pal. des Beaux-Arts	Brussels
	10.01–04.02.74	**13th Copper Cardinal, 14th Copper Cardinal, 25th Copper Cardinal**	Wide White Space	Antwerp
	27.01–14.03.74	**Sculpture, Prints and Drawings**	MOMA	Oxford
	08.06–31.07.74	**Carl Andre, Poems**	Lisson Gallery	London
	19–24.06.74	**Eine Ausstellung zur ART 5'74**	Rolf Preisig	Basel
	21.06–20.07.74	**Carl Andre**	Konrad Fischer	Düsseldorf
	07.01–[ ].75	**Carl Andre**	Art & Project	Amsterdam
	02.75	**Carl Andre**	Gian Enzo Sperone	Turin
	06.05–[ ].75	**Group show**	Gian Enzo Sperone	Rome
	06–07.75	**Carl Andre**	Lisson Gallery	London
	08.06–20.07.75	**Carl Andre, Poems 1958–74**	MOMA	Oxford
	20.09–[ ].75	**Carl Andre**	Gian Enzo Sperone	Rome
	04.10–01.11.75	**Carl Andre**	Sper/Westw/Fischer	New York
	22.12–[ ].75	**Group show**	Gian Enzo Sperone	Turin
	1976	**Räume** *(g)*	Museum	Mönchengladbach
	11.01–08.02.76	**Group show**	MOMA	Oxford
	10–20.06.76	**Andre, Judd, Ryman – ART 7'76**	Rolf Preisig	Basel
	26.06–31.07.76	**Neubrückweg von Carl Andre Düsseldorf gewidmet**	Konrad Fischer	Düsseldorf
	07–09.76	**Summer Group show**	Art & Project	Amsterdam
	04.09–30.09.76	**Pläne/Zeichnungen/Diagramme** *(g)*	Paul Maenz	Cologne
	16.09–13.10.76	**Copper Prime Couples**	Yvon Lambert	Paris

ARTIST	DATE	EXHIBITION TITLE	LOCATION	CITY
	04.12–20.12.76	**War Resisters League Benefit** (*g*)	Heiner Friedrich	New York
	12.03–02.04.77	**Andre – Early Work and Minimal Show** (*g*)	Sper/Westw/Fischer	New York
	04.05–28.05.77	**Carl Andre**	Sper/Westw/Fischer	New York
	22.11–[ ].77	**Copper–Aluminium alloy square 1970, Copper–Zinc alloy square 1970**	Gian Enzo Sperone	Rome
Douglas Huebler	15.03–27.04.69	**Op Losse Schroeven, Situaties en Cryptostructuren** (*g*)	Stedelijk Museum	Amsterdam
	30.09–12.10.69	**Prospect 69** (*g*)	Kunsthalle	Düsseldorf
	15.01–31.01.70	**Douglas Huebler**	Konrad Fischer	Düsseldorf
	11.03–18.03.70	**Douglas Huebler, Variable Works**	Yvon Lambert	Paris
	24.03–08.04.70	**Douglas Huebler, Duration Piece**	Gian Enzo Sperone	Turin
	25.04–08.05.70	**Location Piece No. 8, Amsterdam, Holland**	Art & Project	Amsterdam
	06.01–[ ].71	**Douglas Huebler, Variable Works (In Progress)**	Gian Enzo Sperone	Turin
	06.01–21.01.71	**Douglas Huebler**	Konrad Fischer	Düsseldorf
	26.02–[ ].03.71	**Eight proposals** (*g*)	Françoise Lambert	Milan
	22.05–11.06.71	**Variable Piece 1 (January 1971)**	Art & Project	Amsterdam
	29.10–05.12.71	**Actualité d'un bilan** (*g*)	Yvon Lambert	Paris
	16.03–31.03.72	**Douglas Huebler, Variable Pieces: 1, 2, 3, 4, 5**	Yvon Lambert	Paris
	18.03–23.04.72	**'Konzept'-Kunst** (*g*)	Kunstmuseum	Basel
	22.03–22.04.72	**Douglas Huebler**	MTL	Brussels
	25.03–[ ].72	**Das Konzept ist die Form** (*g*)	Kunstverein	Münster
	04.72	**Douglas Huebler, Variable Pieces: 15, 16, 17, 18, 19**	Jack Wendler	London
	13.04–04.05.72	**Douglas Huebler**	Konrad Fischer	Düsseldorf
	28.04–27.05.72	**Douglas Huebler/Sol LeWitt** (*g*)	MOMA	Oxford
	27.06.72	**Douglas Huebler** (mg)	Art & Project	Amsterdam
	17.12.72–28.01.73	**Douglas Huebler**	Kunstverein	Münster
	01.02–[ ].73	**Group show**	Sperone/Fischer	Rome
	21.03–[ ].73	**Douglas Huebler, Variable Pieces**	Sperone/Fischer	Rome
	13.04–18.05.73	**Douglas Huebler**	Jack Wendler	London
	28.04–27.05.73	**Douglas Huebler**	MOMA	Oxford
	15.08–[ ].73	**Douglas Huebler**	Art & Project	Amsterdam
	14.11–[ ].73	**Group show**	Sperone/Fischer	Rome
	1974	**Douglas Huebler**	Jack Wendler	London
	09.04–09.05.74	**Douglas Huebler, Duration Pieces and Variable Pieces**	MTL	Brussels
	19–24.06.74	**Eine Ausstellung zur ART 5'74**	Rolf Preisig	Basel
	05–26.09.74	**Douglas Huebler**	Konrad Fischer	Düsseldorf
	10.74	**Douglas Huebler, Variable Pieces**	Yvon Lambert	Paris
	10.04–[ ].74	**Douglas Huebler, Drawings**	Gian Enzo Sperone	Turin
	15.11–20.12.74	**Douglas Huebler**	Rolf Preisig	Basel
	02.75	**Douglas Huebler**	Françoise Lambert	Milan
	06.05–[ ].75	**Group show**	Gian Enzo Sperone	Rome
	22.06–16.07.75	**Auswahl** (*g*)	Museum	Mönchengladbach
	16.09–04.10.75	**Douglas Huebler**	MTL	Brussels
	18.11–[ ].75	**Group show**	Gian Enzo Sperone	Rome
	03.12–24.12.75	**Douglas Huebler**	MTL	Brussels
	22.12–[ ].75	**Group show**	Gian Enzo Sperone	Turin
	22.04–8.05.76	**Douglas Huebler** (with Leo Castelli, NY)	Sper/Westw/Fischer	New York
	07–09.76	**Summer Group show**	Art & Project	Amsterdam
Joseph Kosuth	30.09–12.10.69	**Prospect 69** (*g*)	Kunsthalle	Düsseldorf
	09.11–16.11.69	**Joseph Kosuth**	Gian Enzo Sperone	Turin
	22.11–30.11.69	**Jospeh Kosuth, Art as Idea as Idea**	Art & Project	Amsterdam
	04.07–18.07.70	**Joseph Kosuth, 11 Works from 1965**	Gian Enzo Sperone	Turin
	16.02–05.03.71	**Joseph Kosuth**	Paul Maenz	Cologne
	25.03–[ ].72	**Das Konzept ist die Form** (*g*)	Kunstverein	Münster
	21.12–[ ].72	**Joseph Kosuth, The 9th Investigation. Proposition 2**	Sperone/Fischer	Rome
	12.72	**Group show**	Gian Enzo Sperone	New York
	01.02–[ ].73	**Group show**	Sperone/Fischer	Rome
	17.03–19.04.73	**Art as Idea as Idea, 1967–68**	Paul Maenz	Brussels
	10.04–12.05.73	**Einige wesentliche Beispiele früher Konzpetueller Kunst** (*g*)	Paul Maenz	Cologne
	20.05–24.06.73	**Investigationen über Kunst & 'Problemkreise' seit 1965**	Kunstmuseum	Lucerne
	10.11–09.12.73	**Investigationen über Kunst und 'Problemkreise' seit 1965**	Kunstverein	Münster
	04.07–27.07.74	**13 Projekt '74** (*g*)	Paul Maenz	Cologne

ARTIST	DATE	EXHIBITION TITLE	LOCATION	CITY
Joseph Kosuth	28.09–07.10.73	**Prospect 73 – Malers Painters Peintres** (*g*)	Kunsthalle	Düsseldorf
	28.11–[ ].74	**Joseph Kosuth, The 10th Investigation. Proposition 7**	Sperone/Fischer	Rome
	1975	**Joseph Kosuth, Practice**	MTL	Brussels
	06.05–[ ].75	**Group show**	Gian Enzo Sperone	Rome
	18.11–[ ].75	**Group show**	Gian Enzo Sperone	Rome
	22.12–[ ].75	**Group show**	Gian Enzo Sperone	Turin
	25.02–20.03.76	**Joseph Kosuth and Sarah Charlesworth: Face/Surface** (*g*)	MTL	Brussels
	04.09–30.09.76	**Pläne/Zeichnungen/Diagramme** (*g*)	Paul Maenz	Cologne
	16.02–[ ].77	**Group show**	Gian Enzo Sperone	Rome
	18.05–15.06.77	**Accrochage (Graham, Kosuth, Mees** (*g*)	MTL	Brussels
Sol LeWitt	1968	**Sol LeWitt, Five Cubes**	Heiner Friedrich	Munich
	06.01–03.02.68	**Sol LeWitt**	Konrad Fischer	Düsseldorf
	13.02–08.03.68	**Group show**	Heiner Friedrich	Munich
	20–29.09.68	**Prospect 68** (*g*)	Kunsthalle	Düsseldorf
	17.01–23.02.69	**Minimal Art** (*g*)	Kunsthalle	Düsseldorf
	01.03–31.03.69	**Young American Artists** (*g*)	Wide White Space	Antwerp
	22.04–16.05.69	**Sol LeWitt**	Konrad Fischer	Düsseldorf
	24.04–01.06.69	**The Art of the Real, USA 1948–68** (*g*)	Tate Gallery	London
	30.09–12.10.69	**Prospect 69** (*g*)	Kunsthalle	Düsseldorf
	02.01.70	**Sol LeWitt, Lines and Combinations of Lines** (mg)	Art & Project	Amsterdam
	04.06–27.06.70	**Sol LeWitt, Wall Drawings**	Yvon Lambert	Paris
	12.06–[ ].70	**Sol LeWitt, Wall Drawings**	Gian Enzo Sperone	Turin
	15.06–14.07.70	**Sol LeWitt**	Lisson Gallery	London
	09.70	**Drawings**	Heiner Friedrich	Munich
	09.70	**American Drawings** (*g*)	Yvon Lambert	Paris
	01.71	**Wall Show** (*g*)	Lisson Gallery	London
	04.01.71	**Ten Thousand Lines-Six Thousand Two Hundred and Fifty Lines** (mg)	Art & Project	Amsterdam
	02.71	**Group show**	Françoise Lambert	Milan
	06–07.71	**Sol LeWitt**	Lisson Gallery	London
	03.09–01.10.71	**Sol LeWitt**	Konrad Fischer	Düsseldorf
	07.09–02.10.71	**Sol LeWitt, Proposition for two Wall Paintings**	Art & Project	Amsterdam
	29.10–05.12.71	**Actualité d'un bilan** (*g*)	Yvon Lambert	Paris
	25.03–[ ].72	**Das Konzept ist die Form** (*g*)	Kunstverein	Münster
	28.04–27.05.72	**Douglas Huebler/Sol LeWitt** (*g*)	MOMA	Oxford
	05.07–26.09.72	**Sol LeWitt, Wall Drawings**	MTL	Brussels
	09–10.72	**Arcs and Lines, Lines and Lines**	Konrad Fischer	Düsseldorf
	25.09.72	**Sol LeWitt** (mg)	Art & Project	Amsterdam
	12.72	**Group show**	Gian Enzo Sperone	New York
	09.01–[ ].73	**Sol LeWitt**	Yvon Lambert	Paris
	01.02–[ ].73	**Group show**	Sperone/Fischer	Rome
	27.04–27.05.73	**Sol LeWitt**	MOMA	Oxford
	03–31.05.73	**Sol LeWitt, Wall Drawings and Structures**	Lisson Gallery	London
	03.09–[ ].73	**Sol LeWitt**	MTL	Brussels
	13.11–08.12.73	**Sol LeWitt**	MTL/Art & Project	Antwerp
	27.01–14.03.74	**Sculpture, Prints and Drawings** (*g*)	MOMA	Oxford
	03.74	**Incomplete Open Cubes**	Yvon Lambert	Paris
	04–05.74	**Sol LeWitt, The Location of Lines**	Lisson Gallery	London
	16.05–09.06.74	**Sol LeWitt, Ripped Paper Drawings: Two Series of Fifteen Each**	MTL	Brussels
	16.05 16.06.74	**Hanne Darboven and Sol LeWitt**	Pal. des Beaux-Arts	Brussels
	12.06–[ ].74	**Tre disegni su parete. Posizione di un rettangolo, di un trpezoide e di un parallelogramma**	Gian Enzo Sperone	Turin
	19–24.06.74	**Eine Ausstellung zur ART 5'74**	Rolf Preisig	Basel
	29.11.74–26.01.75	**Sol LeWitt, Prints**	Stedelijk Museum	Amsterdam
	1975	**Incomplete Open Cubes**	Van Abbemuseum	Eindhoven
	1975	**Sol LeWitt, Graphik 1970–75**	Kunstmuseum	Basel
	04.03–15.03.75	**Sol LeWitt**	Art & Project	Amsterdam
	14.03–20.04.75	**Group Show**	Museum	Mönchengladbach
	07.05–07.06.75	**Lines from Four Sides of Four Walls**	Konrad Fischer	Düsseldorf
	22.06–16.07.75	**Auswahl** (*g*)	Museum	Mönchengladbach
	23.09–[ ].75	**Sol LeWitt, Incomplete Open Cubes**	Gian Enzo Sperone	Turin
	18.10–22.11.75	**The Location of Red, Yellow and Blue Lines on Yellow, Red and Blue Wall**	Rolf Preisig	Basel
	18.11–[ ].75	**Group show**	Gian Enzo Sperone	Rome
	22.12–[ ].75	**Group show**	Gian Enzo Sperone	Turin
	11.01–08.02.76	**Group show**	MOMA	Oxford
	10.06–[ ].76	**Sol LeWitt**	Gian Enzo Sperone	Rome

ARTIST	DATE	EXHIBITION TITLE	LOCATION	CITY
	07–09.76	**Summer Group show**	Art & Project	Amsterdam
	04.09–30.09.76	**Pläne/Zeichnungen/Diagramme** (*g*)	Paul Maenz	Cologne
	19.11–15.12.76	**Sol LeWitt, Geometric Figures**	MTL	Brussels
	04.12–20.12.76	**War Resisters League Benefit** (*g*)	Heiner Friedrich	New York
	12.03–01.04.77	**Geometric Figures**	Konrad Fischer	Düsseldorf
	12.03–[ ].77	**Minimal Show** (*g*)	Sper/Westw/Fischer	New York
	12.03–09.04.77	**New Works, Structures and Early Working Drawings**	Lisson Gallery	London
	24.04–29.05.77	**Incomplete Open Cubes**	MOMA	Oxford
Bruce Nauman	10.07–08.08.68	**6 Day Week – 6 Sound Problems**	Konrad Fischer	Düsseldorf
	20–29.09.68	**Prospect 68** (*g*)	Kunsthalle	Düsseldorf
	25.11–15.12.68	**Bruce Nauman**	Ileana Sonnabend	Paris
	1969	**Kompass IV, Westkust USA** (*g*)	Van Abbemuseum	Eindhoven
	01.03–31.03.69	**Young American Artists** (*g*)	Wide White Space	Antwerp
	15.03–27.04.69	**Op Losse Schroeven, Situaties en Cryptostructuren** (*g*)	Stedelijk Museum	Amsterdam
	02.12–[ ].69	**Bruce Nauman**	Ileana Sonnabend	Paris
	05.02–03.03.70	**Bruce Nauman**	Konrad Fischer	Düsseldorf
	25.02–10.03.70	**Bruce Nauman**	Gian Enzo Sperone	Turin
	09.70	**American Drawings** (*g*)	Yvon Lambert	Paris
	1971	**Films**	Heiner Friedrich	Cologne
	02.71	**Group Show**	Françoise Lambert	Milan
	02.03–[ ].71	**Bruce Nauman**	Ileana Sonnabend	Paris
	05.03–01.04.71	**Bruce Nauman**	Konrad Fischer	Düsseldorf
	30.04–06.06.71	**Leucht-Schrift-Kunst (Air Art)** (*g*)	Stedelijk Museum	Amsterdam
	08–17.10.71	**Prospect 71 – Projection** (*g*)	Kunsthalle	Düsseldorf
	06.12.71–05.01.72	**Bruce Nauman**	Françoise Lambert	Milan
	20.01–04.03.73	**Diagrams and Drawings** (*g*)	Kunstmuseum	Basel
	01.02–[ ].73	**Group show**	Sperone/Fischer	Rome
	28.08–23.09.73	**Bruce Nauman, Werke von 1965 bis 1972**	Kunsthalle	Düsseldorf
	12.10–25.11.73	**Light Objects, Environment, Video-Sculptures**	Van Abbemuseum	Eindhoven
	1974	**Bruce Nauman**	Ileana Sonnabend	Paris
	01–03.74	**Bruce Nauman**	Kunstmuseum	Basel
	04.02–06.03.74	**Yellow Body**	Konrad Fischer	Düsseldorf
	26.02–30.03.74	**Artisti della West Coast** (*g*)	Françoise Lambert	Milan
	08.03–11.04.74	**Bruce Nauman, Snaf**	Wide White Space	Antwerp
	19–24.06.74	**Eine Ausstellung zur ART 5'74**	Rolf Preisig	Basel
	08.01–01.02.75	**Drawings** (*g*)	Wide White Space	Antwerp
	16.03–20.04.75	**Spiralen und Progressionen** (*g*)	Kunstmuseum	Lucerne
	18.11–[ ].75	**Group show**	Gian Enzo Sperone	Rome
	16.12.75–24.01.76	**Forced Perspective/Open Mind/ Equal Mind/Parallel Mind (Allegory and Symbolism)**	Konrad Fischer	Düsseldorf
	1976	**Räume** (*g*)	Museum	Mönchengladbach
	07.02–04.04.76	**Functions of Drawings** (*g*)	Kunstmuseum	Basel
	30.10–27.11.76	**Bruce Nauman, The Consummate Mask of Rock**	Sper/Westw/Fischer	New York
Robert Ryman	13.02–08.03.68	**Group show**	Heiner Friedrich	Munich
	10–11.68	**Robert Ryman**	Heiner Friedrich	Munich
	21.11–17.12.68	**Robert Ryman**	Konrad Fischer	Düsseldorf
	15.03–27.04.69	**Op Losse Schroeven, Situaties en Cryptostructuren** (*g*)	Stedelijk Museum	Amsterdam
	30.09–12.10.69	**Prospect 69** (*g*)	Kunsthalle	Düsseldorf
	11.11–12.12.69	**Robert Ryman**	Konrad Fischer	Düsseldorf
	21.11–20.12.69	**Robert Ryman, Drawings and Paintings**	Heiner Friedrich	Munich
	12.69–01.70	**Robert Ryman**	Françoise Lambert	Milan
	12.69	**Robert Ryman**	Yvon Lambert	Paris
	12.69–01.70	**Minimal Art** (*g*)	Kunstmuseum	Basel
	09.70	**American Drawings** (*g*)	Yvon Lambert	Paris
	02.71	**Group show**	Françoise Lambert	Milan
	06.71	**Group show**	Françoise Lambert	Milan
	26.06–27.07.71	**Standart**	Heiner Friedrich	Cologne
	29.10–05.12.71	**Actualité d'un bilan** (*g*)	Yvon Lambert	Paris
	1972	**Group Show**	Heiner Friedrich	Cologne
	06.04–16.04.72	**Group show**	Françoise Lambert	Milan
	06.72	**Robert Ryman**	Heiner Friedrich	Munich
	09–10.72	**31 Trail Proofs**	Heiner Friedrich	Cologne
	05.12.72–20.01.73	**Robert Ryman**	Lisson Gallery	London
	01.02–[ ].73	**Group show**	Sperone/Fischer	Rome
	28.09–[ ].73	**Robert Ryman, Suite of Seven Aquatints (1972) + Nine Unique Aquatints (1972)**	Art & Project	Amsterdam

ARTIST	DATE	EXHIBITION TITLE	LOCATION	CITY
Robert Ryman	28.09–07.10.73	**Prospect 73 – Malers Painters Peintres**	Kunsthalle	Düsseldorf
	11.73	**Robert Ryman**	Konrad Fischer	Düsseldorf
	15.11–23.12.73	**Eine Malerei Ausstellung** (*g*)	Museum	Mönchengladbach
	1974	**Robert Ryman**	Pal. des Beaux-Arts	Brussels
	01.02–24.03.74	**Paintings: survey from 1958 until now**	Stedelijk Museum	Amsterdam
	30.03–28.04.74	**Geplante Malerei** (*g*)	Kunstverein	Münster
	12.05–16.06.74	**Das komplette graphische Werk**	Kunstverein	Münster
	19–24.06.74	**Eine Ausstellung zur ART 5'74**	Rolf Preisig	Basel
	10.74	**Robert Ryman**	Kunstmuseum	Basel
	03.12.74–18.01 75	**Paintings** (*g*)	Lisson Gallery	London
	01–02.75	**Daniel Buren, Robert Ryman, Ian Wilson** (*g*)	MTL	Brussels
	27.02–[ ].75	**Baer, Mangold, Renouf, Ryman** (*g*)	MTL	Brussels
	25.05–22.06.75	**Fundamental painting** (*g*)	Stedelijk Museum	Amsterdam
	10–20.06.76	**Andre, Judd, Ryman – ART 7'76**	Rolf Preisig	Basel
	03.05–[ ].77	**Robert Ryman**	Gian Enzo Sperone	Rome
Lawrence Weiner	15.03–27.04.69	**Op Losse Schroeven, Situaties en Cryptostructuren** (*g*)	Stedelijk Museum	Amsterdam
	10.04–[ ].69	**Lawrence Weiner**	Konrad Fischer	Düsseldorf
	20.06–30.06.69	**Lawrence Weiner**	Wide White Space	Antwerp
	01.09.69	**A Translation from One Language to Another** (mg)	Art & Project	Amsterdam
	30.09–12.10.69	**Prospect 69** (*g*)	Kunsthalle	Düsseldorf
	03.12–10.12.69	**Lawrence Weiner (Statements, Concepts)**	Gian Enzo Sperone	Turin
	19.03–26.03.70	**Lawrence Weiner**	Yvon Lambert	Paris
	25.11–11.12.70	**Lawrence Weiner**	Konrad Fischer	Düsseldorf
	14.12–22.12.70	**Lawrence Weiner**	Gian Enzo Sperone	Turin
	01.71	**Wall Show** (*g*)	Lisson Gallery	London
	03.02–13.02.71	**Lawrence Weiner, 10 works (book)**	Yvon Lambert	Paris
	26.02–[ ].03.71	**Eight proposals** (*g*)	Françoise Lambert	Milan
	08–17.10.71	**Prospect 71 – Projection** (*g*)	Kunsthalle	Düsseldorf
	29.10–05.12.71	**Actualité d'un bilan** (*g*)	Yvon Lambert	Paris
	30.12.71–06.01.72	**And/or: green as well as blue as well as red**	Jack Wendler	London
	1972	**Lawrence Weiner, record plaat 7**	Yvon Lambert	Paris
	18.03–23.04.72	**'Konzept'-Kunst** (*g*)	Kunstmuseum	Basel
	25.03–[ ].72	**Das Konzept ist die Form** (*g*)	Kunstverein	Munster
	04.72	**Lawrence Weiner**	Konrad Fischer	Düsseldorf
	22.04–12.05.72	**Lawrence Weiner**	Art & Project	Amsterdam
	08.05.72	**Lawrence Weiner** (mg)	Art & Project	Amsterdam
	24.06–25.06.72	**Contributions to Newspapers: *Gazet van Antwerpen, International Herald Tribune***	Wide White Space	Antwerp
	9.11–14.11.72	**Lawrence Weiner, Disco 7**	Françoise Lambert	Milan
	16.12.72–07.01.73	**Kunst als Boek** (*g*)	Stedelijk Museum	Amsterdam
	01.02–[ ].73	**Group show**	Sperone/Fischer	Rome
	06.73	**Mailing of a Card, Collection Public Freehold**	Wide White Space	Antwerp
	15.09–14.10.73	**Lawrence Weiner, 50 Arbeiten**	Kunstverein	Munster
	17–30.09.73	**With relation to the various manners with various things**	Jack Wendler	London
	25.09–16.10.73	**Lawrence Weiner**	Jack Wendler	London
	28.09–07.10.73	**Prospect 73 – Malers Painters Peintres**	Kunsthalle	Düsseldorf
	04.10–04.11.73	**8 Arbeiten von Lawrence Weiner**	Museum	Mönchengladbach
	27.11–22.12.73	**Six Works of Lawrence Weiner presented by Wide White Space Bruxelles/Antwerp for Sale and/or Information over a Period of Time**	Wide White Space	Brussels
	29.11–[ ].73	**Presentation of a new record of Lawrence Weiner (Having been done at/Having been done to)**	Sperone/Fischer	Rome
	30.11–[ ].73	**Two Works of Lawrence Weiner**	Gian Enzo Sperone	Turin
	11.12–21.12.73	**Lawrence Weiner**	Art & Project	Amsterdam
	10.05–08.06.74	**With a Relation to the Various Manners of Resonance**	Rolf Preisig	Basel
	19–24.06.74	**Eine Ausstellung zur ART 5'74** (*g*)	Rolf Preisig	Basel
	12.09–26.09.74	**3 works of Lawrence Weiner**	Yvon Lambert	Paris
	28.01–20.02.75	**3 Works in Relation to Place**	Konrad Fischer	Düsseldorf
	26.04–[ ].75	**Lawrence Weiner**	Gian Enzo Sperone	Turin
	22.06–16.07.75	**Auswahl** (*g*)	Museum	Mönchengladbach
	28.11–23.12.75	**Carried to Great Lengths...**	Rolf Preisig	Basel

ARTIST	DATE	EXHIBITION TITLE	LOCATION	CITY
	12.03–26.04.76	**A Selection of Works by Lawrence Weiner with a Commentary by H.R. Fuchs**	Van Abbemuseum	Eindhoven
	07–09.76	**Summer Group show**	Art & Project	Amsterdam
	28.08–03.10.76	**Lawrence Weiner**	Kunstmuseum	Basel
	1977	**Lawrence Weiner, A Work**	Yvon Lambert	Paris
	27.04–13.05.77	**Lawrence Weiner**	Konrad Fischer	Düsseldorf
	04.05–05.06.77	**A Work of Lawrence Weiner Presented within the Context of an Installation**	Wide White Space	Antwerp

Marcel Broodthaers

Modèle: la pipe
(1969, polyester plate)
1969 · Wide White Space, Antwerp
(purchase, 1978)

M.B.
(1973, ink on paper)
1974 · Michael Werner, Cologne
(purchase, 1983)

La plume de l'ange
(1974, ink on cloth and paper napkin)
1974 · the artist (purchase, 1980)

Citron-citroen (réclame pour le mer du Nord)
(1974, screenprint)
1974 · Galerie Seriaal, Amsterdam
(gift, 1995)

The ballad of a star over Reading Gaol (1974, oil on 3 canvases)
1974 · the artist, through Wide White Space, Antwerp (by G.J. Visser)
(purchase, 2000)

Au clair de la lune
(1973, ink and print on paper)
before 1976 · gift from the artist
(purchase, 1987)

Musée d'art moderne dépt des aigles, Service publicité
(1971, polyester plate)
before 1978 · Galerie Seriaal, Amsterdam (purchase, 1978)

La bouteille de lait
(1968, photograph with inscription)
before 1979 · gift from the artist
(gift, 1979)

Piero Manzoni dubs Broodthaers a work
(undated, ink and offset print on paper)
before 1986 · gift from the artist
(gift, 1986)

Daniel Buren

Peinture sur toile
(1970, red and white striped canvas)
1970 · Wide White Space, Antwerp
(purchase, 1981)

Peinture sur toile
(1972, orange and white striped canvas and curtain hooks)
1972 · Wide White Space, Antwerp
(gift, 1984)

Passage
(1972, boxed book)
1972 · the artist (purchase, 1992)

Hanne Darboven

Zeichnung Striche
(1966, ink on graph paper)
1967 · Konrad Fischer, Düsseldorf
(purchase, 1983)

Zeichnung
(1968, ink on graph paper)
1968 · Konrad Fischer, Düsseldorf
(purchase, 1992)

Zeichnung
(1968, ink on graph paper)
1968 · gift from the artist
(purchase, 1983)

Zahlen Zeichnung
(1967, pencil on paper)
1972 · Konrad Fischer, Düsseldorf
(purchase, 1992)

19 Zahlenzeichnungen or Part-19. part 1. book 1
(1973, 20 drawings)
1973 · Art & Project, Amsterdam
(purchase, 1983)

Cover design for the catalogue Funkties van tekenen
(1975, ink on paper)
1975 · gift from the artist (gift, 1980)

Untitled
(1972–73, pencil on paper)
1979 · Galerie Durand-Dessert, Paris
(purchase, 1992)

Zahlenzeichnungen
(1970, ink on paper)
before 1980 · gift from the artist
(gift, 1980)

Zeichnung Plan
(1968, ink and pencil on paper)
before 1981 · the artist
(purchase, 1981)

Jan Dibbets

Merwede
(1970, photo collage with map and text)
1970 · Konrad Fischer, Düsseldorf
(purchase, 1983)

Study for Merwede
(1970, photo collage)
1970 · Konrad Fischer, Düsseldorf
(purchase, 1983)

Gilbert & George

A message from the sculptors
(1969, card, photographs and various leftovers)
1969 · gift from the artists (gift, 1996)

Postal sculpture
(1969, print)
1970 · gift from the artists (gift, 1996)

The sadness in our art
(1970, print)
1970 · gift from the artists (gift, 1996)

To be with art is all we ask
(1970, print and photograph)
1970 · gift from the artists (gift, 1996)

The pencil on paper descriptive works
(1970, print and card)
1971 · gift from the artists (gift, 1996)

The limericks
(1971, 8-part postal sculpture)
1971 · gift from the artists (gift, 1996)

A day in the life of Gilbert & George (1971, printed matter and photographs)
1971 · gift from the artists (gift, 1996)

The Ten Speeches of Gilbert & George the sculptors
(1971, printed matter)
1971 · the artists (by G.J. Visser) (gift, 2001)

A Day in the Life of Gilbert & George the sculptors
(1971, printed matter)
1971 · the artists (by G.J. Visser) (gift, 2001)

2nd Postcard
(1972, printed matter)
1972 · gift from the artists (gift, 1996)

The pink elephants
(1973, printed matter)
1973 · gift from the artists (gift, 1996)

Human Bondage no. 6
(1974, 9 part photo-piece)
1974 · Art & Project, Amsterdam (by G.J. Visser) (purchase, 2000)

The red boxers
(1975, printed matter)
1976 · gift from the artists (gift, 1996)

Angry
(1977, 25 part photo-piece)
1980 · Art & Project, Amsterdam (by G.J. Visser) (purchase, 2000)

Richard Long

Stone sculpture
(1971, pencil on paper)
1971 · Konrad Fischer, Düsseldorf (purchase, 1984)

Twelve Circles of sticks
(1973–74, 701-cm-wide floor sculpture)
1973 · Konrad Fischer, Düsseldorf (purchased by G.J. Visser, 1974; purchase, 2000)

With the River towards the Sea, A Walk down the Riverbed in Joyce's Country, County Galway
(1974, photo collage)
1974 · John Weber, New York (purchased by G.J. Visser, 1984; purchase, 2000)

A line, the length of a straight walk from the bottom to the top of Glastonbury Tor in Somerset. A clay track sculpture
(1973, photographs)
1974 · Konrad Fischer, Düsseldorf (purchase, 1991)

Untitled (A thousand stones)
(1976, ink on transparent paper)
1976 · gift from the artist (gift, 1981)

Untitled
(1976, ink on transparent paper)
1976 · gift from the artist (gift, 1981)

Untitled (41–50)
(1976, ink on transparent paper)
1976 · gift from the artist (gift, 1981)

Untitled
(1976, shirt with embroidery)
1976 · Konrad Fischer, Düsseldorf (gift, 2001)

Two Journeys one road, A Clockwise Walk Summer 1974, A Clockwise Bicycle Ride Winter 1975
(1974–75, pencil on paper)
1978 · Rolf Preisig, Zurich (purchase by G.J. Visser, 1984; purchase, 2000)

Slate stone circle
(1979, 21 part floor sculpture)
1979 · gift from the artist

Carl Andre

Square piece (For Mia and Martin Visser)
(1967, 100 part floor sculpture)
1967 · Konrad Fischer, Düsseldorf (purchase, 1990)

Dutch poem
(1967, ink on paper)
1967 · gift from the artist (gift, 1996)

Poem
(1967, ink on paper)
1968 · Konrad Fischer, Düsseldorf (purchase, 1978)

Copper Ribbon
(1969, sculpture)
1969 · Wide White Space, Antwerp (by G.J. Visser); (purchase, 1995, with support from the Mondriaan Stichting)

Timber piece
(1968, 35 part floor sculpture)
1970 · Konrad Fischer, Düsseldorf (purchase, 1990)

Copper inside-out piece
(1969, 2 part floor sculpture)
1970 · Konrad Fischer, Düsseldorf (purchase, 1990)

Weathering Piece
(1970, 36 part floor sculpture)
1971 · Wide White Space, Antwerp (by G.J. Visser); (purchase, 1995, with support of the Mondriaan Stichting)

Timber Piece, Henge on threshold (Meditation on the year 1960)
(1971, sculpture)
1971 · Konrad Fischer, Düsseldorf (with G.J. Visser); (1977, purchased by Dr C.H. van der Leeuw Foundation; gift, 1977)

Lead Ribbon
(1969, sculpture)
1971 · Wide White Space, Antwerp (purchase, 1989)

101 Brass scallop run
(1972, 100 part floor sculpture)
1972 · Konrad Fischer, Düsseldorf (purchase, 1989)

White chalk run
(1972, 36 part sculpture)
1972 · Konrad Fischer, Düsseldorf (purchase, 1989)

54 part steel cut
(1972, 54 part sculpture)
1973 · John Weber, New York (purchase, 1989)

4 Piece sort
(1972, sculpture)
1973 · Konrad Fischer, Düsseldorf (purchase, 1989)

Quaker Battery
(1973, 5 part outside sculpture)
1973 · gift from the artist (purchase, 1989)

Copper-steel dipole N/S
(1973, 2 part sculpture)
1973 · Konrad Fischer, Düsseldorf (1980, purchased by G.J. Visser; purchase, 1995, with support from the Mondriaan Stichting)

Copper-steel dipole W/E
(1973, 2 part sculpture)
1973 · Konrad Fischer, Düsseldorf (by G.J. Visser); (purchase, 1995, with support from the Mondriaan Stichting)

Four paintings
(1963, 4 paintings)
1976 · Konrad Fischer, Düsseldorf (with G.J. Visser); (purchased by Martin Visser, 1980; purchase, 1989)

Squantum
(1976, 36 part sculpture)
1979 [ ].· Konrad Fischer, Düsseldorf (purchase, 1989)

4 × Untitled
(1972, screenprint)
date unkown · provenance unknown (gift, 2001)

6 × Untitled
(1974, screenprint)
date unkown · provenance unknown (gift, 2001)

Joseph Kosuth

One and three glass
(1965, 1977 version, installation)
1976 · Art & Project/MTL, Antwerp (by G.J. Visser); (purchase, 1995, with support from the Mondriaan Stichting)

Sol LeWitt

Working drawing for 'Serial project set ABCD'
(1966–67, drawing)
1967 · gift from the artist (purchase, 1992)

9 Square grid for sets ABC or D
(1966–67, drawing)
1967 · gift from the artist (gift, 1981)

Working drawing for set A o/o
(1967, drawing)
1967 · the artist (gift, 1977, by the Dr C.H. van der Leeuw Foundation)

Working Drawing for set B c/o
(1967, drawing)
1967 · the artist (gift, 1977, by the Dr C.H. van der Leeuw Foundation)

Working Drawing for set C o/c
(1967, drawing)
1967 · the artist (gift, 1977, by the Dr C.H. van der Leeuw Foundation)

Working Drawing for set D c/c
(1967, drawing)
1967 · the artist (gift, 1977, by the Dr C.H. van der Leeuw Foundation)

Serial project no. 1 (ABCD) set A
(1966, executed 1968, structure)
1967 · Konrad Fischer, Düsseldorf (by G.J. Visser); (gift, 1977, by the Dr C.H. van der Leeuw Foundation)

Serial project no. 1 (ABCD) set C
(1966, executed 1968, sctructure)
1967 · Konrad Fischer, Düsseldorf (gift, 1977, by the Dr C.H. van der Leeuw Foundation)

Untitled
(c. 1966, drawing)
1967 · gift from the artist (purchase, 1992)

6 Part piece for Martin and Mia Visser (1968, drawing)
1968 · gift from the artist (gift, 1977)

6 Part piece for Martin and Mia Visser (1967–68, executed 1969, sculpture)
1968 · gift from the artist (gift, 1977)

Working drawing for eight wall pieces (1968, drawing)
1968 · gift from the artist (gift, 1981)

Wall pieces
(1968, drawings)
1968 · gift from the artist (gift, 1981)

Untitled
(c. 1968, drawing)
1968 · the artist (purchase, 1983)

Working drawing for table with washers
(1969, drawing)
1969 · gift from the artist (gift, 1981)

Working drawing for grid table
(1969, drawing)
1969 · gift from the artist (gift, 1981)

Lines, colors and their combinations
(1969–70, 16 drawings)
1970 · Konrad Fischer, Düsseldorf (purchase, 1991)

Small drawing for Mia and Martin Visser
(1971, drawing)
1971 · gift from the artist (gift, 1981)

Lines in three directions
(1971, drawing)
1971 · the artist (purchase, 1985)

Lines in four directions
(1971, drawing)
1971 · the artist (purchase, 1984)

Wall drawing at Visser residence no. 117, Four part drawing
(1970–75, wall drawing)
1971 · Konrad Fischer, Düsseldorf (purchase, 1992)

Plan for wall drawing for Visser House, Bergeyk, Holland
(1971, drawing)
1971 · Konrad Fischer, Düsseldorf (purchase, 1991)

Working drawings for the first page of the book: Four basic colors and their combinations
(1971, 4 drawings)
1973 · Lisson Gallery, London (purchase, 1985)

Paper torn from the corners towards the center
(1975, paper collage)
1975 · the artist (purchase, 1985)

Paper torn from the sides towards the center
(1975, paper collage)
1975 · the artist (purchase, 1985)

Rip drawing R214
(1974, drawing)
1975 · Art & Project, Amsterdam (gift, 1981)

Rip drawing R216
(1974, drawing)
1975 · Art & Project, Amsterdam (gift, 1981)

Untitled
(1975, drawing on beer mat)
1975 · gift from the artist (gift, 1981)

The location of a quadrangle, a circle and a not-straight line
(1975, drawing)
1976 · Konrad Fischer, Düsseldorf (purchase, 1992)

The location of a circle and a not straight line
(1975, drawing)
1976 · Konrad Fischer, Düsseldorf (purchase, 1992)

The location of a yellow rectangle, blue parallelogram, red circle and black trapezoid
(1976, drawing)
1976 · Konrad Fischer, Düsseldorf (purchase, 1992)

The location of a circle, a square and a straight line
(1975, drawing)
1976 · Konrad Fischer, Düsseldorf (purchase, 1992)

Red lines from the midpoint of the left side, blue lines from the lower right corner
(1975, drawing)
1976 · Konrad Fischer, Düsseldorf (purchase, 1991)

Drawing for a painted woodwall structure
(1977, 3 versions; ink on paper)
1977 · gift from the artist (purchase, 1992)

Working drawing for 7 part piece
(1968, drawing)
date unknown · Dick van der Net (1968); (gift, 1981)

Working drawing for 2 modular pieces
(1968, drawing)
date unknown · Dick van der Net (1968); (purchase, 1984)

Working drawing for open cube and closed cube
(1968, drawing)
date unknown · Dick van der Net (1968); (purchase, 1984)

Working drawing for open cubic cube (1968, drawing)
date unknown · Dick van der Net (1968); (purchase, 1984)

Working drawing for three modular pieces
(1969, drawing)
date unkown · Dick van der Net (1969); (purchase, 1985)

Untitled, or Folded paper piece
(1971, 2 versions; folded paper)
date unknown · Konrad Fischer, Düsseldorf (gift, 1981)

Bruce Nauman

Space under my (steel) chair in Düsseldorf
(1965–68, executed 1968, drawing)
1968 · Konrad Fischer, Düsseldorf (by G.J. Visser; purchase, 1995, with support from the Mondriaan Stichting)

A cast of the space under my chair
(1965–68, sculpture)
1968 · Konrad Fischer, Düsseldorf (by G.J. Visser; purchase, 1995, with support from the Mondriaan Stichting and Vereniging Rembrandt)

First poem piece
(1968, sculpture)
1968 · Konrad Fischer, Düsseldorf (purchase, 1986)

Study for first poem piece
(1968, drawing)
1968 · Konrad Fischer, Düsseldorf (purchase, 1988)

You may not want to be here / tape loop – 1 word each second / 80 second loop
(1968, drawing)
1968 · Konrad Fischer, Düsseldorf (purchase, 1986)

Platform made up of the space between two rectilinear boxes on the floor
(1966, sculpture)
1972 · Nigel Greenwood, London (with G.J. Visser; 1980 by G.J. Visser; purchase, 1995 with support from the Mondriaan Stichting and Vereniging Rembrandt)

Drawing for white/pink/yellow tubes piece
(1971, drawing)
1976 · Konrad Fischer, Düsseldorf (purchase, 1988)

Untitled (Room with partitions)
(1972, drawing)
1976 · Konrad Fischer, Düsseldorf (purchase, 1989)

Forced perspective – concave
(1975, drawing)
1976 · Konrad Fischer, Düsseldorf (purchase, 1988)

Mask of rock II – rhomboidal stone blocks
(1975, drawing)
1976 · Konrad Fischer, Düsseldorf (purchase, 1988)

Plan view – Double ended steel cage
(1975, drawing)
1976 · Konrad Fischer, Düsseldorf (purchase, 1988)

Spilling coffee because the cup was too hot
(1966, drawing)
1977 · provenance unknown (by Martin Visser; purchase, 1988)

Alternate
(1977, drawing)
1977 · Konrad Fischer, Düsseldorf (purchase, 1988)

Study for Untitled (Model for trench, shaft and tunnel)
(1977, 3 versions, drawings)
1978 · Konrad Fischer, Düsseldorf (by Martin and G.J. Visser; purchase, 1988)

Two blocks of lead driven apart by a steel wedge
(1968, drawing)
date unknown · Rolf Ricke, Cologne (purchase, 1986)

Drawing for First hologram series: making faces (I–B)
(1967, drawing)
date unknown · Konrad Fischer, Düsseldorf (purchase, 1988)

Lawrence Weiner

Perhaps after being redone
(1971, statement)
1971 · Art & Project, Amsterdam (purchase, 1993)

Richard Long

Sculpture at Gallery Lambert
(1969, floor sculpture)
1969 · Françoise Lambert, Milan

Sculpture at Konrad Fischer
(1969)
19[ ] · Gian Enzo Sperone, Turin

Untitled Sculpture, June 1968 England
(1967, 2 photographs)
1972 · John Weber, New York

Untitled – England
(1967, 2 prints)
1973 · John Weber, New York

Stone Circle
(1976, 105 part sculpture)
1976 · Lisson Gallery, London

Stone Circle
(1976, 182 part sculpture)
1976 · Gian Enzo Sperone, Turin

Carl Andre

249 Brass Run
(1969, 249 part sculpture)
1969 · Gian Enzo Sperone, Turin

6 × 6 Den Haag Steel Lock
(1968, 36 part sculpture)
1972 · John Weber, New York

2 × 18 Aluminium Lock
(1968, 36 part sculpture)
1973 · John Weber, New York

Fall
(1968, 21 part sculpture)
1973 · John Weber, New York

10 × 10 Altstadt Copper Square
(1967, 100 part sculpture)
1973 · Konrad Fischer, Düsseldorf

Reef
(1966, 75 part sculpture)
1973 · Heiner Friedrich, Munich

5 × 20 Altstadt Rectangle
(1967, 100 part sculpture)
1974 · Konrad Fischer, Düsseldorf

Portland Regulus
(1974, sculpture installation)
1975 · Sperone-Westwater-Fischer, New York

2001 Slope
(1968, 6 part sculpture)
1975 · Gian Enzo Sperone, Turin

Third Copper Triode
(1975, 4 part sculpture)
1976 · Sperone-Westwater-Fischer, New York

Fifth Copper Triode
(1975, 7 part sculpture)
1976 · Sperone-Westwater-Fischer, New York

Seventeenth Copper Triode
(1975, 25 part sculpture)
1976 · Sperone-Westwater-Fischer, New York

Douglas Huebler

Location Piece #9, New England, March 1969
(1969, photo collage)
1969 · Gian Enzo Sperone, Turin
(gift to GM)

Sol LeWitt

Wall Drawing #146, All two part combinations of blue arcs from corners and sides, and blue straight, not straight, and broken lines
(1972)
1972 · John Weber, New York
(gift to GM)

Wall Drawing #262, All one-, two-, three-, and four part combinations of lines in four directions and four colors, each within a square
(1975)
1975 · the artist (to be installed at Panza's residence in Varese; gift to GM)

Bruce Nauman

Lighted Center Piece
(1967–68, neon piece)
1969 · Leo Castelli, New York

Touch and Sound Walls
(1969, wall structure)
1969 · Leo Castelli, New York

Lighted Performance Box
(1969, neon piece)
1970 · Gian Enzo Sperone, Turin

Acoustic Wedge (Sound Wedge – Double Wedge), (Wallboard and acoustic material)
(1969–70, wall structure)
1970 · Ileana Sonnabend, Paris

Sound Breaking Wall
(1969, wall structure)
1970 · Ileana Sonnabend, New York

Performance Parallelogram (Rolling)
(1970–71, installation)
1970 · Leo Castelli, New York

None Sing – Neon Sign
(1970, neon piece)
1970 · Leo Castelli, New York

Diagonal Sound Wall (Acoustic Wall)
(1970, wall structure)
1970 · Konrad Fischer, Düsseldorf

Four Fans Room (Enclosed)
(1970, installation)
1973 · Konrad Fischer, Düsseldorf

Acoustic Corridor (Castelli Gallery)
(1973, installation)
1973 · Leo Castelli, New York

Double Wedge Corridor (with mirror)
(1970–74, installation)
1973 · Ileana Sonnabend, New York

Two Fans Corridor
(1970, installation)
1974 · Konrad Fischer, Düsseldorf

Spinning Spheres
(1970, film)
1974 · Leo Castelli, New York

Pink and Yellow Light Corridor (Variable Lights)
(1972, light installation)
1974 · Konrad Fischer, Düsseldorf

Floating Room (Light Outside, Dark Inside)
(1972, installation)
1974 · Leo Castelli, New York

Yellow Room (Triangular)
(1973, installation)
1974 · Konrad Fischer, Düsseldorf

Compression and Disappearance or Exit
(1974, masking tape)
1974 · Konrad Fischer, Düsseldorf

Acoustic Pressure Piece
(1971, wall structure)
1975 · Leo Castelli, New York

Double Doors – Projection and Displacement
(1973, wall structure)
1975 · Ace Gallery, Los Angeles

False Silence
(1975, installation)
1975 · Ace Gallery, Los Angeles

Forced Perspective II
(1975, sculpture installation)
1976 · Konrad Fischer, Düsseldorf

Triangle Room
(1978–80, installation)
1980 · exchange with the artist
(for Lambert Corridor, 1971)

Parallax Corridor
(1969–70, installation)
19[ ] · Leo Castelli, New York

Video Surveillance Piece (Public Room, Private Room)
(1969–70, installation)
19[ ] · Leo Castelli, New York

Green Light Corridor
(1970, installation)
19[ ] · Leo Castelli, New York

Yellow-Blue-Yellow Corridor on Three Sides of a Room
(1970, wall structure)
19[ ] · Konrad Fischer, Düsseldorf

Parallax Room with Three Horizontal Bars
(1971, installation)
19[ ] · Ileana Sonnabend, Paris

Kassel Corridor: Elliptical Space
(1972, installation)
19[ ] · Leo Castelli, New York

Robert Ryman

Allied
(1966, painting)
1971 · Gian Enzo Sperone, Turin

Aacon
(1968, painting)
1971 · Gian Enzo Sperone, Turin

Classico I
(1968, painting)
1971 · Konrad Fischer, Düsseldorf

Classico IV
(1968, painting)
1971 · Konrad Fischer, Düsseldorf

J. Green 1
(1968, painting)
1971 · Yvon Lambert, Paris

Classico XX
(1968–69, painting)
1971 · John Weber, New York

V
(1969, painting on cardboard)
1971 · Konrad Fischer, New York

Untitled (Four Units)
(1969, 4 paintings on cardboard)
1971 · Gian Enzo Sperone, New York

Untitled (Whitney Revision Painting 3)
(1969, 3 paintings on cardboard)
1971 · Françoise Lambert, Milan

Central
(1971, painting)
1971 · John Weber, New York

Surface Veil II
(1971, painting)
1971 · Yvon Lambert, Paris

Surface Veil I
(1970, painting)
1972 · Yvon Lambert, Paris

Classico II
(1968, painting)
1972 · Konrad Fischer, Düsseldorf

Surface Veil III
(1970, painting)
1972 · John Weber, New York

Empire
(1973, painting)
1973 · Konrad Fischer, Düsseldorf

Zenith
(1974, painting on wood)
1974 · John Weber, New York

Impex
(1968, painting on canvas and wall)
19[ ] · Heiner Friedrich, Munich

Lawrence Weiner

Cat. #029, The residue of a flare ignited upon a boundary
(1969, statement)
1970 · Konrad Fischer, Düsseldorf

Cat. #091, A stake set
(1969, statement)
1970 · Gian Enzo Sperone, Turin

Cat. #151, Earth to Earth Ashes to Ashes Dust to Dust
(1970, statement)
1970 · Yvon Lambert, Paris

Cat. #148, An amount of material placed upon the Ocean North of the coaxial cable. An amount of material placed upon the Ocean South of the coaxial cable (1970, statement)
1970 · [ ]

Cat. #085, A stake set in the ground in direct line with a stake set in the ground of an adjacent country
(1969, statement)
1971 · Gian Enzo Sperone, Turin

Cat. #238, Over and Over. Over and Over. And Over and Over. And Over and Over
(1971, statement)
1971 · Yvon Lambert, Paris

Cat. #278, To See and Be Seen
(1972, statement)
1971 · Yvon Lambert, Paris

Cat. #276, To Have and Have not
(1972, statement)
1972 · [ ]

Cat. #277, To Have and to Hold
(1972, statement)
1972 · [ ]

Cat. #279, To Give and to Take
(1972, statement)
1972 · [ ]

Cat. #280, To Show and to Tell
(1972, statement)
1972 · [ ]

Städtisches Museum, Mönchengladbach

Marcel Broodthaers

Théorie des Figures
(1970–71, box with objects)
1972 · the artist

Untitled
(1966, mural installation)
1980 · donation of the Museums-verein; purchased from H. Rothschild

Narcisse
(1966, mural installation)
1980 · donation of the Museums-verein; purchased from J. von Oppenheim

Un Coup de Dés
(1969, installation)
1980 · Galerie Borgmann, Cologne; with support from the Nordrhein Westfalen Land

Daniel Buren

Von da an/A partir de là
(1975, in situ environment)
1975 · the artist

Hanne Darboven

6 Filme nach 6 Büchern über 1968
(1968, 6 films)
1969 · gift from the artist

Ohne Titel
(1968, 25 drawings)
1970 · the artist

Zu El Lissitzky
(1972, 10 drawings)
1972 · Konrad Fischer, Düsseldorf

Richard Long

Four Weeks Documentation: Evidence from July 26–August 26 Africa 1969
(1969, 10 photographs)
1971 · the artist

Project drawing
(1967, drawing)
1973 · Konrad Fischer, Düsseldorf

Green Stone Circle
(1977, 54 part sculpture)
1977 · Konrad Fischer, Düsseldorf

Drawing for Green Stone Circle
(1977, drawing)
1977 · Konrad Fischer, Düsseldorf

Mario Merz

Cono
(1965, sculpture)
1980 · Konrad Fischer, Düsseldorf; with support from the Nordrhein Westfalen Land

Carl Andre

8001 Mönchengladbach Square
(1968, 36 part sculpture)
1969 · Alfred Schmela, Düsseldorf; with support from the Nordrhein Westfalen Land

8002 Mönchengladbach Square
(1968, 36 part sculpture)
1969 · Alfred Schmela, Düsseldorf; with support from the Nordrhein Westfalen Land

Drawing for Steel Piece, 8001 M. Square
(1968, drawing)
1969 · Alfred Schmela, Düsseldorf

Drawing for Steel Piece, 8002 M. Square
(1968, drawing)
1969 · Alfred Schmela, Düsseldorf

Broken Glass Floor Piece
(1968, drawing)
1980 · René Block, Berlin

Douglas Huebler

Alternative Piece 3 North Paris, France
(1970, photomontage)
1972 · Konrad Fischer, Düsseldorf

Sol LeWitt

Set of Nine Drawings
(1971, 9 drawings)
1973 · Konrad Fischer, Düsseldorf

Vancouver Project
(1969, drawing)
1975 · Konrad Fischer, Düsseldorf

Avalanche
(1971, drawing)
1975 · Konrad Fischer, Düsseldorf

Rochester Piece 3
(1972, drawing)
1975 · Konrad Fischer, Düsseldorf

Page Drawing (Boston)
(1972, drawing)
1975 · Konrad Fischer, Düsseldorf

Bruce Nauman

Forced Perspective #2
(1975, 64 part sculpture)
1975 · Konrad Fischer, Düsseldorf

Drawing for Forced Perspective
(1975, drawing)
1975 · Konrad Fischer, Düsseldorf

Lawrence Weiner

Untitled
(1970, drawing)
1970 · the artist

1) Down a Hatch, 2) Up a Tree,
3) Around a Town
(1973, statement/paper certificate)
1973 · Konrad Fischer, Düsseldorf

Broken Off/Abgebrochen
(1974, statement/paper certificate)
1974 · gift from the artist

Ludwig Museum, Cologne

Hanne Darboven

00–99/100 à 19 = 19 × 42 No/2K–61K
(1970, 40 drawings)
1973 · Rudolf Zwirner, Cologne;
1976 Ludwig donation

1.10.71–31.01.71
(1971, 35 drawings)
1973 · Rudolf Zwirner, Cologne;
1976 Ludwig donation

24 Songs: A-Form 1974
(1974, 596 drawings)
1976 · gift from the artist

Carl Andre

Lock Series (Köln Steel Lock)
(1967, 36 part sculpture)
1969 · Dwan Gallery, New York;
1976 Ludwig donation

Proposal for the Hague Museum – Lock Series October 1967 Carl Andre
(drawing, 1967)
1969 · Dwan Gallery, New York;
1976 Ludwig donation

Timber Piece (Well)
(1964/1970, 28 part sculpture)
1970 · Dwan Gallery, New York;
1976 Ludwig donation

Joseph Kosuth

Titled (art as idea as idea (definition Abstract))
(1967, photographic blow-up)
1972 · Paul Maenz, Cologne
(purchased by the Wallraf-Richartz Museum)

Frame – One and Three
(1965, mural installation)
1973 · Paul Maenz, Cologne;
1976 Ludwig donation

Sol LeWitt

3 Part set 789 (B)
(1968, sculpture)
1968 · Rudolf Zwirner, Cologne;
1976 Ludwig donation

Bruce Nauman

Westerman's Ear
(1967–68, mural sculpture)
1971 · Eugenia Butler, Los Angeles;
1976 Ludwig donation

Kunstmuseum, Basel

Marcel Broodthaers

La Clef de l'Horloge (Un poème cinématographique en l'honneur de Kurt Schwitters)
(1957–58, film)
1974 · deposit of the Emanuel Hoffmann-Stiftung;
Heiner Friedrich, Munich

Histoire d'amour (Dr. Huysmans), 1971 – **Chère petite sœur (La tempête)**, 1972 – **Ah, que la chasse soit le plaisir des rois**, 1972 – **Un film de Charles Baudelaire**, 1971 – **Un jardin d'hiver**, 1974 (films) · deposit of the Emanuel Hoffmann-Stiftung; Heiner Friedrich, Munich

Un poisson, undated – **La pipe (René Magritte)**, 1970 – **La pluie (Projet pour un texte)**, 1970 (films) · deposit of the Emanuel Hoffmann-Stiftung; Heiner Friedrich, Munich

Berlin oder ein Traum mit Sahne
(undated, film)
1974 · deposit of the Emanuel Hoffmann-Stiftung; Galerie Stampa, Basel

Le Corbeau et le Renard (d'après La Fontaine)
(1967, film)
1975 · deposit of the Emanuel Hoffmann-Stiftung; Galerie Felix Handschin, Basel

Jardin d'Hiver I
(1974, drawing)
1975 · gift of Dr. Franz Meyer

Hanne Darboven

Grosse Zeichnung (3/11/7/5/9)
(1967, 2 drawings)
1972 · deposit of the Emanuel Hoffmann-Stiftung;
Konrad Fischer, Düsseldorf

Ein Jahr 1974
(1974, drawings installation)
1974 · Konrad Fischer, Düsseldorf, with support from the Max Geldner-Stiftung

Ein Monat, August 1968
(1968, drawings installation)
1976 · gift from the artist

Jan Dibbets

Untitled
(1974, photo collage and drawing on paper)
1975 · deposit of the Emanuel Hoffmann-Stiftung; Rolf Preisig, Basel

Richard Long

Stone Line
(1977, sculpture)
1977 · desposit of the Emanuel Hoffmann-Stiftung; 1977 exhibition Kunsthalle Bern

Mario Merz

Nymphéas
(1978, installation)
1980 · deposit of the Emanuel Hoffmann-Stiftung; Galerie Jean and Karen Bernier, Athens, deposit since 1979

Sit-in
(1967, neon piece)
1980 · deposit of the Emanuel Hoffmann-Stiftung; Galerie Felix Handschin, Basel

Carl Andre

10 × 10 Altstadt Square
(1967, 100 part sculpture)
1974 · Heiner Friedrich, Cologne, deposit since 1969, with support from the City of Basel

Cedar Piece
(1959/1964, 74 part sculpture)
1976 · John Weber, New York

Sol LeWitt

Large Modular Cube
(1969, sculpture)
1970 · deposit of the Emanuel Hoffmann-Stiftung;
Konrad Fischer, Düsseldorf

Arcs from four sides and four corners (1972, drawing)
1972 · gift of the Karl August Burckhardt-Koechlin-Fonds

Grid & Arcs from two opposite sides
(1972, drawing)
1972 · gift of the Karl August Burckhardt-Koechlin-Fonds

Wall Structure 5 4 3 2 1
(1966–73, wall sculpture)
1975 · Rolf Preisig, Basel

Circles, Grids, Arcs from four Corners and Sides
(1973, wall drawing)
1977 · gift from the artist in memory of Dr. Carlo Huber

Bruce Nauman

Storage Capsule for the Right Rear Quarter of my Body
(1966, iron sheet)
1971 · Bruno Bischofberger, Zurich

Untitled (Drawing for Rotation Glass Walls)
(1970, drawing)
1972 · Rolf Ricke, Cologne

Violining
(1967, film)
1972 · deposit of the Emanuel Hoffmann-Stiftung; Heiner Friedrich, Cologne

Art Make-Up, No 1–4 (White, Pink, Green, Black)
(1968, 4 films)
1972 · deposit of the Emanuel Hoffmann-Stiftung; Heiner Friedrich, Cologne

Bouncing Two Balls between the Floor and Ceiling with Changing Rhythms
(1968, film)
1972 · deposit of the Emanuel Hoffmann-Stiftung;
Heiner Friedrich, Cologne

Playing a Note on the Violin while I walk around the studio
(1968, film)
1972 · deposit of the Emanuel Hoffmann-Stiftung;
Heiner Friedrich, Cologne

Kunstmuseum, Basel

Bruce Nauman

Turned up on End
(1966, drawing)
1973 · deposit of the Emanuel Hoffmann-Stiftung; Richard Bellamy, New York

Cry to Me
(1966, drawing)
1973 · deposit of the Emanuel Hoffmann-Stiftung; Richard Bellamy, New York

Drawing of the Bracket for a Timed 2 part Neon Wall Piece
(1966, drawing)
1973 · deposit of the Emanuel Hoffmann-Stiftung; Richard Bellamy, New York

Functionless Wall Bracket
(1966, drawing)
1973 · deposit of the Emanuel Hoffmann-Stiftung; Richard Bellamy, New York

Untitled
(ca. 1966, drawing)
1973 · deposit of the Emanuel Hoffmann-Stiftung; Richard Bellamy, New York

Untitled
(1966, drawing)
1973 · deposit of the Emanuel Hoffmann-Stiftung; Richard Bellamy, New York

Untitled (Study for Slant Step)
(1966, drawing)
1973 · deposit of the Emanuel Hoffmann-Stiftung; Richard Bellamy, New York

Untitled (Study for Booth Piece)
(1966, drawing)
1973 · deposit of the Emanuel Hoffmann-Stiftung; Richard Bellamy, New York

The Original Slant Step, Wood and Linoleum
(1966, drawing)
1973 · deposit of the Emanuel Hoffmann-Stiftung; Richard Bellamy, New York

Parts for the Booth Piece
(1966, drawing)
1973 · deposit of the Emanuel Hoffmann-Stiftung; Richard Bellamy, New York

Sandwich Sculpture
(1966, drawing)
1973 · deposit of the Emanuel Hoffmann-Stiftung; Richard Bellamy, New York

Sheet Lead
(1966, drawing)
1973 · deposit of the Emanuel Hoffmann-Stiftung; Richard Bellamy, New York

Drawing of the Brown Crayon Box
(1967, drawing)
1973 · deposit of the Emanuel Hoffmann-Stiftung; Richard Bellamy, New York

Myself as a Marble Fountain
(1967, drawing)
1973 · deposit of the Emanuel Hoffmann-Stiftung; Richard Bellamy, New York

Untitled
(1967, drawing)
1973 · deposit of the Emanuel Hoffmann-Stiftung; Richard Bellamy, New York

Seven Wax Templates of the Left Half of my Body spread over 12 Feet
(1967, drawing)
1973 · deposit of the Emanuel Hoffmann-Stiftung; Richard Bellamy, New York

Untitled (Drawing for Corridor with a Parallax)
(1971, drawing)
1974 · deposit of the Emanuel Hoffmann-Stiftung; the artist

Henry Moore bound to fail, Back view
(1967–70, sculpture)
1974 · deposit of the Emanuel Hoffmann-Stiftung; Sotheby's New York

Corridor with a Parallax
(1974, installation)
1974 · deposit of the Emanuel Hoffmann-Stiftung; the artist

The true artist helps the world by revealing its mystic truths (Window or Wall Sign)
(1967, neon piece)
1978 · Bruno Bischofberger, Zurich, anonym depositum since 1972

Robert Ryman

Two Models for Undergound Tunnels, No 1 – Horizontal, No 2 – Vertical
(1978, steel sculpture)
1978 · Ace Gallery, Venice (California)

Aacon
(1968, painting)
1971 · deposit of the Emanuel Hoffmann-Stiftung; Heiner Friedrich, Cologne

Singer I
(1975, painting on wood)
1975 · John Weber, New York; with support from the Max Geldner-Stiftung

Kunstmuseum, Lucerne

Hanne Darboven

Atta Troll (I–VIII, 1117)
(1975, 126 drawings)
1975 · gift from the artist

Stedelijk Museum, Amsterdam

Hanne Darboven

Four drawings
(1972, 4 drawings)
1972 · Art & Project, Amsterdam

1. Buch / 42. Buch
(1972, drawings)
1973 · Art & Project, Amsterdam

24 Gesänge: B-Form
(1974, drawings installation)
1976 · gift from the artist

Jan Dibbets

Perspective Correction – My Studio II
(1968, photographs)
1971 · Gian Enzo Sperone, Turin

Louverdrape horizontal
(1971, photo collage)
1972 · Art & Project, Amsterdam

Perspective correction – diagonal/crossed/diagonal
(1968, photographs)
1972 · gift from Vincent Van Gogh Stichting, Amsterdam; Konrad Fischer, Düsseldorf

Universe/A construction or Dutch Mountain-sea
(1971, photo collage)
1972 · Art & Project, Amsterdam

4 Diagonals
(1970, film; Videogalerie Schum)
1972 · Art & Project, Amsterdam

Film: White Table
(1972, photo collage)
1972 · Art & Project, Amsterdam

Universe/World's platform
(1972, photo collage)
1973 · Art & Project, Amsterdam

4 Points 0–135°
(1972, photo collage)
1973 · Yvon Lambert, Paris

Panorama, my studio
(1971, photographs)
1973 · John Weber, New York

land/sea
(1973, drawings and photo collage)
1973 · Art & Project, Amsterdam

Comet Sea 3°–60°
(1973, photographs)
1974 · Gian Enzo Sperone, Turin

Zeeschap
(1974, photographs)
1976 · Art & Project, Amsterdam

Landschap
(1974, photographs)
1976 · Art & Project, Amsterdam

Monet's dream study
(1975, collage)
1976 · Art & Project, Amsterdam

Untitled
(1973, collage)
1977 · Art & Project, Amsterdam

Color Study 1 (3 parts)
(1976, photographs)
1977 · Konrad Fischer, Düsseldorf

Stone Structure
(1978, photographs)
1978 · the artist; with an anonymous gift of money

Structure Panorama 330°
(1977, photographs)
1978 · the artist; with an anonymous gift of money

Construction 330°
(1979, photographs)
1979 · the artist

Gilbert & George

16 part photo-piece
(1971, photographs)
1972 · Art & Project, Amsterdam

Gordon's Makes Us Drunk
(1972, film; Videogalerie Schum)
1972 · Art & Project, Amsterdam

Autumn ferns
(1973, photo-piece)
1973 · Ileana Sonnabend, New York

In the Bush
(1972, film; Videogalerie Schum)
1978 · Projektion Ursula Wevers, Cologne

A portrait of the artists as young men
(1972, film; Videogalerie Schum)
1978 · Projektion Ursula Wevers, Cologne

Richard Long

Guggenheim Piece
(1971, photo collage)
1973 · Konrad Fischer, Düsseldorf

A rolling stone, resting places along a journey
(1973, photo collage)
1973 · Konrad Fischer, Düsseldorf

Zig-zag. Städtisches Museum Mönchengladbach
(1970, photo collage)
1973 · Gian Enzo Sperone, Turin

17 stones
(1976, sculpture)
1976 · Konrad Fischer, Düsseldorf

Bluestone Circle
(1978, sculpture)
1978 · Sperone-Westwater-Fischer, New York

Mario Merz

Città irreale
(1968, assemblage)
1969 · Ileana Sonnabend, Paris

Fibonacci Napoli (Mensa di fabbrica A.S. Giovanni a Teduccio), Napoli, Agosto, 1971
(1971, photographs)
1973 · Art & Project, Amsterdam

Lumaca
(1970, film; Videogalerie Schum)
1978 · Projektion Ursula Wevers, Cologne

Carl Andre

Twenty-third steel cardinal
(1974, sculpture)
1975 · Konrad Fischer, Düsseldorf

10 × 10 Altstadt Lead Square
(1967/1976, 100 part sculpture)
1976 · Konrad Fischer, Düsseldorf

Douglas Huebler

Alternative Piece no. 4 (s)
(1970, photographs and map)
1971 · Gian Enzo Sperone, Turin

Joseph Kosuth

Five fives (to Donald Judd)
(1965, neon piece)
1972 · Gian Enzo Sperone, Turin

Sol LeWitt

Lines & Lines, Arcs & Arcs
(1972, drawings)
1972 · Art & Project, Amsterdam

Lines & Arcs
(1972, drawings)
1972 · Art & Project, Amsterdam

Fold
(1972, folded paper)
1972 · Art & Project, Amsterdam

Bruce Nauman

My name as though it were written on the surface of the moon
(1968, neon piece)
1969 · Ileana Sonnabend, Paris

Violining
(1969, film)
1973 · Leo Castelli, New York

Eat/Death
(1972, neon piece)
1974 · Leo Castelli, New York

Pursuit
(1975, film)
1979 · Castelli-Sonnabend Tapes & Films, Inc., New York

Dance or exercise on the perimeter of a square
(1971, film)
1979 · Castelli-Sonnabend Tapes & Films, Inc., New York

Art make-up
(1967–68, film)
1979 · Castelli-Sonnabend Tapes & Films, Inc., New York

Walking in an exaggerated manner around the perimeter of a square
(1971, film)
1979 · Castelli-Sonnabend Tapes & Films, Inc., New York

Walking with a contraposto
(1969, film)
1979 · Castelli-Sonnabend Tapes & Films, Inc., New York

Wall/floor position
(1968, film)
1979 · Castelli-Sonnabend Tapes & Films, Inc., New York

Clear vision
(1973, film)
1980 · Galerie Schellman & Klüser, Munich

Robert Ryman

VII
(1969, 7 paintings)
1972 · the artist, through Konrad Fischer, Düsseldorf

Untitled
(1972, painting)
1972 · John Weber, New York

Untitled
(1960, painting)
1972 · John Weber, New York

Untitled
(1973, 5 paintings)
1973 · Konrad Fischer, Düsseldorf

Untitled
(1973, painting)
1973 · Konrad Fischer, Düsseldorf

Classico 3
(1968, painting on paper)
1974 · Konrad Fischer, New York

Monitor
(1978, painting)
1979 · Sidney Janis, New York

Oneida
(1980, painting)
1980 · Konrad Fischer, Düsseldorf

Lawrence Weiner

Beached
(1970, video; Videogalerie Schum)
1978 · Projektion Ursula Wevers, Cologne

Broken off
(1970, video; Videogalerie Schum)
1978 · Projektion Ursula Wevers, Cologne

Stedelijk Van Abbemuseum, Eindhoven

Daniel Buren

Passage
(1974, box and 7 books)
1974 · Gallery Seriaal, Amsterdam

Peinture angulaire
(1975, painting)
1976 · the artist

Peinture sur toile
(1977, painting)
1977 · Wide White Space, Antwerp

Hanne Darboven

Konstruktion 21 × 21 – Zahlen: 1, 3, 5, 7, (+ 5) = 21
(1968, drawings)
1975 · Konrad Fischer, Düsseldorf

Jan Dibbets

The shortest day at the Van Abbemuseum
(1970, photographs)
1971 · Art & Project, Amsterdam

Structure Piece
(1974, photographs and drawings)
1975 · Art & Project, Amsterdam

Unitled (Land)
(1973, photographs)
1977 · Art & Project, Amsterdam

Untitled (Sea)
(1974, photographs)
1977 · Art & Project, Amsterdam

Untitled
(1973, photographs and drawings)
1979 · Art & Project, Amsterdam

Colorstudy C1, C2, C3, C4
(1980, photographs)
1980 · Konrad Fischer, Düsseldorf

Gilbert & George

Are you angry or are you boring?
(1977, 16 photographs)
1978 · Konrad Fischer, Düsseldorf

Richard Long

Crossing two rivers
(1974, photographs)
1976 · Art & Project, Amsterdam

Sixty Stones
(1975, 60 part sculpture)
1977 · Konrad Fischer, Düsseldorf

Wood Circle
(1977, sculpture)
1977 · permanent loan from Mrs A. Korevaar-Visser, The Hague

Peeting Place
(1977, drawings and maps)
1979 · Rolf Preisig, Basel

Circle in Africa
(1978, photographs)
1980 · Anthony d'Offay, London

Throwing a stone around MacGillycuddy's Reeks
(1977, photographs)
1980 · Anthony d'Offay, London

Mario Merz

Igloo Nero
(1967–79, installation)
1980 · Konrad Fischer, Düsseldorf

Carl Andre

Henge on 3 right Thresholds
(1971, sculpture)
1976 · permanent loan from Anton Herbert, Gent; Konrad Fischer

Twenty-Fifth Steel Cardinal
(1974, sculpture)
1976 · Konrad Fischer, Düsseldorf

Douglas Huebler

Variable Piece #111, London
(1974, photographs and stickers)
1977 · Rolf Preisig, Basel

Joseph Kosuth

Art as Idea as Idea (First Investigation)
(1968, photographs)
1977 · Paul Maenz, Cologne

One and Nine A – Description
(1965, paint on glass)
1979 · the artist

Sol LeWitt

Rip, Number 215
(1974, drawing)
1975 · Art & Project, Amsterdam

Rip, Number 220
(1974, drawing)
1975 · Art & Project, Amsterdam

Rip, Number 326
(1975, drawing)
1975 · Art & Project, Amsterdam

Wall Structure
(1972, mural sculpture)
1977 · Konrad Fischer, Düsseldorf

Wall Drawing no. 256
(1975, wall drawing)
1978 · Martin Visser, Bergeijk

Bruce Nauman

Driven Man, Driven Snow
(1976, sculpture and drawing)
1977 · Konrad Fischer, Düsseldorf

Robert Ryman

Untitled
(1974, painting)
1977 · Rolf Preisig, Basel

Lawrence Weiner

On a smooth – Being within the context of (a) place
(1975, statement)
1975 · Konrad Fischer, Düsseldorf

In the rough – Being within the context of (a) place
(1975,statement)
1975 · Konrad Fischer, Düsseldorf

On a rough – Being within the context of (a) place
(1975, statement)
1975 · Konrad Fischer, Düsseldorf

Up (on) in the air. Down (on) in the ground. Being within the context of (a) reaction
(1975, statement)
1975 · Leo Castelli, New York

Being within the context of a reaction: up (on) in the air. down (on) in the ground
(1975, statement)
1975 · Leo Castelli, New York

A second quarter
(1975, film)
1975 · Common Film Produktion GmbH, Berlin

Carried to great lengths. Carries to (relatively) great lengths
(1976, statement)
1976 · Rolf Preisig, Basel

A first quarter
(1973, film)
1976 · Castelli-Sonnabend Tapes & Films, Inc., New York

Done to
(1974, film)
1978 · Castelli-Sonnabend Tapes & Films, Inc., New York

A bit of matter and a little bit more
(1976, video)
1978 · Castelli-Sonnabend Tapes & Films, Inc., New York

Green as well as blue as well as red
(1976, video)
1978 · Castelli-Sonnabend Tapes & Films, Inc., New York

Affected and/or effected
(1974, video)
1978 · Castelli-Sonnabend Tapes & Films, Inc., New York

For example decorated
(1977, video)
1978 · Castelli-Sonnabend Tapes & Films, Inc., New York

Do you believe in water[ ].
(1976, video)
1978 · Castelli-Sonnabend Tapes & Films, Inc., New York

To and from. And to. And to and from. And from and to
(1972, video)
1978 · Castelli-Sonnabend Tapes & Films, Inc., New York

Shifted from the side
(1972, video)
1978 · Castelli-Sonnabend Tapes & Films, Inc., New York

Ian Wilson

Discussion, 25 April 1976
(1976, discussion)
1976 · the artist

Discussion, 27 April 1976
(1976, discussion)
1976 · the artist, through John Weber

Discussion, 30 April 1976
(1976, discussion)
1976 · the artist

Discussion, 30 April 1977
(1977, discussion)
1977 · the artist

Discussion, 14 May 1980
(1980, discussion)
1980 · the artist

Tate Gallery, London

Marcel Broodthaers

Casserole et Moules Fermées
(1964, sculpture)
1975 · the artist, through MOMA, Oxford

Mademoiselle Rivière and Monsieur Bertin
(1975, photographs)
1975 · the artist, through MOMA, Oxford

La Soupe de Daguerre
(1974, collage on paper)
1977 · Nigel Greenwood, London

Je retourne à la matière, Je retourne la tradition des primitifs, Peinture à l'œuf
(1966, sculpture)
1980 · Galerie Isy Brachot, Brussels

Jan Dibbets

Perspective Corrections
(1968, photographs on canvas)
1973 · Gian Enzo Sperone, Turin

Panorama Dutch Mountains 12 × 15° Sea II A
(1971, photographs on paper)
1973 · Konrad Fischer, Düsseldorf

Collage
(1973, collage)
1974 · Leo Castelli, New York

Gilbert & George

Balls: The Evening before the Morning After, Drinking Sculpture
(1972, photographs)
1972 · Nigel Greenwood, London

In the Bush
(1972, film; Videogalerie Schum)
1972 · Nigel Greenwood, London

Gordon's Makes Us Drunk
(1972, film; Videogalerie Schum)
1972 · Nigel Greenwood, London

A Portrait of the Artists as young Men
(1972, film; Videogalerie Schum)
1972 · Nigel Greenwood, London

Richard Long

A Hundred Mile Walk
(1971–72, map, photograph and drawing)
1973 · Lisson Gallery, London

Circle of Sticks
(1973, 76 part sculpture)
1973 · the artist, through Konrad Fischer

Ben Nevis Hitch-Hike
(1967, drawing, photograph and card)
1976 · the artist, through Lisson Gallery

Cerne Abbas Walk
(1975, photograph, map and drawing)
1976 · the artist, through Lisson Gallery

119 Stones
(1976, 119 part sculpture)
1976 · the artist, through Lisson Gallery

River Avon Driftwood
(1976, 80 part sculpture)
1976 · the artist, through Lisson Gallery

Turf Circle
(1966, photograph, card and words)
1976 · the artist (public freehold)

Turf Sculpture
(1967, photograph, card and words)
1976 · the artist (public freehold)

A Line Made by Walking
(1967, photograph)
1976 · the artist (public freehold)

England
(1968, photograph, card and words)
1976 · the artist (public freehold)

Slate Circle
(1979, 214 part sculpture)
1980 · gift of Anthony d'Offay, London

Carl Andre

Ladder No. 2 (Last Ladder)
(1959, sculpture)
1972 · the artist, through John Weber, New York

Untitled (Equivalent VIII)
(1966, 120 part sculpture)
1972 · John Weber, New York

144 Magnesium Plates
(1969, 144 part sculpture)
1973 · Heiner Friedrich, Cologne, through Lisson Gallery, London

Diagram of Reef
(1967, drawing)
1977 · gift of David Novros, through the American Federation of Arts

Drawing for The Perfect Painting
(1967, drawing)
1977 · gift of David Novros, through the American Federation of Arts

Rotor Reflector Review
(1967, drawing)
1977 · gift of David Novros, through the American Federation of Arts

Diagram for Installation of Magnet Pieces 1966, at Tibor de Nagy Gallery, New York
(1966, drawing)
1977 · gift of David Novros, through the American Federation of Arts

Douglas Huebler

Site Sculpture Project, Windham College Pentagon, Putney, Vermont
(1968, photographs, map and documentation)
1973 · gift of Mr and Mrs Joshua A Gollin, New York, through the American Federation of Art;
Leo Castelli, New York

Variable Piece No. 44
(1971, photographs and card)
1974 · the artist

Joseph Kosuth

Clock (One and Five) English/Latin Version
(1965, installation)
1974 · the artist, through Nigel Greenwood, London; Leo Castelli, New York

Sol LeWitt

Wall Drawing, Four Basic Colors (black, yellow, red and blue) and all combinations
(1970, wall drawing)
1973 · the artist, through Lisson Gallery, London

Two Open Modular Cubes/Half-Off
(1970, sculpture)
1974 · the artist, through Lisson Gallery, London

Untitled
(1965–67, wall structure)
1980 · Lisson Gallery, London

On four black walls, white vertical parallel lines, and in the centre of the walls, eight geometric figures (including cross, x.) within which are white horizontal parallel lines. The vertical lines do not enter the figures.
(1980, wall drawing)
1980 · Lisson Gallery, London

Bruce Nauman

Corridor with Mirror and White Lights (Corridor with reflected Image) (1971, installation)
1973 · the artist, through Konrad Fischer, Düsseldorf

Prices of Conceptual art purchased by European museums, 1967–80: Stedelijk Museum, Amsterdam and Tate Gallery, London

Stedelijk Museum, Amsterdam

ARTIST	WORK	PRICE
Hanne Darboven	**Four drawings** (1972, 4 drawings) 1972 · Art & Project, Amsterdam	*f* 1,200 (*f* 300 each, incl. 4% btw)
	1. Buch / 42. Buch (1972, drawings) 1973 · Art & Project, Amsterdam	*f* 18,000 (*f* 17,307 + 4% btw)
	24 Gesänge: B-Form (1974, drawings installation) 1976 · gift from the artist	*f* 147,200 approx. (valued $ 40,000 at Castelli's)
Jan Dibbets	**Perspective Correction – My Studio II** (1968, photographs) 1971 · Gian Enzo Sperone, Turin	*f* 3,650 (*f* 3,509 + 4% btw / $1,100)
	Louverdrape horizontal (1971, photo collage) 1972 · Art & Project, Amsterdam	*f* 10,000 (*f* 9,615 + 4% btw)
	Perspective correction – diagonal/ crossed/diagonal (1968, photographs) 1972 · gift from Vincent van Gogh Stichting, Amsterdam; Konrad Fischer, Düsseldorf	*f* 20,000 approx. (DM 20,000)
	Universe/A construction or Dutch Mountain-sea (1971, photo collage) 1972 · Art & Project, Amsterdam	*f* 10,000 (*f* 9,615 + 4% btw)
	4 Diagonals (1970, film; Videogalerie Schum) 1972 · Art & Project, Amsterdam	*f* 800 (*f* 769.23 + 4% btw)
	Film: White Table (1972, photo collage) 1972 · Art & Project, Amsterdam	*f* 20,000 (*f* 19,231.60 + 4% btw)
	Universe/World's Platform (1972, photo collage) 1973 · Art & Project, Amsterdam	*f* 8,000 (*f* 7,692 + 4% btw)
	4 Points 0–135° (1972, photo collage) 1973 · Yvon Lambert, Paris	*f* 8,450
	Panorama, my studio (1971, photographs) 1973 · John Weber, New York	*f* 9,943.13
	land/sea (1973, drawings and photo collage) 1973 · Art & Project, Amsterdam	*f* 1,050 (*f* 1,137.22 + 4% btw)
	Comet Sea 3°–60° (1973, photographs) 1974 · Gian Enzo Sperone, Turin	*f* 26,514.30
	Zeeschap (1974, photographs) 1976 · Art & Project, Amsterdam	for both works: *f* 2,080 (*f* 2,000 + 4% btw)
	Landschap (1974, photographs) 1976 · Art & Project, Amsterdam	
	Monet's dream study (1975, collage) 1976 · Art & Project, Amsterdam	*f* 15,600 (*f* 15,000 + 4% btw)

ARTIST	WORK	PRICE
	Untitled (1973, collage) 1977 · Art & Project, Amsterdam	*f*1,170 (*f*1,125 + 4% btw)
	Color Study I (3 parts) (1976, photographs) 1977 · Konrad Fischer, Düsseldorf	*f*22,108.15 (DM24,000 – DM3,000 (12%) discount = DM21,000)
	Stone Structure (1978, photographs) 1978 · the artist; with an anonymous gift of money	*f*12,376 (*f*11,900 + 4%btw/gift)
	Structure Panorama 330° (1977, photographs) 1978 · the artist; with an anonymous gift of money	*f*20,020 (*f*19,250 + 4% btw/gift)
	Construction 330° (1979, photographs) 1979 · the artist	*f*49,920 (*f*60,000 – 20% discount = *f*48,000 + 4% btw)
Gilbert & George	**16 part photo-piece** (1971, photographs) 1972 · Art & Project, Amsterdam	*f*7,500 (*f*7,211.54 + 4% btw)
	Gordon's Makes Us Drunk (1972, film; Videogalerie Schum) 1972 · Art & Project, Amsterdam	*f*2,118 (*f*2,065,05 + 4% btw)
	Autumn ferns (1973, photo-piece) 1973 · Ileana Sonnabend, New York	*f*10,416.88 ($3,500)
	In the Bush (1972, film; Videogalerie Schum) 1978 · Projektion Ursula Wevers, Cologne	*f*1,680 approx. (DM2,000 – 20% discount = DM1,600)
	A portrait of the artists as young men (1972, film; Videogalerie Schum) 1978 · Projektion Ursula Wevers, Cologne	*f*1,680 approx. (DM2,000 – 20% discount = DM1,600)
Richard Long	**Guggenheim Piece** (1971, photo collage) 1973 · Konrad Fischer, Düsseldorf	for both works: *f*31,888.45
	A rolling stone, resting places along a journey (1973, photo collage) 1973 · Konrad Fischer, Düsseldorf	
	Zig-zag. Städtisches Museum Mönchengladbach (1970, photo collage) 1973 · Gian Enzo Sperone, Turin	*f*9,092 ($2,500)
	17 stones (1976, sculpture) 1976 · Konrad Fischer, Düsseldorf	*f*22,980 (DM22,000)
	Bluestone Circle (1978, sculpture) 1978 · Sperone-Westwater-Fischer, New York	*f*28,000 ($14,000)

Stedelijk Museum, Amsterdam

ARTIST	WORK	PRICE
Mario Merz	**Città irreale** (1968, assemblage) 1969 · Ileana Sonnabend, Paris	*f*3,240
	Fibonacci Napoli (Mensa di fabbrica A.S. Giovanni a Teduccio), Napoli, Agosto, 1971 (1971, photographs) 1973 · Art & Project, Amsterdam	*f*7,800 (*f*8,500 – *f*1,000 (12%) discount = *f*7,500 + 4% btw)
	Lumaca (1970, film; Videogalerie Schum) 1978 · Projektion Ursula Wevers, Cologne	*f*2,520 approx. (DM3,000 – 20% = DM2,400)
Carl Andre	**Twenty-third steel cardinal** (1974, sculpture) 1975 · Konrad Fischer, Düsseldorf	*f*37,340.51 (DM40,250 – 10% = DM36,225)
	10 × 10 Altstadt Lead Square (1967/1976, 100 part sculpture) 1976 · Konrad Fischer, Düsseldorf	*f*152,531.25 ($64,000 – return of another work = $45,000)
Douglas Huebler	**Alternative Piece no. 4 (s)** (1970, photographs and map) 1971 · Gian Enzo Sperone, Turin	*f*3,193.27 ($ 1,000)
Joseph Kosuth	**Five fives (to Donald Judd)** (1965, neon piece) 1972 · Gian Enzo Sperone, Turin	*f*6,380 ($2,000) + costs of production: *f*3,078
Sol LeWitt	**Lines & Lines, Arcs & Arcs** (1972, drawings) 1972 · Art & Project, Amsterdam	both for: *f*5,500 (*f*5,288.25 + 4% btw)
	Lines & Arcs (1972, drawings) 1972 · Art & Project, Amsterdam	
	Fold (1972, folded paper) 1972 · Art & Project, Amsterdam	*f*320 (*f*307.62 + 4% btw)
Bruce Nauman	**My name as though it were written on the surface of the moon** (1968, neon piece) 1969 · Ileana Sonnabend, Paris	*f*7,200 ($2,000) – costs of production: *f*2,482
	Violining (1969, film) 1973 · Leo Castelli, New York	*f*450 approx. ($150)
	Eat/Death (1972, neon piece) 1974 · Leo Castelli, New York	*f*7,917.15 ($3,000)
	Pursuit (1975, film) 1979 · Castelli-Sonnabend Tapes & Films, Inc., New York	*f*1,000 approx. ($500)
	Dance or exercise on the perimeter of a square (1971, film) 1979 · Castelli-Sonnabend Tapes & Films, Inc., New York	*f*250 approx. ($125)

ARTIST	WORK	PRICE
	Art make-up (1967–68, film) 1979 · Castelli-Sonnabend Tapes & Films, Inc., New York	*f*930 approx. ($465)
	Walking in an exaggerated manner around the perimeter of a square (1971, film) 1979 · Castelli-Sonnabend Tapes & Films, Inc., New York	*f*220 approx. (for seven films incl. those three: *f*1,514.77)
	Walking with a contraposto (1969, film) 1979 · Castelli-Sonnabend Tapes & Films, Inc., New York	*f*220 approx.
	Wall/floor position (1968, film) 1979 · Castelli-Sonnabend Tapes & Films, Inc., New York	*f*220 approx.
	Clear vision (1973, film) 1980 · Galerie Schellman & Klüser, Munich	*f*895.62
Robert Ryman	**VII** (1969, 7 paintings) 1972 · the artist, through Konrad Fischer, Düsseldorf	*f*30,000
	Untitled (1972, painting) 1972 · John Weber, New York	*f*15,000 ($6,000)
	Untitled (1960, painting) 1972 · John Weber, New York	*f*35,524.55 ($12,000)
	Untitled (1973, 5 paintings) 1973 · Konrad Fischer, Düsseldorf	*f*50,340.95
	Untitled (1973, painting) 1973 · Konrad Fischer, Düsseldorf	*f*29,227.50 ($11,500)
	Classico 3 (1968, painting on paper) 1974 · Konrad Fischer, New York	*f*50,026
	Monitor (1978, painting) 1979 · Sidney Janis, New York	*f*40,295 ($20,000)
	Oneida (1980, painting) 1980 · Konrad Fischer, Düsseldorf	*f*46,756.25
Lawrence Weiner	**Beached** (1970, video; Videogalerie Schum) 1978 · Projektion Ursula Wevers, Cologne	*f*1,000 approx. (DM 1,200 – 20% discount = DM 960)
	Broken off (1970, video; Videogalerie Schum) 1978 · Projektion Ursula Wevers, Cologne	*f*1,000 approx. (DM 1,200 – 20% discount = DM 960)
	TOTAL	***f*1,061,330.96 approx.** ($371,094.74)

	ARTIST	WORK	PRICE
Tate Gallery, London	**Marcel Broodthaers**	**Casserole et Moules Fermées** (1964, sculpture) 1975 · the artist, through MOMA, Oxford	£2,300
		Mademoiselle Rivière and Monsieur Bertin (1975, photographs) 1975 · the artist, through MOMA, Oxford	£850
		La Soupe de Daguerre (1974, collage on paper) 1977 · Nigel Greenwood, London	£308.70 (£315 – 10% + 8% VAT)
		Je retourne à la matière, Je retourne la tradition des primitifs, Peinture à l'œuf (1966, sculpture) 1980 · Galerie Isy Brachot, Brussels	£4,000 approx.
	Jan Dibbets	**Perspective Corrections** (1968, photographs on canvas) 1973 · Gian Enzo Sperone, Turin	£3,443 ($8,800)
		Panorama Dutch Mountains 12 × 15° Sea II A (1971, photographs on paper) 1973 · Konrad Fischer, Düsseldorf	£1,175 (DM8,000)
		Collage (1973, collage) 1974 · Leo Castelli, New York	£132 ($350 – 10% = $315)
	Gilbert & George	**Balls: The Evening before the Morning After, Drinking Sculpture** (1972, photographs) 1972 · Nigel Greenwood, London	£1,170 (£1,300 – 10%)
		In the Bush (1972, film; Videogalerie Schum) 1972 · Nigel Greenwood, London	£225 (£250 – 10%)
		Gordon's Makes Us Drunk (1972, film; Videogalerie Schum) 1972 · Nigel Greenwood, London	£225 (£250 – 10%)
		A Portrait of the Artists as young Men (1972, film; Videogalerie Schum) 1972 · Nigel Greenwood, London	£225 (£250 –10%)
	Richard Long	**A Hundred Mile Walk** (1971–72, map, photograph and drawing) 1973 · Lisson Gallery, London	£900 (£1,000 – 10%)
		Circle of Sticks (1973, 76 part sculpture) 1973 · the artist, through Konrad Fischer	£1,100 (£1,000 + 10% VAT)
		Ben Nevis Hitch-Hike (1967, drawing, photograph and card) 1976 · the artist, through Lisson Gallery	£2,160 (£2,000 + 8% VAT)

ARTIST	WORK	PRICE
	Cerne Abbas Walk (1975, photograph, map and drawing) 1976 · the artist, through Lisson Gallery	£2,160 (£2,000 + 8% VAT)
	119 Stones (1976, 119 part sculpture) 1976 · the artist, through Lisson Gallery	£2,160 (£2,000 + 8% VAT)
	River Avon Driftwood (1976, 80 part sculpture) 1976 · the artist, through Lisson Gallery	£2,160 (£2,000 + 8% VAT)
	Turf Circle (1966, photograph, card and words) 1976 · the artist (public freehold)	£50
	Turf Sculpture (1967, photograph, card and words) 1976 · the artist (public freehold)	£50
	A Line Made by Walking (1967, photograph) 1976 · the artist (public freehold)	£50
	England (1968, photograph, card and words) 1976 · the artist (public freehold)	£50
	Slate Circle (1979, 214 part sculpture) 1980 · gift of Anthony d'Offay, London	gift
Carl Andre	**Ladder No. 2 (Last Ladder)** (1959, sculpture) 1972 · the artist, through John Weber, New York	£5,743 ($15,000)
	Untitled (Equivalent VIII) (1966, 120 part sculpture) 1972 · John Weber, New York	£2,297 ($6,000)
	144 Magnesium Plates (1969, 144 part sculpture) 1973 · Heiner Friedrich, Cologne, through Lisson Gallery, London	£16,528.55 (DM90,000 + 10% VAT = DM99,000)
	Diagram of Reef (1967, drawing) 1977 · gift of David Novros, through the American Federation of Arts	£950 approx. (insurance: $2,000)
	Drawing for The Perfect Painting (1967, drawing) 1977 · gift of David Novros, through the American Federation of Arts	£950 approx. (insurance: $2,000)
	Rotor Reflector Review (1967, drawing) 1977 · gift of David Novros, through the American Federation of Arts	£700 approx. (insurance: $1,500)
	Diagram for Installation of Magnet Pieces 1966, at Tibor de Nagy Gallery, New York (1966, drawing) 1977 · gift of David Novros, through the American Federation of Arts	£1,100 approx. (insurance: $2,500)

Tate Gallery, London

ARTIST	WORK	PRICE
Douglas Huebler	**Site Sculpture Project, Windham College Pentagon, Putney, Vermont** (1968, photographs, map and documentation) 1973 · gift of Mr and Mrs Joshua A Gollin, New York, through the American Federation of Art; Leo Castelli, New York	£1,600 approx. ($4,000)
	Variable Piece No. 44 (1971, photographs and card) 1974 · the artist	£2.20 ($100)
Joseph Kosuth	**Clock (One and Five) English/Latin Version** (1965, installation) 1974 · the artist, through Nigel Greenwood, London; Leo Castelli, New York	£1,835 ($4,400 – 10% + VAT = $4,000)
Sol LeWitt	**Wall Drawing, Four Basic Colors (black, yellow, red and blue) and all combinations** (1970, wall drawing) 1973 · the artist, through Lisson Gallery, London	£1,622.72 ($4,000)
	Two Open Modular Cubes/Half-Off (1970, sculpture) 1974 · the artist, through Lisson Gallery, London	£2,230 approx. ($5,000 – 10% + 10% VAT = $4,950)
	Untitled (1965–67, wall structure) 1980 · Lisson Gallery, London	£6,637 ($15,000 – 10% = $13,500)
	On four black walls, white vertical parallel lines, and in the centre of the walls, eight geometric figures (including cross, x.) within which are white horizontal parallel lines. The vertical lines do not enter the figures. (1980, wall drawing) 1980 · Lisson Gallery, London	£13,274 ($30,000 – 10% + 15% VAT = $31,050)
Bruce Nauman	**Corridor with Mirror and White Lights (Corridor with reflected Image)** (1971, installation) 1973 · the artist, through Konrad Fischer, Düsseldorf	£2,400 approx. ($6,000)
	TOTAL	**£82,803.17 approx.** ($35,605.36)

Appendix 2: Documents

2.1 Prospect 68 – Votes of the Jury

DEALER GALLERIES	BOWNESS	DEVELING	HULTEN	MEYER	PEETERS	VISSER	WEMBER	VOTES
Wide White Space (A)*	•				•	•	•	4*
Clert (P)	•		•	•	•		•	5*
Fels & Co. (P)	•		•		•			3*
Iolas (P)	•		•	•				3
René (P)	•		•			•		3
Sonnabend (P)	•	•	•		•	•	•	6*
Y. Lambert (P)	•	•						2*
Fraser (L)	•				•			2*
Kasmin (L)	•	•	•		•	•		5*
Rowan (L)	•	•				•		3
Apollinaire (M)				•		•	•	3*
Dell' Ariete (M)				•		•		2
Del Leone (V)		•			•		•	3
Del Naviglio (M)			•		•			2*
Sperone (T)		•	•			•	•	4*
Tartaruga (R)							•	1
Swart (A)	•	•				•	•	4*
Bischofberger (Z)	•	•	•			•	•	5*
Ziegler (Z)	•	•	•					3*
Bellamy (NY)	•	•	•		•	•	•	6
Bykert (NY)	•	•						2
Castelli (NY)	•		•	•	•	•	•	6
Dwan (NY)	•	•	•			•	•	5*
Fischbach (NY)		•						1
Janis (NY)			•		•	•		3
Pace (NY)	•		•		•	•		4
Wilder (LA)	•	•				•		3
Block (B)			•				•	2
Friedrich (MU)		•	•			•	•	4
OpartMayer (E)				•				1
Müller (S)	•	•		•		•	•	5
Ricke (C)		•				•	•	3
Schmela (D)			•		•	•	•	4
Thelen (ES)						•	•	2*
Zwirner (C)		•	•		•	•	•	5
Warrington (L)	•							1
Axiom (L)	•							1*
Marlborough (L)	•							1
McRoberts + Tunnard (L)		•						1
Büren (ST)			•					1
Schwarz (M)			•					1
Stable (NY)			•					1
Gerber (BE)				•				1
Aktuell (BE)				•				1
Atelier Bettina (BE)				•				1
Krugier (G)				•				1
Alice Pauli (LU)				•				1
Levi (M)				•				1
Bollag (Z)				•				1
Royal Marks (NY)					•			1
Whitechapel (L)							•	1
Grosvenor (L)							•	1
Marconi (M)							•	1
Minami (TO)							•	1
Morelo (MA)							•	1
Fischer (D)							•	1

(* denotes votes of the dealer galleries that took part in the exhibition)

A: Antwerp
B: Berlin
BE: Bern
C: Cologne
D: Düsseldorf
E: Esslingen
ES: Essen
G: Geneva
L: London
LA: Los Angeles
LU: Lausanne
M: Milan
MA: Madrid
MU: Munich
NY: New York
P: Paris
R: Rome
S: Stuttgart
ST: Stockholm
T: Turin
TO: Tokyo
V: Venice
Z: Zurich

2.2.a Prospect 69 – Votes of the Jury

ARTIST	DE CASTILLEJO	CLAURA	DEVELING	RIECHARDT	SZEEMANN	VISSER	WEMBER	VOTES	GALLERY
D'Armagnac Dekker			•			•		2*	18 [wws/Mickery]
Atkinson			•						
Barry					•	•	•	3*	15 [Siegelaub]
Baldwin			•					1	
Becher			•				•	2	
Benglis			•			•		2*	3 [Bykert]
Beuys		•	•				•	3*	[Wide White Space]
Boetti			•					1*	17 [Sperone]
Bollinger						•	•	2	3
Brouwn			•					1*	[Art & Project]
Buren		•			•	•		3*	10 [Y. Lambert]
Christensen	•							1	6
Christo		•				•		2	18
Cooper					•			1*	[ACE]
Darboven		•				•	•	3	
Dibbets		•			•	•		3	
Dupuys									16
Flanagan		•	•					2	13
Gronen	•							1	
Haacke			•				•	2*	[Wise]
Heizer		•			•	•	•	4	
Huebler					•	•	•	3*	15 [Siegelaub]
Humphrey	•							1	
Irwin	•							1	
Kaltenbach		•				•		2	
Keinholz					•			1	
Kosuth			•		•	•	•	4*	15 [Siegelaub]
Kounellis			•			•	•	3*	1 [L'Attico]
LeWitt						•	•	2	5
Long		•			•	•	•	4	
McCrachen							•	1	
Marden					•			1*	[Bykert]
Morris						•		1	
Nauman			•			•	•	3	16
Olitzky	•							1	
Oppenheim			•					1*	[Y. Lambert]
(Panamarenko)		•				•		(2)	(18)
Pascali			•				•	2	1
(Perlstein)						•	•	(2)	
Prini			•			•	•	3*	17 [Sperone]
Rot					•	•	•	3	
Ruscha						•	•	2	
Ruthenbeck		•			•		•	3	
Ryman		•	•					2*	7 [Fischbach]
Sandback					•			1	
Saret						•	•	2	3
Schnyder			•		•			2*	9 [Toni Gerber]
Serra					•	•	•	3	4
Snow							•	1	
Sonnier					•	•	•	3	4
Turrell					•			1	12
Venet							•	1	
(Walther)		•			•		•	(3)	
Weiner		•	•		•	•	•	5*	15 [Siegelaub]
Wheeler					•			1*	12 [ACE]
Wiley			•					1	8
Zaj		•			•	•	•	4*	14 [Seiquer]

(* denotes votes of the dealer galleries that took part in the exhibition)

2.2.b Prospect 69 – Confirmation of the dealer galleries

NO	GALLERIES	CONFIRMATION	SUGGESTION	ANNOUNCEMENT
1	L'Attico (Rome)	•	Kounellis, Pascali	Kounellis, Mattiacci
	ACE (LA)	•	Wheeler	Wheeler, Cooper
	Art & Project (Amsterdam)	•	Brouwn	Brouwn
	Irvin Blum (LA)	/	Ruscha	
	Butler (LA)	•		E.P. Butler, Eric Orr
3	Bykert (New York)	•	Benglis, Bollinger	Benglis, Marden
4	Castelli (NY)	/	Serra, Sonnier	
5	Dwan (NY)	•	Heizer, LeWitt	Ross, Smithson
6	Emmerich (NY)	/	Christensen	
7	Fischbach (NY)	•	Ryman	Ryman, Ohlson
8	Frumkin (Chicago)	/	Wiley	
9	Gerber (Bern)	•	Schnyder	Schnyder, Raetz
10	Y. Lambert (Paris)	•	Buren	Buren, Oppenheim
	Minami (Tokyo)	•		Mitsuo, Toshinobu
12	Pace (NY)	/	Turell, Wheeler	
13	Rowan (London)	/	Flanagan	
14	Seiquer (Madrid)	•	Zaj	Hidalgo, Marchetti
15	Siegelaub (NY)	(•)	Barry, Huebler, Kosuth, Weiner	
16	Sonnabend (Paris)	•	Dupuys, Nauman	Griffa, Prentice
17	Sperone (Turin)	•	Boetti, Prini, Calsolari	Idem + Zandere
18	Wide White Space (Antwerp)	•	D'Armagnac, Dekker, Christo	Lamelas
	Howard Wise (NY)	•	Haacke, Wen Ying Tsai	Haacke

2.3 Kunstkompass Rangliste der Künstler, 1970 (1–50)

NAME	NATION	STIL	PREISE DM	PUNKTE	PPR PREIS/PUNKT RELATION	RANG
Albers	USA	Konstruktivismus	von 40 000 bis 50 000	2340	von 17 bis 21	25
Andre	USA	Minimal Art	bis 40 000	1290	bis 31	62
Antes	Deutschland	Neue Figuration	von 10 000 bis 20 000	2090	von 5 bis 10	31
Anuszkiewicz	USA	Op Art	bis 20 000	870	bis 23	93
Arakawa	Japan	Neuer Realismus	bis 7 500	1245	bis 6	69
Arman	Frankreich	Neuer Realismus	von 20 000 bis 40 000	3495	von 6 bis 11	7
Bell	USA	Minimal Art	von 25 000 bis 30 000	1535	von 16 bis 20	48
Berrocal	Spanien	Plastik	von 20 000 bis 30 000	1270	von 16 bis 24	67
Beuys	Deutscheland	Aktionen, Prozeßkunst	von 60 000 bis 80 000	2000	von 30 bis 40	32
Bill	Schwiz	Konstruktivismus	bis 60 000	1660	bis 36	42
Blake	England	Pop Art	von 8 000 bis 35 000	1090	von 7 bis 32	82
Bontecou	USA	Plastik	von 40 000 bis 65 000	1080	von 37 bis 60	83
Brüning	Deutscheland	Neuer Realismus	bis 12 000	1560	bis 8	46
Bury	Belgien	Kinetik	von 10 000 bis 30 000	1350	von 7 bis 22	59
Caro	England	Plastik	von 80 000 bis 100 000	1275	von 63 bis 78	66
César	Frankreich	Plastik	von 10 000 bis 20 000	1995	von 5 bis 10	33
Chamberlain	USA	Plastik	von 10 000 bis 20 000	1290	von 8 bis 15	62
Christo	Bulgarien	Neuer Realismus	von 10 000 bis 35 000	2100	von 5 bis 17	30
Chyrssa	Griechenland	Lichtkunst	von 10 000 bis 40 000	1230	von 8 bis 33	72
Colombo	Italien	Kinetik	bis 10 000	940	bis 11	91
D'Arcangelo	USA	Pop Art	bis 30 000	980	bis 31	88
Demarco	Brasilien	Lichtkunst	von 2 000 bis 12 000	1050	von 2 bis 11	85
De Maria	USA	Land Art, Conceptual Art	bis 50 000	860	bis 58	95
Dine	USA	Pop Art	von 30 000 bis 45 000	3080	von 10 bis 15	10
Fahlström	Schweden	Neuer Realismus	bis 40 000	1420	bis 28	54
Flavin	USA	Minimal Art	von 12 000 bis 25 000	1910	von 6 bis 13	36
Fontana	Italien	Neuer Realismus	von 35 000 bis 60 000	3820	von 9 bis 16	3
Frankenthaler	USA	Neue Abstraktion	von 20 000 bis 30 000	1365	von 15 bis 22	58
Gaul	Deutschland	Neue Abstraktion	von 3 000 bis 10 000	1155	von 3 bis 9	77
Geiger	Deutschland	Neue Abstraktion	bis 10 000	1385	bis 7	56
Gerstner	Schweiz	Op Art	von 5 000 bis 60 000	860	von 6 bis 70	95
Haese	Deutschland	Plastik	bis 40 000	1105	bis 36	80
Hains	Frankreich	Neuer Realismus	bis 3 000	855	bis 4	98
Hamilton	England	Pop Art	bis 70 000	1825	bis 38	37
Heerich	Deutschland	Minimal Art	bis 22 000	1060	bis 21	84
Hockney	England	Pop Art	von 50 000 bis 60 000	2925	von 17 bis 21	16
Hoyland	England	Neue Abstraktion	von 7 000 bis 14 000	815	von 9 bis 17	100
Hundertwasser	Österreich	Phant. Realismus	bis 100 000	1550	bis 65	47
Indiana	USA	Pop Art	von 12 000 bis 20 000	1665	von 7 bis 12	41
Johns	USA	Neuer Realismus	von 200 000 bis 300 000	3820	von 52 bis 79	4
Jones	England	Pop Art	bis 20 000	2270	bis 9	26
Judd	USA	Minimal Art	bis 80 000	2120	bis 38	29
Kelly	USA	Neue Abstraktion	bis 100 000	2535	bis 39	21
Kienholz	USA	Environment	von 160 000 bis 200 000	1460	von 110 bis 137	50
King	England	Plastik	bis 40 000	1425	bis 28	53
Kitaj	USA	Pop Art	bis 40 000	2465	bis 16	23
Klapheck	Deutschland	Pop Art	von 20 000 bis 30 000	1435	von 14 bis 21	51
Klein	Frankreich	Neuer Realismus	von 60 000 bis 200 000	3335	von 18 bis 60	8
Kramer	Deutschland	Kinetik	von 2 500 bis 5 000	870	von 3 bis 6	93
Le Parc	Argentinien	Kinetik	von 5 000 bis 30 000	1980	von 3 bis 15	34

stil: style
preise: price
von: from
bis: to

NAME	NATION	RICHTUNG	PREISE DM	PUNKTE	PPR PREIS/PUNKT RELATION	RANG
Lenk	Deutschland	Plastik	bis 8 000	1160	bis 7	75
LeWitt	USA	Minimal Art	bis 30 000	1315	bis 23	61
Lichtenstein	USA	Pop Art	von 120 000 bis 150 000	3245	von 37 bis 46	9
Linder	USA	Pop Art	von 140 000 bis 180 000	1420	von 99 bis 127	54
Louis	USA	Neue Abstraktion	von 160 000 bis 200 000	2765	von 58 bis 72	17
Luginbühl	Schweiz	Plastik	von 8 000 bis 50 000	980	von 8 bis 51	88
Mack	Deutschland	Kinetik	von 10 000 bis 20 000	2610	von 4 bis 8	19
Manzoni	Italien	Neuer Realismus	von 15 000 bis 54 000	1190	von 13 bis 45	74
Marisol	Venezuela	Pop Art	von 25 000 bis 30 000	1290	von 19 bis 23	62
Mavignier	Argentinien	Op Art	von 5 000 bis 30 000	1035	von 5 bis 29	86
Morellet	Italien	Kinetik	bis 18 000	1100	bis 16	81
Morris	USA	Minimal Art	von 20 000 bis 40 000	2240	von 9 bis 18	27
Naumann	USA	Minimal Art	von 15 000 bis 30 000	1240	von 12 bis 24	71
Noland	USA	Neue Abstraktion	von 60 000 bis 150 000	2420	von 25 bis 62	24
Oldenburg	USA	Pop Art	bis 180 000	3545	bis 51	5
Paolozzi	England	Plastik	bis 45 000	3035	bis 15	12
Pfahler	Deutschland	Neue Abstraktion	bis 5 000	1115	bis 4	79
Phillips	England	Pop Art	von 6 000 bis 15 000	1270	von 5 bis 12	67
Piene	Deutschland	Lichtkunst	von 7 000 bis 10 000	2560	von 3 bis 4	20
Pistoletto	Italien	Neuer Realismus	von 10 000 bis 12 000	1605	von 6 bis 7	44
Pomodoro, A.	Italien	Plastik	bis 100 000	1285	bis 78	65
Poons	USA	Neuer Abstraktion	von 15 000 bis 20 000	1245	von 12 bis 16	69
Rauschenberg	USA	Neuer Realismus	von 120 000 bis 250 000	5515	von 22 bis 45	1
Raysse	Frankreich	Neuer Realismus	von 10 000 bis 50 000	2485	von 4 bis 20	22
Richter	Deutschland	Neuer Realismus	von 6 000 bis 10 000	1375	von 4 bis 7	57
Rickey	USA	Plastik	von 40 000 bis 100 000	1225	von 32 bis 82	73
Riley	England	Op Art	von 20 000 bis 40 000	1930	von 10 bis 21	35
Rivers	USA	Pop Art	bis 20 000	1620	bis 12	43
Rosenquist	USA	Pop Art	von 24 000 bis 40 000	2950	von 8 bis 14	15
St-Phalle	Frankreich	Neuer Realismus	von 10 000 bis 15 000	1345	von 7 bis 11	60
Segal	USA	Pop Art	bis 80 000	2170	bis 37	28
Serra	USA	Prozeßkunst	von 6 000 bis 26 000	840	von 7 bis 31	99
Smith, R.	England	Neue Abstraktion	von 6 500 bis 13 000	1585	von 4 bis 8	45
Smith, T.	USA	Minimal Art	bis 150 000	1015	bis 48	87
Smithson	USA	Land Art	bis 10 000	960	bis 10	90
Sonnier	USA	Prozeßkunst	von 7 000 bis 32 000	860	von 8 bis 37	95
Soto	Venezuela	Op Art	von 15 000 bis 40 000	3020	von 5 bis 13	13
Spoerri	Schweiz	Neuer Realismus	bis 10 000	1160	bis 9	75
Schöffer	Frankreich	Lichtkunst	von 16 000 bis 160 000	1820	von 9 bis 88	38
Schultze	Deutschland	Phant. Realismus	von 5 000 bis 12 000	1480	von 3 bis 8	49
Stella	USA	Neue Abstraktion	von 80 000 bis 150 000	3050	von 26 bis 49	11
Tilson	England	Pop Art	von 12 000 bis 20 000	1790	von 7 bis 11	39
Tinguely	Schweiz	Kinetik	von 25 000 bis 50 000	3525	von 7 bis 14	6
Trova	USA	Plastik	von 30 000 bis 140 000	1125	von 27 bis 124	78
Twombly	Italien	Neuer Realismus	von 15 000 bis 30 000	1430	von 10 bis 21	52
Uecker	Deutschland	Kinetik	von 5 000 bis 15 000	2685	von 2 bis 6	18
Vasarely	Frankreich	Op Art	von 40 000 bis 50 000	4405	von 9 bis 11	2
Warhol	USA	Pop Art	bis 180 000	2985	bis 60	14
Wesselmann	USA	Pop Art	von 45 000 bis 75 000	1700	von 26 bis 44	40
Wunderlich	Deutschland	Phant. Realismus	von 8 000 bis 36 000	900	von 9 bis 40	92

2.3 Kunstkompass Rangliste der Künstler, 1971 (1–50)

RANG 1971	1970	NAME	NATION	RICHTUNG	PREISE FÜR GRAFIK UND OBJEKTE DM	PREISNOTE	PPR	PUNKTE
1	1	Rauschenberg	USA	Neuer Realismus	1000–5000	preiswert	0,85	5895
2	5	Oldenburg	USA	Pop Art	600–6000	sehr teuer	1,28	4705
3	4	Johns	USA	Neuer Realismus	1600–10000	sehr teuer	2,13	4685
4	6	Tinguely	Schweiz	Kinetik	200–3000	preiswert	0,68	4420
5	8	Klein	Frankreich	Neuer Realismus	5500	sehr teuer	1,29	4260
6	10	Dine	USA	Pop Art	350–1500	billig	0,60	4170
7	7	Arman	Frankreich	Neuer Realismus	150–1200	sehr billig	0,29	4155
8	32	Beuys	Deutschland	Aktionen	bis 3000	preiswert	0,78	3835
9	9	Lichtenstein	USA	Pop Art	280–4500	sehr teuer	1,17	3830
10	11	Stella	USA	Neue Abstraktion	650–5000	sehr teuer	1,31	3820
11	13	Soto	Venezuela	Op Art	280–2000	billig	0,54	3700
12	14	Warhol	USA	Pop Art	500–2600	preiswert	0,71	3645
13	12	Paolozzi	England	Plastik	150–2000	billig	0,56	3585
14	16	Hockeny	England	Pop Art	480–1800	billig	0,59	3405
15	15	Rosenquist	USA	Pop Art	200–2400	preiswert	0,78	3095
16	27	Morris	USA	Minimal	–	–	–	3080
17	18	Uecker	Deutschland	Zero	8–300	sehr billig	0,10	3075
18	30	Christo	Bulgarien	Neuer Realismus	160–800	sehr billig	0,27	2980
19	24	Noland	USA	Neue Abstraktion	1200	billig	0,41	2935
20	17	Louis	USA	Neue Abstraktion	–	–	–	2900
21	22	Rayasse	Frankreich	Neuer Realismus	bis 3000	sehr teuer	1,07	2815
22	21	Kelly	USA	Neue Abstraktion	–	–	–	2725
23	19	Mack	Deutschland	Zero	140–990	billig	0,37	2710
24	20	Piene	Deutschland	Zero	120–200	sehr billig	0,07	2690
25	29	Judd	USA	Minimal	70–900	billig	0,34	2665
26	33	César	Frankreich	Plastik	200	sehr billig	0,08	2650
27	35	Riley	England	Op Art	350–1500	billig	0,57	2650
28	28	Segal	USA	Pop Art	400–4500	sehr teuer	1,71	2635
29	50	Kienholz	USA	Environment	–	–	–	2585
30	26	Jones	England	Pop Art	160–850	billig	0,33	2570
31	23	Kitaj	USA	Pop Art	450–1200	billig	0,47	2555
32	31	Antes	Deutschland	Neue Figuration	160–650	billig	0,27	2425
33	36	Flavin	USA	Minimal	3200	sehr teuer	1,32	2420
34	34	Le Parc	Argentinien	Kinetik	480–2000	teuer	0,86	2330
35	40	Wesselmann	USA	Pop Art	400–2000	teuer	0,87	2305
36	44	Pistoletto	Italien	Neuer Realismus	–	–	–	2285
37	62	Andre	USA	Minimal	–	–	–	2230
38	39	Tilson	England	Pop Art	200–600	sehr billig	0,27	2200
39	41	Indiana	USA	Pop Art	280–800	billig	0,36	2195
40	45	Smith, R.	England	Neue Abstraktion	400–800	billig	0,37	2155
41	37	Hamilton	England	Pop Art	150–4800	sehr teuer	2,24	2145
42	38	Schöffer	Frankreich	Lichkunst	200–350	sehr billig	0,17	2110
43	75	Spoerri	Schweiz	Neuer Realismus	–	–	–	2110
44	59	Bury	Belgien	Kinetik	550–1200	billig	0,58	2075
45	71	Naumann	USA	Minimal	300	billig	0,15	2040
46	61	LeWitt	USA	Minimal	130–400	billig	0,20	1995
47	47	Hundertwasser	Österreich	Phant. Realismus	540–2800	sehr teuer	1,41	1990
48	43	Rivers	USA	Pop Art	185–2000	sehr teuer	1,01	1985
49	60	St-Phalle	Frankreich	Neuer Realismus	400–500	sehr billig	0,25	1985
50	83	Bontecou	USA	Plastik	550–750	billig	0,38	1965

rang: rank
richtung: direction
preise für grafik und objeckte: price for prints and multiples
preisnote: price note
sehr teuer: very expensive
teuer: expensive
sehr billig: very cheap
billig: cheap
preiswert: good value
punkte: points

1971 (51–100)

RANG 1971	1970	NAME	NATION	RICHTUNG	PREISE FÜR GRAFIK UND OBJEKTE DM	PREISNOTE	PPR	PUNKTE
51	52	Twombly	Italien	Neuer Realismus	150–1200	billig	0,61	1960
52	–	Dorazio	Italien	Neue Abstraktion	120–400	sehr billig	0,20	1955
53	–	Chillida	Spanien	Plastik	–	–	–	1950
54	54	Fahlström	Schweden	Neuer Realismus	250–600	billig	0,32	1890
55	48	Bell	USA	Minimal	–			1855
56	51	Klapheck	Deutschland	Pop Art	500–750	billig	0,41	1840
57	66	Caro	England	Plastik	–	–	–	1805
58	53	King	England	Plastik	–	–	–	1795
59	62	Chamberlain	USA	Plastik	–	–	–	1790
60	49	Schultze	Deutschland	Phant. Realismus	120–260	sehr billig	0,15	1750
61	46	Brüning	Deutschland	Neuer Realismus	120–180	sehr billig	0,10	1735
62	72	Chryssa	Griechenland	Lichtkunst	500–1500	teuer	0,90	1675
63	69	Arakawa	Japan	Neuer Realismus	240–1200	preiswert	0,73	1655
64	74	Manzoni	Italien	Neuer Realismus	1000–2500	sehr teuer	1,52	1640
65	56	Geiger	Deutschland	Neue Abstraktion	60–400	sehr billig	0,25	1600
66	58	Frankenthaler	USA	Neue Abstraktion	500–900	billig	0,57	1575
67	67	Phillips	England	Pop Art	100–450	sehr billig	0,29	1560
68	69	Poons	USA	Neue Abstraktion	400	sehr billig	0,26	1535
69	88	D'Arcangelo	USA	Pop Art	240–1100	preiswert	0,72	1520
70	81	Morellet	Frankreich	Kinetik	280–1500	teuer	1,00	1500
71	62	Marisol	Venezuela	Pop Art	900	billig	0,60	1495
72	80	Haese	Deutschland	Plastik	–	–	–	1490
73	65	Pomodoro, A.	Italien	Plastik	700	billig	0,47	1485
74	57	Richter	Deutschland	Neuer Realismus	50–250	sehr billig	0,17	1475
75	82	Blake	England	Pop Art	–	–	–	1400
76	–	Rotella	Italien	Neuer Realismus	–	–	–	1400
77	73	Rickey	USA	Plastik	bis 4000	sehr teuer	2,90	1380
78	87	Smith, T.	USA	Minimal	700	billig	0,51	1375
79	88	Luginbühl	Schweiz	Plastik	bis 280	billig	0,20	1370
80	–	Pomodoro, G.	Italien	Plastik	–	–	–	1355
81	67	Berrocal	Spanien	Plastik	320–6000	sehr teuer	4,44	1350
82	–	Rainer	Österreich	Tadeismus	50–200	sehr billig	0,15	1310
83	95	Sonnier	USA	Prozeßkunst	600	billig	0,46	1300
84	99	Serra	USA	Prozeßkunst	600	billig	0,47	1290
85	–	Ipoustegy	Frankreich	Plastik	–	–	–	1285
86	90	Smithson	USA	Land Art	900–1600	sehr teuer	1,25	1280
87	86	Mavignier	Argentinien	Op Art	170–650	billig	0,51	1275
88	–	Visser	Holland	Plastik	200–1500	sehr teuer	1,22	1230
89	95	De Maria	USA	Land Art	800–6000	sehr teuer	4,92	1220
90	77	Gaul	Deutschland	Neue Abstraktion	60–180	sehr billig	0,15	1215
91	78	Trova	USA	Plastik	800–2000	sehr teuer	1,67	1200
92	100	Hoyland	England	Neue Abstraktion	250–400	billig	0,33	1195
93	79	Pfahler	Deutschland	Neue Abstraktion	60–200	sehr billig	0,17	1195
94	85	Demarco	Belgien	Lichtkunst	800	preiswert	0,70	1140
95	84	Heerich	Deutschland	Minimal	90–500	billig	0,44	1130
96	–	Verheyen	Belgien	Zero	320	sehr billig	0,29	1115
97	–	Rot	Deutschland	Prozeßkunst	bis 2000	sehr teuer	1,80	1110
98	91	Colombo	Italien	Kinetik	250–650	billig	0,59	1100
99	–	Krushenik	USA	Neue Abstraktion	450–600	billig	0,55	1090
100	75	Lenk	Deutschland	Plastik	80–200	sehr billig	0,19	1080

2.3 Kunstkompass Rangliste der Künstler, 1972 (1–50)

RANG 1972	1971	NAME	NATION	RICHTUNG	PREIS-PUNKTE-VERHÄLTNIS	PREIS-PUNKTE-VERHÄLTNIS VON/BIS	PREISNOTE	PUNKTE
1	1	Rauschenberg	USA	Pop Art	50 000/200 000	7/27	teuer	7275
2	2	Oldenburg	USA	Pop Art	50 000/160 000	8/25	preiswert	6395
3	3	Johns	USA	Neuer Realismus	100 000/400 000	16/63	sehr teuer	6370
4	4	Tinguely	Schweiz	Kinetik	25 000/100 000	4/16	billig	6290
5	8	Beuys	Deutschland	Aktionkunst	15 000/100 000	3/17	billig	5760
6	5	Klein	Frankreich	Neuer Realismus	45 000/280 000	8/49	sehr teuer	5750
7	7	Arman	Frankreich	Neuer Realismus	20 000/150 000	4/28	preiswert	5395
8	12	Warhol	USA	Pop Art	30 000/180 000	6/34	sehr teuer	5350
9	9	Lichtenstein	USA	Pop Art	30 000/240 000	6/47	sehr teuer	5135
10	6	Dine	USA	Pop Art	15 000/90 000	3/18	preiswert	4860
11	11	Soto	Venezuela	Optical Art	12 000/120 000	3/25	preiswert	4730
12	10	Stella	USA	Neue Abstraktion	50 000/230 000	11/49	sehr teuer	4680
13	26	César	Frankreich	Neuer Realismus	15 000/50 000	3/11	billig	4365
14	18	Christo	staatenlos	Neuer Realismus	20 000/40 000	5/9	billig	4295
15	13	Paolozzi	England	Plastiker	20 000/100 000	5/23	billig	4280
16	17	Uecker	Deutschland	Zero	10 000/60 000	2/14	billig	4260
17	16	Morris	USA	Antiform	20 000/40 000	5/10	billig	4000
18	19	Noland	USA	Neue Abstraktion	50 000/140 000	13/35	sehr teuer	4000
19	15	Rosenquist	USA	Pop Art	25 000/100 000	6/25	teuer	3980
20	23	Mack	Deutschland	Zero	5 000/45 000	1/12	billig	3830
21	30	Louis	USA	Neue Abstraktion	50 000/150 000	13/39	sehr teuer	3805
22	14	Hockney	England	Pop Art	50 000/80 000	14/22	preiswert	3695
23	21	Rayesse	Frankreich	Neuer Realismus	25 000/90 000	7/25	teuer	3655
24	29	Kienholz	USA	Realismus	35 000/240 000	10/68	sehr teuer	3545
25	24	Piene	Deutschland	Zero	5 000/30 000	1/8	billig	3540
26	41	Hamilton	England	Pop Art	70 000/90 000	20/26	teuer	3505
27	44	Bury	Belgien	Kinetik	24 000/120 000	7/36	preiswert	3365
28	30	Jones	England	Pop Art	10 000/25 000	3/7	billig	3350
29	25	Judd	USA	Minimal Art	5 000/60 000	2/18	billig	3325
30	45	Nauman	USA	Prozeßkunst	12 000/40 000	4/12	billig	3290
31	28	Segal	USA	Pop Art	50 000/60 000	15/18	billig	3275
32	22	Kelly	USA	Neue Abstraktion	45 000/100 000	14/31	teuer	3270
33	37	Andre	USA	Minimal Art	18 000/30 000	6/9	billig	3260
34	35	Wesselmann	USA	Pop Art	35 000/60 000	11/19	preiswert	3230
35	46	LeWitt	USA	Minimal Art	12 000/40 000	4/13	billig	3140
36	42	Schöffer	Frankreich	Lichtkunst	30 000/120 000	10/39	teuer	3065
37	31	Kitaj	USA	Pop Art	40 000/60 000	13/20	preiswert	3025
38	27	Riley	England	Optical Art	20 000/50 000	7/17	preiswert	2970
39	32	Antes	Deutschland	Neue Figuration	10 000/45 000	3/15	preiswert	2965
40	64	Manzoni	Italien	Neuer Realismus	30 000/60 000	10/20	preiswert	2950
41	34	Le Parc	Argentinien	Kinetik	8 000/30 000	3/10	billig	2945
42	52	Dorazio	Italien	Neue Abstraktion	10 000/30 000	3/10	billig	2925
43	33	Flavin	USA	Minimal Art	10 000/35 000	3/12	billig	2890
44	43	Spoerri	Schweiz	Neuer Realismus	5 000/25 000	2/9	billig	2830
45	39	Indiana	USA	Pop Art	5 000/80 000	2/29	teuer	2775
46	36	Pistoletto	Italien	Neuer Realismus	5 000/26 000	2/10	billig	2715
47	56	Klapheck	Deutschland	Pop Art	8 000/40 000	3/15	preiswert	2700
48	38	Tilson	England	Pop Art	15 000/30 000	6/11	billig	2670
49	–	Dibbets	Nierderlande	Conceptkunst	6 000/18 000	2/7	billig	2565
50	40	Smith, R.	England	Neue Abstraktion	8 000/25 000	3/10	billig	2505

rang: rank
richtung: direction
preise für grafik und objeckte: price for prints and multiples
preisnote: price note
sehr teuer: very expensive
teuer: expensive
sehr billig: very cheap
billig: cheap
preiswert: good value
punkte: points

1972
(51–100)

RANG 1972	RANG 1971	NAME	NATION	RICHTUNG	PREIS-PUNKTE-VERHÄLTNIS	PREIS-PUNKTE-VERHÄLTNIS VON/BIS	PREISNOTE	PUNKTE
51	53	Chillida	Spanien	Plastiker	5 000/200 0000	20/81	sehr teuer	2460
52	84	Serra	USA	Prozeßkunst	20 000/95 000	8/37	preiswert	2460
53	57	Caro	England	Plastiker	80 000/120 000	34/51	teuer	2355
54	89	De Maria	USA	Land Art	4 000/30 000	2/13	billig	2320
55	–	Huebler	USA	Conceptkunst	3 000/7 000	1/3	sehr billig	2265
56	83	Sonnier	USA	Prozeßkunst	15 000/40 000	7/18	billig	2260
57	97	Rot	Schweiz	Neue Sensibilität	10 000/40 000	4/19	billig	2240
58	59	Chamberlain	USA	Plastiker	10 000/50 000	4/22	billig	2235
59	49	St-Phalle	Frankreich	Neuer Realismus	10 000/20 000	4/9	billig	2235
60	74	Richter	Deutschland	Neuer Realismus	4 000/15 000	2/9	billig	2205
61	70	Morellet	Frankreich	Kinetik	5 000/20 000	2/9	billig	2180
62	–	Merz	Italien	Prozeßkunst	10 000/60 000	5/28	preiswert	2125
63	58	King	England	Plastiker	20 000/45 000	10/22	billig	2075
64	50	Bontecou	USA	Plastiker	40 000/70 000	19/34	preiswert	2060
65	51	Twombly	USA	Neuer Realismus	8 000/80 000	4/39	teuer	2060
66	54	Fahlström	Schweden	Neuer Realismus	10 000/40 000	5/20	preiswert	2030
67	85	Smithson	USA	Land Art	3 000/5 000	2/3	sehr billig	1990
68	63	Arakawa	Japan	Neuer Realismus	10 000/18 000	5/9	billig	1975
69	48	Rivers	USA	Pop Art	25 000/45 000	13/23	preiswert	1960
70	75	Blacke	England	Pop Art	30 000/50 000	16/26	teuer	1930
71	–	Haacke	Deutschland	Prozeßkunst	5 000/15 000	3/8	billig	1930
72	78	Smith, T.	USA	Minimal Art	50 000/150 000	26/78	sehr teuer	1930
73	61	Brüning	Deutschland	Neuer Realismus	3 000/12 000	2/6	billig	1915
74	–	Long	England	Land Art	8 000/15 000	4/8	billig	1885
75	88	Visser	Niederlande	Minimal Art	5 000/30 000	3/16	billig	1850
76	79	Luginbühl	Schweiz	Plastiker	20 000/80 000	11/43	teuer	1840
77	73	Pomodoro, A.	Italien	Plastiker	50 000/120 000	27/65	sehr teuer	1835
78	76	Rotelia	Italien	Neuer Realismus	7 000/25 000	4/14	billig	1800
79	–	Agam	Israel	Optical Art	40 000/300 000	22/168	sehr teuer	1790
80	–	Heizer	USA	Land Art	3 000/8 000	2/4	billig	1770
81	55	Bell	USA	Minimal Art	20 000/35 000	11/20	billig	1750
82	–	Gilbert & George	England	Selbstdarsteller	8 000/35 000	5/20	billig	1745
83	–	Walther	Deutschland	Aktionskunst	2 500/8 000	1/5	billig	1740
84	–	Kosuth	USA	Conceptkunst	10 000/30 000	6/18	preiswert	1710
85	90	Gaul	Deutschland	Neue Abstraktion	3 000/10 000	2/6	billig	1705
86	71	Marisol	Venezula	Pop Art	25 000/35 000	15/21	billig	1690
87	69	D'Arcangelo	USA	Pop Art	10 000/40 0000	6/24	teuer	1680
88	68	Poons	USA	Neue Abstraktion	25 000/80 000	15/48	sehr teuer	1680
89	–	Hains	Frankreich	Neuer Realismus	7 000/25 000	4/15	preiswert	1675
90	65	Geiger	Deutschland	Neue Abstraktion	3 000/10 000	2/6	billig	1670
91	67	Philips	England	Pop Art	6 000/20 000	4/12	billig	1660
92	–	Weiner	USA	Conceptkunst	3 600/--	2/--	sehr billig	1660
93	85	Ipousteguy	Frankreich	Plastiker	20 000/60 000	12/37	preiswert	1610
94	77	Rickey	USA	Kinetik	10 000/100 000	6/63	sehr teuer	1600
95	80	Pomodoro, G.	Italien	Plastiker	25 000/80 000	16/50	teuer	1595
96	–	Filliou	Frankreich	Neuer Realismus	5 000/30 000	3/18	preiswert	1590
97	72	Haese	Deutschland	Plastiker	10 000/40 000	6/25	preiswert	1590
98	–	Oppenheim	USA	Land Art	3 000/5 000	2/3	sehr billig	1590
99	82	Rainer	Österreich	Selbstdarsteller	3 000/25 000	12/16	preiswert	1580
100	–	Artschwager	USA	Neuer Realismus	3 000/25 000	2/16	preiswert	1550

2.3 Kunstkompass Rangliste der Künstler, 1973 (1–50)

RANG 1973	1972	NAME	NATION	RICHTUNG	MINDESTPREIS FÜR EIN REPRÄSENTATIVES WERK IN MARK	PREIS-PUNKTE-VERHÄLTNIS	PREISNOTE	PUNKTE
1	1	Rauschenberg	USA	Pop Art	100 000	7,5	preiswert	13 420
2	3	Johns	USA	Neuer Realismus	150 000	12,7	sehr teuer	11 770
3	2	Oldenburg	USA	Pop Art	80 000	6,8	preiswert	11 760
4	5	Beuys	Deutschland	Aktionskunst	30 000	2,7	billig	10 980
5	6	Klein	Frankreich	Neuer Realismus	80 000	7,4	preiswert	10 880
6	8	Warhol	USA	Pop Art	150 000	14,2	sehr teuer	10 540
7	9	Lichtenstein	USA	Pop Art	100 000	9,7	teuer	10 270
8	4	Tinguely	Schweiz	Kinetik	35 000	3,6	billig	9 675
9	12	Stella	USA	Neue Abstraktion	70 000	7,4	preiswert	9 410
10	7	Arman	Frankreich	Neuer Realismus	40 000	4,4	billig	9 015
11	10	Dine	USA	Pop Art	50 000	5,6	preiswert	8 955
12	11	Soto	Venezuela	Optical Art	15 000	1,7	billig	8 830
13	14	Christo	Staatenlos	Neuer Realismus	25 000	3,1	billig	8 160
14	21	Louis	USA	Neue Abstraktion	180 000	22,5	sehr teuer	7 995
15	18	Noland	USA	Neue Abstraktion	60 000	7,5	preiswert	7 950
16	19	Rosenquist	USA	Pop Art	60 000	7,7	preiswert	7 750
17	17	Morris	USA	Antiform	20 000	2,7	billig	7 430
18	13	César	Frankreich	Neuer Realismus	50 000	6,8	preiswert	7 385
19	16	Uecker	Deutschland	Zero	20 000	2,7	billig	7 370
20	15	Paolozzi	England	Pop Art	50 000	6,8	preiswert	7 365
21	32	Kelly	USA	Neue Abstraktion	70 000	9,6	teuer	7 270
22	35	LeWitt	USA	Minimal Art	15 000	2,1	billig	7 220
23	27	Bury	Belgien	Kinetik	50 000	7,3	preiswert	6 815
24	29	Judd	USA	Minimal Art	40 000	5,9	preiswert	6 765
25	22	Hockney	England	Pop Art	100 000	14,8	sehr teuer	6 760
26	24	Kienholz	USA	Realismus	100 000	15,1	sehr teuer	6 635
27	43	Flavin	USA	Minimal Art	15 000	2,3	billig	6 600
28	26	Hamilton	England	Pop Art	100 000	15,3	sehr teuer	6 515
29	23	Raysse	Frankreich	Neuer Realismus	50 000	7,9	preiswert	6 305
30	31	Segal	USA	Pop Art	40 000	6,4	preiswert	6 275
31	20	Mack	Deutschland	Zero	12 000	1,9	billig	6 245
32	33	Andre	USA	Minimal Art	25 000	4,1	billig	6 155
33	40	Manzoni	Italien	Neuer Realismus	30 000	4,9	preiswert	6 100
34	30	Nauman	USA	Prozeßkunst	40 000	6,7	preiswert	5 990
35	36	Schöffer	Frankreich	Lichtkunst	30 000	5,0	preiswert	5 985
36	25	Piene	Deutschland	Zero	8 000	1,4	sehr billig	5 910
37	38	Jones	England	Pop Art	30 000	5,2	preiswert	5 790
38	37	Kitaj	USA	Pop Art	60 000	10,4	teuer	5 745
39	34	Wesselmann	USA	Pop Art	60 000	11,1	teuer	5 400
40	46	Pistoletto	Italien	Neuer Realismus	15 000	2,8	billig	5 325
41	47	Klapheck	Deutschland	Pop Art	30 000	5,8	preiswert	5 200
42	45	Indiana	USA	Pop Art	50 000	9,6	teuer	5 185
43	52	Serra	USA	Prozeßkunst	30 000	5,9	preiswert	5 090
44	65	Twombly	USA	Neuer Realismus	60 000	12,0	teuer	5 025
45	38	Riley	England	Optical Art	50 000	10,0	teuer	5 005
46	51	Chillida	Spanien	Abstraction	150 000	30,2	sehr teuer	4 960
47	54	De Maria	USA	Land Art	10 000	2,0	billig	4 950
48	41	Le Parc	Argentinien	Kinetik	12 000	2,5	billig	4 895
49	57	Rot	Schweiz	Neue Sensibilität	25 000	5,2	preiswert	4 840
50	48	Tilson	England	Pop Art	25 000	5,2	preiswert	4 830

rang: rank
richtung: direction
preise für grafik und objeckte: price for prints and multiples
preisnote: price note
sehr teuer: very expensive
teuer: expensive
sehr billig: very cheap
billig: cheap
preiswert: good value
punkte: points

1973
(51–100)

RANG 1973	RANG 1972	NAME	NATION	RICHTUNG	MINDESTPREIS FÜR EIN REPRÄSENTATIVES WERK IN MARK	PREIS-PUNKTE-VERHÄLTNIS	PREISNOTE	PUNKTE
51	53	Caro	England	Neue Abstraktion	40 000	8,3	preiswert	4 815
52	39	Antes	Deutschland	Neue Figuration	30 000	6,2	preiswert	4 805
53	44	Spoerri	Schweiz	Neuer Realismus	15 000	3,1	billig	4 790
54	–	Schoonhoven	Niederlande	Neue Konkrete Kunst	10 000	2,2	billig	4 630
55	60	Richter	Deutschland	Neuer Realismus	10 000	2,2	billig	4 535
56	69	Rivers	USA	Pop Art	30 000	6,6	preiswert	4 530
57	74	Long	England	Land Art	8 000	1,8	billig	4 425
58	55	Huebler	USA	Konzeptkunst	8 000	1,8	billig	4 390
59	79	Agam	Israel	Optical Art	50 000	11,4	teuer	4 380
60	59	Saint-Phalle	Frankreich	Neuer Realismus	20 000	4,6	billig	4 375
61	50	Smith, R.	England	Neue Abstraktion	20 000	4,6	billig	4 355
62	68	Arakawa	Japan	Neuer Realismus	15 000	3,5	billig	4 335
63	49	Dibbets	Niederlande	Konzeptkunst	8 000	1,9	billig	4 325
64	58	Chamberlain	USA	Neuer Realismus	50 000	12,0	teuer	4 170
65	64	Bontecou	USA	Individ. Mythologie	50 000	12,1	teuer	4 130
66	56	Sonnier	USA	Prozeßkunst	20 000	4,9	preiswert	4 070
67	–	Olitski	USA	Neue Abstraktion	25 000	6,3	preiswert	3 940
68	–	Gnoli	Italien	Mag. Realismus	150 000	38,3	sehr teuer	3 920
69	84	Kosuth	USA	Konzeptkunst	12 000	3,1	billig	3 890
70	63	King	England	Neue Abstraktion	30 000	7,9	preiswert	3 805
71	83	Walther	Deutschland	Aktionskunst	3 000	0,8	sehr billig	3 735
72	66	Fahlström	Schweden	Neuer Realismus	25 000	6,7	preiswert	3 710
73	81	Bell	USA	Minimal Art	20 000	5,4	preiswert	3 700
74	87	D'Arcangelo	USA	Pop Art	30 000	8,3	preiswert	3 610
75	72	Smith, T.	USA	Minimal Art	50 000	14,1	sehr teuer	3 540
76	–	Takis	Griechenland	Kinetik	5 000	1,4	sehr billig	3 540
77	–	Kolár	CSSR	Konkrete Poesie	2 000	0,6	sehr billig	3 490
78	76	Luginbühl	Schweiz	Neuer Realismus	50 000	14,8	sehr teuer	3 390
79	–	Ryman	USA	Neue Malerei	18 000	5,4	preiswert	3 340
80	–	Krushenik	USA	Neue Abstraktion	30 000	9,0	preiswert	3 315
81	–	Jensen	USA	Konzeptkunst	12 000	3,7	billig	3 270
82	88	Poons	USA	Neue Abstraktion	50 000	15,4	sehr teuer	3 250
83	71	Haacke	Deutschland	Prozeßkunst	10 000	3,1	billig	3 245
84	–	Heerich	Deutschland	Minimal Art	5 000	1,6	billig	3 220
85	–	Cheyssa	Griechenland	Lichtkunst	20 000	6,2	preiswert	3 210
86	82	Gilbert & George	England	Selbstdarstellung	8 000	2,5	billig	3 195
87	61	Morellet	Frankreich	Neue Konkrete Kunst	15 000	4,8	billig	3 150
88	–	Samaras	USA	Individ. Mythologie	15 000	4,8	billig	3 150
89	–	Darboven	Deutschland	Konzeptkunst	8 000	2,6	billig	3 130
90	–	Heyboer	Niederlande	Individ. Mythologie	2 000	0,6	sehr billig	3 090
91	62	Merz	Italien	Prozeßkunst	15 000	4,9	preiswert	3 085
92	99	Rainer	Österreich	Selbstdarstellung	10 000	3,3	billig	3 070
93	–	Graubner	Deutschland	Neue Abstraktion	12 000	3,9	billig	3 065
94	86	Marisol	Venezuela	Pop Art	30 000	10,0	teuer	3 010
95	–	Alviani	Italien	Neue Konkrete Kunst	8 000	2,7	billig	2 970
96	70	Blake	England	Pop Art	40 000	13,6	sehr teuer	2 960
97	–	Ruscha	USA	West Coast Art	12 000	4,1	billig	2 960
98	73	Brüning	Deutschland	Neuer Realismus	6 000	2,1	billig	2 865
99	–	Davis, R.	USA	West Coast Art	40 000	14,0	sehr teuer	2 860
100	90	Geiger	Deutschland	Neue Abstraktion	5 000	1,8	billig	2 850

2.3 Kunstkompass Rangliste der Künstler, 1974 (1–50)

RANG 1974	RANG 1973	NAME	NATION	RICHTUNG	MINDESTPREIS FÜR EIN REPRÄSENTATIVES WERK IN MARK	PREIS-PUNKTE-VERHÄLTNIS (PPV)	PREISNOTE	PUNKTE
1	1	Rauschenberg	USA	Pop Art	150 000	9,3	teuer	16 200
2	3	Oldenburg	USA	Pop Art	90 000	5,9	preiswert	15 050
3	2	Johns	USA	Pop Art	250 000	16,8	sehr teuer	14 880
4	8	Tinguely	Schweiz	Neuer Realismus	60 000	4,1	preiswert	14 635
5	4	Beuys	Deutschland	Aktionskunst	50 000	3,5	preiswert	14 475
6	6	Warhol	USA	Pop Art	120 000	8,5	teuer	14 090
7	5	Klein	Frankreich	Neuer Realismus	150 000	10,8	teuer	13 850
8	7	Lichtenstein	USA	Pop Art	120 000	9,0	teuer	13 390
9	9	Stella	USA	Neue Abstraktion	80 000	6,8	preiswert	11 730
10	10	Arman	Frankreich	Neuer Realismus	40 000	3,5	preiswert	11 545
11	13	Christo	Staatenlos	Neuer Realismus	35 000	3,1	preiswert	11 225
12	11	Dine	USA	Pop Art	60 000	5,4	preiswert	11 015
13	12	Soto	Venezuela	Op Art	50 000	4,6	preiswert	10 890
14	16	Rosenquist	USA	Pop Art	60 000	5,8	preiswert	10 270
15	17	Morris	USA	Antiform	30 000	3,0	billig	10 120
16	14	Louis	USA	Colour Field	200 000	20,0	sehr teuer	10 040
17	19	Uecker	Deutschland	Zero	30 000	3,1	preiswert	9 730
18	30	Segal	USA	Pop Art	40 000	4,3	preiswert	9 255
19	22	LeWitt	USA	Minimal Art	20 000	2,2	billig	9 220
20	21	Kelly	USA	Neue Abstraktion	70 000	7,6	preiswert	9 180
21	15	Noland	USA	Colour Field	60 000	6,6	preiswert	9 080
22	24	Judd	USA	Minimal Art	40 000	4,5	preiswert	8 825
23	20	Paolozzi	England	Pop Art	50 000	5,7	preiswert	8 705
24	33	Manzoni	Italien	Neuer Realismus	40 000	4,6	preiswert	8 680
25	28	Hamilton	England	Pop Art	100 000	11,5	sehr teuer	8 675
26	23	Bury	Belgien	Kinetik	60 000	6,9	preiswert	8 665
27	18	César	Frankreich	Neuer Realismus	50 000	5,8	preiswert	8 595
28	31	Mack	Deutschland	Zero	20 000	2,3	billig	8 565
29	27	Flavin	USA	Minimal Art	25 000	3,0	billig	8 440
30	34	Nauman	USA	Prozeßkunst	40 000	4,7	preiswert	8 440
31	32	Andre	USA	Minimal Art	50 000	5,9	preiswert	8 405
32	25	Hockney	England	Pop Art	120 000	14,8	sehr teuer	8 095
33	26	Kienholz	USA	Realismus	80 000	10,1	teuer	7 895
34	43	Serra	USA	Prozeßkunst	30 000	3,8	preiswert	7 870
35	29	Raysse	Frankreich	Neuer Realismus	50 000	6,6	preiswert	7 595
36	49	Rot	Schweiz	Neue Sensibilität	30 000	4,0	preiswert	7 520
37	39	Wesselmann	USA	Pop Art	80 000	10,9	teuer	7 320
38	63	Dibbets	Niederlande	Konzeptkunst	15 000	2,1	billig	7 295
39	53	Spoerri	Schweiz	Neuer Realismus	20 000	2,8	billig	7 180
40	47	De Maria	USA	Land Art	50 000	7,0	preiswert	7 150
41	44	Twombly	USA	Abstraktion	100 000	14,3	sehr teuer	6 995
42	55	Richter	Deutschland	Neuer Realismus	20 000	2,9	billig	6 965
43	35	Schöffer	Frankreich	Lichtkunst	40 000	5,8	preiswert	6 855
44	40	Pistoletto	Italien	Neuer Realismus	25 000	3,7	preiswert	6 810
45	41	Klapheck	Deutschland	Magischer Realismus	40 000	5,9	preiswert	6 770
46	38	Kitaj	USA	Pop Art	70 000	10,3	teuer	6 765
47	68	Gnoli	Italien	Magischer Realismus	250 000	38,0	sehr teuer	6 585
48	36	Piene	Deutschland	Zero	15 000	2,3	billig	6 470
49	37	Jones	England	Pop Art	30 000	4,7	preiswert	6 450
50	54	Schoonhoven	Niederlande	Neue Konkrete Kunst	15 000	2,3	billig	6 425

rang: rank
richtung: direction
preise für grafik und objeckte: price for prints and multiples
preisnote: price note
sehr teuer: very expensive
teuer: expensive
sehr billig: very cheap
billig: cheap
preiswert: good value
punkte: points

1974
(51–100)

RANG 1974	1973	NAME	NATION	RICHTUNG	MINDESTPREIS FÜR EIN REPRÄSENTATIVES WERK IN MARK	PREIS-PUNKTE-VERHÄLTNIS (PPV)	PREISNOTE	PUNKTE
51	46	Chillida	Spanien	Abstraktion	150 000	23,4	sehr teuer	6 420
52	79	Ryman	USA	Neue Malerei	45 000	7,1	preiswert	6 295
53	69	Kosuth	USA	Konzeptkunst	12 000	1,9	billig	6 235
54	62	Arakawa	Japan	Konzeptkunst	18 000	2,9	billig	6 145
55	57	Long	England	Land Art	10 000	1,6	billig	6 105
56	60	St-Phalle	Frankreich	Neuer Realismus	20 000	3,3	preiswert	6 005
57	45	Riley	England	Op Art	50 000	8,3	teuer	5 995
58	51	Caro	England	Abstraktion	60 000	10,1	teuer	5 965
59	50	Tilson	England	Pop Art	25 000	4,2	preiswert	5 940
60	59	Agam	Israel	Op Art	80 000	13,6	sehr teuer	5 890
61	42	Indiana	USA	Pop Art	40 000	6,8	preiswert	5 875
62	66	Sonnier	USA	Prozeßkunst	30 000	5,2	preiswert	5 740
63	58	Huebler	USA	Konzeptkunst	10 000	1,8	billig	5 595
64	91	Merz	Italien	Prozeßkunst	20 000	3,6	preiswert	5 495
65	86	Gilbert & George	England	Selbstdarstellung	10 000	1,8	billig	5 485
66	48	Le Parc	Argentinen	Kinetik	15 000	2,8	billig	5 425
67	–	Weiner	USA	Konzeptkunst	5 000	0,9	sehr billig	5 270
68	97	Ruscha	USA	Pop Art	15 000	3,0	billig	5 080
69	71	Walther	Deutschland	Aktionskunst	6 000	1,2	sehr billig	4 965
70	89	Darboven	Deutschland	Konzeptkunst	15 000	3,0	billig	4 935
71	56	Rivers	USA	Pop Art	45 000	9,1	teuer	4 930
72	64	Chamberlain	USA	Pop Art	50 000	10,3	teuer	4 870
73	52	Antes	Deutschland	Neue Figuration	40 000	8,3	teuer	4 805
74	75	Smith, T.	USA	Minimal Art	50 000	10,4	teuer	4 790
75	61	Smith, R.	England	Neue Abstraktion	8 000	1,7	billig	4 755
76	65	Bontecou	USA	Abstraktion	50 000	10,7	teuer	4 670
77	87	Morellet	Frankreich	Neue Konkrete Kunst	15 000	3,2	preiswert	4 660
78	70	King	England	Abstraktion	30 000	6,4	preiswert	4 655
79	–	Martin	USA	Konzeptkunst	120 000	26,0	sehr teuer	4 610
80	–	Broodthaers	Belgien	Individ. Mythologie	6 000	1,3	billig	4 600
81	–	Dekkers	Niederlande	Neue Konkrete Kunst	12 000	2,7	billig	4 470
82	–	Filliou	Frankreich	Neue Sensibilität	8 000	1,8	billig	4 410
83	67	Olitski	USA	Colour Field	25 000	5,7	preiswert	4 390
84	82	Poons	USA	Colour Field	50 000	11,6	sehr teuer	4 300
85	93	Graubner	Deutschland	Neue Malerei	20 000	4,7	preiswert	4 245
86	96	Blake	England	Pop Art	30 000	7,1	preiswert	4 230
87	84	Heerich	Deutschland	Minimal Art	8 000	1,9	billig	4 200
88	76	Takis	Griechenland	Kinetik	20 000	4,8	preiswert	4 180
89	–	Panamarenko	Belgien	Individ. Mythologie	25 000	6,0	preiswert	4 175
90	81	Jensen	USA	Individ. Mythologie	25 000	6,0	preiswert	4 170
91	72	Fahlström	Schweden	Pop Art	30 000	7,2	preiswert	4 140
92	–	Visser	Niederlande	Neue Konkrete Kunst	6 000	1,5	billig	4 080
93	92	Rainer	Österreich	Selbstdarstellung	15 000	3,8	preiswert	3 980
94	74	D'Arcangelo	USA	Pop Art	30 000	7,6	preiswert	3 960
95	95	Alviani	Italien	Neue Konkrete Kunst	8 000	2,0	billig	3 950
96	–	Buren	Frankreich	Individ. Mythologie	7 000	1,8	billig	3 940
97	–	Heizer	USA	Land Art	8 000	2,0	billig	3 930
98	77	Kolár	CSSR	Konkrete Poesie	3 000	0,8	sehr billig	3 930
99	–	Ruthenbeck	Deutschland	Individ. Mythologie	10 000	2,6	billig	3 895
100	83	Haacke	Deutschland	Konzeptkunst	12 000	3,1	preiswert	3 875

2.3 Kunstkompass Rangliste der Künstler, 1975 (1–50)

RANG 1975	RANG 1974	NAME	NATION	RICHTUNG	MINDESTPREIS FÜR EIN REPRÄSENTA-TIVES WERK IN MARK	PREIS-PUNKTE-VERHÄLTNIS (PPV)	PREISNOTE	PUNKTE
1	1	Rauschenberg	USA	Prae-Pop Art	150 000	7,36	teuer	20 370
2	2	Oldenburg	USA	Pop Art	90 000	4,44	preiswert	20 260
3	6	Warhol	USA	Pop Art	120 000	6,39	teuer	18 770
4	3	Johns	USA	Prae-Pop Art	200 000	10,98	sehr teuer	18 200
5	5	Beuys	Deutschland	Aktionkunst	50 000	2,78	preiswert	17 930
6	8	Lichtenstein	USA	Pop Art	120 000	6,79	teuer	17 670
7	4	Tinguely	Schweiz	Neuer Realismus	60 000	3,54	preiswert	16 930
8	9	Stella	USA	Neue Abstraktion	80 000	4,82	preiswert	16 590
9	7	Klein	Frankreich	Neuer Realismus	150 000	9,21	sehr teuer	16 270
10	11	Christo	USA	Neuer Realismus	40 000	2,74	preiswert	14 550
11	12	Dine	USA	Pop Art	60 000	4,20	preiswert	14 270
12	20	Kelly	USA	Hard Edge	70 000	5,03	preiswert	13 900
13	19	LeWitt	USA	Minimal Art	20 000	1,45	billig	13 700
14	16	Louis	USA	Colour Field	250 000	18,34	sehr teuer	13 630
15	15	Morris	USA	Antiform	30 000	2,21	billig	13 560
16	13	Soto	Venezuela	Op Art	50 000	3,72	preiswert	13 410
17	21	Noland	USA	Colour Field	50 000	3,75	preiswert	13 330
18	10	Arman	Frankreich	Neuer Realismus	40 000	3,05	preiswert	13 110
19	22	Judd	USA	Minimal Art	40 000	3,07	preiswert	12 990
20	14	Rosenquist	USA	Pop Art	60 000	4,63	preiswert	12 940
21	25	Hamilton	England	Pop Art	100 000	8,19	teuer	12 210
22	29	Flavin	USA	Minimal Art	25 000	2,05	billig	12 190
23	23	Paolozzi	England	Pop Art	50 000	4,14	preiswert	12 060
24	31	Andre	USA	Minimal Art	50 000	4,15	preiswert	12 020
25	30	Nauman	USA	Prozeßkunst	40 000	3,34	preiswert	11 950
26	18	Segal	USA	Pop Art	40 000	3,37	preiswert	11 860
27	17	Uecker	Deutschland	Zero	40 000	3,49	preiswert	11 460
28	28	Mack	Deutschland	Zero	40 000	3,58	preiswert	11 160
29	34	Serra	USA	Prozeßkunst	30 000	2,69	preiswert	11 120
30	27	César	Frankreich	Neuer Realismus	50 000	4,59	preiswert	10 880
31	32	Hockney	England	Pop Art	120 000	11,07	sehr teuer	10 840
32	24	Manzoni	Italien	Neuer Realismus	40 000	3,72	preiswert	10 740
33	58	Caro	England	Abstraktion	70 000	6,67	teuer	10 480
34	36	Rot	Schweiz	Neue Sensibilität	30 000	2,89	preiswert	10 380
35	38	Dibbets	Niederlande	Konzeptkunst	15 000	1,47	billig	10 140
36	26	Bury	Belgien	Kinetik	60 000	5,99	preiswert	10 010
37	33	Kienholz	USA	Realismus	80 000	8,00	teuer	10 000
38	37	Wesselmann	USA	Pop Art	60 000	6,33	teuer	9 470
39	42	Richter	Deutschland	Neuer Realismus	20 000	2,16	billig	9 220
40	43	Schöffer	Frankreich	Lichtkunst	40 000	4,37	preiswert	9 140
41	52	Ryman	USA	Neue Malerei	50 000	5,48	preiswert	9 120
42	41	Twombly	USA	Abstraktion	100 000	11,16	sehr teuer	8 960
43	35	Raysse	Frankreich	Neuer Realismus	50 000	5,58	preiswert	8 950
44	55	Long	England	Land Art	10 000	1,13	billig	8 820
45	39	Spoerri	Schweiz	Neuer Realismus	15 000	1,74	billig	8 580
46	40	De Maria	USA	Land Art	50 000	5,90	preiswert	8 470
47	46	Kitaj	USA	Pop Art	70 000	8,39	teuer	8 340
48	53	Kosuth	USA	Konzeptkunst	11 000	1,32	billig	8 290
49	44	Pistoletto	Italien	Neuer Realismus	25 000	3,01	preiswert	8 280
50	70	Darboven	Deutschland	Konzeptkunst	15 000	1,82	billig	8 210

rang: rank
richtung: direction
preise für grafik und objeckte: price for prints and multiples
preisnote: price note
sehr teuer: very expensive
teuer: expensive
sehr billig: very cheap
billig: cheap
preiswert: good value
punkte: points

RANG 1975	1974	NAME	NATION	RICHTUNG	MINDESTPREIS FÜR EIN REPRÄSENTATIVES WERK IN MARK	PREIS-PUNKTE-VERHÄLTNIS (PPV)	PREISNOTE	PUNKTE
51	61	Indiana	USA	Pop Art	40 000	4,87	preiswert	8 200
52	57	Riley	England	Op Art	50 000	6,12	preiswert	8 160
53	68	Ruscha	USA	Pop Art	10 000	1,24	billig	8 060
54	54	Arakawa	Japan	Konzeptkunst	25 000	3,11	preiswert	8 030
55	67	Weiner	USA	Konzeptkunst	5 000	0,64	sehr billig	7 750
56	51	Chillida	Spanien	Abstraktion	150 000	19,37	sehr teuer	7 740
57	65	Gilbert & George	England	Selbstdarstellung	10 000	1,29	billig	7 740
58	84	Poons	USA	Colour Field	50 000	6,48	teuer	7 710
59	83	Olitski	USA	Colour Field	25 000	3,24	preiswert	7 700
60	45	Klapheck	Deutschland	Magischer Realismus	40 000	5,22	preiswert	7 650
61	48	Piene	Deutschland	Zero	15 000	1,96	billig	7 650
62	49	Jones	England	Pop Art	30 000	3,93	preiswert	7 630
63	59	Tilson	England	Pop Art	20 000	2,62	preiswert	7 610
64	63	Huebler	USA	Konzeptkunst	10 000	1,31	billig	7 590
65	62	Sonnier	USA	Prozeßkunst	30 000	3,95	preiswert	7 580
66	–	Oppenheim	USA	Video-Kunst	1 000	0,13	sehr billig	7 370
67	60	Agam	Israel	Op Art	80 000	10,86	sehr teuer	7 360
68	80	Broodthaers	Belgien	Indiv. Mythologie	6 000	0,82	sehr billig	7 300
69	50	Schoonhoven	Niederlande	Neue Konkrete Kunst	15 000	2,05	billig	7 300
70	96	Buren	Frankreich	Indiv. Mythologie	7 000	0,96	sehr billig	7 280
71	47	Gnoli	Italien	Magischer Realismus	200 000	27,70	sehr teuer	7 220
72	79	Martin	USA	Minimal Art	120 000	16,68	sehr teuer	7 190
73	75	Smith, R.	England	Neue Abstraktion	10 000	1,42	billig	7 000
74	78	King	England	Abstraktion	30 000	4,31	preiswert	6 950
75	56	St-Phalle	Frankreich	Neuer Realismus	20 000	2,89	preiswert	6 900
76	66	Le Parc	Argentinien	Kinetik	15 000	2,19	preiswert	6 830
77	64	Merz	Italien	Prozeßkunst	20 000	2,94	preiswert	6 790
78	71	Rivers	USA	Pop Art	45 000	6,65	teuer	6 760
79	74	Smith, T.	USA	Minimal Art	50 000	7,40	teuer	6 750
80	89	Panamarenko	Belgien	Indiv. Mythologie	25 000	3,72	preiswert	6 710
81	72	Chamberlain	USA	Pop Art	50 000	7,46	teuer	6 700
82	77	Morellet	Frankreich	Neue Konkrete Kunst	15 000	2,26	billig	6 610
83	–	Bell	USA	Minimal Art	30 000	4,70	preiswert	6 380
84	76	Bontecou	USA	Abstraktion	50 000	8,00	teuer	6 250
85	–	Hesse	USA	Exzentr. Abstraktion	30 000	4,87	preiswert	6 160
86	–	Di Suvero	USA	Neue Bildhauerei	50 000	8,15	teuer	6 130
87	86	Blake	England	Pop Art	30 000	4,95	preiswert	6 060
88	69	Walther	Deutschland	Aktionkunst	6 000	0,99	billig	6 030
89	–	Marden	USA	Neue Malerei	25 000	4,23	preiswert	5 900
90	100	Haacke	Deutschland	Konzeptkunst	12 000	2,09	billig	5 720
91	–	Boltanski	Frankreich	Indiv. Mythologie	3 000	0,52	sehr billig	5 680
92	82	Filliou	Frankreich	Neue Sensibilität	8 000	1,40	billig	5 680
93	73	Antes	Deutschland	Neue Figuration	40 000	7,05	teuer	5 670
94	–	Rinke	Deutschland	Körperkunst	8 000	1,41	billig	5 670
95	97	Heizer	USA	Land Art	8 000	1,41	billig	5 640
96	88	Takis	Griechenland	Kinetik	20 000	3,68	preiswert	5 430
97	–	Fulton	England	Konzeptkunst	4 500	0,83	sehr billig	5 370
98	–	Luginbühl	Schweiz	Neuer Realismus	50 000	9,41	sehr teuer	5 310
99	93	Rainer	Österreich	Selbstdarstellung	20 000	3,76	preiswert	5 310
100	–	Mangold	USA	Neue Malerei	15 000	2,83	preiswert	5 290

2.3 Kunstkompass Rangliste der Künstler, 1976 (1–50)

RANG 1976	1975	NAME	NATION	RICHTUNG	MINDESTPREIS FÜR EIN REPRÄSENTATIVES WERK IN MARK	PREIS-PUNKTE-VERHÄLTNIS (PPV)	PREISNOTE	PUNKTE
1	1	Rauschenberg, R.	USA	Prae-Pop Art	17 000	0,83	preiswert	20 490
2	3	Warhol, A.	USA	Pop Art	20 000	1,03	teuer	19 410
3	2	Oldenburg, C.	USA	Pop Art	12 500	0,65	preiswert	19 170
4	4	Johns, J.	USA	Prae-Pop Art	25 000	1,34	teuer	18 660
5	5	Beuys, J.	Deutschland	Aktionkunst	6 000	0,32	billig	18 320
6	7	Tinguely, J.	Schweiz	Neuer Realismus	3 000	0,17	billig	17 570
7	6	Lichtenstein, R.	USA	Pop Art	20 000	1,18	teuer	16 910
8	8	Stella, F.	USA	Neue Abstraktion	12 500	0,74	preiswert	16 870
9	9	Klein, Y.	Frankreich	Neuer Realismus	25 000	1,49	sehr teuer	16 810
10	10	Christo	USA	Neuer Realismus	4 000	0,26	billig	15 130
11	11	Dine, J.	USA	Pop Art	7 000	0,48	billig	14 620
12	13	LeWitt, S.	USA	Minimal Art	4 000	0,28	billig	14 110
13	18	Arman, F.	Frankreich	Neuer Realismus	5 000	0,35	billig	14 080
14	12	Kelly, E.	USA	Colour Field	12 000	0,91	preiswert	13 180
15	19	Judd, D.	USA	Minimal Art	7 500	0,57	preiswert	13 110
16	17	Noland, K.	USA	Colour Field	15 000	1,15	teuer	13 040
17	14	Louis, M.	USA	Colour Field	**	–	–	12 960
18	20	Rosenquist, J.	USA	Pop Art	18 000	1,40	sehr teuer	12 870
19	15	Morris, R.	USA	Antiform	12 500	0,98	preiswert	12 720
20	24	Andre, C.	USA	Minimal Art	1 000	0,08	sehr billig	12 620
21	16	Soto, R.	Venezuela	Op Art	4 000*	0,32	billig	12 380
22	22	Flavin, D.	USA	Minimal Art	5 000	0,41	billig	12 260
23	21	Hamilton, R.	Großbritannien	Pop Art	8 000	0,66	preiswert	12 170
24	26	Segal, G.	USA	Pop Art	10 000	0,83	preiswert	11 980
25	23	Paolozzi, E.	Großbritannien	Pop Art	4 000	0,33	billig	11 950
26	27	Uecker, G.	Deutschland	Zero	1 500	0,13	sehr billig	11 670
27	31	Hockney, D.	Großbritannien	Pop Art	4 500	0,40	billig	11 240
28	30	César	Frankreich	Neuer Realismus	5 000*	0,44	billig	11 220
29	28	Mack, H.	Deutschland	Zero	1 500	0,13	sehr billig	11 210
30	35	Dibbets, J.	Niederlande	Konzeptkunst	10 000	0,90	preiswert	11 090
31	25	Nauman, B.	USA	Prozeßkunst	10 000	0,92	preiswert	10 860
32	29	Serra, R.	USA	Prozeßkunst	12 500	1,24	teuer	10 090
33	32	Manzoni, P.	Italien	Neuer Realismus	12 000	1,21	teuer	9 950
34	36	Bury, D.	Belgien	Kinetik	10 000	1,01	teuer	9 890
35	34	Rot, D.	Schweiz	Neue Sensibilität	1 000	0,10	sehr billig	9 610
36	43	Raysse, M.	Frankreich	Neuer Realismus	4 000	0,41	billig	9 600
37	37	Kienholz, E.	USA	Realismus	5 000	0,53	preiswert	9 370
38	38	Wesselmann, G.	USA	Pop Art	10 000	1,08	teuer	9 200
39	51	Indiana, R.	USA	Pop Art	5 000	0,55	preiswert	9 120
40	49	Pistoletto, M.	Italien	Realismus	5 000	0,56	preiswert	8 840
41	44	Long, R.	Großbritannien	Land Art	10 000	1,14	teuer	8 720
42	40	Schöffer, N.	Frankreich	Kinetik	10 000*	1,15	teuer	8 670
43	62	Jones, A.	Großbritannien	Pop Art	5 000	0,58	preiswert	8 620
44	33	Caro, A.	Großbritannien	Abstraktion	12 500*	1,47	sehr teuer	8 520
45	39	Richter, G.	Deutschland	Neue Malerei	4 000	0,47	billig	8 500
46	42	Twombly, C.	USA	Abstraktion	16 000	1,89	sehr teuer	8 460
47	52	Riley, B.	Großbritannien	Op Art	2 000	0,24	billig	8 420
48	41	Ryman, R.	USA	Neue Malerei	8 000	0,96	preiswert	8 360
49	82	Morellet, F.	Frankreich	Neue Konkrete Kunst	1 500	0,18	billig	8 160
50	70	Buren, D.	Frankreich	Konzeptkunst	5 000	0,61	preiswert	8 130

rang: rank
richtung: direction
preise für grafik und objeckte: price for prints and multiples
preisnote: price note
sehr teuer: very expensive
teuer: expensive
sehr billig: very cheap
billig: cheap
preiswert: good value
punkte: points

1976
(51–100)

RANG 1976	1975	NAME	NATION	RICHTUNG	MINDESTPREIS FÜR EIN REPRÄSENTATIVES WERK IN MARK	PREIS-PUNKTE-VERHÄLTNIS (PPV)	PREISNOTE	PUNKTE
51	45	Spoerri, D.	Schweiz	Neuer Realismus	1 500	0,18	billig	8 080
52	47	Kitaj, R.	USA	Pop Art	4 500	0,55	preiswert	8 050
53	50	Darboven, H.	Deutschland	Konzeptkunst	1 500	0,19	billig	7 820
54	58	Poons, L.	USA	Colour Field	**	–	–	7 820
55	48	Kosuth, J.	USA	Konzeptkunst	12 500	1,61	sehr teuer	7 750
56	65	Sonnier, K.	USA	Prozeßkunst	5 000	0,64	preiswert	7 720
57	61	Piene, O.	Deutschland	Zero	2 000	0,27	billig	7 640
58	55	Weiner, L.	USA	Konzeptkunst	5 000	0,65	preiswert	7 620
59	66	Oppenheim, D.	USA	Videokunst	750	0,10	sehr billig	7 590
60	83	Bell, L.	USA	Minimal Art	5 000	0,66	preiswert	7 540
61	54	Arakawa, S.	Japan	Konzeptkunst	12 000	1,59	sehr teuer	7 525
62	67	Agam, Y.	Israel	Op Art	6 000	0,81	preiswert	7 320
63	57	Gilbert & George	Großbritannien	Performance	7 500	1,03	teuer	7 310
64	76	Le Parc, J.	Argentinien	Kinetik	1 000	0,14	sehr billig	7 300
65	46	De Maria, W.	USA	Land Art	4 000	0,55	preiswert	7 290
66	73	Smith, R.	Großbritannien	Neue Abstraktion	2 000	0,27	billig	7 280
67	59	Olitski, J.	USA	Colour Field	**	–	–	7 270
68	53	Ruscha, E.	USA	Pop Art	7 500	1,03	teuer	7 270
69	60	Klapheck, K.	Deutschland	Magischer Realismus	9 000	1,26	teuer	7 160
70	56	Chillida, E.	Spanien	Abstraktion	5 000	0,70	preiswert	7 090
71	68	Broodthaers, M.	Belgien	Indiv. Mythologie	1 000	0,14	sehr billig	7 080
72	72	Martin, A.	USA	Minimal Art	10 000	1,43	sehr teuer	7 010
73	64	Huebler, D.	USA	Konzeptkunst	7 500	1,07	teuer	7 000
74	63	Tilson, J.	Großbritannien	Pop Art	2 500	0,36	billig	6 850
75	93	Antes, H.	Deutschland	Neue Figuration	4 000	0,58	preiswert	6 840
76	86	Di Suvero, M.	USA	Abstraktion	7 500	1,10	teuer	6 830
77	81	Chamberlain, J.	USA	Pop Art	15 000*	2,19	sehr teuer	6 820
78	69	Schoonhoven, U.	Niederlande	Neue Konkrete Kunst	2 000	0,29	billig	6 810
79	85	Hesse, E.	USA	Exzentr. Abstraktion	6 000	0,88	preiswert	6 730
80	78	Rivers, L.	USA	Prae-Pop Art	5 000	0,74	preiswert	6 710
81	75	St-Phalle, N.	Frankreich	Neuer Realismus	1 000	0,15	sehr billig	6 680
82	96	Takis	Griechenland	Kinetik	15 000*	2,40	sehr teuer	6 250
83	71	Gnoli, D.	Italien	Magischer Realismus	12 000	1,92	sehr teuer	6 240
84	80	Panamarenko	Belgien	Indiv. Mythologie	1 500	0,24	billig	6 230
85	98	Luginbühl, B.	Schweiz	Neuer Realismus	1 500	0,24	billig	6 220
86	84	Bontecou, L.	USA	Abstraktion	4 500	0,73	preiswert	6 120
87	87	Blake, P.	Großbritannien	Pop Art	3 000	0,49	billig	6 100
88	94	Rinke, K.	Deutschland	Body Art	6 000	1,02	teuer	5 900
89	90	Haacke, H.	Deutschland	Konzeptkunst	12 000*	2,06	sehr teuer	5 830
90	77	Merz, M.	Italien	Prozeßkunst	4 000	0,69	preiswert	5 830
91	74	King, Ph.	Großbritannien	Abstraktion	10 000*	1,73	sehr teuer	5 790
92	89	Marden, B.	USA	Neue Malerei	6 000	1,04	teuer	5 760
93	–	Smithson, R.	USA	Land Art	7 000	1,24	teuer	5 640
94	79	Smith, T.	USA	Minimal Art	15 000*	2,70	sehr teuer	5 560
95	91	Boltanski, Ch.	Frankreich	Indiv. Mythologie	4 500	0,81	preiswert	5 530
96	99	Rainer, A.	Österreich	Body Art	1 500	0,27	billig	5 500
97	–	Flanagan, B.	Großbritannien	Exzentr. Abstraktion	2 000	0,37	billig	5 330
98	88	Walther, F.E.	Deutschland	Aktionkunst	1 500	0,28	billig	5 320
99	100	Mangold, R.	USA	Neue Malerei	4 000	0,77	preiswert	5 180
100	–	Becher, B. & H.	Deutschland	Fotografie	500	0,10	sehr billig	5 170

2.3 Kunstkompass Rangliste der Künstler, 1977 (1–50)

RANG 1977	1976	NAME	NATION	RICHTUNG	MINDESTPREIS FÜR EIN REPRÄSENTATIVES WERK IN MARK	PREIS-PUNKTE-VERHÄLTNIS	PREISNOTE	PUNKTE
1	1	Rauschenberg, R.	USA	Prae-Pop	140 000	6,14	teuer	22 800
2	5	Beuys, J.	Deutschland	Aktionskunst	70 000	3,23	preiswert	21 670
3	3	Oldenburg, C.	USA	Pop Art	70 000	3,35	preiswert	20 870
4	2	Warhol, A.	USA	Pop Art	120 000	5,76	teuer	20 800
5	4	Johns, J.	USA	Prae-Pop	190 000	9,45	sehr teuer	20 105
6	10	Christo	USA	Neuer Realismus	45 000	2,41	billig	18 610
7	6	Tinguely, J.	Schweiz	Neuer Realismus	60 000	3,48	preiswert	17 235
8	7	Lichtenstein, R.	USA	Pop Art	100 000	5,85	teuer	17 075
9	8	Stella, F.	USA	Neue Abstraktion	60 000	3,58	preiswert	16 750
10	9	Klein, Y.	Frankreich	Neuer Realismus	100 000	5,97	teuer	16 745
11	12	LeWitt, S.	USA	Minimal Art	17 000	1,10	billig	15 405
12	11	Dine, J.	USA	Pop Art	40 000	2,64	preiswert	15 120
13	19	Morris, R.	USA	Anti-Form	30 000	1,98	billig	15 110
14	20	Andre, C.	USA	Minimal Art	17 000	1,17	billig	14 420
15	15	Judd, D.	USA	Minimal Art	35 000	2,44	billig	14 315
16	14	Kelly, E.	USA	Hard Edge	90 000	6,29	teuer	14 300
17	31	Nauman, B.	USA	Prozeßkunst	50 000	3,58	preiswert	13 950
18	16	Noland, K.	USA	Farbfeldmalerei	40 000	2,87	preiswert	13 910
19	13	Arman	Frankreich	Neuer Realismus	45 000	3,25	preiswert	13 825
20	17	Louis, M.	USA	Farbfeldmalerei	120 000	8,83	sehr teuer	13 580
21	22	Flavin, D.	USA	Minimal Art	25 000	1,86	billig	13 430
22	18	Rosenquist, J.	USA	Pop Art	45 000	3,50	preiswert	12 855
23	27	Hockney, D.	England	Pop Art	50 000	3,94	preiswert	12 690
24	32	Serra, R.	USA	Prozeßkunst	50 000	4,07	preiswert	12 285
25	24	Segal, G.	USA	Pop Art	40 000	3,26	preiswert	12 255
26	21	Soto, J.	Venezuela	Op Art	40 000	3,29	preiswert	12 125
27	23	Hamilton, R.	England	Pop Art	60 000	4,95	teuer	12 100
28	25	Paolozzi, E.	England	Pop Art	40 000	3,40	preiswert	11 760
29	26	Uecker, G.	Deutschland	Zero Kunst	20 000	1,72	billig	11 585
30	30	Dibbets, J.	Niederlande	Konzeptkunst	14 000	1,21	billig	11 540
31	29	Mack, H.	Deutschland	Zero Kunst	20 000	1,76	billig	11 300
32	28	César	Frankreich	Neuer Realismus	50 000	4,44	preiswert	11 245
33	45	Richter, G.	Deutschland	Neue Malerei	12 000	1,15	billig	10 410
34	34	Bury, P.	Belgien	Kinetik	50 000	4,85	preiswert	10 305
35	37	Kienholz, E.	USA	Environment Art	60 000	5,98	teuer	10 025
36	33	Manzoni, P.	Italien	Neuer Realismus	30 000	2,99	preiswert	10 025
37	41	Long, R.	England	Land Art	8 000	0,80	billig	9 940
38	50	Buren, D.	Frankreich	Konzeptkunst	7 500	0,77	billig	9 635
39	35	Rot, D.	Schweiz	Neue Sensibilität	30 000	3,12	preiswert	9 605
40	63	Gilbert & George	England	Performance	8 000	0,87	billig	9 135
41	36	Raysse, M.	Frankreich	Neuer Realismus	40 000	4,41	preiswert	9 060
42	46	Twombly, C.	USA	Malerei	100 000	11,06	sehr teuer	9 035
43	44	Caro, A.	England	Abstraktion	22 000	2,45	billig	8 970
44	59	Oppenheim, D.	USA	Video Kunst	15 000	1,69	billig	8 840
45	47	Riley, B.	England	Op Art	30 000	3,39	preiswert	8 825
46	58	Weiner, L.	USA	Konzeptkunst	7 000	0,80	billig	8 680
47	52	Kitaj, R.	England	Pop Art	50 000	5,76	teuer	8 675
48	51	Spoerri, D	Schweiz	Neuer Realismus	10 000	1,15	billig	8 650
49	40	Pistoletto, M.	Italien	Neuer Realismus	25 000	2,92	preiswert	8 560
50	42	Schöffer, N.	Frankreich	Lichtkunst	60 000	7,07	sehr teuer	8 485

rang: rank
richtung: direction
preise für grafik und objeckte: price for prints and multiples
preisnote: price note
sehr teuer: very expensive
teuer: expensive
sehr billig: very cheap
billig: cheap
preiswert: good value
punkte: points

1977
(51–100)

RANG 1977	1976	NAME	NATION	RICHTUNG	MINDESTPREIS FÜR EIN REPRÄSENTATIVES WERK IN MARK	PREIS-PUNKTE-VERHÄLTNIS	PREISNOTE	PUNKTE
51	48	Ryman, R.	USA	Neue Malerei	30 000	3,54	preiswert	8 470
52	53	Darboven, H.	Deutschland	Konzeptkunst	16 000	1,89	billig	8 445
53	43	Jones, A.	England	Pop Art	26 000	3,08	preiswert	8 420
54	55	Kosuth, J.	USA	Konzeptkunst	15 000	1,79	billig	8 340
55	49	Morellet, F.	Frankreich	Konkrete Kunst	20 000	2,41	billig	8 280
56	38	Wesselman, T.	USA	Pop Art	25 000	3,04	preiswert	8 210
57	39	Indiana, R.	USA	Pop Art	30 000	3,67	preiswert	8 160
58	56	Sonnier, K.	USA	Prozeßkunst	22 000	2,70	preiswert	8 125
59	71	Broodthaers, M.	Belgien	Neo-Surrealismus	15 000	1,87	billig	7 980
60	65	de Maria, W.	USA	Land Art	55 000	6,93	sehr teuer	7 930
61	62	Agam, Y.	Israel	Op Art	50 000	6,36	teuer	7 855
62	57	Piene, O.	Deutschland	Zero Kunst	15 000	1,92	billig	7 780
63	72	Martin, A.	USA	Minimal Art	60 000	7,73	sehr teuer	7 755
64	67	Olitski, J.	USA	Farbfeldmalerei	18 000	2,35	billig	7 655
65	54	Poons, L.	USA	Farbfeldmalerei	17 000	2,22	billig	7 625
66	69	Klapheck, K.	Deutschland	Mag. Realismus	30 000	8,93	preiswert	7 615
67	93	Smithson, R.	USA	Land Art	20 000	2,65	preiswert	7 540
68	70	Chillida, E.	Spanien	Abstraktion	80 000	10,72	sehr teuer	7 460
69	61	Arakawa, S.	Japan	Konzeptkunst	35 000	4,76	preiswert	7 345
70	73	Huebler, D.	USA	Konzeptkunst	7 000	0,95	billig	7 320
71	91	King, P.	England	Abstraktion	30 000	4,13	preiswert	7 260
72	78	Schoonhoven, J.	Niederlande	Konkrete Kunst	18 000	2,50	billig	7 175
73	64	Le Parc, J.	Argentinien	Kinetik	15 000	2,10	billig	7 115
74	74	Tilson, J.	England	Pop Art	5 000	0,70	sehr billig	7 090
75	68	Ruscha, E.	USA	Pop Art	22 000	3,10	preiswert	7 085
76	66	Smith, R.	England	Malerei	12 000	1,69	billig	7 085
77	88	Rinke, K.	Deutschland	Körperkunst	6 000	0,85	billig	7 010
78	60	Bell, L.	USA	Minimal Art	25 000	3,57	preiswert	6 985
79	80	Rivers, L.	USA	Prae-Pop	25 000	3,59	preiswert	6 955
80	84	Panamarenko	Belgien	Indiv. Mythologie	20 000	2,87	preiswert	6 945
81	75	Antes, H.	Deutschland	Neue Figuration	35 000	5,04	teuer	6 940
82	81	St. Phalle, N.	Frankreich	Neuer Realismus	15 000	2,17	billig	6 905
83	76	di Suvero, M.	USA	Abstraktion	60 000	8,72	sehr teuer	6 875
84	–	Heizer, M.	USA	Land Art	25 000	3,76	preiswert	6 645
85	77	Chamberlain, J.	USA	Pop Art	29 000	4,37	preiswert	6 625
86	96	Rainer, A.	Österreich	Körperkunst	25 000	3,83	preiswert	6 520
87	82	Takis, O.	Griechenland	Kinetik	20 000	3,06	preiswert	6 520
88	90	Merz, M.	Italien	Prozeßkunst	15 000	2,33	billig	6 425
89	–	Frankenthaler, H.	USA	Farbfeldmalerei	36 000	5,63	teuer	6 390
90	92	Marden, B.	USA	Neue Malerei	25 000	3,95	preiswert	6 325
91	95	Boltanski, C.	Frankreich	Spurnsicherung	6 000	0,95	billig	6 265
92	83	Gnoli, D.	Italien	Mag. Realismus	100 000	16,18	sehr teuer	6 180
93	94	Smith, T.	USA	Minimal Art	50 000	8,15	sehr teuer	6 130
94	98	Walther, F.E.	Deutschland	Aktionskunst	12 000	1,99	billig	6 020
95	100	Becher, B. + H.	Deutschland	Fotografie	8 000	1,34	billig	5 970
96	89	Haacke, H.	Deutschland	Konzeptkunst	12 000	2,04	billig	5 880
97	99	Mangold, R.	USA	Neue Malerei	12 000	2,06	billig	5 815
98	79	Hesse, E.	USA	Exentr. Abstraktion	35 000	6,06	teuer	5 770
99	–	Fulton, H.	England	Konzeptkunst	5 000	0,89	billig	5 570
100	85	Luginbühl, B.	Schweiz	Neuer Realismus	40 000	7,18	sehr teuer	5 570

Appendix 3: Chronological lists of exhibitions in European Conceptual art dealer galleries, 1967–77

3.1 Art & Project (Amsterdam)

1968
Charlotte Posenenske (20 September–16 October, Bulletin no. 1: 17 September)
Jan Slothouber & William Graatsma (18 October–20 November, Bulletin no. 2: 14 October)
Gruppe X (22 November–22 December, Bulletin no. 3: 18 November)

1969
Charlotte Posenenske (4 January, no mailing)
Willy Orskov (11 January–9 February, Bulletin no. 4: 6 January)
Paul Schuitema/Aldo van den Nieuwelaar (12 February–5 March, Bulletin no. 5: 10 February)
Gianfredo Camesi (29 March–23 April, Bulletin no. 6: 24 March)
Ed Sommer (26 April–21 May, Bulletin no. 7: 21 April)
This Way (Stanley) Brouwn (31 May–25 June, Bulletin no. 8: 27 May)
Stanley Brouwn (11 July, no mailing)
Summer (Drawings by Jan Dibbets and Bernd Lohaus) (Bulletin no. 9: 22 July, no exhibit)
Lawrence Weiner, A translation from one language to another (Bulletin no. 10: 1 September, no exhibit)
Stanley Brouwn at Prospect 69 (30 September–12 October, Bulletin no. 11: 30 September)
Rainer Giese (18 October–12 November, Bulletin no. 12: 14 October)
Willy Knoebel (15 November–10 December, Bulletin no. 13: 14 October)
Joseph Kosuth, Art as Idea as Idea (22–30 November, Bulletin no. 14: 18 November)
Jan Dibbets (starting 16 December, Bulletin no. 15: 26 November)
Peter Struycken (Bulletin no. 16: 10 December, no exhibit)
Robert Barry, During the exhibition the gallery will be closed (17–31 December, Bulletin no. 17: 12 December)

1970
Sol LeWitt, Lines and Combinations of Lines (Bulletin no. 18: 2 January, no exhibit)
Ger Van Elk (10–24 January, Bulletin no. 19: 6 January)
Gilbert & George, Art Notes and Thoughts (12–23 May, Bulletin no. 20: 1 March)
Yutaka Matsuzawa (Bulletin no. 21: 26 March, no exhibit)
Douglas Huebler, Location Piece No. 8, Amsterdam, Holland (25 April– 8 May, Bulletin no. 22: 17 April)
Keith Arnatt: 1220400–0000000 (30 May–13 June, Bulletin no. 23: 25 May)
Daniel Buren (June–July, for Bulletin no. 24, see the catalogue of Documenta 5, page 17.31)
Emmy van Leersum & Gijs Bakker (31 January 1970, Bulletin no. 25: 23 June)
Hideto Yamazaki (27 June–11 July, Bulletin no. 26: 24 June)
Mel Bochner, Excerpts from Speculation 1969–1970 (Bulletin no. 27: 15 September, no exhibit)
Hanne Darboven, 00/366–1, 99/365–100 (24 October–13 November, Bulletin no. 28: 19 October)
Marinus Boezem (14 November–5 December, Bulletin no. 29: 10 November)
Ian Wilson (Bulletin no. 30: 30 November, no exhibit)
Willy Knoebel (Bulletin no. 31: 16 December, exhibition at Utrechtse Kring, Utrecht)

1971 **Sol LeWitt, Ten Thousand Lines – Six Thousand Two Hundred and Fifty Lines** (Bulletin no. 32: 4 January, no exhibit)
Ger van Elk (9–23 January, Bulletin no. 33: 6 January)
Martin Maloney (6–20 February, Bulletin no. 34: 3 February)
Jan Dibbets, A white wall (Bulletin no. 36: 7 April, no exhibit)
Robert Barry (starting 10 April, Bulletin no. 37: 20 April)
Stanley Brouwn, The total number of my steps (24 March–14 May, Bulletin, no. 38: 20 April)
Douglas Huebler, Variable Piece I (January 1971) (22 May–11 June, Bulletin no. 39: 19 May)
Daniel Buren (Bulletin no. 40: 2 June, no exhibit)
John Baldessari, Art disasters (3–15 July, Bulletin no. 41: 5 July)
Richard Long, Reflections on the Little Pigeon River, Great Smoky Mountains, Tennessee (1970) (17 July–6 August, Bulletin no. 35: 22 March)
Yutaka Matsuzawa (7–21 August, Bulletin no. 42: 3 August)
Sol LeWitt (Folded into 48 rectangles) (7 September–2 October, Bulletin no. 43: 1 September)
A private collector (works by Daniel Buren) (Bulletin no. 45: 9 November, no exhibit)
Jan Dibbets (27 November–18 December, Bulletin no. 46: 23 November)
Gilbert & George, New Photo-Pieces (22 December–21 January 1972, Bulletin no. 47: 28 December)

1972 **David Askevold** (22 January–18 February, Bulletin no. 48: 17 January)
Willem Breuker (19 February–3 March, Bulletin no. 49: 14 February)
Salvo (Bulletin no. 50: 25 February, no exhibit)
Robert Barry (4–24 March, Bulletin no. 51: 29 February)
Hamish Fulton (25 March–14 April, Bulletin no. 52: 22 March)
Bas Jan Ader (15–21 April 72, Bulletin no. 44: 12 October 71)
Lawrence Weiner (22 April–12 May, Bulletin no. 53: 18 April)
Lawrence Weiner (Bulletin no. 54: 8 May, no exhibit)
Ger van Elk (13–27 May, 20 June–7 July, Bulletin no. 55: 10 May)
Jan Dibbets (Bulletin no. 56: 12 June, for the Dutch pavilion at the 36th Venice Biennale)
Douglas Huebler (Bulletin no. 57: 27 June, no exhibit)
William Leavitt (29 July–12 August, Bulletin no. 58: 24 July)
Ian Wilson (Bulletin no. 59: 11 September, no exhibit)
Sol LeWitt (Bulletin no. 60: 25 September, no exhibit)
Salvo (3–8 October (Cologne Art Fair) + 10–21 October, Bulletin no. 61: 29 September)
Alighieri Boetti (Bulletin no. 62)
Stanley Brouwn (25 November–15 December, Bulletin no. 63)
Hanne Darboven (16 December–12 January 1973, Bulletin no. 64)
Robert Barry (November, Bulletin no. 65)
Gilbert & George (Bulletin no. 66)

1973 **8 Italians (Zorio, Anselmo, Boetti, Penone, Salvo, Merz, Paolini, De Dominicis)** (20 January–10 March; concurrent with exhibit at MTL, Brussels)
Marcel Broodthaers, Rétrospective (October 1963–March 1973) (March, Bulletin no. 67; in collaboration with MTL, Brussels)
Douglas Huebler (15 August, Bulletin no. 68)
Stanley Brouwn (4–26 September, Bulletin no. 69)
Robert Ryman (28 September, Bulletin no. 70)
Lawrence Weiner (11–21 December, Bulletin no. 72)
Jan Dibbets
Richard Long

1974 **Ben Ackerman** (January)
Hanne Darboven, '73, 1973; '74, 1974 (12–23 March)
Daniel Buren, Transparency (March)
Rainer Gise (March–April)
Brouwn, Fulton, Van Elk, Berghuis & others (July–August)
Robert Ryman, Suite of seven aquatints and **Nine unique aquatints** (1972) (Bulletin no. 70: 28 September 1973)
Richard Long, Circle in the Andes (Bulletin no. 71)
Gilbert & George (The Tuileries) (Bulletin no. 73)
Rainer Gise (September, Bulletin no. 77 + no. 79)
Japp Berghuis (Bulletin no. 78: September)
Jan Dibbets (October)
William Leavitt (Bulletin no. 80: 1–19 October)
Alan Charlton (Bulletin no. 81: 29 October–16 November)

1975 **Barry Flanagan**
Alan Charlton
Carl Andre (7 January, Bulletin no. 85)
Hamish Fulton (21 January–8 February, Bulletin no. 86)
Jan Dibbets (11 February– 1 March, Bulletin no. 87)
Sol LeWitt (4–15 March, Bulletin no. 88)
Richard Long, River Avon Driftwood, Crossing Two Rivers/Minnesota/ Wiltshire (18 March–15 April, Bulletin no. 89)
Stanley Brouwn (9 December–3 January 1976, Bulletin no. 94)

1976 **Antonakos**
Berguis and Carel Visser
Hanne Darboven, Roy Colmer (6–24 January, Bulletin no. 95)
David Tremlett (27 January–14 February, Bulletin no. 96)
Robert Barry (17 February–6 March, Bulletin no. 97)
Daniel Buren (18 April)
Richard Long, A Line in the Himalayas (Bulletin no. 99)
Summer group show (Akkerman, Andre, Antonakos, Barry, Berghuis, Breuker, Brouwn, Buren, Charlton, Darboven, Dibbets, Flanagan, Fulton, Gilbert & George, Huebler, Leavitt, LeWitt, Long, Nonas, Rajlich, Rosenthal, Rückriem, Ruppersberg, Tremlett, Visser, Weiner) (July–September)

1977 **Alan Charlton**
Ben Akkerman, Paintings and Drawings (January–February)
Richard Long, Two Stone Lines (8 February–5 March)
Alan Charlton (Bulletin no. 101: 5–30 April)
Gilbert & George, New Photo-Pieces (1–26 November, Bulletin no. 103)
Barry Flanagan, Light pieces (7–31 December, Bulletin no. 104)

3.2 Nigel Greenwood Inc. Ltd. (London)

1970 **Gilbert & George, Underneath the Arches** (10–14 November)
Gilbert & George, To be with art is all we ask (starting mid-November)
Robert Barry (organised by David Lamelas)
David Tremlett

1971 **David Tremlett**
Edward Ruscha, Books (7–30 January)
Jack Goldstein (starting 23 August)
Barry LeVa (starting 1 October)
Joel Fisher (starting 1 November)
Publication (Arnatt, Barry, Brouwn, Buren, Burgin, Claura, Gilbert & George, Latham, Lippard, Maloney, Reise, Weiner) (23 November–6 December, organised by David Lamelas)
Gilbert & George, The Ten Pieces (29 November–December)

1972 **David Lamelas, Film Script** (starting 18 January)
John Stezaker (starting 25 February)
Group show (starting 15 March)
Richard Hamilton (starting 24 May)
Gilbert & George, Books (starting 4 July)
Keith Milow (starting 16 July)
The Book as Art Work 1960–1972 (20 September–14 October, organised by Germano Celant)
Gilbert & George, Videos (starting 27 September)
Rita Donagh (17 October)
Gilbert & George, The Evening before The Morning after (20 November–December)
Bernd and Hilla Becher (14 December–January 1973)

1973 **John Walker** (starting 1 February)
Bill Beckley (starting 21 March)
Edward Ruscha, Paintings and Drawings 1973 (26 April–22 May)
David Tremlett (23 May–15 June)
Alan Charlton, 7ft square canvases in varying shades of grey (20 June–15 July)
Gilbert & George, Recycling Drunk (16–21 July)
John Walker, New graphics (25 July–11 August)
Ed Herring, Acts 3 (3–20 October)
John Stezaker, Mundus (23 October–10 November)
Keith Milow (13 November–1 December)
Moholy-Nagy, Photographs, photograms and 'fotoplastikes' (4 December–January 1974)

1974 **Gallery Artists and Video Prints from Keith Sonnier** (starting 1 February)
Alan Johnston, New paintings (starting 12 March)
Ger van Elk (18 April–11 May)
Gilbert & George, Dark Shadow (5 June–5 July)
Group show (starting 18 July)
David Tremlett, Cool Clear Water (16 September–October)
Keith Milow (starting 31 October)
Richard Tuttle (10 December–January 1975)

1975 **John Walker: New Paintings** (starting 28 March)
Alan Johnston: New Work (starting 10 April)
John Stezaker (starting 8 May)
Bill Jacklin: Paintings 1975 (starting 3 June)
Joel Fisher and Group Show (starting 14 July)
Ger van Elk (starting 1 October)
Marcel Broodthaers, Ceci Cela ou Rien (1 October–31 January 1976)
Artists and Photographs (starting 1 December)

1976 **John Stezaker** (starting 4 March)
David Tremlett (starting 6 April)
Keith Milow (starting 7 June)
Group Show (starting 24 July)
Anne Pullinger and Adrian Hall (starting 10 August)
Alan Johnston (starting 16 September)
Joel Fisher (starting 12 October)
Ger van Elk (starting 16 November)

1977 **Presentation of Dark Shadow by Gilbert & George** (starting 6 January)
Bill Beckley (starting 11 January)
Accrochage – Gallery Artists (starting 8 March)
Marcel Broodthaers, The complete editions on paper and books (5 April–14 May)
John Stezaker (starting 25 May)
Bernd and Hilla Becher (starting 12 July)
Ian McKeever (starting 13 September)
Marc Chaimowicz's Book Dream, and Additions to New Editions (starting 18 October)
Richard Tuttle (starting 1 December)

3.3 Françoise Lambert (Milan)

1969 **Richard Serra** (June)
Dennis Oppenheim (July)
David Diao (October)
A Sculpture by Richard Long (15 November–1 December)
Robert Ryman (December–January 1970)

1970 **Brice Marden** (February)
Jan Dibbets, Shadows, Krefeld '69 (26 February–March)
Alain Jacquet (April)
David Lamelas (May)
Nagasawa (May, one week show)
Antonio Trotta (June, one week show)
Gilbert & George, Frozen into the Nature for your Art (June)
Daniel Buren (July)
Edward Keinholz (September)
Mario Merz, Sciopero generale azione politicy relative proclamata relativamente all'arte (1 October–3 November)
Fred Sandback (November)
Christo (November–December)
Salvo (December–January 1971)

1971 **Group show (Brouwn, Dibbets, Flavin, LeWitt, Merz, Nauman, Oppenheim, Ryman, Salvo)** (February)
Eight Proposals (Barry, Buren, Burgy, Dibbets, Huebler, Kienholz, Hidetoshi, Nagasawa, Weiner) (26 February–March)
Maurizio Mochetti (March–April)
Louis Cane (April)
Stanley Brouwn (May)
Group show (Arakawa, Cane, Long, Marden, Ryman) (June)
Emilio Prini (July)
Denis Oppenheim (November)
Bruce Nauman (6 December–5 January 1972)

1972 **Hans Haacke** (January)
Andy Warhol, Electric Chairs (January, one week show)
Vincenzo Agnetti (2–20 February)
David Lamelas, Reading of an Extract from 'Labyrinths' by J L Borges + Film Script (24 February–3 March)
Bruce McLean (6–19 March)
Peinture Cahiers Théoriques: Présentation de la Revue (21 March–3 April)
Group show (Buren, Dibbets, Flavin, Lamelas, Paolini, Ryman) (6–16 April)
Marcel Broodthaers, Au delà de cette limite vos billets ne sont plus valables (19 April–5 May)
Steve Reich, Drumming (9–20 May)
David Lamelas (June)
David Askevold (October)
Bill Beckley (October–November)
Lawrence Weiner, Disco 7 (9–14 November)
Tania Moraud (November–December)
Maurizio Mochetti (December–January 1973)

1973 **Marcel Broodthaers, Fumer–Boire–Copier–Parler–Ecrire–Peindre–Filmer** (January)
Giulio Paolini, Collages 1961–71; Les Promenades d'Euclide, 1968; Il Vero, 1971–72; Ennesima, 1972 (February, in collaboration with Galleria Toselli, Milan)
Niele Toroni (March)
Edward Ruscha, Drawings: Stains (April)
Edda Renouf (May)
Christo (June)
Richard Tuttle, Drawings (June–July)
Allen Ruppersberg (September)
Brice Marden (October)
Van Schley (November)
Record as Artwork (December, organised by Germano Celant)

1974 **Books by Edward Ruscha + Premium movie** (January)
Jack Goldstein, Films (January)
Braco Dimitrijevic (February)
Artisti della West Coast (Nauman, Ruppersberg, Ruscha, Van Schley) (26 February–30 March)
William Wegman (March)
David Askevold (April)
Bernard Joubert (May)
Robert Grosvenor (June)
William Leavitt (June–July)
Edward Ruscha, Paintings (October)
Gilberto Zorio (October–November)
David Lamelas, Cumulative Script (November–December)

1975 **Thomas Rajlich** (January)
Douglas Huebler (February)
Dennis Oppenheim (March)
Edda Renouf (March–April)
Dan Flavin (April)
Luciano Bartolini (May)
Niele Toroni (June–July)
Katharina Sieverding, New Screens (October)
Bill Beckley (October–November)
James Collins (December)

1976 **Laura Grisi** (January)
André Cadéré (6–13 February)
Salvo (February–March)
Paolo Icaro (March)
Alain Middleton, Concerto (March)
Lucio Pozzi (April)
Jacques Charlier (May)
Nam June Paik (June–July)
Hans Haacke, Seurat's *Les Poseuses* (October–November)
Edda Renouf, Otto Disegni (December)

1977 **Michele Zaza** (January)
Bernard Joubert (February–March)
Luciano Bartolini, Pensando all'Oriente (April)
André Cadéré (25 May–June)
James Bishop (October–November)
Lucio Pozzi, Paint works on woods (November–December)

3.4 Yvon Lambert (Paris)

1966 **Robert Malaval**
Claude Gili
André Cadere

1967 **André Cadere**
La Figure Humaine (Baszkowski (Pologne), Bîelutin (URSS), Campi (France), Csernus (Hongrie), Jordan (Yougoslavie), Key Hiraga (Japon), Lebenstein (Pologne), Neizvestny (URSS), Stancie (Youg.), Tomlison (Etats-Unis), Zuka (Etats-Unis)) (4 October–4 November; concurrent with FIAC)

1968 **Tony Smith**
D'Arcangelo

1969 **Joseph Helman**
Dennis Oppenheim
Daniel Buren, Interruption (May)
David Lamelas (May)
Richard Long, Sculpture (5–26 November)
Robert Ryman (December)

1970 **Fred Sandback**
Arakawa
Richard Long
David Lamelas, Interview
Douglas Huebler, Oeuvres variables (11–18 March)
Jan Dibbets (starting 19 February)
Lawrence Weiner (19–26 March)
Niele Toroni (March, April and July)
Sol LeWitt, Wall Drawings (4–27 June)
American Drawings (Nauman, Ryman, Sandback, Tuttle, LeWitt, etc) (September)
Daniel Buren (2 December– 5 January 1971)

1971 **Joseph Helman**
Bruce McLean
David Lamelas, Reading of an Extract from *Labyrinths* by J.L. Borges
Cy Twombly (before summer)
Lawrence Weiner, 10 Works (3–13 February)
Carl Andre (3 February–1 March)
Robert Barry Presents Three Shows and a Review by Lucy R. Lippard (April)
Daniel Dezeuze (starting 21 May)
Jeunes peintres japonais (29 September–30 October; concurrent with FIAC)
Edward Keinholz (October)
Actualité d'un bilan (29 October–5 December; organised by Michel Claura)
Marcel Broodthaers, Au delà de cette limite vos billets ne sont plus valables (starting 15 December)

1972 **Hamish Fulton**
Richard Long, Look the Ground in the Eye (starting 3 May)
Lawrence Weiner, Record plaat 7
Jan Dibbets (starting 3 February)
Douglas Huebler, Variable Pieces (16–31 March)
Richard Tuttle (October)
Marcel Broodthaers (October)

1973 **Sol LeWitt, All combinations of black lines in four directions superimposed on a red circle (15 parts)** (starting 9 January)
Robert Barry (February)
Edward Ruscha (spring)
Robert Mangold (March)
Hanne Darboven (ends 18 May)
Marcel Broodthaers, A, B, C – Paysage d'Automne (14–20 June)
Brice Marden, Ink drawings and paintings (October)
Deux Films de Marcel Broodthaers (6 November)
Daniel Buren (starting 10 November)
Daniel Dezeuze and Robert Barry (November)
Hamish Fulton (December)

1974 **Robert Barry**
Richard Tuttle
Sol LeWitt, Incomplete Open Cubes (March)
Cy Twombly (April–May)
Tomas Rajlich (May–June)
Richard Tuttle (July–August)
Lawrence Weiner, 3 works (12–26 September)
Douglas Huebler, Variable Pieces (October)

Jan Dibbets, Comète (November)
Dan Flavin (December)

1975 **Bill Beckley**
Joseph Helman
David Lamelas, A Fiction (6–30 March)
Richard Long (24 April–20 May)
Dennis Oppenheim (September)
Niele Toroni (October–November)
Daniel Dezeuze (November–December)
André Cadere (23 November–7 December)

1976 **Richard Tuttle, Two Days**
Bernard Joubert (January)
Brice Marden (January)
Lucio Pozzi (February, in collaboration with the Galerie Rencontres)
Giulio Paolini (March)
Richard Long (March–April)
Carl Andre, Copper Prime Couples (16 September–13 October)
Michèle Zaza (October)

1977 **Lawrence Weiner, A Work**
Richard Tuttle
Joseph Helman
Robert Barry
Gordon Matta-Clark
Dennis Oppenheim
Jan Dibbets (starting 12 May)
Daniel Dezeuze (starting 25 November)

3.5 Lisson Gallery (London)

1967 **Terence Ibbott, Derek Jarman, Paul Martin, Keith Milow, Paul Riley** (12 April–14 May)
Jene Highstein (25 August–11 September)

1968 **Peter Schmidt** (7 November–24 December)

1969 **Rolph Brandt, Timothy Drever** (6 June–31 July)

1970 **Sol LeWitt** (15 June–14 July)
Llewellyn Jones, Gerald Newman (1 July–22 August)
John Latham: Least Event, One Second Drawing, Blind Work, 24 Second Painting (11 November–6 December)

1971 **Wall! Show (Arnatt, Arrowsmith, Edmonds, Flanagan, Ginsborg, Hemsworth, Hilliard, Latham, Lew, LeWitt, Louw, Munro, Newman, Palermo, Rinke, Sirrs, Stezaker, Tremlett, Weiner, Wentworth)** (January)
Robert Medley (5 February–4 April)
Peter Joseph (4–30 May)
Sol LeWitt (June–July)
John Hilliard, Roger Cutforth (September)
Martin Maloney (6 October–[ ])

1972 **Dan Graham** (starting 25 February)
Carl Andre, Sorts (starting 9 May)
Robert Ryman (5 December–20 January 1973)

1973 **Richard Long** (23 January–24 February)
Robert Mangold (March)
Dorothea Rockburne (30 March–28 April)
Sol LeWitt, Wall Drawings and Structures (3–31 May)
John Hilliard, Recent Photographic Pieces (19 June–7 July)
Vaughan Grills, An Indo-Chinese Pan Sculpture (ending 20 October)
Art & Language (16 October–10 November)
Dan Flavin (November–22 December)

1974 **Dan Graham**
Art & Language (January)
Don Judd (January–February)
Tim Mapson (13–30 March)
Sol LeWitt, The Location of Lines (April–May)
Victor Burgin, New Work (May–June)
Carl Andre, Poems (8 June–31 July)
Richard Long (1–30 November)
Paintings: Jo Baer, Alan Charlton, Bob Law, Robert Mangold, Robert Ryman (3 December–18 January)

1975 **Robert Hunter** (7 January–8 February)
Art & Language (February)
John Hilliard (10 March–5 April)
Ulrich Rückriem (15 April–10 May)
David Dye (13–31 May)
Carl Andre (June–July)
Don Judd (September)
Robert Law, New Paintings (7 October–15 November)

1976 **Alan Charlton**
Hans Haacke
Jo Baer (13 January–17 February)
Daniel Buren (2 March–3 April)
Roger Ackling (20 May–12 June)
Richard Long, Stones (24–26 June)
Roger Ackling (4 August, one day exhibition)
Stephen Cox (20 August–September)

1977 **On Kawara, Date Paintings**
Giulio Paolini
Fred Sandback
Ackling, Art & Language, Charlton, Cox, Cragg, Hilliard, Joseph, Law, Long, Mapston, Willats (8 February–5 March)
Sol LeWitt, New Works, Structures and Early working drawings (12 March–9 April)
Richard Long (21 May–18 June)
Roger Ackling (21 June–9 July)
Bat Wasserman (16 July–21 August)
Bob Law (21 September–8 October)
Stephen Cox (23 November–17 December)

3.6.a MTL (Brussels)

1969 **Guy Mees**
Yves de Smet

1970 **Marcel Broodthaers, MTL–DTH** (13 March–10 April)
Niele Toroni (spring, probably May)
Daniel Buren, A partir de/Vanaf (13 June–1 July)
Jacques Charlier, Paysages Professionnels (5–25 September)
Philippe Van Snick (most likely October)
Guy Mees (29 October–29 November)
Martin Maloney, Intervention (mid-December–mid-January)

1971 **Bernd Lohaus, Tableaux/Sculpture** (February)
Yves De Smet, Contenant/Contenu (8 April–6 May)
Gerard Hemsworth (Summer)
Stanley Brouwn, Steps (IX–100X) (26 November–14 December)
Jan Dibbets, Venetian Blinds (18 December–15 January 1972)

1972 **Ian Wilson** (21–23 January)
Hanne Darboven (1–29 February)
Barry, Defining of it... 1971–72 (slide pieces) (7–20 March)
Videotape, W. Knoebel, Projektion X 1972 (Videogalerie Schum, 21 March)
Douglas Huebler (22 March–22 April)
John Baldessari (28 April–15 May)
Marcel Broodthaers, Tractatus Logico-Catalogicus (18 May–17 June)
Alighiero e Boetti (18–30 June)
Sol LeWitt, Wall drawings (5 July–26 September)
John Baldessari, Floating: Stick (one figure), Version 1 (19 September)
Gilbert & George, videotapes (In the Bush, 15 min, 25 ex; Gordon's Makes Us Drunk, 14 min, 25 ex.; Portrait of theArtists as Young Men, 7 min, 25 ex.) (October)
Jan Dibbets (18 November 1972–14 January 1973)
Mel Bochner (25 November; shown concurrently at MTL and Galerie Le Bailli)
Dan Graham
Hanne Darboven
Stanley Brouwn
Giovanni Anselmo

1973 **Guy Mees** (26 January)
Sol LeWitt
8 Italians (Zorio, Anselmo, Boetti, Penone, Salvo, Merz, Paolini, De Diminicis) (20 January–10 March; concurrent with exhibition at Art & Project)
Gilbert & George, Richard Long, Hamish Fulton (17 March)
Marcel Broodthaers, Petrus Paulus Rubens (starting 20 March, at MTL and Le Bailli; in collaboration with Art & Project who showed a Flemish version at the same time)
Robert Barry (March–April)
Giovanni Anselmo (5 May)
Sol LeWitt (3 September)
Guy Mees (21 November–7 December)
Jan Dibbets (17 October)
Ian Wilson
Dan Flavin, Carl Andre, Donald Judd

Tony Shafrazi (starting 22 October)
André Cadere, Six Pièces (16–21 November)
Joost E Romeu
Gilberto Zorio (15 December – 10 January 1974)

1974 **Présentation d'une édition de Gilles Richard: Traces de feu dans la forêt d'Auxonne, Edition Hossmann Hambourg 1973** (8 February)
Stanley Brouwn, Fichiers (7–25 March)
Hanne Darboven, '73, 1973; '74, 1974 (26 March–6 April)
Douglas Huebler, Variable Pieces and Duration Pieces (9 April– 9 May)
Sol LeWitt, Ripped Paper Drawings: Two Series of Fifteen Each (16 May–9 June)
Gilberto Zorio
Guy Mees, Installation Shot Galerie MTL November 1973
John Baldessari (2–26 September)
Marcel Broodthaers, Cinq Séries de neuf tableaux dont une reste la propriété de l'artiste (Série Culture Internationale) (27 September–24 October)
Dan Graham, 6 Films 1969–74 (31 October–17 November)
Edda Renouf, Peintures récentes (19 November–7 December)
Jacques Charlier, Photos de la Biennale de Venise de 1972 (7 December–4 January 1975)

1975 [*in April 1975, the gallery was taken over by Gilbert Goes*]
Buren, Ryman, Wilson (January–February)
Jan Dibbets, Autumn Structures (7–27 February)
Stanley Brouwn, 100.000 mm (28 February–14 March)
Art & Language (15–29 March)
Niele Toroni
Andre Cadere, noir, blanc, jaune, orange, rouge, violet, bleu, vert (16–30 April)
Gilbert & George, Bad Thoughts (30 May–25 June)
Joseph Kosuth, Practice
John Baldessari
Douglas Huebler (16 September – 4 October)
Daniel Buren, Morceler, Traverser, Limiter (3–29 November)
Douglas Huebler (3–24 December)
Marcel Broodthaers, Les Poissons–De Vissen (4–20 December)
Marcel Broodthaers, La Conquête de l'Espace (Atlas à l'usage des artistes et des militaires) (4 December–10 January 1976)

1976 **Joseph Kosuth and Sarah Charlesworth, Art & Language New York** (25 February – 20 March)
John Baldessari (23 March–10 April)
Bernd Lohaus, Sculptures et dessins (6–31 May)
Art & Language, A critique of virtue without terror, choruses from a musical comedy (17 June–10 July)
Guy Mees (9–30 September)
Sol LeWitt, Geometric Figures (19 November–15 December)
Stanley Brouwn (21 December–17 January 1977)

1977 **Gilbert & George, The Red Sculpture**
Accrochage (Barry, Charlier, Shafrazi, Wilson) (1–15 February)
Presentation of Dark Shadow, a new book by Gilbert & George (16 February)
André Cadere (24 March–20 April)
Robert de Boeck, Portraits 1976–77 (21 April–10 May)

Edda Renouf, Dessins récents (15 May–15 June)
Accrochage (Dan Graham, Joseph Kosuth, Guy Mees) (18 May–15 June)
Sarah Charlesworth, Fourteen Days (18 October–4 November)
Marthe Wery (16 December–3 January 1978)

3.6.b Art & Project/MTL (Antwerp)

1973 **John Baldessari** (17 September–10 October)
Gilberto Zorio (October)
Sol LeWitt (13 November–8 December)
Hamish Fulton (December)

1974 **Robert Barry** (January)
Gilbert & George, Dark Shadow (February)
Hanne Darboven, '73, 1973; '74, 1974 (12 March–6 April)
Stanley Brouwn (April)
Gilbert & George, Drinking Sculptures
Guy Mees
Allen Ruppersberg
Dan Graham (October–10 November)
Edda Renouf (12 November–1 December)
Jan Dibbets (2 December–4 January 1975)

3.7 Rolf Preisig (Basel)

1973 **Stanley Brouwn** (23 November–22 December)

1974 **Ulrich Rückriem, Skulpturen** (4–24 January)
Ulrich Rückriem, Eine neue Skulptur, 10 Zeichnungen (25 January–15 February)
Daniel Buren: Triptyque, Division I (22 February–3 March)
Daniel Buren: Triptyque, Division II (4–13 March)
Daniel Buren: Triptyque, Division III (14–23 March)
Jan Dibbets, Land 9°–81° (29 March–27 April)
Lawrence Weiner, With a relation to the various manners of resonance (10 May–8 June)
Eine Ausstellung zur Art 5 '74 (19–24 June)
Vivian Suter (1–27 July)
Robert Barry: 16th century (2–28 September)
Ian Wilson, Discussion (20 September)
Reiner Ruthenbeck (2–31 October)
Douglas Huebler (15 November–20 December)

1975 **Daniel Buren, From one space to the other** (14 January–8 February)
Stanley Brouwn (11 February–1 March)
Ulrich Rückriem: Teilung und Ergänzung (6–27 March)
Hamish Fulton (3 April–3 May)
Gerhard Richter, 4 graue Bilder (13 May–7 June)
Richard Long (12 June–12 July)
Lothar Baumgarten (18 September–14 October)

Sol LeWitt (18 October–22 November)
Lawrence Weiner: Carried to great Lengths (28 November–23 December)

1976 **David Tremlett** (8–31 January)
Robert Barry, Neue Zeichnungen (3–21 February)
Edda Renouf, Paintings (24 February–27 March)
Bernd and Hilla Becher (6–30 April)
Ian Wilson, Discussions (2–4 May)
Andre, Judd, Ryman, Teilnahme an der Art 7 '76 (10–20 June) NB*** diff. title
Alan Charlton (10 September–2 October)
Stanley Brouwn (5–30 October)
Lesley Foxcroft (12 November–4 December)
Daniel Buren, Exercises (7–31 December)

1977 **Hamish Fulton** (11 January–6 February)
Ulrich Rückriem, 3 Steinskulpturen (8 March–2 April)
Bob Law, 5 Paintings (14 April–14 May)
Urs Raussmüller (9 May–4 June)
Richard Long, Meeting Place (17 May–21 June)
James Lee Byars, The Hundred One Page Book (1–23 July)
Robert Barry, Celebrate, a Soundpiece (6 September–1 October)
On Kawara, 13 Date Paintings (11 October–5 November)
Rémy Zaugg: L.B. Alberti (11 November–10 December)

3.8 Ileana Sonnabend (Paris)

1967 **Andy Warhol, The Thirteen Most Wanted Men**
Piero Gilardi (January)
Arman (March)

1968 **Robert Morris** (starting 20 February)
Robert Morris, 'Feutres' (starting 21 November)
Bruce Nauman (25 November–15 December)

1969 **Giovanni Anselmo**
Gilberto Zorio
Mario Merz (22 April–June)
Donald Judd (June)
Bruce Nauman (starting 2 December)

1970 **Tsoclis** (starting 6 February)
Lichtenstein, Sculptures (starting 3 March)
Dan Flavin (starting 29 October)

1971 **Bruce Nauman** (starting 2 March)
Pier Paolo Calzolari (starting 18 September)
André Cadere (13–21 October)
Sarkis, Le Troisième Reich, des origines à la chute (starting 18 November)

1972 [ ]

1973 **Bernd and Hilla Becher**
Gilbert & George, Any Port in a Storm (Autumn)

Cecil Beaton (September)
John Baldessari (October)
André Cadere (3–21 October)
Anne and Patrick Poirier (6–7 November)

1974 **Bruce Nauman**
Christian Boltanski (February)
Andy Warhol (February–March)
Horst (April)
Sarkis (September)
Christian Boltanski (December)

1975 **Roy Lichtenstein, New Paintings** (January)
Robert Rauschenberg (February)
Bernd and Hilla Becher (25 February–18 March)
Gilbert & George, Bloody Life (starting13 March)
Jim Dine (April)
Vincenzo Agnetti (starting 29 April)
Robert Rauschenberg (starting 15 May)

1976 **Mel Bochner, Drawings 1973–75** (7–28 February)
Horst (15 May–5 June)

1977 **Anne and Patrick Poirier** (Paris)
Robert Rauschenberg (Paris)

3.9 Jack Wendler (London)

1971 **Lawrence Weiner, And/or: green as well as blue as well as red** (30 December–6 January)

1972 **Robert Barry**
Daniel Buren (February)
Jan Dibbets (25 February–9 March)
Ian Wilson, Conversation (March)
Douglas Huebler, Variable Pieces: 15, 16, 17, 18, 19 (April)
John Baldessari, Videotapes (7–21 April)
Mario Merz, A real sum is a sum of people (2–16 May)
Hanne Darboven (23 May–6 June)
Marcel Broodthaers (1–22 December)

1973 **Peter Downsbrough** (5–31 January)
Douglas Huebler (13 April–18 May)
Daniel Buren, Manipulation (9–30 March)
Ian Wilson, Conversation (March)
David Lamelas, A Film (June)
John Murphy, Bruce Robbins and Darcy Lange – Video (July)
Lawrence Weiner, With relation to the various manners with various things (17–30 September; flyers and posters)
Lawrence Weiner (25 September–16 October)
Scheduled exhibition (November)
Jan Dibbets (December)

1974 **Douglas Huebler**
Robert Barry, Slide Piece (4–28 February)
Mario Merz (February)
Ian Wilson (March)
Gerard Hemsworth (April)
John Baldessari (3–24 May)
David Lamelas, The Desert People (films) (May–June)
Mario Merz, It is possible to have a space with tables for 88 people as it is possible to have a space with tables for no one, Tables from drawings of Mario Merz (Fibonacci tables) (14 June–5 July)

3.10 Konrad Fischer (Düsseldorf)

1967 **Carl Andre** (21 October–28 November)
Hanne Darboven, Konstruktionen (starting 5 December)

1968 **Sol LeWitt** (6 January–3 February)
Palermo (6 February–1 March)
Reiner Ruthenbeck (11 March–6 April)
Fred Sandback, Plastische Konstruktionen (18 May–11 June)
Richard Artschwager (18 June–9 July)
Bruce Nauman: 6 day week – 6 sound problem (10 July–8 August)
Jan Dibbets, Rasenrolle, Holzbündel, Wasserpfütze (15 August–17 September)
Richard Long (21 September–18 October)
Hanne Darboven (22 October–15 November)
Robert Ryman (21 November–17 December)
Robert Smithson (20 December–17 January 1969)

1969 **Dan Flavin, Fluorescent Light** (24 January–14 February)
Klaus Rinke, Begehbares Wasser (24–28 February)
Reiner Ruthenbeck (6 March–3 April)
Lawrence Weiner (starting 10 April)
Sol LeWitt (22 April–16 May)
Mel Bochner, Measuring Room Series: 48" Longitudinal Projection (22 May–6 June)
Hamish Fulton (10 June–1 July)
Richard Long (5 July–1 August)
Panamarenko (starting 15 August)
Bruce McLean/Richard Sladden, Luggage/Handgepäck (3–29 September)
Daniel Buren, Position–Proposition (20 September–7 October)
Carl Andre, Alloy Squares (12 October–11 November)
Robert Ryman (11 November–12 December)
Ulrich Rückriem (16 December–9 January 1970)

1970 **Douglas Huebler** (15–31 January)
Bruce Nauman (5 February–3 March)
Mario Merz (7–31 March)
Palermo (7 April–2 May)
Gerhard Richter (11 April–7 May)
Gilbert & George (11 May–5 June)
Richard Long (11 May–9 June)
Sigmar Polke (9 June–2 July)

Donald Judd (3–30 July)
Hanne Darboven, Das Jahr 1970 (3–30 July)
Robert Law (4 August–4 September)
Reiner Ruthenbeck (8 September–9 October 1970)
Klaus Rinke/Monika Baumgartl, Fernost, Far East (5–18 November 1970)
Ian Wilson, Oral Communication (November 1970)
Lawrence Weiner (25 November–11 December)
Bernd and Hilla Becher (7–31 December)
Stanley Brouwn (14–31 December 1970)

1971 **Hanne Darboven, One Century in One Year** (1 January–31 December)
Douglas Huebler (6–12 January)
Alighiero Boetti, 16 Drawings (26 January–15 February)
Bruce Nauman (5 March–1 April)
Jan Dibbets (6–22 April)
Hamish Fulton (23 April–12 May)
Brice Marden, Bilder und Zeichnungen (18 May–7 June)
Carl Andre, Four Meditations on the year 1960 (12 July–12 August)
Sol LeWitt (3 September–1 October)
John Baldessari, Ingres and other Parables (8–22 October)
On Kawara, One Million Years made in New York from 1970–1971 (14 October–10 November)
Ulrich Rückriem (6–30 November)
Sigmar Polke (2–20 December)

1972 **Gilbert & George (Christmas of 1971)** (starting 3 January)
William Wegman (14 January–10 February)
Ian Wilson (25–27 January)
On Kawara, 15 paintings of the TODAY series (18 February–17 March)
Lothar Baumgarten, Amazonas – Kosmos (20 March–8 April)
Douglas Huebler (13 April–4 May)
Lawrence Weiner (April)
Carl Andre, Small Floor Pieces (May)
Brice Marden (June)
Hamish Fulton, Porridge, Bacon and Eggs, Toast and a Pot of Hot Tea (June)
Sol LeWitt, Arcs & Lines, Lines & Lines (September–October)
Alan Charlton, Paintings (20 October–17 November)
David Tremlett, The Spring Recordings (10 October–17 November)
Reiner Ruthenbeck (1–30 December)
Gerhard Richter (December)

1973 **Stanley Brouwn, Constructed Walk, Constructed Distance, Construction** (16 January–15 February)
Robert Morris (17 February–16 March)
Jan Dibbets (16 March–15 April)
Roger Welch (9–29 March)
Bill Beckley (3–27 April)
Sigmar Polke (8–25 May)
Richard Long, A Rolling Stone (29 May–25 June)
Carl Andre, Dipoles Al-Cu-Fe (1–28 June)
Brice Marden (July)
Bernd and Hilla Becher (July)
Alan Johnston (August)
John Baldessari (August)
Lothar Baumgarten (25 September–13 October)
Robert Ryman (November)
Alan Charlton, Channel Paintings (11 December–15 January 1974)

1974 **Bruce Nauman, Yellow Body** (4 February–6 March)
Gilbert & George (17 March–17 April)
Robert Mangold (19 April–18 May)
Lesley Foxcroft (26 April–18 May)
Lothar Baumgarten, RABE (starting 22 May)
Edda Renouf (21 June–22 July)
Carl Andre (21 June–20 July)
Imi Giese (July)
Douglas Huebler (5–26 September)
Ulrich Rückriem (21 September–17 October)
Jan Dibbets (19 October–16 November)
Hamish Fulton (23 November–19 December)
Robert Hunter (December)
Richard Long, River Avon Driftwood (20 December–19 January)

1975 **Lawrence Weiner, 3 Works in Relation to Place** (28 January–20 February)
Alan Charlton, A Series of 6 Paintings each with a Central Vertical Division (27 February–24 March)
On Kawara (8–30 April)
Sol LeWitt, Lines from four sides of four walls (7 May–7 June)
Hanne Darboven (starting 10 June)
Brice Marden, Shape Book, 8/73–8/75 (2–23 September)
Lothar Baumgarten (2–23 September)
Gerhard Richter (27 September–21 October)
Louis Cane (15 November–10 December)
Bruce Nauman, Forced Perspective/Open Mind/Equal Mind/Parallel Mind (Allegory and Symbolism) (16 December–24 January 1976)

1976 **Daniel Buren, Vice Versa** (31 January–14 February)
Katharina Sieverding (21 February–18 March)
Stanley Brouwn (20 March–12 April)
Robert Mangold (14 April–6 May)
Richard Long, River Avon Driftwood (15 May–11 June)
Carl Andre, Neubrückweg (26 June–31 July)
Gilbert & George, Die rote Skulptur (2–3 July)
Bernd and Hilla Becher (27 August–17 September)
Joseph Beuys, Drei Teile des Aktionssockels von '24 Stunden', 5 Juni 65, 0–24 Uhr (9–30 September)
Gerhard Merz (25 September–28 October)
Mario Merz, La Natura è l'Arte del Numero (11–17 November)
Lothar Baumgarten (1 November–2 December)

1977 **Jan Dibbets, Color Studies 1976** (12 February–10 March)
Sol LeWitt, Geometric Figures (12 March–1 April)
Silvia Wieczorek, Zuordnung III, 1 (2–22 April)
Maria Nordman (18 April–18 May)
Lawrence Weiner (27 April–13 May)
Carel Visser (27 May–16 June)
Horst Schuler (18 June–1 July)
Alan Charlton (2–21 July)
Ulrich Rückriem (9 September–5 October)
Gerhard Richter (22 October–22 November)
Gilbert & George, The Dirty Words (26 November–23 December)

3.11.a Heiner Friedrich (Munich)

1967 **Franz Erhard Walther, Teile aus dem 1ten Werksatz und Diagramme/Werkzeichnungen**
Demonstrative 1967 (Blinky Palermo, Sigmar Polke, Gerhard Richter, John Hoyland, Konrad Lueg, Reiner Ruthenbeck, Cy Twombly)
Blinky Palermo, Bilder, Stoffbilder, Objekte (13 June–11 July)
Sigmar Polke, Bilder (4–23 April)
Gerhard Richter, Neue Bilder (2 May–4 June)
John Chamberlain, Skulpturen (26 October–14 November)
John Hoyland (16 November–5 December)
Alain Jacquet (7–31 December)

1968 **Sol LeWitt, Five Cubes**
Fred Sandback, Sculptures
Andy Warhol, Marilyn Monroe (15 January–9 February)
Group Show (13 February–8 March)
Carl Andre, 22 Steel Row (16 March–18 April)
Dan Flavin, Two Primary Series and One Secondary (9 May–5 June)
Walter De Maria, Dirt Show, 50 m³ (1600 Cubic Feet) Level Dirt (18 September–10 October)
Robert Ryman (October–November)
Blinky Palermo, Wandzeichnungen, Variation der Zahl 5 (12 December–20 January 1969)

1969 **Group Show**
Franz Erhard Walther, Teile aus dem 1ten Werksatz
Reiner Ruthenbeck, Skulpturen
Michael Heizer (April)
Mel Bochner, Measurements (9–31 May)
Hanne Darboven, 1968 + Ein Jahrhundert (3–17 June)
La Monte Young/Marian Zazeela, Dream House: A continuous frequency environment in sound and light with singing from time to time (6–12 July)
Robert Ryman (21 November–10 December)

1970 **Fred Sandback**
Gerard Richter, Städtebilder
Ed Ruscha
Sigmar Polke
Gilbert & George, Underneath the Arches, Singing Sculpture (4 May)
Sol LeWitt, Drawings (September 1970)
Group Show, Drawings (September or December)
La Monte Young/Marian Zazeela, Dusk Adaption Environment (22–25 September)
Michael Heizer, Land Drawings (October)
Dan Flavin, Three near-square cornered installations (3–21 November)
Brigid Polk (November)

1971 **Group show**
Reiner Ruthenbeck
Donald Judd, Zeichnungen (January)
Fred Sandback, 8 Variationen für die Galerie Heiner Friedrich München (January–February)
Blinky Palermo, Wandmalerei, Positiv-Negativ (5 February–3 March)
A.R. Penck, Bilder (April)

Imi Knoebel, Drachen (14 May–16 June)
Carl Andre, 39 part Retrograde Invention (June–July)
Zeichnungen von Künstlern der Galerie (October–November)
Franz Erhard Walther, Teile aus dem 1ten Werksatz, Werkzeichnungen und Prozessaufzeichnungen (December–January 1972)

1972 **Imi Knoebel**
Blinky Palermo, 3 weiße Objekte
Jörg Immendorff, Bilder und Zeichnungen
Fred Sandback
La Monte Young, Concert
Knoebel, Palermo, Polke (March)
Gerhard Richter, Bilder nach Polaroids von Brigid Polk (April–May)
Marcel Broodthaers, Zeichnungen, Dias, Filme (6–25 May)
Robert Ryman (June)
Georg Baselitz, Vogelbilder (July)
Editionen der Galerie (August–September)
Donald Judd, 18 Skulpturen (November–December)
Blinky Palermo, Objekte (Tür, Wand, Wand) (5 December–15 January)

1973 **Franz Erhard Walther, Achtundzwanzig Entwürfe, 1962**
Maurizio Mochetti, Installation
Donald Judd, 18 Cubes
Richard Tuttle, Wire Pieces
Imi Knoebel, Projektion/Fotoedition
Fred Sandback, Skulpturen

1974 **Laszlo Moholy-Nagy, Fotoeditionen**
Gerhard Richter, Atlas
Luigi Veronesi, Fotoedition
A.R. Penck, T.M. Serie
Robert Whitman, Zeichnungen
Fred Sandback, Zeichnungen
Blinky Palermo, Komplette Grafik (July–August)
Marcel Broodthaers, Die Lorelei (December)

1975 **Fred Sandback, Graphik**
Antonius Höckelmann, Bilder und Zeichnungen
Georg Baselitz, Neue Zeichnungen (1–10 April)
Blinky Palermo, Multiples, Lithographien, Aquarelle, Handzeichnungen. Arbeiten zum Thema 'Happier than the Morning Sun...', gewidmet Stevie Wonder (13 November–30 December)

1976 **Gerhard Merz, Bilder**
Imi Knoebel
Gerhard Richter, Atlas. Entwürfe. Fotografien. Skizzen (295 Blätter von 1962–73)
Dan Flavin, Donald Judd – Grafik
Georg Baselitz
Arnulf Rainer, Radierungen (December–January 1977)

1977 **Michael Heizer, Zeichnungen, Collagen und Plakate**
Georg Baselitz, Der Neue Typ, Zeichnungen und Radierungen
Imi Knoebel, 10 Serien 5-teiliger Mennigearbeiten
Fred Sandback, Neue Druckgraphik und Skulpturen (1 December–14 January 1978)

3.11.b Heiner Friedrich (Cologne)

1970 **Gilbert & George, Underneath the Arches, Singing Sculpture** (October)
Gilbert & George, Frozen into the Nature for your Art (October)
Dan Flavin (October–November)
Brigid Polk (November)

1971 **Gregory Markopoulos, Film**
Andy Warhol Chelsea Girls, Blue Movie, Nude Restaurant
Gerhard Richter
Group Show, Films (Nauman, etc)
Blinky Palermo, Projekte 68/70 (January–February)
Dan Flavin, Arbeiten (March)
Blinky Palermo, Wandmalerei und Skulptur (21 April–5 June)
Franz Erhard Walther, Vorstellung des 1. Werksatzes (25 May–19 June)
Robert Ryman, Standard (26 June–7 July)
Carl Andre, John Chamberlain, Dan Flavin, Walter De Maria, Robert Rauschenberg, Frank Stella, Cy Twombly, Andy Warhol (20 July–29 August)
Soziologisches Experiment mit Arbeiten von Beuys, Darboven, Flavin, Long, F.E. Walther/Accrochage mit Chamberlain, Rauschenberg, Stella, Twombly, Warhol (September)
Dan Flavin, Quartett im Lichthof (October–November)
Imi Knoebel (December)

1972 **Imi Knoebel**
Gerhard Richter, Bilder nach Polaroids von Brigid Polk
Sigmar Polke, Zeichnungen
Group Show (Ryman, etc)
Hanne Darboven, Ein Jahrhundert (14 January–13 February)
Blinky Palermo, Bilder (18 March–12 May)
Willy Knoebel (March–May)
Maurizio Mochetti (June–July)
Walter De Maria (September–October)
Robert Ryman, 31 Trial Proofs (September–October)

1973 **Franz Erhard Walther, Diagramme/Werkzeichnungen**
Imi Knoebel, Installation
Blinky Palermo, Objekte. I für eine Tür, II für eine kleine Wand, III für eine große Wand (April)
La Monte Young/Marian Zazeela, Dream House, a time installation in sound and light (5 July–5 September)
Dan Flavin, In memory of Barbara Schiller, 1973, with some diagrams for Circular Fluorescent Light, 1972–73, from Dan Flavin (9 November–7 December)

1974 **Imi Knoebel**
Fred Sandback, Eine von 6 horizontalen Linien
Donald Judd, 18 Skulpturen (1 June–10 July)

1975 **Imi Knoebel**

1976 **Franz Erhard Walther**
Imi Knoebel
Blinky Palermo, Zeichnungen
Fred Sandback
Blinky Palermo, Metallbilder (17 September–20 October)

1977 **Group Show, Drawings**
Franz Erhard Walther, Schreit- und Standstücke, Körperräume, Werkzeichnungen
Donald Judd (May–June)
Georg Baselitz (9 September–11 October)
Imi Knoebel, 14 Farben (14 October–15 November)
Andy Warhol (18 November–31 December)

3.12.a Paul Maenz (Cologne)

1971 **Hans Haacke** (16 January–13 February)
Joseph Kosuth (16 February–5 March)
Peter Roehr (starting 6 March)
Carel Visser (9–27 March)
Robert Barry, Some places to which we can come... (30 March–8 April)
Martin Maloney (13 April–7 May)
Ulrich Rückriem (8 May–2 June)
Salvo (5–25 June)
Victor Burgin (3 July–4 August)
Roelof Louw (7 August–2 September)
Willi Knoebel (4–30 September)
Peter Roehr (2–30 October)
Mark Boyle (6–30 November)
Giulio Paolini (3–22 December)

1972 **Robert Barry, Invitation Piece**
Will Insley (8–29 January)
David Askevold (4–23 February)
Robert Barry (1–16 March)
Carel Visser (17 March–13 April)
Salvo (18 April–10 May)
Anne and Patrick Poirier (13 May–10 June)
The Art and Language Institute (15 June–1 July)
Giuseppe Penone (8–29 July)
Heidi Bochnig (2–16 September)
Victor Burgin (19–30 September)
Hans-Peter Feldmann (2–28 October)
Mark Boyle (4–30 November)
Peter Roehr (2–30 December)

1973 **The Art & Language Institute** (13 January–7 February)
Anne and Patrick Poirier (9 February–9 March)
Salvo (10 March–7 April)
Einige wesentliche Beispiele früher Konzeptueller Kunst analytischen Charakters : Atkinson, Baldwin, Burgin, Burn, Kosuth, Ramsden (10 April–12 May)
Giuseppe Penone (15 May–16 June)
Victor Burgin (19 June–21 July)
Art & Language (Philip Pilkington/David Ruschton) (11 September–20 November)
Art & Language (Ian Burn/Mel Ramsden) (23 October–17 November)
Marthe Wéry (27 November–20 December)

1974 **Robert Barry** (15 January–9 February)
Hans-Peter Feldmann (12 February–2 March)
David Askevold (5–30 March)
Giulio Paolini (6 April–3 May)
Ulrich Rückriem (4 May–1 June)
Salvo (8–29 June)
13 Projekt '74 artists, Art & Language, Joseph Kosuth, etc. (4–27 July)
Hans Haacke (4–31 July)
Mark Boyle (19 October–2 November)
Peter Roehr (9–29 November)
Marthe Wéry (30 November–21 December)

1975 **Anne and Patrick Poirier** (11–30 January)
Giuseppe Penone (15 February–8 March)
Hans-Peter Feldmann (11–26 March)
Jean-Marie Bertholin (5–26 April)
Carel Visser (29 April–16 May)
Noël Dolla (23 May–14 June)
Künstler der Galerie (24 June–26 July)
Giulio Paolini, Idem (v) (6–25 September)
Marthe Wéry (26 September–25 October)
Salvo (15 November–5 December)
Victor Burgin, Hussonet (6–20 December)
Rune Mields (10–20 December)

1976 **Daniel Buren, Vice Versa** (31 January–14 February)
Paul Maenz présente sa galerie de Cologne à Paris chez Eric et Xiane Germain (28 February–20 March)
Niele Toroni (3–30 April)
Peter Roehr (5 May–4 June)
Robert Barry (9 June–3 July)
Paolo Mussat Sartor (6–30 July)
Pläne/Zeichnungen/Diagramme, Carl Andre, Art & Language, Daniel Buren, Hanne Darboven, Jan Dibbets, Joseph Kosuth, Sol LeWitt, etc. (4–30 September)
Jean-Marie Bertholin (2–22 October)
Giulio Paolini, Idem (vi) (2–27 November)
Claude Rutault (11 December–22 Janaury 1977)

1977 **Anne and Patrick Poirier** (29 January–25 February)
Daniel Buren (1–26 March)
Hans-Peter Feldmann (2–23 April)
Robert Barry, Almost (Sound Piece) (26 April–21 May)
Duane Michals (5–25 June)
Peter Roehr (1–31 July)
Claude Rutault (16 September–15 October)
Carlo Maria Mariani (26 October–15 November)
John Hilliard (19 November–15 December)
Giulio Paolini, Ebla (17 December–24 January)

3.12. b Paul Maenz (Brussels)

1973 **Art and Language** (17 February–2 March)
On Kawara (3–16 March)
Joseph Kosuth (17 March–19 April)
Hans-Peter Feldmann (26 April–12 May)
Hans Haacke (19 May–9 June)
100 Avant-Garde Publications (13–29 June)
Victor Burgin (11 September–13 October)
David Askevold (17–27 October)
Piero Manzoni (30 October–24 November)
Peter Roehr (28 November–20 December)

1974 **Heidi Bochnig** (8 January–2 February)
Art & Language (5 February–8 March)
Salvo (9 March–27 April)
The Last Tango (starting 30 April)

3.13. a Gian Enzo Sperone (Turin)

1967 **Joe Raffaele, Lowell Nesbit** (starting 18 March)
Flavin, Rosenquist, Chamblerain, Warhol, Fontana, Pistoletto, Gilardi, Piacentino, Fabro, Pascali (starting 26 April)
Tom Wesselmann (starting 24 May)
Marisa Merz (starting 30 June)
Arman (starting 17 October)
Gilberto Zorio (starting 14 November)
Con temp l'azione (Pistoletto, Mondino, Nespolo, Simonetti, Boetti, Piacentino, Alviani, Scheggi, Fabro, Zorio, Anselmo) (starting 4 December)
Michelangelo Pistoletto (starting 22 December)

1968 **Mario Merz** (starting 19 January)
Mario Ceroli (starting 13 February)
Dan Flavin (starting 14 March)
Giovanni Anselmo (starting 11 April)
Gianni Piacentino (starting 8 May)
James Rosenquist (starting 5 November)
Jannis Kounellis (starting 22 December)

1969 **Giovanni Anselmo** (starting 14 January)
Gilberto Zorio (starting 29 January)
Pier Paolo Calzolari (14 February)
Mario Merz (March)
Robert Morris (10 March)
Alighiero Boetti (starting 19 April)
Disegni progetti: Anselmo, Boetti, Calzolari, Merz, Penone, Zorio (starting 22 May)
Carl Andre (29 September–12 October)
Lo Zoo scopre l'uomo nero alla galleria Sperone (starting 15 October)
Anselmo, Boetti, Calzolari, Griffa, Maini, Merz, Penone, Prini, Zorio (starting 29 October)
Joseph Kosuth, Second Investigation. Part 3–11 (starting 9 November)

Giorgio Griffa (starting 7 November)
Lawrence Weiner (3–10 December)
Giuseppe Penone (starting 11 December)
Robert Barry (starting 10 December)

1970 **Bill Bollinger** (starting 14 January)
Salvo (starting 7 February)
Bruce Nauman, Audio/Tactile Separation Piece (starting 25 February)
Michelangelo Pistoletto (starting 6 March)
Douglas Huebler, Duration Pieces (starting 24 March)
Giovanni Anselmo (10 April)
Pier Paolo Calzolari (starting 22 April)
Robert Watts (starting 6 May)
Alighiero Boetti (starting 22 May)
Sol LeWitt, Wall Drawings (starting 12 June)
Walter De Maria, Hard Core 1969 (starting 13 June)
Joseph Kosuth, 11 works from 1965 (starting 4 July)
Hamish Fulton, One Week Event (starting 9 September)
Dipinti/Paintings di Johns, Pistoletto, Warhol, Twombly, Arman, Dine, Stella (starting 1 October)
Mel Bochner, Degrees (starting 29 October)
Hanne Darboven (starting 14 November)
Robert Barry (starting 1 December)
Lawrence Weiner (starting 14 December)

1971 **Douglas Huebler, Variable Works (in Progress)** (starting 6 January)
Gerry Schum, Identifications (Weiner, Gilbert & George, Buren) (6 February)
Jannis Kounellis (starting 11 February)
Cy Twombly (starting 22 February)
Jan Dibbets (13–23 March)
Mario Merz (starting 27 March)
Richard Long, Project for Rocky Mountains (starting 13 April)
Giovanni Anselmo (starting 27 April)
Gilberto Zorio (starting 14 May)
Plagio, Michelangelo Pistoletto, Vettor Pisani (May)
Gilbert & George, There were two men (starting 28 May)
Brice Marden (starting 11 June)
Art & Language Press (starting 22 June)
Alighiero Boetti (starting 3 July)
Giuseppe Penone (November)

1972 **Richard Long, A Hundred Mile Walk** (January)
Hamish Fulton (January)
On Kawara, One Million Years (March)
Giovanni Anselmo (April)
Mario Merz, Torino, Ristorante della Spada da 1 a 55 persone (starting 12 April)
Giorgio Griffa (starting 31 May)
Daniel Buren, Invito a leggere come indicazione de quello che c'è da vedere (starting 12 June)
William Wegman (starting 31 October)
Peter Roehr (starting 21 November)

1973 **Cy Twombly** (starting 8 January)
Hans-Peter Feldmann (starting 20 February)
Ettore Pistoletto Oliviero, Michelangelo Pistoletto, Padre e Figlio (June)
Gilbert & George, New Decorative Works (starting 27 June)
Donald Judd (starting 29 September)
Art & Language (starting 12 October)
Giuseppe Penone (starting 22 October)
Jim Dine (starting 6 November)
Two works of Lawrence Weiner (starting 30 November)
Carl Andre, Copper Cardinals (starting 4 December)
Gilberto Zorio (starting 21 December)

1974 **Alan Charlton** (starting 15 January)
Jan Dibbets, Constructions of Land and Sea (starting 15 February)
Cy Twombly (starting 12 March)
Douglas Huebler, Drawings (starting 10 April)
Hanne Darboven (starting 15 May)
Robert Barry (starting 29 May)
Braco Dimitrijevic (starting 31 May)
Sol LeWitt, Tre disegni su parete, posizione di un rettangolo, di un trapezoide e di un parallelogramma (starting 12 June)
Hamish Fulton (starting 14 September)
Gilberto Zorio (starting 5 October)
Daniel Buren, Suite n.1 nello spazio dato (starting 20 November)
Alighiero Boetti (starting 12 December)

1975 **Carl Andre** (February)
Giuseppe Penone (starting 5 March)
Lucio Pozzi (starting 26 March)
Lawrence Weiner (starting 26 April)
Giovanni Anselmo, Particolare del tutto (starting 28 May)
Giovanni Anselmo, Particolare di infinito (starting 18 June)
Sol LeWitt, Incomplete Open Cubes (starting 23 September)
André Cadere (starting 6 October)
Bruno Martinazzi (December)
Drawings of Andre, Anselmo, Barry, Boetti, Calzolari, Darboven, Dibbets, Gastini, Griffa, Huebler, Kosuth, Kounellis, LeWitt, Merz, Paolini, Penone, Salvo, Schifano, Twombly, Zorio (starting 22 December)

1976 **Paolo Mussat Sartor** (starting 27 January)
Francesco Clemente (starting 25 February)
Braco Dimitrijevic (starting 12 March)
Mario Merz (starting 7 April)

3.13.b Sperone & Fischer (Rome, 1972–74), Gian Enzo Sperone (Rome, 1975–77)

1972 **A new sculpture by Gilbert & George** (starting 7 December)
Joseph Kosuth (starting 21 December)

1973 **Salvo** (starting 15 January)
Group show (Anselmo, Andre, Art & Language, Barry, Boetti, Buren, Darboven, Dibbets, Fulton, Gilbert & George, Huebler, Kosuth, LeWitt, Long, Nauman, Paolini, Penone, Pisani, Ryman, Weiner) (starting 1 February)
Giulio Paolini (starting 24 February)
Donald Judd (starting 8 March)
Douglas Huebler, Variable Pieces (starting 21 March)
Jan Dibbets (starting 6 April)
Hamish Fulton (starting 27 April)
Alighiero Boetti (starting 12 May)
Lothar Baumgarten (starting 29 May)
Robert Barry (starting 14 June)
Group Show (Anselmo, Art & Language, Baumgarten, Boetti, Buren, De Dominicis, Dibbets, Gilbert & George, Huebler, Kosuth, Judd, Penone, Pisani, Zorio) (starting 14 November)
Prezentatione di nuovo disco di Lawrence Weiner (starting 30 November)
Giuseppe Penone (starting 14 December)

1974 **Gilberto Zorio** (starting 11 January)
Luciano Fabro (starting 31 January)
Alan Charlton (starting 21 February)
Giovanni Anselmo (starting 30 April)
Gilbert & George, Cherry Blossom. No. 10 Sculpture (starting 14 September)
Joseph Kosuth, The Tenth Investigation, Proposition 7 (starting 28 November)
Daniel Buren, Suite n.2 nello spazio dato (starting 14 December)

1975 **Michelangelo Pistoletto** (starting 14 January)
Giorgio Griffa (starting 14 February)
Jim Dine (starting 14 March)
Lucio Pozzi (starting 14 April)
Group show (Andre, Anselmo, Boetti, Buren, Darboven, Gilbert & George, Huebler, Kosuth, Penone, Salvo, Zorio) (starting 6 May)
Alighiero Boetti (starting 20 June)
Francesco Clemente (starting 28 June)
Carl Andre (20 September–18 October)
Giovanni Anselmo (starting 21 October)
Group Show (Boetti, Darboven, Flavin, Kosuth, LeWitt, Merz, Nauman, Paolini, Zorio) (starting 18 November)
Bruno Martinazzi (December)
Vettor Pisani (starting 5 December)

1976 **Robert Barry** (starting 15 January)
Marco Gastini (starting 30 January)
Mario Merz (starting 22 February)
Richard Long (starting 16 March)
Clemente, Merz, Pisani (starting 14 April)
Jan Dibbets (starting 29 April)

Tano Festa, Storia familiare degli utensili (starting 18 May)
Sol LeWitt (starting 10 June)
Cy Twombly (starting 23 November)
Francesco Clemente (starting 17 December)

1977 **Sandro Chia** (January)
Group show (Anselmo, Beuys, Chia, Clemente, Kosuth, Long, Mario Merz, Marisa Merz, Ontani, Paolini, Pisani, Salvo) (starting 16 February)
Gilbert & George, The Red Sculpture and Dark Shadow (starting 23 February)
R C Theatrum, Vettor Pisani (12 April)
Robert Ryman (starting 3 May)
Carlo Maria Mariani (starting 29 May)
Hoh! Sandro Chia 1977, Ebla Giulio Paolini 1976–77, I giganti fulminati da Giove Salvi 1977 (starting 12 October)
Group show (Carl Andre, Giovanni Anselmo, On Kawara) (starting 22 November)
Brice Marden (starting 17 December)

3.14. a Wide White Space (Antwerp)

1967 **Accrochage (Appel, Beuys, Broodthaers, Fontana, Gaul, Hennemann, Heyrman, Manzoni, Palermo, Panamarenko, Tàpies, Van Severen, Vasarely** (29 January–16 February)
EPO Show (24 February–15 March)
Hisachika Takahashi (29 Marc–6 April)
Christo (18 April–4 May)
Gotthard Graubner, Kissenbilder (9 May–15 June)
Group Show (Arakawa, Arman, Beuys, Broodthaers, Christo, Engels, Flavin, Fontana, Gilardi, Heyrman, Hiltmann, Klein, Manzoni, Mees, Palermo, Panamarenko, Richter, Schultze, Spoerri, Van Severen, Vasarely (19–30 June)
Arakawa, Arman, Beuys, Broodthaers, Christo, Engels, Flavin, Fontana, Gilardi, Graubner, Heyrman, Klein, Manzoni, Mees, Palermo, Panamarenko, Richter, Spoerri, Vasarely (22 September–10 October)
Gerhard Richter (13 October–14 November)
Panamarenko (24 November–20 December)

1968 **Arakawa, Arman, Beuys, Brauner, Broodthaers, Bury, Christo, Engels, Fontana, Graubner, Klein, Manzoni, Panamarenko, Richter, Scultze, Spoerri** (5 January–7 February)
Joseph Beuys and Henning Christiansen, Eurasienstab, 82', Fluxorum Organum (9 February–3 March)
Marcel Broodthaers, Le Corbeau et le Renard (7–31 March)
Carl Andre, Clastic (3–25 May)
Beuys, Panamarenko, Christo, Lamelas, Lohaus, Palermo, Panamarenko, Ruthenbeck, Venet (16 October–14 November)
Reiner Ruthenbeck (15 November–15 December)

1969 **Daniel Buren** (17 January–6 February)
Ben d'Armagnac, Gerrit Dekker (7–27 February)
Young American Artists (Andre, Artschwager, Bollinger, De Maria, Dan Flavin, LeWitt, Nauman (1–31 March)
James Lee Byars (18 April–7 May)

Christo (9 May–6 June)
Lawrence Weiner (20–30 June)
James Lee Byars (summer)
Carl Andre (19 September–16 October)
Panamarenko, Multimilionair (24 October–21 November)
Marcel Broodthaers à la Deblioudebliou/S, Exposition littéraire autour de Mallarmé (2–20 December)

1970 **David Lamelas** (31 January–28 February)
Paul Joostens, 1889–1960 (25 March–25 April)
Edward Keinholz, Watercolours (11 May–10 June)
Accrochage (Andre, Beuys, Broodthaers, Christo, Kienholz, Panamarenko, Warhol) (29 September–31 October)
Georg Baselitz (7 November–3 December)
Multipels en grafische werken (4–23 December)

1971 **Panamarenko** (15 January–15 February)
Filiou, Kopcke, Panamarenko, Vercammen (8–20 March)
Carl Andre, Weathering Piece (22 April–6 May)
Daniel Buren (11 May–5 June)
Marcel Broodthaers, Figures anciennes et modernes (27 September–27 October)
Robert Filliou (4 November–3 December)
Edward Keinholz (6 December–16 January 1972)

1972 **Andy Warhol, Electric Chair** (20 January–1 March)
Broodthaers, Christo, Panamarenko (21 March–15 April)
A.R. Penck (15 April–13 May)
David Lamelas, Cummulative Script (22 May–2 June)
Daniel Buren (2–15 June)
Marcel Broodthaers, Edition Le Corbeau et le Renard (1967–72) (17–30 June)
Lawrence Weiner, Contributions to newspapers (24–25 June)
Robert Filliou (12 October–15 November)
Christo, Works 1958–72 (15 November–7 December)
Philippe van Snick (12 December–12 January)

1973 **Marcel Broodthaers, Fig.1, Programme** (13–28 January)
James Lee Byars (10 February–10 March)
Richard Long (15 March–12 April)
Ger van Elk (14 April–9 May)
David Lamelas (22 May–20 June)
Daniel Buren (22 June–28 July)
Lawrence Weiner, Mailing of Card (June)
Joseph Beuys (12 September–15 October)
Niele Toroni (19 October–25 November)
Six works of Lawrence Weiner (26 November–22 December)

1974 **Carl Andre, Thirteenth Copper Cardinal, Fourteenth Copper Cardinal, Twenty-fifth Copper Cardinal** (10 January–4 February)
Lothar Baumgarten (4–25 February)
Bruce Nauman (8 March–11 April)
Daniel Buren (23 April–June)
Marcel Broodthaers, Ne dites pas que je ne l'ai pas dit, Le Perroquet (19 September–3 November)
A.R. Penck (21 November–23 December)

1975 **Drawings (Baselitz, Beuys, Broodthaers, Byars, Kienholz, Nauman, Panamarenko, Penck, Van Snick** (8 January–1 February)
Peter Downsbrough (3–22 February)
Travail Peinture de Niele Toroni (26 February–15 March)
David Lamelas (19 March–14 April)
Richard Long (15 April–16 May)
Philippe van Snick (18 May–15 June)

1976 **Richard Long, Driftwood** (25 May–10 June)

1977 **A work of Lawrence Weiner presented within the context of an installation** (4 May–5 June)

3.14.b Wide White Space (Le Bailli, Brussels)

1973 **Ger van Elk** (24 April–20 May)
David Lamelas (22 May–20 June)
Joseph Beuys (11 September–15 October)
Niele Toroni (20 October–26 November)
Panamarenko (30 October–25 November)
Lawrence Weiner (27 November–22 December)

1974 **Carl Andre** (8 January–4 February)
Lothar Baumgarten (5–25 February)
Philippe van Snick (12 March–29 April)
Henryk Stazewski (30 April–31 May)
Marcel Broodthaers (25 September–3 November)
A.R. Penck (20 November–23 December)

Appendix 4: Conversations

4.1 Conversation with Jean-Christophe Ammann

Frankfurt, 4 October 2004

SOPHIE RICHARD *As Director of Kunstmuseum Lucerne, which galleries have you worked with in Switzerland and Europe?*

JEAN-CHRISTOPHE AMMANN Leo Castelli, New York; Gian Enzo Sperone, Turin; Art & Project, Amsterdam; Ileana Sonnabend, Paris; Annemarie & Gianfranco Verna, Zurich; Elisabeth Kaufmann, Zurich; Toni Gerber, Bern; Konrad Fischer, Düsseldorf.

SR *In the 1970s Kunstmuseum Lucerne included a lot of Conceptual artists (Buren, Gilbert & George, Darboven, Art & Language) in its exhibition programme. How did that come about?*

J-CA When I was appointed to the Kunstmuseum Lucerne in the autumn of 1968, I visited Leo Castelli in New York, a man I greatly admired, and told him what exhibitions I had planned, and at the same time asked him for financial support because funds were tight. That's how we ended up doing this series, as well as the first major retrospective of Joseph Kosuth. The shows with Anselmo, Art & Language, Boetti, Buren, Barry, Darboven and Dibbets were held in a small space. (Joseph Beuys had shown his *Clock-room* in the same space in 1969). Gilbert & George had a big exhibition with the paintings *With us in Nature*. They both also spent a week in Lucerne and performed *Underneath the Arches* every afternoon for five hours. The little exhibitions came to an end in 1972–73, with the recession. Some of the exhibitions were small, but always accompanied by a catalogue.

SR *In the 1970s the museum in Lucerne bought hardly any works by Conceptual artists. According to my research, only two works by Darboven and one by Gilbert & George entered the collection between 1970 and 1980. These three were gifts from the artists. How do you explain that? Was Conceptual art already too expensive, or was the museum's budget too small?*

J-CA We had no money. Darboven gave us her work. Nothing by Gilbert & George came into the museum. Zorio and Penone gave us outstanding works. Just imagine, our purchasing budget before the end of 1977 was 16,000 SFr!

SR *What do you think of the idea of a progressive European microcosm leading to the recognition of Conceptual art in the 1970s? Which European galleries and museums were in your view the most committed to Conceptual art in the 1970s?*

J-CA The influence of American art in Europe came to an end in 1973. When Conceptual art spilled over from the USA to Europe, that was the last stylistic trend in the twentieth century. (Buren, Toroni, Mosset, Parmentier saw themselves as painters.) Conceptual art was essentially an Anglo-Saxon trend in art. In the mid-1970s a particular direction in art, music and theatre came to an end. I'm referring to the historical avant-gardes. But at that time there was no longer an array of styles. Each artist had to work out for himself where to find back and front, left and right. I think all the open-minded museums throughout Europe were committed to Conceptual art.

Translation from German: Shaun Whiteside

4.2 Conversation with Jacques Charlier

Luxembourg, 5 October 2005

SOPHIE RICHARD *I'd like to start our discussion by talking about the situation in the art world in Belgium in the 1970s. In those days, there was a dynamism in commercial galleries, particularly MTL and Wide White Space, and there was also a dynamism where collectors were concerned: people like Herbert, Daled or Matthys. But where museums are concerned, apart from a few exhibitions at the Palais des Beaux-Arts, they seem to have had no commitment to the new artistic trend of Conceptual art.*

JACQUES CHARLIER After the early 1960s, the situation in Belgium was like this: in the southern, French speaking part, they were still tied to the Paris School. In the northern part, Antwerp was a pretty consistent international magnet. That's why I did my first two exhibitions there. When I went to that city, I visited the Hessenhuis, where you could find Group Zero, as well as people like Manzoni, Yves Klein, the Nouveau Réalistes. Antwerp also welcomed people like Lucio Fontana, who did some actions. Not only at the level of the visual arts, but also at the level of Anglo-Saxon musical culture, Antwerp was a very important magnet. I'd say that the most advanced among the American Minimalist artists headed towards Conceptual art, including LeWitt. It wasn't a matter of change. It's quite natural that there should have been a perfect affinity between Conceptual art and Minimal art from the moment they started to make their approach more theoretical and to believe that the plan was enough. As Lawrence Weiner put it, each work could be fabricated by someone else, or not built at all; the project is the driving force. Well, you could say that formulas and attitudes like this on the part of different American artists, including Kosuth, established contact much more easily with certain landing spots, not in Germany, not in Holland, not elsewhere – they did it in Belgium. They found not only welcoming gallery owners, but also collectors who took an interest in that formula. I think the first one, which might not have been the most purist, but was the most intuitive, was Wide White Space. Even in the 1960s, the protest movements and happenings that took place in Antwerp would influence the whole of the Belgian context. Because Bernd Lohaus was close to Beuys, it was easy to bring in a whole series of willing artists, both Expressionist and Minimalist. So everything was going very well internally at the gallery, and had a definite resonance with all the collectors and gallery owners, who gradually became familiar with the formula. Given that they felt there might be potential clients, people started opening new galleries. MTL was one of those. You couldn't say that French speakers were left out of the climate completely. In the late 1960s/early 1970s the Yellow gallery would over time become a publishing house, and would also give rise to the activities of the *Cirque d'hiver*; all of that formed a central point in the French speaking region, especially in Liège, but everything revolved around the Fluxus movement, for which Ben Vautier acted as a kind of mainspring. Obviously there's no comparison with what was going on in Brussels and Antwerp ...

SR *Plus Kern.*

JC Plus Kern, quite. He and Debruyn tried to get set up and in a sense acted as intermediaries for the other galleries desperate to seduce the Belgian collectors ... This adventure would only last a little while, though. Even the Xone Gallery and Marc Poirier would work with Spillemaeckers, but Debruyn was the intermediary for the Sonnabend Gallery. If, for example, you look at shows at Fernand Spillemaeckers's first gallery, MTL, between 1969 and 1975 [*he refers to a list of these exhibitions*], you see people like Guy Mees who's from Antwerp, Yves de Smet from Gent, Broodthaers from Brussels, Niele Toroni and Daniel Buren, who are French. So even there you can see the kind of direction he was headed in ... The Sonnabend Gallery, which wouldn't touch photographs – they're not made by the artist, they're so radically ordinary that you can't imagine they're art. So Spillemaeckers shows Philippe van Snick, Guy Mees again, Bernd Lohaus ... and then he invites the gallery that's going to be his rival, Wide White Space, Yves de Smet again, Gerard Hemsworth. Then in 1971–72 you sense that it's getting more and more radical, with Stanley Brouwn, Ian Wilson, Hanne Darboven, Jan Dibbets, to try and get the trade going. Robert Barry, Douglas Huebler, Boetti, Broodthaers again, LeWitt ... He was showing what was important right then, and he was clearly trying to make acquaintance with Gerry Schum, etc., from whom we have videos of Gilbert & George, Imi Knoebel and Baldessari. In 1972–73, you sense the influence of the gallery owner on the way the artists put together their exhibitions. Mel Bochner puts down his little stones, his accountancy work on the ground, on the windows of the gallery; you see Baldessari, still a radical, doing very edgy stuff. Dan Graham, Darboven, Brouwn, Anselmo, LeWitt again, Broodthaers, Mees, Dibbets, Wilson and Barry ... But there are new things as well, because he tries to get hold of American Minimalists, but they're not so much a part of that radical tendency: Flavin, Andre, Judd, Gilbert & George, Long, Fulton ... Then a whole flock of Italians: he shows Zorio, Anselmo, Boetti, Penone, Salvo, Merz, Paolini and De Dominicis. In 1973–74 it goes on, but things are evolving. So he meets Cadere. He takes Cadere and finds very quickly that there's this element of tension and polemic between Cadere and Buren. I went to this gallery almost every weekend, and for the full duration of its activity, Spillemaeckers acted in such a way that not only the works by the artists put him in danger, but they put the gallery in danger and created a critical set of problems.

SR *Put the gallery in danger in what way?*

JC From the moment Cadere came to do his stuff, he knew very well it would affect his affinity with Buren, who didn't support Cadere. Spillemaeckers liked Cadere because there was something purely mental and very provocative about him. It's beyond Minimalism, the act of strolling towards a place with a guy holding a stick that becomes an exhibition. That rhetoric is very naïve – but the impact was immediate. People threw him out, people couldn't bear him being there because it became an exhibition within an exhibition, so it turned into a direct polemic. What Buren created within the city, within a gallery, is one thing, but here it becomes a truly direct and physical relationship. It becomes a conversation. So you find Wilson, whose verbal support constitutes the work. People like Huebler, Darboven, Brouwn, LeWitt, even Zorio ... he made them do things that were basically taking it to the extreme. The gallery was small – it was a little corridor – not the kind of space where you can organise theatrical events and stuff to strike the eye. You've got hardly anything. So when Kosuth comes, he doesn't put paintings everywhere, he sticks up posters with questions. He sticks them up on the walls in half an hour and then we go off and spend the rest of the night drinking in bars and setting the world to rights. He was going more and more for the critical, philosophical side of the things to be shown. In 1974–75, the business was working less and less. It wasn't bringing in any money. He wasn't a good businessman. Back come Baldessari, Broodthaers, Graham, Eda Renouf, Charlier, Buren, Ryman – who will come and paint on-site – Wilson again, Dibbets, Brouwn, Art & Language and Toroni. So that's the field that the Belgian side – other galleries like Krivine, like Debruyne and the galerie D, like Plus Kern or galleries like Richard Fonck in Gent, and particularly Antwerp with Wide White Space – aren't going to feel an extreme amount of sympathy with ... You're getting public funds, it's very difficult to convince the elected bodies to devote cash to putting completely incomprehensible things on the walls, which aren't at all spectacular, when basically ... they only have one desire, which is to see the Hyperrealists.

SR *But that was possible in other countries, like, for example the museum in Eindhoven, which wasn't so far from Belgium. Rudi Fuchs was able to buy Ian Wilsons and so on.*

JC You're right, but you'll understand why straight away: They're Protestants – we're among Calvinists! The fact that there's no picture reassures everybody. It was much easier for the Eindhoven museum, the Stedelijk, etc. All the Dutch museums made that journey easily. You won't come across a Stanley Brouwn here in Belgium, for example. But in the Netherlands there was a kind of radicalism on the part of some people. They reacted to the physical invasion of Minimalism, the flagrant imagery of Pop – they rejected it in favour of something more meditative, more philosophical, more critical, more purist.

SR *While in Belgium they tend to prefer...*

SR We're among Catholics. The home of Rubens! Pop was inevitably going to cause a stir ... In the mid-1970s, for a year, Yves Gevaert and Michel Baudson were in charge of the Palais des Beaux-Arts, Brussels. Gevaert, who'd already made a breakthrough with the exhibition of Belgian artists at MOMA in Oxford in 1974, showed his great understanding of the network, having a very good idea of how to arrange the works, and he was appointed for a year, which would be a year of transition. Because the Society of the Palais des Expositions couldn't make their mind up to appoint anybody, Gevaert got some freedom of movement to set up some spectacular exhibitions that were entirely in line with what was happening in the advanced German, English, Dutch positions – not in France yet, because France was still stuck in the mud.[1] You just have to look at the few shows he organised, including the one I took part in with On Kawara. But there were other shows, where the whole gang came together, with Andre as well as Gilbert & George and Richter.[2] He did what he could within a very short space of time. I don't know what tricks he pulled, but we knew it didn't go down too well. I remember there was even a whole wall of Ryman that was damaged by graffiti. That wasn't very well received by the few collectors in the Société des Expositions who'd acted as intermediaries for Pop apart from people like Daled, Herbert ... Except for a few of them, like Matthys ... You have a very clear sense that the way (and this is a personal opinion) the Flemish collectors bought up Minimalism and Conceptual art was a kind of religious transference. It was very violent. They saw them as meditative spaces. Religion was collapsing in Flanders, so it became the central pillar. And art is an outlet – less radical than it is for the Dutch, but there's a bit of that going on.

SR *In Belgium most of the collectors are of Flemish origin – they're more in the Flemish part of the country. Isn't it true to say that there's more of a tradition of collecting among the Flemish than among the Walloons?*

JC ... The Flemish have a tradition of pictorial art, which is down to the fact that they produced some original artists. Painting has an extremely well-anchored tradition but you'd have to admit that it suffers from a number of identity complexes. The first of these lies in the fact that these artists have never become internationally known. So, there's this complex: the art that we like by our artists doesn't make it to the outside world. And then you've got these Francophones imposing the Paris School – all those writers who have to write in French!

SR *It's partly to do with the language barrier.*

JC Yes, it's there, it's huge. So, you've got this whole system. But what's interesting is that all this is happening at the same time as the industrial collapse of Wallonia and the ascendancy of the Flemish capitals. In Antwerp during this time, the diamond industry was at its peak. So you've got this whole gang that's there taking risks and buying things, but you also have people in the region of Gent ... they did something that never happened in Wallonia: they bought works in common, and passed them from one to the other. They said to themselves: 'We'll buy a big Christo and put it in storage until we've got a modern art museum.' It was the Société des Expositions, the Gent literary circle, they're doctors, lawyers and so on, around Karel Geirlandt and Matthys. That created a kind of elixir of youth for people, who said to themselves: 'We understand English, we understand German, we've got to show that we're open to the world.' That's how it was!

SR *But it's also a consequence of the partition of the country.*

JC Yes, but the partition of the country was based on its industrial division. You mustn't forget that you've got millions of Flemings coming to work here in Wallonia when business is good. But when the 1960s came and it was plain that the industrial sector was in meltdown. That's why they bought works collectively. They were pooling forces, but around something inter-national; they found a global vision of the world. What's the vision they aimed for primarily? Well, it's the Americans. Pop art fits the bill exactly. It's plain that Rauschenberg, Dine and all those people were still successful, but also the Nouveau Réalistes, that openness to Group Zero ... They said, 'Now as for us, we're brave enough to buy that, while you people are still stuck in your language, which is busy dying'. Unconsciously, that's how it worked. Obviously, you've got the people of Brussels, who are bilingual and who have certain connections with the Flemish, and they all worked together. You mustn't forget them, because Brussels and Flanders was the crucible of everything that happened.

SR *There was also the Conceptual Art Congress at La Cambre, which played a part in opening up the situation.*

JC What happened was that given that there was a lot of theory that came with Minimalism, etc., and that the most extreme aspects of Conceptual art were able to find an audience in Belgium, Spillemaeckers said to himself: 'Let's really break away from the countries adjacent to ours and set up a Conceptual Art Congress.' It was interesting in terms of the artists who got involved, in terms of the idea, but you shouldn't imagine that it found any kind of resonance amongst collectors and curators. It was something that passed almost unnoticed.

SR *What about the public?*

JC Listen, hardly anyone came! From the outset, you could say that it was the party around Spillemaeckers, who was already a brilliant self-taught philosopher, who published a little magazine that was the epitome of radical hipness. But there were also people who were less well known, like Nicole Daled's brother, Paul Verstraeten. There was a whole flock of people who came to those openings, but were not talking about art. These were philosophical fights! It wasn't Dan Graham any more – it was Althusser, it was Deleuze – that was what fed into the basis of it. Lohaus and De Decker said to me: 'We were the intellectual side, but political, too.' Running through all that there was a kind of radical leftism, that desire to make things that could effectively bring people closer to the work, and give them art that they had a right to, with a kind of whiff of revolution.

SR *That intellectual milieu particularly developed around MTL, while Wide White Space had a very practical side. Anny De Decker doesn't seem to be an extremely intellectual person. She told me that herself.*

JC No, it was turned towards a kind of esoteric poetry, a kind of symbolism of objects, something more physical and certainly not cerebral: Beuys, Lohaus, James Lee Byars, Baselitz, Penck, from his good periods ... of course, they also introduced Buren, Toroni, etc. But let's say that the very essence of the gallery, even when Broodthaers came and did things, was something less mental and less critical. Bruce Nauman was less radical as well. She did exhibitions with Christo, who's radical as well, but it's more physical with her.

SR *It's more a gallery as place for exhibitions than a place for debate, perhaps?*

SR Oh, yes, absolutely. It wasn't a place for debate. Besides, that scares away people who are interested in things like that, who are touched by them but can't explain why. There's always a way of sweet-talking them, but if you explain it to them, it will never get below the surface. If you cease to see art as an object of contemplation, but rather as a place of action, a place of reflection, a place of analysis and a place of contradiction ... All the possibilities of putting works on the wall, putting them in public, will be analysed. All possibilities for pushing the idea into its furthermost nooks by getting rid of more and more materials will be put into effect. It's a kind of extreme and often ridiculous purification and radicalism.

SR *What surprised me, looking at the list of exhibitions that you did during the 1970s, was that in 1970 your 'Professional Landscapes' were shown both at MTL and in Wide White Space. Wasn't that a rather unusual situation?*

JC You see, Spillemaeckers forced the door very clumsily so that there was not an association, but a complicity. We were going to do something about professional photographs, but I could see very clearly that they were doing it out of politeness. Not only did they know nothing about it, but they saw it as something dangerous. I understood that very clearly. It's an interrogation of the social order, it's a reaction, an analysis with regard to the found object, which I would tirelessly continue, and I think that now we're right in the middle of the outcome of what I predicted during those years. The whole world has become a revived found object, religion has become thoroughly involved in art. I was the first to point that thing out!

SR *What was the position of the Galerie Véga in Liège?*

JC It was the only almost commercial outpost. Spillemaeckers criticised me because there was no outpost of his gallery in Liège. We drank a lot and fought around the Étangs d'Ixelles ... because with Spillemaeckers you couldn't just say something; it was really serious. So I went home, and by some strange coincidence, during the week I was contacted by Monette Moureau who was a saleswoman at Galerie Véga, which had just started, and was showing Folon, Pierre Alechinsky, Alberto Burri, Monori, Robert Delaunay ... She wanted to recreate what l'APIAW (Association pour le progrès intellectuel et artistique de la Wallonie) could no longer supply. She really wanted to do exhibitions. She'd shown enormous enthusiasm at the time of the exhibition *Absolute Zone*, which I'd organised and which Broodthaers had inaugurated. She'd told me it was fantastic. The gallery owner was Manette Repriels. So she came to see me and said: 'Listen, Manette Repriels would like to buy your *Absolute Zone*.' It was very different from nowadays, when you mix everything together. Back then it was really pretty clear-cut – you didn't go over to the enemy! So I said, 'I'm happy to sell it to her, as long as she changes her programme, and I want to supply her with the weapons to change her programme easily.' She said to me, 'Let's get together on neutral terrain.' I went to see this saleswoman and her architect husband. We met up at their house. I had *Absolute Zone* with me: it's a roll of paper. I say, 'OK, I agree to sell it to you, on condition that you do much more serious, much more edgy exhibitions than what you're doing at the moment. What do you think about a show with Broodthaers, Gilbert & George, Dibbets, Baldessari, LeWitt, and so on?' And she says to me, 'Oh, that would be fantastic!' I ask her if it would be possible in three weeks. She says: 'We'll do it like that.' I phoned Spillemaeckers, and bang, it was done. I have to say, we did some pretty incredible shows. I saw Dan Graham's best exhibition there.

SR *And that was in the mid-1970s?*

JC Yes, around the mid-1970s. So she did Denis Oppenheim, LeWitt, Gilbert & George ...

SR *So it became a kind of outpost gallery for Conceptual art in Wallonia?*

JC Yes, you could say that, but not entirely Conceptual, partially Conceptual. As I had connections with Konrad Fischer, she developed contacts with him. She wanted to do the Bechers with Sonnabend, and so on. She went to a lot of trouble and for a few years she did establish a programme. But obviously the main customers weren't French speakers. They were Flemish.

SR *What interests me is the contact between the different galleries in Belgium, and also the contacts that those galleries had with galleries abroad. You put on exhibitions with Anka Ptaszkowska and Eric Fabre in Paris, with Françoise Lambert in Milan, with Kiki Mayer-Hahn in Düsseldorf. How did that happen?*

JC I met Anka Ptaszkowska through Daled. She was a Polish immigrant. She was supported by Michel Denizot and Michel Claura. She asked me to do an exhibition and I did. With Mayer-Hahn, Fischer phoned me one day and said: 'You've got to go to Kiki Mayer-Hahn, you'll have an exhibition there.' I went there and managed to bring in Toroni and a whole crowd of people; it was a gallery that was starting up. One day, Françoise Lambert saw my cartoons somewhere, perhaps at Konrad Fischer, and she wanted to do an exhibition of the cartoons. Franco Toselli tried to do something as well. It didn't really work. The humour was too bound up with the milieu; it was geared too much at a limited audience. On the other hand, there were others who decided not to show me at the last minute, because of the content of the drawings and so on.

SR *The cartoons were seen as a kind of polemic?*

JC Yes. They'd noticed that in the art world, unlike the political world, a caricature has incredible effects.

SR *Meaning?*

JC You do a caricature that's quite edgy in spirit, and they take it very badly. I'm talking about those years.

SR *The caricatures are pretty cutting, but I don't think they're especially mean.*

JC There's nothing worrying about them. That's the weird thing. And I really think it's a problem of context. The proof is that now everyone's interested in them.

SR *People didn't like being portrayed like that in those days?*

JC That's right. I did a drawing of Schum, showing him with wings just after he died. The Dutch artists, Jan Dibbets at their head, said I was the worst kind of creep. It was weird. For me, it was a nice kind of tribute. Michael Sonnabend introduced me to Leo Castelli, saying: 'This is Jacques Charlier, the nastiest artist in the art world.' I mean come on ... What are you going to do? It was because I'd drawn Ileana Sonnabend knitting (she liked knitting) and the ball of wool went all the way to New York and her ex-husband Leo Castelli. It was the truth! I'd also drawn Warhol, fat, eating Campbell's Soup. Michael Sonnabend told me whatever I did not to show it to Warhol. 'That's Charlier all over, doing things like that.' You see? Whereas if they were politicians it would be the opposite ...

SR *Perhaps because there's more of a tradition of caricatures in politics.*

JC There was Ad Reinhardt, who was very polemical and paid heavily for it. You can look at the drawings he did about the art world, and they're unusually violent. It's interesting. He took it all the way.

SR *I was struck by two caricatures in particular. The first series concerns ten drawings that represent Fischer's journey from artist to powerful gallery owner. The final picture shows him sitting on a throne with a sceptre in his hand. The second drawing shows him walking and smoking with an eagle on his shoulder. His shadow is Napoleon's. Was Fischer really as powerful as that?*

JC He was! He was. Listen, joking aside, he was! He wasn't the kind of decent bloke you could have a laugh with all the time. He said 'bang' [*hits the table with his fist*] ... A frustrated artist – it's a killer! He was a painter – a good painter. But he was authoritarian. The first of those cartoons went down very badly.

SR *But the work he did for the artists he defended was positive ...*

JC I'm willing to believe that. I never did caricatures of nobodies. You can't imagine the number of people who wanted me to do caricatures. I only ever drew interesting people.

SR *By way of contrast, there's a caricature of Gian Enzo Sperone that makes him look a bit of a dreamer ...*

JC A cowboy of the old west.

SR *...When you look at some of the correspondence, concerning his sales to the Tate Gallery, you can see that the museum was reluctant to do deals with him.*

JC He's a killer. He's a cowboy. He's very much a cowboy.

SR *Those drawings are a terrific source of information about the art world of the day.*

JC At the same time, for me, it's also a failure because I imagined the art world would have enough of a critical, humorous, self-mocking spirit to accept that kind of thing. Most of the drawings were bought by the Antwerp Museum, when Florent Bex was there. Some went into private collections. Daled bought the drawing of the party at his place. But it's very strange; it wasn't seen as an interesting phenomenon at the time. As far as I was concerned, the cartoons were to dip my toe in the water and make everyone laugh. I sent out a hundred photocopies – everyone knew about it. You sent out a hundred invitations, and if your index cards were up to date, it was everyone. So if you compare that milieu, that international microcosm with now ... The *Art Diary* was tiny at the time – it's huge now! ... It's like a kind of Roman Curia.

SR *It's fashionable.*

JC Yes, it's fashionable, but for reasons of spiritual inflation ... lots of blind faith. They believe in it! Everything's magic, it's all superstition. You can imagine the damage ...

SR *The cartoons were a way of commenting on the art world of the time. What about the photographs of the* Vernissage des Expositions *in 1975. Were they done in the same spirit?*

JC I had the idea, of choosing the medium that suits the subject. That's one thing. I also choose the style that suits it. Yves Gevaert told me about On Kawara, who was doing this obsessive work about himself every day: he's still alive, he got up at a particular time, etc. I initially showed the audience that was looking at that kind of art, for a year, all over the place: Amsterdam, Cologne, Düsseldorf, Brussels ... I took photographs, in medium shot ... For me, the basic concept was: you've got to take photographs almost in a Cubist way, so that you've got the reverse of the art ... I started to arrange them in the same way that I did my professional photographs, in groups of nine so that they were transportable. And then Gevaert said to me, 'What are we going to do for a catalogue?' And I said 'let's do a catalogue, but post-exhibition. On the day of the opening I want the bar to be on my side of the room. We'll photograph people looking at the photographs.'

SR *It's a kind of mise-en-abîme.*

JC Yes, that's it, a mise-en-abîme. It was extremely interesting, because my room was the place where everyone stayed – that was where the bar was. But there were also the photographs. They were looking at the photographs, asking, 'Why am I not there? That person's dead now', and so on and so forth. And then it was very funny, because on the On Kawara side you had two or three people wandering in, and that was it. I wasn't trying to win some kind of game by doing that. It was really to show how the art world worked in those days. And what's moving about it is that those photographs over time became more and more interesting for some people, due to the fact that more and more people have died and a few people you see in them have become stars. But at the time, in 1975, that wasn't the case. [*He flicks through the catalogue.*] Everyone is there.

SR *You can clearly see Benjamin Buchloch.*

JC Yes, with Isa Genzken, Annick Herbert, André Cadere, Albert Baronian, Peter Downsbrough, Lynda Morris ...

SR *Was there always going to be an On Kawara–Jacques Charlier exhibition?*

SR That was the choice of Yves Gevaert. I saw Yves recently, and he reckons it's one of the most consistent things I've done ... He now realises what the issue really was. I'm not sure he understood it straight away. But I'm grateful to him for trusting me, because when it was fresh, it was a report on the year. It didn't have the same impact as it does now. I had this idea of putting it on the page when I saw Pietro Lunghi's paintings in Venice. They were always social studies; you can see everyone, as many people as possible, in the shot. You see the faces of the people talking, who is talking to whom, etc.

SR *The people who were at the opening that day, were they flattered, or what was their attitude?*

JC We took the photographs in such a way that they didn't notice particularly. But the people who were in the photographs and recognised themselves, they told everyone else: 'Hey, I was there in Cologne for Projekt '74, so-and-so was there.' But then what was very funny is that when the catalogue with the photographs was launched, they did it in this rough club, The Black and White, where I did a guitar concert and then people were given the catalogue.

SR *That was after the exhibition closed?*

JC Yes, that was how we closed the exhibition.

SR *That catalogue is really a great source of information. It's entirely in the spirit of my research into the milieu of northern European art in the 1970s. It puts its finger on that little group of people who were all associated with each other.*

JC It was a sect. That's the weird thing: the 1960s, the

few Belgian artists doing anything other than sub-Pop and trying to go beyond the norm. There was just a handful of them. There was Broodthaers, who wanted to meet me because I'm from Liège, Panamarenko, Jef Geys, and a few like that, but not many. So that was how it worked. In the 1970s it didn't have much to do with our neighbouring countries. Then the Americans came; they knew each other and the other galleries ...

SR *To get back to the 1975 exhibition, I saw in* Flash Art *that you'd also taken photographs of Mimmo Rotella in Milan and the museum in Bologna. It's the same concept, reproduced in a magazine.*

JC Absolutely. It was after the exhibition in Brussels. I think I did that when I was showing cartoons at Françoise Lambert. I did two or three things like that and I said to myself that that was enough. It could have become a system. I could have turned it into a system ...

SR *And there's also the fact of reproducing it in a magazine, which is a completely different kind of support from an exhibition.*

JC With *Domus*, I was able to include some cartoons, because Lisa Licitra Ponti wanted me to. But she didn't dare include too many. What I dreamed of was doing a humorous magazine about art. Doing jokes all the time would have been funny! I'd have loved to do a kind of Hara-Kiri of the art world. It would have been hilarious! But you can't do that kind of thing; you don't laugh at sacred things.

SR *Perhaps also because it was a very small milieu. As Anton Herbert says, you had to keep your elbows pulled in.*

JC He's right. From the moment you show the heart of the matter ... Yes, it's the eternal problem of faith.

Translation from French: Shaun Whiteside

1 [Editor's note: See a selection of Jacques Charlier's *Vernissage des Expositions* photographs on pp.269–289.]
2 [Editor's note: *Carl Andre, Marcel Broodthaers, Daniel Buren, Victor Burgin, Gilbert & George, On Kawara, Richard Long, Gerhard Richter*, Palais des Beaux-Arts, Brussels, 9 January–3 February 1974, organised by Yves Gevaert.]

4.3 Conversation with Anny De Decker

Antwerp, 16 November 2004

SOPHIE RICHARD *I'd like to start our conversation by discussing the difficulty involved in finding an appropriate term to describe the artists whose careers began in the late 1960s. 'Conceptual' is the term most often used.*

ANNY DE DECKER Yes, for example, someone like Gerhard Richter isn't Conceptual. He was already successful at that time. We thought what he was doing then was a kind of European Pop art. We didn't see it as a particularly personal thing. At first, basically, we saw everything through the art of the United States. That was the newest thing. There was also a Hyperrealist tendency during the 1970s. But I wasn't interested in that.

SR *A whole set of new galleries opened up in the late 1960s, like Wide White Space, MTL (Belgium), Art & Project (Amsterdam), Yvon Lambert (Paris), Sperone (Turin), Konrad Fischer, Paul Maenz (Germany), Lisson and Nigel Greenwood (London). In your eyes, what distinguished this new generation of gallery-owners from their predecessors?*

ADD We were all young; we weren't yet 30. All those galleries started at the same time. There was also Rolf Ricke. What was different was that we didn't base ourselves on other galleries. Before, there was a kind of tradition that you continued. But now it was quite different. We had a relationship with the artists, because they were from our generation. There was something like a spirit of adventure. We were very optimistic. We thought that everything that was new was better. That optimism was in the general mentality of the 1960s. There was also a feeling of freedom. The 1950s were still very closed, you can see that in the films of the day. In the 1960s, in all the universities, there were rebellions. The students wanted something else. They were against authority, against the established order. All those new galleries were of that generation. We wanted to create a different spirit. The gallery owners defended the artists, not just for their art, but also to allow them to have a livelihood. (Of course, there have always been gallery-owners who are preoccupied with their artists.) In general, we were very good friends with the artists. It was difficult art to sell, but we wanted to let them have a livelihood. Obviously, we wanted to sell their works, but there's a difference between dealer and gallery owner, particularly in Germany. A gallery owner is much more involved with the artists; he follows them from year to year, while a dealer buys works more for his customers and to get a commission, and it's less to support the artist. We chose the artists first and then tried to find customers. But obviously there were very few.

SR *Did you know about the opening of other galleries at that time? You were one of the first to open in 1966.*

ADD I knew Konrad Fischer because he'd been at the Düsseldorf Academy with my husband, Bernd Lohaus. Sometimes Fischer travelled around Belgium with another gallery owner, Alfred Schmela. They would usually visit a collector, and so on. When we opened the gallery, they came to see us. So we knew each other. Then one day Konrad told us he was going to open a gallery in two months' time. We'd been to see Art & Project in Amsterdam, but I don't remember how we knew they'd opened a gallery. They must have sent an invitation. In some magazines such as *Art International*, there were lists of galleries. In Paris it wasn't difficult, because even though it's a big city, the galleries were listed in the newspapers. It was easy. Perhaps it was like that – looking at the list of galleries in magazines – that we discovered Art & Project.

SR *Were the art magazines a good way to keep up to date with what was happening in the art world?*

ADD Yes, *Art International* most of all. But we didn't really read the articles, we just looked at the reproductions. The Palais des Beaux-Arts in Brussels published a little magazine, *L'Journal des Beaux-Arts*, in French and Dutch. There, too, there was a list of exhibitions. There was a paper in Antwerp that reported all the exhibitions that were going on, because there was an art critic who was interested in what we were showing. From that point of view, we were spoilt; no other newspaper carried reviews of the exhibitions.

SR *So you gradually came to know all these new galleries?*

ADD Yes, we looked. The collectors told us where they went as well. We very quickly met Martin Visser, for example, who came from Bergeyk in Holland. He came to see us, because he'd had an invitation. Christo had an exhibition at the Eindhoven Museum in 1966; it was the first museum to show artists like him. Maria Broodthaers had told me she'd read in a Dutch paper that a collector called Visser had lots of Christos. She showed me the paper and I immediately noted the name. I must have asked the museum for his address. He and his wife Mia became great friends of ours. They told us where the galleries were. The group of people involved in the avant-garde was very small; we had lots of contact. We all knew each other – there was a kind of solidarity. Some people think it was the plan that all the artists would go round all those galleries. But it wasn't like that at all. I've never taken an artist because he was at another gallery. I went and looked in the galleries and if I liked something I contacted the artist. For example, when Andre showed at Konrad Fischer for the first time, I thought it was so fantastic that I immediately decided I wanted to show him, too. But it wasn't because he was at Konrad's that he was inevitably going to come to me. I was never really interested in LeWitt, for example. We often made the same choices. Konrad showed Panamarenko several times, and later Broodthaers. Broodthaers put people off because he used the French language a lot and it was very intellectual. There was also Prospect, an exhibition organised by Fischer. All the galleries came together there. We ended up knowing one another because we saw each other often.

SR *But there was also collaboration between the galleries – for example, when it came to sharing an artist's travel costs to bring him to Europe.*

ADD Yes, once we'd decided on an artist, that was what we did. At the time it was very expensive to come from the States. It costs almost 15,000 fr. at the time, which would be more or less 150,000 fr. today. That's really very expensive.

SR *If, for example, you take the case of Weiner, he was first shown by Fischer in April 1969, then in June the same year in Wide White Space, in September at Art & Project and in December at Sperone. Then in March 1970 he was shown at Yvon Lambert, then again in December 1970 at Fischer and so on – a really quick succession.*

ADD We'd met Weiner at Seth Siegelaub in New York. He'd talked about these four artists he was showing at the time (Barry, Kosuth, Huebler, Weiner). I couldn't really make my mind up and suggested showing the four together. Siegelaub didn't want me to do that, because he wanted it to be a solo exhibition. And anyway I couldn't take the four of them! In the end Lawrence Weiner was the one I found most interesting. We met and talked, and that persuaded us we wanted to show him.

SR *Is the affinity with the artist very important?*

ADD Yes, absolutely. For example Barry came to Antwerp and he almost wanted to force me to do an exhibition with him. It was at a point when I was fed up with the gallery – sometimes it was really too much work, with two children and so on. He was working on a project called *During the exhibition the gallery will be closed*. I got angry and said, 'If I want to close the gallery, I'll do it myself!' He got on my nerves because he didn't understand that it wasn't the right time. Once the first moment has passed, you meet other artists and you don't always go back on your decisions.

SR *When an artist starts being shown by several galleries in Europe, doesn't a certain competitiveness come into it?*

ADD It's a two-sided blade. It's great publicity for the artist: the more he's shown, the better he's known. It's better for the artist and for his work. But obviously it's also more difficult, because you all have works by the same artists. When the Cologne Art Fair was on, for example, all the galleries were there, competing. It's somewhere between the two, good and bad. There was nothing to be done. In the beginning, I was alone as far as Belgium was concerned, then afterwards there was the MTL. But Fernand Spillemaeckers took on the artists I hadn't shown (Darboven, Huebler, Barry, etc.). So it wasn't a problem because we didn't have the same artists. Fischer was there for the Rhineland, Art & Project for Holland, etc. Basically we all covered big territories. Obviously the Dutch collectors came to us. The Belgians always went to Paris. People tended to buy abroad, because when they were travelling they had more time and it was more pleasant.

SR *In Paris you were in contact with Anka Ptaszkowska's gallery in particular.*

ADD Yes, she started a gallery, but she didn't want it to have a name. So the first exhibition was *Galerie 1*, then the second *Galerie 2* etc. That project was Buren's idea. I'd met Anka at the Galeries Pilotes in Lausanne in 1970. We'd set up next to the Galerie Foksal in Warsaw. We immediately became friends. She lived in Paris and knew Buren and Toroni very well.

SR *There was also Sperone in Italy.*

ADD Yes, but that was further away. He was closely connected with Ileana Sonnabend and took on a lot of her artists. Sonnabend was always very tricky where we were concerned. I'd asked her to let us show Lichtenstein and Warhol, and she always refused. Maybe she thought the gallery was too small and not well-known enough and those artists were so famous. While Sperone showed all those artists and others as well. They never wanted to work with us. I think it was because they had a lot of clients in Belgium and there was nothing in it for them. Sperone was a bit loftier. Then he worked with Konrad Fischer.

SR *To come now to the trade in Conceptual art, I can't imagine that selling Weiner's phrases or Long's walks could have been an easy business.*

ADD At that time, a Weiner, for example, cost 1,000 dollars. For the same price, you could have a nice object by Beuys. Luckily there were collectors who had the same mentality as us and thought it was interesting; they thought it was a brilliant idea to have a Weiner phrase. I also think they really wanted to support the artist and the gallery at the same time.

SR *How was contact made with interested people?*

ADD Some of them came to see us of their own accord. In those days, when there was an exhibition by an artist, the collector's name often went in the catalogue. When the Palais des Beaux-Arts in Brussels put on an exhibition by Arman, by Martial Raysse or Broodthaers, all the collectors' names were listed in the catalogue. That never happens nowadays. Often the artists and curators don't want it because it's as if they depended on the collectors. There's a kind of pride in not mentioning the buyers, so as not to make them too important. But sometimes the collectors made demands. For example, they demanded that a particular piece be shown, or lesser-known artists from their collection to be shown as well, or else they threatened not to lend any works. Some collectors did little bits of blackmail for the exhibitions and sometimes the galleries were the same. There's always a good bit of scheming in big exhibitions like that. In those days, artists were proud to be able to say they were in some private collection or other. It was a bit like a confirmation for the artist. When I saw an artist in Panza's collection, I said to myself that we had to keep an eye on that artist and it might be worth contacting him. That has a part to play – you're influenced by collectors.

SR *Who were your first collectors?*

ADD There was Isi Fiszman, who lived in Antwerp at the time and came every week. (Now he lives in Brussels.) Some people even thought he was the director of the gallery. There were the Vissers, and Daled, whom we saw regularly, but who didn't buy much. The Herberts came later; they bought a Richard Long, but that was in around 1974–75 [*Driftwood*, 1975]. It made a huge difference in 1968 or 1974, particularly in terms of what had been accepted in the meantime.

SR *Do you remember any of your first major sales to a collector, when you said to yourself that the gallery was starting to work?*

ADD It's hard to say, because we always sold a minimum. Fiszman was really a very assiduous customer. He often bought several works at the same time, but his bargaining could go on all night. It's more when two or three people bought things that I had the sense that the gallery was working. In Belgium, Panamarenko has always sold. His pieces were sold six months or a year after they were shown. It was mostly Germans, Belgians and Dutchmen who bought, especially the Vissers. The first really well-known artist I had was Christo. That was quite early on. His work was in the stores of the Eindhoven Museum, and through Schmela we were able to organise an exhibition by him. What he did was always very spectacular. He was already much better known than my other artists. He was of an older generation than the Conceptual artists. At the time of his exhibition, lots of people bought, especially Dutch collectors. It was a kind of affirmation of the gallery. For the Andre exhibition in May 1968, there were only two pieces. I think one piece was sold to Fiszman. For the second it took a few years.

SR *I read that Panza bought Weiner's work at the time of his exhibition in 1969, when the gallery space was completely empty and the only thing on show was the invitation card.*

ADD Panza bought an Andre, but I don't remember a Weiner. Panza bought from us, but not much. He never came to Belgium. I even think the Andre was done through correspondence, with photographs.

SR *You sold a number of works by Andre to Mia and Martin Visser, notably* Copper Ribbon *(1969) and the* Weathering Piece *(1970).*

ADD Yes, but the *Weathering Piece* was bought by Martin Visser's brother, Geertjan Visser. They bought two ribbons, one in lead and the other in copper.

SR *Generally speaking, did the collectors contact you directly for the purchase of a work?*

ADD Yes, they came of their own accord; they came to look. Sometimes, of course, we also contacted them to talk about the exhibitions we were doing. I hated that, but you've got to wake people up. Often they knew the artists already. When I showed Filliou, for example, I sold five or six pieces very quickly. People didn't know his work, but they liked it and they were used to objects of that kind. I was amazed to see that it worked pretty well, even though Filliou was almost unknown. People knew that he existed, but they didn't really know his work. I think it was Ben Vautier who talked to us about him; we saw him often.

SR *Do you think that private collectors in some way prepared the ground for getting these artists into museums?*

ADD I think so. The museum directors and the younger people who worked in the museums visited the collectors anyway. Jan Leering in Eindhoven put on an exhibition called *Three Blind Mice* in 1968, about the collectors Visser, Peeters and Becht. So he understood the work of the collectors. Panza's collection was frequently shown in different museums. There was a kind of aura surrounding Panza; his collection was very big. It must have been a model for the museums, because he had big works, exhibited in huge rooms. It wasn't a living room with a few objects.

SR *Were there museums in Europe who bought works by Conceptual artists?*

ADD At first there weren't really any museums. But later on, there were the Eindhoven Museum and the Stedelijk Museum in Amsterdam which bought regularly. The Director of the Stedelijk Museum, Edy de Wilde, was very grand, while the Director of the Van Abbemuseum, Rudi Fuchs, was much simpler. Obviously it depends on the people. When De Wilde came to Antwerp, the gallery had already existed for five years. But he didn't want to lower himself by setting foot in a little known gallery like ours. At the time, there was a lot more prestige surrounding museum people. Some assistants came. For example, Wim Beeren, who later became the Director of the Amsterdam Museum [1985–93], visited us regularly. Otherwise, the Rotterdam museum bought as well. The Dutch museums were really a model. In Belgium, there was nothing. The museum in Brussels was the first to have a Modern Art Department, with Phil Mertens. Then there was Jan Hoet at the museum in Gent, but that was later, in about 1975. But we were nearly finished by then. In Paris, the Musée d'Art moderne had already bought a Panamarenko. The Moderna Museet in Stockholm had bought things as well. In Germany, there was of course the Mönchengladbach museum. And there was the Kunsthalle in Düsseldorf, where Jürgen Harten was, but obviously, he didn't buy anything. But it was an important place where artists could exhibit. There was also the Krefeld museum with Paul Wember, but he was mostly interested in the Nouveaux Réalistes. He bought three works by Bernar Venet from me when I showed him at the gallery [1968]. So there were a few museums who bought, but that was mostly in the 1970s.

SR *According to my research into the 1970s, you sold a work by Buren,* Peinture sur toile *(1977) to the Van Abbemuseum in Eindhoven. Fuchs was the Director at the time. Can you tell me about that sale?*

ADD It was a work with blue stripes, if I remember correctly. I think it was the first Buren we sold to a museum – perhaps the only one. We sold about ten or 15 Burens in the end, but mostly to private collectors. We knew Fuchs before he was the Director of the Eindhoven museum. He was a bit younger than us. I think he was an art critic. In any case, he'd already come to the gallery. He was someone we knew. At that time, for example, Nick Serota came to see us as well. He was a bit younger as well. Fuchs came to see us about the Buren, but I think he also bought the series of nine canvases with French authors by Broodthaers [*Série de neuf tableaux*, 1972].

SR *According to Lynda Morris, the galleries tended to give better prices to private collectors than to museums. Is that true?*

ADD At my gallery, at any rate, the museums didn't pay more. In fact, I tended to give a museum a better percentage, because it's important for an artist's prestige to have a work in a museum. Maybe afterwards, things changed, because there was a period in the late 1970s when museums paid very slowly. It sometimes took a year, even more. So there, yes, there was a price difference.

SR *Was there a difference in the choice of works made by private collectors and museums?*

ADD Yes, museums are more thoughtful. Generally, they wanted quite a considerable work, very representative of the artist. Museums are also answerable. So they wanted representative pieces so that they could explain them to their committees. I think that's less the case nowadays, because everyone knows the representative pieces nowadays, and they look for slightly different works. But at the time, museums wanted typical pieces, like Andre's squares. A collector is usually more intuitive. But not all of them. Someone like Anton Herbert could wait months and months to find the piece he wanted. People are very different. Some of them buy spontaneously because they like the work, but there are also some who think about their whole collection. Some of them think of the space they've got and how they're going to be able to show it. Others don't immediately think of that at all.

SR *What was the reaction from the public when a museum bought a work?*

ADD There was an awful lot of mockery. Sometimes even in the gallery itself. They came to the gallery just to mock – it was incredible! Sometimes students from the art schools came to see it. But it was very difficult to get that art accepted. In the end, I'd had enough of having to explain it to people. At first I didn't care, but in the end it's irritating: a public that doesn't understand anything.

SR *At the art fairs, like Prospect or the Cologne fair, did the public come more just to find out about things or to buy?*

ADD I'd say more to buy. Not at Prospect – that was more of a group of galleries, where everyone had his own space. There were very few people who came there to buy. From the beginning, the Cologne Kunstmarkt was more a commercial event. For collectors, it was the first time they'd seen so many things together. Otherwise, they had to go from one city to another and those were long distances without a motorway. It was very important for Wide White Space to be represented there, although I've always had a lot of clients from the Rhineland, because Bernd is from Düsseldorf and we went there often. The Germans often went to the Belgian coast on holiday and passed through Antwerp. When they went to Paris or Amsterdam, they passed through here as well. In that sense, Antwerp is in a good location. England was isolated for a long time. It was a lot more complicated to get there. You had to take a four-hour boat trip.

SR *Did you go to the United States to see the galleries?*

ADD I went there only once while we had the gallery, in 1969. There wasn't really much trade with the American galleries. In New York we chose Weiner and James Lee Byars. Afterwards, we showed Nauman, but he'd always been seen at Konrad's and it was done through his intermediary. Sometimes we bought pieces, then we showed them and sold them, as we did with Flavin, for example. But we didn't work directly with him. We also had some Warhols. We tried to go to the Factory, but it never worked. It wasn't easy to get in there.

SR *You opened Wide White Space in 1966. Between 1973 and 1974 you had a kind of branch in Brussels in the commercial gallery Le Bailli. Can you tell me a little about that collective of galleries?*

ADD It was a Brussels gallery. It was Spillemaeckers who told me there were two of them in that gallery and that they did openings together. He asked us if we'd like to join them. I told myself that if they were doing things together, I had to be there; otherwise, I'd be forgotten. The rent was practically nothing, something like 5,000 fr. In those days, it was very easy to go regularly to Brussels. So I hired a space, then Paul Maenz came along a few months afterwards and also the Plus Kern gallery and the Galerie Oppenheim (Dadaism and Russian Constructivism). In the end there were seven or eight of us. For a year it went very well because we did all the openings together and lots of people came. Once, it was very funny, because while everyone was in this kind of big corridor, we stared papering the walls with big stripes by Buren. But Buren wasn't there and no one knew who'd ordered it. It was Daled, and at all his openings, the wall was papered in another colour. I took part in Le Bailli, but basically I lost a huge amount of energy in it. It didn't really bring much to the gallery. I sold a few pieces, but I would have sold them in Antwerp anyway. But I'd convinced myself I had to be there, because everything happens in Brussels and no one comes to Antwerp. But in the end it wasn't all that clever.

SR *All the galleries started more or less at the same time. Then they stopped a year and a half, or two years later.*

ADD At that time there was an economic crisis. We were selling hardly anything; it was disastrous. I remember that Bernd had been in Cologne in a kind of 'Galeriehaus', where there were four or five galleries together. They only turned on the light when a customer came into the gallery. They said that no one had been buying before, and that now they no longer even asked the prices. It was around 1974–75, after the oil crisis, and economically it was very hard. We left Brussels in 1974. We'd just bought a house in Antwerp and there were problems with building work. I was very tired, too.

SR *In May 1969 you took part in the opening of an institute of alternative art, A 379089 in Antwerp. Can you tell me about that initiative?*

ADD It was basically the inspiration of Byars, who did a lot of things in Belgium, especially happenings. He was living with us during that time. He was very good friends with people from Flemish television, who made a long documentary about him. Fiszman was very enthusiastic as well. Byars always told Fiszman that he wanted to set up a kind of institute. Fiszman wanted to set up a private museum, but Byars wanted to do an 'institute'. To cut a long story short, the idea came about at Filliou's opening in Mönchengladbach [June–July 1969]. There was Fiszman and Broodthaers, and people from Flemish television, particularly Jef Cornelis, who made very good films about contemporary art and also about the Documentas. A whole crowd of Belgians travelled to the opening. Kasper König was there. He was very young, 20 or 22, and he'd just come back from New York, where he'd been living for a few years. He couldn't make up his mind where in Europe to go and live. Then Fiszman suggested that he become the coordinator of this kind of new centre in Antwerp. Kasper thought it was a fantastic idea. I think Fiszman then phoned Peeters to tell him he had to participate in that project.

SR *Peeters was a Belgian private collector?*

ADD Dr Peeters lived in Bruges. He was older than us, and he mostly collected Pop. We knew him because he'd come to the gallery, but he thought it wasn't the same quality as the American artists. He had pieces by all the American artists, particularly some magnificent Warhols and some Segals that he'd bought at Sonnabend. Fiszman liked him, so he suggested that he come to Antwerp and get involved in his new centre. Instead, Peeters invited us all to Bruges, where there was a very big house with a garden. It was there that we set up A 379089 with about 15 other people. The first thing we did was to hire a space in Antwerp. There was an empty house not far from the gallery; someone phoned the owner to rent it.

SR *What happened in that institute?*

ADD The first thing that was organised was a big champagne breakfast to celebrate the moon landing in July 1969. We spent all night there watching television, and at about 4am we saw the astronauts coming down from their rocket. For the morning of the landing, Fiszman had hired a caterer and we'd set up some big tables. There were lots of artists from Antwerp, but from other cities as well. About 60 people were there to celebrate the moon landing. It was pretty crazy. It had nothing to do with art or criticism. Broodthaers was against it. He was anti-American and he thought going to the moon was pretty ridiculous. Later, Kasper invited three artists, Robin Page, Thomas Schmitt and Addi Koepke. They made objects in the spirit of Fluxus and they weren't very well known. Kasper said we'd send them an air ticket and they'd work on site. It was a completely new concept. It was summer, the heat was awful and they didn't do a thing. After three weeks, they figured they ought to get moving. They often went to a café called Amadou. They decided to continue what they'd been doing so far. So they installed the café in the space. They copied the sign and the tables, and invited people to come in and have a drink. König's girlfriend made soup and various kinds of food. You could eat and drink, but for free. So the institute's money disappeared at a terrible rate!

SR *How was the institute financed?*

ADD It was all financed by collectors, and other people who were in Bruges to see it being set up, who had agreed to give a certain sum per month. The collectors gave about 10,000 fr., and people like us between 1,000 and 2,000 fr. The total budget was 50,000 fr. per month. But given the speed with which people were invited, it wasn't working at all. It wasn't enough, and after a while there was a terrible hole in the budget. The third activity involved a musician, La Monte Young, who came to Antwerp. He couldn't make music without rugs, so they came to our house in search of Persian rugs. He and his wife sang for hours and hours; it was great. Afterwards there was no money left at all. König finally hung a list of all the outgoings on the front door so that people could see how much it really cost. Some of the founders thought it couldn't go on. König did it for six months and it all came to an end around the end of 1969, the beginning of 1970. Then Panamarenko said he wanted to become the coordinator of 'A'. He made his balloon, which didn't cost anything. He even changed the locks so that König couldn't get in, because König spent hours on the phone to the United States, and at that time it was very expensive. Panamarenko used it a bit like his studio. People could come in and talk to him, and so on. Afterwards, a group of people came, but they weren't artists and it was less interesting. They formed the basis of the Green Party. Still, König did show films by Warhol and by Jean Genet, things you couldn't see in other places.

SR *Would you say that in Belgium at the time, the main galleries for the avant-garde were MTL and Wide White Space?*

ADD Yes, absolutely. Plus Kern, too, but it was more provincial; the programme wasn't international.

SR *What was your relationship with Galerie MTL? Were you in contact?*

ADD *(hesitantly)* Sometimes it was OK and sometimes we were angry ... It wasn't easy, because there weren't many collectors. There was a rivalry, and we were in strong competition with each other. There was a huge row about the exhibition at the Musée Dhont-Dhaenens, which was played out in public in the papers. I thought that was completely out of order. We sent each other open letters. There was a whole business about that exhibition, which never took place in the end. There were documents, but no objects. So as far as I was concerned, it wasn't an exhibition. It was mostly Buren's fault; he was against Cadere and didn't want him to take part. But I can't remember exactly what happened in the end. Afterwards the collectors told me they'd been extremely embarrassed, because they didn't want to take sides with either of us. And they didn't know what the whole thing was based on and they didn't care. So they went abroad instead! I found that whole row completely idiotic.

SR *You opened Wide White Space in the middle of a period of anti-authoritarianism.*

ADD And particularly of euphoria. In 1966 it wasn't yet anti-authoritarian; later, yes, in 1968. We had a sense that everything was permitted. In Knokke there was an experimental festival where, for example, Yoko Ono stayed under a blanket for two hours, and films were shown that you couldn't show now, involving sex with animals. We saw all kinds of things! That didn't really exist afterwards.

SR *To what extent was politics important for you at that time? Did that influence your way of managing the gallery?*

ADD I've always stayed on the visual art side. I don't understand anything about the scheming in politics, and politics is all about scheming. I thought you had to be on the left; all the artists were on the left. For me, coming from a very traditional background, that wasn't easy. Nor for Bernd. We both come from very Catholic families. We weren't in favour of Communism, but we were in favour of Socialism.

SR *Nonetheless, some of the gallery's artists, like Buren, Broodthaers or Beuys, were very strongly committed politically.*

ADD Yes, but Beuys was very different. Broodthaers was suspicious of Beuys. I didn't understand it at all at the time; I do a bit better now. I thought Beuys had very good ideas. He wanted something new, but so mystical that other artists were clearly frightened of him. He also had so much charisma – he had a kind of power over people. That's dangerous! Beuys wasn't yet talking about politics in 1966. That came later, in about 1968–69. Every year was very different. For me, 1966 is very different from 1968. It was then that Broodthaers started getting suspicious of him. I thought people like Broodthaers and Buren were right.

SR *You said in the catalogue devoted to Wide White Space that you wanted anti-authoritarian change. Did you mean the authority of the art world and its established structures?*

ADD It was on every level. At that time, we'd just become parents and it was something that interested us greatly. In Germany, people on the left had created all kinds of communitarian structures into which they placed their children. There were very few places in official nurseries. That way, mothers and fathers looked after between 15 and 20 children. The children could do absolutely anything; the parents didn't intervene, unless it became very dangerous. You saw naked children sprawling on the ground, hurting themselves and so on. They thought that children should regulate themselves. We were very interested in all that. There was also the authority of the museums, the museum directors. Artists wanted to have their say about these structures. In 1968 the artists occupied museums like the Palais des Beaux-Arts in Brussels. They wanted to intervene in the choice of programmes and exhibitions, and so on.

SR *In the gallery, did you have a sense of supporting artists who challenged that artistic authority?*

ADD Yes, they all did. Broodthaers very strongly, Filliou as well. It was an obvious and natural thing at that moment. I think people today don't realise how much the idea of authority is impressed on us in our education. You had to be quiet, you had to listen, be polite and so on. When someone was older or had a higher position, you could never speak freely or say what you wanted. It was a terrible burden. If you spoke to someone higher up or older as one equal to another, you were being really rude. You had to listen and very cautiously try to say something, or else you were sent away.

SR *So there was a common desire among gallery owners and artists to find a different way of operating?*

ADD Yes, absolutely. Lots of artists, like Weiner and Kienholz, tried to change the art market. Kienholz did an exhibition of a series of watercolours [May–June

1970]. On the first he wrote 'For one dollar', then 'For two dollars', 'For three dollars' and so on. The exhibition had about 30 watercolours, each of which cost one dollar more. He also put his thumbprint on each. Then he carried on in that direction and we put on an exhibition with a hundred watercolours, a whole wall. People were still buying, but for a hundred dollars. It was always the same thing, and always more expensive. It was showing how the art world worked. Broodthaers also did a lot of things with his initials, 'M.B.', and finally sold his signatures.

SR *Creating works of art, even ones that question the art world, is still creating objects that have a value and will be sold on the market. Isn't that playing the game of the art world you're trying to criticise?*

ADD Yes, they tried, but they didn't succeed. Siegelaub tried to impose a contract to protect artists. But most of the artists themselves wanted nothing to do with it. For example, at his first exhibition, Buren had stuck up his papers, then said we had to do a price list. I asked him if it was for sale. If anyone wanted an intervention at their own house it would be done for a fixed sum, whether it was big or small. It was like a kind of fee. Weiner asked about 1,000 dollars for a medium-sized work. It stayed at 1,000 dollars for a long time; then it was 1,200 or 1,500. But for each phase, it was the same price, whether it was big or small. But obviously you can't escape the art market.

Artists tried to counter the art market with multiples, too. The multiples ended up increasing in price, but not in the same way as the original works. At first, people were very frightened of multiples; they thought they had no value. In the end, artists have never managed to change the market. Often in museums, artists now are paid to put on an exhibition. That does take a lot of work. In the 1960s, an artist didn't even get his expenses paid. He had to be happy to be shown in a museum. Still, much of that has changed to the artist's advantage. It's always difficult for an artist to live off his art, unless he's very well known. It's very hard to resist money and fame. An artist can say to himself that another artist's works have been sold at a particular price, and he has to sell for at least the same price, because he's just as good, and so on. That's how prices are set, by comparison. The price of a work of art is never set in relation to the production costs or the hours put in. That's pointless.

SR *That's also something that distinguished you from earlier galleries. The artists came and created directly in the gallery.*

ADD Yes, absolutely. Also, it was always the artist who decided. Previously, the gallery went to the studio and made the choice of works. The artist didn't have much say in the matter. We've always been able to allow the artist to act. There were also artists who brought pieces, like Richter. The set-up of the exhibition was done together with the artist. Someone like Beuys did it all by himself, but there wasn't much to do. Once he did a performance and he wanted to put his drawings on the windowsills, not on the walls. So there wasn't very much work. The important thing was that the artists were invited to a gallery and they could do what they wanted, even if it wasn't saleable. At that time, we learned that basically everything is saleable, even a phrase, even a piece of clothing worn during a performance. There was adventure, too. As a gallery, you had no idea what the artist was going to do and what you were going to do with his work.

SR *Most collectors in Belgium, and the gallery owners too, tended to come from Flanders. What do you think about that?*

ADD Yes, especially at that time. I think it was a cultural question. A lot of things were happening in Germany, especially in the Rhineland, and the Flemish were able to go there easily. They very quickly felt at home. It was a lot harder for the French speakers, because they didn't speak German. They tended to go to Paris. But at the time the most interesting things were happening in Düsseldorf and Cologne. That was why Broodthaers settled down there. People in the art world tended to speak German and English, and the Flemish often speak more languages.

SR *It's also interesting to note that most of the European gallery owners who opened galleries in New York in the 1970s were of German origin.*

ADD Yes, one of the first was René Block. He was very isolated in Berlin [1964–79], behind the wall. He was the first to show Beuys in the States with the performances of *Coyote* [May 1974]. The Germans were the hardest workers and the most organised. The rhythm of work in America was different from that in Europe. The Germans were also heavily influenced by the postwar American occupation.

SR *Have you ever regretted giving up the gallery?*

ADD Sometimes yes, when I see a good exhibition. But it was a complicated life. Bernd, as an artist, couldn't bear it at all. He showed people to the door when they asked stupid questions. We always made our decisions about the gallery together because he has a very good eye. But later I thought maybe I should have found another partner. If I'd found a good collaborator I could have gone on. But that didn't happen.

Translation from French: Shaun Whiteside

4.4 Conversation with Jan Dibbets

Amsterdam, 28 April 2005

SOPHIE RICHARD *Could we start our discussion by talking about your first show with Konrad Fischer in 1968?*

JAN DIBBETS If I'd never shown with Konrad Fischer, it wouldn't have changed my work. But all my life would have probably been spent teaching. You might find a young genius in music or poetry; sometimes someone writes beautiful poetry at 15 or 16 – that happens. But in art, that doesn't exist. The only exception I've seen in my whole life is Richard Long, who knew at the age of 23 exactly what he wanted. But there you see that a person who's already so secure at such a young age is doomed to stick with his thing. It's almost like autism. I don't mean to say that Richard Long is autistic, but it's clear that in general things develop from age 25 on. That's the age that you can begin to speak about authentic work. Indeed, between 25 and 26, that's the time I turned away from doing paintings. They were already totally minimal and monochromic. It was the same for Lawrence Weiner and for many other artists. That's the dead end, and then you realise: 'There's nothing for me in painting.' What can you do after monochrome painting? There were already Robert Ryman's white paintings; you can't do a red painting – that's ridiculous. So the feeling was very strong that there were many more possibilities in art if you could move away from painting. It wasn't so much a general feeling, but it was a belief among those artists who'd accepted the idea that they wanted to be radical. My last paintings were just stacks of white canvases. What can you do after that? From that point on, a lot of things happened. There'd been an exhibition in 1967 in September, organised by Paul Maenz ...

SR *The* Dies alles Herzchen *exhibition?*

JD Yes, *Dies alles Herzchen wird einmal dir gehören.* That exhibition was ahead of all the others of that type. It was the first of the first. I knew Paul Maenz, because of the *Serielle Formationen* show. That was the sort of thing many artists were doing in 1965–66.

SR *How did you meet Paul Maenz?*

JD I was hitchhiking and Paul Maenz and a friend picked me up and they took me to Cologne. We started to speak in the car. They knew about my work, strangely enough. They were very much into these *Serielle Formationen*. That was in 1965 and they made that exhibition in 1966 or early 1967, and I participated in it. So I went to see them in Frankfurt and I said that I had a grant to go to England. They came to see me when I was in England. I told them that I'd met a few people who were doing quite interesting things and that there was a total change in mentality, something totally new in the air. Paul Maenz decided to make an exhibition from that information. I'd choose the English artists and he'd choose some German artists. And that was that exhibition, which was planned just for one evening. It was something brand new and particularly interesting because part of it came from London. Paul Maenz made this possible. It was the first time that Richard Long showed. George was invited, although he was not yet with Gilbert. There were Barry Flanagan, Konrad Fischer and Gerry Schum. And some others: Konrad Fischer was there under his artist name Konrad Lueg. He told me at the exhibition that he was very interested in what he saw and asked if I knew more about all this. He also told me that evening that he was going to open a gallery. He asked me if I wanted to show, if I had the address of Richard Long and that he wanted to go to England to meet him. I advised him to go to see George (Pasmore) too. Gerry Schum decided that evening to stop filming for the WDR and to start working only with artists. So all these decisions were made that evening. There was already something in the air. Later on, Konrad Fischer had a great gallery; Paul Maenz had a great gallery; Schum gained influence later with his 'videogallery'. All these interconnections were there that evening. From then on, something started to grow. I think you can't overestimate the importance of that small show: that's where it all came from. If it hadn't happened, it would probably have taken much longer to bring this attitude to light. Konrad Fischer wouldn't have been aware of anything, except from what he knew in America. He had Hanne Darboven, Carl Andre and Sol LeWitt.

SR *Did you meet Konrad Fischer at that show?*

JD Yes, while he was still an artist. That was in September 1967.

SR *The fact that you went to Germany and to London, did that convince you even more to turn away from painting and to do other things?*

JD I'd stopped painting before. Strangely enough, although I'd stopped, I wasn't desperate about not knowing what to do. I couldn't care less. I'd fulfilled my idea about painting, which I'd always greatly admired. So it was very good for me to go to London, because it was very avant-garde at that moment. I came from a small provincial town, so my contacts were non-existent. Holland had nothing to offer, except for, let's say Ad Dekkers. But that was it. I knew Ad Dekkers, that was all.

SR *It was quite conservative.*

JD Yes, it was called 'modern'. I thought it was ridiculous. I could not find any roots in Holland. That means that you're very open to other things. I came to St Martin's, but not to study, because I knew what I was looking for. I'd finished art school years before, but I had to register at an art school in order to get my grant. For that reason, I went to St Martin's to see what was going on, especially the sculpture class, which was run by Anthony Caro. It was an extra year that you could do after you'd finished. It was uninteresting. They were all doing Caros and classical polyester bubbles, typical of that period, full of colours: green, yellow ... The only one who immediately made an impression on me was George, because he was the only one who did nothing. He was always reading smelly books, already dressed as he is now. He was reading smelly, humid books from the basement. His clothes had a mothball smell. He did two things that impressed me enormously. One morning Caro came and he said to George: 'You haven't done anything yet? Next time, you must have a sculpture.' – 'Yes sir.' You have to understand that the respect for Caro was already zero. For my part, it was absolutely ridiculous. All these sculptors who'd surpassed new ideas – it was business as usual. George had exactly the same ideas. So he said: 'Next week I'll have a sculpture.' The following week, on Thursday at 11 o'clock' – that was the time Caro came in – George was there at a quarter to 11 and there was nothing there. In a little corner, he had a little table for himself and a chair. He put a piece of blue plastic fabric (what they use for gardens and balconies) on his table. The moment Caro came to his table, George took out of his pocket three little boats, which you got round the corner from a Greek ice-cream shop. From the other pocket he took a little piece of paper, which said 'The Sea'! [*Laughs*] Caro came and got very angry: 'This is ridiculous! You're making a fool of yourself and you're trying to make a fool of me. But you can't fool me. Next time you come up with something more serious.' The next week, just before Caro came in, he had a plate of glass on which there were two flows of plaster, two wide circles. He made a little more plaster and put it on top of the circles. So there were two little bubbles. When Caro came in, he got a little tube of paint, took a brush and painted the two bubbles yellow! It was called *The Eggs*. [*Laughs*]. That was the end of Caro teaching George, of course. At the time it made an enormous impression on me: somebody not just making fun of his teacher, but also doing something very serious. I learned a lot from that. The teacher failed desperately to understand, or didn't want to understand, what was done there.

SR *So it was after being in London that you participated in the* Dies alles Herzchen *exhibition?*

JD Yes.

SR *What kind of work did you show?*

JD The exhibition was held at a farm outside of Frankfurt. At the entrance there was an external open space which was surrounded by stables. It was quite big; let's say about 40 by 40 metres. I put sawdust all over that space and I made an enormous oval by cleaning the space. Like this [*pointing at the big oval table*]. If you came in, you saw a circle that wasn't a circle. It was like a *Perspective Correction* actually, but it was just that the whole space went like this because the circle wasn't the circle that you expected. If you came in from a distance, you saw a circle, but it wasn't a circle in perspective. That means that the whole thing made you visibly insecure: you don't recognise an ellipse, you recognise a circle. You reconstruct the circle and then you see the whole thing. So that was the thing you saw, when you were entering that outside space. That was my sculpture. The oval was 12 by 6.5 metres.

SR *Was that the first time you publicly exhibited this kind of new work?*

JD Yes. That was the beginning.

SR *After that you had your first show at Konrad Fischer.*

JD That was in 1968.

SR *Could you talk about that show?*

JD That was actually confusing because I had a grass roll, which was about 2 by 2 metres, in a corner. In diagonal it was this wide [*showing the width with his hands*]. I'd made sculptures of wood with neon in them. I had one *Perspective Correction*. I could have done a whole exhibition of *Perspective Corrections*, but I decided not to do it with Konrad. But actually, many, many years later, I thought that was a mistake. You always learn from your mistakes. I should have done what I thought I should have done: just *Perspective Corrections*. But Konrad thought the other thing was more interesting. After that, the shows became more precise. In 1969, I was already using shadows etc.

SR *From that moment on, your work was shown in a network of galleries: Art & Project, Yvon Lambert, Françoise Lambert, Sperone,* MTL, *Jack Wendler ...*

JD Yes. You have to see it happening from this point: the moment Konrad Fischer turned up. That was at the same moment that there was this big change in art. 1968 was, with the student revolt, absolutely radical. In 1967 it was already bubbling, but it was in 1968 that the explosion happened. Everything became clear. The thing was there were very few people who created this explosion. Now it seems so clear when you look back. It was very simple: everybody knew everybody; there were only 25 people. It turned out that these 25 people could change things much more than anybody had ever expected – this chain of people who understood that a big change was taking place. Since nobody helped these people, they helped each other. It was that simple. [*Laughs*]

SR *It seems to have been a small group of people who stuck together.*

JD Yes. It's like when I went to New York in 1969. I'd met Harald Szeemann just before, in early 1968, because he was in Amsterdam to organise a show on Dutch art at the Bern Kunsthalle. This was long before he made the exhibition *When Attitudes Become Form*. He was doing an exhibition on Dutch art. I was, of course, not on the list of important Dutch artists, because they didn't understand what I was doing. Lucassen, a Dutch painter, who was a friend of mine, at that time had a studio next to mine. He didn't speak English. So he came to me, I think at the beginning of 1967, and he said: 'Could you translate something for me? There's someone from a museum in Switzerland, but I don't understand what this person is saying to me. That person told me I got this list of artists from the Stedelijk Museum. I should see their work. Could you explain when I ask questions, what he replies, etc?' I said: 'OK, no problem.' Just out of sheer politeness, I think, just to be kind, he said to me: 'Can I see your studio?' I took him to my studio next door where I had a grass and neon table. On the wall there was a big square of a *Perspective Correction*. He didn't say a word for 20 minutes at least. Then he looked at me and asked: 'Do you know other people who are doing work like this?' I said: 'Yes, I know people.' I told him about Ger van Elk and so on. He said: 'You're in the show. I'll phone you tonight. I need the address of these two other artists.' I said: 'One lives outside Amsterdam, the other lives in Amsterdam.' He phoned me later that day and said: 'I've seen their work. The most interesting room in the museum is the entrance hall. That's for the three of you.' This, of course, changed the way curators like Wim Beeren saw Dutch artists. Szeemann turned it all explicitly upside down, because he suddenly realised that he could deal with far more interesting artists, when he did not just do what they told him to do. That's also the beginning of the network. That's in Szeemann's notes on his exhibition *When Attitudes Become Form*, where he writes that it all started from a visit to the studio of Jan Dibbets.

SR *That's in his diary?*

JD Yes, it is. It's interesting because there you see how these little incidents change things. But then something happened that you absolutely won't know about. I came back from London to Enschede, before I moved to Amsterdam. Around that time, Wim Beeren came to Enschede to see a sculptor who was living in the same house that I was living in. He invited him for an exhibition. This person, who had no idea what to do, and was informed about modern sculpture by me. He could make anything, but he had no ideas. Beeren was very enthusiastic about his sculptures and he gave him an exhibition. The artist said: 'Upstairs is an artist who's very interesting, maybe you should see his work. It's Jan Dibbets.' – 'Oh yes, I know Jan Dibbets and his work at Galerie Swart.' – 'No, he's making something totally different. He went to London and came back with totally new works'. So Beeren went upstairs and saw the *Perspective Corrections*. I showed him sand sculptures, which I'd made at the beach, and the pieces of grass, which were from 1967. He laughed and said: 'Oh, you're crazy!' That was his mistake. But the thing is that from that moment, he never could forgive me for the fact that he laughed at me. He became a very good friend of Ger van Elk, and he tried to keep me out of exhibitions or of purchases. De Wilde, (the Director of the Stedelijk Museum at that time) said all the time: 'But I like his work!' but he kept saying no. Then something very interesting happened. I spoke with Ger van Elk: 'You have a very good contact with Wim Beeren. I have a very good contact with Harald Szeemann. If you go to Wim Beeren and explain that making an exhibition on this new art in his museum, he would be the first one ever in the world and it would be very prestigious for him. I'll do the same with Harald Szeemann. Then we'll see what happens.' They were very good friends, Szeemann and Beeren. So, I spoke to Szeemann about this exhibition and he was very enthusiastic. He came to Holland. I was in Arnhem with Ger van Elk. I remember that evening very well. As we were talking, the three of us, we convinced him that an exhibition like that would be easy to do. He said: 'I'm going to do this.' We gave him names, told him where to travel, where to go, etc. Ger van Elk did the same with Wim Beeren, who thought it was a great idea. He started his *Op Losse Schroeven*. And there you have these two friends who travelled the world, visiting the same studios, and none of the artists said: 'Yesterday there was somebody here with the same idea.' Nobody! It was a miracle that they didn't know. By the time the shows were totally set, it turned out that they'd both planned the opening for the same day. An enormous quarrel erupted between the two, about who was the first person to have thought about that exhibition. So it turned into a fight between those two prestigious people! So you see how things can speed up in no time.

SR *1969 is also the year when you did your* Project for Art & Project. *The work that later on had been shown in the* Conceptual Documents *show that Catherine Moseley organised in Norwich.*

JD Yes, it was in the Norwich show. The work was really about networks. It was the network of contacts worldwide. The show was four maps: Amsterdam, the Netherlands, Europe, and the World. People were asked to return the invitation to Art & Project gallery and every answer was indicated on one of the maps. There were quite a lot of lines.

SR *Which gallery do you feel helped you most to develop your work in the late 1960s, early 1970s?*

JD For me *the* gallery was Konrad Fischer. The gallery that made the most money was Sperone. Sperone was the Seller and Fischer was the Thinker. Sperone was the businessman. Fischer never liked business at all. Sperone had a lot of collectors whom he convinced that that sort of art was the thing to buy. A lot of Italians at that time bought that sort of art. I think these were the two most important galleries at that time.

SR *There were also some Dutch collectors who bought your work, like the Vissers or the Van Eelens.*

JD Not the Vissers. They bought just two works of mine, I think. They had these meetings on Sundays where people came and had a coffee or whatever. They invited me several times and I never went. I made a work for them *Merwede* [1970], which is now at the Kröller-Müller Museum. She liked it and he didn't like it. He told me that he didn't like it. That was the end of the collecting, as you'll understand. I always felt – and I still do – that you shouldn't get involved in your own country. I live here, because I have nothing to do with Holland. If I'd been too much involved in the Dutch art scene, it would have paralysed me. I try to keep as great a distance as possible. That's why I was happy that it didn't work out with the Vissers. And it's also the same reason why I quit Art & Project in 1975. I still think it was wise to do that. There's a lot of my work in museums in Holland, but privately there are maybe fewer than ten people who have a work of mine.

SR *Why was it important to keep a distance from Holland?*

JD If you live in Holland, it becomes quickly very homey.

SR *I know that from Luxembourg.*

JD Yes, I think Luxembourg would be the ideal place to live, and not to deal with anybody. For that reason I bought this place in Amsterdam. My home is my castle. And by the way, part of the year we live in Italy. On a certain moment you know all the museums, the art world is very small. With my students, whether they're in Amsterdam or in Düsseldorf, it's always the same: they say, 'I spoke to this person, he's got an exhibition there, this person is opening a little gallery, etc.' They're obsessed with exhibitions and becoming world famous. I always tell them: 'You have to keep one thing in mind: every minute there are exhibition openings, in Tokyo, in Milan, or Rome or Madrid or Barcelona, Palermo, Athens, Brussels, London, Edinburgh ... If you start to think about this, you get so nervous that you can't even think about any small gallery. Either you do fantastic work and they'll pick you up, even if you have nothing to do with them, or you'll do the wrong work and it will never happen. So, that's the choice you have.'

SR *Why do you think that the public collections and museums in Eindhoven and in Amsterdam, even early on, were quite open to your work, whereas private collections weren't? The museum in Amsterdam bought at least 20 or 25 works by you in the 1970s, which is huge.*

JD Yes, they bought a lot. If it was something new, De Wilde bought. Rudi Fuchs did the same. Why was that? We have a long tradition in our museums of buying avant-garde work. It doesn't happen too often that you have something in your country that you seriously consider avant-garde. Another reason for sure is that a certain amount of the budget had to be used to buy Dutch art. It's that simple.

SR *Dutch museums, in comparison to the Tate or to museums in Switzerland or Germany, bought a lot of Conceptual artworks. In the 1970s, the Dutch museums were very open to this new art.*

JD That's what I'm saying. It's a consequence of the *Op Losse Schroeven* exhibition. Another consequence is Harald Szeemann's *When Attitudes Become Form* and the Documenta of 1972. It was just like exploding bombs, so it kept going on. This didn't happen for Pop art or for Minimal art. It's specific to Conceptual art, just as it happened to Dada. That also exploded in everybody's face. It exploded and then it went away, but it had an enormous influence.

SR *In 1970–71, you had two major one-man shows in Eindhoven and Amsterdam. That was also quite important.*

JD Yes. It was a very exciting time, but it also became quickly very heavy. There were not only museums but also the pressure of galleries like Konrad Fischer, Art & Project, who had the same program, MTL in Brussels, Yvon Lambert in Paris, Sperone in Turin and Bykert in New York.

SR *So Art & Project and Konrad Fischer were in competition?*

JD No, Fischer was so much stronger, he was more helpful to them.

SR *How was the situation in America as compared to Europe in your experience?*

JD I had a show with Bykert in New York in 1972. That was a very interesting show and there was a piece that I think is still one of my favourites. There was a beautiful space, about five by eight metres I guess, that was the main room of the gallery. Behind this space, there was a little corridor. I had a film that was called *Venetian Blinds*. (The work is from 1971). The projector should not be in the main space, so we made a hole in the wall. The room was completely dark, with a projection on the wall showing a window with opening and closing blinds. What I found out is that if you project a completely black image, then before you can see it, you see this grey surface on the wall. It takes two little pins before this starts to show up in your eyes, before your eyes adjust to the dark. The loop was from opening the blinds to closing them. So you see a bit of light, stripes, and then the room lights up. And it was like in a dream. It was an incredible sensation. It was really about asking what is an image, what is a film, what is a loop? It was a reason for me to immediately stop making films, because I thought this was *the* film. There's no better idea than the image representing what it really is and doing what it's made for: the notion of light, the ray of light. What happened was really there but, at the same time, it was not real because it was a film. That was an exhibition, which nobody understood at the time. It was a non-success in New York. For people, there was nothing to see. Maybe there was also one *Perspective Correction*, I don't remember

SR *Was this your first trip to New York?*

JD No, I'd been there before. I was already friends with Robert Ryman and Sol LeWitt. I went there in 1968 for the first time. I went in 1969 twice and in 1970, two or three times.

SR *What was your impression of the art world on you first trip, in comparison to the European art world?*

JD Well, I realised that nothing of what we're speaking about was to be found there. Minimal art was getting a certain recognition. The main art was the same as here. Here was Cobra, there was something else, but the same. It wasn't so different. There were only a few artists who were doing something else, and I knew them.

SR *Because they were showing in Europe?*

JD Yes, they were in Europe too: Ryman, Robert Mangold, Carl Andre, Sol LeWitt, Donald Judd ... Nauman didn't live in New York. There were Conceptual artists like Weiner, Kosuth and Barry. But in New York you hardly could see their work, before they joined with Leo Castelli like I did too in 1973.

SR *So when you travelled there it was more to see those artists who were your friends?*

JD Yes, that's the reason I went. And to see what was going on or what could be done, or to see an exhibition or discuss a piece that somebody wanted me to make for a group show. For a European there wasn't so much to do since art markets are very chauvinistic. I always say, it's about a thousand times more difficult for an artist from Luxembourg (I always say Luxembourg, as the smallest country in Europe) to become a world-famous artist. He really has to be a genius to make it, in comparison to a person from America. Because the one from America is supported by 250 million people and the one from Luxembourg by 400,000. The problem is that they have no economic entity behind them. In Europe, everything is divided, so who should be considered the best artist in Europe, a German or an

English or a French artist. American artists are for that reason in the better situation.

SR *You also participated in the Project Class, organised by David Askevold at the Nova Scotia College of Art and Design, Halifax, in 1970. Could you talk about your experience there?*

JD I think I was there for two months. The teaching in the Project Class was very different from that in the other classes. There was no painting there, of course. The people who did the Project Class were into Conceptual art. David Askevold and Richard John headed the course. I remember, for example, that I took the students on a trip, and the trip was the work of art for everybody. We'd started by thinking about what we could do as a work of art. So I said: '25 of us will go on a trip for five days. We won't know where we're going and we'll see what happens. Everybody will think about himself and register what he does. Later, we'll make an exhibition about all the things we created during the trip.' That's the sort of thing we did. The work that I did during the trip was a photograph of me sitting on the train from Halifax to Toronto every hour. That's quite a long train ride – terribly long. Somebody had to take a photograph of me sitting in the train every hour. That meant that during the night somebody had to get up. I had a clock on top of my head, which rang every hour. So you have photographs of me like that [*makes funny faces*]. It starts at the station in Halifax with the clock and then you have photographs for every hour. The other work was postcards of landscapes grouped together. I gave everybody a blank postcard with the school's address. So everybody had to mail one card from wherever they wanted. The postcards were all put together in the end. That was the work. It was that kind of thing. They saw what you did and you saw what they did and everybody could compare. It was quite an interesting situation there, actually.

SR *So it was basically a course where foreign artists would come and teach for several months?*

JD It wasn't even teaching, I'd say. It was like I was young, they were young, and we were doing all sorts of things together.

SR *Were the students mostly Canadians?*

JD I have no idea. It's so long ago. It was probably mostly Canadians. It was famous in the art world, but when you're a young student you don't know the art world. Probably, they were the students who didn't want to do painting anymore. Probably at that time it involved the more interesting and intelligent students.

SR *You often use the term 'Conceptual art'. Would you consider yourself a Conceptual artist?*

JD No, no ... I use it as an easy vehicle, but I don't feel at all part of Conceptual art.

SR *It's difficult to find an appropriate term.*

JD To make it easy, we say Conceptual art. But I think there's much more to it than concepts. I must say, strongly, that Concept art has moved away from what it claimed to be. People like Joseph Kosuth or Weiner – I've had conflicts with them about the presentation of art. For example the *Konzept-Kunst* exhibition that Konrad Fischer organised in Kunstmuseum Basel in 1972, with that yellow catalogue. Lawrence Weiner, Hanne Darboven, etc., had convinced Fischer to make a catalogue with no pictures in it. That had never been done before – just texts. It was a real hardcore Conceptual art exhibition. I said to Konrad: 'If I have to make a statement in this catalogue, you have to allow me to have a colour photograph reproduced.' Black and white photography was considered serious at the time, but colour photography was considered dull. Black and white photography was considered the newest of the new ways to make art; colour was considered kitsch. Anyway, I said to Konrad that I wanted a colour photograph. That wasn't done: it was a statement because it was visual – you could see it. Konrad said: 'Well, if I tell them this, they'll explode. Let's see what happens. I'll tell them, because I can't do it without saying a word. But at the same time, I promise you that you'll be the only one to get a colour photograph. What the others will do, I don't know.' Well, the moment Konrad told them that I wanted to have a colour photograph in the catalogue, everybody wanted to have one. There was this incredible clash and discussion, especially with Weiner and Kosuth, about how the work should be presented. Kosuth thought that he could make a blow-up and that was it – the photograph. But Weiner thought that it was all bullshit, that there was only one way – the way he did it: take a piece of paper and write a concept – or type it, which is even more anonymous – and put it on the wall. I said that I disagreed completely, because the artist has the responsibility to visualise what he wants to say. Weiner made an exhibition in the Stedelijk Museum in 1997 or 1999, and he'd already moved so far from that position that the whole museum, to my total amazement, was yellow walls with red letters, and circles on the floor with green letters. I couldn't believe my eyes! I said: 'Lawrence, you're the man who's against presentation.

You're showing off your concepts from 1967 to 1970. You're changing history. You're making fashionable art.' He got so fed up. The same happened to Daniel Buren: the switch of an idea that's said to be extremely consequential. But in fact, there is no consequence. That's the strange thing.

SR *In an interview with Catherine Moseley, you said: 'If there is a period which is very extrovert, you can be sure that underneath, the art will become more hidden and introvert.' Could you develop that idea a bit?*

JD The art reacts to the society, just as it reacts to what was created beforehand. My main idea not to paint anymore came from the idea that everything was Cobra. The next thing that I admired was monochrome painting. So there was no space for me. Everything is a reaction to something, what to do? That means that you also react to society. Art reflects society. It puts a mirror in front of society in a way society doesn't want to see itself. Society doesn't have a place without art. It's art that gives a face to society. Whether you think about Greek art or Roman art or the art of the sixteenth or eighteenth centuries, you have an idea about those societies because of their art, the buildings, the tables etc. You have an idea from what you see (art), hear (music), read (literature) and from buildings (architecture).

SR *But in a period like the late 1960s, which was very political, the art from that period isn't political.*

JD No. In my opinion, the only political artist at that time was Hans Haacke. That was very boring. There was an issue in the early 1970s with Lucy Lippard and the women's liberation movement. There were a lot of people who were pressing the artists to be more politically involved. I remember talking with Ryman and LeWitt about that. We thought that was total bullshit. You could be against the war, you could donate a work to support something, but to involve your work in the war or political ideas or women's lib, that was totally crazy. Because that doesn't reflect anything; or that's too direct a reflection. What the mirror shows isn't what you want to see. It's difficult to involve politics in art. That's a one-to-one situation. That's flat; there are no dimensions, no future, no perspective.

SR *Still, I suppose that you were at least discussing political issues with other artists and dealers? You were meeting regularly and had to discuss something.*

JD Yes, but we didn't speak about that sort of thing.

SR *It was more about art?*

JD Well, with Konrad Fischer, you couldn't speak two serious words. That doesn't mean that he wasn't a serious person. He was extremely serious, severe and precise. If you had that sort of political discussion, it was always due to fashion. It was something totally artificial. I think that's logical, because 'revolution' isn't planned. You can't speak about it unless you do something. What you do if you don't see yourself as revolutionary ... that comes later on.

4.5 Conversation with Rudi Fuchs

Amsterdam, 25 April 2005

SOPHIE RICHARD *The Stedelijk Museum in Amsterdam and the Stedelijk Van Abbemuseum in Eindhoven were the European museums that collected the most Conceptual work in Europe during the 1970s. How would you explain that? Do you think it has to do with budgets, or with a sort of open-minded situation in the Netherlands, or both?*

RUDI FUCHS I think it's the latter. I also think that in the late 1960s the Stedelijk collected following the exhibition *Op Losse Schroeven*. That was 1969. There were all these artists exhibiting there. It was usual for a museum to buy something from an exhibition. In Eindhoven, I think the collecting started somewhat later. I did that. Before me, they didn't really collect. That was late 1974.

SR *So you think there was an openness to the most up-to-date art?*

RF Yes. I think also, the budget was reasonable and Conceptual art was not expensive. The Tate and other museums at that time, for instance MOMA in New York, were much more traditional. In Germany it was the same thing. It seemed the natural thing to do, to buy these works. In Eindhoven, the building was very small and the collection never became very large. Apart from the Dutch art it had acquired, there were also works by Donald Judd and Robert Morris, Frank Stella and a beautiful Ellsworth Kelly painting. Then other artists of the time, like Lawrence Weiner, came along and were from roughly the same generation – although Judd, Morris and Andre, I think were a little older than Weiner – but they were the same group of people, the same galleries, the same bars, the same occasions where you met most of them, in Düsseldorf, in Basel, in Brussels, in Paris, in London. We travelled quite a lot at the time. There were small shows, mostly in galleries, that we went to. Düsseldorf was close by, it was an hour by car from Eindhoven. Brussels was close, Amsterdam too. So there were these openings of exhibitions that were completely different from now. To continue collecting in Eindhoven, after Judd or Andre or Stella, it seemed the logical thing to go to Conceptual art. There was a strong feeling, which I still have, that it was a very decisive movement in art, because of the redefinition of many things. The 'Conceptual' idea was very broad. It goes from Robert Ryman and Alan Charlton to Ian Wilson, from Bruce Nauman to LeWitt. Even if there are many differences between Minimal and Conceptual art, it redefined everything in art. Paintings like those of Baselitz would be impossible without the ideas of Conceptual art; the same goes for Gerhard Richter, of course. You could no longer just paint a picture after Conceptualism. It had to be motivated at some point. I compare it with the moment in Florence in the early fifteenth century when the Renaissance began. It was profound and also so simple. The entire conception of art, everywhere, was changed. We saw this happen with Conceptual art. I was thinking at the time, probably quite consciously, that we should collect it, because it was going to be very important.

SR *And also show it, because you did a lot of exhibitions of these artists.*

RF Yes. That came out of the same thing. I thought it was very important. I was in a position in this museum, in this country, to do it. Nobody asked me to explain why it was important.

SR *You didn't have trustees to whom you had to explain your choices?*

RF Yes I did. Their role was to basically approve the Director's choices. They *could* question what you did and so we talked. They had the same kind of interests. My most important trustees were Rudolf Oxenaar, the Director of the Kröller-Müller museum, and Martin Visser, the collector. Also there was much later Anton Herbert. Formally, they had to see if the price you paid was right. They had to check that you weren't paying too much money. So there was no problem. There was this idea that you should accept it. And of course, in the museum itself, we were very autonomous.

I've always found that when you're collecting with a focused interest, making an exhibition is the best way to check things out. It's the best way to find out how certain things work, what it could be. You put it to the test in a sense. And of course, I thought it was important to make all those things more public. There was this small museum in this provincial area, besieged by all these artists. I'd been an art critic for a newspaper before I joined the museum, and I'd met many people before.

SR *Where did you meet them?*

RF I met Jan Dibbets in the late 1960s and in 1972. I did the catalogue text for his Biennale show there in Venice. I also met Sol LeWitt and others. Lawrence Weiner had a boat in Amsterdam where he often stayed. Then there were the exhibitions at Art & Project. I was teaching at the University of Leiden and I was writing as a critic. So I also went to these shows. I went regularly to Konrad Fischer, to Spillemaeckers in Brussels, Wide White Space, to Paul Maenz in Cologne ...

SR *So you went to all this new generation of dealer galleries.*

RF Yes. Also Rolf Preisig in Basel.

SR *Do you have the impression that some of these dealer galleries were more important or more influential than others? For example, to set up the Conceptual art collection in Eindhoven, were there galleries with which you particularly collaborated?*

RF I think Fischer and Spillemaeckers were important. It depends ... At the time, there was no market, it had to be created. There was a market in the end. Very quickly, there were people who began to collect. These you knew as well: Herman Daled, Anton Herbert (that was later); then there were a few colleagues: Johannes Cladders, Jean-Christophe Ammann, Johannes Gachnang ... The artists were travelling all the time. The nice thing was that the works had to be made on the spot. They had no studios, except Ryman. Maybe Bruce Nauman had one. Bruce came to Europe only very rarely. He had this idea that the neon pieces he did with figures should be made from life-size drawings. So Konrad Fischer would take the large drawings and send them to a factory somewhere in Germany and have the figures made. But Nauman seldom came. There was this idea that art could be made by post. Eindhoven owned Nauman's *Driven Man, Driven Snow* [1976]. Nauman made drawings for his sculptures and he also made a drawing of how they should be placed in the room. He'd send that and they'd be made in Europe. I saw them at Konrad Fischer and I bought them for Eindhoven. There were two drawings: a large one for the disposition, which you could use as instructions, and a smaller one. The others were always there: Carl Andre, Sol LeWitt, Lawrence Weiner, Richard Long, Robert Barry, Daniel Buren ... They'd always be there for a week or more – contact with artists at work was quite intense.

Of the dealers, I think Konrad was the most important one, because he was the most artistic one. Fernand Spillemaeckers was also very important. But other galleries like Art & Project, eventually became fussy, formal – they became like dealers. Konrad was a good laugh. He was artistic; he'd been an artist. He was a player; he played the horses for money – his wife as well. That's how they made money – betting on horses. It was always an adventure in that sense. Fischer was never chic or fashionable. Now it's a little bit more chic, but it's still pretty much the same. Art started at home then. He was very good at doing all these things, producing things. I did that as well. Many shows we did were produced on the spot. It was nice to invent things with the artist. I was convinced it was a very important aspect of the art.

SR *It was a collaboration with the artist, rather than going to his studio and choosing works to exhibit in the museum.*

RF I went to some studios. I once went to Alan Charlton's studio, which was quite interesting because he had a place in the backyard where criminals would store stolen cars. [*Laughs*] I went to many studios. Also, when they came to Eindhoven, they mostly stayed at my house. I had a room and bathroom upstairs, and that's where many of them stayed.

SR *So you got to know them very well.*

RF Yes. Once, Michael Asher turned up at the station in Eindhoven. I was away. Michael was ill and he felt very bad. He had the flu or something. He was travelling in Europe. During his trip, he came to Eindhoven and called me from the station. He got my wife on the phone. This was 11 o'clock in the evening. She told him to take a taxi to come to us and she put him into bed. He was really ill, so he stayed for a few days. My daughter didn't know he was there as he'd come late in the evening. The next morning, she was there in the kitchen with a girlfriend before they went to school. He came down completely groggy and he asked for some milk. So she gave him milk and he stumbled back up the stairs. The girlfriend asked 'Who was that?' And my daughter said, 'Oh, I don't know. We call him Michael.' [*Laughs*] That's how it was.

SR *What about Ian Wilson?*

RF Ah, Ian Wilson! In Eindhoven, we have the world's largest collection of Ian Wilson! [*Laughs*]

SR *Exactly. You were also practically the only museum to organise his 'Discussions'.*

RF And to publish his books.

SR *Yes. So how did that came about?*

RF Ian Wilson is an extremely charming man. He's

Scottish, I think. He was a swimming champion at school. Very strong. I thought that Ian was the ultimate expression of Conceptual art. I think the best thing he did was the *Circle of Chalk*, one metre in diameter. In Eindhoven, I would pay a fee for a 'Discussion', and what we got was a piece of paper on which there was the date, a description of the discussion ... There were always slight differences. I think we had ten or 11. Then there were the little books he did. He made these books which are phrases or arguments. It gave me satisfaction to exhibit these. If this is serious art, you have to support it. We paid, I think, about 500 dollars at the time, plus expenses, which were always very low. He ate very little; he only drank tea. I was interested. It was outrageous in a sense, but on a very small scale. Then eventually, I think I made a room containing his works in the museum. He had this editor, who published his catalogues. At the time it cost nothing. It was beautiful and small.

On a large scale was the Michael Asher exhibition. In Eindhoven he worked on the glass ceilings. All the rooms were empty and he removed the plates of the glass ceiling. Because of that, it could really change the atmosphere. The light had changed; it was much more intense. The museum was 'empty' but full of strong light. The show was open for one month. There was 'nothing' to see. Not in one room, but the entire museum. These shows were major shows. In some cases, the first major show of an artist.

The dealers were important. They were important because their galleries were where the artists were working. Everybody was very nice. There was no fashion, no hype, no nothing. Nobody had any money. For an opening at a gallery like Fischer's, it would be on a Saturday afternoon, there'd be some people and we'd drink some beer – that's it. Later, we'd go to a cheap restaurant. It was a pleasant moment, because it wasn't about fashion, about hype, about who's the best one; it was very much about artists discussing each other's work. That's how they met, in a very different way from now. In a way, they still do, that generation. They have fewer shows, but they're still in touch with each other, Ryman, Nauman, LeWitt ... I'm in touch with them too.

SR *It was a group of friends.*

RF Yes.

SR *Did you work with other public institutions in Europe to organise exhibitions? Or did you work on your own in Eindhoven?*

RF We produced most things ourselves. But occasionally there were collaborations with the Kunsthalle in Basel, the Kunsthalle Bern, the Whitechapel Art Gallery in London, the Musée d'Art moderne de la Ville de Paris with Suzanne Pagé in France. That was a bit later, with the part of the museum called ARC, which is on the top floor of the building. I was called 'Arc-en-chiel' and I called them 'Suzanne et ses anges' [Suzanne and her angels]; there were four or five women working with her. I think the Lawrence Weiner exhibition, which was in 1975–76, went to Basel. The catalogue was translated into German. We did it because it was always nice to find another venue. So there was this small network.

People often ask why there was an interest in this kind of art in this country. I always thought it was because the Dutch like and are used to abstraction: De Stijl, Gerrit Rietveld, Mondrian, but also the contemporaries of Dibbets. Painters like Ad Dekkers, Peter Struycken, Jan Schornhoven. Abstraction was normal. Abstraction was seen as art in Holland, and taken more seriously than Expressionist art, especially in those years. I remember I wrote a review of a Karel Appel exhibition, I think, in 1972. I wrote that although Appel was a major painter, which he is, it wasn't interesting for art at that moment. Something that's abstract, that needs your mind, that brings a sort of discovery, that wasn't so unusual. It was much more unusual for the Germans or for countries like England. In England, I think, they always say that art is funny. There's a long tradition of visual art, as well as theatre. Museum art is serious, but modern painting is funny.

SR *So, in the Netherlands the public response to, for example, the Ian Wilson shows in Eindhoven was rather good?*

RF Yes. There was no complaining. People respected the museum. Of course, the other thing is that in those days, nobody asked how many visitors you got. We weren't counting.

SR *There was no pressure.*

RF For Eindhoven, it was very simple. It was a town where there was little: Philips, DAF cars and one museum. That was it. It was a town that people in the rest of the country laughed about. There was a small public, but there were people out there who knew about Eindhoven because of the museum. My predecessor Jan Leering also had the idea that this museum should be very special. To be special, it needed to be avant-garde at the time, outrageous in a sense.

Because doing shows of Cézanne was too expensive,

it was very simple: Conceptual art cost nothing. The entire Rückriem show, with the transport of the stones and the catalogue, cost 16,000 Guilders, which is maybe 7,000 Euros. It was very little. From a practical point of view, you could have a first-class programme with something new, never seen before. I was, and still am, completely convinced that this was a very important moment in art. For many, it doesn't yet have the importance of, let's say, early Picasso or early Da Vinci. But that will change. It takes time. You see beautiful things, but it takes time for people to understand – to see the beauty of an Alan Charlton painting, for instance. They have so many things to get out of their minds first. People always said they were all just grey. But each painting has a different grey.

SR *It's a kind of art that involves the participation of the viewer.*

RF Also, you need to believe in it. That's a very important element in art anyway, always. It's very easy to ridicule a cube by Sol LeWitt. It's always easy to ridicule art. Art is always fragile in that sense. So you need to believe. What's important is the idea of believing, of giving it credit, and pushing it to the extreme. There was nothing else. It wasn't beautiful in the sense that maybe you could find a painting by Gerhard Richter beautiful. But in the end, a Sol LeWitt is very beautiful. Although it can take years to see it. Also, when you get closer to these artists, you feel less embarrassed and more respectful. I remember writing that LeWitt had a very comical talent. It is very comical to take a piece of paper and to note that you have to do this and this and that. It's very funny, isn't it, if you think about it? I like the idea that he was funny. But at the same time, Sol is a very quiet and reticent person. In a way, he's very serious and also very funny.

SR *You've talked several times about your writings and articles. How did you get involved with* Studio International*?*

RF You don't decide these things. I was very happy that I worked on it, because it was a major magazine. What happened was that there was a critic called Barbara Reise. She was an American living in London. She was quite exuberant. She knew about Marcel Broodthaers and so on. I knew her through Jan Dibbets. I think she was on the Board of *Studio* or something like that. Anyway, when *The New Art* show was on in London, which Anne Seymour curated, they were looking for someone to review it. I can't remember why, but Peter Townsend, the Editor, called me and asked if I'd review it for them. He couldn't find an English critic; there was no one in England who could do it for some reason. Some were friends of the artists, perhaps. I was kind of distant. So I went to London to see the show. I stayed for four days and I wrote a review. That's it. I think that's how I got involved with them. Then I wrote a few other things for them, about Sol, Dibbets ... *Studio International* was eventually sold to somebody called Michael Spens, an architect.

SR *Was there an equivalent art magazine in the Netherlands?*

RF The only one was called *Museumsjournaal*. That's all there was, but it was interesting, because it was non-commercial. It was published by all the museums together. They were advertising their shows. It was also quite amateurish and had a very small circulation. It was in Dutch and had summaries of the articles in English, which is always pointless in the end. That's always a problem in this country. There are some serious writers, but no magazines. Also, I decided at some point that I should learn to write in English, because, there's never money for translations and no time. I've found that writing in English is not a big problem. There's some peculiarity for the readers, because they notice that someone isn't writing in their first language. It isn't wrong, just curious sometimes; it becomes nice. At first, the Editor-in-chief tried to correct it and rewrite it in proper English. But it didn't work. So they left me alone. So now I can write anywhere in the world.

There's another thing in Holland, apart from this interest in abstraction, out of the De Stijl tradition: there's also a tradition of being closed within yourself, in your own circle and of complaining about not being recognised by the outside world – blaming the outside world for not seeing the genius of the Dutch nation. The same happens in Belgium; it's always like that in small countries. It's very strong in Austria. There's a joke that says 'Who is avant-garde?' The answer: 'The first one who imitated it in Vienna.' [*Laughs.*] That's very true. So what happened in Holland was always low-key in a sense. We could never capitalise. We didn't know how to present the work, how to prophesise. In London they know how to do it; they are masters in that area. Tate Modern is a very traditional museum, but it has this ability; it's very spectacular. In Holland they think that the Tate is far beyond anything in the world. They think that the Tate is really up-to-date. So that's really about perception. A big country is special because it can create shivers by saying: 'The greatest thing on earth is this and that!' We could never say 'This is the greatest artwork'. We're raised in a context of modesty. You have to pretend. We have this discussion in Holland, where we all say that art here is quite plain and modest, and that one should go to England. But when people come over from London, they're surprised by what's out here and they like Dutch art. So on the level of art, it's quite different. But the critics here are convinced that Dutch art is very modest and that the real stuff is in London. Until it's somewhere else, which they'll find out ten years later.

Another thing in this country, and this is a weakness and a strength at the same time, is that there's no special feeling about foreignness, and at the same time, there's no idea of nation, of national art. In many other countries, where it's French art, German art, etc, it's the other way around. They say it's a legacy of the past. The merchants who went out into the world in the sixteenth century couldn't afford to make distinctions between the Turks and the Spanish, the Catholics, etc. They had to make money. So there's a kind of practical attitude towards nationality.

SR *Isn't the openness also to do with the important fact that there's a tradition of private collecting in the Netherlands?*

RF Not particularly. In Holland there are few collectors. Another thing is that the collectors aren't willing to go beyond a certain point. They get to a certain limit and then they stop collecting. So maybe they bought an early Sol LeWitt or an early Bruce Nauman, but at the time when Judd and Nauman pieces were fetching $200,000 or more, the museums stopped. We couldn't afford it. If you look at Eindhoven very carefully, you'll find that the collection consists of the early works of great artists. At that time, it was so cheap. There was one beautiful Kelly, and I remember we could not afford to continue with his art. So you'd never build on one artist. When you had two or three works by Carl Andre, you had to find something else, quite different, that could add to it and connect to it, which would be maybe a Dan Graham or a sculpture by Rückriem or something very different. When you haven't got much money, the collecting has to be more intelligent. I remember that we bought one painting by Robert Ryman, which was made of 11 or 12 small panels painted white, of course, on plastic sheets. I saw it in Rolf Preisig's gallery in Basel. It had been made for an exhibition organised by Yves Gevaert in Brussels. At that time, the Stedelijk already had quite a beautiful collection of paintings by Ryman, six or seven works. I'd thought it wasn't worth us buying another one. But then I saw this Ryman and I thought it was the perfect one, because it's the most conceptual; it's about making the same thing 12 times. It was very small, very conceptual and also serial in a sense. So it connected very well to Sol LeWitt and to other things in the collection. And of course, he was part of the movement. So you cannot have a Robert Ryman if you have all these other things. You need some kind of reference. I never bought another Ryman, but this one really functions. It's also very different from the ones in Amsterdam. I know why, De Wilde bought them because he has an eye for painting. De Wilde dislikes Conceptual art. He likes painting and he has this kind of sensual vision. The Rymans he selected are very pictorial, they have a physicality. Whereas the one I bought is this dry, conceptual thing. For De Wilde, that would be a bad Ryman. So it was perfect. That's how it went.

Rudi Fuchs would like it acknowledged that this transcript is the result of a very informal conversation.

4.6 Conversation with Charles Harrison

Banbury, 19 May 2003

SOPHIE RICHARD *How did you get involved in the* When Attitudes Become Form *exhibition that you curated for the Institute of Contemporary Arts (ICA) in London in 1969?*

CHARLES HARRISON Initially, I had proposed to the ICA an exhibition of English artists: Vic Burgin, Barry Flanagan, Bruce McLean, Roelof Louw and Richard Long. I arranged with the ICA that each of them would be paid a certain amount of money to install their work. The ICA was short of money at the time. They were offered the *Attitudes* show by Philip Morris, with some heavy sponsorship. The only problem was they didn't have a gap in the programme. So, I was called to the office of a guy (Harry Kissin) who was a sort of banker to the ICA, and he made me an offer. Instead of putting on the show of English artists, I could put on the *Attitudes* show. They would pay me the same money. At the beginning I refused, because I thought it was a disgraceful thing to do, to tell the artists their show had been cancelled. Kissin then told me that if I wouldn't do it, the ICA would cancel the show anyway. So, I talked to the artists concerned to see if they would accept for their work to be included in the *Attitudes* show. Part of the idea of this show was that it should change from venue to venue. Several of the English artists had been in the *Attitudes* show anyway – all but Burgin, I think. Finally, all the artists agreed to be included in the show. In fact, for most of them it was better to present their work in a more competitive setting. The condition was that they got paid the money they would have had anyway and got to install the work they'd planned.

Vic Burgin and Roelof Louw particularly had large pieces. The Vic Burgin piece was a 'photo-path' on the floor. Louw had a rope piece. That took up two large areas of the exhibition. Bruce McLean did a piece with sheets of painted paper on the floor. These were three artists who really had to be in the show. Richard Long didn't want to do anything particular for the show. He wanted to be represented by his work in Gerry Schum's *Land Art* film. Barry Flanagan had three large pieces in the show. So four of these artists were finally given very large spaces in the exhibition. I think, if I remember correctly, that I decided those areas first, then everything else was exhibited around them.

SR *Did you hear of the Bern* Attitudes *show before it came to London?*

CH I heard about it through Barry Flanagan, who was a close friend. I met Barry in 1967, while I was working for *Studio International*. He was very much a part of the group that then composed a sort of 'Anti-Form' avant-garde. Barry came back from the Bern show, talking about what a great show it was. I also heard about Joseph Kosuth from Barry Flanagan. Barry had met him, I don't know where. I heard about *Op Losse Schroeven* as well, which opened in Amsterdam just before the Bern show. Barry, Roelef Louw, Long and Bruce McLean were in both shows, so far as I remember. They were all associated with Saint Martin's in London, where I was teaching.

SR *What did you think when you first saw the works from the Bern show? Was it a surprise or a shock?*

CH I can't remember if I had seen the Bern exhibition catalogue before. The reason why it wasn't a shock was that in the spring of 1969, I had gone to New York. I met Joseph Kosuth there and he introduced me to Lucy Lippard, Seth Siegelaub, Lawrence Weiner, Bob Barry, probably also Douglas Huebler. I met Kosuth in a Ken Noland exhibition in Larry Rubin's gallery. I was in conversation with the receptionist of the gallery. I told her I was in New York to have a look at art and meet American artists. She said, pointing at Kosuth, that he was an artist. I told him we had a mutual friend in Barry Flanagan. So we went out for a coffee. He discovered I was working as Assistant Editor for *Studio* and he took me around to some shows in New York and introduced me to some people. Kosuth also showed me his work and I was fascinated and very impressed by it. In fact, part of my brief for the trip to New York was to find new material for *Studio International*. So, I asked Joseph to write a piece for *Studio*, which turned out to be 'Art after Philosophy'. I went to America for two reasons. Principally, I wanted to meet Clement Greenberg, which will tell you a bit about the state of my enthusiasms. But I also wanted to see some more American art. I was also, I suppose, a sort of youngish art critic. I was looking for the avant-garde art of my generation. Before I went to New York, probably the year before, I got to know an American woman, who lived in London, Barbara Reise. She was a graduate student who came to the *Studio International* office, which was a kind of contact point for artists and critics passing through London. We shared an interest in contemporary art. Barbara had a part-time job, teaching Art History at Coventry College of Art, which was where the Art & Language people were. So I first heard about Art & Language from Barbara Reise. She told me about the strange Conceptual art they were making. So I had a sort of interest in knowing more about that. Then, two of the Art & Language people, Terry Atkinson and Harold Hurrell, showed up at *Studio*, with some examples of their work. This must have been late 1968 or early 1969. I was interested, not so much in the works, but in them. They were people who were not like normal artists; they were different.

SR *What made them different?*

CH They were not making a pitch in the same way artists tend to do. They just had a completely different social style. To some extent they were more serious. I had already, at that point, started to feel very uncertain about what I was doing, writing articles, and being an art critic. I felt very uncertain about the basis from which I was making judgements. I also felt very unsure about the sociology of the world I was working in. It just seemed very unpleasantly corrupt. I can't remember having talked so much about their art with Barbara Reise. She worked for *Studio* on a special issue on Minimal art in 1969, and one on Barnett Newman the next year. She was very interested in Minimal art. I must have talked a bit with her about these artists. You have to remember, Minimal art wasn't shown in England before 1969. I think the first showings came after April 1969, when *Studio* published its special issue about Minimalism. Before that, there was no Judd, no Morris, no Andre, no LeWitt. None of them was shown in London before 1969.

I actually have to go back a bit to 1967. There were two things that really brought me up to date. One was meeting Barry Flanagan and getting interested in the kind of work he was doing. The other was reading *Artforum* and particularly the summer 1967 issue. Because what that made clear was that there was a real split, not just between American and European concepts of modernism, but also a split within American modernism itself. On the one hand you had articles on sculpture, like Caro's. On the other hand, you had the 'soft' sculpture of Robert Morris, but also Sol LeWitt's 'Paragraphs on Conceptual art' and so on, all in the same issue. I can remember very clearly feeling jealous that there was a debate going on in America, whereas in England it was very quiet. The English magazines were working in a way which made things appear very provincial.

SR *What about* Studio International, *which seemed, at the time, to be the only magazine in England that was open to 'new' art?*

CH It was, but not to that extent. There was also a sense that the new things *Studio* was open to were going on somewhere else. As a writer I wanted to be writing for *Artforum* and not just for *Studio International* (under Phil Leider's editorship, *Artforum* was a very different journal from the mess of advertisements and cultural froth that it is today). I wanted to be where things were happening and where the critical arguments took place. There was a kind of passion, particularly in the sense that art mattered, which was very attractive. Whenever American art came to England, I wanted to write about it.

SR *So you went to New York and met Kosuth and other artists, in order to get to know American art better?*

CH Yes, I met Carl Andre, Robert Morris, probably also some others. I can't remember exactly. My original contact with Conceptual art was with the Americans.

SR *Could we go back to when you met Kosuth for the first time, in spring 1969. What kind of work did he show you, that you found so interesting and radical?*

CH I remember very clearly, 'Definitions'. Almost entirely 'Definitions', in fact, and a few pieces with glass with letters on. He didn't have then any of the pieces that were later shown as early works – or 'proto investigations'. I think he didn't have any of those made by that time. So, it was mostly 'Definitions'. I can't remember very clearly how he presented his work to me. I wasn't so much surprised by his work as fascinated by his personality and his conversation. He was a very energetic and amusing person then. I liked his extremism. He was very young. I liked his courage, his determination, his ambition. Joseph was a very unusual person. When I look back at it, I find it very hard to explain why I thought his work was important. And I am still not sure. Maybe it's just a feeling of something radically new, something you couldn't have imagined.

SR *At that time, what did you think of the work of other Conceptual artists, like, for example, Lawrence Weiner?*

CH It was much more whimsical, light and poetic,

almost romantic. Barry's I was less sure about. Weiner and Kosuth were the two I thought were the most interesting. What I liked with Kosuth was something to do with why I started feeling insecure with writing art criticism. I'm now making sense of things that weren't so clear for me at the time. One of the problems with trying to write art criticism in the mid-1960s, was that modernism was dying on its feet. A whole system of criticism that was based on a significant discrimination between forms and colours was becoming more and more unreal. It was as though the discriminations had less and less of the world behind them. The job for a standard art critic at the end of the late 1960s was to stand in front of a painting–let's say a Ken Noland–and talk about the incredible balance between the colours within the stripes, and about why he got it right and somebody else got it wrong. There was a very high degree of arbitrariness in that. At the same time, a very high degree of rationalism inside the critical system. With the work that Kosuth was doing in 1969, this just wasn't an issue. It raised questions that just weren't there before. You either had to say, 'It's not art at all', and just dismiss it–which I refused to do–or you had to say that you didn't want to worry about colour and so on anymore. The problem had changed and that's why it was so interesting.

SR *So, you met all these artists in New York and then came back to England for* When Attitudes Become Form*?*

CH It came a bit later. I was only in New York for two weeks. The first thing I had to do was a Ben Nicholson show at the Tate. That opened in mid-June. The *Attitudes* show came soon after, in September. It was quite strange. Ben Nicholson was such an important figure in my graduate work as an art historian. So, doing the *Attitudes* show after that was really weird.

Art & Language wasn't in the *Attitudes* show. My contact with them was separate. I barely knew them and the kind of work they were doing at the time. The only artists I added in the show were those I was already committed to. I didn't have a sense of my potential power as a curator. I didn't know I had the authority to include other artists. I must have met Terry Atkinson again, as soon as I came back from New York, and I told him about Joseph Kosuth. Kosuth had heard about Art & Language – the first issue of *Art-Language* was spring 1969 – so he was keen to make contact anyway. In fact, when Terry arrived in New York, Joseph was waiting for him at the airport. He took him straight back to his loft and Terry stayed with him during his trip to New York.

When I came back from New York, I felt very changed by what I'd seen; I had a different sense of myself. I felt more impatient about the art I'd been interested in. I was very keen to discover other artists of my generation, very keen to meet other artists who might be part of this movement.

When I came back from the States, somebody – I think it was an organization called the *Artists Information Registry* (AIR) – published a large directory of artists living in London, with descriptions of their work. I went through this, looking for artists that might be doing the kind of work I had seen in New York, and I found one. That was Vic Burgin, and I phoned him up, asking if I could see his work. He was quite astonished to get a call from anybody. I found his work very interesting and I asked him if he wanted to be in the show I was proposing for the ICA. That's why he was in the *Attitudes* show. I must have proposed the show of English artists to the ICA after I came back from New York, as an attempt to try to make something out of the things I found out when I was there. I wanted to put on a kind of avant-garde show. But I wanted to put on a show of English artists. I think partly because I wouldn't have known how to organize a show of any other artists.

SR *Was it Philip Morris or Harald Szeemann, the Director of the Kunsthalle in Bern, who proposed the show to the ICA?*

CH It was Philip Morris and I suspect they must have proposed the show to many other places. The show went to Krefeld after coming to London. The ICA accepted the show mainly for financial reasons. I doubt they knew anything about the kind of art involved. There was nobody at the ICA knowing much about that kind of art. The director of the ICA was a theatre person and he had no idea about the work. They hired me, partly because I had already proposed an avant-garde show. Partly also because, apart from Barbara Reise, I was probably one of the few people in London who knew much about the kind of work at that time.

SR *Did you know before the* Attitudes *show the work of other avant-garde artists, like the Italian Arte Povera movement for example, with artists like Mario Merz?*

CH I knew some of the works slightly, through working at *Studio*. Catalogues and other magazines were coming to the office, also artists and curators. There was a lot of gossip going around and you heard about a lot of stuff. That's partly why I wanted to work there. About really knowing the stuff, having a real understanding ... Their work was very different from the avant-garde I was interested in. I never liked second-hand enthusiasm and I was never confident of my interest until I saw the stuff for real. I may have seen some at Prospect 68. But I don't remember having known a lot about the Arte Povera stuff until the *Attitudes* show came over from Bern. My first contact with the *Attitudes* show was in the warehouse when it arrived. There was a lot of junk. A lot of work had been packed up in a lot of paper, etc. In some cases, it was hard to tell the difference between the original material of the work and the packing material. But I had a set of photographs and illustrations, and I became a sort of instant expert. There was a lot of stuff which was not properly installed at the ICA. There were two Eva Hesse works for which I had no adequate instructions. So it wasn't easy.

SR *Didn't a few artists come over to London to install their work?*

CH Yes, part of the package from Philip Morris included paying for a trip for some of the artists. For Bern, a lot of artists had been paid to come over, as for *Op Losse Schroeven*. It was one of the important characteristics of the movement as a whole that certain artists had to come over do their pieces directly in the museum. Part of the deal with Philip Morris was that they would pay for a certain amount of artists to come over to London, with accommodation. I asked Robert Smithson, who came over. Jan Dibbets came too. Also Richard Artschwager and Ger van Elk. Of the Arte Povera artists, I could only invite one, and I chose Giovanni Anselmo, but they shared the money and all came together. Alain Jacquet, that was a mistake. I invited him because I had seen some paintings of his I quite liked. But when he came he did some stuff on the wall, which was just stupid. A lot of 'first choice' artists turned down the invitation to come – London probably wasn't important enough for them at the time.

SR *Did Szeemann come?*

CH Szeemann came to the opening. He made a silly mock speech, where he made a lot of gestures and pretended to talk but without actually speaking – a sort of avant-gardish thing. I hardly talked to him. But I got along fine with the artists!

SR *Can we talk a bit more about the artists?*

CH Reiner Ruthenbeck was one of the artists who came over to London. We had to get some ashes in London for him to make his piece, which was a work about German war guilt, with ashes and wire. They could only deliver wet ashes in sacks, which were very heavy. The way Ruthenbeck made the piece was to tangle up the wire and then to pour the ashes over it. But because the ashes were wet, he couldn't lift the sack. He is very short, very small. Jan Dibbets is very big, he's a Dutchman. So, Dibbets picked up the bag and did it, and it was over in a couple of seconds. And that was it, that's why Ruthenbeck came all the way over from Germany, and Jan Dibbets did it for him.

There was a piece by Kounellis, which was a series of sacks of different kinds of grain which we installed by the staircase on the way in. This was the 1960s. The hippies were coming in to the ICA and taking some grains to chew as they walked around. But they would throw some away and a lot of the grain landed in Reiner Ruthenbeck's ash heap, which was still damp and humid – the perfect conditions for germination. So, after about two weeks of the exhibition, it went green. It bloomed. It wasn't really what the piece was about.

There was also a shaved cactus by Ger van Elk. He came over to London and shaved a cactus. And I got into trouble because of that. They wanted to film him while he was shaving the cactus. So we had to get a camera crew and get him some shaving cream. We bought, I think, Persona shaving cream. And they filmed him doing this. Then, the public relations woman from Philip Morris said, how could I have done that to her, because they owned Gillette! So we had to do it again. Eva Hesse did a piece which I didn't install properly. I am not quite sure how it was supposed to be. It was composed of rubber mats and they were supposed to be flipped over. People walked on the Burgin piece, despite the fact there was a sign saying 'Please don't walk on the work'. But I don't remember people kicking the stuff around. People were rather careful.

SR *How did you manage the hanging of the exhibition? How did you place the works?*

CH Burgin and Louw came and installed their own pieces. The Flanagans more or less placed themselves. Bruce McLean had a group of large works, which he called 'Landscape Paintings'. He went to Scotland, with a lot of wallpaper, which he sort of dragged over the landscape and he painted whatever was underneath the paper on the top. I remember being anxious he wouldn't turn up with them in time, but I must have reserved space for him next to Louw's piece. After that

I had photographs from the Bern show. Sometimes things had to go on the wall, others on the floor. Some pieces had neon, so they needed to be in a safe place and near electric points, etc. There was a very good team and a very good gallery manager. They were very good at putting the stuff up and they did all the technical work.

Ger van Elk wanted to polish the pavement outside the ICA and he had to get permission from Buckingham Palace, which was refused, so we installed the application and the refusal. The 'wall removal' of Lawrence Weiner wasn't done. He sent a new piece, *A River Spanned*. I just got the title printed on a card and stuck it on the wall. There was a piece by Keith Sonnier that was originally done in Bern with latex and flocking directly on the wall. It didn't make a great deal of sense in the ICA. A lot of the work which came over from Bern didn't make a great deal of sense in London. It was in a different installation, so it had a different status in a way. I came to feel that putting these strange looking objects into a room was not very radical. What was more critically powerful was giving people nothing to look at, or giving them a text to read – requiring people to construct the object out of what they read. The work becomes animated from the moment when someone is thinking about it and actually engages with it.

I see Art & Language's *Documenta Index* as the most clearly sorted out piece for those kind of circumstances. We had a lot of material sorted out in such a way that it worked as an installation. Even there, I think, that very few of the people who visited Documenta actually had much sense of what it was about. The *Art-Language* journal was a sort of complement to the work. One of the important things about the situation at the time, was that it was never clear where the art was; whether the text was something that pointed you in the direction of the object, or whether the text itself was the object. Conceptual art was in some ways made of that very uncertainty. You don't really know if the text you are reading is an essay about art or an essay as art. In some ways, that uncertainty stayed – with Art & Language anyway. The recognition of a border line, between something you call text and something that you call a work of art, is an administrative battle. A huge number of issues got raised at that time. I think we are still living with the consequences of some of these questions. Not all have clear and easy answers. Certainly that question – where the edge of an artwork is – remains.

SR *The press in Bern and in Krefeld seemed to have been totally shocked by the* Attitudes *show. But this doesn't appear to have been the case in London. What do you think of the press and people's reaction to the show? Especially with regards to the postscript of your catalogue text, where you point out how closed London galleries were to the avant-garde.*

SR Actually, I can't really remember what had been shown before the show in London. Barry Flanagan had a contract with a gallery. I think he was the only British artist who had a gallery. Gilbert & George were taken over by Nigel Greenwood. The Lisson Gallery showed more Op art at that time. Not all the works from Bern were shown in London. The choice was made largely by me. The galleries of the ICA were a lot smaller. Basically, I installed the work that travelled from Bern. A lot of the works went back to the artists, directly from Bern, for instance the big rubber installations by Serra. Some artists came to Bern to do special pieces there and didn't come to London. Other artists came to London and did special pieces which weren't in Bern.

SR *So there wasn't a sort of 'political' choice of avoiding certain works, that might have caused trouble?*

SR Absolutely not. No, the only case where things might have been very difficult was with Joseph Beuys, who I invited. I heard about his work in Germany, I think at a Prospect exhibition in Düsseldorf. In fact now I think of it I'd seen him on a trip to Germany in 1968. He was cooking Schweinhaxl at Daniel Spoerri's restaurant in Düsseldorf – with his hat on – and taking forever over each order. I tried to get hold of Beuys to invite him to the ICA and instead got his agent, who proposed a great new work for the show, which was the Volkswagen Microbus with twenty-two sledges with fat and felt. We just needed to pay for the work to be brought over to England, with four assistants to install it! This would have taken the entire budget, and also we wanted Beuys and not his assistants! I didn't want something so 'powerful' for the ICA. So finally, Beuys was not represented. This piece was shown in the 1982 Documenta. It would certainly have been a scoop for the ICA show, but it would have dominated it – which was presumably the intention.

SR *Do you remember the general reception of the exhibition in London? What did people tell you?*

CH I remember a sort of anti-climax. The response was typically English. It was fairly open, but there was no sense of enthusiasm or commitment. I had felt completely absorbed in the exhibition and the work.

I had a sort of missionary feeling about it. I took it very seriously, very earnestly. Too much so probably. I wanted everybody to see that it was the most fantastic exhibition there had ever been, the most wonderful art that ever was. So, I was disappointed by the reception. The other people didn't take the work as seriously as I did. This is one reason why I learned that I shouldn't do things like organising exhibitions. I was frustrated, and I was deeply suspicious of the press. I had to do an interview with someone from the *Sunday Times*, and I insisted that he showed me what he was going to publish. I was just not very good at these public relations. I felt confused by the response, and in a way also by my own commitment. For me personally it was great, to meet the artists and so on. I enjoyed very much working with artists. I had to learn that artists were just like anybody else. You learn that some are great, some are nice, some are interesting, some are boring ... I think I was quite idealistic, then. I certainly believed very powerfully that this was a new movement, that it was historically very important. Which I still do, in some ways, though I think, inevitably, the major artists of the movement were only a small number.

For me, within less than a year, this sort of art became identified with Art & Language. Or certainly with Conceptual art. So, after the *Attitudes* show, I got to know Art & Language much better. I liked what was so radical about their work. I organised also another show, *Idea Structures*, in 1970 at the Camden Arts Centre. I went back to New York in the autumn of 1969, just after doing the *Attitudes* show, in order to further my contacts with people there – I talk of contacts, but the people who mattered were friends. I also went back in 1970. When I went back in the autumn of 1969, Joseph came back with me to stay in London. Then we went to Düsseldorf together for a show there.

SR *Was it at that moment that Kosuth became the American Editor of* Art-Language*?*

CH No, that happened before. Terry Atkinson went in summer 1969 to New York and he stayed in Joseph's loft. They got on and established common cause there. Terry invited Joseph to be American Editor then.

SR *Would Düsseldorf have been, for you, the place to go in Europe, culturally speaking?*

CH Yes, definitely. Also Cologne, at the Paul Maenz gallery. I met Maenz through Art & Language. He was their dealer. He published a collection of Art & Language articles in 1972. In Paris, Art & Language were shown by Daniel Templon. He came to England and just asked Art & Language to exhibit in his gallery. I think it was 1970–71, it might have been later.

About that time also Bruno Bischofsberger came to England. He bought a large amount of Art & Language work. He also negotiated the sale of the Art & Language *Index* from the 1972 Documenta.

SR *Can we talk a bit more about this European network around Conceptual art, which was becoming embedded at that moment, around 1969. Were you aware that you were part of this network?*

CH Yes. In 1969, there was a sense that if you went to New York, you had only to meet one person in the network and they would pass you on to everybody else. Then, when I went to Amsterdam, I visited Dibbets. In Paris, it would be Michel Claura. In every town, there would be somebody who would introduce you to the key figures and would offer you a place to stay.

At the time, my first wife and I had a large house in London and I wanted to be the person in London that people could contact. So, when I went to New York, I told everybody I met that they could stay at my place in London. A lot of people travelled to London. Konrad Fischer stayed, Weiner too. Joseph stayed with us in London, Seth Siegelaub and Lucy Lippard. Also, Gerry Schum.

SR *Did you work a lot with Seth Siegelaub? He seems to have been a major figure regarding American Conceptual art.*

CH What happened is, when I went over for the second time to New York, with my wife and young son, Seth let us stay at his place, on Madison Avenue. He had an apartment and he let us stay there for two weeks. He was very generous. The place was full of the art he showed. There was a Carl Andre in the bedroom – one of the *Equivalents*. My son stomped all over it and did some damage. That piece is now in the Tate I think, though I assume that the bricks have been replaced! Seth had a reason for giving us a place to stay, and that was me being Assistant Editor of *Studio International*. He wanted to publish a sort of manifesto. So it turned out that part of the deal was that I could stay at his place if I would publish an interview with him in *Studio*. That was 'On Exhibitions and the World at Large', published in December 1969. I felt a bit iffy about it, but this doesn't take away from Seth's generosity. And I'd have to say that he was quite open about it. I've always seen the interview as his text, though, not mine. After that, the 'July/August 1970' issue of *Studio* was set up, when Seth came to stay with us in London, which must have been in spring 1970. He set that up with Peter Townsend, who was the Editor of *Studio*. It was certainly a very good opportunity.

SR *What about the* Art-Language *publications?*

CH The publication of the first issue of *Art-Language*, as well as Kosuth's 'Art after Philosophy,' changed things in England and in America, within that avant-garde. It made for distance between a sort of 'analytical' Conceptual art group and the rest. This was what Joseph wanted, he wanted to be *the* Conceptual artist. In America, Weiner, Huebler, Barry and him were seen as a group, until Kosuth published 'Art after Philosophy'. He advertised himself as the person who made the first Conceptual artwork and relatively disregarded the work of the others. So, there were a lot of mixed feelings about that. He also allied himself to the group in England, partly as a way to distinguish himself from the other Americans. Similarly, the English group was happy to identify themselves with an American artist. So for a while, there was a mutual interest. Joseph would come over to England and stay with the English group. He got on very well with Michael Baldwin, until it became clear that Joseph's ambitions were really personal ambitions, and at the expense of Art & Language. Joseph couldn't work with a group. He never really was the 'American Editor'. It began and ended with the second issue of the journal, when he wrote his introduction. That was the only thing he ever did. Then what he would do is stamp his address on the inside front cover of the issues we sent over and he would just give them away, not even trying to sell them. That was actually all the work he ever did. But of the American Conceptual artists, Kosuth was the one Art & Language was most interested in. I still think that the work he did in 1967–69 was very important. But then, at one point, it became clear that it was just impossible to collaborate with him anymore.

SR *Can one say that something changed for the network at Documenta 5? A sort of disillusionment?*

CH Yes, there was a sense of division – not just with Art & Language, but generally in the movement. Conceptual art became business, commercial stuff. With Documenta 5, Conceptual art got its official recognition. It was the end of the 'pure' Conceptual art movement – if there was ever such a thing. After that, two things happened. On the one hand, certain dealers had a market for a kind of picturesque Conceptual art, and for what Paul Maenz called 'classic Conceptual art'. There were collectors who saw a potential avant-garde. The other thing is that Conceptual art became intellectualized and academicized. It was absorbed into a more standard intellectual life, particularly through semiology. It turned into a kind of university art. There came to be a sort of political, intellectual fashion for a kind of new political art. And it became sort of transparent, in the sense that Socialist Realism is transparent – transparent in its content, in its ideology. For me, what was always fascinating with Conceptual art was that it was opaque. It shared the opacity of poetry, while not having the same artistic pretensions. It was very dry in one sense, but it just wasn't transparent, not simple. At one point, in the early 1970s, Conceptual art just became less interesting. It was more consumable. The art historians and art critics loved it.

SR *Were the artists aware of that change?*

CH I think so, but I am talking from the Art & Language point of view. Certainly, that was the perception within Art & Language. And this is partly why the group abandoned Conceptual art for something else. After Documenta 5, there was a change in the personnel of Art & Language. Terry Atkinson and Joseph Kosuth became less engaged. Michael became more clearly the dominant figure. Mel Ramsden and I became more involved. The implications of the indexing system also changed the work of Art & Language. It's not easy to distinguish between the art world changing and the changes in terms of practice, in how you actually make the work. The publication of *Art-Language* didn't change, that was always crucial for the movement. One thing that made things change within Art & Language was the fact that after Documenta there was a group of people in England and there was another set in New York. The people there increasingly felt they were not properly represented by Art & Language, in opposition to those in England. The New York art world was very different from the one in London. There was a sort of tension, which led in the end to the publication of *The Fox*. Joseph wanted a journal of his own, though it was Mel who did most of the real work on it.

SR *After Documenta 5, did Art & Language and Kosuth have anything in common?*

CH After Documenta, Mel Ramsden became the major figure in New York. He worked a lot on the *Index*. He came over and did a lot for the installation of the work at Documenta. He became quite close to Michael and to a certain extent to me and to my then wife. Then, after the exhibition, he went back to New York. He set up a sort of indexing system in New York, a collaborative conversational practice, which included Joseph. So, a group developed then in New York. Joseph was a kind of figurehead there, but Mel was doing much of the actual work. Also, he and Ian Burn had their separate history of collaboration. So, it was a strange and messy situation, with tensions within the group in England with Terry Atkinson pulling away, and tensions between the English and New-York-based groups. There were also tensions between the people in New York. We don't have any contact with Kosuth now. We met him in Barcelona for an exhibition in 1999; that was the last time.

SR *What were then the questions you had to ask yourself as an art critic?*

CH Well, it took me a lot of time to try to figure that out. At the time I didn't really know. I made some terrible blunders. With Kosuth's art, the question you would have to ask is how does it change the definition of art? That's how he represented it himself in 'Art after Philosophy'. I suppose I would have gone along with that at the time. Now I think that's wrong or limited. I think it's not enough, because, in a way it assumes that art can survive without content. Which is what 'Art after Philosophy' means, that art doesn't draw its content from outside itself; it operates only on its own definitions. But any definition would actually be made under particular circumstances, and those circumstances are part of its content. I still ask myself those questions and I still don't have good answers. Art is a part of the social system, not just of the artistic one. You have to consider all the changes that are happening in the society, not just the ones in the art world. They're part of what you make your culture from. But it doesn't follow that you can just read the papers or watch TV and go ahead and make critically significant art. At the time I was definitely very confused. Writing about Conceptual art is extremely difficult. Anything I wrote about Conceptual art during the 1970s was rubbish. I didn't really know what I was dealing with, or how to sort it out.

SR *Do you feel more comfortable now?*

CH I feel more comfortable now in writing on its history. I write about it in relationship to what else was happening at the time. I am much clearer about that relationship than I could have been at the time, though I hope I'm still learning. In a way, what Conceptual art was made of was a sort of crisis in modernism. You can't make any sense of Conceptual art without considering the condition of modernism in art and culture generally: what had happened to it, why it didn't work anymore, why it had become ineffective. In a way, Conceptual art was inescapable – but very much as a transition. Nobody knew at the time what it was a transition to, but it certainly wasn't more Conceptual art. One of the things that I would now criticise about Joseph's work, is that he treated his practice as if it could be non-transitional, as if it was sufficient for itself, as if it could be justified as a continuing style. He was in a way considering that his work was the only and last possibility for art.

SR *What about the big comeback of figurative painting in the late 1970s and beginning of 1980s?*

CH It was a big release for the dealers! But there was no getting round the fact that modernism had lost its intellectual content. Conceptual art was a way of reintroducing an intellectual depth into art and thereby keeping it alive somehow. But I don't think that that life came back with the figurative painting of the 1970s and 1980s.

4.7 Conversation with Annick and Anton Herbert

Gent, 15 November 2004

SOPHIE RICHARD *I'd like to start our conversation with the new galleries that opened in Europe in the late 1960s, which were committed to the innovative artistic tendencies of the day (Minimal, Conceptual, Arte Povera). You were particularly close to Konrad Fischer and Fernand Spillemaeckers in the 1970s. Could you talk about them? How did you meet them, and to what extent did they influence the choices you made in your collection?*

ANTON HERBERT Konrad Fischer and Fernand Spillemaeckers had galleries that strongly made their mark on us. They were two characters who influenced us a lot. Both immediately took us out of our local perspective, a typically Belgian and Flemish situation. With them we entered into an international context: Carl Andre, Art & Language, Daniel Buren. Although each artist had also his own local character: Buren – French, Gilbert & George – English, Carl Andre – American, they presented together an overall perspective, a common vision. Precise activities gave a value to the whole. Fernand had held a symposium on the art situation of that time at La Cambre in Brussels, followed by an exhibition at the Museum Dhont-Dhaenens in Deurle. The location of Fischer in Düsseldorf and Spillemaeckers in Brussels was of no importance whatsoever. On a whim we'd jump in the car to go and see either one of them.

ANNICK HERBERT We didn't differentiate. For example, we bought an Andre with Spillemaeckers from Fischer. Their choice of artists – you can see that in the collection – matched up.

SR *So Fischer and Spillemaeckers knew each other?*

ANTON H They knew each other very well. There's that famous piece from 1973 by Robert Barry called *Invitation Piece*, which explains very clearly that these artists were nomadic, and the galleries in a sense joined in with that nomadic spirit. There was Art & Project, Jack Wendler, Yvon Lambert, Sperone, Paul Maenz, Nigel Greenwood, Konrad Fischer, MTL, Wide White Space, Leo Castelli and Toselli. The art world was so small and these galleries had to make huge efforts to get a few people in.

ANNICK H The artists moved from one gallery to the other. When American artists came to Europe, they went around all these galleries. They did the circuit.

SR *How was the circuit established? You realise that there were tensions between MTL and Wide White Space. As a result the circuit probably didn't work very well between those two galleries.*

ANTON H Those tensions weren't the essential thing. There were tensions and there weren't. At some points, the tensions were very powerful. There were misunderstandings between Paul Maenz and Konrad Fischer in Germany, too. And between Herman Daled and Anton Herbert! But we had to show, and did show, solidarity to the outsider.

ANNICK H We were so convinced that we were on the right track!

ANTON H There weren't that many of us and there was no way of doing anything other than grouping together, because of the superficiality of the people against us. So we had to group together to defend ourselves. Anyway, we were fanatical, defending the truth and the essence of our beliefs. For that group of people – artists, critics, galleries and collectors (the museums weren't involved so much) – it was vital to stay together, even if there were sometimes small misunderstandings. It was important to group together to define and defend what really mattered, and also to perfect strategies of ideas. We were the opposition.

ANNICK H You mention strategies, but not everyone held that view. You are talking on behalf of yourself and Spillemaeckers, who had that same vision.

ANTON H Yes, there were people, collectors and others, who were part of this group without realising how important it was to defend those artists. For us it was an opposition to the common view from that time: Support/Surface or Pattern Painting. No one talks anymore about Pattern Painting, but it was extremely important at that point in those years. There was also Body Art with Gina Pane and some others. All those movements were as important as the one we thought was essential.

ANNICK H We were a tiny core of people who'd made that choice.

ANTON H That core went on to become essential. Don't forget that at the time there were as many wrong tracks as right ones. Everything was possible. The museums were given little or no support. There were hardly any contemporary art museums, none in Belgium.

ANNICK H You had to go to Holland: Eindhoven and Amsterdam.

ANTON H Yes, there were only a few exceptions. The Van Abbemuseum in Eindhoven did a lot already from the beginning of the 1970s onwards. That museum had of a number of people around Rudi Fuchs who dealt with these artists. There was also Martin Visser – a private collector working in a museum structure – at the Museum Boijmans van Beuningen in Rotterdam. It was a little core of people who launched a battle. In Germany, in Mönchengladbach, Johannes Cladders was very good. It is well known, he made these cardboard boxes by way of catalogues, because it was less expensive. The least expensive catalogue you could make then was a cardboard box. And now it's probably the most expensive!

SR *You said in 2000, 'To choose this art is also to choose your friends'. Do you agree with the idea that it was a small group of dynamic, enthusiastic and committed people who led people to the recognition of the movement across Europe?*

ANNICK H Yes.

ANTON H We worked out, very early on, who the people were who weren't our friends, through the fact that it's intellectually very demanding to commit yourself to a work by artists such artists as Daniel Buren or Ian Wilson or Douglas Huebler. You could tell immediately who was superficial and who was sincere.

ANNICK H You had to commit yourself.

ANTON H Yes, you really had to show your commitment, persuade people that it wasn't something lightweight or whatever. It was clear that the list of people who did the defending, who were very committed to these values, was very short.

SR *When you say 'commit yourself', in concrete terms for you as collectors, what did that mean?*

ANTON H Already from the beginning, for us, it was extremely clear how to work. We wanted to participate in that movement. Perhaps this was different from what others were doing. In France, for example, people who were committed weren't collecting. This is the French mentality. French intellectuals lived out their ideas, pure and noble but without direct engagement. We could not 'not' collect. We could not 'not' commit ourselves.

ANNICK H It was our wish to participate.

ANTON H To commit oneself was to participate and to participate was to collect. And what was collecting? It was buying a Buren fabric or a Lawrence Weiner phrase!

ANNICK H Certainly not collecting in the sense that you buy paintings to hang on the wall.

ANTON H So we went to Konrad Fischer and came home with a phrase in our pocket and then we had to pay for it! It was pretty crazy, all in all.

SR *Do you remember the first Conceptual work you bought?*

ANNICK H The very first work we bought were some drawings by Sol LeWitt, four small drawings as a group. It was the first timid commitment we made. They're magnificent! That was at MTL when they were in Antwerp with Art & Project. We did that one week and then the next we already started buying something else. That left its mark on me.

ANTON H Everything speeded up very quickly. This didn't happen from one day to the next. There was a long preparatory period of discussions, a 'battle of words' with Spillemaeckers, with Fischer and with the artists. We wanted to know exactly what we were dealing with. We wanted to test the ground. For us, it was a fast-track training. In three or four months, we'd completely changed our way of seeing, which had been fairly bourgeois and local. Let's say we'd been passively prepared by the spirit of 1968. We had a particular attraction to this new world.

ANTON H We were well informed. We travelled a lot. We went to all the exhibitions, till then, without doing anything, without committing ourselves. Our meetings with Spillemaeckers and the discussions we had with him and Konrad put us on the right road.

SR *How did you keep yourselves informed?*

ANNICK H All kinds of ways.

ANTON H There were, at the time, some specific art magazines, like *Avalanche*, which we were able to find un-regularly.

SR *Where did you find copies of* Avalanche *in Belgium?*

ANNICK H There were addresses, you had to find your copy.

ANTON H You had to write to get them. You found some in galleries like Fischer's. There were also *+–0*, *Art-Rite* and *Art Vivant*. Irmeline Lebeer wrote for *Art Vivant*. Her articles were fantastic. Later there was *The Fox*, by Kosuth and Art & Language. There was also *Interfunktionen*. And this incredible magazine, *Museum Journaal*, a small brochure published by the Van Abbemuseum in Eindhoven, the Stedelijk in Amsterdam and the Rotterdam Museum. Certain issues of *Museumsjournaal* are absolutely essential. Also *Opus International*, *VH 101* and *Studio International*, which all published extraordinary issues at that time.

SR *So, art magazines were a way of staying up to date?*

ANTON H Yes, but some set off on the wrong track.

ANNICK H You had to make a choice.

ANTON H In France, some magazines wandered off into Body Art in a deplorable way, like *Artitudes*. We realised we were being badly informed.

ANNICK H What was absolutely exceptional was the Documenta 5 in Kassel in 1972, curated by Harald Szeemann.

ANTON H Before that, there was *When Attitudes Become Form*, and a whole series of exhibitions which changed our way of seeing things. In particular, there were two exhibitions by Paul Maenz, *Serielle Formationen* and *Dies alles Herzchen*. And the two first Cologne Kunstmarkt of 1967 and 1968. There was Prospect 68 in Düsseldorf. Also the exhibition in Eindhoven, *Three Blind Mice*, showing the collections of Martin Visser, Hubert Peeters and Frits Becht in 1968. There was the *Xerox Book*, of Seth Siegelaub in 1968 and all the Art & Project *Bulletins*. And the book that Germano Celant wrote about Arte Povera. There was the exhibition *Konzeption/Conception* in Leverkusen, the different shows of Siegelaub in 1968–69, and *Op Losse Schroeven* in Amsterdam. Not to mention *Information*, which took place in New York in 1970 at the MOMA, and the *18 Paris IV* organised by Michel Claura in Paris, as well as the special issue of *Studio International* in summer 1970.

SR *Did you go and see all those exhibitions?*

ANTON H Yes, but only from 1971 on, not before. We were on the road all the time. There was Lucy Lippard's book *Six Years* in 1973, which brought a complete overview of all the essential events of those years. My list of important books and catalogues between 1967 and 1977 comes to 87 items. This archive is our Bible today.

ANNICK H From 1976, 1977 on it was the end. When Paul Maenz showed his painting exhibition in 1976 the movement was quickly going down.

ANTON H With *Projekt 74, Kunst bleibt Kunst* in Cologne, in July 1974, we already had a sense that the content had started to change.

SR *When you went to the early Kunstmarkts in Cologne, did you go to see what was happening, or also to buy?*

ANTON H We never travelled to fairs with the intention of buying.

ANNICK H You didn't do that in those days. It wasn't the way people thought.

ANTON H The first people who did that later on were the Americans. They 'made' their 'shopping tour'.

ANNICK H They came to Europe to do their 'shopping tour', going to the fairs to see what they could buy. But that didn't exist before. Art fairs were places where galleries showed works of art and provided information about what is going on.

ANTON H In those days, you had plenty of time to go back home, talk and think. Now people are under incredible stress. They have their chequebooks and they want to buy straight away. The spirit is completely different.

ANNICK H Art fairs were places where you could meet the galleries and even the artists.

SR *When you wanted to buy a work for your collection, did you go to galleries?*

ANTON H Yes, absolutely.

ANNICK H But we didn't go to buy an object for the collection. It was the culmination of a discussion, after a long preparation. It was a whole ritual.

ANTON H First of all you had to be in perfect harmony with the artist. You had to know him and have at least three or four serious discussions with him to see if it held water or not. People don't really do that any more.

SR *So you didn't go to galleries to choose from the works shown in exhibitions?*

ANNICK H We went to see what new things the artist was showing. It was a meeting place for the artist. Then we came back home and the next day talked together about all these works. We took our time.

ANTON H Mostly, nothing was ready at the vernissage. You would get to an opening and would not see anything: the artist hadn't yet arrived, or he hadn't managed to get his work ready. It was chaotic. The idea was to participate in something that was going to happen. When Dan Graham showed his films at Spillemaeckers, he was mostly always crouching under the table trying to get the machine to work. While we waited, we chatted and had a drink. If nothing worked, and it happened all the time, they told us to come back the next day. It was all very good-natured. In fact it wasn't professional. But even if it didn't work, we all went out to dinner together and had some good talks. The discussions were very important.

ANNICK H The content was essential. Now it's superficial and worldly.

ANTON H Today, you have to dress up to go to an

opening. In those days, you'd dress as normally as possible. Today, sometimes you barely dare to go into some galleries, they're so chic.

SR *In your view, what distinguished that set of new galleries from the previous generation of galleries? For example, Castelli, which opened much earlier?*

ANTON H Castelli was part of the movement.

ANNICK H Sonnabend too. They were really precursors.

ANTON H They who started their galleries with Pop art. What you might ask instead is, what distinguishes these two from the others, from Denise René or Claude Bernard?

SR *For me, Castelli and Sonnabend are slightly separate, in the sense that their reputations as gallery-owners were already established when they took on Conceptual artists. Whereas the new generation of European galleries built up their own reputations on the basis of those artists.*

ANNICK H Yes, they're separate. But the Conceptual artists, in those early years, didn't have other galleries in New York. Sonnabend and Castelli were their galleries in the States, while in Europe they were all new.

ANTON H Castelli and Sonnabend are the two exceptions who managed to round the cape of Pop art without problems. They found straight away who was important in the next generation of artists. They had open minds. Castelli showed Lichtenstein, but also Kosuth, Rauschenberg but also Nauman. Look to the historical group photographs of the Castelli Gallery's artists: you see Ruscha, who wasn't at all well known at the time, beside Lichtenstein, or Oldenburg next to Weiner.

ANNICK H In the States, at that time, there wasn't a gallery for those younger artists. And American collectors weren't at all interested in it.

ANTON H Castelli kept all those artists alive. They didn't sell anything.

SR *So it tended to be the Americans who showed at Castelli?*

ANTON H No, not only: Hanne Darboven and Jan Dibbets, both had very important exhibitions at Castelli.

ANNICK H Castelli and Sonnabend were very European. They had a European mentality.

ANTON H An American artist like Baldessari wasn't shown anywhere in the United States. Only at Sonnabend. And Sonnabend tended to Baldessari's career in an extraordinary way. Before, he hadn't sold anything at all.

ANNICK H She was able to support those young artists with the money she made with Pop art.

ANTON H Fischer had huge respect for Castelli and Sonnabend. Castelli was a God for those European galleries.

ANNICK H They both were the American counterpart for all the young European galleries.

SR *What did they admire about Castelli?*

ANTON H His commitment, his way of giving carte blanche to artists, his generosity, his professionalism with collectors, also his commitment to his artists' survival. He always managed to give the artists their monthly cheque. Castelli and Sonnabend were very correct. For lots of young galleries like Spillemaeckers and Sperone, Castelli was their absolute model. It was often said that Konrad Fischer was Castelli's heir apparent. And he died first! Castelli was a great man, a great gentleman.

ANNICK H Sonnabend started her gallery in Paris in the late-1960s. In comparison, Denise René was really the old guard, the old style, the 1950s.

SR *What's the old style?*

ANTON H People who showed kinetic art in those years in Paris. There was nothing to see in those galleries. You were wasting your time. When we went to New York we would first stop off at Castelli's to see what was happening there. If he was showing Pop art, we respected it, because this was part of his trade. But we knew that a month later he would be showing Douglas Huebler with just as much attention. He was extremely professional and I think people clung on to that. If you received the blessing of Castelli and Sonnabend, it gave an incredible amount of added value. All the artists we were interested in needed a nudge in the right direction in this way. I remember Kosuth talking to us about Castelli in the most incredible terms.

They didn't make any mistakes. There are some galleries that did make huge mistakes. When Cucchi and Clemente showed up, some galleries switched sides directly. They turned to painting and forgot about everything else. Fischer, on the other hand, remained a hard-liner. Those were very bad years for him. Castelli, in good or bad times, had a kind of grandeur, a European panache in New York. You received a kind of consecration from him, even as a collector. For many people, Castelli's name was like a guarantee of quality. Sonnabend too, but Castelli most of all.

SR *Did you go regularly to the States in those days?*

ANNICK H Yes, we went there regularly. From 1971–72 on.

ANTON H I remember we went to Castelli to see work of Nauman and bought our first drawings there and the same week we also bought some Nauman pieces from Angela Westwater who worked close to Castelli. From 1971 onwards, Nauman was extremely important to us. Konrad had told us we had to go and see it. We listened.

ANNICK H We talked about the whys and hows of all those artists, and made up our own minds afterwards.

ANTON H We also could have collected lots of other artists. We had to choose. We didn't have unlimited funds, so we had to be careful. We met the artists and the people running the galleries, some critics too. But we didn't meet any American collectors apart from the Vogels, whom we visited in their little apartment. People in the States were mostly talking about Scull, the big taxi magnate, who was the most important collector from Castelli. He bought large amounts of Pop art but was not at all interested in Conceptual art. In Europe his counterpart at that time was the Ludwig Museum in Cologne.

ANNICK H For us, in New York, Heiner Friedrich's art foundation, later the Dia Art Foundation, was essential and our first priority. They were involved with our artists.

ANTON H There was a system to our visits there. We had a list of addresses and went to see those people who were in the same mode: a small group. At the front of the *When Attitudes Become Form* catalogue, Harald Szeemann printed a photo of his address book: 40 to 45 names. That was how he did his exhibition. Szeeman didn't know anybody at the beginning of his Bern project. Dibbets told him some names, so did Richard Long and Nauman, and then others. He was intelligent enough to ask the right questions and to know where to go. This inspired us in our contacts. It was a close-knit little circle of people.

SR *Some people were very committed politically, like Spillemaeckers, for example. He wrote texts that were very committed and political. To what extent was he radical and critical?*

ANNICK H We used to discuss a lot in those days.

ANTON H These discussions were essential and exciting. They started for us in the wake of May 1968.

ANNICK H One evening, Spillemaeckers showed us a work by Sol LeWitt telling us how extraordinary it was, and he went on and on, for hours and hours, making a masterpiece of that specific work, far into the night. Then he came all the way down and gave all the arguments that said the piece was absolutely worthless. You had to construct and deconstruct. Radical and critical.

ANTON H Before midnight we bought the work and by the end of the night it wasn't worth anything!

ANNICK H He was critical in the sense that he was able to construct and deconstruct. He saw exactly the strengths and the shortcomings.

ANTON H He was a hard-line intellectual. A leftist. But everyone was somewhere on the left in those days. He had no sense of the bourgeoisie. He scorned conventional bourgeois norms that led nowhere. Every discussion was a calling into question, an in-depth examination of what one has and what one doesn't have. He tried to give as many arguments for as against, to get a complete vision of the problem, whether it was Andre, Judd, LeWitt, Ryman, Mangold or Marden. You had to find out who was the most radical. The idea of figurative art was completely impossible. After Minimal and Conceptual art, going back was out of the question. On the contrary, art was opening windows to other horizons.

ANNICK H Spillemaeckers said there was nothing more beautiful than Stanley Brouwn's metre line! He was really a utopian!

ANTON H It was magnificent! We were open-mouthed. We thought it was incredible and drank in his words.

SR *How did you meet Spillemaeckers?*

ANNICK H It was at the Museum Dhondt-Dhaenens in Deurle, which at the time was very local and very bourgeois.

ANTON H We'd received an invitation to an exhibition that was going to take place there. It had all the names of the artists we were interested in.

ANNICK H This was strange and we had to go along to see for ourselves.

ANTON H That was in 1973. The invitation card mentioned Andre, Art & Language, Askevold, Baldessari, Barry, Beuys, Broodthaers, Buren, Cadere, Graham, Huebler, Kosuth, LeWitt, Paolini, Penck, Ryman, Weiner and Wilson. We turned up and there was absolutely nothing to see, a large empty room and hardly anyone there. There was Madame Rona, Spillemaeckers, his wife Lili Dujourie, Philippe van Snick and the two of us. We asked where the exhibition was and they told us it was laid out on the table: a few covers with paper sheets. We were astonished! The exhibition had been boycotted by Wide White Space and by Paul Maenz.

ANNICK H They'd cancelled all the invitations except ours. They'd forgotten about us! After that 'opening', we spent a long night in discussion with Spillemaeckers. And went to Brussels the next week to be 'brainwashed' in a short time!

ANTON H We were attracted by those people who were 'outside the norm'. They led us to radical points of view. We were interested in extreme directions.

SR *When did you meet Fischer?*

ANTON H At around the same time. All those things happened together. Spillemaeckers brought us to Fischer a few months later. Daled came to Gent to take a look at those collectors who were starting to move in. He was already collecting actively many years before us and wanted to hang on to his territory.

SR *You said Spillemaeckers was very intellectual. What was Fischer like?*

ANNICK H He didn't say anything. He had another way of communicating but we knew very well what he meant. We didn't have the kind of discussions with him that we had with Spillemaeckers.

ANTON H No, you had to be present. It was a silent communication. We were on the same wavelength, but there was no music! It was through his exhibition programme that we knew what he thought. He expressed himself in little touches, like a painter. He had a very strong physical presence.

ANNICK H When he looked at works of art, you knew exactly what he was thinking.

ANTON H Sometimes he came out with a phrase. With just a few words he was straightforward and absolutely right. Fischer was the first to show Carl Andre in Europe in October 1964. It was even the first show of his gallery. And also the last one: in September 1992.

ANNICK H He was the one who stuck to his guns when painting arrived, with the Neuen Wilden, Cucchi and Clemente. It was terrible. We had to phone him up and give him our support. The arrival of painting was just as dramatic for his artists.

ANTON H In total Konrad did more than 300 exhibitions!

ANNICK H Fischer was the most complete gallery in Europe. He had all the best artists. Here in Belgium they were shared out between Spillemaeckers and Wide White Space.

SR *Fischer was also the one who sold most to European museums.*

ANNICK H That's interesting. I didn't know that. Yes, he did a great job!

ANTON H Obviously, at the time, this art wasn't worth much.

Annick H: No, but after all, museums had to buy works anyway, and it was his job to guide them.

SR *Do you think the private collectors somehow 'validated' this art for the museums, in the sense that the collectors' choices reassured the museums?*

ANTON H Yes and no. We did notice, at the Van Abbemuseum in Eindhoven, that the fact that we made some acquisition decisions had a certain influence. We looked at what they were doing and they looked at what we were doing. When in 1984 we showed the collection in this museum, we made a kind of deal. Rudi Fuchs wanted to show our collection, and we were of course interested in the collection of the Van Abbemuseum. So Fuchs told us to choose works out of the museum collection and he chose works from our collection. We put on a mixed exhibition, *L'architecte est absent*. Alongside artists like Weiner, in the same room and mixed in, were historic artists like Mondrian and Beckmann whom, of course, collectors can't buy. It was a symbiosis of two collections at the Van Abbemuseum.

ANNICK H All the same, I don't think museums are influenced by the choice of collectors.

SR *Or reassured?*

ANTON H Museums looked at what the private collectors were doing. For example, Martin Visser had a huge influence on the Rotterdam museum's collection. They even asked him to be on the board. That's an important point. Museums collect a bit later, when they have confirmation that they are not making a mistake. Apart, perhaps, from Cladders, who was already buying for Mönchengladbach, with very limited funds, in the beginning.

SR *Lynda Morris suggested that gallery owners offered different prices to museums and private collectors. Is that true?*

ANTON H Yes, I think private collectors were able to be more demanding to galleries. More demanding on the price as they wanted to buy more works and made fast decisions. Museums often took a long time to decide and they paid late. I remember a discussion with Fischer about the big Richter we have in the collection. The Kröller-Müller Museum had that work in storage for six months with a free view to its possible acquisition. But they couldn't make up their minds and Fischer got fed up waiting. He told us he would give us an incredible price if we decided within the week. He thought that if the museum had really been interested they would have paid full price straight away. Konrad was positive to us as we went to see him quite often and usually made our minds up quickly, so he gave us special prices. Fair enough. Museums are public institutions, they have to move slowly. Museum directors have to present the work to their committees, and that take time. We didn't have those problems.

SR *Was Willi Bongard's* Kunstkompass *of any importance to you?*

ANTON H It was a small newsletter. We thought it was unhealthy, as money strategies in contemporary art were spread out. On the other hand, Cadere liked Bongard because his ranking system was so iconoclastic. Bongard proposed a formula to calculate how famous artists are and then marked the first hundred on the basis of economic success. He based his formula on various parameters which meant that each artist rose or fell a notch in the annual *Kompass* list.

ANNICK H It was very fashionable at the time.

ANTON H It has its importance as a first model to try out how to rank power in art. On the other hand, and in ethical opposition, there was Siegelaub's Transfer and Sale Agreement. This 'sale contract' is the hard-line vision, in which the added value has to be shared between the collector and the artist. Those two aspects, Bongard and Siegelaub, came out at the same time and are completely opposed to each other.

ANNICK H Everyone, in those years, read *Kunstkompass* and nobody worked with the Sieglaub agreement.

ANTON H Someone should study the relationship between power and money in contemporary art. In the November 2003 issue, *Art Review* started its first annual 'Power 100', a list ranking the top 100 people in the art world who are considered to have the most power: collectors, galleries, artists, critics and curators. The first of them was Charles Saatchi!

SR *As regards to the value of art, do you agree with the idea that Conceptual artists have challenged the art world and its established system?*

ANTON H I think these artists have partially succeeded. They've set the record straight. They came after the happy years of Pop art, pure merchandise! With Conceptual and Minimal art, starting after Prospect in 1968 and 1969, you discovered complete change. These two catalogues were breathtaking. Wide White Space, Art & Project, Yvon Lambert, Konrad Fischer, all those people showing together at the Düsseldorf art fairs: there was so little to sell but all to show. These were the times of ideas and content. That's when we turned up.

SR *There was a kind of rejection of capitalism?*

ANNICK H Yes, all this came out of the counter-culture of May 1968, which was a complete rejection of the existing system. But look what that's given us now!

ANTON H We now have reached far-right extremes in the art world. You travel from Miami to Basel and from Basel to Miami, but what for? It's all lightweight and superficial. Alongside that, a new generation will certainly come up, certainly, more thoughtful and aggressive which takes the debate to a different level. But first we will need a large market crisis.

ANNICK H In the 1960s and 1970s, all the necessary changes were made even if you couldn't see the result as a whole. The basic work, the basic thinking was there, so there's nothing new to do today. The new generation can begin on the basis of the work that's been done already. Even that's a skill.

ANTON H Absolutely. If people like you study these early years, the 1960s and 1970s, new opportunities will arise. It's not lost.

ANNICK H You don't realise today what it was like in the years around 1968. At the level of art, but also, for example, for women: I had to ask my husband's permission to open a bank account. That was in 1972. Can you imagine?

ANTON H The shift in mentality in May 1968 was huge.

ANNICK H Young people today do not realise that these important changes happened through the new spirit of 1968. There have been huge social changes. This was an extraordinary achievement. After those essential years, women were at least able to have a say.

ANTON H In any century, there are one or two fascinating periods. In the twentieth century, there were the years around the 1920s and the 1970s, both periods were incredible.

ANNICK H In 1968 we knew very well what we were doing and we were sure that we were right. We knew it was important. What happened in May 1968 was a great challenge.

On the other hand, I remember a lunch with Lawrence Weiner and Carl Andre in Eindhoven in the late 1970s at the time when painting was coming back again. They were all exhausted. They wondered what they'd been doing all those years and what was going to become of them. This new movement was like a great bulldozer slashing all down. Galleries were swallowed up by it. That was after 1976–77. It was like a funeral.

ANTON H Fischer was abandoned. He was an inch away from bankruptcy. It was a disaster.

SR *So in the end, the art world that those artists had wanted to reject ends up bringing them back in. What about the technological advances that happened during the period, like the fax for example?*

ANNICK H I really can't remember. That was more for offices. It did not have a great impact. At the time, we didn't think that way at all. We didn't even talk about Xeroxes. They were machines that you used and that was it.

ANTON H It's more or less the opposite with the internet and mobile phones of today. Now, you get so much information you can't even deal with it. It's total zapping. Somewhere along the line it stops you being able to think. In Spillemaeckers's time, no one could distract us from our essential concern.

Translation from French: Shaun Whiteside

4.8 Conversation with Klaus Honnef

Bonn, 21 March 2005

SOPHIE RICHARD *In the 1960s you worked first of all as a journalist and exhibition organiser in Aachen. Then you were appointed director of the Westfälischer Kunstverein in Münster. How did that come about?*

KLAUS HONNEF That happened in 1970. I'd already put on exhibitions in Aachen in a centre for contemporary art. Gegenverkehr – Zentrum für aktuelle Kunst was set up by some friends of mine. I was a co-initiator but not a co-founder for various reasons. From October 1968, we put on exhibitions of the advanced art of the time in that art centre, and they quickly attracted attention. First of all, it was younger or more important German artists. It started with Peter Brüning, Winfred Gaul and Rupprecht Geiger. The fourth exhibition was Gerhard Richter's first exhibition outside of the private gallery scene. After that I showed artists from the sector of 'Concept art', as it was called in those days – Jan Dibbets and Lawrence Weiner. This was Weiner's first exhibition outside of the private galleries. These exhibitions caused a great sensation among the members, particularly the committee members of the Kunstverein. There were contacts between a partner of mine, Rune Mields, and Münster. The Münster collectors were interested in the programme in Aachen. When I was fired from the newspaper in Aachen, the position in the Westfälischer Kunstverein happened to be free. I was asked whether I was interested. I was, and I wrote a pro forma application and drove to Münster one Saturday to introduce myself. That was how I was appointed Director of the Westfälischer Kunstverein in Münster.

SR *How did you first come across the work of artists like Dibbets and Weiner, whom you showed in Aachen?*

KH I came across them through my work as cultural editor of the *Aachener Nachrichten*, for the arts section, and through my work as an art critic. Apart from film, my main area of interest at the time was art, and above all the much-talked-about contemporary art. I came across it in the wake of this critical activity, at press conferences, too. I must have seen their exhibitions in the galleries and come across them there, as well – above all in Düsseldorf, which was at the time the centre of advanced contemporary art in West Germany, the old Federal Republic.

SR *When you started in Münster, did you want to go on showing the same artistic trends there?*

KH Yes, but in a modified form. I never had any kind of complete register of ideas. I was too curious and too open, and I had no artistic concept apart from showing art that revealed new perspectives. To that extent, of course, I was able to refer to my work as an art critic and exhibition organiser in Aachen. I extended my range of ideas in that way, not least according to the principle of 'learning by doing'. The thing people valued most highly was making accessible to the public artistic methods or ideas that broke with traditional methods of mere picture-making. In Monschau in 1970 I held the first big exhibition of 'Außenkunst' (Art outdoors) in Germany, *Umwelt-Akzente: Die Expansion der Kunst*, with Peter Brüning, Daniel Buren, Michael Buthe, Jan Dibbets, Günther Uecker, Klaus Rinke, Lawrence Weiner ... In Münster I had more opportunity to show these unusual trends in the avant garde than in Aachen because artists were breaking away from art forms that had been current until then – painting and sculpture – and completely different forms, and tending to intervene more in reality. I went on to pursue these trends further in Münster, but along with other directions in art that were engaging with the whole environment of the mass media. That was always very important. The so-called 'Concept' artists should be considered against the background of commercial art.

SR *Does a different form of art bring with it a different form of curating? Was an exhibition a dialogue with the artist?*

KH I stopped looking for works from the studio or from private collections as I'd done before. Now the works often didn't even exist, or where they did exist new pieces were made as well. It was always a collaboration with the artist, largely relating to the spaces which some of the artists already knew. Then we developed a concept together, for which the artists were partly responsible. During those years, the position of the art critics changed completely. Art critics like me, along with the great young critics of the time like Georg Jappe, Laszlo Glozer, Bernd Lohse, Hans-Peter Riese, stopped writing about exhibitions like traditional art critics, who had said 'Those are good or bad, interesting or uninteresting pictures'. Instead, we wrote so-called 'empathetic' reviews – we no longer paid any attention to what we thought were bad, but to what we considered interesting. Things we thought had a future, we wrote about with a more empathetic attitude, and not from the outside – we entered the world of the artist's imagination and reviewed them from the point of view of artistic vision. That's something quite different from before. For all the differences between artists and critics, or exhibition organisers, we had the common goal of intervening in reality and changing it, even if it only concerned the way the public saw the products of contemporary art. It was changing people's attitude to reality through art, not in terms of the Fascist, National Socialist or Communist ideologies, but more pragmatically in terms of a more or less idealistic idea of art. But it wasn't with the goal of making better people; it was to perhaps find more conscious and sensitive people than before at the end of this whole process of influence. The quest for this socio-political goal brought us together, even if the goal was very vague. To that extent, our relationships with artists were quite different. It wasn't the critic judging the artist; it was relationships based on dialogue. You might even call it a partnership. Many of us became curators or exhibition organisers, which was also a partnership. What the artists brought to the project was their ideas and what they made or didn't make, and we brought along our professionalism in the realisation of artistic ideas within the spaces that had been made available to them.

SR *Was this partnership also partly borne out by the fact that artists and critics belonged to the same generation, even in terms of producing a different artistic idea?*

KH I'd agree with that. Because we were more or less the same age, we were shaped by the same experiences. We were the first generation to have grown up in the Third Reich, but not to have been involved in acts of war, and we therefore didn't have such a sophisticatedly critical view of the past as the people who were five or six years younger than us, the later generation of 1968. We were also the first generation with a cosmopolitan orientation. My generation looked first to France and then to the USA. What we sought out more than anything, of course, was American culture, in the form of film, literature and advertising. That great variety of cultural influences, which were simultaneously rejected, was set against those traditions that had been discredited by the Third Reich, and also by a pretty mouldy bourgeoisie that was busy reconstituting itself. These all created the conditions that meant we could work on the same wavelength.

SR *You've previously mentioned the cosmopolitan character of this generation. During this time in Europe in general a little network of dynamic and committed people had met up. You get the impression that different galleries and museums were producing a new dynamism.*

KH That's true, too. Today you'd call it a network. We travelled a lot, all crammed into the back of our rickety cars. That way we developed a kind of network, because none of us had much money and we could always sleep on someone's floor. This created a terrific exchange of ideas. When I was in Aachen, and after that in Münster, I would drive to Düsseldorf at least once a week. I'd go to Zur Uel, which was Konrad Fischer's favourite bar. Whenever you got there, there were always artists – Gerhard Richter, Bernd und Hilla Becher, Lawrence Weiner, Carl Andre, Sol LeWitt, Hanne Darboven and so on. There were people sitting together and talking, mostly about art and hardly ever about football. I remember art being discussed more than anything else. That also created a little community all across Europe. Buren was part of it, of course, and Michel Claura. There were lots of people in Holland; not just artists like Jan Dibbets, Stanley Brouwn and Ger van Elk, who was rather on the fringes, but also curators and museum people. Holland was very important at that time. Some of the Italians came to Düsseldorf too, Prini and Sperone. The Rheinland was the focus for everything. It was a very small number of people, a few dozen at the most, who completely changed the picture of art in Europe and the US in the 1960s and 1970s. The first major exhibitions to come out of this sector of ephemeral arts, or 'Concept' art, which wasn't manifested in tangible objects, were in Europe, above all in Düsseldorf, in Krefeld, in Mönchengladbach, in Amsterdam or Bern.

SR *The importance of meeting artists and discussing these issues with them is something I'm hearing over and again. Can you tell me in quite concrete terms what you talked about?*

KH We talked in general. Of course someone was always about to have an exhibition. We talked about that. It was also playful. It was important that it happened in pubs. Zur Uel is a simple Düsseldorf bar. Opposite it was the Ratinger Hof, where Peter Brüning and Sigmar Polke went. It was only a street away. We made jokes and laughed a lot. It wasn't as if we were a conspiratorial society that had to achieve something. We were convinced that what our artists were doing, and what we were doing as exhibition organisers or critics, was the future. We weren't short of self-confidence. We'd rejected everything else, although there were still the negotiations for power. We talked about details and problems, and the strategies for occupying positions. It was all rather playful. It wasn't a laboratory – that would be a false idea. The network had great communicative value, in that we met up and then arranged to meet up again. As exhibition organisers or critics we then met the artists individually and talked intensively about the works. We weren't interested in very much else. At the time it was an idea of art that was realised in people's minds, and to some extent also through ephemeral objects, most of which had a transitory character which was quite at odds with what the public thought and also with what the established art business thought. We were against the established modern art business of the time.

SR *What distinguished the old established art business from the new, progressive one?*

KH The first Cologne Kunstmarkt had just been held. Pop art was a massive success in Germany and the art market was starting to be commercialised. All the people who met in Düsseldorf – artists, museum directors, art dealers and collectors – were rather anti-commercially minded. But not in the sense of the political left; we all found that suspicious. Many of us were also looking for new channels for communicating art, which weren't reconcilable with the usual commercial ways through objects in galleries and museums. It was also what was already being called the 'new media', using the most modern techniques to communicate art. That was an essential part of non-object art. Travelling had also been identified as their programme by some artists. Ian Wilson absolutely refused to make anything that was an object. His art consisted of being invited to particular places and discussing art with people there – not his art, because discussing art was his art. Joseph Kosuth saw his art as a kind of definition of art. At the same time, there was also something theoretical going on in artistic practice, to give a stronger definition of what one saw as art, through artistic practice. It sounds very contradictory, but for us it wasn't. There was artistic practice, but it consisted of theory. It was a matter of brings theory back into artistic practice. Of course, you can see it as an unrecognised romantic concept running through this whole story. But you can also relate it to purely narcissistic art. That's always existed in art. Theory, what has been thought and written about art, was no longer completely separate from what was going on in artistic practice, what artists did.

SR *Wasn't it precisely because it was no longer an object art, because it was theory as artistic practice, that the discussions were so important?*

KH Yes, of course. That's also where you have to narrow down the question a little. The discussions were important, but not in the individual case of what we discussed on Friday the 13th 1970 in Düsseldorf. Of course we discussed things, and we sometimes wrote things down or whatever. But as a rule, it tended to be rather playful in character. You can call that communication – funny conversations. Alcohol helped too, of course. We weren't just drinking mineral water; it was 'Düsseldorfer Alt'! We talked and chatted in an incredibly lively way – we didn't have discussions. Sometimes we did have discussions, but in my memory the communicative effect was much more important. By and large, there was no fundamental disagreement between the artists, let's say between Richter and Carl Andre, who was almost in the extreme position in that group. Andre had written the first essay about Bernd and Hilla Becher in the States, in *Artforum*. There were no major disagreements in their fundamental ideas. The disagreements were with the others who lay in Fischer's orbit. Otherwise, there were more or less affiliations within a fundamental attitude based on the change from what people had previously seen as art. It was the establishment of a very particular concept of art that, when I look back at it, I see was stabilised through the old Kantian, idealistic concept of art, and became Conceptual art, Process art, Minimal art or whatever you want to call it. Actually, we all knew what was art or what wasn't art, or whatever we were defining.

SR *How important were politics in discussions in this sphere? It was in 1968–69, when so many student movements were happening.*

KH Not at all. For us it wasn't important at all. I can't remember us having big discussions about it. In my case you could say, and this was true of the others as well, that we rejected these politically committed students, or the ones who were also involved in the art business, as elitist. In the 1970s I was often invited to talk about art – above all, the function of art, what art has to do in contemporary society. And I was always invited effectively as a Fascist pig, as the 'far right', even though at the time I was already a Social Democrat. I never had anything to do with Fascism, not the slightest sympathy for Fascism or National Socialism. But it was already very discriminatory. The main thing that united us all was our opposition to any kind of instrumentalisation of art. We represented a concept of art that was completely autonomous, which asserted its total autonomy. We rejected any kind of experiments for art to change society, in the sense of introducing a different society, a better one. In our view, that instrumentalisation of art had absolutely nothing to do with art.

SR *It was art for art's sake.*

KH Yes.

SR *But the art world was a small sphere; isn't a little network elitist anyway?*

KH We had nothing against elitism. That completely distinguished us. And then the 'lefties' as we called them attacked us all the more. We were much, much more dangerous for them, because we had influence. We gained more and more influence with our attitude towards the non-instrumentalisation of art. The paradox at the time was that we too wanted change. Perhaps we were pragmatists, and to that extent also more realistic, in that we were aiming initially at a change in the concept of art, stating the concept of art more precisely and defining it, rather than in changing society. I can't remember us talking about it. We were more skeptical about it. We liked to quote that phrase of Dan Flavin about how the avant-garde should be given back to the military.

SR *So running an institution like Westfälischer Kunstverein was a way of showing that change in a practical way.*

KH Yes, of course. In the Kosuthian sense – Kosuth was of course a controversial figure; there were some problems between him and Fischer; he was with the Paul Maenz Gallery in Cologne – we were all more or less aware of this question about art being a matter of definition and working towards that. It was also the chief goal, but that's not to say that it was always intended to run counter to the intellect, or within that narrow circle; it was supposed to radiate outwards as well. We were aware of the meaning of a concept of artistic-social unification, while at the same time we were setting about defining it – artists through their practice, we through our texts or through our exhibitions. We wanted to bring that whole work to the public eye through what today you would call a 'platform'– with the help of the institutions we ran, galleries, Kunstvereine and museums.

SR *If you look at the exhibition programme of various institutions, like the ones in Basel, Lucerne, Amsterdam, Eindhoven or Münster, you see that it's always the same artists being shown in the institutions.*

KH Yes, it was Cladders in Mönchengladbach, Paul Wember in Krefeld, I was in Aachen and later in Münster, in Düsseldorf it was the Konrad Fischer Gallery and in Cologne the Paul Maenz Gallery. In München there was Heiner Friedrich, who then went to Cologne; he was focused on Minimal art and Land art.

SR *At that time, smaller regional institutions were developing international reputations. The regions seem to be coming into the open.*

KH Yes. That's to do with the fact that the organisation of exhibitions with ephemeral art or art 'in the head' as Harald Szeemann called it, was much simpler. You don't need big budgets. If you were supported by the institution, whether by influential people on the city council or the committee of the Kunstvereine; you could work quite independently. A factor that's always overlooked in Germany itself, but explains why Germany was the centre from which it spread, is that the big newspapers were on our side. Critics like Georg Jappe, Laszlo Glozer, Bernd Lohse, and Hans-Peter Riese at the *Frankfurter Allgemeine Zeitung*, then Lohse went to the *Süddeutsche Zeitung*, so that those two big newspapers and to some extent *Die Zeit* as well, gave a great deal of space to these unusual artistic trends which compared with the significance it had in the art world, was disproportionately large. Because of this, the much more significant trends that became better known to the wider public seemed smaller than they actually were in Germany. For me, and also for Johannes Cladders, if we got a big review in the FAZ, for example, there would suddenly be this great outcry among the high-ups. We'd answer the letters of protest ourselves. The coverage on the radio was also very important. The early days of television were already starting. Our contemporary Gerry Schum infiltrated the television and Wibke von Bonin was a television editor with WDR in Cologne. The times were extremely favourable because there were people in the media who were interested in what we were doing.

SR *Was that coverage also influenced by the editors of the newspapers?*

KH No, by the arts editors who gave those critics that space. In Frankfurt you had Eva Maria Demisch. No one remembers her nowadays, but she was a very fashionable editor, and the newspaper's art editor. She gave Jappe, Lohse and Riese, all three of whom started with her, enough space to develop their ideas. That was done at the expense of other kinds of artistic pictorial expression, so for painting, that meant Tachisme and Pop art, which was starting to become established. But Pop art was seen only in a critical way. So Conceptual and Minimal art somehow looked more serious because these critics argued clearly and rationally for it. Above all, because they also broke down that idea that people had of art. Nor can you forget what a centrally important role Joseph Beuys played at that time, not just his art but as a man.

SR *What was the attitude of the art magazines in comparison to that of the newspapers?*

KH *Das Kunstwerk* was rather critical, although I wrote about exhibitions like that in it from time to time. Hans Alexander Baier's and Dieter Bechtloff's *Magazin Kunst* was very enthusiastic. I wrote a whole special issue about Concept art in 1970 delivered the stuff for my book. *Concept Art* was the first book on this subject in the world. The special issue contained interviews with the individual protagonists. *Magazin Kunst* very openly backed all these trends. There wasn't much more than that.

SR *What about the international art magazines, such as* Studio International *from England?*

KH *Studio International* was a bit reticent. *Art and Artists* opened up the interest in Concept art when it started. Then *Studio International* came later, when Charles Harrison was there. In America there was *Artforum*. Willoughby Sharp did *Avalanche*. It spread very quickly, even though the group was very small. For three-four-five years it was very, very small, before the commercial side of it came in the late 1970s and Weiner and those people made objects and writings that ended up in collections. In the 1970s everything was still very barren for the artists; ten years, and then that Renaissance of painting returned. Only 20 years later, did those Conceptual trends and Minimalist trends reappear, and become commercially interesting.

SR *In 1973 you organised an exhibition in Westfälischer Kunstverein in Münster,* Avalanche: the development of an avant-garde magazine.

KH I don't remember that. If I did, it was a small exhibition.

SR *Another exhibition that interests me is* Das Konzept ist die Form, *in 1972.*

KH That was the book! [*laughs*] The book was the exhibition. The exhibition was at Konrad Fischer, where we presented the book and nothing on the walls. I do repeat it again: the book was the exhibition. We showed the materials for the book in vitrines, what the artists wrote, the drafts, the telegrams from On Kawara, the instructions from Sol LeWitt, or leporello I still have hanging up by Jan Dibbets. There was nothing on the walls because the exhibition was the book. That was the realised form, or one of the possible realised forms, of the artists' thoughts. It was also the idea. The third part of the exhibition of the book was, so to speak, a book exhibition, conceived not as an artist's book, but really as an exhibition. I had written to all the artists and sent them the layout to ask for a suggestion of how they'd like to realise an artistic idea in the form of this book.

SR *That was also part of the trend of the time; Seth Siegelaub also made exhibitions in the form of books and the special issue of* Studio International.

KH Yes, of course. Another project was the retrospective exhibition of Lawrence Weiner (*Lawrence Weiner. Retrospektive – 50 Werke*) that I did in Münster in 1973. It was a poster and then just a book. There was nothing more than that. The poster and the book are two forms of the exhibition. The book isn't the catalogue of the exhibition, it's the exhibition. Another form of this was with Jan Dibbets, which was a normal exhibition with his 'Perspectiv-Korrekturen' [Perspective Corrections] in Aachen (1970) and so on, but he did a photographic project rather than a catalogue [*shows the project*]. It wasn't hung on the walls. That's one of the artists' programmes in the context of those catalogues that I was doing at the time. It was an exhibition, it wasn't an artist's book and it wasn't a catalogue. It was the new form that Seth Siegelaub was the first to do. The ideas were in the air, to some extent only the published forms were the artistic reality. Weiner's famous quotation: 'The artist may construct the piece; the piece may be fabricated; the piece need not be built; each being equal and consistent for the intent of the artist, the decision as to condition rests with the receiver upon the occasion of receivership.' This is the central motto of the whole thing, although Weiner also saw it as an art piece. To that extent it was also important that we wanted to get away from the established channels of artistic communication, the transfer of objects. Books, phone-calls, or even television and video could be used; they were all natural ideas that made up Concept art. All those directions were finally much more political than attempts by painters like Jörg Immendorff to mobilise through paintings the workers in the Ruhr to demonstrate on the first of May.

SR *There were also the technological developments that gave the artists the opportunity to work with video.*

KH Of course. Unlike the previous generation, the Informel artists, the Tachistes, they took the perspective away from traditional demonstrations of art, meaning painting. In the end they conceived drawings only as sketches, and then turned their eye to photography. This finally brought photography into the museum, through Concept art; Video and film, too. Super-8 was a very popular medium then, not least for alternative cinema. There was also the telephone, and the mail, as with On Kawara's telegrams and postcards – all strands of communication and means of transmission, all media, so to speak, were used. It was the first time the concept of media came up in the discussion of art.

SR *How did the book project arise? What made you decide to publish the book as an exhibition?*

KH The impetus came from the publishing house.

SR *The publishing house contacted you?*

KH Yes. Phaidon, a German company at the time, wanted to do a new programme, but it so far hadn't been successful. Alexander Schleber, was a man full of ideas, full of enthusiasm, who wanted to break away from the picture in art publishing. He knew my *Magazin Kunst* and asked me if I fancied doing a book for him on Conceptual art. So I did that. How the idea arose to conceive the third part as an exhibition, I can't remember. But as you can see, it was in the air. It wasn't actually such a great feat. Here's the letter that Schleber wrote to the artists [*shows the letter reproduced in the book*]. Emilio Prini went on to use it as his suggested object. It was then the cover. They were both by Prini.

SR *Your book was published in 1971. Were you already aware that other books about Conceptual art were in production, such as the book by Ursula Meyer or the one by Ermanno Migliorini in Italy?*

KH I can't remember. I might have known something about Lucy R. Lippard's book. But I didn't go to New York until 1972. So I don't think I did know anything about it. Definitely not about Ursula Meyer's, but I don't think I knew anything about Lippard either. I only met her in 1972. I never met Meyer.

SR *What did you think about those books when you read them later, in comparison to the ideas in your book?*

KH If I remember correctly, Lippard was more limited to a collection of material. Meyer I can't remember now. I was a bit disappointed by them, because I didn't actually find out anything that I didn't know already. What I'd have wanted to do would be the whole prehistory, starting with Erwin Panofsky, from a European perspective, to try and get close to this phenomenon of an art of ideas or idea-art. I would have hoped for an academic version of that from an American point of view, something more fundamental. I was very disappointed by those books and I never read them again. I can't even really remember what was in them.

SR *One idea that interested me a lot in your book is in your last chapter. You write, and it's something we've just discussed, that the emphasis of the idea as an artistic factor has extended the boundaries of art. You write that this was having considerable consequences for the art trade. Since an idea can't be sold, dealers were becoming publishers and film producers. They were the only ones who could connect these new artistic trends directly with the art market.*

KH I'm always a bad prophet! None of those things happened. It all went back to the art trade [*laughs*]. What I find important, though, is that historically you can see how political we really were – misunderstood in the sense of party-political or ideologically political.

SR *So were there American artists' ideas and European artists' ideas?*

KH No. Perhaps that has to do with the fact that Marcel Duchamp was being re-elevated at that time as one of the central founding fathers. So the American who was a Frenchman, but naturalised of course, had the same ideas that we agreed upon. Therefore the ideas weren't influenced so much by the different cultures, the American and the European. The American artists weren't successful in the States themselves, quite the contrary. They were, if not exactly discovered as artists, then at least known, by Europe, by the Dutch and the Germans. They had initially felt much more at ease in Europe, because their ideas, in relation to an art that had a conceptual character, where planning was foregrounded over actual physical realisation, had seemed to be better understood, at that time. It's remarkable that Germany, with its Expressionist tradition, and the USA with the great age of Abstract Expressionism which was about to come to an end, were so united in their rejection of that emotionally divested form of art. Even more than one might have expected. Then of course there were connections, like Hanne Darboven who was discovered in America as a German, by Sol LeWitt and people like that. And then there were personal points of contact. Since this community was initially very small, personal acquaintances were very, very important.

SR *The American artists weren't successful in America. It's as if America only started to see the US Conceptualists as artists when they were successful in Europe.*

KH Yes, of course. Very soon, of course, there were curators in the USA who started taking an interest in the new trends, or art critics like Lippard. She'd previously written and edited a very influential book about Pop art. She also wrote intensively about some of the Conceptual artists like LeWitt and so on. There was also Willoughby Sharp, who was very close to Zero art, and who, as an American, brought out a magazine, *Avalanche*, that was influential. Among the *Artforum* people I can't remember who the contacts were. John Coplans was also a very open-minded man. Then in New York – New York was always the bridge to Europe and we Europeans had less to do with America than you might imagine – there were people like Kynaston McShine and the big Minimal exhibition in the Jewish Museum, or Pontus Hulten's work on the art of the machine, in which Duchamp had been recently re-established. There was a whole series of points of con-tact that weren't in the mainstream of artistic dis-cussions, but which were already appearing as the future crystallisation points. The travelling back and forth began at that time. It was getting a bit easier to get to the USA from Europe, and also from Germany, than it had been ten years before. The Netherlands were, you might say, a kind of mainstay in communication between America and Germany. The Dutch played an extraordinarily important role.

SR *So in the US the art scene was in New York?*

KH At the time it was exclusively in New York. Then Weber came from Los Angeles. I can't remember any more. Even today, those trends have been restricted more or less to New York. The Concept artist Ed Ruscha, in California, has an approach that's a bit different from the rather more intellectual attitude formulated by people like LeWitt, Weiner and Barry, who was already a bit mystical.

SR *When you travelled to the US in 1972, did you think the art scene was very different from the one in Europe? Was there also a small Conceptual sphere there?*

KH For me, it was a step or two backwards. I was in New York for Documenta, for our 'Ideen-Kunst' section, and of course I was dealing with the artists from that circle. They were all, more or less, not established. There were no galleries that they showed at. I can't remember where ... Leo Castelli, of course, but I don't think he specialised in Conceptual art at the time. There were other galleries ... I visited Klaus Kertess and I remember Mary Boone was his secretary. It wasn't happening so much in the galleries as in the artists' apartments. In fact, the centre was Max's Kansas City bar. The Pop artists all went to that bar, as well as the Minimalists and the Conceptualists. That was the meeting point. After I'd checked into my hotel, Andre, Smithson and Darboven came and said hello. My first appearance in New York was at Max's Kansas City.

SR *So you went to New York for* Documenta, *where you curated the section called* Idee+Idee/Licht *with Fischer. How did that come about? Did Szeemann contact you?*

KH Yes. Szeemann asked me if I felt like joining the team. I said yes. He came to my flat in Münster with Jean-Christophe Ammann and asked me what I'd like to do. I had the alternative of doing that *Idee+Idee/Licht* section, as it was called at the time, with Fischer or on my own. I decided I didn't want to do it on my own. By now I had three, four, five years of practice as an exhibition organiser. My feeling was that I could still learn a few things and I opted to work with Fischer. I think it was the right decision. So we did it together. It was a very intense collaboration. I worked very intensively with him on exhibitions in Münster, and he cooperated with me very closely on the book. Those were four exhausting weeks in Kassel and we'd put that section together very carefully.

SR *Documenta 5 has the reputation of being very important. What was the position of that section in relation to Documenta as a whole?*

KH On the margins at first. It wasn't Szeemann's favorite section. He wasn't wild about it, he thought it was a bit too cerebral. Harry Szeemann already had different ideas. They weren't opposed to ours, but he had different preferences, let's put it that way. He later invented *Individuelle Mythologien*. It was never planned as a section in that sense, it became heterogeneous. He worked very spontaneously. We were actually much more settled than he was. The section with the most publicity was Jean-Christophe Ammann's section on photorealism. Of course, the specialists, the insiders, thought that our section – that big room with the *Circle* by Richard Long in the middle and Hanne Darboven and Sol LeWitt opposite, and also Agnes Martin – was the cathedral of Documenta, along with Richard Serra, who was in the next room. For the serious art business, which was more interested in innovative things, things that pointed to the future, that was the section that mattered. I think the most photographed room was the one with Long in the middle. The reaction to Documenta was rather poor, with the exception of the photo-realism, which went down well. Everything else was pretty much dismissed, which was usual at the time; it's different today. We ourselves didn't have any problems. Szeemann went on to have a lot of problems with Documenta; the state even brought proceedings against him. It was all very unpleasant. Fischer was very meticulous about the budget. We only had a little bed-and-breakfast on the edge. He wasn't a great eater, so we generally ended up eating fish and chips in a little kiosk in the Nordsee or the Bilka Kaufhaus, but apart from that I have only very good memories. It was a brilliant collaboration, with Szeemann and Ammann too. At first we didn't get on well at all. Then we met up properly, and Szeemann came along as if nothing had happened [*laughs*]! There was a very peculiar atmosphere, but we changed that too and this conception emerged that became the section we showed later on. The night before the press conference, I spent the night on the desk in Szeemann's office, which was up at the top next to the Neue Galerie [*laughs*]. That was a very intense time, but it was also a companionable time: those conversations, the communicative, playful stuff. After Documenta 5 it got a lot harder with rivalries and hostility. At Documenta 5 I can't remember any rivalries. I can remember discussions, minor conflicts and disagreements, but that's all part of big projects. But otherwise it was a very good event; everything went smoothly with the artists as well. I just remember playing boules; Fischer was a big boules fan, and we all played boules in front of the Fridericianum.

SR *It was also a good opportunity to present this new artistic direction to a big audience.*

KH Yes, of course. It was a way of putting across Conceptual art or Idea art as a central manifestation of the time. There were also consequences with bigger exhibitions in Basel and Leverkusen, in Holland ... After that, the artists started having individual careers. Buren worked with Cladders in Mönchengladbach, Dibbets showed with Wember and in Aachen, Weiner in Aachen too, and Barry and Kosuth, and then there was the big LeWitt exhibition in Holland, Sonsbeek. A lot happened in the wake of Documenta. The initial spark was *When Attitudes Become Form* and *Op Losse Schroeven* in Amsterdam, Documenta, Sonsbeek in the Park ... There were artistic events going on everywhere, showing Concept art and Land art – all those trends that didn't take their bearings from the 'white cubes', as they were coming to be known. With the activities, the emanations with Conceptual strategies or manifestos for changing the environment in terms of Land art, the differences merged; they levelled out.

SR *You said the Documenta artists went on to have their own careers. Did anything change in that respect?*

KH That all fell apart, yes. It got too big. Then the focus in Germany moved from Düsseldorf to Cologne. The Kunstmarkts brought the galleries to Cologne, and lots of artists (Sigmar Polke, Gerhard Richter and so on) moved from Düsseldorf to Cologne. I moved in the end from Münster, in 1974, to Bonn. I started spending more time in Cologne than in Düsseldorf. That focus on Düsseldorf stopped somehow with Documenta 5.

SR *So the intense period was from 1967 until 1972.*

KH You could say that. It was a brief and a very intense time. I'd put on a big Darboven exhibition in 1971 before Documenta. After Documenta came *Das Konzept ist die Form* and the Weiner retrospective. Those were my last exhibitions in the field of Conceptual art. I didn't do any more after that, at least not in Münster. Boltanski (1974 in Münster) and then in Bonn the double feature Boltanski/Messager (1976) belongs more to the direction Harry Szeemann labelled as *Individual Mythologies*, it wasn't what Konrad Fischer liked so much. And later in Bonn the Bechers with their first retrospective I cooperated only with Bernd and Hilla and with this show I extended my interests to the realm of photography in general.

SR *Did you do a lot of work with Fischer for the programme in ... ?*

KH Yes. But only Darboven in fact. The Weiner, I did with the artist. The collaboration with Fischer actually ended with Documenta 5.

SR *For the exhibitions that you went on to organise in Münster, did you tend to contact the artists directly, or the art dealers?*

KH Not always, but generally the artists themselves, because I knew many of them. Sigmar Polke I did with Polke. Hanne Darboven, that was because my exhibition had fallen through and I didn't know how to fill the date quickly, and by chance Darboven was there and I asked her. Reiner Ruthenbeck I did with Ruthenbeck. Yes, I did everything with the artists. In Münster I didn't have much to do with the art business. In 1974, I went to Bonn, and I kept Münster going as well until 1975.

SR *Did you show Conceptual artists in Bonn as well?*

KH Yes, the second or third exhibition that I did there was a retrospective of Bernd and Hilla Becher, if you want to call them Conceptual. Then I did the big exhibition with Hanne Darboven, then Christian Boltanski and Annette Messager, that's a bit Conceptual too. Those are the Conceptual exhibitions that I remember.

Translation from German: Shaun Whiteside

4.9 Conversation with Nicholas Logsdail

London, 21 February 2005

SOPHIE RICHARD *When you decided to open the Lisson Gallery in 1967, were you aware that several other dealer galleries interested in the same kind of art were opening all over Europe? I'm thinking, for example, of Konrad Fischer.*

NICHOLAS LOGSDAIL No, because Fischer opened several months after me. And I didn't decide to open a gallery. In a way, the gallery was decided for me, because I was an artist. The first exhibition ... well I suppose to some extent I organised it, but in fact it was a joint collaborative effort in the way in which young artists organise their own exhibitions. I had a building, in very bad condition, but I had both ground floor and basement space that wasn't being used. One of the other artists said, 'Why don't we do this show in your place?' So we all came together and painted it white, put in some light and things that students do.

I suppose I'd been aware for about 18 months to two years of the so-called 'Conceptual' activities, partly through *Artforum*, which I arranged for the Slade librarian to get. When the principal discovered that we were getting *Artforum*, he told them to cancel the subscription because he thought it would be too subversive for the students. I was also doing photography and I was very interested in the way in which artists were using photography. Whether I was already aware that it had the label 'Conceptual art' attached, I don't know. I was very young, 19 or 20 years old. I think at that age you're very instinctive, but unknowing. People of that age can be very sharp on those things, but very unaware of bigger issues. Art students are like that and it's where a lot of talent comes from: conscious-unconscious, not through teaching. I learnt more in a year or two making the gallery than I have ever learnt through my studies. The empirical knowledge is always the best.

I had no intention of having a gallery; it was just to have one show. I got thrown out of university because I wasn't going to class or studying. But then I had a gallery and I discovered I maybe could do that for the rest of my life. For me, there was this excited feeling of 'Let's do some more shows!' There was so much interest in it and it was a lot of fun. It was, however, very difficult because there was only a small trickle of money. The generation of other gallery people who started at that time, were nearly all seven, eight, nine, ten years older. Konrad was seven years older I think, and so were the others: Paul Maenz, Sperone, John Weber. There was no one of my age at that time. So I was the junior and was treated in that way by some people. I wasn't taken seriously by the other galleries for the first two to three years, until we got the programme going and they saw what was being done. Then it started to become a little bit successful and the whole attitude changed. Some even started to be a little bit jealous. Basically, in about 1970–72, everybody was friendly. Then it started to become a business and a lot of friendships became rather difficult. We were competing with each other over the same artists, sometimes at the same time.

SR *There were, however, some dealer galleries with which you collaborated?*

NL Yes, absolutely: with Konrad Fischer, with Art & Project, with Paul Maenz a little later, a tiny bit with Sperone on one or two deals, and very much with MTL in Brussels. Fernand Spillemaeckers was a very good friend. I introduced Art & Language to him. So in a sense I introduced Art & Language to Belgium.

SR *Was working with an American counterpart different from working with a European one?*

NL Well don't forget that at that time – although I'd describe it as the first period of internationalism – Sol LeWitt would say that it wasn't important where an artist came from, but what mattered was whether the artist was any good. I thought that was brilliant and I always had that in the forefront of my mind. I still do to this day. In a way, Conceptual art, more than Minimal art, was born out of that ethos. But having said that, it was still centred around New York. We Europeans like to believe that it was an international thing, but the fact is if you didn't go to New York, you were out of the loop.

SR *But still, at least in the beginning, Conceptual artists had a voice in Europe and not so much in America.*

NL Well, the really interesting thing was that it was focused on New York. The dialogue, the conversations, the intercourse between artists was either done by mail, postcards or telegrams. (There was On Kawara, but there were also many other artists using telegrams.) In my experience, the shop talk was in New York, and a little bit in Germany, and in the bars of Cologne and Düsseldorf. There would be local artists and an American artist, say, who had a show there, all getting smashed. There was a bar near Konrad's gallery where we went.

SR *What kind of relationship did you have with other dealers in London? I'm thinking particularly of Jack Wendler and Nigel Greenwood.*

NL With Nigel it was always very good. With Jack, well, I didn't know him and he came to London with a lot of money, so it was quite hostile. I think Jack was so innocent about it all and didn't realise why some of the other galleries dealing in the same territory were being hostile to him. He came in with relatively a lot of money, which we didn't have, and also with ready-made contacts from New York. We found that we lost some ground there, in the sense that he was showing artists whom we'd planned to show. At the end of the day, it didn't really matter because he closed and we became very dear friends. We still are very good friends.

SR *One of the artists I'm researching is Richard Long. I wondered if you could talk about the first show you organised with him in 1973, since it was the first time he exhibited in a dealer gallery in Britain.*

NL I think my first contact with Richard Long was in 1968 or 1969. He was already quite close to Konrad. Konrad didn't really want him to show in London. I sensed that there was this kind of battle going on, where he was referring to Konrad and Konrad would say 'You don't need a London gallery, you have me!' Konrad was very like that he wanted to be the number one person for the artists, especially in the early days. He maintained relationships with the artists he represented and the artists would always refer to him before doing anything. Konrad turned it a little bit into a joke: 'Maybe you should show with Nigel, maybe you should show with Jack, maybe you should show with Nicholas.' So in fact, he was playing a little bit of a game. It was a kind of strange humour, it was like turning something quite serious into humour and thereby creating confusion.

SR *So finally, you convinced him. How did it happen?*

NL I paved the way and he kept coming to the gallery. He kept sending me postcards. This is Richard's way of saying, 'I'm paying attention to you. Don't forget me, I'm here.' What convinced Richard to do a show is that we'd started to do little artists' books. Nobody was doing artists' books. So we did a book together, which unfortunately we were all terribly amateur about as we did not have enough experience in making books. The printing wasn't very good and Richard wasn't happy with it. So we had it reprinted and it was to his liking.

SR *Were there any people collecting at that time in England?*

NL Basically, there were only two serious collectors. There were a few people hanging around, but you couldn't take them that seriously in this field. Of course there were collectors, but they were collectors of good old English roast beef kind of art, with the Yorkshire pudding and gravy. In fact, some of the art even looked like that, like Leon Kossof. What we were doing was understood only by artists or curators of my generation, like Anne Seymour, and one or two art critics. Art critics were very good, although if you look at press cuttings of the time, you see that they were also pretty naive. They were very enthusiastic, but they could badly misinterpret the work, even though you talked to them and explained it. They didn't want your explanations, they wanted to interpret the work themselves.

SR *From which magazines were they?*

NL *Studio International*, which was Charles Harrison and Peter Townsend; Nigel Gosling for *The Observer*, John Russell in the *Sunday Times*. There was also Richard Cork at the *Evening Standard*, who was really amazing. He had a very enthusiastic way of describing things, but he was very supportive. Well, there were a number of other characters who were interested. Also, I was very accessible. I was here all the time. Anybody who came in would be very, very welcome, because there were very few visitors, I had one or two a day.

SR *Who would come to the gallery?*

NL Mostly artists and the sort of early professionals of my generation, like Nicholas Serota. There are still a number of people around today who were regulars then. The openings were very lovely and friendly affairs, with a few bottles of wine and maybe five artists and one collector, a young curator or two.

SR *So the public response wasn't aggressive to the kind of art you were showing?*

NL Sometimes a little bit. But we didn't target that art audience. I just thought it was a new area, a new way of thinking, a new kind of gallery; we weren't even really thinking business. We were thinking about how we were going to get money for the next show. The only way to do that, of course, was to sell something. So the search for collectors and museums was a primary concern.

SR *You were talking before about two Conceptual art*

collectors.

NL Oh yes, in the late 1960s in London the only informed collectors were Ted Power and Alan Power, the father and son. Ted Power was coming to the end of his collecting and he bought Donald Judd and Sol LeWitt from me. He walked in and bought a whole show! They were London-based. Alan Power was in some ways less adventurous than his father. And then a couple of years later, he got it and started buying good work. Collectors in this field were mostly on the continent and before there were any significant American collectors for this kind of work. Let's face it, even today, for the purist-of-the-pure Conceptual art, there still aren't many collectors. There are many more collectors for Anish Kapoor, Jeff Koons or Damien Hirst, to mention a few very obvious names.

SR *Why do you think this is the case?*

NL Well, because the work wouldn't do it. For most collectors the motivation is the materiality of the object, a painterly painting or a material sculpture. That's the fact; there's no denying that. It's always been the case and it will always be the case. The Conceptual art collectors are the connoisseurs. It will always be insiders who understand why it's important to buy such art: its significance being greater than its materiality, wall drawings, etc. These types of work were not very material. Early Art & Language wasn't very much more than that either. The artists at that time, as you well know, it's even a cliché, were trying to make work that was immaterial, on the basis that it remained pure and couldn't really be sold. This was a very strange contradiction, because all the artists, however cool they were trying to be, actually were in need of selling works, to a greater or lesser extent.

SR *So on the one hand they wanted to make something immaterial, and on the other hand they needed something material to sell.*

NL That's what I'm trying to say, yes. I think Lawrence Weiner or Art & Language would make a joke out of this. Of course, what we didn't understand at the time was that if you're creating an art object, if you're working with art galleries, it's their job to create the market. Actually, if you try hard enough, you can probably create a market for anything. You could create a market for a glass of water! And for the last twenty years, this has finally been a very good business.

SR *From 1972–73, there were a number of museums in Europe that would collect.*

NL There was Mönchengladbach, the Van Abbemuseum, the Stedelijk, the Tate Gallery, a little bit ...

SR *You sold to the Tate?*

NL We sold a little bit. We probably sold more than anybody else to the Tate Gallery, mostly through my friendship at the time with Anne Seymour. Actually, the Victoria & Albert Museum were actively buying in the late 1960s, there was a brilliant curator there, Carol Hogben. Well, institutionally, what else was there?

SR *In the Netherlands ...*

NL The Kröller-Müller Museum, a very big museum. We also sold to Edy de Wilde, notably a Ryman painting, which is still there I believe. In 1972–73, the Belgian collectors became very important: Herman Daled, and maybe a little later, Anton and Annick Herbert and others especially in Belgium.

SR *Was the Lisson Gallery represented at the Cologne art fair or the Prospect shows? Was it important to go abroad?*

NL Yes, it was. It was very enlightening. It gave you a length and depth to the panorama, the landscape of the art world from a more European perspective.

SR *Do you feel that England was a bit isolated?*

NL Yes. Certainly because it's an island, certainly because it had less of a modernist intellectual art history connected with it. Except, of course, that there were very important artists coming out of here at the time. But they kind of came to the attention of the emerging British audience either through America or through Germany, through people travelling. So English museum curators and directors or very young emerging British collectors would see their first Richard Long in Düsseldorf or New York, not in London. I think it's still the case today. To see what's on our doorstep, we have to go somewhere else.

SR *How would you define Conceptualism? Is it a type of artwork produced or a group of artists who were seen as such?*

NL Well, I think both. If you look at something like the Kynaston McShine *Information* show in 1970, or Szeemann's *When Attitudes Become Form* exhibition, which wasn't exactly Conceptual art, or Lucy Lippard's book *Six Years*, most of the artists who were doing anything interesting are in those books and catalogues. It was really a new way of thinking. It was like a big international family. For those who were interested, over a very short period of time, collectors, artists, and most of the other players involved, became aware of each other. They'd make it their business to find out more. If I went to New York or Germany, I'd have phone numbers, and I'd make it my business to go and see the people I'd heard about. In some cases, I wouldn't even know whether it was interesting or not, but it was something I'd seen in a catalogue. It was through those encounters that I learned the most through conversations with artists. I really enjoyed these conversations with artists, and I still do. Many collectors are very knowledgeable and fun to be with. So Conceptualism was a family of people who were thinking and believing, in a way, that we were part of a new way of thinking, a new way of doing things, a new way of communicating.

This also coincided with the beginning of inexpensive jet travel. I think this was an incredibly important component in making it all happen. If I hadn't been able to fly to New York the first two or three times, although very inexpensively, I wouldn't have been able to do what I've done: to establish the gallery and to put on Conceptual shows. I think that applies to everybody else as well. No one would have been able to fly artists over for their first shows. It was affordable and the artists weren't complaining. Few were thinking about serious money in those days; they were thinking about art and how to function. It really had to do with discovering uncharted territory. Artists would go through great pain to discover a new territory, a new way of thinking, and they'd claim that territory as theirs. It was like pioneers going out to the Wild West and staking their claim, but on an intellectual level.

SR *Conceptual art is quite intellectual anyway.*

NL Well, some of it is also pretty dull, to be honest. But its dullness is part of its quality. They love to call it irrational. Some of it's very rational and very logical. But it's as much about one as the other. There was nothing else in between.

SR *There was also the 1968–69 spirit and the youth movements.*

NL Yes. There was much scandalous discussion about artists stealing ideas from each other and so on. There were a lot of discussions about that, about origins. That's how certain artists such as Richard Long and Hamish Fulton gained a lot of respect, because they really invented their own territory without any doubt. I remember an argument about Smithson and Long, that Smithson had actually stolen the spiral from Long – although he was from a slightly older generation – some claimed that Smithson saw Long's work and that out of it came his early work. Would *Spiral Jetty* [1970] have been done without Long's work? I know there were some great debates about that at the time. In New York, especially, people would take sides.

SR *And not so much in Europe?*

NL In a different context. There were deep, loving friendships between artists. There were core artists who were the kind of glue to those friendships, for example Sol LeWitt, Dan Graham, Lawrence Weiner, Art & Language in their independent alternative way. It had to do with the artists' attitudes and approaches. I think that Art & Language were so intense that they were often regarded as too smart. Art & Language in turn were trying to defend their position with an intellectual barrage, like a smokescreen. The early writings of Art & Language are a lot like smokescreens that they could hide behind. You know what they say, 'Where there's smoke, there's fire.'

SR *Could you talk about the 'wall drawing' show you did with Sol LeWitt in June–July 1970?*

NL It came about through my initial contact with Sol. It wasn't my first show with him. The first show was with Don Judd as well in 1969. It was through my contact with Sol and his commitment to doing a show. It came about through visiting him in New York and an exchange of letters. You didn't use the telephone in those days. Phone calls to New York were astonishingly expensive and you didn't use the telephone very much unless it was very urgent. It was probably cheaper flying there than having a very long phone call.

SR *So did Sol LeWitt come over for his show in 1970?*

NL Absolutely, yes. We got together a very interesting bunch of people to make the wall drawings, which was a combination of my artist friends, in some cases from my student days. I wanted to try and give them a new experience and get them out of their old thinking. Sol was incredibly generous. He said something very endearing that I'll never forget. When he left, he said: 'By the way, I've given you a lot of drawings to sell. I know the wall drawings are very difficult to sell. People don't seem to get it, because they're immaterial. When people buy the drawings, just keep the money and use it to do more shows, and pay me when you can.' This was one of the sweetest and most endearing things any artist could have said at that time to me. I really worked so extra hard, a) to sell them and b) to pay him. My relationship with Sol has always been a little like that. He seldom really wants the money; he likes to trade works with other artists. I sometimes feel it as an embarrassment, because the money is there.

He wants to figure out what to do with it. Sol was very supportive of British artists if he liked them.

SR *So it was really getting the artist over from America and doing a show with him on the spot.*

NL The other thing about that era that made everything possible, was that communication became faster, mostly through word of mouth, through people travelling. Some people were travelling all the time from one show to another. Americans, especially, would come to Europe and line up four shows with different galleries. It was much more economical for them to do that. They'd literally come with the work in a suitcase or they'd make the work in situ. So there were none of these transportation costs that have become very expensive, especially today.

SR *It was much more dealing with artists rather than with works.*

NL Yes. It was the relationship you had with the artist. The fondest memories I have of those ten years, I'd say, were the friendships with artists. They'd stay for one or two weeks in my house with my wife Fiona, you'd hang out with them. It was the same when you went to stay with them. You were really getting into each other's heads!

SR *A lot of artists are uncomfortable with the term 'Conceptual art'.*

NL Well, I think they are, because I think in the beginning they thought of it as a label. You could argue that virtually all artists are conceptual anyway. Whatever kind of art it is, there has to be some kind of an idea about doing something, even if it's putting a paint brush into a pot of paint and applying it to the canvas.

SR *What is the terminology to use?*

NL My definition of Conceptual art was that it was always predetermined, even if the idea of the work had to do with chance. The idea of chance in the work was predetermined by the series of actions that the artists would take. Often the idea was to be surprised by the result, but knowing that because the idea was good, the result would turn out to be interesting, visually or conceptually or intellectually.

SR *In those days, what was the terminology the artists used to describe themselves?*

NL Artists, that's all! [*Laughs*]

SR *But did they see themselves as a group or a new generation of artists?*

NL Absolutely, as a new generation, yes. As a new, thoughtful, intelligent, and for the first time, an international generation. For sure, this was the first generation of artists who would become known internationally among a small group of people in different cities and different countries. They'd become well known within a matter of months or years. Prior to that, artists would work hard for half a lifetime before they'd get any kind of local recognition, let alone international recognition.

SR *There was a network in which the information was getting around very fast.*

NL Yes. You were either part of that network or you weren't. There were some people who would have killed to be part of that network! I was very fortunate in a way, because I had the knowledge. By the late 1960s, I really had the knowledge. I was an insider, and still very young. In 1970, I was twenty-five years old, and by that time, I was pretty well informed. Of course, there are many things I now know that I wasn't completely clear about at the time. But, you couldn't be clear about it, because you were right in the middle of the most productive phase of the work of those artists.

I've always maintained that there was a landmark year, which was 1966, a year before I started. 1966 had the feel of being the truly formative year, when things started to come together. It gave a flavour and set the stage for what was to come. That wasn't clear at that moment, but it became clear very soon afterwards, within four or five years, that it was a landmark, a historical year. As you became aware of what had happened, most things would lead back to 1966–67. Those were the key dates. For artists who started later, it was already too late.

SR *A lot of people say that by the end of the 1970s, this kind of network spirit disappeared.*

NL Yes. All you were left with were the key figures, the real die-hards.

SR *What changed, from the point of view of your gallery, from the late 1960s to the late 1970s?*

NL I remember that by about 1975, 1976, there was another group of artists here, who were more or less of the same generation, but they were on the tail end of it. Tony Cragg is a good example of this. Cragg's first work goes back to the early 1970s, from 1972 onwards. He was quite close friends with Richard Long in those days. I met him around 1974, although we didn't do a show until 1979. I remember Tony felt excluded because he was too late with this sort of graphic work and photographic work that had the look of that era. They're from the early Conceptual period, but they don't go back before 1972. So they were too late to be early. I remember having long conversations with him; he realised that he couldn't be one of them. He had to create his own territory. He paved the way for a convincing new generation of sculptors. Artists such as Anish Kapoor, Bill Woodrow, Richard Deacon, Richard Wentworth, Shirazeh Houshiary and Julian Opie. I think that's something that people today don't understand at all. That's what I mean about authenticity as well, the authenticity of the origins, where one thing leads to another thing. It has always been a very competitive game, especially with this generation. Why were they all so obsessed with football and sports, like playing boules?

SR *Were they really?*

NL Oh absolutely, yes. Sitting in pubs watching boxing matches on television.

SR *You said before that at the beginning, your gallery was run with very little money. From what moment on did it start to go well?*

NL Well, gradually. It was just growing slowly but solidly. I was lucky in a way, because this street [Bell Street, London NW1] was a very inexpensive street in those days. I was able to buy the building. This gave me some security. I didn't start with any capital, but I could go to the bank and borrow. Buildings, like art, have greatly increased in value. So one could borrow money against it and build and develop the gallery. I did that from about 1972 onwards. I couldn't have funded the activities of the gallery without doing that. That is now a long time ago and this gallery has flourished. But it has somehow always kept some of the innovative spirit of those early days. That's how things go.

4.10 Conversation with Paul Maenz

Berlin, 6 October 2004

SOPHIE RICHARD *The progressive European galleries that encouraged Conceptual art in the 1970s were all founded in the late 1960s. For example, Wide White Space (1966), Yvon Lambert (1966), Konrad Fischer (1967), Gian Enzo Sperone (1967), Paul Maenz (1970). How do you explain that?*

PAUL MAENZ The gallery owners were from the same generation as the artists and were interested in the art of their time.

SR *Do you agree with the view that your gallery encouraged above all 'intellectual' and 'analytical' Conceptual artists in the 1970s, such as Buren, Kosuth and Art & Language?*

PM Yes.

SR *Which European galleries and museums were, in your view, the most progressive in the 1970s? Which did you visit, and which did you trade with?*

PM Konrad Fischer, Düsseldorf; Art & Project, Amsterdam; Wide White Space, Antwerp; MTL, Brussels, Gian Enzo Sperone, Turin; Yvon Lambert, Paris and Daniel Templon, Paris.

SR *Which private collectors were most committed to Conceptual art? Which were your most loyal customers?*

PM Herman Daled, Brussels; Mia and Martin Visser, Bergeyk; Anton Herbert, Gent; Panza di Biumo, Varese; Friedrich Erwin Rentschler, Laupheim.

SR *How did the Paul Maenz Gallery in Brussels come to be founded in 1973–74? Why did you choose Belgium for your second gallery? Was Belgium one of the most important artistic centres in Europe?*

PM The artists from my Cologne gallery weren't represented in Belgium.

SR *Did you also look towards America at the time? What in your view were the differences between the European and the American art scenes as regards Conceptual art??*

PM The American art scene only became interested in Conceptual art after those artists were successful in Europe.

Translation from German: Shaun Whiteside

4.11 Conversation with Rolf Preisig

Berlin, 6 October 2004

[Preisig is commenting on a folder containing all the invitation cards from the Galerie Rolf Preisig, 1973–79]

ROLF PREISIG The Weiner exhibition was a tape, spoken by a woman in four languages. So there was nothing to see. The piece consisted of this invitation and the tape only.

SOPHIE RICHARD *David Tremlett...*

RP Then Robert Barry drawings. I designed the invitation card out of a list of words that now hangs on the wall in my toilet! Edda Renouf: I have no idea what she's doing now. You don't hear anything from her any more.

SR *Ian Wilson ...*

RP This was during Art Basel 1976 ... a little special exhibition with three works of Carl Andre, Donald Judd and Robert Ryman, all serial works: white paint on polyester with sticky bits, a long copper line on the floor and then a 'stack' by Judd. It was wonderful.

SR *At that Art Basel you also had a stand with Konrad Fischer.*

RP Yes, exactly. In 1978 I was there with Konrad again. We showed Richter's first abstract pictures, those smear paintings, at prices of around 25,000 Francs. Seven or eight paintings, and we didn't sell a single one. Now they go for millions, that's life!

SR *Alan Charlton ...*

RP At that show he presented four '4 part paintings'. ... Leslie Foxcroft is Alan Charlton's wife. She does very interesting things, all with paper ... Daniel Buren, Hamish Fulton, Ulrich Rückriem ...

SR *What was Buren's project?*

RP This here was his second exhibition [*shows photographs*]. He covered parts of the windows with pink and white striped paper, and repeated the pattern on the inside gallery wall. The space was a former stable, about 10.5 × 6 metres, the ceiling 4 metres high. Good proportions, but without heating, and freezing cold in winter!

SR *In a courtyard?*

RP The building was U-shaped. First I could rent the left wing, years later also the opposite wing. I specially liked the ceiling: iron joists vaulted with bricks. For the opening show in this space, Buren extended the arches of the ceiling into intersecting circles to form a sort of garland. This 'reflection' of the ceiling was projected to the opposite wall, partly covering the windows.

SR *The gallery's first exhibition with Stanley Brouwn, what was shown there?*

RP Simply a table with filing cabinets, and in the filing cabinets cards with pace measurements! It was a pretty chilly start of a gallery! But I absolutely wanted Brouwn, one of the really good guys, to set the standard.

SR *Richard Long, On Kawara, James Lee Byars ...*

RP Byars' show was *The Hundred One Page Books*, black books piled up on a black table. At the opening Byars, dressed in black and wearing a top hat, entered the room, picked up a book, whispered the one word or the sentence printed on the one page, set the book back down, until he'd gone through the hundred books, and walked out. Very magic and mysterious!

SR *Rémy Zaugg, Sol LeWitt ...*

RP *Geometric Figures*, his second show after the *Wall Drawing* in 1975 ...

SR *And Wilson did his 'Discussion' in the gallery?*

RP Yes. He was present and the people came or did not come! There were never many participants, and they were completely baffled. Two years ago, Ian was invited by Urs Raussmüller for a 'Discussion' in Schaffhausen, and he was just the same as 30 years ago – incredible.

SR *Lawrence Weiner ...*

RP *A work of Lawrence Weiner presented within the context of an installation and a book*. So there was also this publication, beside the piece itself that was carved into the gallery wall [*shows photograph*].

SR *So it wasn't stuck on to it.*

RP Not at all, it was hammered in by an art student. And the wall was to be freshly plastered after the show!

SR *Here's an artist I didn't know.*

RP That's Vaclav Pozarek, a very interesting character, originally from Prague, now living in Bern.

SR *... Are those books?*

RP No, those are wooden slabs. On the concrete floor of the gallery he placed them in circles. In the other gallery space with a parquet floor, he put granite stones one on another in a contra-rotating circle.

SR *So that was on the other side of the courtyard?*

RP Exactly, in the right wing of the building. I had it

restored, adding a little office.

SR *You were always on Rheinfelderstrasse?*

RP I moved there in January 1975, for the first year the gallery address was Wettsteinallee 6. I showed in two rooms on the ground floor of the house I lived in with my family ... Pozarek, then Federico Winkler, a Basel artist, followed by Wolfgang Laib – with one of his first exhibitions, certainly his first in Switzerland ... And to end it all, a double English final: Long and Fulton!

SR *Long's invitation card is beautiful, with the* Milestones.

RP Thank you! Another announcement card I like very much is the one for *4 Graue Bilder* by Richter 1975: photographic papers exposed by the artist himself, each one in a slightly different grey, and mounted on cardboard. So each announcement became an original Richter! I don't know how many people realised it!

SR *Let's start at the beginning. How did the gallery come to be opened?*

RP I'll first have to tell you about my life. I was quite interested in art, but started working as a copywriter in the Swiss advertising agency GGK. In October 1967 I moved from Basel to Düsseldorf, where GGK just opened a branch office. At exactly the same time, Konrad Fischer started his gallery there with Carl Andre. When I first saw this space with those steel slabs on the floor, I was completely thrilled! Only a few weeks later I met my future wife Barbara, a former gallery assistant at Schmela. By then she was collecting a bit and I was collecting a bit. We made friends with Konrad and Dorothee Fischer, they had two children practically at the same time as we did. 1973, after six years in advertising the idea of returning to Switzerland and starting a gallery came up – of course with a stock of Fischer artists we'd met and also bought works of. I wondered whether to go to Basel or to Zurich. As at that time the Basel Kunstmuseum was simply better – directed by the legendary Franz Meyer – and the Basel Kunsthalle was an interesting place too, I decided for Basel.

SR *Are you from Basel?*

RP I was born in Basel and grew up and went to school there. I'd actually always lived in Basel until I went to Düsseldorf in 1967.

SR *Did you have a deal with Fischer that allowed you to take on his artists?*

RP No, it was a thing between friends. I didn't have to pay Konrad fees or anything. Of course, we were always interested in what the other one was doing. I also went to Düsseldorf a lot at that time, all happened there and in Cologne and Holland ... I was most interested those days in what was called the 'Fischer school', but there was also a 'Michael Werner school'. I can still hear Konrad say: 'Oh, that Penck! Lüpertz, oh no!' On the other hand, Werner was more or less ignoring Fischer's artists. Only very few people knew to integrate both 'schools'. Like Rudi Fuchs in Eindhoven, or Johannes Gachnang in Bern, who died recently. They had no problems mixing shows of Brouwn, Long, Judd or Andre and shows of Baselitz, Byars, Immendorff or Penck. So one day I said to myself: 'Why not show Penck? Or Byars? They are interesting artists!' That became important to me, also as a small act of emancipation.

SR *You were actually almost the only gallery in Switzerland to show those artists. There was also Bruno Bischofsberger, but he was more Art & Language and Kosuth.*

RP Bischofsberger in Zürich was a great dealer, of course, and he still is. To my horror he'd shown Alan Charlton before me in Switzerland, but he'd asked Fischer many years ago. Very strange to see Alan in the gallery of Warhol, Twombly and Basquiat! In Basel there was Galerie Stampa, which still exists. And in Zürich Annemarie Verna, working with Judd, Ryman or LeWitt, for example. As her space was smaller than mine, I could go for the big wall drawing 1975, when Sol decided for two simultaneous shows in Switzerland. But we also joined forces to publish the book *Lines & Color*, with additional help of Marilena Bonomo – 3,000 Swiss Francs for each, an almost incredible amount of money then!

SR *Did you go on working in advertising?*

RP No, I didn't want to be a part-time dealer for full-time artists. That was important for me. But I had to right at the end, because financially it was getting worse and worse. So I started freelance jobs again, but got into troubles soon: When there was an artist on visit or an exhibition to put up, there was also an urgent presentation to be written. An impossible situation! And as the gallery needed to be completely rebuilt, I was forced to close for at least a year and to move somewhere else. This and upcoming private problems made me decide: 'Draw a line under it and go back to advertising!'

SR *What was the situation for art collectors in Switzerland? Were there some people who were interested?*

RP There was a very small group of interested people. I had perhaps 60 visitors a month at the most, sometimes only five ... Some 'small' collectors in Basel bought some 'small' works from time to time. Others found it more chic to go and buy art in New York or Paris. They were wonderfully well-informed – there was always exciting stuff on show in my gallery. But since I did not have the real money to buy and keep the works, they were no longer available when these people had worked out three or five years later how great these pieces were. Then I also had to accept that I wasn't really viable as a dealer. Being honest by nature, I always paid the artists first, and they thought highly of me for that. But this principle of mine, on the other hand, obviously reduced my financial flexibility. So there was ever only just enough to put on the next exhibition. Even in those days, transport was not cheap, and the artists had to get their tickets, they always liked to come to Switzerland ... Yes, collectors belonged to a rare species! ... I was glad Rudi Fuchs started to buy stuff from me.

SR *But that was more museums.*

RP Yes, sure. But in terms of private collectors, I wasn't lucky enough to enjoy the permanent support of someone like Panza!

SR *So there was no private interest in Switzerland?*

RP Not very much indeed. I had no entrée to Zurich too, not even to the museums there. It was all quite difficult.

SR *Did you also work with museums like the Kunstmuseum in Basel, for example, to put on an exhibition of one of your artists?*

RP That did happen. There was a little Fulton show we did together. They also bought a Charlton painting once. But the famous Emanuel Hoffmann Foundation that dealt with contemporary art was hard to approach. The decision-makers then were more Paris-oriented and good clients of Yvon Lambert! But I remember to have finally sold at an Art Fair a wonderful, large Dibbets to the Emanuel Hoffmann Foundation. But no Barry, no Weiner, no Bob Law, no Buren – what a pity!

SR *So you think the art scene in Switzerland was perhaps not all that committed?*

RP It was quite a barren landscape, I'd have to say.

SR *How do you explain the fact that there was no interest?*

RP The crazy thing was that Basel had an international reputation based on the Art Fair and the Kunstmuseum. Franz Meyer there collected wonderful works, by Beuys for example. But with Long, things became difficult! At some point the Emanuel Hoffmann Foundation bought a *Stone Line* of his, out of Long's Bern exhibition. I had worked hard for that show, organised most of the material in the Jura, lifted tons of stones with Richard, helped to build up the exhibition with him and Gachnang. And at the end the work that goes to Basel is handled by some other dealer – not Konrad Fischer! – and I don't see a single Swiss Franc. There comes a point when you start to think: 'What exactly am I doing here?'

SR *What happened with the Crex Collection?*

RP The Crex Collection was the result of a collaboration of a lot of money made on the stock market by an anonymous group of investors and Urs Raussmüller! As an art adviser to Migros, the big Swiss retail chain, Raussmüller had already built up a collection primarily of Swiss art. Now he persuaded some successful people to heavily invest in international contemporary art and bought all that great, important stuff, that is today so wonderfully presented in the Hallen für neue Kunst in Schaffhausen.

SR *Was the Crex Collection always supposed to be open to the public?*

RP Yes, now it's open to the public in Schaffhausen.

SR *Yes, but was it then?*

RP No, in the beginning it was more of a warehouse collection. In 1978 Raussmüller opened InK, Halle für internationale neue Kunst in Zurich. It was supported by Migros, and was an ideal tool for presenting works from the Crex Collection, mainly in group shows of four artists. I remember having seen there Penck, Ryman, LeWitt, Kounellis, Long, Nauman, Richter, Baumgarten, Mangold, and many others. The last exhibition at InK was Beuys's 'Das Kapital' in 1981, afterwards the city of Zürich transformed the building into a school or whatever. But soon Raussmüller found in Schaffhausen this great location and turned it into Hallen für neue Kunst.

SR *Did you have anything to do with the Crex Collection when you were running your gallery?*

RP Yes, they bought Richard Long's *192 Pieces of Wood*, from my Penck show a group of three large paintings, a grey painting by Richter, and in 1975 the LeWitt wall drawing. Those were actually my biggest sales. Since prices were still very moderate at the time, and famous collectors like Panza or Raussmüller asked for discounts – and got them! – they didn't make me rich! But it was important for the artists to be represented in these well-known collections.

SR *Was Art Basel an important event?*

RP Of course it was important to the extent that it was a window on the world. Compared to what happens there today, it was completely provincial, small and cosy. We, Fischer and I, took part in the eighth and ninth edition of Art Basel, still right at its beginnings though. The exhibition hall wasn't air-conditioned yet; we almost suffocated. But nevertheless we had some cool ideas: one year we invited Gilbert & George to perform *Red Boxers* once a day at the Fair!

SR *At that time did you also do a lot of travelling through Europe, to the museums and other galleries?*

RP Well, not that much. I travelled quite a lot to Holland, and to Düsseldorf and Cologne. But I was hardly ever in Paris, for example. I also went to Italy, Milan, Venice and so on. Don't forget that I had a wife and two small children, and I was on my own in the gallery. I painted the gallery walls, I hung the pictures, I had the announcements printed and mailed, I dealt with the artists. I was a real one-man show. Nice, but exhausting. I drove from Basel to Amsterdam and back on a weekend, crazy!

SR *And you went to America as well?*

RP I was in New York a few times, once a year, mostly in autumn when the season started. Fischer Sperone Westwater gallery had a guest-room where I could stay very comfortably.

SR *Did you meet mostly artists there?*

RP Artists above all. But I also visited galleries like John Weber, Leo Castelli, Ileana Sonnabend of course, then René Block, Paula Cooper, Dia Art Foundation and so on. I went so see artists in their studios and apartments, and I remember many drinks in all the bars!

SR *Was it important that you were in Switzerland, so geographically in Europe, but not politically?*

RP I had the feeling it was time for this kind of art to arrive in Switzerland also. I thought you couldn't just show here only Tinguely, or Max Bill, or Dieter Roth, although I knew some of them personally. Karl Gerstner, a co-owner of GGK advertising agency I worked for and an artist himself, had many artist-friends. Travelling a lot at the time we went to see them whenever possible. In London we met Roth and Dorothy Iannone, and went to Richard Hamilton's house. When we opened the GGK office in Düsseldorf 1967, we lured Daniel Spoerri to set up his Eat Art restaurant at the Altstadt. Roth then moved to Düsseldorf too, André Thomkins lived in Essen, Robert Filliou followed. There was something happening! ... But I've always been more interested in reduction in art, in art that leaves things out. If you look now on what I was showing in my gallery, that wasn't always pure 'process art' or 'Conceptual art'. It was always art with a concept, but what you may understand as 'Conceptual art' isn't pure theory all the time. Otherwise, I'd only have been able to show Wilson and maybe Brouwn.

SR *And Lawrence Weiner.*

RP Well, Weiner's works are sculptures of a sort ...

SR *In your opinion, which artists identified most closely with the gallery?*

RP I showed certain artists several times. Barry, for example, quite strongly identified. Larry Weiner and I are still good friends. Then I think also of Rückriem, Brouwn ... Long had three shows over the years. That makes very close and intensive relations.

SR *Were those also the exhibitions you found most interesting?*

RP Every exhibition was an adventure. That's why I've always been more interested in the making of exhibitions and installations than in telling a collector how good a work would look in his bedroom or office. I was very bad at that. But working with art and artists, seeing art come to life ...

SR *Did the artists also make the exhibitions in the gallery themselves?*

RP Yes and no! Penck, for example, at the time still living in the former GDR and not allowed to travel, was sent a floor plan and a proposal for the hanging ... LeWitt for his wall drawing sent me colour patterns in red, yellow and blue, and I painted the gallery walls accordingly. Then Sol came along and together we located and drew the lines on the wall ... Others, like Winkler, were working for days totally alone on their installations ... Buren is known to always work in situ ... Long often used material he'd found in the Basel area. The wood pieces for his first work in my gallery he picked up in a nearby forest, and for the stone works we found a quarry half an hour's drive from the gallery.

SR *Do you have photographs of all the exhibitions?*

RP Yes, more or less. Some prints and Ektachromes got lost, like those of Sol's wonderful wall drawing. [*Shows a folder of all the photographs*] This documentation in alphabetical order starts with Barry and his work 'At Last' 1979, a slide projection in a totally darkened room ... Here we have the Stanley Brouwn exhibition 1978. He showed books and card indexes on shelves for you to flick through and some drawings.

SR *Wasn't there an office in this first room?*

RP No, there was just a table in a corner and two or three chairs. The gallery was open in the afternoon only. I lived 50 metres away, and office work was done there ... Here is a picture of an exhibition during Art Basel 1974, taken in the first gallery space at Wettsteinallee, before I moved to Rheinfelderstrasse.

SR *Starting there with a Daniel Buren exhibition?*

RP Exactly. The first Buren exhibition in 1974 was titled *Triptyque* and used the frame of a door between two rooms. Striped cloth was tacked onto the frame separating or dividing the rooms: *Division I* white and blue, *Division II* white and red, and *Division III* white and grey stripes. Each 'Division' was installed for ten days, and announced separately ... In Alan Charlton's first show 1976 we presented four large 4 part paintings. I was happy to sell one work of this series to the Basel Kunstmuseum! In his second exhibition in 1978 he showed seven paintings, single rectangles in different greys. No sales this time! ...

SR *Were there articles in the press at the time about the exhibitions you put on?*

RP Yes, some shows were reviewed, mostly in the local press only. But nothing to really collect! ... Ah, here's Hamish Fulton. He showed photographic works, first in 1977, and again in 1979. This was to be the last exhibition before I closed down the gallery! ... Robert Law. He drew those fine pencil lines on natural canvas, right at the edges, but also painted a few very dark, almost black pictures, irritating as well as poetic! Law was collected by Panza, I've no idea what he is doing now ... Sol LeWitt's *Geometric Figures* in 1978, circle, square, triangle, rectangle, trapezoid and parallelogram put in a row on the longest gallery wall. Unfortunately the photos of the 1975 wall drawing *The location of yellow, red and blue lines on yellow, red and blue walls* are missing. ...

[*Fetches a second folder of photographs.*]

Here's another of my favourites: Wolfgang Laib. A 'milkstone' and a pollen work, these two works made in 1978 his very first exhibition in Switzerland. Every morning I had to pour in fresh milk, very carefully and slowly, and to remove it again every evening. Quite a meditative job! The hazelnut pollen Laib scattered on a sheet of glass at the time, today he'd put it directly on the floor ... *Meeting Place* was the title of Richard Long's 1977 exhibition and also a work within: *Two walkers walk in opposite directions around a circular road until they meet. Six walks in Wales* was the second map-piece on show, going with the sculpture *Sandstone Circle* on the floor. The greenish stones from a demolition we've found in 'our' quarry. I very much appreciate Long's work, he's a great artist! ... *Red Stone Circle* was the main piece in Richard's third and last show. Red stones with bright green flecks; a very compact, beautiful work. On the walls four photo-pieces plus the great five-part work *Milestones*. I tried so hard to sell it to the Basel Kunstmuseum – another unfulfilled dream! ...

... Vaclav Pozarek, photos of his 1978 show, wood on stone, stone on wood, we talked about already ... An installation view of Edda Renouf's show in 1976 ... Richter. ... Ulrich Rückriem's show 1975 was titled *Teilung und Ergänzung* and was all about division and completion. Three stone sculptures on the gallery floor, real heavy weight lifting. Ulrich found in the courtyard two sandstone slabs and immediately transformed them into a work of art to remember Blinky Palermo who had just died. It was taken away and obviously destroyed when rebuilding work was done in 1979 ...

... This installation view of 1976 shows you David Tremlett's, *The Orient I, II, III*. Each part with four frames, each containing eight red or black chalk drawings, sort of shorthand notes of landscapes in Java, if I'm correct. The complete show went to the Panza collection! In Germano Celant's book on the Panza collection the piece is illustrated, funny enough, with my installation instruction! ... To finish the view back, here's Rémy Zaugg. His show in 1977 was dedicated to L.B. Alberti. There is not much to recognise in the photos, but here you can see one original of the two works that were exhibited at the time! [*Shows four paintings leaning against the wall.*] Sad to say that Rémy died recently.

SR *It's interesting to see all these photographs.*

RP And pretty incomplete, I'm afraid ...

4.12 Conversation with Sir Nicholas Serota

London, 24 January 2005

SOPHIE RICHARD *You headed the Museum of Modern Art in Oxford from 1973 to 1976. I'd like to start our discussion with the position of the Museum in relation to other progressive art museums in Europe. In an interview with Lynda Morris about the MOMA Oxford, published in* Studio International *November–December 1975, you said that Johannes Cladders influenced your attitude and programme. Could you tell me how you came to know Cladders' work and to what extent he influenced you?*

NICHOLAS SEROTA The first thing that I should say is that when I went as a Director to the Museum of Modern Art in Oxford, I was 26 years old. So I was quite young. Probably such an appointment would be impossible now, because one would have to be able to demonstrate much more experience than I had. But it tells you a little bit about the innocence of those times. It also tells you that the museum structure in the United Kingdom wasn't very developed in terms of exhibition spaces. It would be true to say that in the late 1960s and early 1970s, there was really only one institution that had regular contact with European counterparts and that was the Whitechapel Art Gallery. From the mid-1950s and through the 1960s it was the institution that was on a circuit, which took some of the big travelling shows. Many of those came from America, organised by the Museum of Modern Art and the Guggenheim Museum in New York. Those exhibitions would be seen at the Whitechapel and then they went on to other institutions in Europe. The difference, however, was that the Whitechapel at that time was simply one stop on a circuit. It wasn't originating exhibitions and it didn't have special relationships with particular museums in continental Europe. When I went to Oxford, one of the things that I perceived in continental Europe was that because of an equivalence in size or equivalence in geographical location in relation either to centres of production, or because of a shared interest on the part of individual directors, there were certain institutions that worked quite frequently together. I therefore resolved that Oxford should become one of those institutions and join that network. Peter Isben, who preceded me, and made some very interesting shows with individual artists, such as Boltanski and Buren. However, these were 'one offs' and I looked first of all for models that seemed to me to be productive and I also looked for partners to collaborate with. A model that seemed to me to be extremely productive was the one used by Johannes Cladders.

SR *What do you mean by 'productive'?*

NS Productive in the sense of displaying initiative, imagination and ability to present new work, sometimes by new artists, in a way that artists themselves found engaging and constructive. That's to say, generally speaking, involving the artist and not simply putting his work in a show. I looked on the one hand for models and on the other hand for partners. Among the models I saw was, of course, the Museum of Mönchengladbach. What I saw was a very small institution close to large cities, Düsseldorf and Cologne, where an individual had, by inviting the right artists, created a programme that had an internal coherence and which, through the involvement of the artists, had resulted in some memorable exhibitions. He'd also given the artists the opportunity to do something that they hadn't previously done. Cladders seemed to me, from 1966–67, to be one of the people who'd done this most strongly. Another, in a different way, was Harald Szeemann at the Kunsthalle Bern. Those two impressed me most. I suppose also Eindhoven, because of what had happened, particularly in the late 1960s with Jan Leering, before he lost his engagement with contemporary art. Or, as he would put it, found an engagement with another kind of art.

SR *You just said that you wanted the Museum in Oxford to be part of this network of progressive European museums. Wasn't it rather difficult to do that in England, because it seems that there was very little interest in or support for contemporary art, as well as a complete lack of knowledge of what was going on abroad?*

NS I think there was significant interest, but very little manifestation of it, except in some of the commercial galleries. Part of that interest was stimulated by the magazine *Studio International*, edited at the time by Peter Townsend. There was also a very influential Deputy Editor, Charles Harrison, who later became part of Art & Language. From 1966–67 onwards, *Studio International* brought very regular reports on what was happening in continental Europe. A series of significant articles on some of the artists was beginning to emerge. I remember, for instance, a cover by Richard Long published in 1968. This was an artist who at that time was 23 years old. It was quite risky. I don't think there would be many magazines today that would publish a cover by an artist of only 23. But it wasn't the only thing: there was a series of projects. There was Charles Harrison, but also the American critic Barbara Reise, who was writing for *Studio International* at the time. There were small manifestations. For instance, Lynda Morris was working for Nigel Greenwood and later at the Royal College of Art. She made one or two exhibitions for them. So there were some small manifestations in public institutions.

SR *It also seems that those small manifestations happened later in England than in continental Europe. To stay with the example of Richard Long, he had his first one-man show in Mönchengladbach in 1970, whereas he had shows at the Whitechapel and in Oxford in 1971. How do you explain this delay?*

NS You're completely right, England was slow. There were a number of factors. One of them was the success of the preceding generation. Between 1962 and 1966, there was a generation of artists in England, including David Hockney, Anthony Caro and Bridget Riley, known then as The New Generation. Many of them were shown in an exhibition of that name at the Whitechapel Gallery in London in 1964. These were artists who looked very strongly towards America rather than to continental Europe. They had some immediate success both in America and in Europe. They also had success with some British collectors and they were showing at the Kasmin Gallery and at the Waddington Gallery. This success and the fact that they were making works of art that could be bought by collectors, put on the wall, and that were decorative in the best sense, meant that it was quite difficult for the next generation and for younger artists, like Barry Flanagan, Richard Long and others, to establish themselves on the English scene. It didn't help that there were very few galleries and museums that were interested in showing their works. What I wanted to do in Oxford was to provide such a space.

SR *In Oxford, you first looked at Mönchengladbach and Bern. How was the connection made to other institutions with whom you worked, like those in Münster, Brussels and Eindhoven?*

NS It came about because I'd bring artists to show in Oxford and I'd discover that they already had an invitation or were in conversation with another museum. For instance, I remember in 1975, the first time I met Rudi Fuchs. He'd recently gone to Eindhoven as a director in 1974. He'd contacted a British artist, Alan Charlton. This was an artist whom I already wanted to show in Oxford and we decided to make a collaboration. It was by those means that these contacts were established.

SR *In Oxford, how did you contact an artist for a show? Did you contact him directly or did you contact his dealer first?*

NS Generally speaking, I found then the most successful way of working with an artist was to contact him directly and to inform the dealer. In any event, for many of these artists, they either had no dealer in England or they had several dealers on the continent. For instance, they'd show with Yvon Lambert in France, Konrad Fischer in Germany and Fernand Spillemaeckers in Belgium or Art & Project in the Netherlands. The best contact was always with the artist. But obviously, I had to respect certain dealers and I came to know the work sometimes by seeing it at the dealer galleries. I'd also obviously be friends with certain of those dealers.

SR *Like who?*

NS Like Konrad Fischer, whom I knew from quite early on. When I went to the Netherlands, I'd always visit Art & Project. There was a certain phase, from 1974–75, when I was spending some time in Belgium, so I'd see Anny De Decker and some of the dealers there. And then inevitably one meeting leads to another.

SR *Were there any private collectors interested in Conceptual art in Britain at that moment in time?*

NS In the early 1970s, very few. The only person whom you could regard as a serious collector at that time was Jack Wendler. But he was also a dealer. He was in between a collector and a dealer. He was buying pieces from time to time, but not only by the artists he was exhibiting, but also by other artists. It depends on how you define Conceptual art. Alan Charlton isn't really a Conceptual artist, but on the other hand, he was in a certain group that was seen in this way. There were one or two people in the country who occasionally bought pieces, like E.J. Power or his son, Alan Power. They'd previously been collecting a form of art that had an intellectual discipline. They responded to some extent, but they didn't acquire works extensively. So there was no one comparable to the Daleds or the Herberts, building up a collection of Conceptual art in Britain.

In the late 1970s and early 1980s, such people emerged, but not at that time. England was slow. But if it hadn't been slow, I wouldn't have had the opportunity to do what I did.

SR *At the museum in Oxford, among the many Conceptual artists whom you showed (Long, LeWitt, Huebler, etc), why did you never show Gilbert & George?*

NS One of the reasons why Gilbert & George never showed in Oxford is that in this period there were showing very frequently at Nigel Greenwood and at the Situation Gallery. They had dual representation in London and so their work was very present. There didn't seem to be the need to make another big show. I wanted to show the work of artists who weren't that present.

SR *Did you also have contacts with the Lisson Gallery, which seems to be, along with Nigel Greenwood, the other important dealer gallery at the time?*

NS I had close contact with Nicholas Logsdail from the Lisson, Nigel Greenwood and also with Robert Self, who was running the Situation Gallery. It was quite active between 1968 and 1974. Then later there was also Jack Wendler. Those were the four galleries that were the most active during that period.

SR *Although MOMA Oxford has no permanent collection, it did sell works of art. In 1975 the Tate Gallery bought two works of Marcel Broodthaers during his one-man show in Oxford. Isn't it quite unusual for a temporary exhibition space to sell works to a museum? How did this sale happen?*

NS First of all, the exhibition in Oxford was the first serious presentation of the work of Marcel Broodthaers in England. Secondly, the exhibition included a large number of new works that he'd made in Berlin. He'd had a DAAD fellowship in Berlin and I saw him there to select pieces for the exhibition. The show in Oxford was a variation of an exhibition that he'd made in Berlin to mark his stay there at the end of the DAAD fellowship. So a version of this exhibition was made for Oxford, and Marcel added quite a large number of pieces. At that time, he was living in England, but he had no commercial representation. What happened was that one of the Tate curators came to Oxford and then Norman Reid, the Director, came to see the exhibition. He was very taken with certain works. I think he saw an immediate connection to Magritte and Belgian Surrealism. He decided to make the acquisitions. The works were sold through Oxford but I don't think the Museum took a percentage. We just acted as an agent.

SR *How did the public in Oxford, which isn't the same public as in London, react to the quite avant-garde artists that you showed at the museum?*

NS The response was very surprisingly positive. There were two reasons for that. First of all, that it was a university city: the art that was dealing with ideas was immediately engaging to philosophers and thinkers and to people of other disciplines. Secondly, there was a young student population – not completely, of course – but among such a population you find young people with no preconceptions about what art should be, who become immediately engaged with the art they're presented with. They didn't come with the expectation that art would be oil painting on canvas. They were prepared to photograph and interrogate it, then examine it and see it and finally consider it as art. There was a surprisingly strong engagement, although we're not talking about large numbers. Of course, there was also hostility. There were people who came in, especially some of the more conservative academics, who said art had to be painting. Some people saw this art as being rather threatening to accepted values and conventions of art – not so much decadent, as not substantial enough. I remember in 1971, before I went to Oxford, I was responsible for taking an exhibition of sculpture to Norwich. Included in the exhibition were some younger British artists, like Tim Head. During the course of the opening, we had a seminar with some students from the Norwich School of Art. One of the professors was a disciple of Anthony Caro and he said 'I don't recognise this as a sculpture because you cannot kick it.'

SR *Speaking about England being slow, what's quite surprising is that if you look at the Tate Gallery in the 1970s, the museum had a very strong purchasing strategy for Conceptual artworks, but there were absolutely no exhibitions of those artists. How do you explain this?*

NS There's a very clear reason for that. A new director was appointed at the Tate in 1964, Norman Reid. He was someone who'd already been working at the Tate for a long time. When he became Director, he immediately turned the museum into a much more professional institution than it had previously been. He established for the first time a department that was concerned with what was called 'Twentieth-century International Modern Art'. He appointed some younger curators, Michael Compton (who later became Keeper of Exhibitions), Richard Morphet and Anne Seymour (who later became Anne d'Offay). Those three people made recommendations for acquisitions. It was at a time when Norman Reid was rather successful in persuading the government to give the Tate quite large additional sums for purchasing. In the context of those large additional sums, it was possible for the Tate to buy Conceptual art, giving a certain licence to these younger curators, while actually spending very little money. What Reid did was to respond to the proposals made by some young curators, by spending a limited amount of money to reflect what was happening now. By 1976, and especially after the so-called 'Tate bricks affair' in the press, the number of purchases dropped significantly. Even before this, by 1973, Reid was already losing his appetite for buying this Conceptual material.

SR *But if you buy so many artworks, why not show them?*

NS Well, they were showing the works, but they weren't making exhibitions. In 1970 the Tate took on, for the first time, responsibility for organising its own exhibitions in a serious way. Before that, most exhibitions that took place at the Tate were organised by the Arts Council. In 1968, the Arts Council opened the Hayward Gallery and thereafter made their exhibitions there. When the Tate started its own programme of exhibitions, they were testing the water. They felt that they had a number of responsibilities. They wanted to show classic British art and classic modern art, in which the collection wasn't strong enough. Then there was a small space in the programme to show contemporary art. They interpreted that obligation to show contemporary art by showing artists who were aged between 50 and 60, rather than between 30 and 40. They saw that younger artists were shown more readily by the Whitechapel Gallery, by the new Serpentine Gallery or by the ICA. That's where they thought these artists should be shown. There were exceptions with the Robert Morris exhibition in 1971 and in 1972, when they had a cancellation of an exhibition. Michael Compton made a show called *Seven Exhibitions* with Michael Craig-Martin, Bruce McLean, Joseph Beuys, David Tremlett, etc. Most of the exhibition was shown in the Duveen Galleries. It was an important manifestation. It took place about five or six months before *The New Art* exhibition, which Anne Seymour organised in 1972 at the Hayward Gallery.

SR *Had the situation in the British art world evolved in the years between your arrival at the museum in Oxford in 1973 and your arrival at the Whitechapel Art Gallery in 1976?*

NS Not a great deal.

SR *But what you did in Oxford did some good?*

NS It did some good. I was able, much to everyone's irritation, to make two exhibitions simultaneously for my opening presentation at the Whitechapel: one of Richard Long and one of Stanley Brouwn. From the point of view of some people, this was quite a tough beginning. There had been a significant advance, but it depends again on how you define Conceptual art. The activity of the Lisson, Greenwood, Wendler and also *The New Art* show made by Anne Seymour had changed the climate. There was more acceptance and more interest. In the late 1970s there was a renewed interest in art that had some kind of social purpose. So, for instance, an artist like Steve Willats or Hans Haacke. This kind of art really began to gain currency. By that time, there was a general recognition that something new had happened and that the terms of art had changed.

4.13 Conversation with Seth Siegelaub

Amsterdam, 27 April 2005

SOPHIE RICHARD *One thing I'm particularly interested in discussing with you is the transatlantic relations in the late 1960s and early 1970s. How did Americans involved in the art world see the European art world? What did you know about the European art world?*

SETH SIEGELAUB I don't know what I knew, but I do recall that travel was becoming a possibility for many people: the cost of travelling, the facility of travelling. Many people from my generation, from the lower-middle class, were the first to go to Europe, apart from an uncle who came over to fight in the Second World War. So that opened up things tremendously.

But what was perhaps most important is that, because much of the work was so dematerialised, you could see lots of it. You could get a feel and appreciate what was going on. Traditionally, when you were dealing with painting or sculpture, artists would have to be relatively successful to be able to pay for the transport of the work. So you wouldn't see as much work, except for people who were doing the grand tour, as in the eighteenth century, or rich people who could travel, or even rich artists who could travel. But I think one of the emphases was that there was immediately a community of artists working in a certain way, thinking about certain problems, or dealing with certain problems. It's difficult to say what the appreciation was, what we were looking at. One thing was very clear, which is still the case 30 or 40 years later, is that most of the financing, most of the collecting, did take place in Europe: in Holland, Germany, Italy, France. It didn't take many people to create a big activity.

The first thing was, although I lived and worked in New York, half of the exhibitions I did took place in Europe. One, because the environment was there; two, because I wanted to go there. If you can do your trips and visit other countries, why not? Let's go to Cologne. Let's go to Paris. Maybe there's also someone in Nice. Let's go to Italy ... But it was also because that's where the interest was. This is even the case today. You could say, talking on an institutional or even a collecting level, that everyone has an Andre or a Kosuth or a Weiner now. Everyone sort of has to have one of these works, because it does mean something somehow. But no one has been really interested in it in that way, except for one or two – well, one in fact – museum attempts in California. So it was a logical thing for me to go to Europe, because that's where the interest was. I had a few collector-friends who'd pay for various projects, and whom I was able to call upon to do things, but they were very few. I was totally isolated.

SR *How do you explain this lack of interest from America?*

SS Well, America is very materialistic. There's a very materialistic culture. If you look at the collectors in Europe, and even the very rich collectors, there's a certain intellectual stimulation. There's a certain culture. Even though someone may be rich, he – occasionally she – did philosophy at university or something like this. It wasn't just a collecting thing, it was like sharing ...

SR *Friendships with the artists.*

SS Friendships too, but also on the basis of a certain kind of equality. Americans very rarely have this kind of relationship. They want an object that they can hang on their wall, talk to people about, etc. At that time, very few people were interested in this kind of work. I think that's really the reason.

SR *I read somewhere that because the American art market was completely dominated after the Second World War by Pop art and Abstract Expressionism, there was no room for Conceptual art. Do you agree with that idea?*

SS No. You could say that about any period. You could say that about the Surrealists, etc. There was certainly enough room, even though maybe in a restrained community, for people to buy things and not to be afraid to buy things. And, even on a speculative level, to spend $500 and see that it could later be worth $10,000. That spirit is very American, too. It isn't like anyone was forced out because there wasn't enough room. You make your room in a way. Much of the relative lack of interest comes from a very hard-ass materialistic attitude. People expect to buy a painting, a physical object that they can pass on, give away or whatever they do; they want to have it there. They don't want to worry about things like public freeholds, things that can exist in multiples, without definitions, without a clear material life. The European collector in general is much more open to that experience.

You just have to meet people like Herman Daled, even Giuseppe Panza. You've probably met far more than I ever met. I had very little connection with collectors, unlike Konrad Fischer, Sperone or Yvon Lambert. I don't think I even knew any collectors. Or if I did, it was on a friendship level, like with Herman. I'd see him regularly (and I still do in fact at openings and things like this). But I never saw him in the art world. He was very helpful for the Artist Contract that I made in 1970, for example. That's the kind of activity that European collectors, without any sense of merchandising or profit, would finance: the production of something like that.

SR *Are you talking about Herman Daled or Herman van Eelen?*

SS I'm talking about Herman Daled. Herman van Eelen is very nice, too. I'd see him and his wife here in Amsterdam. (I lived here in Amsterdam for six months when I was doing some projects. It must have been 1969–70.) But I don't think he was typical of the kind of collector who was hanging around. When you look at the kind of level of interest many of these people have, it's totally different from the general American collector. There were collectors, like Jack Wendler in London, Stanley Grinsten in California, who were very supportive and who put up money not just to buy works, but to realise various projects, but it was definitely not something that would characterise the American collector, and with it the American institutions – the collectors would influence or would be influenced by the institutions.

There was interest here immediately: people like Konrad Fischer, who was very active, and Hans Strelow, who at that time was a journalist for the *Frankfurter Allgemeine*. He'd write articles about what we were doing in *Der Spiegel*! You'd never see that in the United States. And then other people would respond to it. Public collectors would line up. Konrad had a kind of active business going on in Düsseldorf, as did Sperone, as did Yvon Lambert.

SR *Isn't it also that in Europe, the art world was much more international than in America? It seems that in America everything was focused in New York, whereas in Europe there were a number of cities in different countries.*

SS That's absolutely true. Maybe it was to introduce more local people into their sort of local environment, to support their local artists. So yes, you can say that. In the United States, everything was centred around New York, but that was in large part because of me. But also, there were people in California doing similar things. There was Allen Ruppersberg out there, and there were other people who were doing things. They didn't have the same gallery focus. Well, there was Eugenia Butler in the 699 Gallery. Maybe she wasn't around long enough to do enough shows. Maybe there was never the gallery focus, but there were folks out there who were interested too. New York was the centre of the world we were living in: Jackson Pollock, Abstract Expressionism, Pop art, whatever. Also, the Minimal art, especially Carl Andre and Sol LeWitt, was particularly close to all of us (and still is), although their work is very different. They maintain their roots in the same period, with the same people. Carl is certainly the most successful in that sense. But again, it's not in the context of what we call Conceptual art. He's a sculptor making sculptures.

SR *It's difficult to find a proper term to categorise all those artists. 'Conceptual art' is a kind of jack-of-all-trades term.*

SS Yes, exactly. But that's what it was like. I did this project called *The Context of Art* in 2004. It was published in an English/German edition. Yes, it was really a mess, a *pot-pourri*, a *foutoir*, whatever you want to call it. But that was the feel of it at the time. You get Panamarenko, Reiner Ruthenbeck, Beuys, Lawrence Weiner, Richard Tuttle, Bob Ryman, Brice Marden, all in the same room, sharing a sort of *l'air du temps*, a certain *esprit*, a certain questioning, a sort of theme for the art-making process. Today, one could think of Bob Ryman or Brice Marden as coming out of a very traditional painting history. But at that time, it wasn't the case.

It was also the period of agitation, particularly of socio-political agitation. There was the Vietnam War and the student movement. All this was going on around us. New York was particularly active; the Art Workers Coalition and other groups were protesting in one way or another. Artists wanted control over their work. Even I made an Artist Contract in 1970, which tried to grapple with some of the problems that were raised. There were many other attempts and problems that were going on – living standards and things like this. It was a period of great agitation and a lot of people had hegemonic ideas, which had to do with contestation. Everyone was doing and thinking about this, whether they were making paintings or ... Ryman was making paintings that criticised painting, the paint process, the physicality, the illusion and things like this. Lawrence Weiner, Robert Barry, Gilbert & George, Art & Language etc, were dealing with things in another way. All these things were going on. So yes, it was a *foutoir*. Certainly it was a very unclear mess. You just have to look at any of the exhibitions, whether it was Wim Beeren here, with *Op Losse Schroeven*, or Harry Szeemann in Switzerland or any of my larger exhibitions. We all shared a space, we all knew each other, we were all interacting, friends on various levels and degrees. It was difficult to separate the strands of these types of activities. In a certain way, it's the job of the art historian to try to do that, for better or for worse, to try to make sense of very complex, very confused, very chaotic kinds of activities.

SR *You mentioned the Vietnam War, had any of these artists actually fought in Asia?*

SS No, I don't think so. Not that I'm aware of. I was in the Air Force, but it was a little earlier. When I was in the Air Force, they were just doing flights to Vietnam, about 1963, 1964, 1965. There was no declared war. I remember our sergeant was sending over ships and materials, so-called experts or whatever, to set up the war. It may have been that many of the people were just a little too old. Or if they did see any military activity, it was just slightly earlier. In other words, by the time the Vietnam War came into existence, I'd already finished my military duty in the National Guard. Also, you have to remember the social background of many of the artists, too. They were from upper-middle-class families. A lot of them could avoid becoming real soldiers, going out to war. There were probably a number of artists in the officer class, training in officer courses, things like this. Douglas Huebler was in the Second World War! He was a marine. He was born in 1924, so was definitely older. He was closer in age to my parents than to me. He was older than Sol. He didn't appear older – he had a vitality and a spirit that was contemporary with us. I'd think: 'Hey, wait a minute, this guy is a friend of mine, but is as old as my parents.'

SR *So he fought in Europe?*

SS I think he fought on the Asian front on one of the islands. He was a sort of caricature of the Marine sergeant. He came from Michigan, with a sort of farm-boy past. But that was well before, of course. I can't think of anybody who actually fought in Vietnam. Maybe there were some who did but didn't say. But in a certain way, I wouldn't know because when I was active in the art world, it was at the height of the resistance to the Vietnam War. So all the art world people I'd know were in Europe or something. So if there were people who fought, I wouldn't have met them. They weren't around. But I'd be surprised. Everyone would have something to say about it. Everyone would talk about it in bars. It was a major source of conversation, the war, the battles ...

SR *Do you think it was more a subject of conversation in America than in Europe?*

SS That I don't know. I can't really tell you how it was in Europe. Europe was very much absent in the US–Vietnam War. That's for sure. But it was also compounded by a much more active student movement. In Europe, you'd be storming the barricades at the Boulevard Saint-Michel or the follow-up to that in 1968–69, in which people like Daniel Buren and probably other artists *de gauche* would be identified with that. That was certainly a very important force in Europe, far more important probably than for us, because of Vietnam in a way. Of course, we had Columbia University, Berkley; we had other things. Those two fronts were sort of different on both sides of the Atlantic.

SR *So there was a difference between the social and political engagement of American versus European artists? It must have been slightly different.*

SS Yes, it was probably slightly different. But I wouldn't overestimate its effect on the art-making process, or on the art world. There's no direct affiliation, no direct line between those things and the art that people made. It was only because these larger social issues and activities – protests, marches, fundraising – were essential to the art-making process that they opened up larger questions in the art world: institutional critique and things like selling to Mr X, who made all his money in in the munitions industry. People would go through [these issues], as Hans Haacke did, slum lords, real-estate tycoons, etc. It was more in that sense that a lot of questions were raised, which led to different kinds of answers by different kinds of artists at the same time. It wasn't like people were making political art. Haacke may be one of the few people who directly confronts it. Arte Povera is difficult to imagine without that political background. Even dematerialised art itself is a response to the possibilities of making art economically, without big means, without material in the sense of canvas, paint. So it's not like people were so much involved in protest with their art.

SR *So it was simply talking about it?*

SS Yes, talking. I remember we were always talking in bars about the tactics and this and that, the function of the news, the activities of the week or the day. It was never about making political art. There was a criticism of something, but it would be opportunistic to appropriate a political situation to make art.

SR *Can one say that the statements of Lawrence Weiner, which were completely dematerialised, were a sort of political gesture, because they're difficult to sell?*

SS The problem is posed as a response to political questions. I don't think Lawrence or any other artist would consciously say: 'Let's make something that's difficult to sell.' They were certainly very much aware of the idea of artists' property, of questioning that, the control over the work, the private sphere, etc. So all those words come up. But I don't think that Lawrence or anybody else would set out to make an art that can't be bought. That would be Fluxus or a Surrealist kind of thing. I don't think it was that kind of overt thing, but it was definitely fed by those kinds of questions. You have to remember that the democratising aspect of so-called Conceptual art opened up the field to many kinds of actors, even though it was an art period dominated by Anglo Saxon men. The horizon opened up to all sorts of other actors – women, black, yellow, white people – all sorts of other actors who could make art.

SR *It opened up to women and other actors, but it seems to be a small group of intellectual people who come together. In that sense it's not open to everyone.*

SS Yes, that's true. But that model confuses the difference between the art world and the art-making possibilities. It is true, but today, there are many more collectors, many more galleries, many more possibilities, quantitatively, a sort of democratisation of collecting. At that time (and even within today's context, but on another scale), that wasn't to be confused with the context of art. There's a relationship, that's for sure, although it's not clear what that relationship was at the time. What I was referring to within the art was that possibility to open up: to be interviewed, to become famous because you were shown by Seth Siegelaub. One could be in the middle of nowhere and still make art and do it very well. Perhaps you could say that this was the case with Minimal painters, too, working in small cities in Mexico all their lives. I think the material aspect of it, or the relative lack of material, as well as the opening up of the art world to other actors, was itself a political act. It made it possible to bring in, to appreciate or to understand (or try to understand) other people who lived in New York, London, Paris or wherever. Although it's definitely true that if you really want to have your work seen, you do have to be living in Berlin, New York or Paris. You have to be in proximity to power and money, or at least the concentration of power. The possibility for artists to be able to work outside the system, or on the edge of the system, is definitely primordial.

SR *The work of these artists set up a new system of values, in the sense of what can be art, what art is worth. Objects with apparently no value, like Andre's brick sculptures, were becoming art objects. How would uninitiated people recognise those objects as art, because apparently they're just a pile of bricks?*

SS You mean that it creates a very elite audience of informed people?

SR *Yes.*

SS Yes, in a certain way, that's true. But that's not intrinsic to the properties of making the pile of bricks or any other kind of work. In other words, those are the cultural problems of the work coming into the world. The world adds money to it. The fact is that it's given economic values well beyond any artist's decision. It's a collective decision of forces, where value is determined within the art world. But maybe it's just a pile of bricks. Maybe that's what tributes look like ... we understand it as what it's made of. Carl, as an example, has always been about materials, about their beauty, about the specific character of those materials. And that's all they are: bricks. The fact that someone is going to pay a million dollars for them, that's a fact that's well beyond Carl's control or that of any of his dealers or anybody else. You may find some sucker who spends maybe ten million dollars on it. In a certain way, you can say it's not beyond his control to be able to spend it. Maybe it is just bricks; maybe it is just a pile. The work is telling you that's what it is. You should understand it or try to appreciate it as being just that. The fact that it becomes very valuable and very sought after, and becomes something else along with this material appreciation and its economic appreciation in terms of increase in value, that's certainly not directly related. Even if an artist – Carl, Lawrence, Bob – wanted their work to be worth as much as possible, it's still obviously not a good idea for any particular artist to talk like that. He or she could try to manoeuvre the strings of art values to be able to situate themselves in a certain group.

Obviously many artists do that. All these competitive artists try to create value for their own system of things.

SR *Do you agree with the idea that in America there was a strong sense of the object (Andre, Ryman) and that in Europe, there was more of a challenge to the object?*

SS Oh, absolutely. There's definitely more of a spiritual side to the European collectors in general. People who collected this kind of work have a much more intellectual and spiritual sense. In other words, I have the impression that the European collectors are more spiritual, much more open, much more adventurous. They may also want to buy things very cheap; I'm not denying that. Also, I'm not saying that all American collectors are hard-ass materialists. But it's from Europe that, I'd say, 90 percent of the interest, the exhibitions, the money, the support, the galleries, etc, have come. I'm not talking just about 40 years ago; I'm talking about even today, where you'll find the same kind of appreciation of the work and the same kind of interest in the work. Everyone says that it's a very important movement – it's all this, it's all that – but if you look at who's really done something with it, or committed himself to the period ... for each middle-range painter there are more books that have been written than on this whole subject.

SR *But there were some early exhibitions of those artists in America – for example, the different shows you organised at universities in Massachusetts and in Vermont.*

SS Yes, but that was me! That wasn't an institutional large-scale interest. You also have Canadians up in Nova Scotia; they were very active.

SR *That was all in universities and art schools, so there's a kind of sense that it was happening in places that are intellectual anyway.*

SS Yes. That's where the interest was. I never heard anybody say: 'That's a beautiful stain on the floor', or 'That's a beautiful brick.' It's a whole series of art-aesthetic values that are at play here. It would probably be a little different today, because these people are a recognised force; art has moved on in the last 30 to 40 years, they're more or less respected, etc. So it's not quite the same now. But it's close enough. If you ask any of these artists where they spend their time doing shows and doing commissions, they'll tell you 90 per cent or 75 per cent in Europe.

SR *One has the feeling that the interest in America starts with shows like* Information *at MOMA, New York in 1970, when the artists' reputations were already established in Europe.*

SS Absolutely. I don't want to underestimate that show of Kynaston McShine and of what influenced him into doing that show. But I don't know the motivations behind why he or the museum made that decision.

SR *There have been several other shows, like* Conceptual Art and Conceptual Aspects *at the New York Cultural Center [1970], and they were all in the early 1970s. So there's some response, but slightly later and maybe not on the same scale.*

SS Yes, not on the same scale and not backed up with the same kind of general interest. I don't have any specific data to supply, but there were others like in Vermont or at the Finch College in New York in 1969–70. There were some exhibitions also in Oberlin, Ohio. I'm not saying that there were no exhibitions, but I think we'd be looking at mostly individual curators who were close to the artist and interested in doing a show. That was part of the network of interest that was going on. You could also say, but in a much lesser way than in Europe, that there was also economic, institutional, large-scale support for the work. Even though people weren't getting rich, I'm sure, many of them had the possibility to make works, with a ground-level living here in Europe, whereas it was almost impossible to do that in the United States. There may be the work, but you can't earn a living unless you have a job in the United States. Granted, it's difficult here; it's not paradise, but it's possible for someone to do that.

SR *In the early 1970s, there were several Americans involved in the art world who moved to Europe, like yourself, Jack Wendler and Lawrence Weiner. Slightly later, by the mid-1970s, there seemed to be Europeans going to America, like Sperone and Fischer, who opened a gallery in New York. There were also René Block and Reinhard Onnasch.*

SS That's different. I can't comment on Enzo and Konrad going to New York. That was later. I'd just walk into their gallery when I was in New York.

SR *And they're nearly all German. I find that very interesting.*

SS Yes, all except for Sperone. What exactly motivated them? Of course, they connected with Angela Westwater. But it's difficult for me to say. That all took place later, after I left the art world. Of the three people you mentioned, Jack Wendler and I are the only ones who actually moved here, who actually left the United States. Lawrence bought a boat (and he still has it). They live here, but they don't live here all the time.

They're here for a few months a year and they use it as a *point de chute*. But Lawrence and Alice live in New York. That's where they work from; that's their headquarters. When they come here, sometimes for a few weeks, it's really just passing through, as a base from which to go off to other places. When I first came here in 1969, I found that this is an incredibly useful place to be in contact with the rest of Europe and even the rest of the world. It's very close to Düsseldorf, to Cologne, to Paris and major cities. So there were only two of us. There wasn't a great exodus. In my case, it was purely a personal feminine reason, a personal romance story. It happened in a moment in my life when I was finishing with the art world. It happened at a moment when I was already well into thinking about journalism, research and things like that. It wasn't like a political protest at all. I can't speak for Jack, although he's definitely on the progressive left side, but I'm sure it wasn't an expatriation. One might think that because of his background, but no.

SR *But I'm sure they could also get involved with drugs in Europe.*

SS Absolutely. But they felt it was stronger in New York. They had the means to be able to make that shift with a certain style. Jack opened a gallery and has become an active member of the art world in London. It wasn't a political movement either on his part or on mine and Lawrence never left New York. You hear people complaining; many artists would talk about leaving New York. Now there's Bush, before there was Nixon …

SR *When did you first travel to Europe?*

SS It was in 1969.

SR *Was that when you participated in Prospect 69?*

SS Yes, it was probably that. I certainly paved my own way to come over. So it wasn't like someone suggested that I should come. I remember staying at Konrad's for one of the Prospects. It must have been around that time, and then I'd probably come over at least once a year, maybe more frequently because I was doing shows. People were very excited to see me, very happy. In New York, although I had an active bar life, with my friends and all that stuff, I wasn't taken seriously. And then you'd come over here and people like Konrad, Sperone, Germano Celant, Daniel Buren, Michel Claura or Herman Daled were really excited about what they were doing. They were really happy to see your work and what you were doing. You had very little of that in America. So it was a really nice place to be.

SR *Would you go mainly to Germany?*

SS It would probably have been Germany more than anything, and France. (France was very nice and very cheap.) I don't think I ever went to Portugal. I went to Switzerland for the Szeemann show. That was probably one of the first times. It would have been 1969.

SR *So you knew Konrad Fischer quite well?*

SS I knew him, but I wouldn't say quite well. Again, I didn't have any business with any of these people. I was just like a free spirit sort of floating through, doing exhibitions more or less thought out. In any case I was very happy to see these people, and they were very happy to talk to me. I remember staying at Konrad's house several times. I remember spending time with Daniel in Paris, in Italy at the Sperone gallery. These would be the people I'd see. In Amsterdam, I spent time with Jan Dibbets. They were very good hosts. Everyone was living very simply, modestly. Tough times, one would say. Everyone was coming along, doing their work, so it was a good place to be. It's nice to go anywhere, as long as you're not brutalised, beaten up or shot at or poisoned or something. So it's nice to go to any place for a few weeks, or a few months just to see a different place; even just to travel without any specific purpose in mind. Coming over to Europe, seeing specific people you knew about or you were in touch with by telephone was doubly exciting. You experienced new cultures, you ate new food, you hung around with people you knew or had heard of, so it was very easy and pleasurable. I probably didn't go over more than twice a year. But I did come over – it must have been the winter of 1969–70 – and I did stay in Europe for six months. I was living in Amsterdam, but also preparing the catalogue for Michel Claura's exhibition *18 Paris IV.70*. I remember hanging around until the beginning of the summer.

SR *You also did the special July/August issue of* Studio International *in 1970.*

SS Yes, that was another thing. I hung around there with Peter Townsend, who was my host. I stayed at a B&B. I was in London for a very long time: six weeks or so. I spent a month with Mario and Marisa Merz in Italy. It was very nice to meet all these people, see all these cities.

SR *Did you also meet Lynda Morris at that time?*

SS I'd have met Lynda in London, probably with Jack. It would have been in the early 1970s. I saw a Lamelas film somewhere with Lynda.

SR *She worked at Nigel Greenwood's.*

SS I don't know. I barely remember Nigel. I knew who he was, and that he was involved with books and publishing and various activities. I have a very slim and unclear memory of him. I don't think I met Lynda when I first came to Europe in 1969. It would have been later, probably with Jack Wendler when he had moved there, in 1972–73. I'd go and visit Jack, because I was living in France. So every four months or so, I'd go to London and stay with Jack. He was quite active in the art world, and, of course, I wasn't active at all in Paris. So it was nice to see an old friend, and it still is.

SR *How did the Europeans know what you were doing in America?*

SS Well, because of the publications and the *bouche-à-l'oreille*. Again, the community was relatively small. There was little interest in this kind of art. It was relatively easy to get in touch. There were certain people, like Germano Celant, and probably myself in a certain way in the United States, who knew everybody, who were around all the time, were in touch with different kinds of people, different places and stuff like this. As a matter of fact, it still is that way. You'd hear about people like that and they'd hear about you in the same way. I think it was mostly through catalogues and announcements, the *télégraphe arabe*, people just talking to each other.

Another very important fact is that because of the nature of the art, it was always cheaper to send artists around than to send works around. If you wanted to do a show, very often what you did was put things in an envelope, send instructions or make a telephone call. Even the artists could be sent around for less money than the cost of the shipment of paintings. (That's even true today, in fact.) So there was a lot of movement of people if you were doing a show, and even with a relatively limited budget, people moving around was the second-best way. The best way was to put things in an air-mail envelope and post it. A lot of work was sent around that way. If that couldn't be done, the travelling artist was the next best thing. Artists would be going around meeting other artists that they wouldn't have met otherwise. They wouldn't necessarily have done that with Pop art or painting or sculpture. There wouldn't be quite the same feeling. A number of artists flew out and created what came to be called 'site-specific work' (the term probably didn't exist then, of course). I think that the show that we did at Windham [*Carl Andre, Robert Barry, Lawrence Weiner*, Windham College, Putney, Vermont, 1968] was one of the first exhibitions ever where artists went out and actually worked on a site and built something for that particular place. It was at a university or a college. Someone pointed out to me that four of the places where I arranged exhibitions no longer exist. The physical places have dematerialised. Once, I did a show for Congressman Ed Koch, who later became Mayor of New York, who held a fundraising show. There's absolutely no record of what happened and what was there. I have a vague memory. It was at the Bradford Junior College, Massachusetts, and included Carl Andre, Robert Barry and Lawrence Weiner. That's no longer there. The Windham College, which was the outdoor exhibition, that's no longer there. The building where we did the *January* show on 52nd Street, that's gone, too. I didn't realise it until someone mentioned it to me. So it was a perfectly logical thing for artists to travel around to do their art. Now it's so standard that you don't even think about it.

SR *Is this one of the reasons why you closed down the gallery you had?*

SS No, the gallery I had was completely unrelated. I had it from the fall of 1964 to the spring of 1966. It was very unsuccessful and I was very unclear about what I was doing. I did show Lawrence Weiner twice and maybe one or two interesting exhibitions. But really, I didn't like it at all. So I closed. It wasn't to make money.

SR *But you continued to work with the same artists?*

SS No, the artists had nothing to do with it, because the only artist I was working with at the time was Lawrence. I met Huebler through Dore Ashton and she mentioned his work to me. I went up to see his work at that time, but I never showed him at the gallery. I knew Bob Barry because he was in a cooperative gallery just up the street. He'd come over with people to chat. I met Joseph Kosuth probably through Lawrence. Carl was around with Barry, *et voilà*! So I wasn't involved with these other people until 1966. It would have been from 1967 onwards that I began to go along with them. Art projects didn't start to materialise until the end of 1967 and then I started with the exhibition in January 1968, which was the Bradford Junior College. I did that for three years until 1971 and I did 21 shows.

SR *After you closed the gallery, you did 21 shows?*

SS Yes. The artists with whom I'm now associated, all that only came together in around 1967. So it was after the gallery closed, with the exception of showing Lawrence two times in 1964 and 1965. I was just beginning to know Huebler and Barry, and I began to know Carl during 1967. I started to do exhibitions in January of 1968 until the fundraising political exhibition in the United States. The fund was for the war and soldiers. That was my last project for the art world, until I did this *Context of Art* thing, which is something that just popped up in about 1999.

SR *What was that?*

SS It was a questionnaire sent to artists. Marion Fricke and Roswitha Fricke asked me at the precise moment when the idea occurred to me, to do a show.

SR *Basically, from the moment you moved to Europe, you stopped doing shows.*

SS Absolutely. I was involved in publishing. I was doing research on media and doing left-wing political publishing for about ten years in Paris from around 1972–74. Then I got involved in this textile research, which was something I was doing even before I left the art world. I started to collect books and textiles. I've been working on that for the last 20 years. I've finished now and published two volumes about it. I'm now bringing out a CD-Rom, which is the second edition, but searchable, etc. It's the searchable thing that's absolutely wonderful. So I'm working on that. I've hired someone to set up the programme. I hope to finish soon.

SR *To go back to what we were saying before, how did you meet all these other artists?*

SS Well, you'd see them all the time. People would come to a bar, go to openings, you talk, you look, the same way you meet anybody. There was a special bar that we went to, quite famous, called Max's Kansas City. Everyone would go there to drink. (I didn't drink.) But people would go there and spend lots of time there. The owner also collected art, so that was important. The artists could afford to have a good meal and keep warm. People would hang around there all hours of the night, including myself. So you'd meet everybody. Max's was a central point. The owner was very sympathetic and careful. He'd maintain an environment that allowed us to sit and hang around. I used to go there and maybe have a beer or a cup of coffee and spend four or five hours there, doing nothing except talking. I recall an English collector, Alan Power, coming into town one night and we went to Max's and we fell asleep on the benches. The tables are worth a lot of money to the bar owners on a Saturday night. We slept there for two hours and we didn't order anything. He knew his regulars and he was very careful.

SR *Who was the owner of the bar?*

SS The guy who ran it was Mickey Ruskin. He died (it's a long story), probably in the early 1970s.

SR *Where was the bar situated?*

SS The bar was on Park Avenue South and 14th Street, just off Union Square.

SR *It was well situated.*

SS Yes, but it would have been well situated no matter where it was. He maintained such a good and congenial environment for the art world that if he was in the middle of nowhere, people would have gone there anyhow. In fact he did open several bars over the years. I think he had four or five at different times. Wherever he was, people would go there.

SR *I've heard of that bar from several people.*

SS It was very important. Maybe other art movements in other cities had their own bars.

SR *I've heard about the Ühl and the Cream Cheese in Düsseldorf.*

SS I remember, when I was in Düsseldorf, Daniel Spoerri had a place not far from the museum. It used to be crowded with people; people would hang out outside, and you'd have mussels. As I said, I'm not a big drinker. It was just social. But there were big drinkers – a lot of them were. Of course, if someone bought one of your pieces, you had enough money to enjoy good meals for six months. A lot of artists used to go out every night and drink and eat, eat and drink. It was very seductive.

4.14 Conversation with Harald Szeemann

Maggia, 22 July 2003

SOPHIE RICHARD *I'd like to start by talking about the exhibitions* When Attitudes Become Form *(1969) and Documenta 5 (1972), particularly with regard to the choice of artists. How did you discover the artists you ended up showing?*

HARALD SZEEMANN Some people from Philip Morris came to Bern when Christo wrapped the Kunsthalle while I was Director. It went all the way round the world; it was in all the papers. They suggested doing an exhibition and giving me money. Since I never had funds at Bern Kunsthalle, I told myself I'd finally be able to show artists working with light from the East coast of the States. At the same time, the Stedelijk Museum in Amsterdam wanted to show young Swiss artists, while I wanted to show young Dutch ones. I always had good relations with Amsterdam. When I needed something from the States, they were the ones who brought it over. I was having a lot of problems in Bern, because the Society of Painters always thought I liked young artists too much, and so on. So of course, when the Stedelijk said it wanted to show young Swiss artists, I thought it would be much better if the exhibition was shown first in Amsterdam and then in Bern. That way, the artists would have the validation of one of the best-known museums in the world. It was a little bit strategic. In return, I said I'd show young Dutch artists in Bern. While Christo was wrapping the Kunsthalle, I went to Amsterdam. I told De Wilde I was going to get some money from Philip Morris, and I'd like to show Turrell, Irwin, Weiner ... He told me he'd already booked them. At that time, we were visiting Dutch artists and Lucassen asked me if I'd like some work by his assistant. That was Jan Dibbets, who was watering turf arranged on two tables in his studio. I thought it was extraordinary, and the work was shown in the exhibition of young Dutch artists. I asked him if there were any other artists like him, and that was how everything started moving.

In 1967, I'd also put on the exhibition *Science Fiction* in Düsseldorf, and it was also the start of the Konrad Fischer programme. That was where I met Carl Andre, and that was how things happened. I'd shown Fischer as an artist in 1968, and we were in constant contact. It was a network. I knew Joseph Beuys and Reiner Ruthenbeck already.

SR *You left for the States anyway?*

HS In 1968 I was in New York, where there was a sense that something new was happening. I set off after the Christmas exhibition in December. As the exhibition was planned for March 1969, I had to go to the States to have time to bring the works over on loan. I went to America to visit the artists and they sent me to each other. The whole thing snowballed. [*Refers to his list of addresses published in the* Attitudes *catalogue.*] Of course, I went to see Leo Castelli. He was showing the exhibition *9 at Castelli* [December 1968], which included Serra, Sonnier and so on. I also went to the Green Gallery, to prepare the exhibition *Happening & Fluxus* [November 1970–January 1971].

SR *Finally, in 1969, there were two very similar exhibitions,* When Attitudes Become Form *and* Op Losse Schroeven *in Amsterdam.*

HS I didn't know that Wim Beeren wanted to do the same thing as me in Amsterdam. De Wilde should have told me. We'd have done it together. I even gave all the artists the chance to come via Amsterdam, because Beeren insisted on starting his exhibition a week before me. Beeren later asked me to make a contribution to the catalogue. In the end, people talked much more about mine, even though his started a week before me. People talked about it more, because it was more anarchist. Obviously there were almost the same names in both exhibitions. In Bern, the exhibition took the artists as its starting point. There weren't rooms with works hanging in them. It was fairly chaotic; it was more innovative. In Bern, you could do a lot more things. Everyone could do what he wanted. At the Stedelijk, you couldn't take a bit of wall down for Weiner's intervention, or destroy the pavement for Heizer's work, or make Serra's lead, or have the whole Kunsthalle put under radiation by Barry.

SR *Did you have contact with the people who ran the artists' galleries?*

HS We really did the exhibition directly with the artists. Of course, when we went to Turin to talk to the artists, Sperone was there; he wanted his name to be in the catalogue. That was logical, because everyone knew something was going to happen. In Turin, all the artists depended financially on Sperone. When you had lunch with him and the artists, the artists didn't say a word. Afterwards, I went to see them in their studios and we talked.

SR *Were the works in the exhibition sold to museums?*

HS A Fred Sandback and a Richard Tuttle were sold to Franz Meyer, the Director of the Basel Museum. He wanted to buy them for the museum, which didn't want them, and then after a few years they took them. Apart from that, nothing was sold. Most of the works weren't saleable. You couldn't buy the Sonnier, or the Ruthenbeck. Everyone wanted the Nauman, but it wasn't for sale because I'd only made one copy with his authorisation. He was worried that the neon would get broken during transport. Then the installation was done according to his design. The Beuys installation was bought later by the Bodenmann Collection in Basel. But that wasn't through the Kunsthalle; it was done through the back door.

SR *You've said that* Attitudes *influenced the choices of certain private collectors, even if that took a bit of time to get going.*

HS Yes. The insurance values at the time weren't high at all. In Krefeld, the insurance was five times as much as it had been. At the time, there was Mr Bongard with his *Kunstkompass* of the hundred best artists. When I did an exhibition, he'd always give three times as many points to the artists. Of course, people read the magazine. All of a sudden, Serra was involved and everything happened very quickly. I've always worked directly with the artists. If the gallery owner wanted to give something to support the project, so much the better. I never see the gallery owner; I always go to see the artist. Obviously, if a gallery owner has very beautiful works that haven't been sold yet, and I'd like to have them for an exhibition, I'm going to pay him a visit. In the end, I don't care; what I want to do is good exhibitions. For example, when I did *Science Fiction*, it was Beuys himself who'd brought the work. There was no intervention by a gallery. The Düsseldorf Kunstverein almost always took the exhibitions I did at the Kunsthalle in Bern.

SR *You were talking just now about a network of people who introduced you to the* Attitudes *artists. Did you go on working with those people?*

HS No, because for *Happening & Fluxus* there were different channels; it wasn't the same artists. For Documenta 5, I brought each artist to Kassel to talk to him directly. I didn't go and choose things from galleries. But obviously, it's always like that in those contemporary art exhibitions: the gallery owner always ends up talking to the artist about his project. The preparation for Documenta was quite long and the artists were happy to be part of it. So they talked to other people about it and all of a sudden there were several pieces that had been bought by Mr Ludwig. He bought works by the Nouveau Réalistes before the opening of Documenta, so Documenta had to pay for their exhibition and their transport. So I preferred to give up; either he gives something to Documenta or we give up.

SR *How was contact made with the collaborators on Documenta 5, like König or Konrad Fischer, who did the exhibition* Idee+Idee/Licht*?*

HS At that point, Claes Oldenburg, whom I hadn't planned to include in Documenta, was starting his Mickey Mouse Museum. That project came to Documenta very late, because Spoerri's plan to make the whole history of twentieth-century art in cake had been cancelled. He'd planned to make the classics like Picasso, then Pollock and the Pop artists in cake. The sponsor, Motta, didn't want to participate any more. I wanted to scrap that history of the twentieth century and start with the revolution of 1968. In the end, that led to the idea of doing artists' museums with Duchamp, Broodthaers, Ben Vautier, etc. At that point, the artists were also starting to control their own presentations, so they were doing museums. It was then that I was contacted by König who was working on Oldenburg's *Mouse Museum*. Obviously, I said yes immediately, even if that blew the budget. At Documenta, everything was built in wood, but then the project evolved with corrugated iron, which meant it could be dismantled, and so on. Oldenburg suggested that König should be the curator to travel to America, and it was König who took care of it. Where Fischer was concerned, I didn't want him because he was a gallery owner. I'd asked Honnef [Kunstverein, Münster] if he could deal with Conceptual art. In the end it was Honnef who asked me if he could collaborate with Fischer, so I said of course; he was, after all, best-placed for that kind of art. I was happy for someone who worked in museums to work with Fischer.

SR *Were there any other projects that you had to give up, for budgetary or other reasons?*

HS I wanted to put up a tent in front of the Fridericianum. I'd noticed that the public as a whole, particularly in Germany, was into kinetic art. They were always wanting things to move. So I asked Jean Tinguely, and Hagam with his flame, as well as Sai and Vassilakis Takis, with his magnetic works, to take part, but as something of a preamble. It was a matter of showing people art that they knew before they came into the Fridericianum where there was art that they didn't know. But later on, with all the budgetary discussions, the project was abandoned. I also gave up doing things that were too big in the park. In 1968, there'd been Christo's installation, and I didn't want to compete with those memories. So I told myself it was better to do temporary things in the park. There were people who did performances, like Rinke, and also Rebecca Horn for the first time. She'd never had an exhibition before. So I did ephemeral things and gave up on the monument. It was fine, because that reduction gave me the chance to do a big installation etc. There were a huge numbers of things: there were the concerts by Fluxus and Keith Sonnier; there were also performances at the little theatre of the city of Kassel. In the middle of the exhibition we brought in Terry Fox, Howard Fried and James Lee Byars to do performances. At first, what I really wanted to do was an exhibition of events. But in Kassel, that horribly tedious town, we had to do an exhibition that held together. There always had to be an exhibition to see. Everything that came afterwards, like the ephemeral things, could be done later on if the budget allowed.

SR *Were there sales of works after Documenta?*

HS I'm not really interested in that in the end. What interests me is the exhibition. I know very well that when I do an exhibition, prices go up, people start buying. But I actually had no idea about sales. All I know is that Ludwig tried to buy works by the Nouveau Réalistes. Obviously institutions have a kind of obligation, but I'm not interested in that. I'm working with public money. The Cologne gallery-owners, like Zwirner, attacked me during the preparation of Documenta. For them, it wasn't art and it didn't validate art. They rented the ground floor and the first floor of the skyscraper in Kassel and installed themselves in there to compete with me. But my Documenta was so new for young people that after a few weeks they realised that they weren't selling anything and left.

Translation from French: Shaun Whiteside

4.15 Conversation with David Tremlett

Bovingdon, Herts, 23 February 2005

SOPHIE RICHARD *Could you talk about how in the late 1960s and early 1970s, as an artist in England, you networked with dealer galleries across Europe?*

DAVID TREMLETT It was very different from today, in the sense that nobody needed or wanted to network (or knew what it meant). The whole idea of meeting people was in fact considered rather low level. Today, everyone goes to the museums and galleries, and they want to meet everybody. Artists now just have no fear. I never did an exhibition unless I was invited. To ask for an exhibition was really out of the question. If I wasn't invited, I didn't do anything. Most of the artists in that period were very private people. That's a generalisation because Gilbert & George weren't private; they were great socialisers. Yet, at the same time, they were very private and shut themselves off completely from what they didn't want. But, in England, I live here in Hertfordshire, and others who I found were in similar group shows were living outside the London area. It's not that everybody would go to a pub in the evening like in London, where many lived, although I remember many a wobbly night with G&G and others around the West End. I think this had to do with the fact that England did not have a big gallery structure for artists, except Nicholas Logsdail and Nigel Greenwood. Outside this, there was little. The result was that we worked with Konrad Fischer or Art & Project or the interesting galleries in Europe. The rest of Europe had Fluxus and all that stuff with Joseph Beuys and the Düsseldorf art scene. Italy had its past with Futurism and everything that then led to Arte Povera. There was a Parisian School in some ways, but it was never so strong. Daniel Buren tended to dominate. (Others seemed to struggle like Niele Toroni, who is a great artist; I don't know why but the French need a king.) I haven't made a gallery exhibition for years in this country. I made one in the Serpentine Gallery maybe ten years ago, and I've made them in other public spaces like Manchester and Bristol. And the reality is that I am always in Italy, France, America and Japan. So I found in general England was not so easy and went outside.

SR *Was Nigel Greenwood your first dealer in London?*

DT No, the very first gallery show I made was with Grabowski Gallery in Chelsea just after I left the Royal College. There were just the Royal College and St Martin's which had anything of interest at the time. St Martin's was a bit more radical because it didn't have the sort of snobbish attitude of the Royal College. The Royal College was considered the place where the best fashion designers went, the best photographers. It was the 'trendiest' place in London. I didn't notice this at all, to be honest. I came from Cornwall; I was the son of a farmer and they (my parents) emigrated to Australia when I was at Birmingham College of Art. That was two or three years earlier. So once they'd gone to Australia, I was here alone and I was able to move from Birmingham to the Royal College. I did sculpture, as Gilbert & George, Richard Long and Bruce McLean did. We were all sculptors. Nobody did painting courses at all. There was this big thing about being a sculptor.

After the Royal College, I had a studio in South London. It was a railway arch. It was then, when my grandfather died. He left me £500, which at the time was quite a lot of money and at the end of the second year at the College, I decided not to attend. I still received the grant and then found a railway arch as a studio where I continued to work. Of course, that caused a problem with the Royal College because they said that if I didn't come to the courses, they'd write to my local council who in turn would ask for grant money back. They were really very heavy and didn't like me being independent. So I appeared at the end and did a sort of diploma show. I remember I was one of the failing members of the class. [*Laughs*]. But I did at least have a studio. That's when Mr Grabowski came to see me. He had a small gallery where he showed several artists, and he gave me my first exhibition. Nigel Greenwood came to the opening. He said, 'Would you like to come and join the gallery?' I was innocent and didn't know who he was, but he clearly had a decent reputation. So I ended up doing some strange exhibitions with him, in the sense that they'd only lasted one or two days.

SR *When was your first show with Nigel Greenwood?*

DT I'm not quite sure. I'd have to check – around 1970, I think. I took boxes with cabbages, and I put them in an ordered way into the gallery [*laughing, looks in his files*]. There were very few installation shots made at the time. I also exhibited photographs and with a short texts underneath. It was like a passage from one place to another place to another place. So always moving. They were really just a shot from a tree or a hedge, completely anonymous, almost minimal, textual. I also did some very early graphite wall drawings with Nigel. These were rectangles of graphite drawn on the wall. Sometimes, it involved just the drawings and sometimes adding photographs to them. I'd draw on the floor with chalk and sometimes put boxes and objects directly into the forms. This was at Nigel Greenwood's [*shows photograph*]. It's like a table, and once or twice I used to use a workman's boiler suit as part of my pieces. There were some objects, like in the boxes, which I put on the table. This was a tape recorder with a loop tape with the sound of water: dripping. So the whole room sounded wet. I used sound more in the early days. There's a piece at the Tate that was made of cassettes.

SR *Yes, the* Spring Recordings.

DT On each of them is the sound of one county in England. But all you hear is the water or the wind or the rain. That's it. Sometimes you hear the sound of a bird. In essence, it's something with no mechanical sounds 'it was a silent sound landscape'. I made several sound pieces, I knew Gavin Bryars at the time. Gavin is an interesting musician, who's still producing great material and also had met Steve Reich. Then there was a piece where I worked with a tap dancer. She tap danced and I made recordings. Charles Harrison from *Studio International* and Art & Language took an exhibition to New York of some artists [*The British Avant-Garde*, 1971]. It was an important exhibition for the time. I showed musical paper and drew some ideas on it. I recorded Karen Bernard tap dancing. These recordings I still have. She'd dance, let's say, for one minute. This was then put on a loop. Some of the exhibitions that were made were just this noise of Karen's dancing coming from one corner of the room. Maybe in another corner, there'd be another sound of tap dancing. So there was a room with the history of a person dancing. It was somewhere between music, writing, sound and installation. Then slowly, because I'm not so involved with electronic material, I changed. I've always been interested in very simple ways of doing things. Tap dancing was a very simple idea. That's when I started to draw more and more on the wall, because it was a simple way of operating. I could put all materials in a small bag and draw anywhere.

This was, I think, the essence of that period. Many artists were able to put an exhibition in a suitcase and go to 'somewhere', then install. This was why many 1970s galleries were great, because in fact, that's all they expected. They didn't want lorries turning up with huge things. Many of the artists at the time had little money. The galleries didn't have so much money, so everything was sensible budgets. That's where for me 'the travel' was important. We hardly ever flew to Europe. We all went by train. I used to hitchhike sometimes. In 1972 – I think after I'd done my first show with Konrad Fischer – I hitchhiked to Australia. It took me eight months. I did it as a work and I sent postcards back to certain people. There was a gallery here, in the UK, Situation Gallery that gave me £100 and this is what I travelled on for eight months, and I got to Australia on it. In return, I sent them postcards as I was travelling. Now it exists as a piece and is in the collection of the Henry Moore Foundation. There were always these light, inexpensive ways of working.

Artists didn't hang out so much, although I knew Gilbert & George and Alan Charlton well. I don't know how I got to know them at the beginning, but I did see them when I was at the Royal College, when they did their first performance. We just got to know each other. We were pretty good friends and they were my best men when I first got married, for example. I have some works by Gilbert & George because we exchanged work. Fulton – he and I were at the Royal College together – he was there for one year, but afterwards we lost contact, till later. Long I didn't know so well. The familiar ground was the similar galleries we worked with. I worked with Marilena Bonomo Gallery in Bari, who was very close to Sol LeWitt and the American School: Richard Tuttle, Mel Bochner, Carl Andre and these people. I met her in the very early 1970s and have worked with her ever since. I still work with her in a loyal way. There's a very interesting gallerist in Milan, who you probably don't know, Massimo Valsecchi. Valsecchi has been working since before the 1970s. He's extremely private with an incredible collection.

SR *Is he a private collector?*

DT He's a gallerist. It's called Massimo Valsecchi Gallery. He's really hard to find. He worked with very specific people. He did one of the first shows of Gerhard Richter in Italy, for example. He worked for a long time with Bernd and Hilla Becher. He has a great early collection of works by the Bechers, plus early Richter, which he bought early on, of course. But before that, he worked with the Fluxus group a lot. Then he worked with Fulton, Gilbert & George, and with me since 1974–75. Massimo would buy the whole exhibition before he put it up. He'd visit the studio, choose the works for the exhibition and he'd buy it all. He'd buy for the artist's price, maybe take a little discount, but what he did was basically to give you an income. He did this for Gilbert & George, for Fulton and for other artists. Then he'd put on an exhibition; he had to sell some works to keep the business running and retain the rest.

SR *So at the time, was 50 per cent the kind of percentage that dealers would generally take on sales of works?*

DT Always. I'd say, that's the common rule. Most of the artists realised that the galleries needed to produce some money as well. There's a misconception sometimes that galleries have huge amounts of money. Of course, they can produce a lot of money. But most of the galleries, like Fischer, were just art students. Adriaan van Ravesteijn, from Art & Project, was also a student, I don't exactly remember of what. Geert van Beijeren, his partner, was working at the Stedelijk Museum. Geert was able to introduce the Stedelijk to this cross-section of work. Art & Project have a very interesting archive of work. The relationship between the artists and these galleries was often a really good one. Everybody was in a way in the same boat. There were not large sums of money, but there were collectors like Giuseppe Panza, who maybe was going to buy something sometime.

Of course, the German market was strong at the time. I never made numerous exhibitions in Germany, but did enter some of the collections. I found myself more in France or Portugal and Italy. The interesting thing for me is that because it was a severe period, like Stanley Brouwn working with pinpoints, some artists got stuck. They didn't ease up at a certain point. Others sort of put behind them a rigid philosophical position that Conceptual art took. Then, everybody got drunk, some leant to the left politically, rejecting consumerism, etc. But the reality is, now I meet some of these guys and they've got gold watches on! [*Laughs*]

SR *Well, that happens a lot don't you think?*

DT If you're an artist or a writer, or whatever you're doing, clearly what you want to do is to continue to work. I need to work in a way that has a constant revolution in it. All I can say is that I hope I've managed to do it, because I still have these new projects coming up on walls and ceilings and in the most amazing places – churches, castles, expensive homes, subway stations ... And still there's that sort of momentum, which keeps me going. It's not just focusing on the past, and trying to do it again in another way. I always felt I had a sort of personal revolution inside myself. I never sat still.

Of course, travelling made a difference. I was in Africa, many times, in the Middle East, South America and Australasia. Unlike others, who are more like explorers, who need to climb mountains. I sat on railway stations for two days waiting for a train, or I went into some strange hotel and wrote and drew, then took a bus somewhere else. It was travel that was less programmed. I think it taught me to diversify, but always within my own world.

In those days, with small amounts of money, I made things like this [*shows photographs*]. This is in Africa. These are beer cartons. There are thousands of them, and I built this structure up a tree with some local children. It was an idea with cheap and inexpensive materials. [*Shows more photographs.*] That was at the old Greenwood gallery. I was installing it at the time. I filled the complete corner of the gallery space with cabbages and boxes. There was a palette, and it had an old engine on it, which came from my studio under the railway arch. Next to the studio were mechanics mending the London taxis. To make money to pay my studio rent, I used to work as a mechanic. So that's why my materials became engines and old boxes, which were all rejected material, this I used for my art. So this was an installation of materials, which were the simplest things I could find at the time to use. I then, in 1972, went for the first time to Iran and Afghanistan and my work changed as I started to draw. My shows in Germany involved sound and drawing. The Art & Project shows were drawing and a form of poetry.

SR *You also showed with Rolf Preisig in Basel?*

DT Yes. His gallery didn't last for very long – around two or three years. The show I made for Rolf was works on paper with simple line drawings, very similar to those in the show at Nigel Greenwood. All of them were purchased by Panza. It's one of those great exhibitions where the telephone rang and the dealer said 'I sold everything, all at once to Giuseppe Panza.'

SR *Was Panza the private collector who bought the most of your works in the 1970s?*

DT Yes. There was also a collector in Bari called Angelo Baldassare, who bought. This was always through Marilena Bonomo. Panza was famous for buying a lot of pieces by one person and bought from quite a large cross-section of people, but then concentrated on certain artists. I remember he had a private collection of skulls in his house. He has this strange fascination – it's not death, but it's something very minimal. Alan Charlton's work was perfect for him in some ways. Another collector in Udine, called Egidio Marzona, has an incredible collection. He's in Bielefeld, Germany, most of the time, but his collection is in Udine. He has a collection covering that period. He came back to me recently, saying 'David, I missed out on you in this collection. You have to come in and do something for me in the near future.' So he missed out on some things but now he's sort of creating a collection in totality.

SR *What about Belgian collectors, like Herman Daled and Anton Herbert?*

DT Daled was very active. But I didn't have a gallery in Belgium until much later on. I never showed in Wide White Space, and then they closed. I never really started to work in Belgium until the early 1980s. Consequently, it was too late for Daled and Anton Herbert. He has some great works, but it's not like he has everybody from that particular period. I sell in Belgium, but not necessarily to those people. I did some museum shows there, at the Palais des Beaux-Arts in Brussels, and also in Gent where some of the collectors have work, like Pannier and Iserbyt collections.

SR *In Germany, the main collectors were Dr Peter Ludwig and Reiner Speck.*

DT In fact, the best collectors of mine were in Italy. That's because they didn't have any public institutions mainly private collections, which still exist today. For example Valsecchi in Milan, who rarely shows his collection. His collection is broad; not just art, but also glass. He has an excellent collection of Lalique, Daum, Tiffany and furniture from the Wiener Werkstätte. And the art is exceptional.

[*Looks back at the photographs.*] So the Preisig show consisted of works with lines. The frames were red and the drawings would be red, or the frames black and the drawings black and so on. Preisig was a good friend of Fischer. Fischer was an influential gallerist, because he was an inspired man and he was the first to show so much, and he did it so generously. He drank as much as the artists; he did everything because he was an artist, too. The last time I saw him was in Norwich where he asked me to join him in judging the *East* exhibition in 1993. Lynda Morris asked him and he asked me. We were the first ones of this 1970s period, to do the judging for this exhibition. Afterwards there were Nicholas Logsdail, Lawrence Weiner, Richard Long and so on. He and I spent three days locked in a room with hundreds and hundreds of slides. He was ill at this time and under treatment. I remember going to see him one month later in Düsseldorf. We were arranging a new show. And then, he died [in 1996], so it was very dramatic. Konrad was a real mentor for many people. Only Art & Project, who started roughly at the same time, were as important. But they did it in a very different way; they were very Dutch, very pure, they didn't get drunk. They were exacting; were just very good at doing everything. They'd pay your train fare, find you a little hotel, buy you lunch, they'd arrange to buy a work in advance. Very precise, very honest and really charming. Art & Project always had that link with the Mondrian tradition in Holland, a sense of design and so on. They were like that, very minimal, very pure and extremely simple.

SR *What was the relationship between Fischer and Art & Project?*

DT I don't think they collaborated very much. It's the same old story. Even the artists, generally, didn't collaborate very much. They all wanted to do their own thing. As an English artist, I got on well with a German artist or an Italian one. For example, I remember meeting Alighiero Boetti in Afghanistan in 1971–72. I didn't know much about Boetti at the time and I didn't know much about Arte Povera. I'd just seen in *Flash Art* that some strange things were coming from Italy. I first met him in Afghanistan. He'd bought a building in Kabul, and he was trying to make it into a hotel and called it Number 1 Hotel. I met him and thought, 'This man's somewhere on the same road as me plus what am I doing in Kabul with someone who seems to have a similar vision'. Anyway, we remained friends right up to the day he died. But in England, apart from Alan Charlton, with whom I occasionally do collaborative shows, I haven't had any close artist friends. I admire a lot of what Sol LeWitt has done in his sort of systematic, mathematical and mystical way. We have collaborated on a chapel together and often communicated.

SR *What about the museum shows and purchases in the 1970s? You were talking before about the* Spring Recordings *purchased by the Tate.*

DT That was from Konrad Fischer.

SR *Were you aware of other sales?*

DT Well, for me, few museums bought at that time. The Stedelijk bought when I did a show for them. The Centre Pompidou was a bit later; that goes a bit outside of your period: 1982–83. But before then, there was just the Tate, who bought several works and MOMA in New York that bought a small drawing. That was because being involved in the 'Project' series, they purchase. There were some small museums in England and Germany that bought occasionally. In France, there was the FRAC who occasionally acquired, but that was in the 1980s. I sold little to museums at the time. There were pieces here and there, but only once or twice a year.

SR *Did you see that as official recognition or was it more important for you to be in a private collection?*

DT I'd say the private collections were much more interesting. It's a more private relationship. I remember the galleries didn't want you to meet the collectors. They kept you apart.

SR *Why was that? Were they afraid that you'd sell directly to the collector?*

DT No, no. It was more a case that they felt if you kept the artists distant, the collectors would always be curious. It's like cat and mouse. Now it's different, but at that time, it was really keeping the two apart. So private collections were more interesting, as the galleries depended on them and not on museums. That relationship between the gallery and the private collector was close. The artists represented the gallery's thinking. Therefore I felt much closer to the gallery and the collector, even if I didn't meet the collector. The museum was more of a grand purchase. There was a curator called Jenny Licht, she was at the Museum of Modern Art with Kynaston McShine. She was responsible for people like Long, Barry Flanagan and myself being in the museum's collection. She was quite special.

SR *In 1973, you had a show at the MOMA in New York.*

DT Yes, that was the 'Project' series, which I just mentioned.

SR *Did you feel at the time that there was a difference between doing shows in Europe and in America?*

DT Yes. America was like a new place I'd never been to. I knew it from Elvis Presley and James Dean, Marlon Brando films and so on. Plus all those famous artists I had seen and heard about came from New York, so I was excited. The idea for me to go America to make a show was amazingly scary but challenging. At that time I knew few American artists but only the one or two I had met in Europe, such as Steve Reich, LeWitt, Andre. I remember well being invited to fish and chips at Carl Andre and Angela Westwater's apartment when first in New York, they for some reason wanted to make me feel 'at home'.

SR *What was also quite different, I guess, was that as an artist in Europe, you could have shows all over the continent – in Italy, in Germany and in England. Whereas, in America, everything was centralised in New York.*

DT Yes, there's also that cross-language element Italian, English, German, French, Spanish. As in America, everything was in English at that time. And many of the really interesting ideas were still coming out of New York.

SR *So how would you define Conceptual art? Is it determined more by the kind of artwork produced or by a group of artists that became known at the same moment in time?*

DT I think there's a very specific definition. The real, true Conceptual art is probably that of Lawrence Weiner and the thinking of Sol LeWitt. Art & Language, Hanne Darboven, who's wonderful mathematical, philosophical, strange language, I loved. I never really understood what Art and Language were up to, but those huge areas of incomprehensible texts were great to see, and I always remember someone saying that their German collectors would only want an English version or a French collector, a German version, that tells a lot about art!

I knew Terry Atkinson fairly well because he taught me when I was at Birmingham, in the Painting Department. Before Terry got involved with Art & Language, he was making sculpture and for me was the member who was of the greatest interest. Then Terry got completely obsessed with the First World War and was doing all these strange drawings.

SR *At the time, did you consider yourself as being part of Conceptual art?*

DT To be honest, I don't think I knew what it meant. For me, 'Conceptual art' is art where an artist writes or speaks a concept for a work, and it can be made or not. That's what Weiner was making. I don't know who invented that term and I still am not sure, but that's its magic.

SR *There were many terms used at the time, like ABC art, for example. But now, Conceptual art is the term used to categorise the art of that period.*

DT I think you accept what remains. But Conceptual art was another way of working, it was a way that as a young artist we grew up with, and I hope that even my contribution was a small part of a very interesting period. Sometimes artists didn't appear to be doing too much but in the end the less they did often the better and the more historical it became. Jack Wendler who ran a gallery in London was a good example of someone who exposed much of the art of Ian Wilson, Peter Downsborough, Huebler, Weiner, etc. and gave a good feel of the period, he of course went on to do *Art Monthly*, a direct consequence of the art he loved. Also many of us were in Documenta 1972 which had a great impact.

SR *That was the 'Idee' section.*

DT That's right, it was a special time, two good artists paid my airfare!

SR *That's where you showed the* Spring Recordings*?*

DT No, I showed work and photos on paper. They were like small photographs of gypsies with texts. But it was the same period as the *Spring Recordings*, that was at the Fischer gallery at roughly same time from where the Tate purchased it. [*Smiles*] That's how it went. Lynda Morris was working in London at that time. Lisson Gallery was a good gallery at that period with many of the interesting group of artists. I guess, in the 1970s, a lot of battles happened. Artists wanted to make it alone as individuals and not as a group. For the galleries, it was the same. There were people who talked badly about the others, but drank in the same bars. It could be quite tough as an environment. It wasn't that sweet! [*laughs*], but Art never is!

4.16 Conversation with Herman and Henriëtte van Eelen

Amsterdam, 27 April 2005

SOPHIE RICHARD *Could we begin our discussion by talking about the current situation with your collection?*

HENRIËTTE VAN EELEN The 35 pieces in our collection are in storage at the Kröller-Müller Museum in Otterlo. We're negotiating the sale of the works.

HERMAN VAN EELEN The Museum's Director, Evert van Straaten, promised that the works in the collection would stay together, as they've done for Martin Visser. They're a 'collectors' museum. But private collectors, other museums and galleries are also interested, as are auction houses. They're all waiting to see what will happen. Rudi Fuchs wanted to buy our collection for the Stedelijk Amsterdam. But it never happened. The Konrad Fischer Gallery bought a *Perspective Correction* by Jan Dibbets from us before we were in contact with the Kröller-Müller Museum. That's the only work missing.

HENRIËTTE VE But we haven't agreed on the price yet.

HERMAN VE But the problem isn't the money. All the artists in our collection, we know them very well, we write letters. They know that everything is on hold [with the Kröller-Müller].

HENRIËTTE VE They say they have to find more sponsors.

HERMAN VE It started with On Kawara. Van Straaten saw our On Kawara series [*I got up*, 1970 and 1973] in an exhibition in Munich. Then Kasper König, from the Ludwig Museum in Cologne, wrote to us to ask if he could have the work from Munich for an exhibition. I said: 'Yes, yes, take the work from Munich to your museum.' Then he said that he wanted to keep the On Kawara, because it would be so nice for their museum. I said: 'Yes, but it will cost you money.' Maybe he thought we were giving works away!

HENRIËTTE VE Here are all the postcards by On Kawara [*shows a folder with photocopies of the postcards*]. It's the *I got up* piece. This series is the only one in the world to have so many postcards. 126 and not one missing!

SR *This first series is from 1970.*

HERMAN VE Yes. The first series was sent from New York, from May until August 1970. There was one card missing. After several months, it arrived, because it was sent to Bermuda by mistake.

HENRIËTTE VE The second series is a smaller piece. There are seven postcards, which were all sent in Europe. On one of the postcards, the stamp is missing. Somebody took it.

SR *The postcards from the first series were sent first from America and then from Canada.*

HERMAN VE Yes. Van Straaten says that it's the most important piece in the collection.

HENRIËTTE VE Would you like to hear stories about Conceptual art? That's why you're here.

HERMAN VE You want to know the story of the On Kawara?

SR *Yes, of course!*

HERMAN VE Jan Dibbets always talked about On Kawara, On Kawara ... Then we went to see Konrad Fischer and he said, 'Herman, you're a nice person, but On Kawara only gives art pieces to rich collectors and famous museums, so it's not for you.' During the Second World War, I was in a prisoner-of-war camp in Indonesia for three and a half years; there was a Japanese camp there. The Japanese gave us postcards to send with a Japanese text already written on them: 'The Japanese are nice people, they treat us well, the food is good, etc.' My mother was in a women's camp. My father was in a prison camp. I got these cards and I put the address of my family and my name on them. After the war, my mother said, 'Herman, I still have three of those cards. I was so happy to get them. I know you got them from the Japanese, and it was nothing, but it was a sign of life.' So I wrote a nice letter to On Kawara: 'Dear On Kawara, you're a famous artist, we're collectors, etc. I was in a Japanese prison camp for three-and a half years and I always sent my mother these cards. My mother gave them to me after the war. Now, I appreciate your work so much, that I'm sending them to you.' Jan Dibbets, who was a good friend, said: 'He received your cards and put them into a golden frame!' He was fascinated.

HENRIËTTE VE He wrote the story in his diary.

HERMAN VE After 14 days, the On Kawara postcards arrived! The postman asked why there were always these same postcards. I explained to him and he said: 'Oh, I'll look for them!' Sometimes a postcard was late and he said that he knew where it was: at the back of the office somewhere. He made sure that we got the 126 postcards. And it all started because I was in a prison camp. I wrote to Kawara and thanked him very much. But I never met him. He doesn't come to openings of his works. Jan Dibbets said, 'What you did with that card is incredible!' Kawara felt guilty, of course, as a Japanese. I told the story to Konrad Fischer and he said, 'You're a big guy. You're incredible!'

HENRIËTTE VE Those cards from the prison camp are so similar to the cards that Kawara makes: pre-printed in Japanese, the same size ...

HERMAN VE It was a good trick! [*Laughs*]

SR *So this was in 1970. When did you start to collect Conceptual art?*

HENRIËTTE VE In the late 1960s. I don't remember exactly when.

HERMAN VE The exhibition of Conceptual art that Rudi Fuchs did [*Conceptual Art in the Netherlands and Belgium 1965–1975*, 2002] took 1965 as the starting point. The opening was fantastic. All the collectors, and also Catherine Moseley from the Norwich Gallery, were there. Afterwards there was a big meal. There were 200 or 300 people. Rudi Fuchs gave a speech and talked about our collection, and other people talked, like Edy de Wilde. At the end, Rudi Fuchs said 'Applause!' All the people stood up [*gets up and claps his hands*]. We were like pop stars! Afterwards, several collectors and dealers came up to us: 'Here are our cards, please contact us.' Anton Herbert gave me his card and said: 'Here, here, take my card. I'm open for you 24 hours a day.' He did visit us, as well as the other Belgian collector Herman Daled. His collection is fantastic. While we started with Jan Dibbets and other people, he started with Marcel Broodthaers. He told us that he was in his gallery and that a strange man was always walking up and down and looking in. One day he jumped outside, asked the man who he was and invited him in. It was Broodthaers.

SR *So Jan Dibbets was your first contact with this group of people?*

HERMAN VE Yes. But we started to collect with Karel Appel. We were too late for Cobra, though. By the time we started, everything was very expensive.

HENRIËTTE VE But we bought some famous Cobra painters.

SR *Looking at the catalogue of the 2002 exhibition, I noticed that you have mostly early works by all those artists, from the late 1960s and early 1970s.*

HERMAN VE Yes. And also, as a collector, you have to buy things that you can put in your house. Carl Andre, Donald Judd, Beuys: their works are so big. We have small things from Andre, from Judd ...

SR *You had everything in your living room?*

HENRIËTTE VE Yes, everything.

SR *So it was completely full.*

HENRIËTTE VE Yes. But we didn't have them all on the wall. We put them in a little room and then we changed them around. Otherwise it was too much.

HERMAN VE I have another story. In 1968 Enno Develing organised the *Minimal Art* show in The Hague with Sol LeWitt, Carl Andre, etc. Develing said: 'After the opening, there's a nice feast with all the artists. You can come if you like.' He made this typical Dutch soup with herbs in a big pot, *Herbesoup*. So there was this big feast, everyone was eating the herb soup and then after one o'clock, I started to feel a bit fuzzy. I said: 'Henriette, I think it's time to go.' I was looking for my car, but I couldn't find it. Henriette asked: 'Where did you put it?' and I said 'I don't know.' Finally we took a taxi to look for the car and found it. But I said that I couldn't find the way out of The Hague to go back to Amsterdam. I asked the taxi driver to go ahead and I followed him back to Amsterdam. Jan Dibbets couldn't find his car either, so he stayed in a hotel in The Hague. Other people said the same thing. What happened was that Sol LeWitt and all the Americans, thinking that the Dutch eat *herb* soup, put hashish in the soup! So we couldn't concentrate. We were all crazy from the soup!

SR *This is something that I hear very often: that it was a small group of people who became friends and met frequently. Did you also travel to openings in Germany and Belgium?*

HERMAN VE Yes.

SR *Did you go to America at the time?*

HERMAN VE No. We got our Robert Ryman through America, but that's it. We owned the first Ryman [*Orrin*, 1967] in Europe. It was hanging there [*points to a wall in the living room*].

SR *How did you get to know Robert Ryman?*

HERMAN VE Through Jan Dibbets. He said: 'Write to him, write to him. I know him. I visited him in New York.' I told Konrad Fischer that I wanted a Robert Ryman. He said: 'I'll go to New York next week and I'll come back with a Robert Ryman.' I always wanted to buy one, but Henriette was more careful.

HENRIËTTE VE I always wanted to sleep one night before buying.

HERMAN VE Then Konrad phoned and said: 'I have

a nice Robert Ryman. Come to Düsseldorf.' So we went to the gallery for the opening of Lawrence Weiner [April 1969]. He said: 'You came from Amsterdam for me?' He was very happy. We said: 'Yes for you!' Afterwards we went to Konrad's house, where we saw the Robert Ryman. There was a letter from Ileana Sonnabend saying: 'Konrad, I know that you visited Robert Ryman, what you have and what you paid for it. I'll pay double!' It was a difficult piece. You had to put nails on the wall, draw lines around them; that was the framing. It was typical that for every piece of Conceptual art, you had a working paper, about how to mount it, its support. For the Ryman, we had nothing. So I phoned Ryman and said: 'We have a piece from you, but no working paper.' Ryman said: 'You're contacting me for a working paper? I'll make a nice letter for you, explaining how to make the piece, how to put it on the wall.'

SR *So it was a sort of certificate as well as an explanation?*

HERMAN VE Yes, a kind of certificate.

SR *Was Konrad Fischer particularly influential for your collection?*

HERMAN VE Yes, very much. Professionally, I was an actor, so I travelled to several places in Europe. I'd always go back home via Düsseldorf. I'd go to the gallery and Konrad would say: 'I have another piece for you.' I'd reply: 'But Konrad, I have no money.' He'd respond: 'Am I talking about money? You need this piece. You have to have it.' One day, I went there and told Konrad: 'I have to put this work down, I can't pay.' It was two drawings by Bruce Nauman. Konrad said: 'For you, 500 Marks each.' 1,000 Marks for two Bruce Naumans. I asked him how he got the drawings. He said: 'There was en exhibition of Bruce Nauman in the gallery [March–April 1971]. I told the artist: "Bruce, I love your work, but I don't understand what you make. I have to sell something to the public, but this I can't sell. Here's a piece of paper, here's a pencil. Explain to me, what's in the exhibition.' So Nauman was drawing and explaining to Konrad. He asked: 'Do you understand?' Konrad said: 'No.' So Nauman took another paper and did it again. At the end, Konrad said: 'You have to sign it.' Nauman looked at him and understood that he wanted to sell the drawings.

SR *So did Fischer sell the drawings to you?*

HERMAN VE Yes, this is what Konrad would do. He'd say: 'Now you have a Robert Ryman, you have a Nauman ...' Then I'd ask him: 'Who else do I need in my collection?' He'd reply: 'Richard Long.' He explained and we finally bought the work before actually seeing it. A week later, Adriaan van Ravesteijn said: 'Martin Visser phoned. He wants the same piece as you.' We said: 'But we're number one!' Jan Dibbets was a good friend of Konrad. Dibbets had difficulties with Art & Project, and he said: 'I'm going to Konrad Fischer.' But Dibbets sold most things through Art & Project. He saw them every day; they'd eat together.

SR *Was Art & Project the most influential dealer gallery in the Netherlands during the 1970s?*

HERMAN VE Yes. Stanley Brouwn started there, and Dibbets too. All these people were with Art & Project.

HENRIËTTE VE Geert van Beijeren died not so long ago – just a few months ago.

HERMAN VE Art & Project gave a lot of works in their collection to the provincial museum Twenthe [Rijksmuseum Twenthe, Enschede].

SR *Were Art & Project and Konrad Fischer part of the same network?*

HERMAN VE They were in competition, but in contact with the same artists. Artists were going from Konrad Fischer to Art & Project, from Art & Project to Konrad Fischer. There was also Anny De Decker. We bought several things from Anny De Decker.

SR *Antwerp wasn't so far away.*

HERMAN VE No.

SR *What about MTL in Brussels, with Fernand Spillemaeckers?*

HERMAN VE No, we didn't buy from him. In Belgium, it was Anny de Decker. And we didn't buy from any galleries in England. That was the circuit: there was Art & Project, Konrad Fischer – maybe he was a bit more important than the others – and Anny De Decker. That was also the circuit of the artists.

SR *American artists, especially, seemed to be involved with a circuit of dealer galleries whom they'd show with when they came over.*

HERMAN VE American artists are very interested in our collection, because it contains mostly American artists. Carl Andre started here in Amsterdam. We bought the first work from Lawrence Weiner.

HENRIËTTE VE I remember we were sitting in Jan Dibbets' house and Lawrence Weiner was there ...

HERMAN VE He told us he'd make one of his statements for us and we thanked him. We asked Dibbets: 'He's an artist, he has to live. What do we have to pay for it?' He said: 'Nothing, but he'd be very happy with a ticket back to New York. If you pay for his ticket, he'd be extremely happy.' We told Weiner that we knew that he had to go back to New York and that we'd pay for his ticket. He was extremely surprised and happy. We were one of the first to own a statement by Lawrence Weiner. For the *Minimal Art* exhibition in The Hague, the one with the hash in the soup, Carl Andre made *64 Bent Nail Run*. When the exhibition was over, Konrad said: 'There's no interest in the Carl Andre piece. It's now in my gallery.' I said: 'Konrad, this isn't difficult, I'm here.' He said: 'You get it. But you have to pay a little bit.' So I paid a little bit.

SR *You also acquired* Project for Art & Project, *the maps that Jan Dibbets did in 1969. What interested you about this piece?*

HERMAN VE The process. It was beautiful to send those cards all over the world. The maps are from Amsterdam, the Benelux, Europe and the world.

SR *It also reveals this network of people.*

HERMAN VE Yes, the network of people involved with Conceptual art. Also, I like the bit where Dibbets stands on his balcony and puts his thumb up. He sends cards all over the world saying: 'At that time, I'll stand there and do this' [*puts his thumb up*]. What's nice is that it spans the whole world.

SR *It's also interesting to see who sent the postcards back.*

HERMAN VE Yes.

SR *In 1972 your collection was shown in Utrecht with that of Mia and Martin Visser in an exhibition entitled* Conceptual Art From Two Private Collections. *Was that the first time that your collection was shown publicly?*

HENRIËTTE VE I think so. Evert van Straaten was selling art in Utrecht at the time. He saw the postcards from On Kawara for the first time there.

HERMAN VE It wasn't in a museum, but in a school, in an Academy. Franz Hachs was the Director there. He visited us here to talk about Conceptual art.

SR *At the time, did you know Mia and Martin Visser well?*

HERMAN VE Yes, we were working on the same things.

SR *Apart from yourselves and the Vissers, were there others collecting Conceptual art in the Netherlands?*

BOTH No. There was Martin Visser and us. We and Art & Project were here, and he was in the provinces. Martin Visser had a lot of money. He was a friend of Sol LeWitt and owned big works by him; also, big pieces by Judd. Martin Visser is a designer and a big collector.

SR *What did you like initially about the works of all the artists you collected: Andre, LeWitt, Nauman?*

HENRIËTTE VE You have to think about it and to invest yourself in it. There's a story behind everything.

HERMAN VE That's what Jan Dibbets always said: 'You can be in contact with all these people, but look for a piece [*knocks on the table*], a thing, not something too abstract. Look for a real piece, look for material.' Jan Dibbets was the motor; he knew all these artists. We contacted the artists and so we got together. Richard Long made his wood piece in the lounge [*Wooden sticks*, 1968]. We have a photograph of him doing it. We took him to a park nearby and he took branches from there.

SR *Your collection is now held at the Kröller-Müller Museum. What about your archive?*

HENRIËTTE VE We'll give the documentation that belongs to the works to the museum if they buy the collection; maybe also the correspondence. But they haven't asked for it yet.

HERMAN VE We sold part of it to the American art and book dealer Steven Leiber. He was a gallerist, and now he buys the archives of artists, collectors, etc. He makes books of them for universities and libraries in San Francisco. He didn't pay so much for the archive, but there were big packs of material. For every artist we collected, we have a letter or something, a personal contact.

SR *Was it also important to know the artists whose work you were buying?*

BOTH Yes.

4.17 Herman Daled interviewed by Catherine Moseley

Brussels, April 2000

Reproduced from *Conception: The Conceptual art Document 1968 to 1972*, Norwich Gallery, Norwich School of Art and Design, 2001.[1]

CATHERINE MOSELEY *Could you tell me how you became involved in collecting Conceptual art?*

HERMAN DALED I was always involved in visual art through a family tradition. In my family, my parents, my grandparents, there were no books, there was no music, but there were paintings everywhere. So that's a long personal and family history. I went to study medicine but still had an interest in the visual arts. At that time (the 1960s) I was in my thirties and my main question was 'what is art?' and 'what isn't art?'. What's the difference between a Sunday painter or '*un peintre du Dimanche*' and what is recognised as high art, and things like that. At that time, Post-Minimal and Conceptual art arrived and I supposed I would find the response to my question with Conceptual art.

CM *Where were you living at that time?*

HD In Brussels. When I was starting to buy some art and I had the chance to buy very early in 1967 a work by Marcel Broodthaers. And so we started to become friends. I was one of his very first buyers. At that time the Conceptual artists came from America to Europe where there was much more interest than in America. They showed with galleries like Art & Project in Amsterdam, Konrad Fischer in Düsseldorf, Yvon Lambert in Paris, Nigel Greenwood in London and at Wide White Space run by Anny De Decker and Bernd Lohaus in Antwerp.

But there was nothing like those galleries in Brussels (MTL started later). So visiting artists all stopped by Marcel Broodthaers'. At that time, my house was also really an open house. Nearly each night for three or four years, there were artists at the house for dinner, nearly always brought round by Marcel. And so I have had the opportunity to know most of the artists personally.

CM *How did you meet Marcel?*

HD I bought this first piece of Marcel Broodthaers from the Galerie Cogeime that does not exist anymore, without knowing who he was. It has completely disappeared now. It was a gallery here in my neighbourhood in Brussels. Coming back from my office and going on my way home, I just stopped by, saw a work of art and I bought the work – as I usually do, very fast! I was the only visitor, the only buyer, and for the dinner after the show there was Marcel, the owner of the gallery, Mr Lechien and myself. So I met Marcel after I bought the piece. Later on I met many other artists like Bob Ryman, Daniel Buren, Niele Toroni, Douglas Huebler, On Kawara, Lawrence Weiner, David Lamelas, Carl Andre, Robert Barry, Mel Bochner, James Lee Byars, André Cadere, Jan Dibbets, Dan Graham, Hans Haacke, Sol LeWitt and many others.

CM *Was it quite usual for people to travel long distances, say to an opening in Amsterdam, Antwerp or Paris or Düsseldorf?*

HD Yes, at that time it was meaningful to do it because there would be just one or two exhibitions a year per artist. So you could follow the activity of Marcel or someone else and go to their openings. Also, at that time there were no magazines at all for this art. So information was quite hard to get; you must always have had personal contacts, that was something very important. But you should note there were newsletters from a German, from Cologne, Willi Bongard. You had to make a subscription and he sent to the people who had their subscription a newsletter of all that was going on in the art world. They are interesting documents if you are making some historical research.

CM *The document also existed as the art work; it could also be the medium supporting the art and the information as well, making it communicable over a wider geographic area. For example, Art & Project bulletins and magazines such as* Studio International. *That magazine is interesting, particularly in this period from 1968 to 1972, for the diversity of art forms that it represented. Instead of just now and again there was an enormous amount of Conceptual art in the magazine. Was* Studio *accessible in continental Europe?*

HD Yes we had *Studio International*, also *Flash Art* and *Parachute*. And the bulletins of Art & Project. That was not much information but it was a very interesting document.

CM *And the Prospect shows.*

HD Prospect was very important ... fantastic. It was at Prospect that I met Daniel Buren for the first time and Niele Toroni too. I found out about the Düsseldorf art scene through Prospect, and Robert Filliou. Marcel Broodthaers moved from Brussels to Düsseldorf and then went from Düsseldorf to London. Then from

London to Berlin, I think, still maintaining a house in London. He died in Cologne. So I used to drive at night, back and forth, to Paris, Amsterdam or Düsseldorf. It was a good period of my lifetime.

CM *Did you visit Konrad Fischer's gallery many times?*

HD Yes.

CM *There was something I read about Anny De Decker, and she said that people would share six to a car, to drive to openings in Düsseldorf or Amsterdam. What about London, obviously it was less easy to get to?*

HD Yes, I went very few times to London, visiting Nigel Greenwood and Jack Wendler. I bought pieces from Jack Wendler of Lawrence Weiner and Marcel Broodthaers, around 1970–71. I went to Marcel Broodthaers' exhibition at the ICA in London. But London was more difficult to get to, you had to take a boat or a plane and it was more expensive, so that was really a problem to go to London.

CM *The activities of the London galleries seem to be taking off just a couple of years after those in Europe. You talked about Conceptual art in particular giving you the response or answer to your question when you saw it. Do you think this relates to there being certain factors in society more generally, that prompted artists to move towards using documentation? For example, ideas about the dematerialisation of the object, or rejecting the idea of art as a commodity, or a greater emphasis on the process of art making?*

HD I think that the art movements are always following very closely political and literary movements. So at that time, in the art of the late 1960s and 1970s, there was this kind of hostile attitude towards all the belonging of the consumer's society, and I think that has had an influence. That was very well illustrated in the exhibition at the Whitney at the end of 1999, where they showed the *American Art of the Twentieth Century*. This very clearly demonstrated how the art movements followed the Vietnam War, and how they were influenced, by all those political and economic facts. I think it was also a reaction to abstract expressionism. It was a reaction to all those huge paintings and pop art, but I am not an art historian!

CM *Artists were obviously interested in coming over from America to Europe, and there was a lot of political activity in Europe in the late 1960s, simultaneous to America. However, the European artists did not go over to America so much as the Americans came here. Why do you think that was?*

HD That's only because Europe was much more welcoming. They found the people here interested in what they were doing and they were rejected in the States. There was no audience for them, but they knew there was an audience here in Europe. Perhaps the mind of the European collector is different, not only collectors but the general public who were interested and wanted to see the works.

CM *And were there a lot of people that wanted to see the work? I know that there was an incredibly strong network of individual artists and collectors and curators, but in terms of a big public audience... How did artists and dealers survive financially? Do you think that economic factors influenced the form of the artwork in any way, such as a set of typed instructions and no object?*

HD It was not cheap at all to buy. It was absolutely normally priced. It's very interesting, this work by Huebler (*Variable Piece #70*, 1971). I had to go and seek in my files, when I bought it, where I bought it, and now I know exactly: in 1971 I bought it for 70,000 Belgian Francs, and that means now around 250,000 BEF or £4,000, so that's not inexpensive. Stanley Brouwn was selling for 100,000 BEF, so around 400,000 BEF or £6,000.

1 Editor's note: Sophie Richard makes a number of references in the text to the interview with Herman Daled by Catherine Butcher (née Moseley) first published in *Conception: The Conceptual Document 1968 to 1972, op. cit.* Reproduced with the permission of Herman Daled and Catherine Butcher (née Moseley).

References

Primary sources

a) Institutional archives

Archive Städtisches Museum, Mönchengladbach (ASMM)
Archive Kunsthalle Düsseldorf, Stadtarchiv, Düsseldorf (AKDSD)
Archive Städtische Kunsthalle Düsseldorf, Düsseldorf (ASKDD)
Documentation Department, Museum Ludwig, Cologne
Archive Kunstverein Münster, Westfälisches Archivamt, Münster (AKMWAM)
Zentralarchiv des Internationalen Kunsthandel, Cologne (Zadik)
Stadtarchiv, Leverkusen
Archive Stedelijk Museum, Amsterdam (ASMA)
Archives de l'Art Contemporain en Belgique, Brussels (AACBB)
Tate Library and Archive, London (TLAL)
Getty Research Institute, Los Angeles (GRILA)
Archives of American Art, Smithsonian Institute, Washington

b) Personal archives

Archive Konrad Fischer Galerie, Düsseldorf (AKFGD)
Harald Szeemann Archive, Maggia (HSAM)
Jacques Charlier Archive, Liège
Herman and Henriëtte van Eelen Archive, Amsterdam
Lisson Gallery Archive, London
Lynda Morris Archive, Norwich (LMAN)
Françoise Lambert Archive, Milan

c) Interviews

1 Artists: Art & Language (Banbury, 19 May 2003, notes), John Baldessari (Graz, 10 June 2006, notes), Jacques Charlier (Liège, 18 May 2004, notes; Luxembourg, 5 October 2005, audio tape recording), Peter Downsbrough and Kaatje Cusse (Brussels, 29 October 2004, notes), David Tremlett (Bovingdon, Herts, 23 February 2005, audio tape recording), Jan Dibbets (Amsterdam, 28 April 2005, audio tape recording), Daniel Buren (Luxembourg, 28 May 2005, notes) and Lawrence Weiner (Graz, 10 June 2006, notes).

2 Dealers: Paul Maenz (Berlin, 6 October 2004, faxed questionnaire), Françoise Lambert (Paris, 21 October 2004, notes), Lili Dujourie (Lovendegem, 27 October 2004, notes), Anny De Decker (Antwerp, 16 November 2004, audio tape recording), Nicolas Logsdail (London, 25 February 2005, audio tape recording), Dorothee Fischer (Düsseldorf, April 2005, notes) and Rolf Preisig (Zurich, 27 October 2005, digital recording).

3 Curators/Museum Directors: Harald Szeemann (Maggia, 22 July 2003, audio tape recording), Jean-Christophe Ammann (Frankfurt/Main, 4 October 2004, manuscript questionnaire), Yves Gevaert (Brussels, 28 October 2004, notes), Sir Nicholas Serota (London, 24 January 2005, audio tape recording), Barry Barker (London, 22 February 2005, audio tape recording), Klaus Honnef (Bonn, 21 March 2005, audio tape recording), Johannes Cladders (Krefeld, 13 April 2005, audio tape recording), Rudi Fuchs (Amsterdam, 25 April 2005, audio tape recording) and Seth Siegelaub (Amsterdam, 27 April 2005, audio tape recording).

4 Private collectors: Sylvain Perlstein (Paris, 20 October 2004, audio tape recording), Annick and Anton Herbert (Gent, 19 April 2003, notes; Gent, 15 November 2004, audio tape recording) and Henriëtte and Herman van Eelen (Amsterdam, 27 April 2005, audio tape recording).

5 Critics: Charles Harrison (Banbury, 19 May 2003, audio tape recording) and Marlis Grüterich (Cologne, 3 March 2005, audio tape recording).

Secondary sources

ALBERRO, Alexander, 'The Turn of the Screw: Daniel Buren, Dan Flavin, and the Sixth Guggenheim International Exhibition', *October*, no.80, Spring 1997, pp.57–84.

ALBERRO, Alexander and Stimson, Blake (eds), *Conceptual Art: A Critical Anthology*, Cambridge, Mass.: The MIT Press, 1999.

ALBERRO, Alexander and NORVELL, Patricia, *Recording Conceptual Art, Early Interviews with Barry, Huebler, Kaltenbach, LeWitt, Morris, Oppenheim, Siegelaub, Smithson, Weiner*, Berkeley, Los Angeles and London: University of California Press, 2001.

ALBERRO, Alexander, *Conceptual Art and the Politics of Publicity*, The MIT Press, Cambridge, Mass. and London, 2003.

——— 'One year under the mast: Alexander Alberro on the Fox – history of periodical devoted to art-related practice', *Artforum*, June 2003.

ALLEY, Ronald, *Catalogue of The Tate Gallery's Collection of Modern Art, other than works by British artists*, London: Tate Gallery and Sotheby Parke Bernet, 1981.

AMMANN, Jean-Christophe, 'Schweizer Brief', *Art International*, vol.3, no.5, 20 May 1969, pp.47–50.

ANCONA, Victor, 'Video art: Castelli-Sonnabend, a gallery geared to new art forms', *Videography*, 2 January 1977, pp.41–43.

André Cadere, Histoire d'un travail, Gent: Herbert-Gewad, 1982.

'Anka Ptaszkowska', *Ohm: Un petit journal de l'art contemporain*, Caen: L'école régionale des beaux-arts Caen la mer, no.22, February 2004.

'Art Aktuell', *Avalanche*, no. 8, November 1973, p.62.

Art of the Fifties, Sixties and Seventies, The Panza Collection, Milan: Antique Collector's Club, Jaca Book, 1999.

Art & Language, Documenta Memorandum (Indexing)/Alternate Map for Documenta (Based on Citation A) (exh. cat.), Cologne: The Art & Language Institute/Paul Maenz, 1972.

'Art & Project', *Flash Art*, no. 54–55, May 1975, p.2.

Articides Follies, J. Charlier, 1969–75, Brussels: Daled & Gevaert, 1975.

ASKEVOLD, David, 'The Projects Class', in *Conceptual Art: The NSCAD Connection, 1967–1973* (exh. cat.), Halifax: Nova Scotia College of Art and Design, 1994, pp.38–39.

AUPETITALLOT, Yves, *Wide White Space, Hinter dem Museum, 1966–1976, Behind the museum* (exh. cat.) Brussels and Düsseldorf: Palais des Beaux-Arts and Richter Verlag, 1994.

Ausstellungen bei Konrad Fischer, Düsseldorf Oktober 1967–Oktober 1992 (exh. cat.), Bielefeld: Edition Marzona, 1993.

BAKER SANDBACK, Amy, 'Virginia Dwan, l'aventure d'un marchand d'art', *Art Press*, special issue fiac 90, no.151, October 1990, p.40–46.

BALDWIN, Michael, HARRISON, Charles and RAMSDEN, Mel, *Art & Language in practice, Illustrated Handbook* (exh. cat.), Barcelona: Fundacio Antoni Tapies, 1999.

BATTCOCK, Gregory (ed.), *Idea Art: a Critical Anthology*, New York: Dutton, 1973.

BAUDSON, Michael and GEVAERT, Yves, 'Aspects of the Avant-Garde in Belgium', *Studio International*, vol.188, no.970, October 1974, pp.142–143.

BEEREN, Wim, '"Op Losse Schroeven" Pro Memoria, An exhibition at the Stedelijk Museum, 15.3–27.4.1969', in *'60–'80, Attitudes/Concepts/Images, A Selection from twenty years of visual arts* (exh. cat.), Amsterdam: Stedelijk Museum, 1982, pp.51–55.

BEHRMAN, Samuel N., *Duveen*, London: Hamish Hamilton, 1952.

Bestandsverzeichnis der Zeichnungen, Graphische Sammlung Museum Ludwig, Cologne: Museum Ludwig, 1986.

'Big Cologne Exhibition Seeks to Focus German Art Market', *The New York Times*, 19 September 1967.

BIK, Liesbeth and VAN DER POL, Jos, *'Proposition for Reclaiming a Space'*, Norwich: Norwich Gallery, Dispatch no.36, 1997.

Bilder–Objekte–Filme–Konzepte: Sammlung Herbig (exh. cat.), Munich: Städtische Galerie im Lehnbachhaus, 1973.

Birnbaum, Daniel, 'Art and the Deal, Daniel Birnbaum on Konrad Fischer/Lueg', *Artforum*, February 2000, pp.17–21.

BLOEM, Marija (ed.), *Lawrence Weiner, Works from the beginning of the sixties towards the end of the eighties*, Amsterdam: Stedelijk Museum, 1988.

Blinde wehrte Euch! Arbeiten aus der Sammlung Speck (exh. cat.), Düsseldorf: K21 Kunstsammlung Nordrhein-Westfalen, 2004.

BLOCK, Carel, 'Letter from Holland', *Art International*, vol.3, no.5, May 1969, pp.51–53.

BLOK, Cor, 'Holland, a change of atmosphere at the Van Abbemuseum', *Studio International*, January–February 1977, vol.193, no.985, pp.30–31.

BLOTKAMP, Carel, 'Sculpture at Soonsbeek', *Studio International*, vol.183, no.936, September 1971, pp.70–73.

BOETTGER, Suzaan, 'The lost contingent: Paul Maenz's prophetic 1967 event and the ambiguities of historical priority', *Art Journal*, vol.62, no.3, Spring 2003, pp.34–47.

——— 'Behind the earth movers: the adventurous support of dealer Virginia Dwan allowed earthwork artists Michael Heizer, Walter De Maria, Robert Smithson and others to realize their pioneering projects–Patronage–Biography', *Art in America*, April 2004.

BONGARD, Willi, 'Capital Kunst Kompass', *Das Capital*, vol.9, no.11, October 1970, pp.148–156.

——— 'Willy Bongard Sammlerporträt: Dr. Wolfgang Hock', *Kunstforum International*, September 1973, vol. 4, no.5, pp.49–51.

Books, Prints, Objects published by Yves Gevaert (exh. cat.), Eindhoven: Van Abbemuseum, 1992.

BRANDT CORSTIUS, Liesbeth, 'Holland', *Studio International*, vol.187, no.964, March 1974, pp.4–5.

BRAUNSTEIN, Peter and DOYLE, Michael William (eds), *Imagine Nation: The American Counterculture of the 1960s and 70s*, New York and London: Routledge, 2002.

BROOKS, Rosetta, 'Prospect', *Studio International*, vol.186, no.959, November 1973, p.194.

—— 'Projekt '74', *Flash Art*, no.48–49, October–November 1974, p.15.
BROOKS, Xan, 'Emails reveal Ofili's cash deal from Tate', *The Guardian*, 24 October 2005.
BROWN, Milton W., *The Modern Spirit, American Painting 1908–1935*, London: Arts Council of Great Britain, 1977.
BUCHLOH, Benjamin H.D., 'Avant-Propos zu Re(tro)spect', in Jürgen Harten (ed.), *Prospect/Retrospect, Europa 1946–1976* (exh. cat.), Düsseldorf: Kunsthalle, 1976, pp.6–8.
—— 'De l'esthétique d'administration à la critique institutionnelle (Aspects de l'art conceptuel, 1962–1969)', in Claude Gintz (ed.), *L'art conceptuel: une perspective* (exh. cat.), Paris: Musée d'Art moderne de la Ville de Paris, 1989, pp.25–59.
BUCK, Louisa, 'Diary of a London dealer: Nicholas Logsdail', *The Art Newspaper*, no.131, December 2002, p.41.
BUREN, Daniel, *Limites Critiques*, Paris: Yvon Lambert, 1970.
—— 'The function of an exhibition', *Studio International*, vol.186, no.961, December 1973, p.216.
—— 'Notes on Work in connection with the Place where it is installed', *Studio International*, vol.190, no.977, September 1975, pp.124–129.
BURNHAM, Jack, 'Alice's Head: Reflections on Conceptual Art', *Artforum*, February 1970, pp.37–43.
BUTIN, Hubertus 'When Attitudes Become Form – Philip Morris Becomes Sponsor: Arts sponsorship in Europe against the background of developments in America', 2000, from www.societyofcontrol.com/research/butin_engl.htm.
Carl Andre (exh. cat.), Mönchengladbach: Städtisches Museum, 1968.
Carl Andre (exh. cat.), New York: Solomon Guggenheim Museum, 1970.
Carl Andre, Marcel Broodthaers, Daniel Buren, Victor Burgin, Gilbert & George, On Kawara, Richard Long and Gerhard Richter (exh. cat.), Brussels: Palais des Beaux-Arts, 1974.
Carl Andre, Sculpture 1958–1974 (exh. cat.), Bern: Kunsthalle, 1975.
'Carl Andre', *Audio Arts*, vol. 2, no.2, 1975.
Carl Andre (exh. cat.), Den Haag: Gemeentemuseum and Eindhoven: Stedelijk Van Abbemuseum, 1987.
Carl Andre, Sculptor 1996, Krefeld at Home, Wolfsburg at Large (exh. cat.), Stuttgart: Oktagon Verlag, 1996.
CELANT, Germano, *Arte Povera* (exh. cat.), Bologna: De' Foscherari, 1968.
—— *Arte Povera, Conceptual, Actual or Impossible Art?*, Milan: Mazzotta; London: Studio Vista; New York: Praeger and Tübingen: Studio Wasmuth, 1969.
—— *Conceptual art, arte povera, land art* (exh. cat.), Turin: Galleria Civica d'Arte Moderna, 1970.
—— 'Book as Artwork 1960–1970', *Data*, vol.1, no.1, September 1971.
—— *The Book as Art Work 1960–1972* (ex. cat.), London: Nigel Greenwood Inc. Ltd, 1972.
—— *Pre-cronistoria, 1966-69: Minimal Art, Pittura Sistemica, Arte Povera, Land Art, Conceptual Art, Body Art, Arte Ambientale e Nuovi Media*, Florence: Centro DI, 1976.
CHERIX, Christophe, 'Un entretien avec les éditeurs du Art & Project Bulletin (Février-Mars 2003)', in Press Release, 'Art & Project Bulletin, Amsterdam, 1968–1989', Geneva: Cabinet des Estampes, Musée d'art moderne et contemporain, 2003.
CHRISTOV-BAKARGIEV, Carolyn, *Arte Povera*, London: Phaidon, 1999.
CLARK, William, 'Katherine Dreier and the Société Anonyme', *Variant*, vol.2, no.14, Winter 2001, pp.4–7.
CLAURA, Michel and DENIZOT, René, '18 Paris IV.70', *Studio International*, vol.179, no.921, April 1970, p.179.
—— *Eine Malerei-Ausstellung mit Malern, die die Malerei in Frage stellen könnten* (exh. cat.), Mönchengladbach: Städtisches Museum, 1973.
CLAY, Jean, 'Art Tamed and Wild', *Studio International*, vol.177, no.912, June 1969, pp.262–265.
COCKCROFT, Eva, 'Abstract Expressionism, Weapon of the Cold War', *Artforum*, June 1974, pp.39–41.
Collectie Becht: Beeldende Kunst Uit De Verzameling Van Agnes En Frits Becht/The Becht Collection: Visual Art from the Agnes and Frits Becht Collection (exh. cat.), Utrecht: Uitgeverij Reflex and Amsterdam: Stedelijk Museum, 1984.
Collection Vicky Rémy (exh. cat.), Saint-Étienne: Musée d'Art Moderne, 2005.
The Collection Visser at the Kröller-Müller Museum, Otterlo: Stichting Kröller-Müller Museum, 2000.
The Collection Visser at the Kröller-Müller Museum, Supplement, Otterlo: Stichting Kröller-Müller Museum, 2001.
COLONNA-CÉSARI, Annick, 'Art Press 30 ans après', *L'Express*, 15 December 2002.
'Concept Art', *Kunst*, vol.10, no.38, 1970.
Concept Art (exh. cat.), Braunschweig: Kunstverein, 1974.
'Conceptual art', *Flash Art*, February–May 1974, p.62.
Conceptual Art from two private collections (exh. cat.), Utrecht: Utrechtse Kring, Neudeflat, 1972.
CONSTABLE, W.G., *Art Collecting in the United States of America, An Outline of a History*, London: Thomas Nelson and Sons Ltd., 1964.
Contemporanea (exh. cat.), Rome: Incontri Internationali d'Arte, Centro Di, 1973.
'Contemporary drawings', *Flash Art*, December 1975–February 1976, no.60–61, p.11.
The Contents of the Nigel Greenwood Gallery, Sold by Order of the Creditors, London: Sotheby's, 15 October 1992.
'Controversy on Bruxelles: Letters and Answers', *Flash Art*, no.43, December 1973–January 1974, p.6.
'Correspondence', *Studio International*, vol.177, no.912, June 1969, p.256.
'Correspondence', *Studio International*, vol.81, no.935, July–August 1971, p.6.
CORRIS, Michael (ed.), *Conceptual Art: Theory, Myth and Practice*, Cambridge: Cambridge University Press, 2004.
Daniel Buren, Mot à Mot (exh. cat.), Paris: Editions du Centre Georges Pompidou, Editions Xavier Barral, Editions de la Martinière, 2002.
'Das Projekt Kammgarn ist eine einmalige Chance für die Region', *Wochen-Express*, 3 February 1993, pp.6–9.
De concert, Oeuvres d'une collection privée (exh. cat.), Carquefou:

Frac des Pays de la Loire, 2002.
DE SALVO, Donna (ed.), *Open Systems: Rethinking Art c.1970*, London: Tate Publishing, 2005.
De Verzameling Tony Herbert (exh. cat.), Eindhoven: Stedelijk Van Abbemuseum, 1999.
DE VRIES, Gerd (ed.), *Über Kunst, Künstlertexte zum veränderten Kunstverständnis nach 1965/On Art, Artists's writings on the changed notion of art after 1965*, Cologne: Verlag DuMont Schauberg, 1974.
——— *Paul Maenz Köln 1970–1980–1990, Eine Avant-garde Galerie und die Kunst unserer Zeit, An Avant-garde Gallery and the Art of our Time*, Cologne: Dumont Buchverlag, 1991.
DEBBAUT, Jan and VERHULST, Monique (eds), *A Companion to Modern and Contemporary Art, Van Abbemuseum*, Eindhoven: Van Abbemuseum and Nai Publishers, 2003.
DELUS, Dieter, 'Kartell am Kunstmarkt', *Saarbrücker Zeitung*, 14 March 1967.
Deurle 11/7/73 (exh. cat.), Brussels: Galerie MTL, 1973.
'Deurle', *Flash Art*, no.44–45, February–May 1974, p.32.
Diagrams & Drawings, Carl Andre, Christo, De Maria, Mark di Suvero, Dan Flavin, Michael Heizer, Don Judd, Sol LeWitt, Robert Morris, Bruce Nauman, Claes Oldenburg, Richard Serra,Robert Smithson (exh. cat.), Basel: Kunstmuseum, 1973.
DIBBETS, Jan, 'Project for Art & Project', *Studio International*, vol.180, no.924, July–August 1970, pp.41–44.
Die Internationale Kunstmesse, Art 6 '75 (exh. cat.), Basel, 1975.
'documenta – documentation', *Interfunktionen*, no.1, 1968.
Documenta 5, Befragung der Realität, Bildwelten von Heute (exh. cat.), Kassel: Bertelsman Verlag, 1972.
DOEHLER, EMESE et al., *Neues Museum Weimar, Die Sammlung von Paul Maenz*, Cologne: Hatje Kantz Verlag, 2001.
Dokumente zur aktuellen Kunst 1967–1970, Material aus dem Archiv Szeemann, Texte von Georg Jappe, Aurel Schmidt und Harald Szeemann, Lucerne: Kunstkreis AG, 1972.
Douglas Huebler: November 1968, New York: Seth Siegelaub, 1968.
Douglas Huebler (exh. cat.), Münster: Westfälischer Kunstverein, 1972.
DREHER, Thomas, *Konzeptuelle Kunst in Amerika und England zwischen 1963 und 1976*, Europäische Hochschulschriften, Reihe XXVIII, Kunstgeschichte BD. 138, Frankfurt am Main: Peter Lang, 1992.
'Drei Stunden-Debatte', *Düsseldorfer Nachrichten*, 23 October 1969.
18 Paris IV.70 (exh. cat.), Paris: Michel Claura and Seth Siegelaub, 1970.
ELGER, Dietmar, *Gerhard Richter, Maler*, Cologne: Dumont, 2002.
Emanuel Hoffmann-Stiftung Basel, Basel: Wiese Verlag, 1991.
'Entretien avec Yvon Lambert', from *paris-art.com*, accessed on 28 January 2005.
ERHARD, Ernst-Otto, *Pop, Kitsch, Concept-Art, Aufsäte zur Gegenwärtigen Situation der Kunst*, Otto Maier-Verlag, Ravensburg, 1974.
'Europa-America', *Art Dimension*, no.2, April–June 1975, pp.3–28.
Everbody knows, Sammlung Dr. Hubert and Marie-Thérèse Peeters, Brügge (exh. cat.), Münster: Landesmuseum, 1972.
'Exklusiv – Interview mit dem Direktor des Kunstmuseums Basel, Dr. Franz Meyer', *Art Aktuell*, June 1973, unnumbered pages.
FELDMAN, Paula, *Made to Order: American Minimal Art in the Netherlands, Late 1960s to Early 1970s*, unpublished PhD, London: Courtauld Institute of Art, 2005.
FRANC, Helen M., 'The early years of the International Program and Council', in *The Museum of Modern Art in the Mid Century, At Home and Abroad*, New York: MOMA 1994.
'Françoise Lambert & Claire Copley Gallery', *Artforum*, October 1973, p.24.
'Françoise Lambert & Claire Copley Gallery', *Flash Art*, no.42, October–November 1973, p.2.
'Franz Dahlem', *Kunstforum International*, vol.104, November–December 1989, pp.242–246.
FUCHS, Rudi H., 'More on *The New Art*', *Studio International*, vol.184, no.949, November 1972, pp.194–195.
'Ganz am Anfang/How it all began: Richter, Polke, Lueg & Kuttner', *Sediment*, Zadik, Cologne, no.7, 2004.
GARRELS, Gary (ed.), *Sol LeWitt: a retrospective* (exh. cat.), San Francisco: San Francisco Museum of Modern Art, 2002.
GEE, Malcolm, *Dealers, Critics and Collectors of Modern Painting: aspects of the Parisian art market between 1910 and 1930*, New York: Garland Pub., 1981.
GEIRLANDT, Karel J., 'Museums, collectors, policies', *Studio International*, vol.188, no.970, October 1974, pp.114–116.
'Gerhard Richter', *Artforum*, September 1973, p.94.
'Gilbert and George: there were two young men who did laugh', *Studio International*, vol.181, no.933, May 1971, pp.220–221.
GILISSEN, Maria and BUCHLOH, Benjamin H.D. (eds), *Marcel Broodthaers, Section Publicité du Musée d'Art moderne, Département des Aigles* (exh. cat.), New York: Marian Goodman Gallery, 1995.
Global Conceptualism: Points of Origin, 1950s–1980s (exh. cat.), New York: Queens Museum of Art, 1999.
GLUECK, Grace, 'Museum presents wide Media Range', *New York Times*, 10 February 1970, p.26.
GMV, Agent d'Art (exh. cat.), Dunkerque: École régionale des Beaux-Arts Georges Pompidou, 1986.
GOHR, Siegfried (ed.), *Museum Ludwig Köln, Gemälde, Skulpturen, Environments vom Expressionismus bis zur Gegenwart, Bestandskatalog*, Munich: Prestel Verlag, 1986.
GOLDSTEIN, Ann and RORIMER, Anne (eds), *Reconsidering the Object of Art: 1965–1975* (exh. cat.), Los Angeles: The Museum of Contemporary Art and Cambridge, Mass.: The MIT Press, 1995.
GOVAN, Michael and BELL, Tiffany, *Dan Flavin, A Retrospective* (exh. cat.), New Haven: Yale University Press, 2004.
GRASSKAMP, Walter, *Johannes Cladders*, Cologne: Kunststiftung NRW, DuMont, 2004.
GROOS, Ulrike, Hess, Barbara and WEVERS, Ursula (eds), *Ready to Shoot, Fernsehgalerie Gerry Schum, videogalerie schum* (exh. cat.), Düsseldorf: Snoeck and Kunsthalle, 2003.
GRÜTERICH, Marlis, 'Switzerland', *Studio International*, vol.190, no.977, September–October 1975, pp.158–159.
——— 'Mönchengladbach', *Studio International*, vol.193, no.985, January–February 1977, pp.27–29.
GUILBAUT, Serge, *Comment New York vola l'idée d'art moderne?*,

Nîmes: J. Chambon, 1989.
'Gurgles around the Guggenheim, Statements and comments by Daniel Buren, Diane Waldman, Thomas M. Messer, Hans Haacke', *Studio International*, vol.181, no.934, June 1971, pp.246–250.
Hanne Darboven (exh. cat.), Mönchengladbach: Städtisches Museum, 1968.
Hanne Darboven, Ein Monat, Ein Jahr, Ein Jahrhundert, Arbeiten von 1968 bis 1974 (exh. cat.), Basel: Kunstmuseum, 1974.
HARRISON, Charles, 'Düsseldorf commentary, Prospect '68 – an international showcase', *Studio International*, vol.176, no.905, November 1968, p.204.
——— *Idea Structures* (exh. cat.), Survey '70, London: Borough of Camden, 1970.
——— 'Educating Artists', *Studio International*, vol.183, no.944, May 1972, pp.222–224.
——— 'The late sixties in London and elsewhere', in *1965 to 1972 – When Attitudes Became Form* (exh. cat.), Kettle's Yard Gallery, Cambridge, 1984, pp.9–16.
HARTEN, Jürgen, '"Documenta 5" at Kassel', *Studio International*, vol.184, no.946, July–August 1972, pp.2–4.
——— *25 Jahre Kunsthalle Düsseldorf*, Düsseldorf: Städtische Kunsthalle, 1992.
HASTINGS, Chris, 'Chris Ofili said artists should give work to the Tate for nothing ... so why has he accepted £100,000 for one of his dung pictures?', *The Telegraph*, 14 August 2005.
HÉMAN, Suzanna, POOT, Jurrie and VISSER, Hripsimé (eds), *Conceptual art in the Netherlands and Belgium 1965–1975: Artists, collectors, galleries, documents, exhibitions, events* (exh. cat.), Amsterdam: Stedelijk Museum and Rotterdam: NAi Publishers, 2002.
HERCHENRÖDER, Christian, 'Collectors', *Studio International*, vol.183, no.941, February 1972, p.86.
HERZOGENRATH, Wulf and LUEG, Gabriele (eds), *Die 60er Jahre, Kölns Weg zur Kunstmetropole – Vom Hapenning zum Kunstmarkt* (exh. cat.), Cologne: Kölnischer Kunstverein, 1986.
HESS, Barbara, '30 Jahre Ausstellungen bei Konrad Fischer 1967–1997', *Sediment*, Zadik, no.2, 1997, pp.17–34.
HESS, Thomas B., 'The Germans are coming! The Germans are coming!', *New York Magazine*, June 1974, p.54.
HIGGINS, Charlotte, 'How the Tate broke the law in buying this £600,000 Ofili work', *The Guardian*, 19 July 2006, p.11.
HILTON, Tim, 'Peter Townsend: he survived China's revolution to start his own as an arts editor in Bloomsbury', *The Guardian*, 26 July 2006.
HONNEF, Klaus, *Concept Art*, Cologne: Phaidon, 1971.
IKI, Internationaler Markt für aktuelle Kunst 1972, Düsseldorf (exh. cat.), Düsseldorf, 1972.
In Another Moment (exh. cat.), Belgrade: Gallery SKC, 1971, unnumbered pages.
'In drei Tagen über 3000 Besucher', *Rheinische Post*, 14 October 1971.
'In drei Tagen 3000 Besucher bei "Prospect"', *Neue Rhein-Zeitung*, 14 October 1969.
Information (exh. cat.), New York: The Museum of Modern Art, 1970.
InK. Halle für internationale neue Kunst. Information, Zurich: InK, Halle für internationale neue Kunst, 1978.
Internationale Kunstmesse, Salon international d'Art, International Art Fair (exh. cat.), Basel, 1970.
Internationale Kunst-und Informationsmesse 1971 (exh. cat.), Cologne: Belgisches Haus, Volkshochschule, 1971.
'Interview with Leo Castelli, conducted by Paul Cummings', *Archives of American Art*, Smithsonian Institute, Washington, 14 May 1969–8 June 1973, from www.aaa.si.edu/collections/digitalcollections/oralhistoriesonline/.
'Jack Wendler Gallery', *Flash Art*, October–November 1974, p.37.
JACOBS, Brigitte, 'Entstehungsgeschichte und Gründungsumstände der Kunstmesse IKI in Düsseldorf 1968–1972', *Sediment*, Zadik, Bonn, no.3, 1998, pp.89–96.
——— 'Galeriehaus Köln, ein Hauch von 57. Straße: Aus dem Zentralarchiv 17', *Frankfurter Allgemeine Zeitung*, 18 August 2001.
——— 'Im Spannungsfeld zwischen Kunstelite und Populärkultur. Der Kölner Kunstmarkt und seine Gegen – und Konkurrenzveranstaltungen in der Medienkritik', *Sediment*, Zadik, Cologne, no.6, 2003, p.34.
Jacques Charlier, Dans les règles de l'art (exh. cat.), Brussels: Editions Lebeer Hossmann, 1983.
Jahresbericht 1972, Lucerne: Kunstgesellschaft, May 1973.
Jahresbericht 1973, Lucerne: Kunstgesellschaft, April 1974.
Jahresbericht 1974, Lucerne: Kunstgesellschaft, June 1975.
JAKOBSON, Barbara, *Leo Castelli, gentle snapshots: An exhibition in honour of the twenty-fifth anniversary of Leo Castelli Gallery* (exh. cat.), Zurich: Galerie Bruno Bischofberger, 1982.
Jan Dibbets (exh. cat.), Amsterdam: Stedelijk Museum, 1972.
January 5–31, 1969 (exh. cat.), New York: Seth Siegelaub, 1969.
JAPPE, Georg, 'Bodenplatten und Neon, Düsseldorfer Galerien im November', *Frankfurter Allgemeine Zeitung*, 20 November 1967.
——— 'Projection: the new trend at Prospect 71', *Studio International*, vol.182, no.939, December 1971, p.258–261.
——— 'Young artists in Germany', *Studio International*, vol.183, no.941, February 1972, pp.65–73.
——— 'Gemalt, dass sich die Balken biegen', *Frankfurter Allgemeine Zeitung*, 1 October 1973.
——— 'Art fairs–vanity fairs?', *Studio International*, vol.186, no.961, December 1973, pp.244–245.
'Joachim Kreibohm im Gespräch mit Egidio Marzona', *Artist Kunstmagazin*, February 1994, no.20, pp.12–15.
JOCKS, Heinz-Norbert, 'Einseitig muss man sein, damit etwas weitergeht', *Kunstforum*, vol.127, July–September 1994, pp.402–404.
JOOSTEN, Joop M. (ed.), *20 Years of Art Collecting. Acquisitions Stedelijk Museum Amsterdam 1969–1984. Painting and Sculpture*, Amsterdam: Stedelijk Museum, 1984.
Joseph Kosuth, Zettel 1–3 (The 8th Investigation, Proposition 2) (exh. cat.), Cologne: Paul Maenz, 1971.
July–August–September 1969 (exh. cat.), New York: Seth Siegelaub, 1969.
'July–August 1970', *Studio International*, vol.180, no.924, July–August 1970.
KANTOR, Sybil Gordon, *Alfred H. Barr, Jr., and the Intellectual*

Origins of the Museum of Modern Art, Cambridge, Mass.: MIT Press, 2002.

KARSHAN, Donald (ed.), *Conceptual Art and Conceptual Aspects* (exh. cat.), New York Cultural Centre, New York, 1970.

——— 'The seventies: post-object art', *Studio International*, vol.180, no.925, September 1970, pp.69–70.

KELLEIN, Thomas, 'It's the Sheer Size: European Responses to American Art', in Christos M. Joachimides, *American Art in the 20th Century*, Munich: Prestel Verlag, 1993, pp.187–194.

——— *Ich nenne mich als Maler Konrad Lueg* (exh. cat.), Bielefeld: Kunsthalle, 1999.

KERBER, Bernhard, *Bestände Onnasch* (exh. cat.), Bremen: Neues Museum Weserburg, 1992.

KIESSLING, Astrid, *Die Galerie Dorothea Loehr in Frankfurt am Main, Das erste Jahrzehnt*, unpublished Master's dissertation, Frankfurt/Main: Kunstgeschichtliches Institut der Johann Wolfgang Goethe-Universität, 1995.

KIMPEL-FEHLEMANN, Sabine (ed.), *Städtisches Museum Abteiberg Mönchengladbach, Bestandskatalog, Gemälde, Skulpturen, Aquarelle, Zeichnungen* (2 vol.), Mönchengladbach: Städtisches Museum Abteiberg, 1981.

KKM '71, Kölner Kunst Markt, Cologne Art Fair, Cologne Foire d'Art (exh. cat.), Cologne: Verein Deutscher Kunsthändler, 1971.

KLAPHECK, Anna, 'Blick in die neue Kunstszene', *Rheinische Post*, 20 September 1968.

KLÜSER, Bernd and HEGEWISCH, Katharina (eds), *L'Art de l'Exposition*, Paris: Editions du Regard, 1998.

KÖLLE, Brigitte, *Die Kunst des Ausstellen. Untersuchungen zum Werk des Künstlers und Kunstvermittlers Konrad Lueg/Fischer (1939–1996)*, unpublished PhD, Hildesheim: University of Hildesheim, 2005.

'Konrad Fischer interviewed by Georg Jappe', *Studio International*, vol.181, no.930, February 1971, pp.68–71.

'Konrad Fischer', *Kunstforum International*, vol.104, November–December 1989, pp.277–281.

'Konzept'-Kunst (exh. cat.), Basel: Kunstmuseum, 1972.

KOSUTH, Joseph, 'Art after Philosophy', *Studio International*, vol. 178, no.915, October 1969, pp.134–137; vol.178, no.916, November 1969, pp.160–161; vol.178, no.917, December 1969, pp.212–213.

——— 'Art after Philosophy', *Art Press*, no.1, December 1972–January 1973.

KOZLOFF, Max, 'American Painting during the Cold War', *Artforum*, May 1973, pp.43–54.

KREIS, Elfie, 'Wem gehört das Kapital? Besitzrechtstreit um Beuys-Installation in den Hallen für neue Kunst Schaffhausen.', *Informationsdienst KUNST*, no.325, 28 April 2005, pp.6–10.

'Kunstmarkt Köln '67, Entstehung und Entwicklung der ersten Messe für moderne Kunst', *Sediment*, no.6, Cologne: Zadik, 2003.

Kunstmarkt 1967 (exh. cat.), Cologne: Verein progressiver deutscher Kunsthändler, 1967.

Kunstmarkt 1968 (exh. cat.), Cologne: Verein progressiver deutscher Kunsthändler, 1968.

KUNZ, Martin, 'Der Galerist Rolf Preisig – Ein Porträt eines leisen Bahnbrechers, Er inszeniert gegen den Strich: cool', *National-Zeitung Basel*, no.404, 28 December 1976, p.25.

L'Architecte est absent – Works from the collection of Annick and Anton Herbert, Répertoire (exh. cat.), Eindhoven: Stedelijk Van Abbemuseum, 1984–1985.

L'art au Futur antérieur, L'engagement d'une galerie, Liliane et Michel Durand-Dessert, 1975/2004 (exh. cat.), Arles: Actes Sud and Musée de Grenoble, 2004.

LANCIONI, Daniela (ed.), *Roma in mostra 1970-1979, Materiali per la documentazione di mostre azioni performance dibatti* (exh. cat.), Rome: Palazzo delle Esposizioni and Edizioni Joyce and Co., 1995.

Lawrence Weiner, Statements, New York: The Louis Kellner Foundation and Seth Siegelaub, 1968.

LEGG, Alicia (ed.), *Sol LeWitt* (exh. cat.), New York: The Museum of Modern Art, 1978.

LEWITT, Sol, 'Paragraphs on Conceptual Art', *Artforum*, vol.5, no.10, Summer 1967, pp.79–84.

——— 'Sentences on Conceptual Art', *0–9*, no.5, January 1969, pp.3–5.

'Lies mich, Baby. Hippie-Zubehör.' *Der Spiegel*, vol.12, no.8, 19 February 1968, p.76.

LIPPARD, Lucy and CHANDLER, John, 'The Dematerialization of Art', *Art International*, vol.2, no.12, February 1968, pp.31–36.

LIPPARD, Lucy, 'The Art Workers Coalition: Not a History', *Studio International*, vol.180, no.927, November 1970, pp.171–174.

——— *Six Years: The Dematerialization of the Art Object from 1966 to 1972: a cross-reference book of information an some aesthetic boundaries: consisting of a bibliography into which are inserted a fragmented text, art works, documents, interviews, and symposia, arranged chronologically and focused on so-called conceptual art or information or idea art with mentions of such vaguely designated areas as minimal, anti-form, systems, earth, or process art, occurring in the Americas, Europe, England, Australia, and Asia (with occasional political overtones)*, Berkeley: University of California Press, 1997 (2nd edition, 1973).

'Lord Palumbo', *The Tatler*, vol.290, no.9, September 1995, p.149.

LUBBERS, Frank, HAKKEN, Anna and GILISSEN, Maria (eds), *Marcel Broodthaers, Projection* (exh. cat.), Eindhoven: Stedelijk Van Abbemuseum, 1992.

MAENZ, Paul, *Art is to change ..., Skizzen aus der Umlaufbahn*, Regensburg: Lindinger + Schmid, 2002.

'The magnificent 100', *Flash Art*, no.38, January 1973, p.17.

Many coloured objects placed side by side to form a row of many coloured objects, Works from the collection of Annick and Anton Herbert, Programme (exh. cat.), Luxembourg: Casino Luxembourg-Forum d'art contemporain, 2000.

Marcel Broodthaers (exh. cat.), London: The Tate Gallery, 1980.

Marcel Broodthaers, Cinéma (exh. cat.), Barcelona: Fundacío Antoní Tàpies, 1997.

MARCELIS, Bernard, 'Ils savaient ce qu'ils voulaient', *+–0*, no.23, 24 October 1978, pp.4–5.

——— 'Forcer l'utopie/Utopia the Only Option', in 'Paroles de Collectionneurs', *Art Press*, supplement to no.305, October 2004, pp.10–14.

The Marzona Collection, Ostfildern: Hatje Cantz, 2002.

MDD *Jaarcatalogus 2004*, Deurle: Museum Dhont-Dhaenens, 2004.

MELLOR, Philip, 'Whichever way you look at Britain's latest work of art ..., What a load of rubbish', *Daily Mirror*, 16 February 1976.

MERZ, Mario, *Fibonacci 1202*, Turin: Gian Enzo Sperone, 1970.

MEYER, Franz, 'Die Sammlungspolitik des Kunstmuseums im Bereiche von Malerei und Skulptur, 1968–1977', *Öffentliche Kunstsammlung Basel, Jahresbericht 1977*, Basel, 1977, pp.38–52.

——— *Minimal und Conceptual Art aus der Sammlung Panza* (exh. cat.), Basel: Museum für Gegenwartskunst, 1981.

MEYER, James, *Minimalism*, London: Phaidon, 2000.

MEYER, Ursula, *Conceptual Art*, New York: Dutton, 1972.

MIGLIORINI, Ermanno, *Conceptual Art*, Florence: Il Fiorino, 1972.

MIGNOT, Dorine (ed.), *Gerry Schum* (exh. cat.), Amsterdam: Stedelijk Museum, 1979.

MILES, Barry, *Hippie*, London: Cassell Illustrated, 2003.

MILLET, Catherine, 'L'art Conceptuel comme sémiotique de l'art', *VH101*, no.3, autumn 1970, p.3–21

Minimal Art (exh. cat.), The Hague: Haags Gemeentemuseum, 1968.

MINOLA, Anna, MUNDICI, Maria Cristina, POLI, Francesco and ROBERTO, Maria Teresa (eds), *Gian Enzo Sperone, Torino Roma New York, 35 anni di mostre tra Europa e America* (2 vol.), Turin: hopefulmoster editore, 2000.

'Mönchengladbach', *Flash Art*, no.46–47, June 1974, p.73.

MORGAN, Robert C., *The Role of Documentation in Conceptual Art: an aesthetic Inquiry*, unpublished PhD, New York: Department of Art, New York University, 1978.

——— *Art into ideas, Essays on Conceptual Art*, Cambridge: Cambridge University Press, 1996.

MORRIS, Lynda, *Art-Art Education-Education, Three titles for a discussion of fine art education*, unpublished MA thesis, London: Royal College of Art and Design, 1973.

——— 'Projekt '74', *Studio International*, vol.188, no.969, September 1974, pp.7–8.

——— 'Carl Andre Poems 1958–1974', *Studio International*, vol.190, no.977, September–October 1975, pp.160–161.

——— 'The Museum of Modern Art in Oxford 1965–1975', *Studio International*, vol.190, no.978, November–December 1975, pp.238–242.

——— *The Story of the Artists' International Association 1933–1953*, Oxford: Modern Art Oxford, 1983.

——— 'Recollection: Joseph Beuys', *Art Monthly*, no.284, March 2005, pp.42–43.

MOSELEY, Catherine, *Conception: Conceptual Documents 1968 to 1972* (exh. cat.), Norwich: Norwich Gallery and Article Press, 2001.

MOURE, Gloria (ed.), *Behind the facts: Interfunktionen 1968–1975* (exh. cat.), Barcelona: Poligrafa, 2004.

'MTL, Antwerp', *Flash Art*, no.60–61, December 1975–February 1976, p.6.

'MTL, Brussels', *Flash Art*, no.66–67, July–August 1976, p.2.

MÜLLER, Grégoire, *The New Avantgarde, Issues for the Art of the Seventies*, London: Pall Mall Press, 1972.

Museum für Moderne Kunst und Sammlung Ströher, Frankfurt/Main: Museum für Moderne Kunst, 1991.

NAIFEH, Steven, *Culture Making: Money, Success, and the New York Art World*, Princeton: Princeton University Press, 1976.

NETTER, Maria, 'Mit aller Konsequenz auf die Moderne ausgerichtet, Zur Einkaufspolitik des Baseler Kunstmuseums.', *Handelsblatt*, 12–13 September 1975, p.16.

The New Art (exh. cat.), London: Hayward Gallery and the Arts Council of Great Britain, 1972.

New Research into Conceptualism in Europe, Dispatch 114, Norwich: Norwich Gallery, 2005.

NEWMAN, Amy, *Challenging Art: Artforum 1962–1974*, New York: Soho Press, 2000.

NEWMAN, Michael and BIRD, Jon (eds), *Rewriting Conceptual Art*, London: Reaktion Books, 1999.

NYLEN, Leif, 'Suddenly last summer', *Art and Artists*, vol.4, no.5, August 1969, pp.58–61.

'Obituary: Peter Townsend 1919–2006', *Art Monthly*, no.299, September 2006, pp.14–16.

Op Losse Schroeven, Situaties en Cryptostructuren (exh. cat.), Amsterdam: Stedelijk Museum, 1969, unnumbered pages.

OSBORNE, Peter, *Conceptual Art*, London: Phaidon, 2002.

OXENAAR, Rudolf W.D., 'On art and museum policies in the Netherlands', *Studio International*, vol.185, no.955, May 1973, pp.203–205.

Painting and sculpture of a Decade, 1954–1964 (exh. cat.), London: Calouste Gulbenkian Foundation and Tate Gallery, 1964.

PALLISTER, David, 'The hot bricks floor the Tate', *The Times*, 17 February 1976.

The Panza Collection, Villa Menafoglio Litta Panza – Varese, Milan: FAI, Skira, 2002.

Paul Maenz Köln 1970–1975, Cologne: Paul Maenz, 1975.

'Paul Maenz', *Kunstforum International*, vol.104, November–December 1989, pp.282–288.

PHILLPOT, Clive and TARSIA, Andrea, *Live in Your Head. Concept and Experiment in Britain, 1965–75* (exh. cat.), London: Whitechapel Art Gallery, 2000.

POLITI, Giancarlo, 'Prospect '73, Which painting', *Flash Art*, no.43, December 1973–January 1974, p.5.

Proposals from Halifax: an Exhibition of Selected Typescripts, Flyers, Posters, Catalogues, Books, Mailers and Postcards of a Conceptual Nature Produced from 1969 to 1999 by Affiliates of the Nova Scotia College of Art and Design (NSCAD) (exh. cat.), Ottawa: National Gallery of Canada, 2000.

Prospect 68, Katalog-Zeitung zur internationalen Vorschau auf die Kunst in den Galerien der Avantgarde (exh. cat.), Düsseldorf: Städtische Kunsthalle Düsseldorf, 1968.

Prospect 69, Katalog-Zeitung zur internationalen Vorschau auf die Kunst in den Galerien der Avantgarde (exh. cat.), Düsseldorf: Städtische Kunsthalle Düsseldorf, 1969.

Prospect 73, Malers, Painters, Peintres (exh. cat.), Düsseldorf: Städtische Kunsthalle Düsseldorf, 1973.

RATTEMEYER, Volker and PENZINGER, Renate (eds), *20 Jahre Kunstmarkt 1967–1986*, Cologne: Bundesverband Deutscher Galerien, 1986.

'Record as Artwork', *Flash Art*, no.43, December 1973–January 1974, p.6.

REISE, Barbara, 'Aspects of art called "minimal"', *Studio International*, vol.177, no.910, April 1969, pp.165–189.

——— 'A tail of two exhibitions: the aborted Haacke and Robert Morris shows', *Studio International*, vol.182, no.935, July–August 1971, p.30–34.

——— '"Incredible" Belgium: Impressions', *Studio International*, vol.188, no.970, October 1974, pp.117–123.

Rendez-vous, Collection Lambert, Arles: Actes Sud, 2000.

'René Block', *Kunstforum International*, vol.104, November–December 1989, pp.254–264.

'Research in Art and Public Institutions: the Dutch Case', *Flash Art*, May–June 1977, pp.14–16.

REUST, Hans Rudolf, *Aus dem Musée éclaté an dem Ort des Werks, Kunsthalle Bern 1969–1993*, Kunsthalle, Bern, 1993.

'Review, News and Notes', *Studio International*, vol.187, no.962, January 1974, p.35.

'Review', *Studio International*, vol.188, no.972, December 1974, p.R3.

Richard Long (exh. cat.), Städtisches Museum, Mönchengladbach, 1970.

'Richard Long', *Avalanche*, no.1, Fall 1970, pp.18–47.

RICHARD, Sophie, *Harald Szeemann et les expositions d'art contemporain*, unpublished MPhil thesis [D.E.A.], Université de Paris I Panthéon-Sorbonne, Paris, 2000.

ROEHR, Peter and MAENZ, Paul (eds), *Serielle Formationen* (exh. cat.), Frankfurt/Main: Studio Galerie, Studentenschaft der Johann Wolfgang Goethe Universität, 1967.

ROHR-BONGARD, Linde (ed.), *Kunst = Kapital, Der Capital Kunstkompass von 1970 bis heute*, Cologne: Salon Verlag, 2001.

'Rolf Preisig', *Art Aktuell*, vol. 3, no.22, 30 November 1973, p.4.

RORIMER, Anne, 'The Exhibition at the MTL Gallery in Brussels, March 13–April 10, 1970', October, no.42, Fall 1987, pp.101 Milan: FAI 125.

——— *New Art in the 60s and 70s, Redefining Reality*, London: Thames & Hudson, 2001.

RUHRBERG, Karl (ed.), *Alfred Schmela, Galerist, Wegbereiter der Avantgarde*, Cologne: Wienand, 1996.

Sale of Contemporary Art 1945–1974, London: Sotheby & Co, Part 1, 3 April 1974; Part 2, 4 April 1974.

Sale of Contemporary Art 1945–1974, London: Sotheby & Co, Part 1, 4 December 1974; Part 2, 6 December 1974.

Sale of Contemporary Art 1945–1976, London: Sotheby's, 2 December 1976.

Sale of Contemporary Art 1945–1977, London: Sotheby's, 30 June 1977.

Sale of Modern and Contemporary Art 1945–1979, London: Sotheby's, 5 December 1979.

Sammlung Hahn, Zeitgenössische Kunst (exh. cat.), Cologne: Wallraf-Richartz Museum, 1968.

Sammlung Hahn (exh. cat.), Vienna: Museum für Moderne Kunst, 1979.

Sammlung Heinemann (exh. cat.), Mönchengladbach: Städtisches Museum, 1982.

Sammlung Speck (exh. cat.), Cologne: Museum Ludwig, 1996.

Sammlung 1968 Karl Ströher (exh. cat.), Berlin: Deutsche Gesellschaft für bildende Kunst, Kunstverein and Nationalgalerie der Staatlichen Museen preußischer Kulturbesitz in der Neuen Nationalgalerie and Düsseldorf: Städtischen Kunsthalle, 1969.

'Sammlungsziele', *Sammlungsleitbild*, Luzern: Kunstmuseum, undated, unnumbered pages.

SAUER, Christel, 'InK – die Halle für internationale neue Kunst', *Du*, April 1980, pp.6–11.

SAUERLÄNDER, Katrin (ed.), *Karl Ströher. Eine Sammlungsgeschichte*, Frankfurt/Main: Revolver, 2005.

SCHMIDT, Katharina and URSPRUNG, Philip (eds), *White Fire, Flying Man, Amerikanische Kunst 1959–1999 in Basel, Werke aus der Öffentlichen Kunstsammlung Basel und der Emanuel Hoffmann-Stiftung* (exh. cat.), Basel: Museum für Gegenwartskunst, 1999.

SCHMIED, Wieland, 'Kunsthändler als Historiker', *Frankfurter Allgemeine Zeitung*, 27 October 1976.

SCHNECKENBURGER, Manfred, 'Wer kauft die (fast) unsichtbare Kunst?', in *7. Kölner Kunstmarkt, 29.9–6.10.73*, Cologne, 1973, pp.28–29.

——— *Documenta, Idee und Institution, Tendenzen–Konzepte–Materialien*, Munich: Bruckmann, 1983.

SCHWARTZ, Therese, 'The Politicalization of the Avant-Garde', *Art in America*, November–December 1971, pp.97–105.

SCHWARZ, Dieter, *Lawrence Weiner, Books 1968–1989, Catalogue raisonné*, Cologne: Verlag der Buchhandlung Walther König and Villeurbanne: Éditeur Le Nouveau Musée, 1989.

SCHWEIGHÖFER, Kerstin, 'Der Fuchs im Hühnerstall hatte zu grossen Appetit und Lust aufs Reisen: Rudi Fuchs hinterlässt in Den Haag Millionen-Schulden', *Art: Das Kunstmagazin*, no.5, May 1993, p.139.

Sculpture by Richard Long, made for Martin & Mia Visser, Bergeyk, publication no.9, Bergeyk: Martin and Mia Visser (sponsors) and Cologne: Fernsehgalerie Gerry Schum, (ed.) 1969.

SEROTA, Nicholas, *Experience or Interpretation: The Dilemma of Museums of Modern Art*, New York: Thames and Hudson, 1997.

——— 'Nigel Greenwood: influential gallerist who helped shape contemporary British art', *The Guardian*, 21 April 2004.

SEWALL-RUSKIN, Yvonne, *High On Rebellion: Inside the Underground at Max's Kansas City 1965–1981*, New York: Thunders Mouth Press, 1998.

SHIREY, David, 'Impossible Art – What Is It?', *Art in America*, May–June 1969, p.39.

SIEGELAUB, Seth and PROJANSKY, Bob, 'The Artists' Reserved Rights Transfer and Sale Agreement', *Studio International*, vol.81, no.932, April 1971, pp.142–144 and pp.186–187.

SIMPSON, Colin, 'The Tate drops a costly brick', Business News section, *Sunday Times*, 15 February 1976.

SINGER, Suzanna (ed.), *Sol LeWitt, Wall Drawings 1968–1984* (exh. cat.), Amsterdam: Stedelijk Museum; Eindhoven: Van Abbemuseum; Hartford: Wadsworth Atheneum, 1984.

'Six Friedrich', *Kunstforum International*, vol.104, November–December 1989, pp.246–249.

6. Kölner Kunstmarkt 1972 (exh. cat.), Cologne: Kunsthalle, Kunstverein, 1972.

6. Raüme (exh. cat.), Mönchengladbach: Städtisches Museum, 1976.

6th Guggenheim International Exhibition 1971 (exh. cat.), New York: The Solomon R. Guggenheim Museum, 1971.

SMETS, Francis, *Een lectuur van discursus van Pop Art en Conceptual Art over de Ready-Mades van Duchamp als bijdrage tot de studie van de ideologie in het laatkapitalisme*, unpublished PhD, Belgium: Catholic University of Louvain, 1978.

SMITH, Roberta, 'Review', *Artforum*, vol.14, no.5, January 1976, pp.61–62.

Sol LeWitt (exh. cat.), Bern: Kunsthalle, 1972.

'Some Concerns in Fine Art Education', *Studio International*, vol.182, no.937, October 1971, pp.120–122.

Sonsbeek 71 (exh. cat., 2 vol.), Arnhem: Centrum Park Sonsbeek, 1971.

SPALDING, Frances, *Roger Fry, Art and Life*, London: Granada Publishing, 1980.

SPECK, Reiner, *Peter Ludwig Sammler*, Frankfurt/Main: Insel Verlag, 1986.

SPILLEMAECKERS, Fernand (ed.), *Ooidonk 1978: Belgische kunst 1969–1977*, Brussels, 1978.

STAVITSKY, Gail, 'The A.E. Gallatin Collection: An Early Adventure in Modern Art', *Bulletin of the Philadelphia Museum of Art*, no.89, 1994, pp.3–47.

'Strategy: Get Arts', History, *Palermo Restore*, from www.eca.ac.uk/palermo/index.htm.

STRELOW, Hans, 'Hundert Stahlplatten gleich eine Plastik, Konrad Fischer eröffnet seine Galerie mit dem Amerikaner Carl Andre', *Rheinische Post*, 20 October 1967.

SZEEMANN, Harald (ed.), *When Attitudes Become Form* (exh. cat.), Bern: Kunsthalle, 1969.

——— 'Journal et carnets de voyage touchant aux préparatifs et aux retombées de l'exposition "When Attitudes Become Form (Works, Concepts, Processes, Situations, Information)" , et à rien d'autre', *Les Cahiers du Musée national d'art moderne*, no.73, autumn 2000, pp.8–35.

The Tate Gallery, Acquisitions 1968–69, London: Tate Gallery, 1969.

The Tate Gallery 1970–72, published by order of the Trustees, London, 1972.

'The Tate Gallery: acquisitions, exhibitions, trustees, future developments', *Studio International*, vol.185, no.954, April 1973, pp.181–192.

The Tate Gallery 1972–74, Biennial Report and illustrated Catalogue of Acquisitions, published by order of the Trustees, London, 1975.

The Tate Gallery 1974–76, Illustrated Catalogue of Acquisitions, London: The Tate Gallery, 1978.

The Tate Gallery 1976–1978, Illustrated Catalogue of Acquisitions, London: The Tate Gallery, 1979.

The Tate Gallery, Illustrated Catalogue of Acquisitions 1978–80, London: The Tate Gallery, 1981.

The Tate Gallery 1980–82: Illustrated Catalogue of Acquisitions, London: The Tate Gallery, 1984.

TAYLOR, Paul, 'John Weber', *Flash Art*, May–June 1986, pp.66–67.

Terry Atkinson, Norwich: Norwich Gallery, 1996.

36 Biennale di Venezia: Esposizione Internationale d'Art (exh. cat.), Venice: Ente Autonomo 'La Biennale di Venezia', 1972.

Three blind mice, The collectors Visser (Bergeyk, Antwerpen), Peeters (Bruges) and Becht (Hilversum) (exh. cat.), Eindhoven: Stedelijk Van Abbemuseum, 1968.

'Truro, Massachusetts, October 11–14, 1992', in *Douglas Huebler, "Variable", etc.* (exh. cat.), Limoges: FRAC Limousin, 1993, pp.126–127.

TUCHMAN, Phyllis, 'American Art in Germany, The History of a Phenomenon', *Artforum*, November 1970, pp.58–69.

XXe/MNAM/Collections, Une histoire matérielle, Paris: Musée national d'Art moderne and Éditions du Centre Georges Pompidou, 1999.

'Un grand collectionneur européen d'art américain: Giuseppe Panza', *XXe siècle*, vol.35, no.41, December 1973, pp.124–127.

'Unmut über "Prospect" konnte sich nicht entladen', *Rheinische Post*, 23 October 1969.

URBASCHEK, Stefan, *Dia Art Foundation, Institution und Sammlung 1974–1985*, Marburg: Tectum Verlag, 2003.

VAN BEIJEREN, Geert, 'Note on private collections in the Netherlands', *Studio International*, May 1973, vol.185, no.955, pp.233–235.

VAN DAALEN, Piet, 'Uit de dossiers van A 379089 te Antwerpen', *Museumsjournaal*, vol.19, no.1, February 1974, pp.20–28.

VAN DEN BOOGAARD, Oscar, 'Discussion with Annick and Anton Herbert', *A-Priori*, no.1, 1999.

VAN DER MEYDEN, Hans, 'Peter and Irene Ludwig', *Apollo*, June 1989, vol.129, no.328, pp.399–403.

VAN LIL, Kira, *Kurzführer Hallen für neue Kunst*, Schaffhausen: Hallen für neue Kunst, 1999.

Vernissage des Expositions J. Charlier, On Kawara (exh. cat.), Brussels: Société des expositions du Palais des Beaux-Arts, 1975.

Virginia Dwan, Art Minimal et Conceptuel, Earthworks, New York, Les années 60–70 (exh. cat.), Paris: Galerie Montaigne, 1991.

VISSER, Hripsimé, 'Conceptuele Kunst 1965–1975', *Bulletin Stedelijk Museum Amsterdam*, vol. 15, no.3, April 2002, pp.2–7.

VON DER OSTEN, Gert (ed.), *Kunst der sechziger Jahre (Sammlung Ludwig), Hundert Werke im Wallraf-Richartz Museum*, Cologne: Wallraf-Richartz Museum, 1969.

VON WIESE, Stephan, 'Creamcheese – Eine Kneipe als Forum der Kunst', in *Brennpunkt Düsseldorf 1962–1987* (exh. cat.), Düsseldorf: Kunstmuseum, 1987, pp.120–121.

WALKER, John, 'Review, Art-Language at the Lisson Gallery, 16 October–10 November', *Studio International*, vol.186, no.961, December 1973, p.248.

WALKER, John A., 'Internal Memorandum', *Studio International*, vol.192, no.983, September–October 1976, pp.113–118.

WEDEWER, Rolf and FISCHER, Konrad, *Konzeption/Conception, Dokumentation einer heutigen Kunstrichtung, documentation of a to-day's tendency* (exh. cat.), Cologne and Opladen: Westdeutscher Verlag, 1969.

WEINER, Lawrence, *Trace/Traces*, Gian Enzo Sperone, Turin, 1970.

WEMBER, Paul, 'Vorstellungen nehmen Form an', in *20 Jahre*

Museum Haus Lange, Eine Retrospektive der Ausstellungen 1955–1975 (exh. cat.), Krefeld: Kaiser Wilhelm Museum, 1976, p.88.

WENDERMANN, Gerda, 'Paul Maenz – Galerist und Sammler der Avantgarde', in Hans Dickel (ed.), *Die Sammlung Paul Maenz, 1. Objekte, Bilder, Installationen, Neues Museum Weimar*, Ostfildern: Hatje Cantz Verlag, 1999, pp.12–27.

WHITE, Harrison C. and WHITE, Cynthia A., *Canvases and Careers: Institutional Change in the French Painting World*, New York: J. Wiley & Sons, 1965.

WHITFORD, Frank and KUDIELKA, Robert, 'Documenta 4: a critical review', *Studio International*, vol.176, no.903, September 1968, pp.74–78.

'Wim Beeren, Des chevilles carrées dans des trous ronds, Interview par Bart de Baere et Selma Klein Essink', *Art Press*, special issue no.17, 1996, pp.131–139.

WISCHERMANN, Susanne, *Johannes Cladders, Museumsmann und Künstler, Peter Lang, Europäische Hochschulschriften*, Frankfurt/Main: Kunstgeschichte, 1997.

Works from the Collection of Dorothy and Herbert Vogel (exh. cat.), Ann Arbor, Michigan: The University of Michigan Museum of Art, 1977.

Xerox Book: Carl Andre, Robert Barry, Douglas Huebler, Joseph Kosuth, Sol LeWitt, Robert Morris, Lawrence Weiner, New York: Seth Siegelaub and John W. Wendler, 1968.

Yvon Lambert, Actualité d'un Bilan, Paris 1972 (exh. cat.), Paris: Galerie Yvon Lambert, 1972.

Zeichnen/Bezeichnen: Zeichnungen aus der Sammlung Mia und Martin Visser, Bergeyk, mit Beiträgen aus der Sammlung Geert Jan Visser, Antwerpen (exh. cat.), Basel: Kunstmuseum, 1976.

Consolidated references

Art-Language, The Journal of Conceptual Art, vol.1, no.1, May 1969; vol.1, no.2, February 1970; vol.1, no.3, June 1970.

Art & Project Bulletin, no.1, 17 September 1968; no.10, 1 September 1969; no.14, 18 November 1969; no.15, 26 November 1969; no.18, 2 January 1970; no.20, 1 March 1970; no.22, 17 April 1970; no.30, 30 November 1970; no.32, 4 January 1971; no.35, 22 March 1971; no.36, 7 April 1971; no.39, 19 May 1971; no.40, 2 June 1971; no.43, 1 September 1971; no.46, 23 November 1971; no.47, 28 December 1971; no.53, 18 April 1972; no.56, 12 June 1972; no.60, 25 September 1972; no.66, 1972; no.89, 18 March 1975.

Avalanche, no.3, winter 1971; no.4, spring 1972.

Galeriehaus Köln, Lindenstrasse 18–22, no.1–9, March–December 1971.

Index

C

G

N

O

T

U

V

W

X

Y

Z

Acknowledgements

Sophie Richard

This research project would not have been achieved without the constant support, the helpful insights, the intellectual thoroughness and the generosity of my supervisor Lynda Morris. This study owes a lot to her invaluable knowledge of the art world of the 1960s and 1970s.

The advice and guidance of my second supervisor Anna Green and of my director of studies Simon Willmoth were most useful. Their kindness and encouragement helped me constantly during my research.

I also have to thank Peter Osborne, Middlesex University, London, for his valuable comments. At NSAD, I could always count on the help of Jean Betts, Carole Burton, Catherine Moseley, Sally Wade and Karen Young.

I am indebted to the financial support of the following institutions: Norwich School of Art and Design, Norwich; Henry Moore Institute, Leeds; DAAD, Goethe Institute, London; CEDIES, Luxembourg.

For sharing memories and thoughts and for their kindness, I would like to thank:

Jean-Christophe Ammann, Art & Language (Michael Baldwin, Mel Ramsden, Charles Harrison), John Baldessari, Barry Barker, Jacques Charlier, Johannes Cladders, Kaatje Cusse and Peter Downsbrough, Anny De Decker, Jan Dibbets, Lili Dujourie, Dorothee Fischer, Rudi Fuchs, Johannes Gachnang†, Yves Gevaert, Marlis Grüterich, Annick and Anton Herbert, Klaus Honnef, Françoise Lambert, Nicolas Logsdail, Paul Maenz, Sylvain Perlstein, Rolf Preisig, Nicholas Serota, Seth Siegelaub, Harald Szeemann†, David Tremlett, Henriëtte and Herman van Eelen and Lawrence Weiner.

I am grateful to the following people for their assistance in making archive material available and/or for sending me various documents and/or providing information and contacts:

Hannelore Kersting (Städtisches Museum Abteiberg, Mönchengladbach); Swaantje Burow, Carina Plath and Hildegard Vogelsang (Kunstverein Münster); Anette Wohlgemuth (Westfälisches Archivamt, Münster); Gesina Kronenburg and Ulrich Tillmann (Museum Ludwig, Cologne); Corinna Schröder (Ludwig Stiftung, Aachen); Gabriele John (Stadtarchiv, Leverkusen); Stephan Urbaschek (Goertz Foundation, Munich); Thomas Deecke (Neues Museum Weserburg, Bremen); Doris Krystof (K21 Kunstsammlung Nordrhein Westfalen, Düsseldorf); Gerda Wendermann (Stiftung Weimarer Klassik und Kunstsammlungen, Weimar); Ulla Wiegand (Konrad Fischer Galerie, Düsseldorf); Günter Herzog and Brigitte Jacobs (Zentralarchiv des internationalen Kunsthandel, Cologne); Franziska Heuss, Valerie Knoll and Katrin Steffen (Kunstmuseum, Basel); Kathrin Grögel and Heidi Naef (Emanuel Hoffmann-Stiftung, Schaulager, Basel); Cornelia Dietschi and Christoph Lichtin (Kunstmuseum, Lucerne); Mira Preisig (Freunde des Kunstmuseums Basel und des Museums für Gegenwartskunst, Basel); Ines Goldbach (Hallen für neue Kunst, Schaffhausen); Virginie Devilliez (Archives de l'Art contemporain en Belgique, Brussels); Jan(us) Boudewijns (Museum Dhondt-Dhaenens, Deurle); Marijke Knies and Maurice Rummens (Stedelijk Museum, Amsterdam); Diana Franssen, Marleen Gijsen and Margo van de Wiel (Van Abbemuseum, Eindhoven); Monique Biekart (Gemeentemuseum, The Hague); Becky Simms (Modern Art, Oxford); Lisa Cole, Nicola Roberts and Emily White (Tate Library and Archive, London); Elisa Kay (Lisson Gallery, London); Lynda McLeod (Christie's Library, London); James Sutton (Archive, Victoria & Albert Museum, London); Judy Greenwood (London); Emmanuel Zwenger (École régionale des Beaux-Arts de Caen); Massimo Minini (Galleria Massimo Minini, Brescia); Enrico Lunghi (Casino Luxembourg-Forum d'Art contemporain, Luxembourg); Lynne Cook (Dia Arts Foundation for the Arts, New York); Sharon Newfeld (Guggenheim Museum, New York); Laura Addison (Museum of Fine Arts, Santa Fe); Robert Chaney (ICA, University of Pennsylvania); Beth Turk and Alex Wittenberg (The Jewish Museum, New York).

For providing accommodation in various cities, I am grateful to Delphine Haluk, Catherine Kontz, Annick Masselot and Julie Patrois.

I also want to thank my mother and my grandmother for their insightful comments on certain part of this thesis. I should also thank Emma Cowan, Alicia Rainot and Graeme Smart for proofreading my text.

Finally, I want to thank my parents and my grandmother for their constant support and encouragement. By far my greatest debt goes to my husband for his unfailing help in every conceivable way. To express my gratitude, this work is dedicated to him.

SR September 2006

Lynda Morris

I would like to thank Tom Reisen, the late Sophie Richard's husband and the father of her daughter Lucie, for his support with every aspect of this publication. Anton and Annick Herbert generously supported the publication from the earliest moment. Enrico Lunghi arranged the funding from the Luxembourg Government. The Henry Moore Foundation and Norwich University College of the Arts have also generously supported the publication. Karsten Schubert, art dealer and founder of the publishing imprint Ridinghouse immediately spotted the importance of Richard's research. Jacques Charlier agreed with my proposal to publish his 1974–75 *Vernissage Photographs* of the Conceptual art network in its heyday, as a work of art within *Unconcealed*.

Richard could not have completed her work without the generous time and support given to her by many of the key figures of this early history of Conceptual art. I opened my address book to her and I would like to thank my old friends and acquaintances who worked with Richard, and who have more recently reworked their interviews for this publication. Herman Daled and Dorothee Fischer read the text and offered their knowledge and insights on the editing. David Lamelas has also discussed the publication with me on many occasions. One of my earlier Norwich University College of the Arts research students, Catherine Butcher née Moseley, generously shared the taped interviews made when she was working on *Conception: Conceptual Documents 1968–1972*. She and Herman Daled agreed for her interview with him to be republished here. Nadja and Jean-Michel Botquin of the Nadja Vilenne Gallery in Liège provided the scans for Charlier's work. Jo Melvin and Joy Sleeman, Nick Fitch and Maxa Zoller are colleagues I have discussed the research with. They are also working on theses and books on aspects of Conceptual art.

I was invited to give a lecture on Richard's research, 'Out of Düsseldorf', in April 2008 at the Getty Centre in Los Angeles at the Anglo-American Conference organised by Antonia Boström from the Getty and Penelope Curtis and Jonathan Wood from the Henry Moore Institute in Leeds. I also lectured on Richard's research at the *Landmark Exhibitions Conference* held at Tate Modern in November 2008, organised by Anthony Hudek of the Jan van Eyck Academie, Maastricht and Marko Daniel. Koen Brams the Director invited me to lecture in Maastricht. I also lectured on Richard's research at the Sainsbury Centre for Visual Arts at the University of East Anglia during the On Location exhibition organised by Dr Simon Dell.

Enrico Lunghi of the Casino and now MUDAM in Luxembourg, Dirk Snauwaert and staff at Weils Brussels, Nicholas Logsdail and Greg Hilty at the Lisson Gallery, London and Alan Johnston of Edinburgh College of Art are all helping to give Richard's book an appropriately international series of launches.

It has been marvellous to work with Rosalind Horne the Editor at Ridinghouse and her assistant Doro Globus. Mark Thomson has designed a minimalist book that elegantly deals with the complexity of the material. Freddie Checketts indexed the book efficiently.

Professor Michael Corris, Terry Atkinson and Dr Krzysztof Fijalkowski were Richard's examiners, chaired by Professor Nick Godard. They had no hesitation in awarding the Phd. Richard was also indebted to my colleagues at Norwich University College of the Arts who shared the supervision with me: The Director of Studies Simon Willmoth and Dr Anna Green. Tom Simmons the Research Officer has arranged for me to be able to travel to bring this publication to fruition.

I cannot tell you how much I miss the twice termly sessions I had with Sophie Richard between 2002 and 2006, looking through my archives and digging out books, magazines and pouring over my much treasured pieces of paper. I look forward to more new graduate students building on the marvellous tradition of Conceptual art studies Sophie Richard and Catherine Moseley have achieved at Norwich University College of the Arts.

LM Norwich, March 2009

Generously supported by:

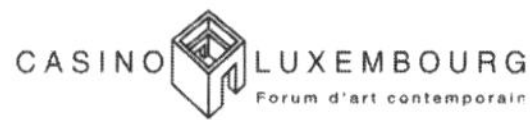

FOCUNA
Fonds Culturel National

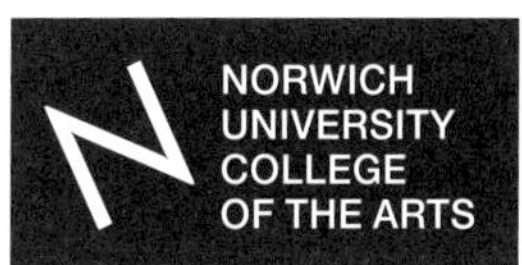

The Henry Moore Foundation

Annick and Anton Herbert

First published in 2009 by Ridinghouse

Produced in association with
Norwich University College of the Arts

Second printing 2010

Ridinghouse
5–8 Lower John Street
Golden Square
London W1F 9DR
www.ridinghouse.co.uk

Distributed in the UK and Europe by
Cornerhouse
70 Oxford Street
Manchester M1 5NH
www.cornerhouse.org

Distributed in the US by
RAM Publications
2525 Michigan Avenue Building A2
Santa Monica CA 90404
www.rampub.com

British Library Cataloguing-in-Publication Data
A full catalogue record of this book is available from the British Library

ISBN 978 1 905464 17 3

Ridinghouse Editor: Rosalind Horne
Assistant Editor: Doro Globus
Copy-editing: Melissa Larner
Translation (interviews): Shaun Whiteside
Designed by Mark Thomson
Set in OT Arnhem
Printed by Samhwa, Korea